UNDERSTANDING PHILOSOPHY

for AS Level

Christopher Hamilton

Published in 2003 by:
Nelson Thornes Ltd
Delta Place
27 Bath Road
CHELTENHAM
GL53 7TH
United Kingdom

04 05 06 07 / 10 9 8 7 6 5 4 3

A catalogue record for this book is available from the British Library

ISBN 0 7487 6560 3

Page make-up by Acorn Bookwork

Printed in Great Britain by Scotprint

contents

Illustrations

To Mimi

Acknowledgements

I am extremely grateful to all those at Nelson Thornes who have been involved in supporting, in different ways, my work on this book. I would especially like to thank Rick Jackman and Carolyn Lee for their tremendous support.

I started writing this book while teaching at Bedales School, and I thank my former colleagues there for their interest in, and support of, my philosophical work. I would like to thank my present colleagues at King's College School for doing so much to create a good and supportive environment in which to work and teach. In particular, I am extremely grateful to Matthew Storey who gives of his time and energy with great generosity in supporting those who work under him.

I am grateful to numerous students at many institutions – among them, Sheffield University, Bedales School and King's College School – who have helped to shape my sense of what philosophy is and what teaching it should be.

I also thank three anonymous readers for Nelson Thornes for their comments on earlier drafts of parts of the book.

My deepest debt is, as ever, to my wife, Mimi. She has read most of the material here at some stage in its production and commented on how to improve it in innumerable ways. Moreover, she has uncomplainingly borne my need to spend a vast amount of time working. But much more important, is that she shows me, as no philosophical argument could, what it might be like to live in the light of the Form of the Good.

The author and publishers wish to thank the following for permission to reproduce photographs and other copyright material in this book:

Digital Stock 6 (NT) p. 311; Hulton Archive/Getty pp. 17, 160, 220, 316, 405; Illustrated London News V2 (NT) p. 372; Mary Evans Picture Library pp. 21, 22, 25, 52, 67, 71, 87, 114, 231, 232, 255, 262, 265, 273, 278, 281, 310, 311, 346, 373, 374, 377; Mary Evans Picture Library/Weimar Archive pp. 191, 204, 368; Mary Evans Picture Library/Ida Kar Collection p. 402; Merton College p. 34; Topham Picture Point pp. 125, 226, 337.

Every effort has been made to contact copyright holders and the publishers apologise to anyone whose rights have been inadvertently overlooked and will be happy to rectify any errors or omissions.

Die Dinge sollten so einfach wie möglich gemacht werden, aber nicht einfacher.

Albert Einstein

(Things should be made as simple as possible, but not simpler.)

Preface

What this book is and how to use it

This book discusses all the topics and texts that are included in the specification for the AQA Philosophy AS Level, though it certainly contains enough material to be of use to others first coming to the subject, such as undergraduates and those with a general interest in how academic philosophers go about their business.

Because the book follows the specification, it is divided into two parts. Part I deals with the topics of the theory of knowledge, moral philosophy and the philosophy of religion; Part II deals with Plato's *Republic*, Descartes' *Meditations*, Marx and Engels' *The German Ideology*, and Sartre's *Existentialism and Humanism*. The aim is to provide the student with everything needed to understand the relevant debates and at least some of the materials needed to learn how to begin to contribute to them. Generally, I have tried not simply to explain what any given thinker thought but also to give his reasons for what he thought; too many introductory books leave out this latter task but the interest of philosophy resides as much in the arguments given for a given view or conclusion as in the view or conclusion itself. Indeed, often the conclusion is of no real interest, what is important lying more or less completely in the arguments given.

There are many review activities along the way. These are basically comprehension exercises and are intended to help students to articulate in their own terms the ideas that have been discussed. This task is very important: often it is not difficult to understand the point being made, but very difficult to put it oneself in a clear way. Students should try to do as many of these exercises as possible; teachers can set them as exercises. At the end of each chapter there are 'some questions to think about'. These can form longer homework exercises and/or the basis for class discussion: they are more difficult and usually require readers to try to think for themselves about the philosophical points made in the main body of the text.

Each chapter ends with suggestions for further reading. It is taken for granted that the works by others referred to in the main body of the text are important for such reading; the further reading sections thus usually add more recommendations to, or comment further on, those to which reference has already been made.

I have tried, in general, to keep my own philosophical views very much in the background, as befits such a book. Occasionally, however, I have allowed myself to reveal something of my own attitudes, sometimes directly, sometimes in the tone of the writing. Nevertheless, when I have done so, I have drawn on the thinking of others and have given the relevant references.

I recommend that, in order to understand the ideas under discussion, readers not only read thoroughly and carefully – that goes without saying – but also take notes as they read.

Despite the fact that there is overlap between some of the topics and texts dealt with in this book, in general each of the chapters is written in such a way as to be self-contained, although students will, of course, find it helpful to have their attention drawn to interconnections between the various chapters and there are occasional cross-references. The only lengthy exception to the self-contained nature of each chapter is in the case of the discussion of the first two of Descartes' *Meditations,* discussion of which is to be found in the chapter on the theory of knowledge. The remaining *Meditations* that are discussed are dealt with in the chapter devoted to them in Part II of the book. It should also be noted that Anselm's version of the ontological argument for the existence of God is found in the chapter on the philosophy of religion in Part I, whereas Descartes' version of the same argument is discussed in the chapter devoted to the *Meditations* in Part II.

A note on references

References to works cited or quoted are, in general, given in the following form: the author of the book, followed by the date of publication, followed by part, page number, chapter or section, as is appropriate. The book may be found under the author's surname in the Bibliography. Thus: Arendt 1958: 22, means: page 22 of Hannah Arendt's 1958 publication *The Human Condition.*

In the case of Descartes, references to the *Meditations* and other writings are given to the translation in the two volumes of Descartes' philosophical writings made by John Cottingham, Robert Stoothoff and Dugald Murdoch (Cambridge: Cambridge University Press, 1985) as in the following example: CSM II: 17/26. This refers to the volume number of their translation, followed by the page number of this same translation, followed by page number (found in the margin of the CSM translation) of the corresponding page of the modern standard edition of the original. In general, where passages by Kant are quoted, a reference is provided to the page number of the relevant English translation and also to the page number of the standard German edition which is to be found in the margin of the English translation. In the case of the *Critique of Pure Reason,* reference is made in the standard way to the first (A) and second (B) editions. References to Plato and Aristotle are given to the standard Stephanus and Bekker editions respectively, found in the margins of all good translations. Any deviation from the way of indicating references explained here should be readily comprehensible.

Where a modern version of an older or classical text is being referred to, the original publication date appears, where appropriate, in square brackets after the date of the modern edition where the book is listed in the bibliography.

PART 1
topics

theory of knowledge

Theory of Knowledge

Key topics in this chapter

- Coherentist theories of justification
- Definitions of knowledge
- Empiricism
- Foundationalist theories of justification
- Perception:
  a) common-sense realism
  b) representative realism
  c) idealism
  d) phenomenalism
- Rationalism
- Scepticism

Introduction

In a very famous sentence at the beginning of his work the *Metaphysics* Aristotle (384–322 BC) writes: 'All men desire by nature to know'. However, what they want to know and how they come to know it differ from person to person and from one time to another. Here are some examples.

- In Conan Doyle's Sherlock Holmes story 'A Case of Identity' a woman, Mary Sutherland, comes to see Holmes about her fiancé who has disappeared. She and Holmes have never met, but their very first conversation goes like this:

  'Do you not find,' he said, 'that with your short sight it is a little trying to do so much typewriting?'

  'I did at first,' she answered, 'but now I know where the letters are without looking.' Then, suddenly realising the full purport of her words, she gave a violent start, and looked up with fear and astonishment upon her broad, good-humoured face. 'You've heard about me, Mr. Holmes,' she cried, 'else how do you know all that?'

  'Never mind,' said Holmes, laughing, 'it is my business to know things.'

  (Conan Doyle 1980: 58)

In fact, Holmes had not heard of Mary Sutherland. Yet he knows that she is shortsighted and types a lot. But *how* does he know what he knows? Does

important terms

Internalism:

a) *in theories of reference:* the theory that what a person means when he says something depends on factors within that person's mind;

b) *in theories of knowledge:* the theory that whether or not a person's beliefs are justified depends on factors within that person's mind.

Necessity: a proposition is necessary if it could not be false – in other words, if it is true in all possible worlds.

Rationalism: the theory that, roughly speaking, reason is much more important than experience in grounding our knowledge.

Synthetic: a proposition is synthetic if its truth or falsity depends on factors besides the meanings of the terms involved, i.e., in which the predicate is not 'contained in' the subject.

he have a reliable method for knowing such things? Later in the story Holmes reveals to Watson how he knew what he knew: he inferred that Mary was a typist from the marks on her sleeves and that she was short-sighted from the marks on either side of her nose from a pince-nez.

- In Joseph Conrad's novel *Lord Jim*, Jim dreams of being a courageous and noble sailor. He longs to show these qualities in great and glorious deeds. However, whilst working as first mate on the *Patna*, a ship transporting 800 pilgrims, the vessel threatens to sink, and Jim jumps overboard, determined to save his own skin. The ship, however, does not sink, and Jim has to try to come to terms with his cowardly behaviour, for which he is put on trial. Jim's predicament is that he does not want to acknowledge being the kind of man he is, that is, a coward. Marlow, to whom Jim tells his story and who is the novel's narrator, says *a propos* of Jim: 'no man ever understands quite his own artful dodges to escape from the grim shadow of self-knowledge' (Conrad 1989: 102). But what kind of knowledge is self-knowledge? And what does it mean to say that one knows oneself? Further, is Conrad right to suggest that we are frightened of this kind of knowledge?

- In *Ecclesiastes*, one of the books of the Bible, we read: 'As thou knowest not what *is* the way of the spirit, *nor* how the bones *do grow* in the womb of her that is with child: even so thou knowest not the works of God who maketh all.' The kind of knowledge being invoked here clearly has some kind of connection with the love of God and a sense of the mystery of things. What kind of lack of knowledge is intended in this sentence? And would it make sense to think one could acquire it?

There are important differences between the kinds of knowledge in question in these three examples.

The Holmes example concerns our knowledge of the external physical world, including those parts of the physical world that are human bodies, and the way in which we interact with it.

The Conrad example has to do with morality or ethics in the broadest sense – it has to do with the kind of knowledge that is relevant to one's sense of leading a worthwhile or meaningful life.

The last example of knowledge involves the issue of religious knowledge. What is it to know God? And, if one thinks one knows God, how will this affect what *else* one knows?

Theory of knowledge also known as epistemology

All of these examples have to do with knowledge, so they can all be treated in the area of philosophy that is called the theory of knowledge. This area is also known as *epistemology* (from the Greek word *epistēmē*, meaning 'knowledge'). In this chapter, however, we shall take our starting point from the kinds of issues that are raised by the first example, that is, from issues concerning our knowledge of the external world. Problems of knowledge in morality and religious thought are discussed in the chapters on moral philosophy and philosophy of religion.

Everyday knowledge and ordinary doubt

If you say to me that you know something I might ask you *how* you know it. For example, if you look out of the window and say that there is a goldfinch in the garden I might ask you how you know that the bird you see is a goldfinch. You might give any number of reasons. For instance, you might say that you were brought up in a place where there were lots of goldfinches and so you learnt to recognise them when you were young or that you have since learnt to recognise them from looking at books of ornithology. In one way or another I shall be asking you to *justify* your knowledge that it is a goldfinch that you see. You have to give me your reasons for knowing that this is a goldfinch.

Everyday justification of knowledge claims

In this case, a claim to knowledge – 'I know that's a goldfinch' – is justified by your previous education. We could put this at least in part in terms of memory because it is the fact that you *remember* what you have learned that means that your previous education is relevant to your justifying your claim to knowledge. However, this claim is also justified by the fact that your eyes are working properly, that the daylight is good enough for you to see the bird, that you know the kind of bird to which the word 'goldfinch' refers, and so on. This kind of justification – roughly, sense-experience plus previous education – is common in everyday knowledge claims. But there are other ways in which, in everyday life, we seek to justify our claims to knowledge: 'I read it in my philosophy book', 'Langshaw told me', 'it says so in the Bible', and so on. All of these are ways in which we seek to *justify* our claims to knowledge.

Everyday mistakes in making knowledge claims

Sometimes, of course, we make mistakes. You look across the field and see a person coming towards you. The figure looks like your friend René and you say to your companion: 'Look, René's coming over'. However, as the figure gets nearer you see that it is not René after all, but Gottfried, who has been out for a walk with Benedict. In this case, your *senses have let you down*. You thought you knew, but you did not. This kind of thing can happen at any time.

However, although we know that from time to time our senses might let us down, we do not ordinarily think that we should distrust our senses altogether. I might wrongly think that Elisabeth is walking towards me, when it is in fact Philippa, as I see when she is nearer, but I can explain my error by noting that it was foggy, or I was tired or whatever. When it is not foggy and I am not tired I might know perfectly well who is walking towards me, and I do not think that, because my senses let me down once, then I should not trust them at all.

Ordinary scepticism

We can put this point this way. We can be *sceptical* about what our senses tell us on a given occasion for specific reasons (it was foggy, I was tired), but this kind of scepticism is *ordinary:* it applies to this *one* occasion on which I use my eyes, and not to all such occasions. Often, I have no reason to distrust my eyes at all.

Descartes' *Meditations*

The *First Meditation*

This last point is made by René Descartes early on in his *Meditations,* one of the most famous works of philosophy.

At the beginning of his *Meditations* Descartes tells us that he has been struck by the fact that as a child he accepted many things that turned out to be false. Moreover, much else of what he believes derives from his childhood, and thus he suspects that he has lots of false beliefs.

Descartes likens this situation to that of a building with rotten foundations. A building in such a state may look sound, but it has no stability and will eventually come crashing down. In the same way, says Descartes, his beliefs are built on rotten foundations. For this reason, he cannot be *certain* of any of his beliefs. He proposes to try to sort out his beliefs, getting rid of the false ones so that he is left with certainty.

Doubt of all that can be doubted

How can Descartes sort out his true beliefs from the false ones? It is no good trying to go through each and every one of his beliefs to see if it is correct, for that would take far too long. What alternative is there? In the case of the building with rotten foundations, clearly the only way to make it safe is to pull it down and rebuild it on secure foundations. This is what Descartes says he is going to do in the case of his beliefs. Hence he says that he will not examine his beliefs individually but, rather, the principles on which they rest.

In order to reach certainty, that is beliefs which cannot be open to the slightest doubt, Descartes says that he will 'hold back' his assent from *every belief that is even capable of being doubted* – in other words, every belief that is not 'completely certain and indubitable'. He will suspend his belief in any and every opinion that has the slightest chance of being false. In this way he hopes to discover those beliefs that *cannot* be doubted, that is, which are *indubitable.* Such beliefs, if he can find them, will constitute the kind of knowledge he is after. He proposes to do this by three successive waves of doubt. This is called Descartes' *method of doubt.*

Witholding of assent

Note that Descartes is not claiming that he will disbelieve everything that is even capable of being doubted. Consider a proposition such as 'God exists'. In this case, one can take up three attitudes to it: a) one can believe it; b) one can disbelieve it; c) one can neither believe it nor disbelieve it. Theists do a); atheists do b); and agnostics are those who do c), for agnostics are those who neither believe nor disbelieve the proposition 'God exists'. Descartes' position with respect to the propositions that are capable of being doubted is like that of the agnostic with respect to the proposition 'God exists': he will neither believe nor disbelieve, but withhold his assent (cf. Dicker 1993: 13–16).

Global scepticism

Because Descartes is going to withhold his assent from everything that *can* be doubted, his scepticism is not a form of *ordinary* scepticism. However, it is not just what one might call *local* scepticism, either. A local sceptic thinks that we lack knowledge about some specific area of human concern. For example, a local sceptic might say that we lack knowledge about God or about moral truths. Consistently with that, however, he could think that we have knowledge about, say, the external world – that is, tables and chairs and mountains and so on – or about mathematics. Descartes' scepticism is more radical than local scepticism: it is *global scepticism,* a scepticism about everything, for, as we have seen, it is a scepticism about the principles on which his knowledge rests.

The search for the indubitable

Before seeing how Descartes proposes to set about his task, we should pause for a moment and note something of interest (cf. Williams 1987: 45ff.). This is that, as we have seen, Descartes thinks of his search for knowledge as a search for the *indubitable.* Yet, very often, perhaps always, in everyday life we think of knowledge in a way that has little, if anything, to do with indubitability. There are often *practical* reasons why this is so. For example, if I want to drive across town I might check the petrol gauge to assure myself that I have enough petrol. If it indicates that the car has half a tank of petrol, then I know that I have enough petrol for my journey. However, if someone insisted that I did not know this because there is always the possibility of error and that I should take the car to the garage to get the petrol gauge and the electrical system of the car checked then I should dismiss this as absurd; to take the car to the garage would mean I should never make the journey across town. For everyday practical purposes we set a limit on how much time and energy we want to invest in any specific enquiry before we say that we know what we wanted to know. In the case of checking the petrol, most of us will invest very little time and energy (unless, say, we are making a trip across the Sahara). There will be different limits for different enquiries: some people might want more checks than others about any given enquiry (you might have a special fear of running out of petrol and so check the petrol gauge twice, for example). However, it seems clear that we do set such limits.

Similar considerations apply to the fact that we often rely on one another for knowledge. For example, if I wish to find out, say, the answer to some simple question in history which might be relevant to a philosophical view about which I am thinking, it will be rational for me to take the say-so of an historian who tells me what I want to know. In general, it would be impractical for me to spend much time checking out whether the historian really knows because, were I to do so, I should be inhibited from following up my philosophical reflections, which provided the reason in the first place for me wishing to find out the answer to my question. There is what one might call a 'division of labour' so far as knowledge is concerned in everyday life: it makes sense, for *practical* purposes, for us to rely on each other for providing us with knowledge.

The irrelevance of practical concerns to Descartes' project

In Descartes' case, such practical considerations are irrelevant to his search since he has devoted himself to the acquisition of knowledge wholly independently of all such concerns. This why he says at the beginning of the *First Meditation:*

> [T]oday I have expressly rid my mind of all worries and arranged for myself a clear stretch of free time. I am here quite alone, and at last I will devote myself sincerely and without reservation to the general demolition of my opinions.
>
> (CSM II: 12/17–8)

Descartes' situation is thus one freed of all practical concerns. And this is why his search for knowledge is the search for the indubitable: the practical considerations that normally make this absurd do not apply to him.

review
activity

1. Explain in your own words why it is that Descartes proposes to seek knowledge by withholding his assent from everything from which it is possible to do so.

2. What does it mean to say that Descartes withholds his assent in this way?

3. Why is Descartes' search for knowledge a search for the indubitable?

The first wave of doubt

Scepticism about the senses

Descartes begins his search for indubitable knowledge by reminding himself that a large part of what he has accepted as true has been so accepted on the basis of what his senses have revealed to him. It is on account of what he sees, feels, hears, tastes and smells that he believes a lot of what he believes. However, he then notes that his senses have often deceived him. Here, in the *First Meditation*, Descartes does not give an example of this. However, he does so in the *Sixth Meditation*.

> *Sometimes towers which had looked round from a distance appeared square from close up; and enormous statues standing on their pediments did not seem large when observed from the ground.* (CSM II: 53/76)

From reflecting on such cases Descartes is tempted to think that 'it is prudent never to trust completely those who have deceived us even once'. However, Descartes rejects this idea. As we have already seen, just because the senses deceive us occasionally, this is no reason to think that they always do or that we should never trust them. For example, they have only ever deceived him about small or distant objects. There surely can be no question of them deceiving him about the fact that he is sitting by the fire, wearing a dressing gown and holding a piece of paper in his hands. Similarly, your senses may have deceived you at times in the past – in the fog, or when you were not wearing your glasses, or when you were tired – but there surely can be no doubt that you now have a book in front of you that you are reading. Thus, the first wave of doubt is not very radical: reflection on the workings of the senses does not lead Descartes to doubt all that could be doubted. Hence, he turns to another line of reflection.

The second wave of doubt

Dreaming and doubt

Descartes next reflects upon the fact that he has often dreamed whilst asleep and that, in his dreams, he has often been convinced that he was sitting by the fire, dressed in a dressing gown, holding a piece of paper in his hand. But if this is so, how can he be sure that he is now awake and not asleep in bed, dreaming? Does not this possibility lead to the total doubt he is pursuing – to what he calls 'philosophical' doubt or 'hyperbolical' doubt? For, he says,

> *I see plainly that there are never any sure signs by means of which being awake can be distinguished from being asleep. The result is that I begin to feel dazed, and this very feeling only reinforces the notion that I may be asleep.* (CSM II: 13/19)

Some philosophers have argued that Descartes' reasoning concerning this second wave of doubt is mistaken.

Austin's reply to Descartes

One challenge to Descartes' view that it impossible to find any signs by which being awake can be distinguished from being asleep has been made by J.L. Austin.

He writes:

I may have the experience ... of dreaming that I am being presented to the Pope. Could it be seriously suggested that having this dream is 'qualitatively indistinguishable' from actually being presented to the Pope? Quite obviously not. After all, we have the phrase 'a dream-like quality'; some waking experiences are said to have this dream-like quality ... If dreams were not 'qualitatively' different from waking experiences, then every waking experience would be like a dream.   (Austin 1964: 48–9)

In other words, Austin is claiming, it is just not true that we cannot distinguish dreaming from waking states.

Curley's reply to Austin

Austin's view has been challenged by E.M. Curley (Curley 1978: 60ff.). Curley notes that, if Austin's claim is to work against the dreaming hypothesis, it will have to be the case that *all* dreams are distinguishable from waking experience. However, if this is not the case, then this will leave it open for Descartes to say that one cannot distinguish at least *some* dreams from waking experience. That will be enough for Descartes' argument at this stage.

So, is it the case that some dreams cannot be distinguished from waking experience? Curley says that probably some people have such dreams and others do not. Perhaps, he suggests, Descartes was one of the former and Austin one of the latter. In any case, Curley goes on to argue that it may be that we all have such dreams but that some of us forget them, or tend to forget them or their true vividness when we wake, whereas others remember them. The evidence for this is provided by psychological experiments that show that dreaming occurs in conjunction with a physiological state known as the REM state. It seems that those who usually or always say that they do not have dreams or do not have very vivid dreams report that they dream very vividly when woken during REM sleep. This suggests, says Curley, that it may be that we *all* have *very vivid* dreams. The difference lies in that some of us forget them whereas others do not. If this is so, says Curley, Descartes may well be right and Austin wrong about distinguishing dreaming from waking states.

Williams's comments on dreaming

There is, however, another objection to Descartes' line of reasoning, which is related to Austin's point. Recall that Descartes believes there to be a complete *symmetry* between dream-filled sleep and waking life: in both we have experiences, and in both we take those experiences to be veridical. But Bernard Williams has argued that it is a mistake to see a symmetry here. There is, in fact, he argues (Williams 1987: 313) an *asymmetry* between dream-filled sleep and wakefulness, namely, that 'from the perspective of waking we can *explain* dreaming ... Such features are part of our way of telling, when we are awake, that we are awake'. What Williams means is, for example, that we can, during our waking life, investigate sleep and dreaming, try to understand why we dream (what function it fulfils, if any), compare the dreams of different people, and so on. This makes sleep and dreaming something quite different from waking life. It is true, as Williams says, that whilst we are dreaming we cannot do anything to establish that we are dreaming by using our knowledge gained in waking life about the nature of dreaming but, he says, this does not matter, for this 'is a consequence of things we understand when we are awake, about dreaming'.

Descartes' rejection of the dreaming hypothesis

Whether Descartes would have been worried about the objections that Austin and Williams raise to his project is a moot point, for Descartes himself goes on to reject the dreaming hypothesis as inadequate to lead to the hyperbolical doubt he is pursuing. He does so for two reasons. The first is that he likens dreams to paintings. The things painters represent, even if they are wholly imaginary, nevertheless are modelled on features of real life, for example, 'corporeal nature in general, and its extension; the shape of extended things' (CSM II: 14/20) and so on. In other words, the images of dreams, just like the images of painters, are as they are because they are modelled after really existing things, for example, the shape of objects, and this means that those things – namely, shape – must really exist. So the doubt is not sufficiently radical enough.

Descartes' second reason why the dream hypothesis is not radical enough is that even when he is dreaming there can, he says, be no doubt about the truths of arithmetic or geometry. 'For whether I am awake or asleep, two and three added together are five, and a square has no more than four sides' (CSM II: 14/20).

Can one make judgements whilst asleep?

There are at least two reasons why Descartes' comments here might be open to criticism. First, it is unclear why when dreaming one could not dream that, for example, $2 + 3 = 6$ (cf. Kenny 1968: 32ff). Second, Norman Malcolm has argued that it makes no sense to think that one can judge *anything* whilst asleep, and thus, *a fortiori*, one cannot judge such things as that $2 + 3 = 5$ when one is asleep (Malcolm 1977b: ch.9).

However, according to John Cottingham, research shows that it is, after all, possible to make judgements whilst dreaming. This is possible, according to Cottingham, if one experiences so-called 'lucid dreams', although not everyone does (Cottingham 1986: 32f).

In any case, Descartes, as we have seen, rejects the second wave of doubt for it does not, he believes, allow him to doubt all that can be doubted, and he goes on to consider a third.

The third wave of doubt

A deceiving God

This final wave of doubt is the most radical. Here Descartes imagines that a deceiving God, who is omnipotent (all powerful) and can thus do anything, has brought it about that 'there is no earth, no sky, no extended thing, no shape, no size, no place' whilst all the time ensuring that it seems that there are such things. Indeed, this deceiving God might be leading Descartes to make mistakes even in matters of mathematics, such as getting it wrong every time he adds two and three or counts the sides of a square (CSM II: 14/21).

The malicious demon

To make the hypothesis of the deceiving God more vivid – although not changing it in any substantive way – Descartes then imagines this God to be a malicious demon. This demon, like the deceiving God, is systematically leading him astray. He writes:

> *I shall think that the sky, the air, the earth, colours, shapes, sounds and all external things are merely the delusions of dreams which he [the malicious demon] has devised to ensnare my judgement. I shall consider myself as not having hands or eyes, or flesh, or blood or senses, but as falsely believing that I have all these things.* (CSM II: 15/22–3)

The brain in a vat

A modern version of this is the so-called 'brain in a vat'. Imagine that you are not reading this book but are actually a brain in a vat. Into this brain is being fed a huge amount of information by an evil scientist, information such as the idea that you are reading this book. In other words, everything you experience is not really happening to you: you only think it is, whereas really you are no more than a brain in a vat, connected to a mass of wires through which are being passed electrical pulses that lead you to believe that you really are having certain experiences. The evil scientist, it seems, could make you believe *anything* by passing the relevant electrical pulses into your brain. But is that right? Is there, after all, something over which he has no control, something with respect to which he could not trick you?

Before we move on, we should look very briefly at the question of just how radical Descartes' doubt is. After all, there seem to be many things that he does not doubt. These include his very capacity to reason and the basic structure of thought itself. In fact, Descartes was ready to grant that such things could not be called into doubt, for if they were then the mind would be totally emptied and thinking would have to be abandoned altogether.

review activity

1. What is Descartes' first wave of doubt and why does he reject it as not being radical enough?

2. What is Descartes' second wave of doubt and what two reasons does he give for thinking it not radical enough?

3. Explain in your own words the dispute between Austin and Curley. If Curley is right, why does this support Descartes?

4. What is Williams's criticism of the 'dream hypothesis'?

The *Second Meditation*

In his struggle to find some kind of foothold, some belief that cannot be doubted, Descartes' doubt is brought to a halt at last by the following recognition: even if the malicious demon is deceiving Descartes in every possible way, the demon cannot deceive Descartes into believing that he does not exist. This is because Descartes must exist in order to be deceived. If Descartes did not exist, then the demon could not deceive him. In Descartes' own words:

The Cogito

> *[T]here is a deceiver of supreme power and cunning who is deliberately and constantly deceiving me. In that case I too undoubtedly exist, if he is deceiving me; and let him deceive me as much as he can, he will never bring it about that*

I am nothing so long as I think that I am something. So after considering everything very thoroughly, I must finally conclude that this proposition I am, I exist, is necessarily true whenever it is put forward by me or conceived in my mind.
(CSM II: 17/25)

So the indubitable piece of knowledge at which Descartes arrives is that he exists just so long as he is thinking.

Notice that Descartes does not use in the *Second Meditation* the famous form of words 'I think, therefore I am', in the Latin, *cogito ergo sum* – known itself as 'the Cogito'. Rather, he uses this form of words in Part Four of his work *Discourse on the Method* and in Part One, Section 10 of his work *Principles of Philosophy*. In fact, the formulation used in the *Second Meditation* seems preferable to the others for the following reason. The Cogito has the form of an *inference* of *sum* ('I am', 'I exist') from *cogito* ('I think' or 'I am thinking') – hence Descartes' use of *ergo* ('therefore'). We can set this out this way:

Premise 1: I am thinking
Conclusion: I exist

If this argument is to be valid, however, we need a second premise to complete the argument, thus:

Premise 1: I am thinking
Premise 2: Everything that is thinking, exists
Conclusion: I exist

However, Descartes himself says in the *Second Set of Replies* that Premise 2 is not something to which he is entitled at this point of the *Meditations*. The reason he gives for this is that Premise 2 is a *general* proposition and that it is 'in the nature of our mind to construct general propositions on the basis of our knowledge of particular ones' (CSM II: 100/141). And Descartes does not yet know anything in general about the world in his *Meditations*: he only knows about his own condition.

The denial that the Cogito is an inference

In fact, Descartes does at times deny that the Cogito is an inference, and thus the formulation of the *Second Meditation* – I am, I exist, is necessarily true whenever it is put forward by me or conceived in my mind – makes this clear. What Descartes means is that if a person says to himself 'I am thinking, therefore I exist' then he grasps his own existence not as the conclusion of the kind of argument we have just looked at but as something *self-evident*, as he makes clear when he says: 'When someone says "I am thinking, therefore I am, or I exist", he does not deduce existence from thought by means of a syllogism, but recognises it as something self-evident by a simple intuition of the mind' (CSM II: 100/140; cf. CSM II: 271/205).

Is the Cogito an inference after all?

The problem in this is that at other times Descartes seems to grant that there is, after all, some kind of inference going on in the Cogito. For example, he writes in the *Principles*:

And when I said that the proposition I am thinking, therefore I exist is the first and most certain of all to occur to anyone who philosophises in an orderly way, I did not in saying that deny that one must first know what thought, existence and certainty are, and that it is impossible that that which thinks should not exist, and so forth. But because these are very simple notions, and ones which on their own provide us with no knowledge of anything that exists, I did not think they needed to be listed. (CSM I: 196/8)

Here it is clear that Descartes is claiming that, for the Cogito to work, the thinker has to have the general proposition 'what is thinking, exists' as a premise. This would mean that the Cogito was an inference after all. It seems, then, that Descartes wants to say that the Cogito both is and is not an inference. How are we to make sense of this?

One possibility is to say that, although the Cogito relies on the premise in question, this premise need not be explicitly grasped by the meditator in the Cogito. Rather, the conclusion of the Cogito is grasped in a single intuitive act, but later, when we reflect on how the Cogito works, we see that it implicitly contained the premise in question.

One way or another, Descartes knows he exists, but he does not yet know what he is. He asks himself what it was he used to think he was, that is, before he embarked on his doubt. Well, he says that he used to think that he had a body that could be perceived by the senses; but now, still imagining that the malicious demon is deceiving him, he cannot know that he has a body, or that he is seeing the real world with his senses, for he would only have senses were he to have a body. So what is he? Eventually, Descartes alights on thought itself. He is, he concludes, a *thing that thinks*.

'What am I? A thinking thing.'

At last I have discovered it – thought; this alone is inseparable from me. I am, I exist – that is certain. But for how long? For as long as I am thinking. For it could be that were I totally to cease from thinking, I should totally cease to exist. (CSM II: 18/27)

Descartes, then, says that he is a thinking thing and that he exists just so long as he is thinking. Does this mean that he does not exist when he stops thinking? In fact, it seems that Descartes would accept this conclusion. So Descartes insists that the human mind never stops thinking. He makes this point in the *Fourth Set of Replies* when talking of the mind of an infant in the womb: 'I do not doubt that the mind begins to think as soon as it is implanted in the body of an infant, and that it is immediately aware of its thoughts, even though it does not remember this afterwards' (CSM II: 171-2/246).

Descartes' explorations into his own nature are not yet at an end, however. For he has yet to enquire what it is to be a thinking thing. What, he asks, is a thing that thinks? Descartes believes that quite a lot goes to make up a thinking thing. He includes here doubting, understanding, affirming, denying, willing, imagining and the having of sensory perceptions.

Substances, essences and modes

This is quite a long list of rather different mental events, and what Descartes is getting at can, perhaps, best be seen by noting that he is relying on a distinction between the notions of *substance*, the *essence (principal attribute) of a substance* and the *modes of a substance*. Although Descartes' use of these terms is not always completely clear, we can give the following basic account of them. A *substance* is, for Descartes, something that is capable of existing independently or on its own (except for the sustaining power of God). Mind is such a substance. It is non-material and its *essence* or principal attribute is thinking. The *modes* are the various ways of thinking, such as those Descartes mentions – doubting, affirming, denying and so on. These are modes of thinking because, although the mind must always be thinking (that is its essence), it can be thinking in now one way and now another.

The wax Descartes goes on from here to compare our knowledge of the mind to that of material objects. In order to do this he considers a particular material object, a piece of wax. He does so because he thinks that most people would suppose that they understand very well what a piece of wax is simply by looking at it. What could be clearer to the understanding than grasping the nature of this piece of wax, which still has some taste of honey and scent of flowers; which has a colour, shape and size that all can see; which is hard and cold and can be handled with no difficulty; and which makes a sound if struck with the finger? But, says Descartes, things are not so simple. For if you bring this piece of wax close to the fire it loses its taste and scent; changes colour, shape and size, even melting if it gets warm enough; and no longer emits a sound when struck. Clearly the same piece of wax remains, but it is changed profoundly. So two questions arise: What, really, is the wax? And, how do you know the wax?

Descartes' answer to the first question is that the wax is a material substance that can change in various ways. I shall say a little more on the notion of material substance below and in the chapter in Part II devoted to Descartes' *Meditations*.

The wax is known by the intellect Descartes' answer to the second question is that it cannot be through the senses that one knows the wax, for what is presented to the senses changes radically from one moment to the next in the way we have seen. He therefore says that the wax must be known by the *intellect*. What does this mean?

Part of what Descartes is saying is that because what is presented to the senses – the wax – is at one time hard, of a certain colour and so on, and a little later soft, of a different colour and so forth, the senses have a *confused* or *unclear* conception of what the wax is. The intellect, however, has a clearer understanding of what it is. This clearer understanding is one that leaves out those properties of the wax that confuse the senses and lead them to have an unclear perception of the wax. Those are, of course, the properties of being a certain colour, hard and so on. So what remains if these are left out? Descartes says that the intellect has a conception of the wax as 'extended, flexible and changeable'. Our true knowledge of the nature of the wax is of it as something that is extended – it occupies space – and is flexible and changeable – for example, it can take on different shapes or sizes. But this is not something that we learn from the senses. We learn this only from the intellect. And this is why Descartes says that the wax 'is perceived by the mind alone' (CSM II: 21/31). He does not mean that the eyes play no role in sensory perception. He means that the purely sensory element in perception cannot constitute our perception of the *nature* of the wax. A judging mind is needed for that, along with eyes.

Descartes gives a second example of the need for a judging mind in perception. It is that of the men whom he sees from his window. What he actually sees on a cold day when people walk around outside tightly muffled up in clothing are coats and hats. Why does he say that he sees men and not hats and coats walking about? It is because he *judges* that what he sees are men. To recognise something as what it is therefore, requires mental judgement beyond experiencing through the senses.

Descartes thinks that what he has argued for the wax and the men also goes for all material objects: we know them better through the intellect – through 'the mind alone' – than through the senses. (Note that Descartes denies that animals are capable of the kind of judgement in question (CSM II: 22/32). Thus, no animal could perceive the nature of the wax, for animals lack the intellect to do this.)

At least two points of interest arise from Descartes' discussion of the perception of material objects. I shall mention them briefly here – they are dealt with at greater length in the chapter on Descartes in Part II of this book.

The material world and geometry

First, because, according to Descartes, material objects are only properly understood by the intellect and this shows them to be extended and nothing more – it shows that they have no properties other than to occupy space – Descartes arrives at the conclusion that matter 'can be characterised in strictly geometrical terms, and hence our reasoning concerning it can enjoy the simplicity, precision and certainty of a geometrical demonstration' (Cottingham 1986: 83).

Descartes' claim that there is only one material substance

Secondly, a related point is that because Descartes holds to the idea that material objects are extended and nothing more, he can say that fundamentally the material universe consists of just *one* single, indefinitely modifiable extended thing. So he ends up claiming that there are just two substances – mind and matter – the *essence* or principal attribute of the former being thought, that of the latter being extension. Further as the *modes* of thought are doubting, willing and so on, so the modes of matter are size, shape, position and local motion.

The human mind better known than material objects

One of the conclusions Descartes draws from his consideration of the piece of wax is that the nature of the human mind is better known than is that of material objects. The reason he gives for this is somewhat obscure. He says that 'every consideration whatsoever which contributes to my perception of the wax, or of any other body, cannot but establish even more effectively the nature of my own mind' (CSM II: 22/33). What does Descartes mean?

In the *Fifth Set of Replies* Descartes says, when discussing the wax:

> [W]e can distinguish many different attributes in the wax: one, that it is white; two, that it is hard; three, that it can be melted; and so on. And there are correspondingly many attributes in the mind: one, that it has the power of knowing the whiteness of the wax; two, that it has the power of knowing its hardness; three, that it has the power of knowing that it can lose its hardness (i.e. melt) and so on … The clear inference from this is that we know more attributes in the case of our mind than we do in the case of anything else. For no matter how many attributes we recognise in any given thing, we can always list a corresponding number of attributes in the mind which it has in virtue of knowing the attributes of the thing; and hence the nature of the mind is the one we know best of all.
> (CSM II: 249/360)

What Descartes seems to mean is that mind is better known than body 'in so far as any judgement I make about the nature of a body provides grounds for recognising one or more facts about me (my mind) – e.g., that I make the judgement, and consequently have the "power" to make it, or to recognise the facts contained in the judgement' (Wilson 1986: 96). In other words, the mind is better understood than body because, in judging a material body (for example, judging that it is hard or cold and so forth), I recognise the powers my mind has and thus learn about the mind in making that judgement about the body.

What is odd about this, as Margaret Dauler Wilson has pointed out (Wilson 1986: 96f.), is that Descartes has already argued that we cannot know the nature of the wax simply by listing its properties or attributes (hardness, coldness and so forth). Yet he seems to suggest that we can know the nature of the mind by listing *its* properties or attributes (in the case Descartes discusses, its powers).

review activity

1. What reason does Descartes give both for denying and for affirming that the Cogito is an inference?

2. What, according to Descartes, does reflection on the wax show about a) the wax itself and b) the human mind?

3. Why is there a puzzle concerning Descartes' belief that reflection on the wax can tell us about the human mind?

Scepticism

Descartes' arguments have decisively shaped mainstream philosophy. In the light of his work, philosophers have returned repeatedly to discuss the issue of scepticism about the external world.

The philosophical problem of scepticism

The problem of scepticism about the external world can be put this way. The evidence we have about the existence of the external world falls short of what is needed for knowledge. It is consistent with that evidence that we are in error. This is what Descartes' device of the malicious demon or its modern version of the brain in the vat is intended to suggest. Even though I seem to have the very best evidence I could have for thinking that I am sitting here writing a book – that is, that there is a computer in front of me, that my fingers touch keys on a keyboard, that I can see books on my desk, that I am in the familiar surroundings of my study and so on – do I really *know* I am writing a book? Am I *certain* I am? All the evidence I have for believing that I am sitting here writing a book is consistent with my being in error: a malicious demon might be deceiving me or I might be a brain in a vat. According to scepticism I do not know I am sitting here writing a book. The sceptic is the person who challenges us to see if we can find conclusive reasons for believing that we do know such things after all.

The philosophical problem about scepticism is thus: What, if anything, can we say to the sceptic to show that he is wrong?

review
activity

Explain in your own words the philosophical problem of scepticism.

Response 1: Moore

Moore's defence of common sense

G.E. Moore is famous for arguing that the sceptic is mistaken because he denies the common sense view of the world.

Moore argues that there are certain propositions that he knows to be true of himself. For example, he says that he knows that

> [t]here exists at present a living human body, which is my body. This body was born at a certain time in the past, and has existed continuously ever since ... Ever since it was born, it has been either in contact with or not far from the surface of the earth ... Among the things which have ... formed part of its environment ... there have ... been large numbers of other living human bodies.
>
> (Moore 1959: 33)

Moore goes on to say that each of us can assert of ourselves the propositions he asserts of himself; that each of us knows those propositions to be true in our own case; and that he knows them to be true of each of us. Moore then says that some philosophers have denied that some of these propositions are true and others have denied that we *know* these things to be true.

Against those philosophers who have denied that these things are true, he says that if this denial were true then there have never been any philosophers at all. For philosophers are, of course, whatever else they are, living human bodies; so if the propositions in question are not true, then there have never been any philosophers. Further, Moore argues that those philosophers who have claimed that the kinds of propositions in question are false have been unable to conceal the fact that really they knew them to be true. For example, he says that they allude to the existence of other philosophers in their work. We might put Moore's point this way as a rhetorical question: if a philosopher writes a book arguing that the propositions in question are false, for whom is he writing the book?

G.E. Moore was brought up primarily in London and in 1892 won a scholarship to Trinity College Cambridge to read classics. He remained at Cambridge after he graduated, and in 1898 was elected a fellow at Trinity. Accordingly, he spent most of his life teaching at the University of Cambridge, although he had strong links with the group of writers and artists known as the 'Bloomsbury Group', so called because they often met together in rooms at Bloomsbury in London. He contributed mainly to ethics and epistemology. He was famous for adopting a 'common sense' approach to problems in philosophy, and was, along with Bertrand Russell, one of the key founders of the style of philosophy – known as 'analytic philosophy' – which was pursued throughout the English-speaking world in the twentieth-century and is still the dominant force in philosophy in the UK, the US and Australia.

G.E. Moore (1873–1958)

Moore offers a different argument against those who deny that we know the kinds of propositions he is discussing are true. He says that if a philosopher denies that we have such knowledge then he must be asserting that there are many other people besides himself who have believed what he says that no one knows, that is, that there are living human bodies and so on. But if that is the case, then, says Moore, such a philosopher is contradicting himself, because he is asserting that there are other people whilst denying that we know there are.

One way we could put Moore's response to the sceptic is to say that, in Moore's opinion, the sceptic cannot take his own scepticism seriously. It is merely an intellectual position in which it is impossible really to believe.

However, Moore's most famous argument against scepticism is to be found in his paper 'Proof of an External World' (Moore 1959: ch.VII). Moore holds up first one hand and says 'Here is one hand', then another and says 'Here is another'. These are the premises of his argument. He says he knows them to be true. Then he concludes that 'Two human hands exist at this moment'. He says, therefore, that he knows that two material objects exist.

Why should one not accept this argument? According to Moore, the sceptic will wish to reject the argument because he, the sceptic, will say that Moore has not proven his two premises. Moore grants this. In fact, he says that he has no idea how he might *prove* that he knows he has two hands. If the sceptic wants such a proof, Moore says, then scepticism cannot be answered. But this does not alter the fact, he says, that he knows he has two hands and that his argument can therefore stand.

Response 2: Wittgenstein

Wittgenstein and the emptiness of scepticism

Ludwig Wittgenstein was deeply interested in Moore's argument concerning his two hands, and he discussed it and scepticism more generally in his book *On Certainty*. However, he thought something was wrong with Moore's

Ludwig Wittgenstein
(1889–1951)

Ludwig Wittgenstein is considered by many to be the greatest philosopher of the twentieth century. He was born in Vienna in 1889 and in 1908 went to Manchester to carry out research in aeronautics. There he became interested in the mathematics behind aeronautics, and then in the philosophical foundations of mathematics, an interest that led him to contact Bertrand Russell, who was, along with G.E. Moore, one of the leading philosophers of the day. He published little during his lifetime, one exception being the *Tractatus Logico-Philosophicus*, which came out in 1921 and is still regarded as a classic work. A restless and in some ways tormented man who possessed a deep integrity, Wittgenstein usually found academic life shallow, and he worked during the 1920s as, amongst other things, a schoolteacher and a gardener. He returned to philosophical work towards the end of the 1920s, and eventually became Professor of Philosophy at the University of Cambridge, something which he described as 'a living death'. His late work, the central text of which is the *Philosophical Investigations*, published one year after his death in 1952, differs in many ways from the work of the *Tractatus* and has been extremely influential in contemporary philosophy. He also exerted great influence as a teacher of philosophy, some of his pupils going on themselves to make significant contributions to the discipline.

argument. Nonetheless, he did not think that this simply left scepticism triumphant.

Central to Wittgenstein's reflections on this topic is the idea that words have a place and a sense only in certain contexts. For example, suppose a person has had an accident and he is lying in hospital, his hands all bandaged up. He is unconscious. He then comes round and, seeing all the bandages, fears that he has lost his hands. He then checks and sees that he still has his hands. He might say to himself, 'I know I have two hands' – for example, as an expression of relief. According to Wittgenstein, in this context, to say one has hands makes sense. It makes sense because there can be *real doubt about whether one has got hands.* Outside of such a context, however, just to say 'I know I have two hands' makes no sense. It no more makes sense than it makes sense to say, in the middle of a conversation with a friend, 'I have known all the time that you are so-and-so' or 'good morning'. It is not the case that just anything, said at any time, makes sense. According to Wittgenstein, when Moore asserted that he had two hands there was no context in which what he said made sense. There was no room to doubt whether he had hands in the first place.

However, Wittgenstein does not think that this means that the sceptic wins the argument. For he thinks that, although there can, of course, be situations in which it makes sense to say: 'I have no hands', the philosophical context of discussions of scepticism is not one of them – no more than it is an appropriate context for saying 'I have two hands'. In fact, that human beings have hands is, according to Wittgenstein, one of a number of empirical facts which we do not *learn* as children but which we simply accept as part of a whole way of looking at the world. Other examples Wittgenstein gives include: 'There is a brain inside my skull' and 'Motor-cars do not grow out of the earth'. Someone who seriously doubts such things, says Wittgenstein, is not, as one might suppose, being especially rigorous, but has lost a proper sense of what can and cannot be doubted. Similarly, someone who seriously doubts that an old friend to whom he has been speaking for the last half an hour really is his friend has lost all grip on what it is to doubt and what it would be to settle doubt. 'Here doubt would seem to drag everything with it and plunge it into chaos', writes Wittgenstein in *On Certainty* (Wittgenstein 1969: § 613). And again, if I were to say in all seriousness that I am *not completely sure* that my name is C.H. then I would probably have started to lose grip on my sanity – certainly I would have also to doubt that I know what 'true' and 'false' mean, and there would be nothing I could rely on to settle that doubt.

If this line of reflection is correct, then it gives us a reason for suggesting that if we think we can doubt such propositions as 'Motor-cars do not grow out of the earth' when doing philosophy, then this shows that, when we are doing such philosophy, we have lost a sense of serious thought and reflection. We reflect within a system that we simply accept and *have* to accept if doubt, knowledge, certainty and so forth are to make sense at all. Outside of that system is not more rigorous reflection but no reflection at all.

Hence, according to Wittgenstein, the existence of the external world – of material objects – is one of the fundamental conditions of existence that it makes no sense to doubt, as it makes no sense to doubt whether one has a brain in one's skull. Material objects form, as Wittgenstein says, the scaffolding of our world, and we should not even be able to think about the world without them. Scepticism, then, according to Wittgenstein, is neither true nor false, but, as we have seen, lacking a proper sense of what counts as doubt, knowledge, enquiry and the like. In this sense, scepticism is not false but *empty*. This may be why, as Moore and others have remarked, no one who has called himself a sceptic on philosophical grounds has ever been able consistently to live out his scepticism.

I return briefly to these reflections from Wittgenstein below.

review activity

1. Explain in your own words Moore's response to scepticism.
2. In what way did Wittgenstein take issue with Moore's answer to scepticism?

Response 3: Putnam

Earth and Twin Earth

Suppose that there is a planet that is just like Earth except in one respect. On that other earth – called Twin Earth – there is stuff that looks like water, tastes like water, behaves like water (boils at 100° C, can be drunk, is used to make tea, when heated provides hot, relaxing baths and so on) but that has a chemical composition unlike water here on earth. Here on Earth water is H_2O whereas on Twin Earth the stuff that is otherwise like water has the chemical composition XYZ. The water on Twin Earth we can call 'twater' to distinguish it from water (though the Twin Earthers just call it 'water').

Suppose now that Marcel lives on Earth. Suppose also that there is a Twin Marcel who lives on Twin Earth. They are molecule-for-molecule identical. However, when Marcel uses the word 'water' what he refers to is H_2O, whereas when Twin Marcel uses the word 'water' (the one *we* translate as 'twater') he is referring to XYZ. Apart from that, there are no differences between the cases. So Marcel and Twin Marcel mean different things, despite the fact that they both use the word 'water'. And they mean something different even if neither of them has any idea what the chemical composition of water is (whether it be H_2O or XYZ). This is because their physical environments are different.

'Meanings aren't in the head.'

What does this thought experiment show? According to its inventor, Hilary Putnam (Putnam 1975: ch.12), it shows that what one means in saying something cannot be understood in terms of what is before one's mind when one says it. The environment alters what one means. Putnam sums this up by saying: 'meanings aren't in the head'.

This view is called *externalism*, because it claims that the meaning of what one says depends on the external environment.

Putnam uses his thought experiment as an argument against scepticism. He puts things in terms of the sceptical hypothesis of brains in a vat (Putnam, 1981). His argument runs as follows. Let us suppose that you are a brain in a vat. In that case, although you think you are sitting reading a philosophy book, in fact you are just a brain in a vat being tricked into thinking that you are reading a philosophy book. Put briefly, Putnam then argues as follows. If it is true that meanings are not in the head, then when you refer to books, or tables and chairs or to any other material objects, you are *not*, in fact, referring to books and tables and chairs. This is because what you are really referring to are your images of books, tables and chairs, that is, the images that are being fed to you as your brain sits in its vat. Of course, you *think* you are referring to real books, tables and chairs: that is part of the sceptical hypothesis. However, you are not *really* so referring, because there are no books and tables and chairs in your world for you to be referring to. *Really* to refer to such things requires that you *actually* come into contact with them in the kind of way that we normally take ourselves to come into contact with them, that is, in a situation that is *not* subject to the sceptical hypothesis. Meanings, remember, are not in the head, so a person who has contact with books, tables and so forth is referring to something different from that to which someone is referring who does not have this contact but only *thinks* he does (because he is a brain in a vat).

Now imagine that a brain in a vat says to itself: 'I am a brain in a vat'. To what do the words of such a brain refer? Just as the thoughts that a brain in a vat has about books, tables and chairs cannot be about real books, tables and chairs, so thoughts it has about vats cannot actually be about real vats. If it says: 'I am a brain in a vat', it is *not* referring to real vats. Rather, it is talking about its image of a vat, that is, the image of a vat that is being fed into it as it sits in its vat. However, this means that the proposition: 'I am a brain in a vat' said by a brain in a vat is false. So, generalising, if we were brains in a vat, then, were we to say: 'We are brains in a vat' this would be false. So the proposition: 'We are brains is a vat' is false. So it is false that we are brains in a vat. Thus, we are not brains in a vat. Therefore, scepticism is false.

It should be noted that Putnam's argument moves from the assumption that one is a brain in a vat to the conclusion that this actually makes no sense at all. This form of argument is a *reductio ad absurdum* (a 'reduction to absurdity'). In this case, the argument works by taking as a premise (assumption) some proposition *p* (in this case, 'I am a brain in a vat') and showing that this premise together with other previously established premises (here, most crucially, the premise that 'meanings aren't in the head') leads to the negation of *p*, that is, 'not *p*' (–*p*). Thus, *p* is reduced to absurdity.

review

activity

1. What does Putnam mean by saying that 'meanings aren't in the head'?

2. Explain in your own words why it is that Putnam thinks that, because meanings are not in the head, scepticism can be refuted.

Of course, one might dispute Putnam's claim that meanings are not in the head, in which case his argument might fail. In general, whether any of the arguments against scepticism is successful is, of course, a matter of great debate amongst philosophers. However, at this point we shall leave scepticism to look at some other issues in epistemology.

Rationalism

We have seen that Descartes believed that material objects are known better by the intellect than by the senses. This is one expression of the fact that Descartes is one of a number of philosophers who are known as *rationalists*. Other important rationalists in the history of philosophy include Spinoza and Leibniz.

The term 'rationalist', as well as its opposite 'empiricist', can be understood in a variety of related ways but, roughly speaking, what rationalists believe is that reason is of much greater importance than sense experience (seeing, hearing and so on) in grounding our knowledge, whereas empiricists believe that it is fundamentally experience that is the source of knowledge.

Innate ideas Given this way of describing rationalism, we can see why it is that Descartes' discussion of the wax and his claim that it, along with the rest of the material world, can best be understood in geometrical terms, is an expression of his rationalism. However, Descartes' rationalism also finds expression in other ways. Central to these is his belief in *innate* ideas. Descartes' account of innate ideas is not always clear but, roughly, what he meant by innate ideas was ideas that are present in the mind from the beginning of its existence. For Descartes, one such idea is that of God. But, according to Descartes, there are other innate ideas. He includes here, for example, the truths of geometry and mathematics. There are, he says, certain further propositions that he says are self-evident, that is, which we simply have to consider in order to see them to be true. These, too, are innate. For the baby in the womb

> *has in itself the ideas of God, itself, and all truths which are said to be self-evident; it has these ideas no less than adults have them when they are not paying attention to them, and it does not acquire them afterwards when it grows up.*
>
> (Quoted in Kenny 1968: 102)

Baruch (Benedictus)
Spinoza (1632–77)

Spinoza was one of the leading rationalist philosophers of his day. He was Dutch, being born in Amsterdam, where there was a large Jewish community, and dying at The Hague. His ancestors were Portuguese crypto-Jews, that is, Jews who had been forced by the Inquisition outwardly to profess Christianity, but who remained, in fact, faithful to their own religion. He was a Hebrew scholar and, by profession, a lens maker. As a young man, he was deeply impressed by the scientific advances that were proceeding apace all over Europe, and this led him to clash with the Jewish community in which he lived, principally because he felt it impossible to reconcile the Bible with those new advances. At the age of 24 he was excommunicated. He became the leading member of a small group of enlightened Christians with whom he discussed philosophy and theology, although he led a basically secluded life and generally avoided publicity, largely because he felt that he could only pursue his thinking if free of official commitments, which might not allow him to express himself freely. This is why, in 1673, he turned down the offer of the Chair of Philosophy at the University of Heidelberg. He longed always to be utterly independent. He died at the age of 44: he was consumptive from an early age, and his condition was probably aggravated by the glass dust from his lenses. His work remained largely ignored until the end of the eighteenth century.

Such self-evident propositions include: 'The same thing cannot both be and not be at the same time'; 'What is done cannot be undone'; 'If equals are added to equals, the result is equal'; and 'Every event has a cause'.

We shall discuss Descartes' own notion of innate ideas in more detail in the chapter in this book on his work, but it is worth now referring to one or two other thinkers who believed in the existence of innate ideas.

Plato and innate ideas

One of the most important philosophers who have believed in innate ideas is Plato (c. 428–348 BC). In his dialogue *Meno* there is a famous episode involving a slave boy. Such a boy would have had no education, but Socrates, the dialogue's central character, asks the boy a series of questions about the relative proportions of the sides of a square, using a diagram drawn on the ground to help him. He correctly answers the questions put to him, and Socrates claims that, precisely because the boy had no education, the only proper explanation of what is going on is that he has innate knowledge of the answers to the questions, knowledge that Socrates draws out of him through his questioning.

Chomsky, language and innate ideas

A modern argument for innate knowledge occurs in the work of the linguist and philosopher Noam Chomsky. One thing that is extremely puzzling is language acquisition. A child very rarely has explicit language teaching, and yet by the age of about four is able to speak his native language to an extremely high level, correctly formulating sentences he has never heard, using the correct word order, correctly conjugating verbs, using the passive voice as it should be used, and so on. This is remarkable by any standards, especially when it is remembered that the child will have been exposed to feedback from the world that is sometimes contradictory, fragmentary and variable from speaker to speaker. Chomsky argues that the child must possess an innate knowledge of language structures (a universal grammar) that can explain the rapidity of correct language acquisition. Thus the claim is that the child's knowledge of a universal grammar, which all languages share at the deep level, is activated on exposure to any natural language, and this explains how it is that infants can learn their native tongue so efficiently.

Gottfried Wilhelm Leibniz (1646–1716)

Leibniz, like Descartes and Spinoza, is considered to be one of the greatest of the rationalist philosophers. Moreover, like Descartes, he was a brilliant mathematician. He was born in Leipzig and studied philosophy, mathematics and law at the Universities of Leipzig and Altdorf. He was about as far from embodying the clichéd image of the secluded philosopher as one could imagine. On the contrary, he was actively engaged in politics and had long associations with some of the most significant men of power of his time, such as the Elector of Mainz, who employed him as a lawyer and diplomat. It was in this latter capacity that he was sent to Paris in 1672 as part of a diplomatic mission to Louis XIV. In Paris he came into contact with many of the leading French intellectuals and 'natural philosophers' (scientists): Leibniz was always as interested in natural science as he was in philosophy, and at various times of his life he worked on a number of mechanical devices (such as hydraulic presses, clocks and water pumps), and on a calculating machine. In 1673 he travelled to England where he was elected a member of the Royal Society. From around 1677 he lived in Hanover, to which city he had been called by the Duke of Brunswick who employed him as his librarian. The later part of his life was spent in some obscurity, something that did not suit his active, power-loving temperament, and he died miserable and unsatisfied.

A priori and *a posteriori* knowledge; the analytic and the synthetic; the necessary and the contingent

A priori *knowledge*

Consider again the proposition 'every event has a cause'. For a rationalist philosopher such as Descartes (although not for empiricists, as we shall see below) we can know this proposition to be true without considering evidence from experience. We can express this by saying that, for the rationalist, we can know this proposition *a priori*: it is not justified on the basis of experience. Other propositions often thought to be *a priori* include the truths of mathematics. For example, you do not have to investigate the world to establish whether 7 + 5 = 12, although you do, of course, have to learn some basic arithmetic. The truths of logic are also usually thought to be knowable *a priori*. Examples include the law of identity: 'A is A', for example, 'This book is this book'. One does not need to look at the world to establish that.

Note that, to say that some proposition is *a priori*, is not to say that one does not have to *acquire* the relevant concepts – for example, mathematical concepts – in order to know the proposition. As I have already noted, one cannot know that 7 + 5 = 12 unless one has learned some mathematics. The point is rather that, once one has the needed concepts, it is one's grasp of their relations, and not the experience that was needed in order to acquire them, that is the basis of one's knowledge of the proposition.

A posteriori *knowledge*

The opposite of *a priori* knowledge is *a posteriori* knowledge. For example, if the front door of your house is green then you know *a posteriori* that it is green, for you need to go and look at it to find this out. You cannot just inspect the proposition: 'My front door is green' to see that it is true (or false, as the case may be).

Analytic propositions

There is another group of truths, which are known as *analytic* truths. These are propositions that are true in virtue of the meanings of the terms. For example, 'all bachelors are unmarried men' is usually given as an example of an analytic truth because a bachelor is an unmarried man and therefore the proposition is true in virtue of the meanings of 'bachelor' and 'unmarried man'. Another example is 'all material bodies are extended', which is true in virtue of the meanings of 'material body' and 'extended'. The idea is that if you understand the meanings of the terms you will see that these propositions are true.

Synthetic propositions

A *synthetic* proposition is defined as being any proposition which is not analytic. An example is 'all crows are black'. In a synthetic proposition the predicate ('black') is not 'contained' in the subject ('crows'). Another way to put this is to say that a synthetic proposition is one in which the predicate 'goes beyond' what is mentioned in the subject.

Necessity

Finally, we should note that some propositions are normally taken to be *necessary*. That is, they *must* be true. Another way of putting this is to say that they are true in all possible worlds: there is no world where they would be false. The truths of mathematics are usually thought of as being necessary truths, and others include: 'nothing can be red all over and green all over at the same time' and 'two material objects cannot be in the same place at the same time'.

Contingency

The opposite of necessary truths are *contingent* truths. For example, it is a contingent truth that you are reading this book for, although it is true that you are reading this book, you might not have been. You might have been doing something else instead. Or again, it is a contingent truth that Mahler died before finishing his Tenth Symphony – he might have lived to complete it.

What is the relation between the various classifications of propositions mentioned here? On the traditional account analytic truths are knowable *a priori*. Thus, 'all bachelors are unmarried' is analytic and knowable *a priori*. However, this proposition tells us nothing about the world. We do not learn from it which men are bachelors and which are not, for example.

Further, according to the traditional picture all necessary truths are knowable *a priori* and all *a priori* truths are necessary. It is not difficult to see why necessity and the *a priori* are often thought to be so related. After all, 7 + 5 = 12, an *a priori* truth, surely could not be false anywhere: in every possible world it is true, which means it *must* be true.

Synthetic a priori *propositions*

If all *a priori* truths were analytic then all claims to *a priori* knowledge would either be trivially true – true in virtue of the meanings of the terms the propositions contain – or false. However, there are some propositions that some philosophers have thought were synthetic *a priori* propositions. The truths of arithmetic and geometry have been thought to be synthetic *a priori*. For example, it has been argued that $7+5=12$ is knowable *a priori* yet the concept of 12 is not 'contained in' the concepts of 7 + 5. Or, as Immanuel Kant (1724–1804) put it:

> [T]he concept of the sum of 7 and 5 contains nothing save the union of two numbers into one, and in this no thought is being taken as to what that single number may be which combines both. The concept of 12 is by no means already thought in merely thinking this union of 7 and 5.
>
> (Kant 1985: 52–3 [B15])

Synthetic *a priori* truths, unlike analytic *a priori* truths, are not trivially true, or true in virtue of the meaning of the terms that the relevant propositions contain. On the contrary, they give us genuine information, and yet we know them without having to investigate the world to see if they are true.

However, not all philosophers agree with Kant in saying that 7 + 5 = 12 is a synthetic truth. For example, A.J. Ayer disagreed with him, as we shall see below.

Kripke on the contingent a priori *and the necessary* a posteriori

Since the work of Saul Kripke, there has been a great deal of new debate concerning the relations between the *a priori*, the *a posteriori*, necessity and contingency. This is because Kripke argued that there are contingent *a priori* propositions and necessary *a posteriori* propositions.

Kripke argues that there are contingent *a priori* propositions as follows (Kripke 1984: 54ff.). Suppose someone sets up the metric system of measurement. He takes a stick, S, and he says that S at that time, t_0, is 1 m long. How did he know that it was 1 metre long? He knew it *a priori*, because he did not have to investigate the world to find out that S was 1 metre long: after all, he is setting up the metric system. He could have chosen any stick he liked.

However, even though the person in question knows *a priori* that S is 1 metre long at t_0, it is not necessary that S is 1 metre long. Rather, it is contingent. This is because S might have been longer or shorter at t_0 than it in fact was. For example, if heat had been applied to S at t_0 then S would have been longer. So, it is a *contingent* matter that S was one metre long at t_0. If Kripke is right, then, there can be contingent *a priori* truths.

Kripke's argument that there are necessary *a posteriori* truths is easier (Kripke 1984: 116ff.). Consider the fact that we now know that gold has the atomic number 79 (assuming that we *do* know this – that our physics and chemistry are correct on this score). Kripke argues that it is a *necessary* truth that this is so: anything that did not have this atomic number would not be gold, and anything with that atomic number is gold, even if turns out not to look much like gold as we now think of it (for example, if it turned out that some substance had the atomic number 79 but was blue it would still be gold). Gold, in other words, could not turn out not to have the atomic number 79. However, we had to find out through experience (experiments and the like) that gold has the atomic number 79, and therefore this is an *a posteriori* truth.

Empiricism

We noted earlier that some philosophers are rationalists. Such philosophers are often contrasted with empiricists, amongst whom the greatest are John Locke, George Berkeley (1685–1753) and David Hume (1711–76).

In their view, as I mentioned earlier, it is sense-experience that is fundamentally the basis of our knowledge. Thus Locke wrote in *An Essay Concerning Human Understanding*:

Locke on the source of ideas

> *Let us then suppose the Mind to be, as we say, white Paper, void of all Characters, without any Ideas; How comes it to be furnished? Whence comes it by that vast store, which the busy and boundless Fancy of Man has painted on it, with an almost endless variety? Whence has it all the materials of Reason*

John Locke (1632–1704)

John Locke was born in a Somerset village in 1632 and died at Oates in Essex in 1704. He was educated at Westminster School and at Oxford University where he studied philosophy and medicine. His knowledge of the latter led to an acquaintance with Lord Ashley, who was, from 1672, the Earl of Shaftesbury. Indeed, Locke became a member of Shaftesbury's household and in 1668 Shaftesbury underwent a major operation on his liver, which was supervised by Locke. The operation was, against all odds, a success and it confirmed Locke's position in the household. For the next 14 years Shaftesbury remained Locke's patron, and Locke assisted him in all manner of domestic and political matters. Shaftesbury was deeply involved in the political life of the times, and he was at different stages the most powerful political figure in Charles II's court and the leader of a national political opposition to that court, which threatened a revolution to overthrow it. Locke was probably not involved in Shaftesbury's schemes, but he felt it prudent to flee to Holland in August 1683, returning to England in 1689. His major works include the *Essay Concerning Human Understanding* and the *Two Treatises of Government*.

and Knowledge? To this I answer, in one word, from Experience: *In that, all our Knowledge is founded; and from that it ultimately derives it self.*

(Locke, 1984, II, i, 2)

Locke's denial of innate ideas

Because he believed that all knowledge comes from experience, Locke argued against the idea that there were innate ideas, such as that of God, or of principles such as 'it is impossible for the same thing to be and not to be' or 'whatsoever is, is'. He argued against such ideas by claiming that children, idiots and many adults do not know such truths as are alleged to be innate, which makes it absurd to think they are, in fact, innate. If it is replied that when children grow up and can reason they come to accept the kinds of principles in question and that this shows they are innate, Locke replies that all this really shows is that they can discover these truths by reasoning, not that they are innate. Further, he argues that there is nothing like universal assent on which principles are supposed to be innate, but that if they were innate we should not expect such disagreement. As far as God is concerned, he says that there are and have been whole nations ignorant of God, which would hardly be explicable if the idea of God were innate. Locke thus concludes that it is from experience that we acquire the kinds of ideas in question, and this is, as I have said, central to the empiricist outlook.

Hume, as I noted, was also an empiricist, and he is often thought to have taken to its limit the idea that we derive knowledge from experience. We can see this very well in his discussion of the concept of causality.

Hume and causality

When modern philosophers discuss causation what they have in mind is usually the relation between different events and how it is that we should understand one event causing another. For example, one event (E1) is the throwing of a brick towards a window and this *causes* another event (E2), namely, the shattering of the glass. Or E1 might be the lighting of a match and E2 the exploding of the gas – in this case, the lighting of the match *causes* the exploding of the gas. And so on for other examples. Usually, when one event causes another, we think that the second event *had* to take place, that it was *determined* to take place. Another way to put this is to say that, given that E1 took place, E2 was *necessitated*. That is, it was necessary that E2 took place. For example, if you throw a brick against the window then the window must break, the breaking of the window is necessary.

In his *A Treatise of Human Nature* (1739–40) and *Enquiries Concerning Human Understanding and the Principles of Morals* (1748–51) Hume discussed causal relations from a strongly empiricist perspective. His question was this: given that we get all our knowledge from experience, where do we get the idea that one event *necessitates* another event? Suppose you throw the brick at the window. What you see is the brick hitting the window and the window breaking. So how should we describe what you have seen? According to Hume you have seen two things: 1) one event's happening before another event, that is, the brick's hitting the window before (just before) the window breaks; Hume calls this *priority*; 2) two objects (the brick and the window) touching each other; this Hume calls their *contiguity*. But this cannot be all that the causal relation consists in, because we have so far left out the fact that the brick hitting the window means that the window *must* break. We have left out the *necessitation* in the relation, or what Hume calls the *necessary connection*. And the difficulty, says Hume, is that we do not see this at all, but we nevertheless have the thought that a necessary connection must be part of the causal relation.

Where, then, could we get the idea of necessary connection if we do not see it? Consider again the brick breaking the window. Suppose, for example, that I see you holding a brick, just about to throw it through the window. What is it that makes me believe that, when you throw the brick at the window, the window will shatter? Hume's answer is that in the past I have often seen bricks breaking windows or, more generally, hard, heavy material bodies shattering frangible bodies. That is, he says that I have seen such events *constantly conjoined*. That is to say, *whenever* I have seen a hard, heavy body impact on a frangible body I have seen the latter break. Hence, when I see you with a brick in the hand about to throw it at the window I expect this *constant conjunction* (hard, heavy bodies breaking frangible bodies) to hold once again, and expect therefore that the glass will shatter. This is why Hume says that if you had never seen a hard, heavy body shatter a frangible body then you would not have this expectation. It is only from the experience of constant conjunction that we get expectations about how bodies in the world will behave.

Hume thus argues that constant conjunction is part of our concept of causation. However, constant conjunction is not the same as necessary connection. It is this latter notion which Hume is trying to understand. What he says is that because we have seen certain events constantly conjoined, for example, hard, heavy bodies breaking frangible bodies, the mind forms the *habit* of expecting frangible bodies to shatter when struck by hard, heavy bodies. So, when I see a hard, heavy body about to strike a frangible body my mind expects the frangible body to shatter. In other words, and speaking more generally: we have the past experience of the regularity of nature – of constant conjunctions. So we become *habituated* to expecting this regularity (these constant conjunctions) to continue. Hume says that it is in '[t]his connexion ... which we *feel* in the mind, this customary transition of the imagination from one object to its usual attendant' that we find 'the sentiment or impression from which we form the idea of power or necessary connexion' (Hume 1985: 75).

However, this might not seem to solve the problem. After all, Hume was looking for a necessary connection between *events in the world*, and he has ended up by telling us of a habit of the mind. If the mind has seen events of type A always followed by events of type B, and it now sees an event of type A, then it expects an event of type B because it has acquired a certain habit. Where is the necessary connection between the events in the world, that is, events of type A and events of type B?

What Hume says about this is that the habit of the mind is so strong and firmly ingrained in us that we project the strength of the association between constantly conjoined events onto the events themselves, and so succumb to the illusion that 'necessary connection' is the name of a relation in which they actually stand to one another. In other words, the mind, so to speak, spreads itself on the external world and attributes to the world a specific character that it fails, in fact, to have.

For our purposes, here, the most important feature of Hume's account of causation is that it is an attempt to explain our understanding of causal relations strictly within *empiricist* terms, that is, strictly within terms of the idea that *we derive our knowledge from experience alone.*

Empiricism and the truths of mathematics

What kind of approach to *a priori* knowledge might an empiricist take – for example, to the truths of mathematics? One possibility, suggested by A.J. Ayer, is the following (Ayer 1990: ch.4). The empiricist could grant that we do have genuine *a priori* knowledge in mathematics, but insist, against Kant, that mathematical propositions, such as $7 + 5 = 12$, are analytic and provide us with no knowledge about the world. They are, says Ayer, tautologies.

Another more radical possibility is suggested by J.S. Mill (1806–73). Mill argued that the truths of mathematics (and logic) are not necessary. He suggested, rather, that we should understand mathematics to be modelled on science. The idea here would be that we should think of the propositions of mathematics as supported by an extremely large number of confirming instances. That is, he thought that we come by, and justify, our knowledge of mathematics by, for example, counting things up again and again and having them confirmed over and over. On this account, the world *could* go haywire in such a way that it turns out that $7 + 5 = 11$, however unlikely this might be.

There is a number of objections to Mill's view. Ayer himself criticised Mill by arguing that if, for example, I were to count what I had taken to be five pairs of objects and found them to be only nine, then I would not say that $2 \times 5 \neq 10$, but that 'I was wrong in supposing that there were five pairs of objects to start with, or that one of the objects had been taken away while I was counting, or that two of them had coalesced, or that I had counted wrongly' (Ayer 1990: 69). Further, if it turned out that whenever I counted five pairs of objects I found nine objects, one might nevertheless argue that it was still true that $2 \times 5 = 10$ but that the world no longer exemplified this truth (cf. Audi 1998: 107).

review
activity

Explain in your own words Hume's account of causation. Why is this view of causation an empiricist account?

Classical foundationalism

Very often in everyday life we justify certain beliefs that we hold by appeal to other beliefs. For example, if I wish to justify my belief that the toast is burning I might do so on the basis of my belief that smoke is pouring out from under the grill. Or again, to justify my belief that I have just become a millionaire I might do so by appealing to a number of other beliefs, such as that the lottery numbers printed in the newspaper are the numbers drawn in this week's lottery and that they match the ones on my ticket.

In each of these cases one belief is more basic than another. The belief that smoke is coming out from under the grill is more basic than the belief that the toast is burning, because the latter belief rests upon the former. Or again, my belief that the newspaper is correctly reporting the numbers drawn in this week's lottery is more basic than the belief that I have just become a millionaire because the latter rests upon the former.

The fact that beliefs can stand to one another in this kind of justificatory relationship raises an interesting question: Are there any beliefs that are the most fundamental beliefs, the ones on which all other beliefs rest in some way? In other words: are there are any beliefs that form the foundations for all other beliefs?

The regress argument

According to *foundationalism* there are such beliefs. In fact, according to foundationalism there *must* be such beliefs. The reason why foundationalists think that there must be foundational or basic beliefs is found in what is called the *regress argument*.

The regress argument, schematically put, goes like this. Consider some belief that *p* (for instance, that I have just become a millionaire). Given that the belief that *p* rests on, amongst others, the belief that *q* (that the newspaper is correctly reporting the numbers drawn in this week's lottery) then what does the belief that *q* rest on? Presumably, it rests on some other belief *r* – for instance, that, in general, this is a reliable newspaper. It seems, then, that every belief is justified by some other belief, which is more basic than the first.

The problem of an infinite regress

However, if this is the case, there seems to be no final stopping place: each belief one has will be justified by some other belief. If there is no stopping place, then we shall be confronted by a regress of beliefs that goes on forever, that is, an *infinite regress*. And if we are faced by such a regress, it seems that we cannot, in the end, provide a convincing justification for *any* of our beliefs. No matter how far down the chain of belief we go, we shall never come to stopping point, a point from which we may see that our other beliefs are justified. In other words, we shall lack *foundations* for our beliefs.

So the foundationalists say that there *must* be some kind of foundations for our beliefs if we are to be justified at all in what we believe. This means, there must be some beliefs that are not justified by any other beliefs.

Inferential and non-inferential justification

We could put the foundationalist position this way. According to foundationalism, there are two ways of justifying beliefs. Some beliefs are those beliefs that are justified by other beliefs. These beliefs are *inferentially justified* because they are *inferred* from other beliefs. For example, my belief that if I turn this switch the light will go on is inferred from other beliefs. These other beliefs are likely to be beliefs about what happened when I turned this switch in the past, about the supply of electricity to the house, the state of the light bulb and so on. Of course, this is not to say that beliefs such as that the light will go on are consciously inferred, but the inference is implicit in my action. However, there are some beliefs that are *non-inferentially* justified. These beliefs stand on their own feet, so to speak, and do not need support from any other beliefs. These beliefs form the foundations for other beliefs.

Clearly, the key question for the foundationalist is going to be: which beliefs form the foundations?

Foundationalism and classical empiricism

One form of foundationalism is found in Descartes' *Meditations*, as we have seen. However, the most influential foundationalist response comes from classical empiricism, according to which foundational beliefs are those a person has about his own present perceptual appearances, plus analytic beliefs. Let us concentrate on the former.

Consider the case where I see a tomato in front of me. Now, I could be mistaken that this is indeed a tomato. Perhaps it is, in fact, a cunning hologram, projected before me and not a tomato at all. Or perhaps it is actually a photograph of a tomato that I mistake for a real tomato. Or maybe it is a novelty candle someone gave me as a present and not a tomato at all. However, although I could make all these mistakes, according to classical foundationalism what I cannot make a mistake about is what the thing in front of me (whatever it is) *looks* like. H.H. Price makes these points clearly:

The empiricist view of present sensory states

> When I see a tomato there is much that I can doubt. I can doubt whether it is a tomato that I am seeing, and not a cleverly painted piece of wax. I can doubt whether there is any material thing there at all. Perhaps what I took for a tomato was really a reflection; perhaps I am even the victim of some hallucination. One thing however I cannot doubt: that there exists a red patch of a round and somewhat bulgy shape standing out from a background of other colour-patches, and having a certain visual depth, and this whole field of colour is directly present to my consciousness. (Price 1965: 110)

Infallibility

So, for classical foundationalists it is our beliefs about our present sensory states that need no justification by other beliefs and that form the foundations for those other beliefs. The reason it is supposed that beliefs about our present sensory states are foundational is that they are usually taken to be *infallible*. They are *indefeasible*. That is, it is thought by foundationalists, as Price suggests, that *one cannot be mistaken about how things seem to one*. Thus you can be mistaken that what you see before you is a tomato, but you cannot be mistaken that things *seem* to you to be a particular way, that is, you cannot be mistaken that it seems to you that there is before you a red colour patch, bulgy and round, and so on.

Sense-data

When the foundationalist focuses on what we are confronted with in present sensory experience, he is focusing on what is called 'the given'. The given is just that which we directly and immediately meet in sensory experience – for example, a red, round colour patch. It is a datum of sense. Hence it is called a *sense-datum*. (Throughout the history of philosophy, philosophers have been attracted to the notion of sense-data, but have sometimes used a different terminology, speaking of 'percepts', 'sensa' 'sensibilia' 'ideas' or 'impressions'. Sometimes the difference of terminology has been used to mark a difference of theory which need not concern us.) We are said, when we perceive the world, to be aware in the first instance of sense-data – red round patches, and so on.

Classical foundationalism gives expression to the empiricist idea that (almost) all our knowledge is derived from experience. It does this by saying that any beliefs not about our present sensory states ultimately rest on beliefs about those states.

review
activity

1.   Explain in your own words the regress argument.

2.   Why have foundationalists typically claimed that it is the immediate objects of one's sense experience that provide foundations for knowledge?

Assessing classical foundationalism

Those who accept foundationalism, we have seen, claim that one has infallible knowledge about one's present sensory states: one cannot be mistaken in one's beliefs about those states. However, they often concede – as A.J. Ayer, who defended a version of foundationalism conceded (Ayer 1965: ch.5; Ayer 1990: 177–8) – that one can make a mistake in one's *description* of one's experience. For example, I might be having a certain sensory experience and not be sure how to describe it: I hesitate between 'magenta' and 'scarlet', for example. I might then describe what I can see as 'magenta' and find that this is a mistaken description by, for example, checking a colour atlas. However, I cannot be wrong in how things *seem* to me. In that sense, my belief is infallible.

Austin's criticisms of foundationalism

J.L. Austin has taken issue with Ayer's line of reflection here (Austin 1964: 113ff). He puts his criticism in terms of whether a given statement one utters, for example, 'That is magenta', when a colour is before one, could be incorrigible. 'Incorrigible' means 'cannot be corrected', and Austin is clearly using it to mean the same as what we have called 'infallible'. He argues that there could be any number of reasons why I might misdescribe something as 'magenta' in such a way as to show that *I actually made a mistake about which colour it was I was seeing*, and *not simply in the words I was using*. For example, I might say '*magenta ... because I was unable to, or perhaps just didn't, really notice or attend to or properly size up the colour before me ... Thus I may be brought to see, or perhaps remember, that the colour before me just wasn't magenta*'. Austin therefore says that there is nothing incorrigible about my statement, for I may see reasons to retract it, having made it. Of course, he grants that there will be plenty of cases where I will not have any reason to retract the statement and in that sense it would be fair to say that they are incorrigible. But he says this is also the case with statements that refer to material objects.

> [I]f I watch for some time an animal a few feet in front of me, in good light, if I prod it perhaps, sniff, and take note of the noises it makes, I may say, 'That's a pig'; and this too will be 'incorrigible', nothing could be produced that would show I had made a mistake.
>
> (Austin 1964: 114)

In other words, there is nothing, as such, incorrigible about statements that refer to sense-data, and there is nothing, as such, especially corrigible about statements that refer to material bodies.

Sellars and the 'myth of the given'

In a difficult but important work Wilfrid Sellars (Sellars 2000: ch.VIII) has also taken issue with foundationalism, challenging the view that statements about one's present sensory states are infallible, even in the case where one correctly describes one's experience. Sellars's argument is roughly as follows.

If I am to be able to describe things in my environment as 'green', 'red' or whatever, then I need to have learned to utter the proposition 'this is green' in standard conditions before objects which are green – for example, in good daylight, before normal healthy grass. This is what learning to use such propositions involves. If I am a competent user of language, that is, I have learnt to use language properly, then my use of 'this is green' has *authority*. For instance, if I am such a user, and you ask me what the colour of some object is, then if I say 'it's green' you can believe me: that is what it is for there to be authority in my use of the colour predicate 'green'. But if there is to be authority in my use of propositions such as 'this is green' then I myself have to know that there is authority in my use of them. However, for me to know this I have to know that uttering 'this is green' is the correct proposition to use when confronted in standard conditions by objects that are green. In other words, when confronted here and now by a green object, I can only know that it is *now* right to say 'this is green' because I know *the general* truth that in the presence of green objects the right thing to utter is 'this is green'.

What this comes to is the idea that knowledge of *particular* matters of fact, for example, that this object is green, depends upon *general* knowledge.

How does one come by that general knowledge? The answer is by being *taught* to utter such propositions as 'this is green' in front of green objects. Gradually one acquires the relevant kind of authority. When one is first learning one does not have that authority, and when, at that stage (say, as an infant), one is confronted by green objects, one does not yet have knowledge that these are green objects. Later, one will be able to say that, as an infant or child, one observed green objects but that this observation did not constitute knowledge.

If Sellars is right then the foundationalist view is mistaken. For that view, as we noted earlier, goes hand-in-hand with the empiricist idea that our knowledge about the world is built up from sensory experience that 'stands on its own feet'. Sellars thinks that it is a myth that there is such a form of sensory experience, which is why he calls the view in question the 'Myth of the Given'. Sellars goes on to say that his argument

> *would be anathema to traditional empiricists for the obvious reason that by making observational knowledge* presuppose *knowledge of general facts … it runs counter to the idea that we come to know general facts … only* after *we have come to know by observation a number of particular facts.*

(Sellars 2000: 76)

review
activity

1. On what grounds does Austin claim that one could be mistaken about the immediate objects of one's present sense experience?

2. What does Sellars mean by saying that observational knowledge presupposes knowledge of general facts?

Coherentism

Some philosophers, convinced that foundationalism must be rejected, have sought to formulate a different conception of the way in which our beliefs can be justified. This is called the 'coherence theory' of justification or simply 'coherentism'.

There is, it should be noted, a distinction between a coherence theory of *justification* and a coherence theory of *truth*, and many theorists talk in terms of truth rather than justification. There are, however, connections between truth and justification, for if we take it that our beliefs are justified, then, presumably, we have good reason to think them true.

The basic idea behind coherentism is that we justify beliefs not by trying to find some about which there can be no doubt at all but by fitting our beliefs together into a set. A simple example will help to make this clearer.

Coherentism: a simple example

Suppose an envelope arrives at my house. I open it and find nothing inside. I form the hypothesis that the only person I know absent-minded enough to forget to put the letter in the envelope is my Aunt Dotty. Aunt Dotty lives in Exeter, so I look at the postmark. However, I see that the letter has come from Edinburgh and I know that Aunt Dotty rarely goes to Scotland. Furthermore, I know Aunt Dotty's handwriting, and this on the envelope is not hers. So my hypothesis that the letter is from her does not cohere with the other things I believe. Then I remember that my brother was going to take Aunt Dotty to the Edinburgh Festival this summer. In addition, I know my brother's handwriting, and the handwriting on the envelope looks like his. So I form the hypothesis that Aunt Dotty wanted to send me a letter from Edinburgh, forgot to put it in the envelope, and got my brother to address it for her. Now I have a coherent set of beliefs and am justified in believing that the envelope came from Aunt Dotty after all.

Holism

This example illustrates the basic idea behind coherentism. The theory is *holistic*. This means that we assess our beliefs as a *whole* group or set, seeing how well they fit together.

Of course, in the example given, we considered only a very few of the beliefs I have. In practice, coherentists will say that, if we want our beliefs to give us a proper understanding of the real world, then the set of our beliefs should be as complete or *comprehensive* as possible. So coherence involves completeness (as far as possible). However, it also involves *consistency*; the beliefs in the set need to be consistent with one another, for there cannot be contradictory beliefs in the same set.

Assessing coherentism

It is important to see that, according to the traditional view of coherentism, what is justified by coherence is each belief in a set of beliefs. It is not the set itself but the beliefs in the set that are justified. However, this leaves the theory exposed to a common objection. It might be said that we could have a number of different sets, each of which is internally coherent – in each of which, therefore, the beliefs are justified. For example, science fiction films and books create coherent worlds, which are often very far from being accounts of the true world. This, so the objection continues, means that coherence cannot provide an adequate account of the justification of beliefs because there can surely only be *one* complete set of justified beliefs about the world, not more than one. So coherentism seems not to provide an adequate account of the way in which beliefs are justified.

Bradley on coherentism

Coherentists usually reject this objection to their view by insisting that there can, after all, only be one coherent set. The reason they give for this is articulated by one coherentist, F.H. Bradley.

Bradley writes:

> My object is to have a world as comprehensive and coherent as possible, and, in order to attain this object, I have not only to reflect but perpetually to have recourse to the materials of sense. I must go to this source both to verify the matter which is old and also to increase it by what is new. And in this way I must depend upon the judgements of perception. (Bradley 1914: 210)

In interpreting Bradley's thought here, Richard Wollheim (Wollheim 1969: 172f.) has written that Bradley intended that coherence should be a test of the justification, not of *any* belief, but of 'those that we have some initial inclination or motive to believe in', so that coherence has the 'function ... to discriminate within those judgements [beliefs] and to eliminate some in favour of others'. A somewhat similar notion has been offered by Jonathan Dancy (Dancy 1984: 364) in a defence of coherentism in which he says that 'in general, if we find ourselves scrutinising something we believe, we retain it unless we find something against it, just on the grounds that it is a belief already'. So the coherentist can, perhaps, reply to the charge that his theory allows for multiple coherent sets of belief that this is not so, as coherence is intended to be a test of the beliefs that we already have (and, of course, of those which we can add to those we already believe).

One interesting feature of Bradley's coherentism is his claim that 'there are no judgements of sense which are in principle infallible' and that 'no judgement of perception [is] more than probable' (Bradley 1914: 202; 211). He makes these claims for the obvious reason that coherentism rejects foundationalism's aspiration to locate infallible beliefs. However, the two claims are not equivalent. It is

F.H. Bradley (1846–1924)

Bradley was born in Clapham in 1846 and was educated at Marlborough and University College, Oxford. His younger brother was A.C. Bradley, the literary scholar and critic, probably best known now for his work on Shakespearean tragedy. In 1870 he was awarded a Fellowship at Merton College, Oxford. He lived there for the rest of his life, although he travelled a great deal, generally spending the winter on the English coast or on the Riviera. In 1871 he suffered a severe inflammation of the kidneys and this left him a sick man for the rest of his life. Indeed, largely on account of his ill health, he was virtually a recluse. He was politically of deeply conservative temperament, and detested liberal beliefs in the equality of human beings and humanitarianism, which he regarded as sentimental. He never married, although he had a close relationship with Mrs Radcliffe, an American living in Paris: she was pretty and vivacious, and claimed never to have read a book in her life. Bradley died of blood poisoning in 1924 and is buried in Holywell Cemetery, Oxford.

possible to agree with the former whilst disagreeing with the latter. And there does, after all, surely seem to be something odd in the thought that it is only *probable* that my computer is in front of me, or that it is only *probable* that you have a book in front of you.

Davidson on coherentism

Donald Davidson, another defender of coherentism, has also responded to the criticism that for the coherentist there could be multiple coherent sets (Davidson 1989). Davidson starts by considering the case of the radical interpreter. Imagine someone, a speaker of English, who is the first to come across a group of people who speak a language, L, which no one outside that group of people knows. How will our speaker of English, the radical interpreter, ever come to understand L? Davidson argues that the interpreter will have to operate with what is called the *principle of charity*. That is, he will have to assume that the beliefs of the speakers of L are, by and large, true. This will, of course, mean *true by the standards of the interpreter*. The interpreter has to assume that he and the speakers of L share roughly the same standards of truth, for otherwise there would not be enough common ground for the interpreter to see where it is that he and the speakers of L do, in fact, disagree.

However, even if the interpreter must assume that he and the speakers of L share more-or-less the same standards of truth, perhaps they are both completely wrong. What guarantee does the interpreter have that his standards, which he extends to the speakers of L, are not mistaken?

Davidson's answer is to imagine an Omniscient Interpreter of our interpreter. If this Omniscient Interpreter is to interpret our interpreter then he will have to extend to him the same standards of truth that the interpreter extended to the speakers of L. That is, the Omniscient Interpreter will have to assume that he and the interpreter share roughly the same standards of truth, just as the interpreter had to assume that he and the speakers of L share roughly the same standards of truth. However, because this Omniscient Interpreter knows everything and everything he knows is true, it follows that *his* standards of truth *could not* be mistaken. It follows, therefore, that the standards of truth of the interpreter and the speakers of L cannot be wholly mistaken.

review activity

1. Explain the key features of coherentism in your own words.

2. How does a coherentist such as Bradley respond to the charge that his theory allows for multiple coherent and consistent sets of beliefs?

3. What does Davidson mean by 'the principle of charity'?

4. How does the principle of charity help establish the claim that there cannot be multiple coherent and consistent sets of beliefs?

If this argument of Davidson's is correct, then it follows that the interpreter must suppose that most of his basic beliefs are justified. He must also think that the body of beliefs of the speakers of L is also justified. There is thus no room here for the thought that there could be more than one coherent set of beliefs – although there can, of course, be room to think that *particular* beliefs need to be investigated to see whether they are justified. So the coherentist can, according to Davidson, rebut the charge against him.

Non-classical (moderate) foundationalism

Wittgenstein as a foundationalist

Before moving on, we should note briefly that there are forms of foundationalism that are more moderate than the classical, empiricist form we discussed earlier. One such form of foundationalism is arguably found in the later work of Wittgenstein, already mentioned above. A key idea behind this foundationalism is that there are certain propositions that need no justification but which justify other propositions. We have already seen examples of such propositions, for example, 'motor-cars do not grow out of the earth' and 'there is a brain in my skull'. Others include 'my hands do not disappear when I look away from them' and 'the earth has existed for more than one hundred years'. In one sense, of course, we believe such things. But in another sense it is rather misleading to say that these are *beliefs* we have: this is because it never occurs to us either to believe these propositions or to disbelieve them. Rather, they are just part of the worldview that we inherit and with which we grow up. They form the foundations of our beliefs and of what Wittgenstein called our form of life.

Searle's account of the 'Background'

Wittgenstein's ideas have been developed by J.R. Searle (see, for example, Searle 1990: ch.5; 1999: ch.8). Searle discusses the idea of what he calls 'the Background'. Roughly speaking, the Background, according to Searle, is a set of capacities and abilities without which one could not do the complex things one does, such as going to the refrigerator and getting a bottle of beer. The Background is a kind of 'know-how'. For example, to open the refrigerator door I have to see the door but I also have to recognise the door when I see it. This ability to recognise the door when I see it is part of the Background.

Searle distinguishes between the 'deep Background' and the 'local Background': the former 'would include at least all of those Background capacities that are common to all normal human beings in virtue of their biological makeup – capacities such as walking, eating, grasping, perceiving, recognising, and … [taking] account of the solidity of things, and the independent existence of objects and other people'. The latter would include such things as 'opening doors, drinking beer from bottles, and the … stance we take toward such things as cars, refrigerators, money and cocktail parties' (Searle 1990: 143–4).

Searle suggests that it is best to study the Background in cases of breakdown. He gives the example of a philosopher who was visiting his university, attending some seminars on the thesis of the Background. He was unconvinced until a small earthquake occurred. This convinced him because he saw that he had never had a belief or conviction or entertained a hypothesis that the earth did not move; he simply took it for granted (Searle 1999: 184–5).

As this example shows, we can get things wrong about the Background. Moreover, the Background can change as our form of life changes. In this sense, if we think of the ideas of Wittgenstein and Searle that have been discussed in this section as articulating a version of foundationalism it will be very different from that of classical foundationalism.

review
activity

1. Explain the key differences between Wittgenstein's foundationalism and classical foundationalism.

2. What does Searle mean by the 'Background'? What is the difference between 'deep Background' and 'local Background'?

The definition of knowledge

Foundationalism and coherentism are theories about the way in which beliefs *hang together* in such a way as to be justified. A separate but related concern is whether we can provide a *definition* of knowledge itself.

Suppose Karl says that he knows that Queen Elizabeth died in 1603. If Karl does know this, then how are we to define his knowledge? Traditionally, the answer is the following. First, it must be *true* that Elizabeth died in 1603. Second, Karl must *believe* that Elizabeth died in 1603. Third, Karl's belief must be *justified*. So we can say that knowledge is *justified true belief*.

The idea behind the definition is that each of three conditions is *necessary* for knowledge and that together they are *sufficient*. That is, if someone knows some proposition *p* (such as that Elizabeth died in 1603), then *each* of the conditions must be satisfied, and *all* must be satisfied.

Is the definition correct?

Are the conditions necessary?

It has been argued by Colin Radford (Radford, 1966) that it is possible to know without believing. Suppose years ago Pierre has followed a course of English history. He is now asked to reply to various questions about English history, such as 'when did Elizabeth die?' He gives an answer – the correct answer – to each question, but, since he has forgotten he took history at school, he considers all his answers to be guesses. He would deny that he believes that, for example, Elizabeth died in 1603, even though he gives the right answer. Radford argues that in such a case we should say that Pierre *knew* the answers to the questions even though he did not *believe* these answers.

In a reply to Radford, D.M. Armstrong (Armstrong 1969) argued that it is possible that Pierre consciously does not believe the answers to the questions set for him, but unconsciously does believe them. This attributes to Pierre contradictory beliefs, but, Armstrong says, people *do* often hold contradictory beliefs, so there is nothing unusual in Pierre in that respect. Radford rejected this reply (Radford 1970) on the ground that is begged the question, for the only reason Armstrong had for saying that Pierre unconsciously *believed* the answers was that he gave the correct answers, and that Pierre believed the answers is just what Radford doubts.

Armstrong argued that Pierre did, after all, believe the answers to the questions set. But both he and Radford agreed that Pierre knew the right answers. So, another strategy against Radford's example is to deny that Pierre *does* know the answers. What reason might one have for that? If Armstrong is right, Pierre holds contradictory beliefs. But if someone believes that p (for example, it is the case that Elizabeth died in 1603) and believes that not-p ($-p$) (it is not the case that Elizabeth died in 1603) then, one might say, it cannot be right to attribute knowledge that p to him.

review
activity

According to Radford it is possible to know some proposition without believing it. What is his argument for this claim?

Are the conditions sufficient?

The main assault, however, on the traditional analysis of knowledge has come not from questioning whether the conditions are necessary but whether they are sufficient. That is, could it be that one fulfils all the conditions for knowledge that the traditional account offers and still not possess knowledge?

In 1963 Edmund Gettier published a famous article in which he argued that this is possible. Consider the following case.

Theodor and Max are interviewees for a job as lecturer in history at a university. As they sit in the waiting room, they start chatting. Theodor has far more qualifications, experience and publications than Max and, moreover, he is friends with the professor who is going to interview them both. Max forms the belief in the light of these facts that Theodor is sure to get the job. Theodor then counts the coins in his pocket. He has 12. Max thus comes to believe the following proposition:

a)   Theodor is the man who will get the job, and Theodor has twelve coins in his pocket.

From this Max infers, correctly:

b)   The man who will get the job has twelve coins in his pocket.

They are both interviewed and, to his astonishment, Max is offered the job (his work is more fashionable than Theodor's). Let us suppose that, by extraordinary coincidence, Max also has 12 coins in his pocket, although he does not know this. So, we can say all of the following:

i)   b) is true;
ii)   Max believes b);
iii) Max is justified in believing b).

However, it is clear Max did not *know* b), even though it was a justified true belief; for b) is true in virtue of the number of coins in Max's pocket, and he bases his belief in b) on a count of the coins in Theodor's pocket, who, he falsely believes, will get the job.

Evidently what has gone wrong in such a case is that Max acquired his justified true belief in the wrong kind of way. It was in this sense an *accident* that he had the justified true belief that the man with 12 coins in his pocket would get the job. He was just lucky.

Here is another example. Henry and William work in the same office. Henry believes that William owns a Ford. He believes this because he has often seen William driving a Ford, William has given Henry lifts in a Ford, and so on. So, the proposition in question, which Henry believes, is:

c) William owns a Ford.

Suppose, now, that Henry has another colleague, Martha, who is out of the office on a business trip and of whose whereabouts Henry is totally ignorant. Henry thinks up some place name totally at random, say Berlin. The following proposition:

d) Either William owns a Ford, or Martha is in Berlin

is entailed by c) and is true. (If you find this hard to see, consider this. 'Or' can be used in two ways: in an *exclusive* way or an *inclusive* way. Here is an example of the former: 'I am going on holiday for a week to Athens or Vienna'. In this case, it is clear that I shall either go to Athens for week or to Vienna for a week. If I go to both, I have not spoken correctly. Going to Athens is *exclusive* of going to Vienna. Here is an example of the latter: 'Every time I go to the sea for the day it is raining or freezing cold'. In this case, using 'or' is not meant to rule out the possibility that it is both raining and freezing cold whenever I go to the sea for the day. Its raining is *inclusive* of its being freezing. So here we have an inclusive use of 'or'. In the simple language of propositions at issue in the Gettier case the 'or' we are considering is inclusive. In this case the proposition 'Either William owns a Ford, or Martha is in Berlin' is true if either disjunct is true – if 'William owns a Ford' is true or 'Martha is in Berlin' is true.)

Imagine now that Henry sees that d) is entailed by c) and proceeds, therefore, to accept d). Therefore, we can say:

i)   d) is true;
ii) Henry believes d);
iii) Henry is justified in believing d).

Henry, of course, has no idea where Martha is.

Let us imagine, however, that William does *not* own a Ford, but that by the sheerest coincidence Martha *is* in Berlin. Then Henry does *not* know d) even though, as we have seen, d) is true, Henry believes d) and Henry is justified in believing d). The problem is clearly that what makes d) true is Martha's being in Berlin, whereas it is because he believes Henry owns a Ford that William (justifiably) believes d).

As was the case with Max, the fundamental problem was that Henry came by the true belief by *accident*. He was just lucky.

Gettier's article provoked, and continues to provoke, a huge number of responses by other philosophers, and has led to the formulation of many interesting accounts of knowledge that seek to circumvent the kinds of difficulties his examples raise. One approach has been to shift attention away from the notion of justification and towards a consideration of the place of the subject in the world and his relations to that world. This shift has been understood in terms of the distinction between reliable and unreliable ways of collecting beliefs. Not surprisingly, the theories of knowledge in question are known as *reliability theories* or, simply, *reliabilism*.

review
activity

Describe in your own words one of the Gettier-type cases and explain why it suggests that knowledge is not justified true belief.

Reliabilism

Consider, for example, a thermometer. What makes a thermometer record, say, a person's temperature correctly is that it is a *reliable* thermometer. This model has been used by some philosophers (for example, Armstrong 1973) to respond to examples of the kind offered by Gettier. It is clear that in the Gettier cases what has gone wrong is that the justified true beliefs were not generated by a reliable method. This is why we say that the person in question (Max or Henry) only *accidentally* reached a justified true belief and hence did not have knowledge.

When is a method for acquiring beliefs reliable?

One difficulty is that the notion of reliability is vague, for it is hard to explain what a reliable method for acquiring beliefs might be. For example, should we say that a reliable method is one which never leads to our having false beliefs? One problem with this suggestion is that we would be left with hardly any, if any, methods for acquiring beliefs, for it seems impossible to grasp what, precisely, a wholly reliable method for acquiring beliefs would be. It seems we should be requiring infallibility, and that is something we cannot suppose our investigative methods to have.

We could suggest, then, that a reliable method is one that does not involve infallibility. After all, a thermometer can be reliable even if it sometimes gives the wrong reading of a person's temperature. But how often must it give the right temperature to be reliable? Nine times out of ten? Or 99 times out of 100? It is unclear what we should say. Moreover, our standards for reliability vary from case to case. For example, it is probably fair to say that a computer that is used everyday is reliable even if it crashes once a year. However, an aeroplane that is flown everyday and crashes once a year is extremely unreliable.

Moreover, it is a problem in explaining the notion of reliability that there can be a reliable method for gaining knowledge which is based on falsehoods. The following example, which I borrow from Adam Morton (Morton 2001: 117), is a case in point. Before it was known that the earth rotates around the sun sailors calculated their latitude by the position of the sun and other heavenly bodies on the assumption that the earth was stationary. Now, as a matter of fact the sailors did things properly and were able *correctly* to compute their latitude on this assumption because their method was reliable. So it seems they had knowledge of their latitude. However, it surely is a problem for reliability theories that there can be a reliable method that gives knowledge but is based on many false beliefs. Such examples show how difficult it is to produce a satisfactory account of reliability.

The causal theory of knowledge

One suggestion for a way in which one might try to make precise the idea of a reliable method for acquiring beliefs is by using the notion of causality.

Consider the following example. Nelson takes a trip to the countryside whilst on holiday in a foreign country. He comes upon an area where there is a great deal of solidified lava strewn all over the countryside, and he forms the belief *p* that a nearby mountain, M, erupted many centuries ago. How does Nelson know that *p*? Central here is that there is a *causal connection* between his belief and M's erupting many centuries ago. There must be a *causal chain* between M's erupting and his belief.

We can see what this means if we construct a situation where the causal chain in question is broken. Suppose that M did erupt many centuries ago and left lava all over the countryside. Suppose then that someone, A, removed all this lava. Even later, let us imagine, someone else, B, who does not know about the original eruption, put a lot of lava all over the countryside to make it look as if M had erupted. Nelson sees this lava and concludes that M erupted. Does Nelson *know* that M erupted? Surely not, for the causal chain linking the eruption of M and his belief that M erupted was broken by the removal of the lava by A.

These examples are due to Alvin Goldman who has accordingly argued (Goldman 1967) that, in order for a person to know some proposition *p*, his belief must be caused by the fact that *p*, as in the lava case, where the belief that M erupted can only be knowledge if it is caused by the eruption of M. In other words, on the causal account, knowledge is appropriately caused true belief, where a belief that is appropriately caused is one that is (in part) produced by the object, event or fact which makes the belief true. For example, I know I am now looking at my computer because my computer plays a part in causing me to believe that I am looking at my computer (other things also play a causal role here, for example, that the light is on).

Such an analysis helps with the Gettier cases, because in such cases the causal chain between the *belief* that *p* and the *fact* that *p* has broken down. For example, in the case of Henry, what caused him to have the belief d) was not the fact that William owned a Ford, but some other facts, for example, that he had seen William driving a Ford. Further, the fact that makes d) true, namely, that Martha is in Berlin, did not cause Henry to believe d), for he had no idea she was in Berlin. Goldman thus says that, if a true belief is to be knowledge, then this belief must be *caused* in the right way by the fact in question.

However, there are certain problems with the causal theory. The most pressing is probably that of knowledge of universal propositions. For example, we might know that all tin-openers are made by human beings but this piece of knowledge does not seemed to be causally supported by the fact that all tin-openers are made by human beings. Your belief that all tin-openers are made by human beings is not caused by the fact that all tin-openers are made by human beings (cf. Moser *et al.* 1998: 96). Further I know that all men are mortal, but this knowledge is not caused by the fact that all men are mortal. The causal analysis must say that what causes it is that this man has died, that man has died and so on. However, it is unclear how my general belief about the mortality of all men can be caused by a belief that this man has died, that that man has died and so on, however many men I believe to have died.

Nozick's tracking theory of knowledge

Another version of the reliability theory, proposed by Robert Nozick (1939–2002), is known as the *tracking theory* (Nozick 1981).

We can start by agreeing that a person *a* knows that *p* if:

1) *p* is true
2) *a* believes that *p*

But now recall that the problem that the Gettier examples exposed in the traditional account of knowledge was that the justified true beliefs were arrived at by luck. Max and Henry came by their justified true beliefs by luck or happy accident. They would still have believed what they believed even if what they believed had been false. For example, Max would still have believed that the man with 12 coins in his pocket would get the job even if that had turned out to be false, for example, if he, Max, had had 11 coins in his pocket.

This means that we should add a third condition to the above two:

3) if *p* were not true, then *a* would not believe that *p*.

However, 1), 2) and 3) are not together sufficient for knowledge. This is because there might be slightly different circumstances in which *p* remains true but *a* no longer believes it. We can see this through the following example, borrowed from Dancy (Dancy 1985: 37–8). Suppose Hannah believes there is a police car outside because she can hear the siren of a police car, and there is in fact a police car outside. However, the siren she can hear is on her son's hi-fi. So, she does not *know* the car is there since, if her son's hi-fi had been silent, she would not have believed it was there – even though it *was* there. We need, therefore, to rule out such cases and can do so by adding a fourth condition:

4) if, in changed circumstances, *p* were still true, *a* would still believe that *p*.

So, on Nozick's account, we can say that *a* knows that *p* if:

1) *p* is true
2) *a* believes that *p*
3) if *p* were not true, then *a* would not believe that *p*
4) if, in changed circumstances, *p* were still true, *a* would still believe that *p*.

This tracking theory is also known as the conditional theory because it depends on the use of conditional propositions ('if *a* were the case then *b* would be the case').

Externalist theories of knowledge

One of the most important aspects of such accounts as Nozick's is that they are *externalist* theories of knowledge. This is because they claim that, when a person has knowledge, his having knowledge will be grounded in elements external to the mind. That is, according to externalism, if he has beliefs that constitute knowledge this will be because his beliefs relate to the world in certain ways – for example, they track the way the world is. The more a theory of knowledge emphasises issues of reliability and the objective conditions under which a person's belief will be true, the more externalist it is as a theory.

Internalist theories of knowledge

Internalism is the opposite of externalism and claims that whether or not a person has knowledge depends on factors internal to a person's mind. The more such factors are emphasised the more the theory is internalist.

Externalist theories tend to emphasise notions such as truth, reliability and tracking; internalist theories tend to emphasise notions such as justification and the reasonability of beliefs.

It should be clear that one attractive option would be to say that an adequate theory of knowledge should incorporate *both* internalist and externalist aspects. Moreover, as Robert Audi has suggested (Audi 1998: 225–6), reliability theories seem to find it difficult to avoid issues of justification. We can see this in the following way.

We have seen that there are difficulties in capturing properly the notion of a reliable method for collecting beliefs. Consider, now, beliefs we form about the external world on the basis of perception. When is such a method reliable? It is so when the subject, for example, sees things in good light, is not drunk, is sufficiently attentive to his surroundings and the like – but how are we to understand the notion of, for example, 'being sufficiently attentive'? The answer is surely something like 'being attentive enough to form *justified* beliefs about the object seen'. So the concept of justification cannot, perhaps, be avoided in a reliability theory, which means that it cannot wholly avoid incorporating internalist features.

review activity

1. Explain in your own words the causal theory of knowledge and the problems it faces.

2. Explain in your own words Nozick's conditional theory of knowledge.

3. What are externalism and internalism when understood with reference to theories of knowledge?

Perception

It is probably fair to say that those who have never studied philosophy know two things about the subject. One is Descartes' famous proposition 'I am thinking, therefore I am'. The other is that philosophers discuss the issue of what happens to the table when we leave the room. Is it still there? And if it is, how do we know it is? In and around these questions are concerns about the nature of perception – that is, about how it is that we see the world of material bodies. Consideration of them takes us to some very interesting, and some very surprising, theories.

Strictly speaking, when philosophers discuss issues of perception they could discuss all five senses – sight, touch, taste, smell and hearing. However, in the main they have concentrated upon sight.

Common-sense realism

According to common-sense (or naïve) realism, when we open our eyes and look at the world what we see is simply the world. It is there, directly open to our inspection. Moreover, common-sense realism says that the reason we see the world when we open our eyes is *because* the world is there. There is, in other words, a *causal relation* between the world being there and us seeing it when we open our eyes: the world's being there *causes* us to see it.

Many philosophers would say that this kind of realism is deeply implausible. The main reason they would say this is that it seems to leave out the way things *look* or *feel* or *sound*. Thus, we all know that a round object can look elliptical – for example, a coin held sideways on; that the quiet ticking of a clock can sound like a loud hammering; and that a bowl of water can feel warm to one of one's hands and cold to the other.

The argument from illusion

These reflections form part of what is known as the *argument from illusion*. Thus, for example, a stick half-immersed in water looks bent even though we know it is not, and people who have had a limb amputated often continue to feel pain 'in' the absent limb even though they know there is no limb there in which to feel pain. Further, consider the fact that light, although it travels at great speed, takes time to get from the source to our eyes. In fact, light from a very distant star can take so long to reach our eyes that, by the time it does arrive, the star itself no longer exists: we see the star as it used to be. Moreover, there are cases where one perceives something that is not there at all and never has been. For example, one might see a mirage in the desert or, as Macbeth did, hallucinate that one is seeing a dagger.

Those philosophers who are attracted to these thoughts usually go on to note that there is no difference in the actual experience or, as it is also called, the *phenomenology* of perception when that perception is illusory and when it is not. That is, they argue that illusory perception and veridical perception are qualitatively indistinguishable: really seeing a bent stick is just like seeing a bent stick in water, for example; and the experience of looking at white walls through green spectacles is qualitatively indistinguishable from looking at green walls (cf. Ayer 1958: 6). From this they infer that, just as in the illusory cases, what we perceive is not the world itself but the way the world looks (sounds, feels and so forth) to us, so even in the veridical case we do not see the world directly. Rather, we see the world *by way of seeing something else*. We have already met that something else – they are, on the traditional account of these things, sense-data.

We shall look in a moment at what kind of theory of perception belief in sense-data leads one to. In the meantime, we should see what can be said in defence of common-sense realism.

review
activity

What is the argument from illusion and what is it designed to show?

Defending common sense

Not all philosophers take the argument from illusion to show that common-sense realism is mistaken. If such philosophers are to defend common-sense realism they have to give an account of perception which avoids the introduction of sense-data in the first place. So how do they respond to the argument?

Strawson's realism

P.F. Strawson has argued (Strawson 1979) that it is simply part of common-sense realism to allow for variation in the way things look. Thus, for example, there seems little that is problematic or puzzling in the idea that, say, a piece of cloth could look purple but actually be green: 'Yes, it looks purple, but take it to the window and you'll see it's really green' (Strawson 1979: 57). Similarly, we might look at blood through a microscope and see that it is mostly colourless, but we quite easily shift back and forth between thinking that blood is red and that it is colourless. This is because what we think depends on the context in which we think and speak: there is nothing surprising about that. The mere fact that some object can look this way to me and that way to you provides no reason to introduce sense-data.

We could add to these thoughts the following reflection. Remember that the sense-data theorist claims that even in the case of veridical perception what one sees directly is the sense-datum and not the object itself. He claims, in other words, that even in veridical perception we should say that the world *looks* to one a certain way. But this seems odd. Suppose, for example, that I see something in the distance and am not sure what it is. I might say, 'Well, it looks like a falcon'. But then I see it close up and say, 'No, I was wrong. It was a kestrel'. Having seen the bird close up it would be strange to insist that it *looks* to me a certain way, for that would suggest that I am not sure that it is a kestrel. But having seen it close up, I am. In such a case, the common-sense realist will say that the world does not *look* to me a certain way: rather, I just see the world.

These arguments might not, however, seem to be enough to confront properly the case of hallucination. After all, when someone hallucinates that there is a tree in front of him his experience is just as it would be were there a real tree in front of him. Does this not show that even in the case of veridical perception of a tree what the perceiver sees is a tree via a sense-datum (or sense-data)?

McDowell's externalism

John McDowell (McDowell 1988) has disputed this. He argues that our account of what it is that is going on in a person who has an hallucination should be different from the account we give of what is going on in someone who really sees a tree. This is possible, he thinks, even though from the point of view of the each person there is no difference in the experience. The hallucinator really thinks he sees a tree and the normal perceiver really thinks he sees a tree. There is no difference 'from the inside'. But from an *external* perspective, there is a great difference: one of them does not really see a tree and the other does. The difference between the two cases is, then, simply this: that in the hallucination there is no tree in front of the perceiver, whilst in the case of the normal perceiver the tree is 'present' in his experience. And this gives us reason to deny that what the person having the veridical perception of the tree is seeing are actually sense-data: we can deny that there is a 'common factor' in the two cases.

McDowell's view is a kind of *externalism*, but it is different from, although related to, the externalism we discussed when considering responses to Gettier type problems in the analysis of knowledge and the externalism that claims that 'meanings aren't in the head'. It is a form of externalism because it holds that the difference between the hallucination and veridical perception is a difference that is not available subjectively to the individuals undergoing the experience but is external to the content of the experience.

review

activity

1. What reasons does Strawson give in favour of common-sense realism?

2. On what basis does McDowell deny that there is a 'common factor' in a veridical and a hallucinatory experience of a tree?

Representative realism

Still, many philosophers have been persuaded by something like the argument from illusion that we should introduce sense-data. As we have noted, they argue that we see the world by way of seeing sense-data. We see sense data *directly* and the world *indirectly*.

Suppose, then, that it is true that we see the world by way of seeing sense-data. This theory is a form of realism, because it says that we see the world, but it is a form of *representative* realism because it says that what we see directly – sense-data – *represent* the world in some way.

The properties of sense-data

What, then, are sense-data? What properties do they possess? They are non-physical; they exist if and only if one is having an appropriate experience (they last just as long as the experience and no longer: there are no unexperienced sense data); they are private (only I have my sense-data); and they have only those properties they appear to have. What this last point comes to is that there is no possibility of me misperceiving my sense-data. This is why there is a strong connection between belief in sense-data and foundationalist thought.

There are certain problems with which representative realism has to deal. The first is this. How can we know that our sense data are anything like the way the world is? If, for example, I look out of my window and have sense-data that appear to come from a field, how can I know that there is indeed a field there? Might there not be something else there altogether? In fact, might there be nothing there at all? Representative realism makes it seem as if we are all shut up in our own private cinema or picture show, having no real contact with the external world. Or, to put it another way, are we not each of us shut up behind a 'veil-of-perception'? If we are, there is no way that we can draw the veil to one side to see what is behind it, so how do we know what is behind it?

The 'veil-of-perception' problem

John Locke, in *An Essay Concerning Human Understanding*, held to the representative theory of perception, though he spoke not of 'sense-data' but of 'ideas' before the mind. Thus he wrote (Locke 1984: II, viii, 8): 'Whatsoever the Mind perceives in it self, or is the immediate object of Perception, Thought, or Understanding, that I call Idea.' Now, Locke was clear that having an idea in the mind does not prove the existence of the thing in question (Locke 1984, IV, xi, 1): '[T]he having the *Idea* of any thing in our Mind, no more proves the Existence of that Thing, than the picture of a Man evidences his being in the World'. So what argument does Locke give to show that there *are* things outside us after all? Here are some of them, from Book IV, Chapter xi of the *Essay*:

a) Those without sense organs never have the experience of ideas belonging to the corresponding senses. Those who are blind never see colours; those who are deaf never hear music, and so on. From this, Locke infers that the sense organs do not produce the ideas we have of colour, sound and so forth on their own: these ideas must be caused by objects outside us.

b) We cannot produce the ideas we have at will. For example, I cannot simply smell the smell of a rose when I wish, or experience the taste of sugar when I want to. Further, when I open my eyes I simply see what is there, and cannot simply see what I wish to be there. The ideas in question must, therefore, Locke concludes, be caused by material objects.

c) Different senses agree in what it is that tells us of the world. For example, if I eat my supper I see, taste and smell my food, as well as feeling it in my mouth. The cause of this agreement is, Locke says, best thought of as the real independent existence of material objects, in this case, my supper.

Notice that these arguments all appeal to the notion of *causality*. That is, Locke is asking what it is that *causes* our perceptions, and he answers that it must be material objects.

However, Locke's arguments can be disputed. a) is weak because it makes an appeal to sense organs, but these might themselves be simply ideas in the mind and not really exist. So to appeal to them to show that material objects exist begs the question. b) Even though we cannot always perceive just what we want to perceive there might be a cause of this other than material bodies. For example, God could make us see what we see, without there being any material objects. c) Similarly, God could be the cause of the fact that 'Our Senses ... bear *witness* to the truth of each other's report', as Locke puts it.

Locke seems aware that his arguments are weak, for he grants that there can be no certainty that there are any material objects. He claims, however, that we have enough assurance that there are for everyday purposes. This, while it may be true, is not really the point.

Mackie on representative realism

In his book on Locke, John Mackie (Mackie 1976) has argued that the representative realist can justify the belief that there is a world of material objects behind the veil-of-perception. However, Mackie prefers not to speak of ideas or sense-data, for he is clear about the kinds of problems that beset any such form of the representative theory (we shall look at specific problems with sense-data below). Instead, Mackie talks simply of the way things look, feel and sound to us, and says that this does not commit us to belief in intermediaries between us and the world. For Mackie, the ways things look and so forth does not involve the idea that appearances of objects are themselves real (non-physical) objects. Nonetheless, there remains the veil-of-perception problem for him as for any representative realist.

review
activity

1. What is the representative theory of perception?

2. What grounds does Locke give for saying that we can be justified in believing that our ideas are caused by material objects?

3. To what problems are Locke's arguments on this exposed?

Mackie notes that one of the things the representative realist has to be able to explain is the order and coherence of our perceptions of the external world. For example, whenever I walk into my study I see my desk, computer, books and so on. Not only that but I see them in the same order in which I left them when I last left my study. Or again, we see a plant over a period of several weeks and it is bigger each time: it seems to have been there and grown even when we have not been looking at it. Mackie says that such things are best explained by the hypothesis that there really are material objects in the world. For that hypothesis 'fills in gaps in things as they appear, so producing continuously existing things and gradual changes where the appearances are discontinuous' (Mackie 1976: 64). Further, Mackie goes on to argue that, once we see that it is a viable hypothesis that there are objects out there, we can build up a picture of the way they *cause* us to have sensations. For example, in an argument very like the one Locke used, Mackie writes:

> [W]hat I seem to be presented with is just that when a feelable cup-shaped object comes to be before my eyes, I begin to have a certain visual sensation, and when the object is removed I cease to have it, the whole set of observations being repeatable in just the ways needed to confirm a causal relationship: I seem to be getting evidence of a real solid object causing sensations.
>
> (Mackie 1976: 65)

It might be wondered why Mackie's appeal in this argument to causality is any more successful than Locke's corresponding version of the same line of reasoning. In Mackie's eyes, there are two reasons why it is more successful. a) If we thought of appearances as (non-material) objects then we should have to explain how it is that, seeing only these non-material objects, we could infer that they are caused by material objects. It would be implausible to think we could because we should have no access at all to the things said to cause our perceptions. The only causal relations we should be able to see would be those between our perceptions, that is, between our sense-data (ideas). Speaking of appearances as simply 'how-things-look', as Mackie does, makes the veil, so to speak, more diaphanous than speaking of sense-data or ideas does. ii) Mackie's appeal to what *causes* our experiences comes *after* the hypothesis that there are objects in the material world. The causal story fills in a hypothesis that, it is said, already has a great deal of plausibility. The causal story does not have to do all the work, as it does in Locke's account.

Mackie is certainly not the only philosopher to think that belief in the external world is some kind of theory or hypothesis. A.J. Ayer, for example, has written that 'in referring as we do to physical objects we are elaborating a theory with respect to the evidence of our senses' (Ayer 1984: 132). But this seems odd. It seems very strange to think that the idea that there are material objects is a theory or hypothesis (cf. Strawson 1979), on a par, as Mackie suggests, with a scientific hypothesis.

review
activity

What are the main differences between the representative theory of perception as offered by Locke and Mackie?

Problems with sense-data

Be that as it may, Mackie is surely correct to be wary of the concept of sense-data. There seem to be significant difficulties with it.

One problem is simply that the notion of sense-data seems to misrepresent the nature of perception. Thus, it seems mistaken to infer from the fact that a material object *appears* to us a certain way that what we perceive is the *appearance* of the thing. There are not things separate from the objects that appear in certain ways that are the appearances of the object. As Chisholm says: 'We do not see, hear, or feel the appearances of things' (Chisholm 1966: 94).

Another difficulty is the following. Suppose an observer looks at a white object. We can say that, to a normal observer under normal conditions, the object will appear white. But suppose we agree that there is a thing – the appearance of the white thing – that itself is white. Then what does it mean to say that it is white? If 'is white' has the same sense when applied to the object and to the appearance, then it seems that to say that the appearance is white is just to say that it – the appearance – will appear white when viewed by a normal observer under normal conditions. But then this will mean that the appearance appears white, and there will thus be another appearance – the appearance of the appearance. Clearly, we could in this way generate an infinite number of appearances, which cannot possibly be the correct account of perception (cf. Chisholm 1966: 95).

The deepest problem with sense-data, however, is probably that it is unclear just what properties they are supposed to have. Remember that they are supposed to be non-physical mental objects. Now, suppose I am looking at a green cuboid box in front of me. On the representative theory of perception what I see directly is a sense-datum (or a set of sense-data). But what properties, then, does my sense-datum have? Is it supposed itself to be green? But does it make sense to think that there exists a non-physical green colour-patch? This seems very unlikely. But it seems even more unlikely that my sense-datum could itself be cuboid, for it surely makes no sense to think that there could be a non-physical cuboid object. Reflections such as these have suggested to many philosophers that the concept of sense-data is too unclear and confused to be of any help.

review
activity

To what problems is the theory of sense data exposed?

Primary and secondary qualities

Our discussion so far of Locke's theory of perception has, however, omitted at least one very important feature. This is that it is embedded within an important distinction that Locke makes – and others have also made it, for example, Descartes – between what are called *primary* and *secondary* qualities. We must, therefore, explore a little what he meant by this distinction, not simply because it is interesting in its own right but also because it came to play a very important role in Berkeley's criticisms of Locke.

Reasons for distinguishing primary from secondary qualities

Consider your experience of looking at a flower – say a buttercup. You see it as yellow. Why is this? There are at least two reasons. Firstly, you are equipped, as a human being, with a certain sensory apparatus that means that you see buttercups as yellow. A bee or a dog or a Martian might see it as having a quite different colour on account of having quite different eyes, brains and so on. The second reason why you see the buttercup as yellow is that the surface of the flower has a particular structure, for example, a particular texture, which causes it to reflect light in a given way. Something else with a different surface structure would reflect light in a different way.

Colour is just one of many properties of objects that seem to depend in this way on the nature of the perceiver and the structure of the object itself. Taste, smell and sound are three. However, there seem to be some properties that objects have in a way that is not at all dependent upon the perceiver. All perceivers will perceive objects as having these properties. These include (according to Locke) shape, size, motion-or-rest, position, number and solidity.

Locke called members of the former group of properties (like colour) 'secondary qualities' and members of the latter group of properties (like shape) 'primary qualities'.

Locke had reasons to draw this distinction that we have not yet mentioned. The most important of these was that the physical sciences, which were emerging at a great rate in Locke's day, had no need of construing material objects as having secondary qualities. Such qualities are redundant from the point of view of explaining, for example, how bodies will act on each other if they collide. For example, if two billiard balls collide, we can explain their interaction without reference to their colour or smell: whether a billiard ball is green or blue will not affect how it impacts on another billiard ball.

Corpuscularian philosophy

Locke thus believed – and he shared this view with many thinkers of the day – that matter, *as it was in itself,* possessed a) the primary qualities and b) the *power* to cause ideas of secondary qualities in suitable perceivers. Thus, an object that we see as a red square would be, in itself, square and would have the power to cause (in us) the idea of red. Thus, along with many at the time, he believed in what is called the *corpuscularian* philosophy, a way of thinking that had its roots in ancient Greek thought. This was the belief that matter was nothing more than atoms in the void. The atoms have the primary qualities and powers to cause secondary qualities in suitable observers, but in themselves have no colour, smell, taste and so on. So a table, for example, according to Locke, was composed of atoms possessing the primary qualities with the power to produce ideas of secondary qualities in observers – and that was all.

According to Locke, our ideas of primary qualities *resemble* the qualities in objects themselves, for objects do, in fact, possess such qualities. However, our ideas of secondary qualities resemble nothing in objects themselves because objects have no secondary qualities in themselves. There is therefore nothing for our ideas of secondary qualities to resemble. This shows that, on Locke's theory, our ideas only *imperfectly* represent the outside world.

This notion of resemblance is very difficult to make clear for reasons we have already seen: if an idea of, say, a spherical object resembles a spherical object, then are we to suppose the idea is spherical? This looks absurd. Jonathan Dancy puts the point well.

> *The sort of three-dimensional shape we attribute to objects is not one which our sensa [ideas] can share. Our sensa can only resemble the way such objects look, not the way they are; but this is no help, since our sensa just are the way such objects look.*
>
> (Dancy, 1985: 167)

However, serious as this criticism is, there have been some critics of Locke after much bigger fish. One of these was Berkeley.

review
activity

Explain in your own words the distinction between primary and secondary qualities.

Idealism

Underlying Berkeley's criticism of Locke is a simple and brilliant idea. Representative realism, according to Locke's version of it leads, it seems, ineluctably to scepticism because it cannot make good the claim that our ideas of material objects are actually caused by material objects. For all we know, there might not be any material objects at all, as Locke conceded. So how can one defeat these sceptical consequences of Locke's theory? Berkeley's extraordinary answer was: by denying that our ideas *are* caused by material objects. If there *are* no material objects then there can be no sceptical problem about the existence of the external world. What one would need to show then would be that there are minds and their ideas – and nothing else. This would bypass the need for material objects at all as anything other than ideas in the mind and would secure human knowledge against scepticism because no one could deny that he has ideas. So Berkeley set himself the task of defeating scepticism by showing that material objects are simply ideas in the mind. This audacious and exciting project he sought to complete in two of his main philosophical works *A Treatise Concerning the Principles of Human Knowledge* and *Three Dialogues between Hylas and Philonous*.

Berkeley called his position 'immaterialism' because it involved the denial that matter exists independently of minds. Later philosophers have called it 'idealism', because it says that matter is nothing more than ideas.

Berkeley's central argument

Berkeley gives one central argument for his view in the following passage, where Philonous articulates Berkeley's view:

> PHILONOUS. *But ... I am content to put the whole upon this issue. If you can conceive it possible for any mixture or combination of qualities, or any sensible object whatever, to exist without [= outside] the mind, then I will grant it actually to be so.*
>
> HYLAS. *If it comes to that, the point will soon be decided. What more easy than to conceive a tree or house existing by itself, independent of, and unperceived by any mind whatsoever? I do at this present time conceive them existing after that manner.*
>
> PHILONOUS. *How say you, Hylas, can you see a thing which is at the same time unseen?*
>
> HYLAS. *No, that were a contradiction.*
>
> PHILONOUS. *Is it not as great a contradiction to talk of conceiving a thing which is unconceived?*
>
> HYLAS. *It is.*
>
> PHILONOUS. *The tree or house therefore which you think of, is conceived by you.*
>
> HYLAS. *How should it be otherwise?*

**Bishop Berkeley
(1685–1753)**

George Berkeley was born in Co. Kilkenny in Ireland. He was educated at Kilkenny College, one of the leading schools in Ireland, and at Trinity College, Dublin. In 1707 he was elected to a Fellowship at Trinity. His *Treatise Concerning the Principles of Human Knowledge* appeared in 1710, but did not gain the attention Berkeley had hoped. He thus recast the argument in a more accessible form in his *Three Dialogues between Hylas and Philonous*, and this time the book was a success. In 1713 he moved to London, and was immediately a great hit on the London literary scene. He spent a year in London and then left for Sicily as chaplain to the Earl of Peterborough. From 1716 to 1720 he travelled in Europe as the tutor to St George Ashe. In 1723 he became Dean of Derry, with an income of around £1100 per annum, an enormous sum in those days. One of the most bizarre episodes of Berkeley's life was the plan he hatched to set up a college in Bermuda to provide a Christian education for young men from America. Astonishingly, he managed to raise a good deal of money for the enterprise and to persuade five fellows of Trinity College to agree to become teachers at the new college. He even obtained a promise from Parliament of public funds to support the project. However, the money never materialised, and Berkeley had to abandon the project, but not before he and his wife had moved to Rhode Island where they had bought a farm which was intended to provide a source of income for the planned college in Bermuda. In 1734 he was made Bishop of Cloyne, where he lived for the rest of his life. He died in 1753 whilst visiting his son at Oxford.

PHILONOUS *And what is conceived, is surely in the mind.*
HYLAS. *Without question, that which is conceived is in the mind.*
PHILONOUS. *How then came you to say, you conceived a house or tree existing independent and out of all minds whatsoever?*
HYLAS. *That was I own an oversight.*

(Berkeley 1998b: 86)

We can see what Berkeley is arguing in the following way.

In Charles Dickens's *Hard Times* there is a scene in Book the Second, Chapter 9 where Mrs Gradgrind lies dying in bed. Her daughter asks her whether she is in pain. She replies: 'I think there's a pain somewhere in the room, but I couldn't positively say that I have got it' (Dickens 1985: 224). Evidently, this is absurd, and a nice joke by Dickens. It is absurd, of course, because there cannot be any such thing as an unfelt or unexperienced pain. If you have a pain, there could not be anything that is *that* thing that is unexperienced. The pain has its only existence as an experienced thing.

Now, consider the case where you smell a smell. Berkeley asks: could there be such a thing as an unsmelt smell, that is, a smell that was not smelt by anyone? Could there be *that* very thing that you smell, unsmelled? Berkeley thinks it obvious that this no more makes sense than does the idea of an unfelt pain. And he thinks the same argument can be offered for all the sense modalities. 'There was an odour, that is, it was smelled; there was a sound, that is to say, it was heard; a colour or figure, and it was perceived by sight or touch' (Berkeley, 1998a: 104 [§3]). There can no more be *that* very thing which you see, the *sight* you have, which exists unseen or unsighted. To suppose otherwise is, Berkeley thinks, just as absurd as supposing that there could be *that* very pain that you feel, unfelt. Sights, smells, sounds and so on exist, just as pains do, *only in the mind.* Everything you see, smell, taste, hear and feel exists only in the mind. But this means, says Berkeley, that trees, mountains, valleys, wheat, roads and houses exist merely as ideas in the mind. The material world is not, after all, a material world, but an immaterial world, a world composed of ideas. So obvious did Berkeley take his argument to be that he could write: 'It is ... an opinion strangely prevailing amongst men, that houses, mountains, rivers, and in a word all sensible [= material] objects have an existence natural or real, distinct from their being perceived by the understanding' (Berkeley 1998a: 104 [§4]). Berkeley says that for all objects of sense, that is, for tables, chairs, books and the rest 'to be is to be perceived': *esse est percipi*.

review activity

1. What does Berkeley mean by saying that 'to be is to be perceived'?
2. What argument does he have for this view?

Abstract ideas

Underlying Berkeley's argument is a claim about what philosophers of his time called 'abstract ideas'. Therefore, if we are properly to understand Berkeley we must attend to what he says about such ideas. What is most important here is Berkeley's rejection of Locke's account of abstract ideas. Accordingly, we must briefly consider Locke's account of abstract ideas and Berkeley's response to that account if we are properly to grasp Berkeley's attack on matter.

We saw in our discussion of Locke that he used the terminology of ideas. Everything that is an object of thought is, for Locke, an idea. Of course, we speak, to ourselves and to others, but if our words are to mean anything they must, Locke thought, ultimately depend upon the ideas in our mind. Thinking is, first and foremost, the having of ideas before the mind. In believing this, Locke was following the mainstream philosophy of the seventeenth and eighteen centuries.

The terminology of ideas as used by Locke and others is in many ways vague and imprecise, but fundamentally it seems that Locke (usually or often) thought of an idea as an *image* before the mind, like a *picture.*

This raises many problems. One of these involves the fact that ideas seem to stand for individual objects. If I have an idea of my cat, then my idea stands for this one cat, who is completely black. If I have an idea of your cat, then I have a different idea before my mind – as it may be, an idea of a tabby cat, or a Siamese. But I might also have ideas of other cats before my mind – for example, of a tiger, a lion, a panther or a leopard. So far, so good. But suppose I speak simply of cats as such, as when I say, for example, 'the cat is a magnificent creature'. Which idea do I have before my mind in this case? It cannot be an idea of my cat, for that is not at all an idea of your cat, or of any other cat. What is the idea, then? Is it some amalgam of all cats? But how could I have an idea before my mind of a cat that was all black, tabby, Siamese, striped like a tiger, with a mane like a lion, the size of a domestic cat as well as of a panther and so on? Clearly, I could not have such an idea. So how, then, do I refer to 'the cat' as such?

The same problem recurs for the theory of ideas with concepts of man, or human being, or tree, or flower and so on.

Locke's account of abstract ideas

Locke's answer was to formulate the notion of abstract ideas. He discusses the notion on more than one occasion in his *Essay.* Here is what he says on one of those occasions.

> [T]he Mind makes the particular Ideas, received from particular Objects, to become general; which is done by considering them as they are in the Mind such Appearances, separate from all other Existences, and the circumstances of real Existence, as Time, Place, or any other concomitant Ideas. This is called ABSTRACTION, whereby Ideas taken from particular Beings, become general Representatives of all the same kind ... Such precise, naked Appearances in the Mind, without considering, how, whence, or with what others they came there, the Understanding lays up ... as the Standards to rank real Existences into sorts, as they agree with these Patterns, and to denominate them accordingly. Thus the same Colour being observed to day in Chalk or Snow, which the Mind yesterday received from Milk, it considers that Appearance alone, makes it a representative of all of that kind; and having given it the name Whiteness, it by that sound signifies the same quality wheresoever to be imagin'd or met with; and thus Universals, whether Ideas or Terms, are made.
>
> (Locke 1984: II, xi, 9)

Mackie on Locke on abstract ideas

According to J.L. Mackie in his book on Locke (Mackie 1976: ch.4), Locke is arguing as follows.

I see chalk and snow and milk and I pay attention to their different properties: chalk is white, hard, porous etc.; snow is white, soft, cold etc.; milk is white, fluid, wet etc. I notice that they resemble one another in all being white. Then, I am able to look at chalk, snow and milk and, by selective attention, ignore all the properties they have but this one they share. Thus, I ignore their shape, fluidity, coldness etc. and focus on the property they have in common. This is their whiteness, and I am thus able and willing to use this word, 'whiteness', of further objects I come across which also share this property, even if these further objects have properties (e.g., sponginess) not shared by the white things I have seen hitherto.

The *abstract idea* of whiteness is, therefore, the idea I have when I have an idea of chalk (or snow or milk and so forth) and selectively attend to its whiteness, ignoring its other properties. 'Whiteness' is the word that goes with this. And a more complex version of the same account could be given of the abstract idea which goes with the word 'cat' or 'human being' or 'tree' and so on.

review
activity

1. To solve which problem did Locke introduce the notion of abstract ideas?
2. According to Mackie, what is Locke's theory of abstract ideas?

Jonathan Dancy has argued (Dancy 1987: 36–7) that, for a variety of reasons, Mackie's account of Locke is inadequate. One central reason Dancy gives for his judgement is simply that Mackie's account does not fit Locke's text. In any case, Berkeley seems to have had an interpretation in mind significantly different from that offered by Mackie. In fact, he seems to have had two interpretations in mind, both of which he thought showed the notion of abstract ideas to be absurd.

Berkeley's first interpretation of Locke on abstract ideas

On Berkeley's first interpretation, Locke is arguing that one could have an idea of some property of an object separate from all its other properties. And, says Berkeley, this is impossible. For example, suppose I have an idea of a piece of paper. I can focus on the colour of this paper, ignoring its shape, thickness and so on. But what I cannot do is have an idea of a piece of paper that *has no properties but whiteness*. But this, it seems, is what Berkeley, at least at times, takes Locke to be arguing (see, for example, Berkeley 1998a: 91 [Introduction: §7]). He thinks that Locke supposes that it is possible to form an idea of whiteness *that has no other properties at all*. But this is not possible. It is not possible to have an idea of whiteness that is not of *some* shape or of *some* thickness or whatever.

Berkeley's second interpretation of Locke on abstract ideas

As I have already noted, Berkeley has a second line of attack on the doctrine of abstract ideas, based on a somewhat different understanding of abstract ideas. This is found in the following passage.

activity

What is Berkeley's first interpretation of, and objection to, Locke's theory of abstract ideas?

> *Whether others have this wonderful faculty of abstracting their ideas, they best can tell: for my self I find I have a faculty of imagining, or representing to my self the ideas of those particular things I have perceived and of variously compounding and dividing them. I can imagine a man with two heads or the upper parts of a man joined to the body of a horse. I can consider the hand, the eye, the nose, each by it self abstracted or separated from the rest of the body. But then whatever hand or eye I imagine, it must have some particular shape and colour. Likewise, the idea of a man that I frame to my self, must be either of a white, or a black, or a tawny, a straight, or a crooked, a tall, or a low, or a middle-sized man. I cannot by any effort of thought conceive the abstract idea.*
>
> (Berkeley 1998a: 92 [Introduction: §10])

In this passage, Berkeley is clearly arguing that to have an idea of, for example, a hand, is to have an idea of a hand of some determinate colour – of, that is, some colour or other. However, he is taking Locke to be claiming that, in forming an abstract idea of a hand, we are supposed to be forming the idea of a hand that has some particular colour and yet no particular colour, and that would just be absurd. Moreover, Locke seems to be playing right into the hands of Berkeley's objection in the following passage.

> *[A]bstract Ideas are not so obvious or easie to Children, or the yet unexercised Mind, as particular ones ... For example, Does it not require some pains and skill to form the general Idea of a Triangle ... for it must be neither Oblique, nor Rectangle, neither Equilateral, Equicrural, nor Scalenon; but all and none of these at once. In effect, it is something imperfect, that cannot exist; an Idea wherein some parts of several different and inconsistent Ideas are put together.*
>
> (Locke 1984: IV, vii, 9)

This passage, which Berkeley quotes in the *Principles*, really does seem to acknowledge that there can be no abstract ideas since the very concept is absurd.

But what has all this to do with Berkeley's argument for idealism?

activity

What is Berkeley's second interpretation of, and objection to, Locke's theory of abstract ideas?

The rejection of abstract ideas and idealism

Commentators disagree about just what the significance is of Berkeley's rejection of abstract ideas for his idealism, but there seem to be at least two possibilities.

Locke, we have seen, has said that, in itself, matter is not coloured and so forth, that is, it is devoid of secondary qualities. But can we form an idea of such matter? Berkeley thinks we cannot, because if we have an idea of any material body whatsoever it must have some colour or other. In this sense, matter is unintelligible, for we can form no idea of it as it is in itself. But if we *could* form abstract ideas of the kind Berkeley takes Locke to believe in then it would look more plausible to suppose that we could have an idea of matter as possessing only primary and no secondary qualities (as we could have an idea of the whiteness of a piece of paper with no other properties). Since Berkeley thinks this impossible, he thinks the very idea of matter is unintelligible, which obviously supports his case (cf. Urmson 1982: 28–9).

A second reason why Berkeley sees a connection between the rejection of abstract ideas and his immaterialism seems to be the following. Recall the fact that Berkeley suggests that the very thing one sees cannot exist unseen, the very thing one hears cannot exist unheard, and so forth, and that he seems to think of this as an analogy with the impossibility of there being an unfelt pain. Now, pursuing this analogy, in some way Berkeley seems to think that, if we could form abstract ideas, we could form the abstract idea of an unfelt pain. But that feat is evidently impossible. And, Berkeley thinks, such abstraction is no more possible in the case of other mental contents – for example, sights and smells – than in the case of pains. So, in general, Berkeley concludes, what the mind perceives can only exist in the mind.

review
activity

In what two ways does Berkeley think the doctrine of abstract ideas relevant to his argument for idealism?

Berkeley's central error

However, for all the ingenuity and brilliance of Berkeley's reasoning, it seems to many to rest on a fundamental mistake or confusion. And this is that, although it is true that *I cannot conceive of a tree without conceiving of it*, it is false that *I cannot conceive of a tree AS existing unconceived*. In other words, although it is quite true that there cannot be an unfelt pain, it is just a mistake to apply the model of pains to that of trees and other such public objects.

Still, Berkeley took himself to have shown that objects are nothing more than ideas in the mind. But there are, of course, problems with his theory. Two of the most urgent are these.

First, I can call up any ideas I like in virtue of the power of my imagination. For example, I can just imagine at will a tree or a house, or some weird and wonderful thing like a unicorn or a griffin. These are, of course, ideas in the mind, but if real, existing trees, houses and mountains are themselves ideas in the mind what is the difference between a tree that I simply imagine and one that really exists? For they are both ideas in the mind, and it looks, therefore, as if there is no significant difference between them.

Berkeley's response to this is that what distinguishes ideas of sense from ideas that are simply the product of the imagination is that a) the former ideas are that are simply the product of the imagination is that a) the former ideas are not subject to the direct exercise of my will, for I cannot, for example, simply choose what to see when I open my eyes; and b) ideas of sense have a stability, coherence and order which ideas that are the product of the imagination do not have. For example, it is never the case that a steam engine suddenly turns into a cat, or sprouts wings and flies, or starts having a conversation with a tree. These are, rather, the kinds of things that might happen in a dream, or in imagination. Part of the stability, coherence and order in question is the fact that the information I receive about the world by one sense is confirmed by that which I receive from the other senses. Thus, when, for example, I see a steam engine at a railway station I not only see it, but also hear it, can touch it and can smell the steam. These experiences from the different senses cohere with one another.

Material objects as ideas in the mind of God

The second problem Berkeley has is to explain what happens to objects when they are not perceived. For if the being of objects consists in their being perceived, what happens to them when they are not being perceived? Do they go out of existence? Berkeley's answer to this is that they do not go out of existence, because they are ideas in God's mind. Monsignor Ronald Knox produced a couple of well-known limericks to sum up Berkeley's position.

> *There was a young man who said 'God*
> *Must think it exceedingly odd*
> *If he finds that this tree*
> *Continues to be*
> *When there's no one about in the quad.'*

> *Reply:*

> *Dear Sir:*
> *Your astonishment's odd;*
> *I am always about in the quad.*
> *And that's why the tree*
> *Will continue to be,*
> *Since observed by*
> *Yours faithfully,*
> *GOD*

Or, in Berkeley's own, more sober words at *Principles* §6: '[S]o long as they [bodies] are not actually perceived by me, or do not exist in my mind or that of any other created spirit, they must either have no existence at all, or else subsist in the mind of some eternal spirit' (Berkeley 1998a: 105).

However, there are traces in Berkeley's work of a somewhat different answer to the question about what happens to objects when they are not perceived by a 'created spirit'. For Berkeley writes:

Berkeley's phenomenalism

The table I write on, I say, exists, that is, I see and feel it; and if I were out of my study I should say it existed, meaning thereby that if I was in my study I might perceive it. (Berkeley, 1998a: 104 [§3])

What Berkeley is suggesting here is a theory of perception which is called 'phenomenalism'. To this theory we now turn.

review
activity

1. What is the fundamental flaw in Berkeley's idealism?

2. With which two further problems does Berkeley's idealism have to cope? How does Berkeley attempt to solve them?

Phenomenalism

Phenomenalists tend to agree that reports of one's present sensory state are reports about sense-data or sensa. This view they share with representative realists. What is interesting and distinctive about phenomenalism is the account it gives of the continued existence of material objects when they are unobserved.

Mill's phenomenalism

We can distinguish at least two forms of phenomenalism. The first is expressed by John Stuart Mill. In a famous phrase, Mill spoke of objects as 'permanent possibilities of sensation'. At any moment, he says, we experience a great number of sensations. For instance, at present I am experiencing sensations of my computer, some flowers in front of me on the windowsill, trees and grass beyond the window and so on. However, at any moment I have the possibility of experiencing many other sensations. For example, I could go into the kitchen and there I would have sensations of the kitchen table, the sink and so on. And if I turn away from my work, I know there is the possibility that I could have the sensations I am at present having if I were to turn back to it. Mill notes, in what is by now a familiar thought, that our sensations – both actual and possible – exhibit coherence, order and stability. Moreover, my sensations agree with those of others: if you and I were to walk into my kitchen we would both see the kitchen table, the sink and so on. All this gives us the notion of a common world ordered according to laws of cause and effect. Hence Mill writes:

'Permanent possibilities of sensation'

> The world of Possible Sensations succeeding one another according to laws, is as much in other beings as it is in me; and has therefore an existence outside me; it is an External World. (Mill 1965: 281)

Problems for Mill's phenomenalism

On this version of phenomenalism, therefore, material objects are collections of actual or possible sensations. The idea of possible sensation looks strange because, as Berkeley argued, the notion of an unexperienced sensation seems confused. However, the basic difficulty that afflicts this version of phenomenalism is something else for it seems to have no explanation of *why* it is that we have the sensations we do, in the order we do. If we say that material objects are permanent possibilities of sensation then we have to ask why it is that they are such possibilities. The common-sense realist can explain why it is that when I go into the kitchen I see the table, the sink and the rest. His explanation is that this is because there is a table and there is a sink in the kitchen. But this is not the explanation that the phenomenalist can give, for according to phenomenalism the unseen table in the kitchen is just the possibility that I should see it were I to go into that room. Why this should be so is unexplained within the phenomenalist's terms.

Ayer's linguistic phenomenalism

Mill's is not the only form of phenomenalism. Another form is that which claims, in A.J. Ayer's words (Ayer 1984: 118) that 'every empirical statement about a physical object ... is reducible to a statement, or a set of statements, which refer exclusively to sense-data'. This is a linguistic version of the phenomenalism we have already examined. What this version of phenomenalism claims concerning the continued existence of objects when they are not being perceived is that this existence is to be analysed in terms of what are called *subjunctive conditionals.* Others refer to these as *counterfactuals.* The basic idea here is that to say that an object continues to exist at a place when not perceived is to say that if a perceiver *were* in that place he *would* see the object in question. For example, I am at present in my study and not in the library. To say that there are unobserved books in the library is to say that if I *were* in the library, I *would* have certain sense-data, normally describable as seeing the books. Similarly, it is to say that if you were in the library you would have certain sense-data (normally describable as seeing the books) and if I were to change my place in the library I would have slightly different sense-data from those I previously had, and so on.

Problems for Ayer's phenomenalism

This version of phenomenalism faces at least two major difficulties. First, if we seek to provide an adequate translation of every material object statement into a statement in terms of subjunctive conditionals, then it is probable that we should have to provide an infinite number of such conditionals. The reason for this can be seen by returning to the example of the books in the library. To provide an account of the existence of the books in the library in phenomenalistic terms we should have to specify what would be seen if I were at this point in the library, at that point in the library, at yet a third point in the library and so forth, as well as what would be seen if you were at such and such a point in the library, at such and such another point in the library and so on, as well as what would be seen if Freddie were ... and so on. It is extremely unlikely that we could give such an analysis.

Secondly, it is not always clear precisely how we are to provide the subjunctive conditionals that phenomenalist analysis requires. This is because it is far from clear just what perceptual experiences would be had in certain circumstances. Thus, to take Jonathan Dancy's example (Dancy 1985: 91), suppose we take the statement 'there is a red rose in the dark'. It is implausible to think that we could specify precisely the subjunctive conditionals that would be required to translate this statement, for we do not know exactly what consequences for perception the red rose's being in the dark would have. In other words, the required translation is likely to be vague, and if this is so then we cannot continue to believe that statements about material objects can be adequately translated by the kinds of subjunctive conditionals in question.

review

activity

1. What does Mill mean by saying that objects are permanent possibilities of sensation?

2. In what way is Mill's phenomenalism open to objections?

3. What is distinctive about Ayer's phenomenalism?

4. To what problems is Ayer's phenomenalism exposed?

some questions to think about

1 Does the fact that Descartes never doubts that he can reason clearly, use language and the like show that his method of doubt is philosophically pointless?

2 What is there to be said for the idea that we cannot distinguish between waking and dreaming experience?

3 Is Descartes' 'hyperbolical' doubt a genuine form of doubt? Would it matter for his argument if it were not?

4 'You know that you are reading this book.' Is this assertion correct?

5 'Wittgenstein's arguments in *On Certainty* show that scepticism is not so much false as empty.' To what extent would you agree with this claim?

6 To what extent do you think it true to say that our beliefs must in some way have foundations?

7 'I can never be mistaken about the way things look to me.' What does this mean and is it true?

8 'The coherence theory of justification can make no real sense of the fact that there can only be one set of truths about the world.' Is this true?

9 'Common sense realism about perception is mistaken since it can make no sense of the fact that material objects can look to us in certain ways.' To what extent would you agree with this?

10 'If scepticism can only be defeated by embracing idealism then this is too high a price to pay.' Do you agree?

11 When discussing Berkeley's idealism, Samuel Johnson (1709-1784) kicked a large stone and exclaimed: 'I refute it *thus*'. Is this an adequate reply to Berkeley? If not, why not?

further
reading

▶ Very good introductions to epistemology include Morton 2001, Audi 1998 and Dancy 1985. The first of these is easily the most accessible to beginners. Extremely useful anthologies are Sosa and Kim (eds) 2000 and Bernecker and Dretske (eds) 2000. Malcolm 1965 and 1977a are very heavily influenced by Wittgenstein and a pleasure to read.

▶ The best, easily obtainable introductory book on Descartes is Cottingham 1986. Among the secondary literature mentioned in the text Williams 1987 stands out, although it is not always an easy read.

▶ Stroud 1984 is a thorough, if somewhat long-winded, discussion of scepticism. The first chapter contains a detailed discussion of Descartes' argument about dreaming. Austin and Moore, amongst others, are also discussed at length in the book. Grayling 1985 is a short, accessible attempt to refute scepticism. Austin 1964 is written in a tone that you will either love or hate.

▶ On Hume, I recommend the very clearly written Stroud 1985. Dancy 1987 is probably the best short modern introduction to Berkeley. Mackie 1976 is a sympathetic reading of Locke.

moral philosophy

Utilitarianism

important terms

Classical (Hedonistic) Utilitarianism: a moral theory according to which one should always act to maximise the happiness and/or to minimise the unhappiness of those affected by one's actions.

Commensurability: two things are commensurable when they can be compared in terms of the same units, concepts and so forth.

Consequentialism: any moral theory, such as utilitarianism, which says that one should always act to secure the best consequences. These consequences might be measured in terms of happiness, satisfaction of preferences or interests, the promotion of welfare or some other unit.

Decision procedure: in morality, a method for determining what one should do in any given case.

Ideal utilitarianism: a form of consequentialism in which ideal goods are promoted.

Negative responsibility: the claim that one is just as responsible for what one allows to happen as for what one does.

Negative utilitarianism: a version of utilitarianism in which one should aim to minimise unhappiness.

Positive utilitarianism: a form of utilitarianism in which one should aim to maximise happiness.

Psychological hedonism: the claim that human beings are always motivated to pursue pleasure and shun pain.

Rule utilitarianism: a form of utilitarianism in which rules to maximise happiness are followed.

Key topics in this chapter

- The nature of a moral theory
- Utilitarianism: act, positive/negative, rule, two-level, ideal

Introduction

Moral philosophy – also called 'ethics' – deals with morality. But what is morality itself? Rather than trying to answer this question directly, the best way to approach it is by considering some examples or situations of a moral nature.

Some examples

- In Shakespeare's *Measure for Measure* Claudio offends the law of Vienna by getting Julietta pregnant. Angelo, who has been installed as the highest power in the city by the Duke, condemns Claudio to death. Isabella, Claudio's sister, pleads with Angelo to save her brother. Angelo says that only if Isabella sleeps with him will he spare Claudio. The situation is particularly poignant because Isabella intends to enter a convent and remain a virgin for life. Further, Angelo has hitherto been thought of, and thought of himself, as one who could not experience the kind of desire for a woman that he now feels for Isabella. What should Isabella do?

- In his autobiography *The World of Yesterday* the Austrian author Stefan Zweig (1881–1942) tells of his meeting as a young man with the Belgian poet Verhaeren, whose work he already knew and admired. Zweig writes:

  [T]o serve this man and his work . . . was a truly bold decision, for this poet . . . was at that time still hardly known in Europe, and I knew in advance that the translation of his monumental poetic work and his three verse-dramas would take away two or three years from my own activities. But even as I decided to give all my energy, time and passion to the work of another, I gave myself the best thing: a moral task. My uncertain seeking and trying now had a meaning.   (Zweig 1999: 149)

  Zweig says that the task of translating Verhaeren's poetry is a *moral* task. What does this mean? What makes a task a moral task?

- In his novel *The Good Soldier* Ford Madox Ford (1873–1939) describes various liaisons which Edward Ashburnham has with different women. At one point he falls in love with Nancy Rufford. Leonora, Edward's wife, is tormented by jealousy. Ford gives the reader Leonora's thoughts:

important terms

Leonora wished to bring the riding-whip down on Nancy's young face. She imagined the pleasure she would feel when the lash fell across those queer features; the pleasure she would feel at drawing the handle at the same moment toward her, so as to cut deep into the flesh and to leave a lasting wheal.

(Ford 1999: 190)

Should Leonora feel guilty at what she imagines? Or does it not matter, because she is, after all, only imaging it, and does not go on to hurt Nancy in the way described? Do thoughts matter, morally speaking, even if they do not lead to action?

What is moral philosophy?

These three examples are all situations that we easily recognise as being moral examples. Yet, although they are in some ways similar, they are nonetheless very different from one another.

The first has to do with a *moral dilemma*, that is, a situation in which a person feels morally obliged to do two things – in this case, care for her brother but also preserve her (sexual) integrity – but in which she cannot do both.

The second is a situation where morality has to do with two things: with *helping another person* and with what a person does to give *meaning* to his life. For it is clear that Zweig thinks that translating Verhaeren's poetry will help the poet. But it is also clear that in translating the work Zweig thinks he will be doing something that is meaningful to himself in some fundamental sense.

The third concerns questions of the *moral significance of the thoughts* a person has, and how they are connected with her character and actions.

Philosophy and the giving of reasons

The fact that the three examples given differ greatly from one another is an indication of how wide-ranging our notion of morality is. That is, many different situations, ideas and the like can properly be thought of as moral situations and ideas. Moral philosophy concerns itself with all of these. It does so by asking just the sort of questions I have already asked in describing the three examples from Shakespeare, Zweig and Ford. Of course, different philosophers will try to answer these and other questions in different ways. However, all philosophical answers will attempt to give *reasons* for those answers. The philosopher is not concerned merely to give his personal opinion or hear the personal opinion of others. He wants to discover what kind of *justification* for a given answer a particular person has.

For example, suppose you think that Leonora should not feel guilty about her fantasies of hurting Nancy. You might give as your reason that it is what people do, not what they think, which matters from a moral point of view. The philosopher might then ask you whether you would feel the same way if you found out that your friend despised you but always behaved as if she cared for you. If that bothers you, then you might want to reassess your view on Leonora. And so on.

The challenge of moral philosophy

Moral philosophy is thus an intellectual discipline that challenges you to formulate reasons for why you believe what you believe on moral issues. You might find, of course, that you have no good reasons for thinking what you think on one or more issues. So you might change your mind. However, philosophy does not require you to do that. What it does require you to do is to step back from what you believe and examine it.

Moral theories

The nature of a moral theory

One common way in which philosophers try to examine what they think about morality is to construct *moral theories*. The word 'theory' comes from the Greek word *theoria*, meaning 'contemplation' or 'sight'. This etymology helps us understand what a moral theory is. A moral theory is a way of *looking* at morality.

In what way does a moral theory look at morality? We have already noted that there are many different kinds of phenomena that have to do with morality. This is so much the case that the whole area might seem a terrible tangle and confusion. For example, some people think that the treatment of animals is a very important and pressing moral problem, whilst others think that we are wasting our time in worrying about animals when so many human beings are leading miserable lives, and that the welfare of animals raises no serious moral issues. Or again, some people think that sexual relations raise lots of difficult and fundamental moral questions, whereas others think that sex does not, as such, raise any serious moral problems. What a moral theory does is to try to bring order to this confusion by telling us which are the most important of the issues with which morality concerns itself, which are of less importance, and which of no real importance at all.

Why should we care about being clear about such issues? One answer that many philosophers would give is that, ultimately, moral philosophy, in constructing moral theories, aspires to give us guidance as to *what we should do* or *how we should live*. Consider, again, the issue of animals' welfare. If a moral theory argues that this really is an important issue, and we agree with the theory, then we shall have a good reason to act in a certain way – say, give up eating meat. Moral philosophy thus takes us right into the heart of the way we lead our lives, day in, day out. It is this that makes it such an important discipline.

Utilitarianism

Moral theories do not, of course, come from nowhere. They must in some way grow out of, or connect with, our ordinary experience. One such theory where we can see this clearly is the theory of *utilitarianism*. The ordinary notion from which utilitarianism grows is that of *happiness*.

Happiness as the ultimate goal of human endeavour

Suppose someone is doing the gardening and you ask him why. Imagine he says that it helps keep him fit. Suppose you ask him why he wants to keep fit. He might say that this means that, in general, he can lead an active life. If you now ask why he wants to lead an active life he might say that to do so makes him happy. Here the questioning seems to come to an end. For it would surely be odd to ask him why he wants to be happy (cf. Hume 1985: 293). Is it not obvious that people aim for happiness? What could be more typical of human beings?

Classical utilitarianism, that is, utilitarianism in its traditional form, starts from such a position. It takes the everyday, common fact that human beings want to be happy and to do things which they think will make them happy and uses this notion of happiness as the key to an understanding of the moral life. How does it do this?

The greatest happiness principle

The central idea, according to utilitarianism, is that one should always act in such a way as to bring about the greatest amount of happiness possible for those who are affected by one's actions. Jeremy Bentham, who is often seen as the founding-father of utilitarianism, put this by saying that when one acts one should aim to produce *the greatest happiness of the greatest number*. Or, if it is not possible to produce happiness, then one should aim to *reduce the unhappiness* of the greatest number. This 'greatest happiness principle' Bentham also called 'the principle of utility'. He defines this as follows:

The principle of utility

> *By the principle of utility is meant that principle which approves or disapproves of every action whatsoever, according to the tendency which it appears to have to augment or diminish the happiness of the party whose interest is in question: or, what is the same thing in other words, to promote or to oppose happiness.*
>
> (Bentham 1962: 34)

So, another way to express the principle of utility would be to say that, according to this principle, happiness is the only thing desirable as an end (that is, for itself) and everything else that is desired is desired as a means to (or as a part of) happiness.

Because utilitarianism is concerned about producing happiness (or reducing unhappiness) it is known as a *consequentialist* theory. That is, what concerns utilitarianism is the idea that *we should act in order to bring about the best consequences* (the most happiness or the least unhappiness).

The basic idea of utilitarianism is clear if we consider an example.

Suppose you have a limited amount of money but would like to buy presents

Jeremy Bentham
(1748–1832)

Jeremy Bentham was the son and grandson of lawyers, and he was meant to follow his forebears into the profession. However, while studying, he became sickened by the law as it stood and turned to exploring how it could be improved. His main interest was thus in public and political life, and he fought for many reforms, going so far as to design a new kind of gaol, the 'Panopticon', of which he was to be the manager. The prison never was built, but he did found University College London in 1817 on a non-religious basis, the first university of such a kind in England. His body may still be seen at the College, preserved in a glass cabinet.

Bentham's design for a new type of prison: the Panopticon

for some of your friends. You could spend all of your money on one particularly lavish gift for one friend and have nothing left over for the others, or you could buy each of your friends a small gift. The utilitarian says that the right thing to do is the action which would create most happiness overall. So the question you should ask yourself is: would more people be happy if I gave everyone a small present, or would there be more happiness overall if I gave a present to just one friend and nothing to the others?

Obviously enough, this is, as stated, a fairly simple example, but it brings out some important features of utilitarianism.

Egalitarianism and impartiality

One of these is its *egalitarianism*. That is, each person who is affected by an action is to count for one, and none for more than one. The happiness of any given person affected by an action cannot be more or less important than the happiness of any other person who is also affected by that action. This includes the person doing the action who may well gain for himself more happiness by doing one thing than another. This makes the theory *impartial*.

Utilitarianism and states of affairs

A second important feature of utilitarianism that comes out in this example is that the happiness of one person can be weighed up against the happiness of other people. This is because what matters to the utilitarian is *bringing about a given state of affairs in the world*. What this means can be seen as follows. Suppose you give a present to each of your friends. Each person, let us say, gets three units of happiness from receiving the present. If you have six friends, then overall the world contains 18 units of happiness by your giving each friend a present. Call this state of affairs S1. Suppose, however, that, instead of giving a present to each friend, you give one big present to one friend and nothing to the others. Let us say that the friend who receives this big present gets 20 units of happiness. Clearly, the others who get no present will remain without an increase in their happiness. In this case, the world contains 20 units of happiness as a result of your giving the present. Call this state of affairs S2. So, the question the utilitarian asks is: does the world contain more happiness in S1 or in S2? Clearly the answer is S2. Hence, you should try to bring about S2. This shows the way in which, for a utilitarian, the happiness of one person can be weighed up against that of others.

review activity

Explain in your own words the 'greatest happiness principle'.

What is happiness?

So far we have been using the notion of happiness to explain the utilitarian theory. But it is unclear at this stage what happiness is. Some people think that happiness is a kind of contentment, a relaxed going-with-the-flow of life. Others think it involves the development of all one's powers to their full capacity. Others have thought it was fundamentally connected with intellectual reflection. Yet others still think it has something to do with being materially comfortable.

Happiness and unhappiness, pleasure and pain

Bentham suggested that we should think of happiness as consisting in *pleasure*. He naturally also thought that unhappiness should be thought of as consisting in *pain*. So, according to Bentham, the more pleasure you experience, the happier you are; and, the more pain you are in, the unhappier you are. This is why a Bentham's utilitarianism, as well being utilitarianism in its classical form, is also sometimes known as *hedonic* or *hedonistic* utilitarianism, from the Greek word for 'pleasure', *hedone*.

Psychological hedonism

One reason why Bentham thought of happiness and unhappiness in this way was that he believed in what is called *psychological hedonism*. That is, he believed that all human beings naturally seek pleasure and shun pain. As he put it:

> *Nature has placed mankind under the governance of two sovereign masters,* pain *and* pleasure. *It is for them alone to point out what we ought to do, as well as to determine what we shall do . . . They govern us in all we do, in all we say, in all we think.*
> (Bentham 1962: 33)

Commensurability

As Bentham thought that happiness consisted in pleasure and unhappiness in pain, he thought that we could compare the happiness of different individuals. For example, you might especially like travelling, reading English novels and sleeping, whereas I might be particularly keen on country walks, listening to music and writing books on philosophy. None of these activities, it seems, has much in common with all the others. They form a very mixed bag, because the experience of, for example, country walks is very different from the experience of reading. However, if we say that the reason you like travelling, reading and sleeping is that these activities give you pleasure, and that the reason I like walking, music and philosophy is that they provide me with pleasure, then we can compare the things you like with the things I like. For, far from being a mixed bag, they will be, at a fundamental level, *commensurable*, that is, comparable with one another in the same terms, namely, pleasure. Commensurability means that even though travelling, reading, sleeping, walking, music and philosophy (and other activities) *look* very different they *are*, in fact, similar, for they are all ways of trying to obtain pleasure.

Bentham was very rigorous in insisting on this commensurability. For example, he famously asserted that if one person gets pleasure from poetry and another gets pleasure from push-pin – a simple children's game – then the only thing to choose between them is the amount of pleasure that each provides for the individual in question. He was only interested in the *quantity* of pleasure an activity provides and made no distinction between poetry and push-pin (or, indeed, anything else) in terms of the *quality* of the pleasure they afford.

It was because Bentham thought of happiness in terms of pleasure that he was able to find natural and plausible the idea of assigning arithmetical units to happiness in the way I did with my example earlier concerning the buying of presents. He drew up a 'felicific calculus' (from the Latin *felix*, 'happy'), which, he claimed, could allow us to measure the degree of a people's happiness or unhappiness (pleasure or pain) in terms of the following factors (Bentham 1962: 64–7):

The felicific calculus

1. intensity;
2. duration;

3.   certainty or uncertainty;

4.   propinquity or remoteness;

5.   fecundity, that is, the chance of a pleasure producing other pleasures and the chance of a pain producing other pains;

6.   purity, that is, the chance of a pleasure producing pains and the chance of a pain producing pleasure;

7.   extent – that is, the number of people sharing in the pleasure or pain.

An example will show the way this is supposed to work. Imagine that a politician has a certain limited amount of money that he can spend on improving conditions in prisons or on improving conditions in hospitals and that he must spend it all on one or the other. First, he considers what would happen if he spent the money on prisons. So, he must try to work out the pleasure that each individual prisoner would get from an increase of expenditure. For this, he uses 1–4. That is, for each prisoner he must work out what the intensity of the pleasure would be that the prisoner would get from the increase in expenditure; how long the pleasure would last, and so on. Then he must factor in 5 and 6 for each individual prisoner. This gives him a measure of the happiness of each individual prisoner. Then he must add together the happiness of each inmate in order to work out the total happiness that would be created by spending the money on prisons – this is 7, above. 1–7 thus gives him a figure for total happiness for prisoners – call it H1. Then he must repeat the process for hospitals, arriving at the total happiness for patients – call it H2. He then compares H1 and H2 and acts to bring about whichever of the two is greater. If they are the same, it makes no difference whether he spends the money on prisons or on hospitals.

review
activity

1.   How does Bentham understand happiness?

2.   What is psychological hedonism?

3.   What does it mean to say that, for Bentham, all pleasures are commensurable?

4.   What are the features of Bentham's felicific calculus? Formulate your own example to illustrate how it is supposed to work.

Mill's utilitarianism

John Stuart Mill, whose father, James Mill (1773–1836), was a friend of Bentham's and brought his son up to be a utilitarian, agreed that all human beings aim at happiness but objected very strongly to the idea that all pleasures are commensurable, that is, that there are no differences in quality as between different pleasures. He did so for a number of reasons, one of which was that he wanted to respond to the objection that utilitarianism, in focusing on pleasure, seemed to many to be a swinish doctrine, that is, for those who simply pursued sensual pleasure and nothing else (Mill 1991: 137ff.).

Higher and lower pleasures

According to Mill, there is a distinction in *quality* between pleasures, and he thus distinguished between what he called 'higher' and 'lower' pleasures. His basic idea was that pleasures of the mind and spirit – philosophy, poetry, conversation and so on – were higher pleasures, whilst those of the body – eating, sleeping, drinking and the like – were lower pleasures. His reason for allotting one type of pleasures to the higher category and one type to the lower was that he thought that those familiar with both sorts would choose to pursue the higher ones over the lower ones. He says:

> If I am asked, what I mean by difference of quality in pleasures, or what makes one pleasure more valuable than another, merely as pleasure, except its being greater in amount, there is but one possible answer. Of two pleasures, if there be one to which all or almost all who have experience of both give a decided preference, irrespective of feeling any moral obligation to prefer it, that is the more desirable pleasure. If one of the two is, by those who are competently acquainted with both, placed so far above the other that they prefer it . . . and would not resign it for any quantity of the other pleasure . . . we are justified in ascribing to the preferred enjoyment a superiority in quality . . . (Mill, 1991: 139)

The test of competent judges

So, Mill's test is one of *competent judges*: those who are familiar with a wide variety of pleasures. For example, if someone is familiar with the pleasures of philosophy and the pleasures of eating then that person will prefer to have the pleasures of philosophy to those of eating. This means that the pleasure of philosophy is a *higher* pleasure than that of eating.

Problems in the distinction between higher and lower pleasures

One difficulty in Mill's distinction between higher and lower pleasures is that it is often unclear just which pleasures are higher and which lower. For example, is the pleasure of drinking a higher or lower pleasure? Mill would certainly have thought it a lower pleasure, but things are not so simple. There is a world of difference between gulping down a pint of water and enjoying a wine so fine that it takes years of cultivating the palate to be able to appreciate it. As Ernest Hemingway wrote in his book on bullfighting *Death in the Afternoon*:

> Wine is one of the most civilised things in the world and one of the natural things of the world that has been brought to the greatest perfection . . . One can learn about wines and pursue the education of one's palate with great

John Stuart Mill (1806–73)

John Stuart Mill, one of the foremost thinkers and social reformers of the nineteenth century, has left a moving record of his life in his *Autobiography*. His father carried out on him an extraordinary educational experiment, teaching him ancient Greek and mathematics from the age of three. He later complained that he had had no real childhood and that all his learning had dried up the sources of emotional response in him. This was somewhat ameliorated by his encounter with the works of the romantic poets, particularly Wordsworth. He was also profoundly helped in this regard, and many others, by Harriet Taylor, whom he met in 1830 and with whom he fell in love. She was, however, a married woman, and it was not until after her husband's death in 1851 that they married.

enjoyment all of a lifetime . . . [A] person with increasing knowledge and sensory education may derive infinite enjoyment from wine.

(Hemingway 1987: 289)

So, perhaps drinking wine is, or is sometimes, a higher pleasure.

However, not only is it difficult to categorise some activities as higher or lower pleasures but it seems also to be the case that whether an activity is higher or lower depends on the other activities with which compares it. Perhaps drinking fine wine is a pleasure higher than drinking water; but it might still be a lower pleasure than, say, the reading of poetry.

Another difficulty in Mill's presentation of the distinction between higher and lower pleasures is that Mill seems to claim that the person who is familiar with both higher and lower pleasures will *always* choose a higher over a lower pleasure. He says that those who are acquainted with both higher and lower pleasures 'give a marked preference to the manner of existence which employs their higher faculties'. He goes on to say that it is only 'from infirmity of character' that anyone familiar with both forms of pleasure ever prefers to pursue the lower instead of the higher (Mill 1991: 139; 140-1). But this just does not seem to be true. We can agree that someone who enjoys philosophy or literature or history will not willingly lose these from his life. Nonetheless, someone who enjoys these things could clearsightedly decide not to pursue them on occasion in favour of, say, swimming or lying in the sun or eating pasta. Mill's implicit thought seems to be that a life that contained only such things as philosophy, literature and history is a better kind of life than one which contained these things *as well as* swimming, lying in the sun and Italian food. In fact, a life that contains *both* these kinds of things is, at least for some people, surely richer than one which does not.

In any case, leaving aside these difficulties, let us consider the nature of the so-called higher and lower pleasures a little further. One thing to note is that, as Mill understands the distinction, the lower pleasures are quite *simple* whereas the higher pleasures are *complex.* To see this, consider the following. Suppose you are hungry and want to eat a cheese sandwich (lower pleasure). Then, if you eat a cheese sandwich your hunger will be satisfied and you will experience pleasure. If, however, you want to understand moral philosophy (higher pleasure), for example, you will have to think and work hard, read books and articles attentively, and generally have to accept and overcome many difficulties before you fully understand the subject. This means that the higher pleasure of studying philosophy brings with it quite a lot of frustration. Nonetheless, Mill still thought that because the pleasures of philosophy are higher than those of eating (and drinking and so on) they are worth pursuing.

Socrates and the fool Animals, of course, can only experience the lower pleasures, whereas human beings can experience both these *and* the higher pleasures. So Mill saw that animals might be more satisfied than human beings: their pleasures are much simpler and thus unlikely to bring frustrations with them. However, because the pleasures of animals *are* only of the *lower* kind Mill thought – as he puts it in a famous aphorism – that it is better to be a human being dissatisfied than a pig satisfied. He also put this by comparing the life of the philosopher with that of the fool – who is familiar with only the lower pleasures – and saying that it is better to be Socrates dissatisfied than a fool satisfied (Mill 1991: 140). The comparison with Socrates (469–399 BC) is especially interesting because his philosophising brought him into conflict with the authorities in Athens and he was condemned to death.

Many philosophers have objected to Mill's comparison between human beings and the pig, and between Socrates and the fool. For, even if it is true that the pursuits of the philosopher are of greater value than those of the fool, the reason for this is not, it seems, that the philosopher is able to judge of the quality of the fool's pleasures by being acquainted with them. For he can, perhaps, no more do so than the fool can judge of the philosopher's pleasures. As Alan Ryan has said (Ryan 1974: 111): 'The philosopher who is a half-hearted sensualist cannot estimate the attractions of a debauched existence, any more than the sensualist flicking through the pages of Hume can estimate the pleasures of philosophy.'

Ryan goes on to offer a second objection to Mill's comparison.

> *An even more powerful objection to the way Mill sets about comparing the lives of Socrates and the fool is that it is very implausible to suppose them both to be acting according to the promptings of pleasure, but different sorts of pleasure. To say that Socrates prefers his way of life, even if he is constantly dissatisfied, is to say that he thinks it better, not that he thinks it more pleasant.*
>
> (Ryan 1974: 111)

Is there, then, nothing in Mill's distinction between higher and lower pleasures? Perhaps we can say something in defence of it. Compare the pleasures of playing the piano with those of eating one's fill. Mill would certainly classify the former as a higher, the latter as a lower, pleasure. Why? Here is a reason. A pleasure like playing the piano is one that involves the exercise of distinctive human faculties of skill, understanding, insight and interpretation and calls on the player to develop distinctive virtues such as patience, dedication and persistence. Further, playing the piano can give a great deal of pleasure to others. None of this seems to apply to eating one's fill or, at best, it does so only to a much lesser extent.

review activity

1. Why did Mill object to Bentham's claim that all pleasures are commensurable?

2. On what basis did Mill distinguish higher from lower pleasures?

3. What are the features of higher and lower pleasures, according to Mill?

4. What difficulties are there in categorising some pleasures as higher and some as lower?

However, this defence of Mill runs into the difficulty in Ryan's second criticism mentioned above. This is that activities that expand and deepen the mind, require skill to be done well, call for insight and the like, can be valued even when they produce no pleasure at all. In other words, if some activity deepens the mind, it is, one might argue, valuable for that very reason, regardless of whether it provides pleasure. Of course, it is true that, if it provides pleasure as well, then this is so much the better. It is also true that, if it *never* provided anyone with *any* pleasure, it is doubtful that anyone would do it. However, it does not follow from this that its value lies in its producing pleasure or that we cannot think it valuable independently of whether it produces pleasure.

Positive and negative utilitarianism

We noted earlier that according to utilitarianism we should aim to increase the happiness of those affected by our actions or seek to reduce the unhappiness of those so affected. We could separate these two out if we wished to. Then we should have two forms of utilitarianism. These are called *positive* and *negative* utilitarianism. A positive utilitarian will say we should aim simply to increase the happiness of all those affected by our actions; a negative utilitarian will say that we should seek to reduce the unhappiness of those affected by our actions.

In practice, few utilitarians wish to distinguish these two forms of the theory. A central reason for this is that it is often unclear whether we should describe an action as increasing happiness or decreasing unhappiness. For example, suppose you wish to learn German and I teach you the language. Then we could say that I am increasing your happiness. However, we could just as easily say that I am reducing your unhappiness by removing your ignorance of German. There seems to be no good reason to insist on the one description rather than the other. As this is so, we cannot properly distinguish positive from negative utilitarianism.

There is, in any case, an important reason why most philosophers would be sceptical about negative utilitarianism. J.J.C. Smart has pointed out that negative utilitarianism seems to have at least one bizarre consequence (Smart in Smart and Williams 1985: 29). This is that if we wished to reduce unhappiness we could effectively do this by blowing up the world and killing everyone. For everyone is unhappy at times, and if everyone were dead then no one would ever be unhappy. This is so even if most people are, in fact, happy most of the time, for the negative utilitarian is not concerned with happiness at all, but with reducing unhappiness. Imagine, for example, that the total world population was ten people and that each person's life contained nine units of happiness and one unit of unhappiness. Then we could reduce the total unhappiness by killing everyone, for we would in this way be removing from the world ten units of unhappiness in total. This is so even though we would also thereby be reducing the happiness of the world by destroying 90 units of happiness. However, the negative utilitarian does not care about that: he is only interested in reducing unhappiness. For this reason not many philosophers think that negative utilitarianism is a plausible theory.

review
activity

1. What is negative utilitarianism?
2. To what major problem is negative utilitarianism exposed?

Advantages of classical utilitarianism

There are several features of utilitarianism which have made it an attractive moral theory to many philosophers. Here are some of them.

Utilitarianism as a secular morality

1. The theory makes no appeal to religious thought or entities. We live in an increasingly secular world and many people feel that our moral thinking should free itself from the dependence on Christianity that has characterised it for 2000 years. Utilitarianism most emphatically aims to do this (cf. Williams 1982: 97).

The connection with human nature

2. As already noted, the theory connects directly with the human desire for happiness and thus appears very much in line with common-sense notions concerning human nature.

A common-sense approach

3. In its aim to maximise happiness, the theory seems eminently 'common-sensical'. After all, if we care about being happy, we surely care about being as happy as possible.

Egalitarianism

4. As we have already seen, the theory is egalitarian and this accords with a moral view that many people share in the modern world, namely that we should treat everyone equally.

Human wellbeing

5. The theory focuses directly on human wellbeing, which surely should be a key notion in any theory of morality. Indeed, the central virtue that utilitarianism seeks to instil in people is benevolence or kindness towards others, and this is very much a central virtue of modern life.

A decision procedure

6. Utilitarianism aims to provide what is called a *decision procedure*. That is, it is a theory which tells us how to act in any given situation. If we are utilitarians, we need never be unsure what to do, from a moral point of view, for we know that we should always act in such a way as to maximise happiness. Many utilitarians take this to be a great advantage of the theory.

review
activity

State in your own words the major advantages of utilitarianism as a moral theory.

Difficulties for classical utilitarianism

As we have seen, there is much to be said for classical utilitarianism. However, there are also reasons to be sceptical of the theory. Here are some of them.

Is psychological hedonism true?

1. One difficulty with classical utilitarianism is its claim that human beings are motivated by the pursuit of pleasure and avoidance of pain. For it just seems to be true that people pursue activities that cannot be rightly thought of as giving them pleasure. Consider, for example, the following comments by Alasdair MacIntyre in an essay on the concept of pleasure:

As I write this essay I can list a dozen activities or experiences that would afford me pleasure. I have no strong reason for abstaining; I do not particularly enjoy writing essays; I am not writing with a great sense of urgency; I have the time and money to indulge myself. Yet I do not rush to open a Guinness or Mr. P.G. Wodehouse's new novel.   (MacIntyre 1971: 171)

In other words, MacIntyre does not obtain much pleasure from writing essays, and there are plenty of other things he could be doing which would given him pleasure. Yet he continues writing his essay. Why? Surely the answer is that writing the essay is part of a lifestyle that helps him find *meaning* in his life or see a *point* to his life. This is surely true for many of the things we do: we do them because we find them meaningful in various ways, not because they afford us pleasure. Indeed, we do many things we find meaningful even though they do not make us happy (except in an extended meaning of the word 'happy', which is more or less equivalent to the meaning we find in things).

Welfare, interest and preference utilitarianism

It is largely owing to such difficulties in the concepts of pleasure and happiness that many modern utilitarians do not speak of maximising happiness but of maximising *welfare* or the satisfaction of individuals' *preferences* or *interests*. Some utilitarians thus think of themselves as, for example, welfare utilitarians or preference utilitarians. For instance, if you want to drink a class of cold water then it promotes your welfare or satisfies your preferences or interests if I give you a glass of cold water to drink. However, the notion of promoting someone's welfare or satisfying his preferences or interests is complicated, and is not the same as satisfying his desires, as the following examples make clear.

Suppose you wish to drink a glass of cold water and see what you take to be a glass of cold water in front of you. You will want to drink this. However, if I know that this is not a glass of cold water but of sulphuric acid, then it promotes your welfare or satisfies your preferences or interests if I stop you drinking the glass of liquid even though you want to drink it. Or, to take another example, children often do not want to learn to read and write but we know that it promotes their welfare if they are made to. This is why we insist that all should be educated to at least a minimal level.

These examples show that if someone's desires are satisfied it does not directly follow from this that his welfare is promoted or that his preferences or interests are satisfied. It might be in his interests to have his desires frustrated, as it is right for me to frustrate your desire to drink what you take to be a glass of cold water when I know it to be in reality sulphuric acid. Basing a moral theory on interests or preferences is, therefore, likely to turn out to be very complicated.

review
activity

Explain the difficulties in psychological hedonism.

Problems in measuring pleasures

2.   A second problem with classical utilitarianism is in its understanding of pleasure and pain. Bentham, as we have seen, suggested that we can

compare pleasures in terms of the felicific calculus. Can we? Is not the pleasure of going swimming quite different from that of watching a good film? Is the pleasure of playing football not very different from that of listening to music? Surely it is just not true that we can measure all of these on one scale. (Cf. MacIntyre 1985: 63–4.)

Knowledge of the consequences

3. A third problem with classical utilitarianism is that we cannot always know what the distant consequences of our actions are going to be, yet, according to utilitarianism, we are supposed to act in the light of the consequences of our actions. But if we do not know what those consequences will be, how can the theory help us to act?

The standard reply to this objection is that usually we *can* have a fairly good idea what the consequences of our actions will be and that, even if we do not, we can, for practical purposes, forget about the very distant consequences.

The difficulty with this response is that it is rather optimistic. Politicians often act in ways that affect millions of people and yet have little idea what the consequences of their actions are likely to be. Or again, consider the inventors of the motor-car, moving pictures or the computer. Could any of these have foreseen the consequences of their inventions?

Utilitarianism as too demanding

4. Many have argued that utilitarianism is an absurdly demanding moral theory. To see this, consider the following example. Suppose you would like to eat an ice cream. Now consider that there are people in the world with insufficient clean drinking water, let alone luxuries such as ice cream. If you were to give your money to Oxfam or some other charity to help provide drinking water to those without it then you would surely be creating more happiness (or promoting more welfare or satisfying more people's preferences or interests) than if you spent your money on an ice-cream. However, there are so many situations like this in life, that really a consistent utilitarian ought to give away everything he has to improve the life of others up to the point where, if he gave anything else away, he would be worse off than those he is trying to help. Indeed, Peter Singer, a contemporary utilitarian, argues just this (Singer 1993: ch.8). Yet surely a moral theory that has the consequence that we should all the time be doing good works (perhaps taking time off to recover our energy to do some more) has an excessively narrow view of what things in life it is worthwhile to do.

Utilitarianism as too impartial

5. This last problem is connected with another. We have seen that it is often thought to be a point in favour of utilitarianism that it is impartial. But some philosophers think that it is *too* impartial. For example, suppose you hear cries coming from a burning house and are brave enough to try to rescue the people inside. You may discover that there are two people there whose lives are threatened, only one of whom you have time to save: your mother, who is otherwise an ordinary woman, and a famous and brilliant surgeon who has saved the lives of many sick people and who will surely go on to do the same if he is rescued. Whom should you rescue? On the utilitarian view it seems that

you should rescue the surgeon, as this will bring greater happiness to world overall. Yet surely you would feel that you have some special bond to your mother that suggests you should save her and not the surgeon (cf. Godwin 1994).

What this example shows is that utilitarianism has difficulty making sense of those special ties and obligations that are important in our lives, such as our relationships with our family and friends. We are asked to consider these as of no special significance at all for morality. Of course, everyone will agree that we are sometimes faced with a clash between moral demands and the demands of personal affection. What utilitarianism asks us to do, however, is to forget all about those demands of personal life when making a moral decision. That, surely, is just to ride roughshod over some of those things that make human life worthwhile.

review
activity

1. Why do some people think that utilitarianism is too demanding? Give an example of your own to illustrate the point.

2. Why might utilitarianism be thought to have an inadequate understanding of personal relationships?

Utilitarianism and obligations

6. Many philosophers think that utilitarianism does not have a proper understanding of the notion of obligation. Consider an example. Suppose you have promised to meet a friend at five o'clock to help her with her philosophy homework. Then someone rings you and asks you to go to the cinema. We normally think that the promise binds you to meet your friend and help with the homework and that your desire to go to the cinema does not alter this: you must keep your promise. However, for the utilitarian the only thing that counts is the consequences. If there will be more happiness in the world in your going to the pictures than in helping your friend, then the promise you made counts for nothing: you are free to ignore it.

The fundamental reason utilitarianism has difficulty making proper sense of the notion of moral obligation is that an obligation is very often *backward looking*. You are obliged to meet your friend because you have promised to: what binds you is what you have done in the past – your making the promise – and the obligation in question cannot be properly understood wholly in terms of the consequences of what might happen or not happen depending on whether you keep it or not. Of course, almost everyone will agree that there are times when you might have to ignore your obligations, but the problem for utilitarianism is that it seems to make incomprehensible the very concept of an obligation as something which binds one *now* to do a particular thing, *not* because of the consequences, but *simply because one does, in fact, have this obligation.*

review
activity

Explain why utilitarianism has a problem explaining the notion of moral obligation.

Using individuals as mere means

7. Some philosophers object to utilitarianism on the ground that it seems willing to countenance the use of individuals as a mere means to increase the happiness of the world. We can see this by considering an example. Dostoyevsky's novel *Crime and Punishment* explores the case of Raskolnikov, a gifted young man who nonetheless lives in penury and hence cannot exercise his talents and gifts. He conceives the idea of murdering a mean old money lender and stealing from her the money that she has hoarded and that is of no use to her. He intends to use the money to do good for himself and for others, in a way that the money lender never would. His justification for the deed is thus fundamentally of a utilitarian nature: what justifies killing her is that overall this will lead to good consequences. However, once he has killed the old woman, he is filled with remorse at his deed, and comes to see that he has done an evil deed in thinking of the old woman as something that merely stood in his way of bringing more happiness into the world. As the philosopher Immanuel Kant (1724–1804), whose thought we shall investigate further below, would put it, the old money lender should never have been treated as a mere means to someone else's good: she has, despite her avaricious nature, dignity as a human being.

Utilitarianism and justice

8. The problems utilitarianism has in the above example come out in a slightly different form in a consideration of the concept of justice.

Suppose that a terrorist has blown up a pub and killed several people. A man is arrested for the crime. The police suspect that he is innocent and they have insufficient evidence to convict him. However, feelings in the general public are running high and it is generally believed that the man is responsible for the deed. In addition, the police themselves feel under pressure to reassure everyone that they are doing their job properly. Further, there is high-level political pressure to convict someone of the crime. The police therefore fabricate evidence, convict the man and cover their tracks so that no one discovers what has really happened. In such a case, it seems that the utilitarian must approve of the actions of the police because everyone is made happy by the conviction, except the man convicted, of course, but his unhappiness is outweighed by the overall happiness created.

In this way, it seems that utilitarianism fails to take seriously our ordinary conceptions of justice because it claims that in some cases it is right to 'punish' the innocent.

The usual utilitarian reply to this is that such a case is likely to happen very infrequently in the real world. However, this kind of situation certainly has occurred and, in any case, the fact that it is a theoretical possibility is still a powerful objection to utilitarianism.

review
activity

1. Why does utilitarianism have a problem explaining our sense of the dignity of human beings?

2. What are the problems that the concept of justice raises for utilitarianism? Give an example to illustrate the point.

Moral agency   9.   We have seen that utilitarianism claims that we should aim to produce states of affairs in which the greatest amount of happiness is present. Some philosophers have criticised utilitarianism as thus having an inadequate understanding of human agency. That is, they have criticised utilitarianism as having an inadequate understanding of the fact that when a person acts it is not just that he is bringing about a state of affairs, but that *he* is the person doing the act.

Jim and the Indians

We can see this through a example offered by Bernard Williams. Williams imagines the following case (Williams in Smart and Williams 1985: 98ff.). Jim is travelling in South America, and one day finds himself in the central square of a small town. Twenty Indians are tied up against the wall and a military captain explains to Jim that they are a random group of inhabitants who are going to be shot: there have been protests against the government recently, and this group of Indians is going to be killed as an example to the general population of the advantages of not protesting. However, the captain says that, because Jim is an honoured guest in the country, he will be allowed the privilege of shooting any one of the Indians, whereupon the other 19 will be released. If he does not shoot one of the Indians, one of the captain's men will kill them all. What should Jim do?

Williams argues that the correct answer for a utilitarian is *obviously* that Jim should shoot one of the Indians, and in this he is surely right. The problem is that, even if one comes to think that the utilitarian solution is right, one's thinking about the case will be a lot more complicated, and deeper, than the utilitarian can allow.

Negative responsibility

The reason for this is that, from the point of view of a utilitarian, the only issue here is that of the resultant state of affairs. Therefore, for the utilitarian the issue is one of how many bodies there are at the end: there will either be 20 bodies or one, and it is clearly better, for the utilitarian, that there be only one. What this leaves out, according to Williams, is that Jim's problem – assuming he is a normally decent person – is that either *he* will kill one of the Indians or he will not. For him, the issue is not one merely of the resultant state of affairs but of what *he* does. If he does kill one of them, there will be something he *does*, and in that sense he will be responsible for the death. However, if he does not kill one of them, then, at most, there will be something that he *allows to happen*, namely, the killing of the twenty. Utilitarianism cannot make sense of this distinction between *doing* and *allowing to happen*. For utilitarianism, one is just as responsible for what one allows to happen (or fails to prevent) as much as for what one does: this is known as the doctrine of *negative responsibility*. Williams says that a moral theory cannot just sweep away this distinction as if it did not matter.

Integrity Williams expresses Jim's predicament in terms of Jim's integrity. But he does not mean that Jim *thinks about* his integrity when thinking about what to do. He means the notion of integrity here merely to pick out the sense that it makes a difference to Jim whether *he* kills anyone or not.

Williams considers the objection that Jim is merely being self-indulgently squeamish in not simply accepting the captain's offer. He rejects this objection on the ground that it simply expresses a utilitarian's way of looking at the situation, and the whole point is that Williams thinks that this is not the correct way to look at it. Jim cannot just discount his feelings that it would be wrong to accept the offer and simply think of them as self-indulgent. Jim does not have 'a possessive attitude to [his] own virtue' as has been suggested by one critic of Williams's view (Glover 1992: 140). Williams says:

> *Because our moral relation to the world is partly given by such feelings, and by a sense of what we can or cannot 'live with', to come to regard those feelings from a purely utilitarian point of view, that is to say, as mere happenings outside one's moral self, is to lose one's moral identity; to lose, in the most literal sense, one's integrity.* (Williams in Smart and Williams 1985: 103–4)

If Williams is right, utilitarianism has thoroughly misunderstood something crucial about human agency.

review activity

1. Explain in your own words Jim's predicament.

2. Explain why Williams thinks that this case shows that utilitarianism has an inadequate understanding of human agency.

Rule utilitarianism

Some philosophers who have been attracted to utilitarianism have tried to amend the theory to cope with such problems as the last two discussed above. In order to see what their attempted solution is we must recognise that the form of utilitarianism we have been discussing is properly called *act utilitarianism* (it is also known as *direct utilitarianism*). This is because the theory tells us to assess each and every act in terms of its consequences without concerning ourselves with any other acts that we have done in the past. *Rule utilitarianism* (also known as *indirect utilitarianism*) alters this somewhat. According to this theory, we learn from experience the kinds of actions that, in the long run, contribute most to human happiness. For example, we learn that not to kill, not to steal and so on contribute to human happiness *in the long run*. This is so even if, *on a given occasion*, killing or stealing were to contribute more to human happiness than not killing or not stealing would. Thus, on utilitarian grounds we can establish the rules 'do not kill', 'do not steal' and so on, and it is these rules that we should follow.

This theory provides an answer to the problem of the man unjustly punished for terrorism. For, on utilitarian grounds we could surely say that the rule: 'do not punish the innocent', if followed, contributes in the long run to human happiness. This is so even if, *in the specific kind of case we have discussed,* to punish an innocent man would create more happiness than not to punish him would. Hence, we should stick to the rule not to punish the innocent man.

There is, however, a problem with this version of utilitarianism. Suppose you are a utilitarian and, further, that you truly believe that a given act would contribute most to happiness on a given occasion. Suppose, for example, that you truly believe that to punish the innocent man would engender more happiness than freeing him would. Then it seems that, if you insist that on this occasion the man should not be punished because to do so would be to violate a rule that in the long run contributes most to happiness, you must be half-hearted in your belief in utilitarianism. For it seems that you are allowing some non-utilitarian moral considerations to influence the way you think about this case. Which ones? Precisely ones concerned with justice from a non-utilitarian point of view. However, in this case you might as well admit that you care about things other than happiness and that your utilitarianism cannot be thoroughgoing; it can be, at best, only a part of your moral outlook.

What this means is that rule utilitarianism as a theory seems to be inadequate as it stands.

Two-level utilitarianism   There is, however, a form of utilitarianism that is related to rule utilitarianism and which may be more plausible. This we can call *two-level utilitarianism.* According to this version of utilitarianism, we can use normal, everyday moral thinking for the most part because experience has taught human beings the kind of ways of behaving that, in general, lead to happiness. Mill makes this point by saying that during

> *the whole past duration of the human species . . . mankind have been learning by experience the tendencies of actions; on which experience all the prudence as well as all the morality of life, is dependent . . . It is truly a whimsical supposition that if mankind were agreed in considering utility to be the test of morality, they would remain without any agreement as to what is useful . . . [M]ankind must by this time have acquired positive beliefs as to the effects of some actions on their happiness.* (Mill 1991: 155–6)

So according to Mill, the first level of moral reflection is that which goes on within the terms of everyday, customary morality. We are brought up to have certain moral feelings, reactions and so on that have, over the course of time, been found to be those feelings and reactions which, if most people have them, will lead those people, on the whole, to act in ways that contribute most, and reliably, to happiness.

However, there will be times when one might find that principles one holds conflict, and then one will have to ascend, so to speak, to a higher level of reflection in order to settle what to do. That higher level is the level of act utilitarian thinking.

'Archangels' and 'proles'

This kind of two-level theory has been defended by Richard Hare (1919–2002). He argues (Hare 1981, esp. ch.3) that, if we were all 'archangels' with, for example, the perfect ability to see all the consequences of any given act, then we could all be act utilitarians all the time, always maximising preference satisfaction. However, because we are, in fact, limited 'proles' we need principles that will work in most situations and we need to be deeply wedded to everyday forms of moral understanding such as that we must not kill, steal, cheat and so on. It is only when, for example, such principles clash that we should try to think like an archangel.

Hare addresses Williams's case of Jim, and he argues that, in this case, as we have seen, the utilitarian would think it right of Jim to shoot one of the Indians. However, he also argues that Williams is right to suggest that Jim – assuming, as before, that he is normally decent – will have a deep repugnance towards the deed. This is because Jim, like the rest of us, is a prole and has been brought up accordingly, that is, to believe in, and act on, specific principles, such as those forbidding killing. Hare claims, therefore, that two-level utilitarianism can explain *both* why Jim ought to feel a repugnance to killing the Indian *and* why he ought, nonetheless, to do it.

review activity

1. Explain rule utilitarianism.

2. To what problem is rule utilitarianism exposed?

3. What is two-level utilitarianism?

4. Explain carefully the difference between rule utilitarianism and two level utilitarianism.

Ideal utilitarianism

So far, we have looked at various forms of utilitarianism. There is another form of utilitarianism that we need to consider. This is called *ideal utilitarianism.*

Ideal utilitarianism is a form of consequentialism – it insists that the only thing that counts in assessing an act for its moral worth are its consequences. Ideal utilitarianism differs from other forms of utilitarianism in claiming that we should not be thinking about promoting happiness or welfare or the satisfaction of people's preferences or interests but rather about promoting certain things that are intrinsically good, good in themselves. What things are these? According to G.E. Moore (1873–1958), a leading ideal utilitarian, friendships and aesthetic pleasures are the two intrinsically valuable things. Thus he wrote in *Principia Ethica*, published in 1903, that:

the most valuable things, which we know or can imagine, are certain states of consciousness, which may be roughly described as the pleasures of human intercourse and the enjoyment of beautiful objects . . . [I]t is only for the sake of these things – in order that as much of them as possible may at some time exist – that any one can be justified in performing any public or private duty . . . [P]ersonal affections and aesthetic enjoyments include all the greatest, and by far the greatest, goods we can imagine. (Moore 1984: 188–9)

Moore's utilitarianism is clear in his claim that it is only if we act in order to bring about more by way of personal affections (friendship) and aesthetic enjoyments that we are fulfilling our duty: what matters for him are the consequences of actions. His idealism comes out in his claim that what we should seek to promote are those very ideals of personal affections and aesthetic enjoyments.

There is something strange in Moore's insistence that it is only personal affections and aesthetic enjoyments that are intrinsically good. For, although few would deny that these are valuable, there are surely many other things that, for an ideal utilitarian, and for others, could be thought of as good. Indeed, ideal utilitarians need not be constrained by Moore's account: they could allow that there are other things that are intrinsically good and that should be promoted. These might include not only friendship and aesthetic enjoyments but also love, knowledge, virtue and no doubt other things.

A problem for ideal utilitarianism

One difficulty with ideal utilitarianism is that it is not always good to promote some of the things that any given version of the theory might consider valuable in themselves. For example, there is little value in knowledge as such; otherwise there would be some value in my coming to know the number of hairs on my forearm by counting them up. Or again, love can very often be possessive and destructive, and in a given case the world might be a better place, morally speaking, for not containing it.

A second problem for ideal utilitarianism

A second difficulty for ideal utilitarianism can be seen in the following way. Remember that classical utilitarianism claimed that we naturally want to be happy and that to ask why someone wants to be happy makes no real sense. Since classical utilitarianism says that we *do* pursue our own happiness anyway, it makes no sense to think the theory ought to provide a reason why each of us *should* pursue our own happiness. However, it is not true that we always pursue those things which ideal utilitarianism claims are intrinsically good. This means that the theory has to give us a reason why we *should* pursue those things. For example, you might agree that philosophical knowledge is intrinsically good but this, as such, does not give you any reason to pursue this knowledge. And the theory does not seem to be able to give each of us any reason why we should pursue those things it deems intrinsically good. It just says they are intrinsically good, and even if we agree, this might leave us unwilling to pursue them. In abandoning the emphasis in classical utilitarianism on happiness, therefore, ideal utilitarianism leaves itself with an unresolved problem about what could motivate anyone to pursue those things it says are good.

Notice, in any case, that both classical utilitarianism and ideal utilitarianism are faced with another problem. This is that, even if I am motivated to pursue my own happiness or the things that ideal utilitarianism tells me are intrinsically good, it does not yet give me a reason why I should be concerned with doing anything to make anyone else happy or promote those goods for other people. However, this kind of problem is not a problem peculiar to utilitarianism. It is the general problem about why one should care about morality at all. The theories are not meant to address that issue. They assume, rather, that the people they are directed at care about morality and they wish to argue those people into looking at morality in a particular way. There is nothing unreasonable in approaching things this way; there might be a general problem about why people should care about morality, but this is not a special problem for utilitarian theories.

review activity

1. What is ideal utilitarianism?

2. To what two problems is ideal utilitarianism exposed?

some questions to think about

1. What do you consider to be the chief problems confronting utilitarianism?

2. Do you agree that it is better to be Socrates dissatisfied than a fool satisfied?

3. Which do you find the most plausible: act-, rule- or ideal utilitarianism?

4. 'Utilitarianism is wholly incapable of explaining what is wrong with the Nazis' treatment of the Jews.' Explain why someone might think this and give your reasons for agreeing or disagreeing with it.

5. Do you think utilitarianism is more useful as a personal morality or as a tool for deciding political policies?

6. 'Utilitarianism fails to understand that it makes a difference not just which states of affairs exist, but who brings them about.' Explain and discuss.

7. Which are the most plausible goods for an ideal utilitarian to suggest we should maximise? Give reasons for your choice.

further reading

▶ Crisp 1997 is a good, clear discussion of Mill's utilitarianism. Parekh (ed.) 1974 contains some useful essays on Bentham.

▶ Good collections of articles on utilitarianism and consequentialism are Scheffler (ed.) 1988, and Sen and Williams (eds) 1984. Singer 1993: ch.1 gives a brief but clear defence of interest utilitarianism. Smart and Williams 1985 is a modern classic on utilitarianism.

▶ Gaita 1991: ch.5 contains some unusual and valuable thoughts on the Jim type case. See also Holland 1980: ch.9, esp. 138–42 on this.

▶ For a tremendously interesting discussion of the concept of pleasure by a literary critic, see Trilling 1967: ch.3.

▶ In my opinion, Mill's *Utilitarianism* does not display his mind at its best. Two essays of his that are, I think, far superior are those on Bentham and Coleridge. The edition edited by F.R. Leavis 1971 is the best because Leavis's introductory essay is also excellent.

Kant's Moral Theory

important terms

Autonomy: the ability to be motivated by reason alone.

Categorical imperative: an imperative not dependent on a desire for its applicability to an agent.

Deontological moral theory: a moral theory whose central emphasis in on rules or principles.

Hypothetical imperative: an imperative dependent on a desire or other inclination for its applicability to an agent.

Maxim: a rule or principle on which one acts.

Universalisation: A maxim can be universalised when it can be willed without contradiction as a maxim on which all act.

Key topics in this chapter

- Categorical and hypothetical imperatives
- The three forms of the categorical imperative
- Causal determinism and moral responsibility
- The relation between reason and inclination
- Autonomy/freedom

I n this chapter we turn to look at the moral theory of Immanuel Kant. In discussing his thinking in moral philosophy we shall concentrate primarily, although not exclusively, on his work *The Groundwork of the Metaphysic of Morals* (also known as *The Foundations of the Metaphysic of Morals* or the *Grounding for the Metaphysics of Morals*). This is the text that is usually taken to express the core of Kant's moral theory.

Earlier we discussed the following example: you have promised to help your friend with her philosophy homework and then you receive an offer from another friend to go to the cinema instead. We would normally say that you are *obliged* to help your friend even if you *want* to go to the cinema. In this case, we have a clash between the demands of morality – your obligation to help your friend – and those of desire – your wish to go to the cinema.

The conflict between morality and desires

This kind of conflict between moral demands on the one hand and desires or wishes on the other is the kind of thing many people think of straight away when they reflect on the place that morality has in life. One way to put this

Immanuel Kant (1724-1804)

Immanuel Kant is, by common consent, one of the greatest, if not the greatest, philosopher of the modern era. He was the fourth of nine children of a poor harness-maker, and was brought up in the pietist faith, a branch of Lutheranism that emphasised the value of hard work, duty and prayer. He spent his whole life in Königsberg, Prussia, where he was born: the life he led there was extremely well disciplined and outwardly uneventful. He published his first major work, *The Critique of Pure Reason*, a work that changed the face of philosophy, in 1781, by which time he was 57. He went on to publish many further works, including two

more critiques (*The Critique of Practical Reason* and *The Critique of Judgement*). An emotionally reserved man, he nonetheless had many friends whom he would entertain at lengthy midday meals. He was also an admired teacher, lecturing not simply on many philosophical areas but also on a great many other topics from geography and anthropology to mathematics and mechanics.

is to say that morality makes demands on us that do not depend upon the desires we happen to have. Whether or not we want to do what morality requires of us is irrelevant; we have to do the morally right deed even if we do not want to do it.

Hypothetical imperatives

This way of looking at things is close to the centre of Kant's moral philosophy. He put it in terms of a distinction between *categorical* and *hypothetical imperatives*.

Categorical and hypothetical imperatives

Suppose you tell me you want to become a great pianist. Then I might tell you that you ought to practise a great deal in order to perfect your skill. Or suppose you want to go to Cambridge on the train and that you want to arrive by midday. Then I might say to you that you ought to leave from King's Cross station by the 10.35 train. In each case I tell you what you ought to do *given* the fact that you want to do something else. You ought to practise a lot *given* that you wish to become a great pianist; you ought to get the 10.35 from King's Cross *given* that you want to be in Cambridge by midday. We can put this in slightly different terms, using an 'if-then' clause:

a) *If* you want to become a great pianist then practise a lot.
b) *If* you want to get to Cambridge by midday then catch the 10.35 from King's Cross.

In both a) and b) I give you a reason to do something if you want to do something else. For if you do *not* want to become a great pianist then my command or *imperative* 'practise a lot' will be irrelevant to you. And, again, if you do *not* want to get to Cambridge by midday then my command or *imperative* 'catch the 10.35 from King's Cross' will not apply to you.

Kant called sentences such as a) and b) *hypothetical imperatives*. This is because the *imperative* in each case ('practise a lot'; 'catch the 10.35 from King's Cross') depends upon the supposition or *hypothesis* that you want to do something else (become a great pianist; get to Cambridge by midday).

Hypothetical imperatives involve what is called an *antecedent* – the 'if' part of the sentence; and a *consequent* – the 'then' part.

Many of the imperatives we use in daily life are hypothetical imperatives. Sometimes the hypothetical nature of such imperatives is *implicit*, that is, presupposed and not explicitly stated. For example, if I say to a friend 'you ought not to smoke' I am assuming that my friend does not want to get lung cancer. Fully spelt out, the imperative is seen to be hypothetical: '*if* you do not want to get lung cancer then you ought not to smoke'. For if my friend for some reason wants to get lung cancer then my imperative cannot apply to him.

Consider now this imperative:

c) You ought not to inflict needless suffering on others.

Is c) an implicit hypothetical imperative? If we say it is, then it might go like this when fully spelt out:

c[1]) *If* you want other people to think well of you then you ought not to inflict needless suffering on others.

However, this does not seem right at all. If someone says: 'well, I don't care whether other people think well of me or not, so I have no obligation not to hurt others' we should feel that something was mistaken in his response. Surely, one should not inflict needless suffering on others regardless of whether one wants others to think well of one or not. The desire that others think well of one is irrelevant to the fact that one ought not to harm others.

Perhaps, then, the imperative should be spelt out like this:

c[2]) *If* you want other people to help you when you need help then you ought not to inflict needless suffering on others.

However, c[2]) is no more correct than c[1]). We should think that someone who said, 'OK, but I'm strong and healthy and I'm prepared to take the risk that I'll never need the help of others, so it's all right for me to inflict suffering on others' had missed the crucial point about causing harm to other people. One ought not to inflict suffering on others whether or not one is prepared to take the risk that one will not need their help in the future.

In general, the same might be said of any desire we specify as being in place in the antecedent. The requirement not to inflict needless suffering on others *does not depend at all upon any desire one happens to have*, and therefore *is not a hypothetical imperative*. We therefore cannot attach any antecedent ('if you want X') to the consequent ('you ought not to inflict needless suffering on others').

Categorical imperatives

Kant expressed this by saying that the requirement not to inflict needless suffering on others is *categorical*. This is because the requirement not to inflict such suffering is a *moral* matter. Hence, Kant argued that each requirement of morality should be expressed in the form of a *categorically binding imperative* – or, more simply, a *categorical imperative* – and all other requirements should be expressed as *hypothetical imperatives*.

review activity

Explain Kant's distinction between hypothetical and categorical imperatives, providing your own examples of each.

Duty and desire

One way in which Kant expressed the idea that moral demands are categorical imperatives was to say that in doing what is morally right, or in abstaining from doing what is morally wrong, we are doing our *duty* or following certain *rules*. We have a duty not to steal, not to lie, not to harm others and so on, regardless of whether we want to do these things or not. For example, if you do not have enough money to buy a ring that you would really like to have, the fact that you want the ring is irrelevant to the fact that you have a *duty* not to steal it. We can also say that you have an *obligation* not to steal it.

Because the demands of *duty*, which are *moral* demands, are *categorical*, and therefore, as we have seen, do not depend upon one's having any particular desire, Kant said that the demands of morality are in general opposed to our desires, inclinations and other similar promptings. Morality appears to us firstly, although not exclusively, in terms of *that which is forbidden.*

Deontological theory

A theory such as Kant's that accords great importance to rules and principles is known in philosophy as a *deontological* theory. Kantianism is not the only form of deontological theory. Any religious set of moral *rules*, such as the Decalogue (the Ten Commandments), is also deontological.

Free will and reason

Causal determinism

Suppose you are playing snooker and you line up your shot. You strike the white ball with the cue, aiming at the blue ball, which you want to go into the pocket. You would be absolutely astonished if, when the white ball hit the blue ball, the blue ball started coming back in the direction from which the white hit it. You would also be astonished if it turned into a rabbit, or if it spread wings and took off. This is because we think that when one snooker ball hits another the behaviour of the second ball can be predicted: if the white ball hits the blue at such-and-such an angle, at such-and-such a velocity, and if each has such-and-such a mass, then the blue ball *must* move off in such-and-such a direction, at such-and-such a velocity. We can say that the blue ball is *caused* to move off in this way by the white ball and that it is *determined* to move off in this way, which is another way of saying it *must* move off in this way. The white ball *causally determines* the blue ball to move in a certain direction, at a certain velocity.

We can say that there is a chain of causes which leads to the blue ball's moving off in a certain way. These causes are, amongst other things: you holding the cue in a certain way; the cue striking the white ball as it does; and the white ball striking the blue ball as it does.

We normally think that everything that happens in the natural world is causally determined in the kind of way that the blue ball's movement is. That is, for every event that takes place – for example, a leaf falling from a tree, a stone breaking a window, a ship sinking – there is a chain of causes that determined the event to take place.

Prediction

Because each event that takes place in the natural world is causally determined we can formulate causal laws that allow us to *predict* what will happen if a certain set of circumstances exists or obtains. For example, Newton's laws of motion allow us to predict that if an object of a certain mass is fired from the surface of the earth at a certain velocity then it will behave in a certain way – for instance, it will fall back to earth at a certain place.

Similarly, the behaviour of animals can also be predicted. An animal is, according to this view, a very complicated mechanism whose movements can be predicted in the same kind of way that those of a projectile can be. Of course, in the case of an animal we have to take into account the fact that it acts on its desires. However, along with the physical nature of a given animal, the animal's desires explain why it behaves as it does. For example, putting it simply, if we know that a cat has the desire to eat some food and we place it in front of a bowl of food that is tasty to cats then we can predict that the cat will eat it.

Now consider the fact that human beings are part of the natural world, just as much as snooker balls, stones, projectiles and animals are. If we can predict the behaviour of snooker balls, stones, projectiles and animals it looks as if we must also say that we can predict the behaviour of human beings. However, this raises a problem. For if the behaviour of human beings can be predicted in just the same way as that of snooker balls and animals can be, then what has become of free human choices? After all, a snooker ball has no choice about how and where to move, given that it is struck in a certain way. A cat has no choice about eating, given that it is in the kind of situation I earlier described. If human behaviour is predictable in just the same kind of way as that of a snooker ball or a cat and there is no further difference except that of complexity, then it seems we must say that human beings also have no choice about what they do.

Responsibility and free will

Why should this matter? It matters because we cannot hold a cat responsible for what it does. It would be absurd to *blame* it for eating the food or think that it *ought not to have eaten the food*. However, then it looks as if we must say the same about human beings. Whatever you do, if your behaviour is as determined as is that of a cat, then I cannot *hold you responsible* for what you did, or *blame* you for what you did, or say that you *ought not to have done* what you did. However, that means that you have no *free will*.

Without free will there is no responsibility at all, and therefore no *moral* responsibility. Just as it would be absurd to hold a cat morally responsible for killing a mouse because it has no free will, if you also have no free will then I cannot hold you morally responsible for killing a living creature – whether it be a mouse or a human being.

The relation between reason and desires

Kant suggested that there is, after all, a way of thinking of human beings as having free will. For he suggested that, unlike an animal, we can *rationally reflect* on our desires. An animal, that is, simply acts on its desires, whereas a person can *think about* whether to act on them. A cat, for example, cannot think about whether to kill a mouse whereas a human being can think about whether to kill a living creature. When we subject our desires to reason in this way, we are free and can after all be held morally responsible for our actions.

Two standpoints

Central in Kant's discussion of our freedom is the idea that we can think about ourselves in two ways or from *two standpoints* (cf. Kant 1983: 118 [458]). If we merely *observe* the behaviour of another person then we can explain this behaviour in terms of natural causal laws, just as we can explain in this way everything that happens in nature. However, if we think about ourselves *from the inside*, then we understand ourselves to be able to act freely. We do not take ourselves to be determined by our desires, inclinations, urges and the like when we act. So, the very same actions seen from one point of view are seen as determined and seen from another point of view are seen as free.

In illustration of his point about how we view ourselves from the inside, Kant provides a very interesting example in the *Critique of Practical Reason*.

Suppose that someone says his lust is irresistible when the desired object and opportunity are present. Ask him whether he would not control his passion if, in front of the house where he has this opportunity, a gallows were erected on which he would be hanged immediately after gratifying his lust. We do not have to guess very long what his answer would be. (Kant 1956: 30 [30])

Kant's point here is, of course, that, even in the face of what seem overwhelmingly powerful desires, inclinations, urges and so forth, it is possible to ignore them and even act contrary to them. Of course, in this example the person in question does not resist his lust for moral reasons but for reasons of self-preservation. Nonetheless, Kant thinks that, just as this man takes himself to be able to resist desires and urges for non-moral reasons, he must also think it possible for him to resist them for moral reasons, that is, to do the morally required act. Hence, Kant continues his example thus:

But ask him [the same man] whether he thinks it would be possible for him to overcome his love of life, however great it may be, if his sovereign threatened him with the same sudden death unless he made a false deposition against an honorable man whom the ruler wished to destroy under a plausible pretext. Whether he would or not he perhaps will not venture to say; but that it would be possible for him he would certainly admit without hesitation . . . [H]e recognizes that he is free. (Kant 1956: 30 [30])

Autonomy and heteronomy

Kant called our *ability* to be motivated by reason alone 'autonomy'; and he said that 'heteronomy' is where the will is motivated by anything other than reason alone, including our own desires, urges, inclinations, emotions and the like. A heteronomous person is, one might say, 'other-directed', and the 'other' will include not simply, for example, thoughtlessly following what others tell us to do, but also following our desires, urges and so on.

Kant granted that he could not *explain* how it is that we possess free will (Kant 1983: 119 [458-9]). However, he thinks that *we have to think of ourselves as free* because otherwise, as we have seen, we could not hold one another responsible for our actions and thus morality itself would collapse. This is what Kant means by calling the belief in our freedom a 'postulate', for we cannot know we are free: we merely have to postulate that we are. Moreover, we do this on the basis of our being *rational* creatures, that is, creatures who can reason.

Freedom as a postulate of pure practical reason

Further, our reason in this context has a *practical* application, that is, it applies to our practice, our activities in the world. Hence Kant called our belief in our freedom a *postulate of pure practical reason.*

review activity

1. 'If we are not free, then morality collapses.' Explain why Kant would agree with this claim.

2. What does Kant mean by saying that there are two standpoints on human action?

3. Why does Kant call our freedom a 'postulate of pure practical reason'?

Reason

For Kant, therefore, reason is extremely important in morality, for it is through the use of our reason that we human beings can subject our desires to scrutiny and freely choose to act on them or not. One way in which Kant expressed the importance of reason in morality was by saying that morality was based on nothing *empirical* (cf. Kant 1983: 55 [389]). What he meant by this was that we cannot derive an idea of what our moral duties and obligations are from our desires or other empirical aspects of our nature such as what it is that makes us happy.

Morality as a priori

The idea that Kant's moral theory is based on nothing empirical can also be expressed by saying that his theory is *a priori*. However, in saying that moral principles are *a priori*, Kant was also claiming that it is 'no more possible to reject or alter a genuine moral demand than it is to refuse to believe that 3 = 1 + 2' (Acton 1970: 31). Moral principles are as necessary and universal as the truths of mathematics. To reject a genuine moral demand would involve, for Kant, a *logical* mistake of some kind. The kind of mistake this is will be discussed below.

We have, of course, already seen one moral theory that is entirely empirical – classical utilitarianism. This theory is based on empirical features of our nature, such as what we desire and what makes us happy. In this respect, utilitarianism contrasts strongly with Kantianism. Further contrasts between the theories will come out later on.

review activity

Explain in your own words what it means to say that, for Kant, morality is *a priori*.

A note on freedom and morality: *Wille* and *Willkür*

A problem in Kant's account of freedom

Before continuing with the exposition of Kant's views, it is worth pausing a moment to consider briefly a difficulty in Kant's reflections on freedom.

Kant, we have seen, argues in the *Groundwork* that if one acts on one's desires, inclinations, feelings and so forth then one is no more free than, say, a cat that acts on its desires, and that one cannot, therefore, be held responsible for one's actions. In acting freely, one is acting according to the *moral law*. It follows from these claims, first, that there can be no free act that is not morally good and, secondly, that one cannot be held responsible for acting badly. Obviously this is absurd, and not the conclusion Kant intended.

In order to remedy this problem in the presentation in the *Groundwork* of the relation between freedom and morality, Kant drew a distinction in other work (for example, Kant 1993; see, 41–2 [213] and 282, fn. 11) between the *Wille* and the *Willkür*. *Willkür* might be translated 'arbitrary will' and it is one's *Willkür* that decides whether one acts according to the moral law or on desires (and so forth), that is, freely to let one's desires (and so forth) determine one's actions. The *Wille*, on the other hand, which is translated simply as 'will', is the good will, the will that acts in accordance with the moral law. The *Wille* is always and necessarily free and is thus not a will that any human being can possess. Only God possesses a *Wille*, because he possesses none of the desires, inclinations, urges and so on that are part of human psychological make up.

For example, I might want to steal a watch from a shop, and here I have a choice: I can act on my desire and steal it, or I can overcome my desire and refrain from doing so. This is an exercise of *Willkür*: it is *Willkür* that chooses between good and evil. God, however, does not experience any desire or temptation to steal things. This is because he possesses *Wille*, the perfectly good will.

review
activity

Explain Kant's distinction between *Wille* and *Willkür* and why he felt the need to introduce it.

Maxims and the categorical imperative

According to Kant, whenever we act, we act on a *maxim*. A maxim is a kind of rule or principle on which one acts. It is not always easy to tell what the rule or principle is on which a person acts, and it need not be the same as the intention on which, or with which, a person acts. Moreover, a given person might be less clear what the maxim is on which he acts than someone else is: in a given situation, you could know the maxim on which I act better than I do.

Here is an example. If you come to visit me I might welcome you by giving you a cup of coffee. But the maxim on which I act is not: 'whenever I have a visitor I shall make him welcome with a cup of coffee', because I might make a visitor welcome with some other drink, or no drink at all. So perhaps the maxim on which I act is: 'whenever I have a visitor I shall make him welcome'. However, even this cannot be right, for if I have a visitor who wishes to pick a fight with me I might wish to make him unwelcome. So perhaps the maxim on which I act is: 'whenever I have a friendly visitor I shall make him welcome' (Cf. O'Neill 1989: ch.5, esp. 84; cf. ch.8, esp. 151).

Anyway, whatever the difficulties are of knowing what the maxim is on which a given person acts, Kant says that *some maxim or other* underlies our actions. He uses this idea to provide a test for the morality of our actions through providing a test for the maxims on which we act or would be willing to act.

The Categorical Imperative as a test of the morality of actions

We have seen that Kant claims that the requirements of morality are expressed as Categorical Imperatives. However, he thinks that there is a supreme principle of morality, which is the categorical imperative. Kant says that it is the Categorical Imperative that we must use as a *test* for maxims of action: if a maxim of action cannot pass the test it must be rejected. It is therefore morally unacceptable.

Kant gives three versions of the Categorical Imperative, which, he says, are equivalent to one another. We shall look at these in turn.

The Categorical Imperative: first formulation

Formula of universal law

The first formulation of the Categorical Imperative runs (Kant 1983: 84 [421]):

Act only on that maxim through which you can at the same time will that it should become a universal law.

Directly after this Kant goes on to say that this is equivalent to acting as though your maxim were to become through your will a *universal law of nature.*

This first formulation of the Categorical Imperative is known as the formula of universal law.

Universalisability

As I mentioned, this formula is intended to give us a test for maxims on which we act or are willing to act. How does it do this? Evidently the fundamental idea is that *one should not make an exception for oneself in moral matters.* The maxim on which I act should be one on which anyone could act – this is what Kant means by 'universal law'. If I am proposing to do some act, then I have to be willing for others to do it: I must be able to *universalise* my maxim. However, clearly what Kant says is intended to go beyond this.

Two forms of contradiction in the maxim of an action

Kant thinks that there is some kind of contradiction in a maxim that cannot be acted upon by everyone. There are two forms this contradiction can take. Kant says:

We must be able to will that a maxim of our action should become a universal law – that is the general canon for all moral judgement of action. Some actions are so constituted that their maxim cannot even be conceived as a universal law of nature without contradiction, let alone be willed as what ought to become one. In the case of others we do not find this inner impossibility, but it is still impossible to will that their maxim should be raised to the universality of a law of nature because such a will would contradict itself.

(Kant 1983: 86-7 [424])

So, there are two kinds of contradiction that Kant has in mind: a *contradiction in conception* and a *contradiction in the will.* We shall focus firstly on the contradiction in conception.

Contradiction in conception

Kant gives two examples of how this kind of contradiction arises (Kant 1983: 85 [421–2]). The examples are: a) when someone is sick of life as a result of misfortunes and contemplates suicide; b) when someone is short of money and borrows some, promising to return it later, but knowing full well that he will never be able to do so. So, how, then, does a contradiction in conception work in these two cases?

Three interpretations of the contradiction

Commentators on Kant are divided about how exactly this is supposed to work. There are at least three interpretations (cf. Korsgaard 1996a: ch.3). These are: the logical contradiction interpretation, the teleological contradiction interpretation and the practical contradiction interpretation. Let us look at these in turn.

The logical contradiction interpretation

The best way to see this is through the false (lying) promise example, where someone 'borrows' some money that he knows he cannot repay. The maxim on which he acts is: 'I intend to make lying promises whenever it is advantageous to me to do so'.

Could this maxim be universalised? In the universalised form we might have: 'I will a world in which everyone will make lying promises, even to me, whenever it is advantageous for him or her to do so'.

Where, then, is the contradiction when the maxim is universalised? Christine M. Korsgaard explains the contradiction thus:

> [W]e are trying to conceive a world in which the agent . . . is making a certain sort of false promise, but at the same time we are necessarily conceiving a world in which no one can be making this sort of promise, since you cannot make a promise . . . to someone who will not accept it.   (Korsgaard 1996a: 81–2)

Here is another way to make the same point. Suppose you make a lying promise. When you do this, you require that you be believed: otherwise there is no point in making the promise. Suppose, further, that the maxim of your act were universalised. In this case, there could be no social world in which people can generally be believed (when they make a promise) because one would have no idea whether someone's promise was a true or a lying promise. And, in fact, such a world would be a world in which there could be no such thing as making a promise. In such a world, nothing could *count* as making a promise. But this is a contradiction: you are *making a promise* in such a way that, at the same time, you will that *nothing could count as making a promise*. Hence, you ought not to make a lying promise. The relevant maxim of action cannot pass the test of the categorical imperative and must be rejected as morally unacceptable.

Note that the issue here is one of the *formal* or *logical* consequences of making a lying promise, that is, that the concept of a promise under such conditions makes no sense. The issue is *not* one of the empirical consequences, that is, one concerning what would happen if everyone followed you in making lying promises.

There is, however, a problem with the logical contradiction interpretation. To see this, consider the following situation. Suppose someone has a baby that cries more than average. This person, let us suppose, contemplates murdering the baby so that he might get a good night's sleep. The maxim might be: 'I intend to kill my baby that cries more than average so that I can get a good night's sleep'. Universalised, this maxim might run: 'I will a world in which any person kills his baby if it cries more than average so that he can get a good night's sleep'.

Can this maxim be universalised? In fact, it can be. Everyone could act on this maxim. Compare the case of lying promises. In this case, promising itself became impossible as a result of universalising the relevant maxim. However, in case of killing the baby no such *logical* impossibility arises: no amount of killing is going to make killing impossible. Yet killing a baby because it cries more than average is clearly evil. However, it passes the test of the Categorical Imperative on the logical contradiction interpretation. So, this interpretation does not 'screen' maxims correctly. Hence, it is not wholly adequate as it stands.

The teleological contradiction interpretation

Consider the fact that each one of us has various instincts. For example, we each have the instinct of self-love. We can think of these instincts as having a goal or a purpose. For example, we could think of the instinct of self-love as having the purpose of self-preservation. That is, we have the instinct of self-love because this is the means of ensuring that we preserve ourselves, for instance, by making us look after ourselves by seeking food, shelter and the like.

If we think of instincts in this way then we are thinking of them as teleological (from the Greek *telos*, meaning 'aim' or 'goal').

Teleology

We can look at things other than instincts in this teleological fashion. We can also look at desires or even actions in this way: they each have a purpose.

The teleological contradiction interpretation uses this way of looking at things to try to show how it is that maxims can be assessed by the categorical imperative. Thus, we 'assign natural purposes to various instincts and types of actions and then find the contradiction when universalized maxims involve uses of those instincts and actions that defeat the natural purpose or perhaps are merely deviant' (Korsgaard 1996a: 88). A couple of examples will help to make this clear.

Suppose we say that the natural purpose of promising is to establish trust and confidence and the co-operation that they make possible. Then, false promising on a universal scale undermines the purpose for which promising exists: it systematically thwarts the purpose for which promising exists. So, false promising has to be rejected.

Now consider suicide. Self-love has, we suppose, the natural purpose of self-preservation. The suicide kills himself, let us suppose, because he cannot bear more pain than he already has experienced. It is out of love for himself that he thus kills himself. So, the maxim on which the suicide acts is that, out of love for himself, he kills himself. If this maxim were now universalised, then the function of self-love – to ensure self-preservation – would be being undermined: the purpose for which self-love exists would be being thwarted under such conditions. Thus, suicide would have to be rejected: it could not pass the test of universalisation.

However, there is a problem with this interpretation. Consider the suicide again. He could grant that there is an instinct of self-love and that this has the purpose of the preservation of life. And it is true that the suicide cannot will this instinct and its purpose and yet commit suicide. However, the suicide could simply reject the instinct and its purpose, and he could do this in the form of a universal maxim: as far as he is concerned, it does not matter if there is such an instinct at all. In other words, he could will that others commit suicide if in his situation.

The practical contradiction interpretation

There is a third way of interpreting the contradiction in the test the Categorical Imperative offers for maxims.

Willing of ends and willing of means

Consider Kant's following comments (Kant 1983: 80–1 [417]): 'Who wills the end, wills (so far as reason has a decisive influence on his actions) also the means which are indispensably necessary and in his power'. In other words, if you want or need to get something and acting in a particular way is necessary to getting that something (and you have no other reason not to want to act in that way) then it is *irrational* not to act in that particular way. For example, if you want to buy a car (your end is to buy a car) then you must will the means to do this. What the means will be will depend on your situation, but let us say that it is getting a job to earn the money. Then, if you have no particular reason not to get a job and getting a job is the only means to getting the money to buy the car then it would be *irrational* of you not to get the job, that is, not to will the means.

Rational constraints on willing

This claim concerning means and ends is one concerning *rational constraints on willing*. That is, it tells us something about what it is that makes willing rational and irrational.

Consider now the case of your making a lying promise. What is the end in this case? That you get the money. Then we can say that the means to this end is the *practice* of promise keeping because you are willing to use this practice to achieve your end: if this practice did not exist you could not make a promise at all and you must, *rationally*, use this practice to achieve your end. However, you are, in fact, making a lying promise. If you universalise this, then you are at the same time willing the *practice* of making lying promises. So, in this case, you are willing: a) the practice of promise keeping; and b) the practice of making lying promises.

However, this involves a contradiction, and hence has to be rejected. You cannot universalise the maxim on which you act and thus you should reject that maxim and not act in the relevant way, that is, not make a lying promise.

Note that the practical contradiction interpretation no more relies on empirical facts than does the logical contradiction interpretation: as we have seen, the former depends upon the irrational use of maxims of action – that is, there is a logical or formal problem for non-universalisable maxims.

The difference between the logical contradiction interpretation and the practical contradiction interpretation

What, then, is the difference between the two interpretations? It is this: that in the case of the logical contradiction interpretation the practice of promise keeping is willed no longer to *exist* by the universalisation of the lying promise; whereas, in the case of the practical contradiction interpretation, what is willed by the universalisation of the lying promise is that the practice of promise keeping will no longer *work*.

The practical contradiction interpretation, however, does not cover all cases. One of these is the suicide case. The reason the present interpretation does not cope with it, that is, does not show, as Kant wanted to show, that it is a breach of the categorical imperative, is that, unlike the promising case, there is here no *practice* to will or not to will: the suicide's end will not be thwarted by universalising his maxim. There is no contradiction in his willing that all commit suicide.

review activity

1. For what is the categorical imperative a test?

2. What does Kant mean by saying that he who wills the end wills the means? Give your own example of this.

3. Explain why a lying promise cannot pass the test of the categorical imperative on

    a) the logical contradiction interpretation;

    b) the teleological contradiction interpretation; and

    c) the practical contradiction interpretation.

There are, then, problems in giving a wholly satisfactory account of the first formulation of Kant's categorical imperative. Nonetheless, it is clear that the basic idea is to find a way of showing that some actions, such as making lying promises and committing suicide, are morally wrong and should never be done.

The categorical imperative is not to be used to assess all our actions

However, we should not suppose that Kant believes that we are to use the categorical imperative in *all* our everyday decisions. If we were to do so, this would lead to absurd conclusions. For example, suppose you wanted to become an artist and you try to do so, for instance, by going to art school. Could you universalise the maxim on which you act? Surely not, because this would just mean that everyone would seek to become an artist. That would be absurd: a world of only artists could not function at all (cf. Sullivan 1994: 42). The point is that what Kant was after in his moral philosophy was a test for the most fundamental principles, rules or policies by which we could live. He was not trying to give a test for every single decision in life.

Permissible actions

Another mistake that is sometimes made in interpreting Kant is to suppose that any maxim that does *not* violate the categorical imperative becomes part of the moral law, that is, is morally obligatory (cf. Acton 1970: 21). Thus, Alasdair MacIntyre has said (MacIntyre 1985: 45–6) that 'many . . . trivial non-moral maxims are vindicated by Kant's test', such as 'always eat mussels on Mondays in March'. This is to misunderstand Kant: as I have said, Kant claims that maxims that do not pass the test of the categorical imperative are ruled out, but not that every conceivable maxim which passes the test is part of the moral law. Such actions which are not ruled out are *permissible*, but not obligatory (Kant 1983: 101 [439]).

Perfect and imperfect duties

Aside from these concerns, we should note that actions that are always morally wrong give us what Kant calls our perfect duties: a perfect duty is one to which there are no exceptions. Perfect duties in this sense are also known as 'narrow' or 'rigorous' or 'necessary' duties. And it is in the case of such duties that *a contradiction in conception* is said to have been generated when a maxim is willed that breaches them.

We have seen two examples of duties Kant considers perfect: never to make lying promises and never to commit suicide. Others that could be derived from the categorical imperative include: never to keep slaves and never to coerce others (cf. O'Neill 1989: 96–7). And, even though there are difficulties, as we have seen, with Kant's argument, it is surely very plausible to think it is right to say that we should, for example, never keep slaves: slavery is, one might say, *always* wrong.

Contradictions in the will

However, Kant wants the categorical imperative to provide us also with imperfect duties. These are also known as 'wide' or 'meritorious' or 'contingent' duties. In the case of such duties a *contradiction in the will* is said to be generated when a maxim is willed that universalises them. That is, such maxims are conceivable in that, although they can be universalised without conceptual incoherence, they are said to be volitionally inconsistent when universalised. They are thus impossible in a different way from contradictions in conception.

Two examples of imperfect duties that Kant gives are: a) to seek our own perfection by developing our talents; b) to promote the happiness of others (Kant 1993: 85–6 [422–3]).

The reason these are known as imperfect duties is that they do not tell us something we should be doing all the time (as the perfect duties tell us we should *never* do certain actions). We cannot be developing our talents *all* the time or be promoting the happiness of others *all* the time. We have to use our judgement about when, how often, and how to do these things: and for that there can be no rules for all, since much will depend here on one's personal circumstances (cf. Kant 1993: 55 [389]).

review
activity

1. What does Kant mean by saying that some maxims cannot be willed because they contain a contradiction in conception and others cannot be willed because they contain a contradiction in the will?

2. Explain the difference between perfect and imperfect duties, giving examples of each.

How might the Categorical Imperative show that a contradiction in the will results when imperfect duties are breached? To see how, consider the example that Kant gives of the person who is flourishing and happy and decides to ignore all others: he will neither help nor harm them and he wills that they treat him in the same way. Kant says that a world of such persons is perfectly conceivable: there is no contradiction in conception here. However, there is a contradiction in the will here (Kant 1993: 86 [243]). Why is this?

The person in the example wills that he help no others, even when they need help. Universalised, this means that he wills that no one help others when those others need help. Hence, he must be willing that no one help him, even if he should be in need of help. So far, there is no contradiction in conception here: as we have noted, a world in which no one helps others is *conceivable*. However, suppose that the person in question comes to need the help of others. That is, he has certain ends, but he cannot will the means to those ends – say, because he has become physically incapacitated in some way. For example, he can no longer go shopping for his food. He has the end of getting food, but he cannot will the means because he is too ill to go to the shops. We have already seen that, if one wills the end then one must, rationally, will the means: this is a rational constraint on willing. However, this means that in this case the person in question must will some such end as that he be helped to get his shopping. So, here he is willing two things: a) that no one help others when they need help; and b) that he be helped when he needs help. In other words, he is willing: c) that he not be helped when he needs help; and d) that he be helped when he needs help.

This is a contradiction. So, the person has to reject his maxim that no one help others.

As I have said, there is a contradiction here in the will, not in the conception. This is because it is only in conjunction with a certain claim concerning the rational constraints on willing that we can generate the contradiction.

Kant and the problem of lying

Is it always wrong to lie?

One problem in Kant's moral philosophy that is often discussed is that concerned with lying. We may, after all, agree that slavery is always wrong, and even, perhaps, that suicide is always wrong. However, it seems implausible to suggest that lying is always wrong. Yet this is just what Kant seems to suggest. In a piece he wrote late in life, Kant imagines that a potential murderer is pursuing his intended victim. The victim is in the house and you know this. The murderer asks you where the intended victim is. Should you tell him or not? Kant says that you should, for it is your duty not to lie. He gives the following as a reason:

> It is indeed possible that after you have honestly answered Yes to the murderer's question as to whether the intended victim is in the house, the latter went out unobserved and thus eluded the murderer, so that the deed would not have come about. However, if you told a lie and said that the intended victim was not in the house, and he has actually (though unbeknownst to you) gone out, with the result that by doing so he has been met by the murderer and thus the deed has been perpetrated, then in this case you may be justly accused as having caused his death . . . To be truthful (honest) in all declarations is, therefore, a sacred and unconditionally commanding law of reason that admits of no expediency whatsoever.
> (Kant 1994: 164 [427])

Certainly Kant's argument seems very weak. After all, if one is going to speculate on consequences as he does in this passage, then there seems no limit to what one can imagine might happen and what this would tell us about the moral acceptability of lying or not. In any case, the conclusion Kant suggests seems unacceptable and most have rejected it. So, how should one respond to Kant's claim?

One possibility, suggested by Ralph C.S. Walker, is simply to dismiss what Kant says here as the product of a mind descending into senility. There is no doubt that Kant's intellectual powers began to desert him as he approached death, and we could say that his thinking on lying was marked by intellectual confusion because it was written so late in his life, that is, when Kant was around 75 years old (Walker 1982: 189, fn 2). Obviously, the problem with this solution is that we do not know how lucid Kant was when he wrote the piece we are discussing, although it is pretty clear that Kant was not then at the height of his powers.

Policies and acts   Roger J. Sullivan suggests another possibility. According to Sullivan, we need to hold in mind Kant's distinction between a *maxim,* on the one hand, and a *specific act* in a particular instance, on the other. Sullivan claims that Kant was actually arguing against the idea that the maxim concerning lying could not be acceptable. That is, Kant was arguing against the idea that a *policy* or *rule* of lying under some circumstances is morally acceptable. So, according to Sullivan, Kant is claiming that the two *policies,* 'never lie' and 'show concern for others' conflict in this case. But, he says, it does not follow from this that the two specific *duties:* 'do not lie, here, now' and 'show concern for this person, here, now' conflict. In fact, Kant denied that there can be any conflict of duties: if it seems that one must fulfil two duties but cannot, then one of them is not a duty after all (cf. Kant 1993: 50 [224]). So, in this case, says Sullivan, Kant is simply denying that the *policy* of lying is acceptable, but not that lying in this case is. Kant would have thought it a duty to lie here in order to help the intended victim (Sullivan 1994: 103–4).

Sullivan's solution looks neat, but it is hard to be completely convinced by it. For one thing, it seems possible to challenge Sullivan's reading of Kant's discussion of conflicts of policies and duties, for it is arguable that he thought that, in the end, there can no more be a conflict between policies than between duties. More directly, and waiving this concern, it is, it has to be said, not easy to interpret Kant's words in the article in question in the way Sullivan suggests: it is natural to read them as saying that one should never lie, that is, that they are about a duty, and not simply about a general maxim (and this is how they have been traditionally read). Further, Kant does seem to think of the ban on lying as like the ban on suicide – as a negative duty, that is, as always unacceptable. So Sullivan's answer might be a good *Kantian* answer, but it does not seem completely plausible that it is *Kant's* answer.

Christine M. Korsgaard has suggested another response to Kant's discussion of lying (Korsgaard 1996a: ch.5: 136). She takes it for granted that Kant really did think that it was always wrong to lie, that is, she rejects (implicitly) such a response as that offered by Sullivan. However, she thinks that, on the universal law formula of the categorical imperative, Kant was mistaken in thinking that it leads to the conclusion that one should not lie to the murderer. She argues that, if the murderer thinks there is any point in asking you whether the person is in the house, then he must believe you do not know he is a murderer. Otherwise, he would know – or, at any rate, be fairly sure – that you would lie and there would be no point in his asking the question.

So, imagine you lie to the murderer. Can we universalise the relevant maxim? Korsgaard supports the practical contradiction interpretation of the categorical imperative, so she takes this to mean 'could there be a universal practice of lying under such conditions'? Her answer is that there could be. This is because the murderer will believe you when you lie precisely because he does not know that you know that he is a murderer. You can universalise your maxim – everyone could lie in such circumstances, because the practice of universal lying will always be efficacious in such circumstances. That is, the practice of lying will *work* in such circumstances because murderers will not know that the persons they question know them to murderers (otherwise they would not ask the question). So universal lying in such circumstances passes the test set by the Categorical Imperative.

The Categorical Imperative: second formulation

Formula of humanity   Leaving aside worries about the issue of lying, let us turn to consider the second formulation of the Categorical Imperative. This runs (Kant 1983: 91 [429]):

> *Act in such a way that you always treat humanity, whether in your own person or in the person of any other, never simply as a means, but always at the same time as an end.*

This is known as the formula of humanity. We have already seen the importance Kant attaches to the fact that we are rational beings, and when Kant speaks of our humanity he is thinking of the fact that we are rational beings. The reason human beings are valuable is that they are rational. This is connected with the fact that rational beings have the power to 'set ends', that is, give themselves goals and the like. Thomas E. Hill, Jr. sums up Kant's idea that we are valuable because we are rational and can set ends by suggesting that this means human beings have the capacity to:

- act on principles or maxims;
- follow rational principles of prudence and efficiency;
- foresee future consequences, adopt long-range plans, resist immediate temptations;
- accept unconditional principles of conduct, that is, categorical imperatives; and
- understand the world and reason abstractly (Hill 1992: ch.2: 40-1).

Kant expressed the sense that human beings (rational beings) are valuable by saying that they have *dignity*. This dignity is something they cannot lose, whatever they do. It has no price or 'market value': human beings, according to Kant, have incomparable worth.

Given this way of looking at human beings, we can see why Kant says that they should never be used merely as a means. What Kant means by treating someone as a means is using him simply to satisfy one's own desires, needs or the like. Thus a slave, for example, is used simply as a means to satisfy his master's desires. Of course, Kant sees that, on occasion, we inevitably treat people as a means to satisfy our desires. For example, if I take my shoes to be repaired, then I am using the cobbler as a means to satisfy my desire for getting my shoes repaired. However, if I pay the cobbler to repair my shoes at a price with which he is happy, then I am not treating him *merely* or *simply* as a means, and as long as I do not treat him *merely* as a means then I do not breach the Categorical Imperative. In this case, I am also treating him as an end.

Treating a person as an end

But then what, exactly, does it mean to treat someone as an end? How are we to acknowledge the dignity of human beings? Hill has suggested (Hill 1992: 50–5) several practical implications that Kant had in mind in saying we should treat human beings as ends. We can acknowledge the dignity of human beings by:

a) refusing to damage another's rationality, e.g., rendering a criminal placid through drugs or a frontal lobotomy;

b) killing them (though killing in war might offer some exceptions and Kant was in favour of capital punishment);

c) trying to develop one's rational capacities;

d) striving to exercise those capacities;

e) appealing to others' reason when talking, discussing etc. and not trying to manipulate them in non-rational ways;

f) leaving others to pursue their own goals as they see fit (within the constraints of the moral law); and

g) displaying certain attitudes and the like whilst avoiding others, e.g., honouring and respecting them, not mocking them.

Let us look at two of these, e) and f), in a little more detail.

The first of these, e), says that one should *respect another person's ability to reason.* Here is an example. Suppose you believe that abortion is wicked and you wish to persuade your friend of this. If you are to treat her as an end in herself, then your attempt to persuade her must not be manipulative: you must seek to give her all the good reasons you have for your view, as well as the areas of doubt you have concerning your view (if any), not conceal any facts concerning abortion of which you are apprised, not try to dazzle her thinking with sensationalised and misleading claims, and so on. Then you must allow her to make up her own mind. The ideal here is of a conversation in which each party is free and equal, respecting the other's ability to think things through for herself.

The second, f), says that it is important in treating a person as an end to respect his desires (providing they are not themselves morally reprehensible). Most fundamentally, this involves respecting his own judgements about how he should seek to find happiness for himself. For it is clear, as we saw when discussing utilitarianism, that human beings seek their own happiness, but it is also clear that we differ greatly in our understanding of the kind of life in and through which happiness is to be found. Even if we think that someone is quite mistaken about where his happiness lies, we should respect his choice, though we may, of course, seek to change his view by giving him our reasons for thinking he is mistaken.

review
activity

1. What does Kant mean by saying that we should never treat a human being merely as a means? Give two examples where someone is treated merely as a means.

2. What does it mean to treat someone as an end?

It is important to note that, for Kant, only rational beings can be treated as ends in themselves because it is only rational beings whose reason can be respected. Furthermore, for Kant, one cannot properly respect the desires of a non-rational creature, such as an animal, because an animal simply acts on its desires without considering whether to act on them.

The Categorical Imperative: third formulation

Kant's third formulation of the categorical imperative runs (Kant 1983: 100 [438]):

Every rational being must so act as if he were through his maxims always a law-making member in the universal kingdom of ends.

Formula of the kingdom of ends

This is known as the formula of the kingdom of ends. This form of the Categorical Imperative brings out something that has been implicit in all that has been said so far about acting on duty. This is that when an agent wills to act only on those maxims that pass the test of the categorical imperative he is *giving the moral law to himself.* That is, he accepts the moral law, but he does not do so simply because, say, he is told to by someone (say, someone in authority) or is frightened into doing so by another. He does so rather because he gives himself the law: he is at one and the same time *legislator* of the law and also *subject* to the law. The law is, so to speak, of his own making for himself through his faculty of reason.

Kant's third formulation of the Categorical Imperative brings out the idea that the ideal community or kingdom is a community of individuals who give themselves the law in this way. In such a community, the individuals will all agree on the basic principles that are to govern their interaction with one another.

We can imagine things this way: a group of individuals who are not members of a community are to come together to decide on the principles that will govern them when they enter a community in order to live together. They will ignore their own particular concerns and interests in striving to agree with one another on the laws that will bind them all (Kant 1983: 95 [433]). As they do come to agree on the laws, they enter the community as free and equal citizens of that community, bound by laws of their own making: they are all legislators and subjects, and no one is subject to laws that he does not recognise as his own, just laws.

In such a community, each member will treat all others never merely as a means but always as an end. This community will be a community or kingdom of ends.

Kant's moral thinking here feeds, and leads off, into his political and religious thought. In the case of the former, Kant's favoured political organisation was that of a republic. In such a republic each person would have as much freedom as was compatible with the same degree of freedom being possessed by all others. As far as the latter is concerned, Kant argued that this republic should be a religious community in which there existed, as Kant expressed it in the title of one of his books, religion within the limits of reason alone. Kant did in fact believe that religion could be defended in such terms, and he argued that, although God could not be thought of as having made the moral law and imposed it on human beings, moral understanding nonetheless could lead, properly understood, to faith in God.

activity

Describe in your own words the idea of a kingdom of ends.

The good will and consequences

Kant saw that sometimes one can will to perform an action that is in accord with the Categorical Imperative and yet things go wrong in the world, for the world is not by any means completely under one's control. The opening of Stefan Zweig's novel *Beware of Pity* provides a good example. Officer Toni Hofmiller has been invited to a party at a grand house. Late in the evening, after having danced with many of the women present, he realises that he has not asked the daughter of the house to dance with him. He sees he has been rude and wishes to make up for this, so he approaches her and asks her to dance. At this point she begins to weep uncontrollably and collapses. It turns out that she is a cripple, but that Hofmiller had no way of knowing this and cannot be blamed for his action. His intentions were entirely honourable and kind.

From a Kantian perspective we could say that Hofmiller's will was good because he willed to do the right thing. Kant would say that, from a moral point of view, this is all that matters. Of course, Kant would agree that what Hofmiller did had bad consequences, but he would insist that, from a *moral* point of view, these consequences do not matter. What matters is the will with which something is done, that is, the intentions and aims of the person acting. Kant is careful to say, however, that when he talks of good intentions he does not mean 'a mere wish, but . . . the straining of every means so far as they are in our control' to do the morally good deed (Kant 1983: 60 [394]).

Only the good will is unqualifiedly good

Kant expresses this by saying that the only thing good 'without qualification', that is, *always* good, is the good will (Kant 1983: 59 [393]). The good will is the will that wills to do the good or right thing, even if, as a matter of fact, as in the case of Officer Hofmiller, something bad results.

Consequences not important for Kant

What this means is that, for Kant, the consequences of an action do not matter from a moral point of view. We can immediately see that Kant's theory is thus quite opposed to utilitarianism, which claims that the *only* things that count from a moral point of view are the consequences of an action.

We can put the contrast between Kant's view and the view of the utilitarians in this way: Kant says that what counts from a moral point of view is the *motivation* that someone has in doing some particular action, whereas for a utilitarian the *motivation* for an action is ultimately unimportant (though not entirely unimportant because having certain kinds of motivations, for example, motivations of benevolence, is more likely to lead to acting according to the utilitarian standard than having other motivations is).

Acting for the sake of duty

Kant does not think that it is enough, however, that one act (will) in accord with duty or the moral law. He thinks that one must act *from* duty or *for the sake of* duty. That is, he thinks one must do the morally right thing because one sees that it is the morally right thing to do: its moral rightness is the reason one has for doing it.

In saying this, one of the most important things Kant had in mind was that, if one acts in accord with one's duty but does so from desire or inclination, then it will just be a matter of *luck* if one does the right thing. For example, suppose I am of a sympathetic temperament and one night I see someone struggling with a heavy load at the back door of the National Gallery. On account of my sympathetic temperament I help him. However, he is, of course, an art thief, and I have done something foolish (cf. Herman 1993: ch.1: 4–5). So, acting for the sake of duty will avoid such cases.

Does Kant think that it is morally better to act for the sake of duty in the *total absence* of a desire to do so? Some interpreters have thought he did. The reason is that he gives the following example. He imagines a man of sympathetic temperament who then experiences such troubles in his life that he loses all sympathy for others: he is indifferent to the situation of others. Kant continues:

> [S]uppose that, when no longer moved by any inclination, he tears himself out of this deadly insensibility and does the action [for example, he helps another] without any inclination for the sake of duty alone; then for the first time his action has its genuine moral worth.
> (Kant 1983: 64 [398])

On the basis of this example, some have read Kant as saying that in *all* cases it is so that *only* if one acts for the sake of duty and without *any* inclination that one's act has moral worth.

Barbara Herman has argued against this view (Herman 1993: ch.1). First, she argues that, in the example, Kant is talking *only* of the man in question: it is only for the kind of man he is in the kind of circumstance in which he finds himself that it is correct to say that actions have moral worth when *no* other inclination is present and the act is done solely for the sake of duty. In other words, his case cannot be generalised. Secondly, she draws a distinction between one's (non-moral) *incentives* to act and one's (non-moral) *motives* to act. An incentive to an action is a reason to act in a given way that is not efficacious, that is, does not actually move one to act. A motive to action, on the other hand, is a reason to act that does actually move one to act. Herman then argues that what Kant means is that (as we have seen) one's act has moral worth only if done for the sake of duty (and not just in conformity with duty) but that the moral worth of such an act is not impugned by the presence of an *incentive* to act in the same way as long as that incentive is not one's *motive*. The motive must be, of course, the motive of acting for the sake of duty.

If Herman is right, the reason Kant focused on a case where there was no incentive or motive present other than the motive of acting for the sake of duty (that is, the case of the unfortunate man) is simply that in this case we can see most clearly what it is to act for the sake of duty and not simply in accord with duty.

However, we could, perhaps, go further than Herman does and argue that, *in the case of wide duties*, Kant would have accepted that desires, inclinations and so on are necessary to motivate us to act well. Roger J. Sullivan has argued just this (Sullivan 1994: ch.8). Consider the wide duty of caring for others. In the case of this duty, as in that of all wide duties, the categorical imperative does not tell us exactly how to care or for whom to care or when to care and such like. Therefore, Sullivan claims, we cannot be motivated when fulfilling such a duty simply by acting in the light of our applying the categorical imperative. Rather, we need to be motivated by something else in order to obey the moral law. This must be our desires, inclinations and the like. If Sullivan is right, this means that, in the case of wide duties, morally good action flows from desires and inclinations. It also means that Kant would agree that a good moral character does not consist simply in our obeying the moral law but in our developing certain 'richer' traits of character, that is, specific ways of feeling, desiring and so on.

Sullivan's is an attractive account of Kant, doing a lot to soften his harsh comments about desires and inclinations. It is as well, however, to be aware that it is a very unusual interpretation of Kant, but it does not follow from that, of course, that it is mistaken.

review activity

1. What does Kant mean by saying that one should act, not simply in accord with the moral law, but for the sake of the moral law?

2. What does Herman mean by the distinction between incentives and motives? Of what use is this distinction in explaining the idea of acting for the sake of the moral law?

Advantages of Kant's moral theory

There is much to be said for Kant's moral theory and it is close to many people's experience of morality. As Alasdair MacIntyre has pointed out: 'For many who have never heard of philosophy, let alone Kant, morality is roughly what Kant said it was' (MacIntyre 1987: 190).

Kant's moral theory and everyday moral experience

1. Despite its complexity, the theory has many points of contact with everyday moral experience. For example, its opposition between acting morally and acting on one's desires is something that is close to the centre of many people's understanding of morality. Many people do take morality to be a constraint on our desires, that is, as something that tells us when and how we should act on our desires, if at all.

Absolute prohibitions

2. Kant's moral theory involves the idea of absolute moral rules. That is, for Kant, since moral rules are categorical, they must *never* be broken. This is something with which one is in many cases likely to agree. For example, it is surely right to say, as we have already noted, that one must never torture another person or inflict needless suffering on him.

The dignity of human beings

3. Kant's idea that we should never treat others as a mere means has much to be said for it. It captures the idea that human beings (that is,

rational creatures) are *worthy of respect* and should not be manipulated. It also articulates well the idea that all human beings possess an inherent *dignity*. This, as we have seen, is the kind of thing Dostoyevsky's character Raskolnikov came to realise after he murdered the old money lender.

Rights 4. The idea that a human being is worthy of respect and possesses an inherent dignity supports the idea that he possesses *rights*, for example, the right to freedom or the right to life or the right to his own opinions. And this, too, is part of the modern moral consciousness.

Difficulties for Kant's moral theory

Acting for the sake of the law 1. Kant's idea that one should always act for the sake of the law is open to question. In criticising Kant on this point, Peter Winch (1926–98) refers to an example provided by Simone Weil (1909–43). Here, a father plays with his child 'not out of a sense of duty but out of pure joy and pleasure' (Winch 1972: ch.9: 181). Winch points out that there is a kind of purity in the father's behaviour, but it is not the kind of purity Kant describes in his theory. Winch goes on:

Kant would have to classify this as a case of acting from 'inclination' rather than from 'practical reason' and hence as possessing no moral value . . . But let us consider the case of a man who finds himself unable to enjoy himself spontaneously with his child; though he goes out of his way to entertain the child out of a sense of his duty as a father. May he not quite well regard his relative lack of spontaneity, vis-à-vis the father in Simone Weil's example, as a moral failing? Can he not, without confusion, regard himself as 'a worse man' than the other?

Evidently, Winch thinks that the father can regard his failing as a moral failing. And surely he is right. After all, although we cannot simply experience emotions at will, we can learn to love better and care better for others. In any case, even if one can do nothing about the fact that one has particular traits of character, such as a tendency to experience certain kinds of desires or urges or inclinations, one can still without absurdity see it as a moral failing to have such traits of character (and one can also judge oneself to have failed morally in failing to have certain desirable traits of character even if one can do nothing about the fact that one does not have them).

It should be noted that the example of playing with one's child is, presumably, one of a wide duty. Granted that, if Sullivan's argument concerning the motivation of wide duties is correct, then Winch's criticism will fall away. However, it would be possible to construct a similar example in the case of a narrow duty. For example, we might think that a shopkeeper who *gladly* treats his customers fairly because he *wants* to is morally better than one who only charges them the right price because it is his duty to do so. As I mentioned just now, we can judge ourselves without absurdity from a moral point of view with regard to the desires, inclinations and so on that we have (or fail to have). It is not only of things that are in our control for which we can be morally judged. This point will also come out in the third criticism, below.

Motivation 2. Kant, we have seen, says that the only important thing from a moral point of view is the motivation from which an action is performed. However, this is something with which one might disagree. For example, in Henry James's novel *The Portrait of a Lady*, Ralph Touchett intends to help his cousin Isabel Archer by persuading his father to bequeath to her £70 000, making her extraordinarily rich. He knows that she wants to travel and learn, and sincerely believes that this is the best way he can help her to do this. However, because she is rich she falls to prey to Gilbert Osmond, who woos and marries her for her money. One of the central points of James's novel is to suggest that Ralph Touchett is morally culpable even though his intentions were entirely honourable. In such a case, Kant's emphasis on motivation to the exclusion of consequences seems mistaken.

Moral luck 3. This last example is connected with something very important for moral understanding. For there is no doubt that Ralph Touchett had *bad luck* when Isabel Archer was wooed by and married Gilbert Osmond. Yet he was still morally culpable. This is something that, one might argue, is often possible in ethics: that one can be morally culpable for something that one could not help doing. For example, a lorry-driver may run over a child even though there was nothing he could do to prevent the accident, but he might nonetheless feel responsible and have a sense of regret. Indeed, if he did not feel such things we should be inclined to regard him as morally questionable in some way (Williams 1986: ch.2, esp. 28). Or again, in Sophocles' play *King Oedipus*, Oedipus kills his father and marries his mother through no fault of his own, yet when he discovers what he has done he blinds himself in remorse.

Kant's moral theory attempts to make human life immune to luck in matters of morality, yet, in doing so, it can be argued that it fails to be sensitive to a fact about life which no theorising will make disappear. Much more than intentions matter in morality.

A common humanity 4. An important criticism of Kant's moral philosophy is suggested by some comments made by Raimond Gaita. Gaita argues (Gaita 1991: ch.3) that Kant's emphasis upon rationality as the most important feature of human beings is misleading. He argues that it is very important that human beings can have a sense of fellowship with one another. However, he suggests, this sense cannot rest upon the fact that we are rational. It involves, rather, something Kant overlooks in this regard, namely, our mortality. For the fact that we all die is not (merely) some empirical fact about us, but is itself part of what gives us a sense of fellowship. Death is central in our understanding of what it is to be a human being and of the ways in which a human life can be fulfilled or wasted (say, through early death). It is also bound up with the fact that we are all born in the way we are: birth and death mark the two ends between which every human life is lived and a proper understanding of each involves, amongst other things, an understanding of the other. Think, for example, of the frailty and of the dependence on others that is similar in both infancy and old age and how the moral sense of one casts light on the moral sense of the other. Thus, a sense of our mortality is bound up with the ways in which we can respond to one another with tenderness, love or pity (or, of course, resentment, anger and the like). In short, when Kant focuses on our rationality as central to our humanity he misses out a great deal of what really does give us a sense of our humanity.

Conflict of duties 5. We have seen that, even if Kant does allow conflicts of principles, he does not allow conflict of duties, arguing that, if one is faced by two duties only one of which one can fulfil, then one of these is not really a duty after all. Yet many philosophers would argue that this is mistaken. In a moral dilemma of this simple kind, it might be argued, even the action one cannot perform remains something one ought to do, and thus one will do some wrong, whatever one does. An example can be found, it could be argued, in Sophocles' *Antigone* in which Antigone is caught between obeying the laws of the state and those of the gods. On the one hand feels she must obey Creon's edict forbidding the burial of her brother, Polyneices, yet, on the other, she believes she must bury him. In either case she does something wrong. If this were not so then the tragedy would not be as deep as it is.

It is possible that a contemporary Kantian could respond to this by simply granting that such moral dilemmas (conflicts of duty) can arise after all.

Morality as a priori 6. Kant's moral theory, as we have seen, is *a priori*. However, there are reasons to think that such a theory is questionable. This is because an *a priori* moral theory is not justified by any feature or features of human nature. Kant's theory, for example, applies to any and every creature as long as it is rational, regardless of how like or unlike us in other respects it is. However, many philosophers believe that any acceptable moral theory must be based in some way on features of the human condition in its empirical aspects. For example, any such theory, they argue, should involve from the first an understanding of the kinds of things that make us happy. We have already seen one theory, namely utilitarianism, of which this is so. Otherwise, they argue, the point or purpose of morality becomes completely unclear. For instance, if leading a morally good life does not in some way lead to our happiness then there is no reason why we should be morally good. This way of looking at things is very important in the moral theory we shall look at in the next chapter, namely, virtue theory.

some questions
to think about

1 If it is true that Kant's first formulation of the Categorical Imperative cannot be made to work fully satisfactorily as a test of maxims, does this mean that Kant's whole theory should be abandoned?

2 To what extent would you agree that Kant is right to say that what matters in morality is the intention with which an action is performed?

3 How far do you agree with the claim that morality appears to us most fundamentally in terms of what is forbidden?

4 Is Kant right to see a profound conflict between duty and desire?

5 'If behaving morally well does not contribute to one's own happiness then there is no reason why one *should* behave morally well.' What, if anything, is there to be said for this claim?

6 'For understanding what a human being is, the most significant thing is reason.' What is there to be said for and against this claim?

7 If someone is cold-hearted by temperament, does it make sense to judge him morally for this?

further reading

▶ For a good, brief general introduction to Kant, which contains a helpful discussion of Kant's moral thinking, see Scruton 1982. Schneewind 1992 gives a good overview of Kant's moral philosophy. Acton 1970, Aune 1979 and Sullivan 1994 are all helpful introductions to Kant's moral philosophy.

▶ Bernard Williams is a well-known critic of Kant's moral philosophy. See, for example, Williams 1985: ch.3.

▶ Rawls 1972 is deeply influenced by Kant and led to a resurgence of work on Kant's moral philosophy. Herman 1993, Hill 1992, Korsgaard 1996a and 1996b, and O'Neill 1989 are all central to the resurgence. Hill's writings are probably the most accessible of these four.

▶ Foot 1978 ch.XI interestingly explores the idea that morality is a system of *hypothetical* imperatives. McDowell 1978 is a reply.

Virtue Theory

Key topics in this chapter

- The rise of virtue ethics in late twentieth century moral philosophy
- The nature of virtue ethics
- The cardinal and theological virtues
- The need for an ethical theory

The background to virtue ethics in modern moral philosophy

Anscombe on moral obligation

In 1958 G.E.M. Anscombe (1919–2001) published a paper entitled 'Modern Moral Philosophy' (Anscombe 1958). In it she argued, amongst other things, that we should abandon the very notions of *moral* obligation and *moral* duty, of what is *morally* right and wrong, and of a *moral* sense of 'ought' (as in Kant's categorical imperative).

Moral obligation and God's law

The best way to see what Anscombe means is, perhaps, in the following way. Suppose a person does something that one judges to be mean and unjust. Suppose further that someone says that what this person did is mean and unjust and morally wrong. What does saying that the action is morally wrong add to the claim that it is mean and unjust? According to Anscombe, there is a way in which it adds something. This is if God has issued a *law* indicating that the (kind of) action in question is not to be done. In this case, to say an action is mean, unjust and morally wrong is to say that that action is mean and unjust and that God has issued a law or commandment forbidding it.

When Western culture believed in a law-giving God the notion that certain actions were morally wrong (morally forbidden and so forth) thus made sense. However, in present-day Western culture few believe in such a God, yet we nearly all of us go on using the notions of the morally wrong, the morally right, the morally obligatory and so on. Why do we do so? According to Anscombe, the reason is that, as a result of centuries of using such notions in a context when they did make sense (when the culture did believe in a law-giving God), these very notions have come to have an 'atmosphere' that makes it *seem* that they do some significant work or have a genuine role to play in moral discourse. However, they do not. They have a mere 'mesmeric force', which is nonetheless illusory. If we do not believe in God as a law giver, to say that someone is *morally* obliged to do something or *morally* ought to do something and the like, is to give the impression of saying something substantive, but is not, in fact, to do so.

Anscombe said that the notions of moral obligation and the rest are thus survivals in modern culture of concepts outside the framework of thought (that is, belief in God as divine law giver) in which they were intelligible and made sense. Now, they are no longer intelligible and no longer make sense. We should, she said, thus drop them altogether.

This does not mean, however, that Anscombe was suggesting we could not or should not ever say that someone ought not to do some particular action. It is just that in using such a notion we should not think of it as having any special *moral* force.

Anscombe pointed out that we do not need the category of 'the moral' in order to do ethics: she noted that Aristotle did extremely powerful and interesting work in this area with no conception of the moral of the kind we have. After all, Aristotle lived long before the advent of Christianity. Moreover, Aristotle had a complex and rich conception of the virtues (and vices), and many philosophers have taken up Anscombe's hint and returned to look at Aristotle's work on the virtues. As a result, reflection on the virtues has become very important in contemporary philosophy, and 'virtue ethics' has emerged alongside utilitarianism and Kantianism as a distinctive moral theory.

review activity

Explain in your own words why Anscombe claimed that we should reject the notion of the moral ought.

How should one live?

Apart from Anscombe's argument, there is another, related reason why virtue ethics has become so prominent in contemporary moral philosophy. This is

Aristotle (384–322 BC)

Aristotle, who is numbered amongst the very greatest of philosophers, was born as the son of a doctor in 384 at Stagira in Chalcidice in northern Greece. At the age of 17 or 18 he entered Plato's Academy at Athens, remaining a member for some 20 years until Plato's death in around 348. On leaving Athens, he went first to Assos on the coast of Asia Minor, where he remained for three years, and then to Mytilene on the island of Lesbos. About 342 he was invited to go to Macedonia as the tutor of the king's son, Alexander (the Great). After a few years he returned to Athens where he founded the Lyceum, his own philosophical school. The kind of philosophy he taught there became known as Peripatetic, owing the name to the covered court (*peripatos*) where the students walked up and down. In 323 Aristotle left Athens for political reasons, going to Chaclis in Euboea where he died the following year. He was twice married and he had a son, Nicomachus, by his second wife. He was something of a dandy, and was accused by his enemies, of whom he had many, of being arrogant. Aristotle worked on almost every imaginable philosophical topic; about a fifth of what he wrote has survived, mostly in the form of what is thought to be lecture notes. His influence on Western philosophy has been enormous and, although his thinking has fallen out of fashion from time to time, he remains a thinker to whom philosophers return again and again, finding in his work tremendous richness, breadth and depth.

that many philosophers have felt dissatisfaction with the two theories we have already considered, utilitarianism and Kantianism. Common to both those theories is an emphasis on what to *do*. Utilitarianism claims, as we have seen, that we *should always act* in such a way as to secure the best consequences in terms of happiness of those affected. And Kantianism claims that we *should always act* for the sake of the moral law.

Many philosophers now feel that this emphasis upon what we should *do* from a moral point of view is somewhat misleading. They have suggested that what this leaves out is how a moral agent *feels* about things – that is, what his *emotions* are – and, more generally, the nature of his *character*.

One way to put this is to say that for virtue theorists the central question for each of us is not, 'what should one do?' but, 'how should one live?' Answering the latter question will, of course, involve issues about what to do, but will go beyond this to involve such issues as those concerning what kind of person one is and could be.

As I have already mentioned, in seeking to provide an alternative to the theories of utilitarianism and Kantianism, virtue theorists have drawn heavily on the work of Aristotle, particularly his work *Nicomachean Ethics*. However, in what follows I shall not discuss Aristotle's own views in particular – although I shall mention them from time to time. Rather, I shall describe virtue theory more generally as it is discussed in modern moral philosophy.

Character

If we reflect on our relations with one another and on what it is that we like or dislike, admire or despise, respect or loathe in ourselves and others then one of the things we shall see quite soon is that it is a person's *character* that is important here. I might admire someone for his kindness or bravery or generosity; or despise someone else for his meanness or laziness or conceit. Virtue theory focuses on a person's character as central to the moral life. According to this theory, the virtues are, roughly speaking, those traits of character that make someone admirable, and the vices, again roughly speaking, are those that make him contemptible.

What are virtues and vices?

Virtues as dispositions to act

A virtue is a trait of character; so is a vice. For example, bravery is a trait of character that is a virtue and cruelty is a trait of character that is a vice. If someone possesses bravery as a trait of character then we say, of course, that he is brave, and we also say that he is *disposed to behave in a brave manner*. What this means is that in situations where bravery is called for, he has a strong tendency to behave in a brave manner. We can also put this in terms of his having acquired an *habitual way of acting*. That is, he has the *habit* of acting in a brave fashion.

How does one acquire the virtues?

The analogy between acquiring the virtues and learning a musical instrument

According to virtue theory, one acquires the virtues through practice. To see what this means, consider the case of learning to play an instrument. If you wish to play the violin you need to practise a great deal. You have to learn how to hold the instrument and bow properly; how to 'warm up' on the instrument each day when you pick it up to play (if you play without warming up you might damage your tendons); you need to practise scales and simple tunes; you need to work repeatedly at the same pieces before you can play them well; and so on. Eventually you will be able to play the violin, but even then your playing will always be capable of being improved, for you will not only have to keep your playing in very good shape technically, but also you will be able to explore different interpretations of the pieces you play.

Acquiring the virtues is similar to learning to play the violin. In order to become brave, for example, or generous or kind, one must do brave or generous or kind things so that one gradually acquires the disposition to do such things, in the kind of way that one must practise scales on the violin until one has the disposition of character which means that one can just play the scale without thinking hard about how to do so.

There are other parallels between learning to play the violin and acquiring the virtues. When you are first learning the violin you might not really enjoy practising and playing the instrument. After a while, however, you will, with a little luck, come to enjoy the instrument, that is, *take pleasure* in playing it. Similarly, even though it is often hard to acquire the virtues, it is possible in the long run to learn to take pleasure in the exercise of the virtues, so that, for example, you enjoy being kind or generous to others. Further, just as you need a teacher when learning the violin to correct you, show how to do things properly, give you inspiration when your spirit is flagging and so on, so you need a teacher to acquire the virtues, for example, your parents or friends. In fact, virtue theorists emphasise the way in which we are helped to acquire the virtues through imitating the good behaviour of others – such as parents or friends – just as we can learn to play the violin better by imitating those who are already proficient on the instrument.

review
activity

What kind of parallels are there between learning to play a musical instrument and acquiring the virtues?

The virtues and the emotions

The virtues and the emotions

As I mentioned earlier, the virtue theorist argues that the emotions are very important in the moral life. For virtue theory, it is important not simply to do the virtuous thing but also to feel the right way. For example, if I see that someone is being treated unjustly by another person it is not simply important for the virtue theorist that I can see this and, if possible, help the person being oppressed but that I feel the right kind of emotions. These might be pity for the oppressed person and anger with this oppressor. Or, to take another example, if you are kind to me then it is not enough that I simply thank you but that I feel gratitude towards you for your help.

Why should one cultivate the virtues?

Peter Geach (Geach 1977: 17) has said that we need the virtues 'as bees need their stings'. What he means by this is that there are certain things that we can only achieve in life if we have at least some of the virtues to some degree. Thus, for example, whatever projects (beyond the easiest) that we might undertake, if we are to do them well we need to have self-discipline to carry them through, courage not to be daunted by the difficulties they present, patience not to give up too soon and the like.

Connected with this is the fact that human beings are subject to all sorts of passions and emotions that can lead them into ruin. For example, if one could never control one's anger or one's appetite then one would be likely to offend other people a great deal or eat and drink so much that one would become physically, and perhaps mentally, sick or even incapacitated. Without the kinds of virtues that guide and structure the emotions and other related psychological drives we could often be led to our own ruin.

Hume's account of the value of the virtues

David Hume (1711–76) suggested that there are basically four reasons why we value the virtues (Hume 1980: III, 3, §1). These are that the virtues are: a) useful to their possessor; b) useful to society at large in that a person who possesses them contributes well to society; c) 'immediately agreeable', as Hume put it, to those who possess them; and d) 'immediately agreeable' to others.

We have already seen how the virtues can be useful to the one who possesses them. They can also be useful to society in that, for example, if I have the virtues of enterprise or industry I shall be likely to do things, for example, my job, that are to the good of those around me or to society more generally.

The virtues can also be agreeable to see in others and agreeable to us if we have them. For example, to be cheerful, witty and light of spirit is pleasing to see in another; and those who possess these qualities are able to take satisfaction in their doing so.

Virtue ethics, human nature and human flourishing

One way of expressing why one has reason to cultivate the virtues is to contrast virtue theory with Kantianism. I mentioned earlier that some philosophers object to Kantian ethics on the ground that, since it is *a priori*, it detaches moral thought from features of human nature in such a way as to make it unclear what the purpose or point of morality is. Virtue ethics is not *a priori*. On the contrary, it is grounded in features of human nature, as we have already seen, such as features of our character. It is also empirical in another way, for it suggests, unlike Kant's theory, that the *point* of acquiring the virtues is the connection of this with human happiness. Of course, virtue theorists point out that you will need things other than the virtues (for example, health) to be happy, and to that extent what counts as the good life will depend to some extent upon one's having good luck. However, leaving that point aside, we can put their view by saying that if you are virtuous you will be happy. The word 'happiness' used in this context is a translation of the Greek *eudaimonia,* and is also sometimes translated by 'flourishing' or 'wellbeing'. So we can also express the virtue theorists' idea by saying that if you are virtuous then you will flourish or enjoy wellbeing.

Of course, when one is first learning to be virtuous, one cannot have a clear understanding of this. For instance, to learn to control one's appetites can be tiresome because it is pleasurable to eat a great deal. It is only when one has acquired the virtues – or has gone some way towards acquiring them – that one can see the real point of doing so.

review
activity

1. What kinds of reason can one give for acquiring the virtues?
2. What is the connection for virtue theory between the possession of the virtues and happiness?

How can one tell which traits of character are virtues and which vices?

The cardinal virtues

This is a difficult question to answer. The traditional 'cardinal virtues' are courage (fortitude or bravery); temperance (self-discipline); (practical) wisdom (or prudence); and justice. They are so called because it has often been thought that these are the central virtues and that if one lacked any of them one could not be happy or flourish. John Casey has devoted a whole book to the cardinal virtues (Casey 1992). I shall say a little about each, drawing for the most part of Casey's discussion: in no case is what I say anywhere near exhaustive.

Courage

Courage can be shown in many circumstances: in the face of grievous disappointment, for example, or in speaking one's own mind or in pursuing a way of life others think absurd. It is, however, most often connected with, and shown in, overcoming fear. This might be fear of pain, as when one is suffering illness, or fear of death. The latter has often been thought of as particularly significant, because many thinkers have regarded the battlefield as the key place where courage is shown. The rewards of showing such courage are public glory and honour. In this form, courage is not commonly highly thought of in the modern world. There are at least two reasons for this. One is that we live in an age of liberal individualism where we value private life – that is, affirm ordinary life, as Charles Taylor puts it (Taylor 1992) – and are sceptical about the public, political realm. The other is that we have objections to war in a way that previous ages did not.

Temperance

Temperance is self-discipline, particularly self-discipline with respect to our physical appetites. The temperate person is not self-indulgent: he knows how to control his appetites and how to enjoy them without becoming their slave. Those who have discussed temperance have often spoken of the fact that lack of this virtue, that is, self-indulgence, is to be 'brutish'. Laziness and gluttony are vices that the intemperate person might have.

Practical wisdom

Possessing practical wisdom is a matter of possessing good judgement. It is not the mere application of rules or principles to a situation but the ability to understand the situation and judge what to feel and think about it and how to act well in it, even if it is a situation in which one has not previously found oneself. To possess practical wisdom is to possess moral imagination. For example, a doctor may never have been in the unfortunate position of having to inform someone of the death of a relative but if he possesses the virtues then he will have the capacity to judge the right kind of way in which to speak and when to remain silent. Or again, a director of a play may have to deal for the first time with a particularly awkward actor, but if she possesses practical wisdom she will have a good sense of how to manage him, placate him when necessary, challenge him when it is appropriate to do so and so on. A person who possesses practical wisdom is the kind of person who *gets things right:* he is not overly specialised and thus good at only a few things. He will have good judgement concerning a range of things: perhaps politics, business matters, assessment of others' characters and so on. He may also have practical skills.

Justice

Justice seems to involve a kind of general harmony in the soul. A just person will not be egoistic and he will be able to listen to others and yield if there are grounds to do so. He will have a high regard for the interests of others, though this does not mean that he will never become angry or assert his own case: the just person is not weak and does not yield to every demand made of him. Indeed, he will make demands for himself when this is appropriate. He will judge like cases in a like manner.

The theological virtues

To these cardinal virtues Christianity added the three 'theological virtues': faith, hope and charity (love). Faith is belief in God; hope is the hope that, through God's grace, we shall eventually partake in an eternal blessedness or happiness; but the greatest of the three theological virtues is love or charity (Greek: *agape*), the striving for the perfect form of which is an ideal even for many today who have no Christian belief. Our understanding of true love as complete selflessness has been decisively shaped by St Paul's famous words in 1 Corinthians 13, part of which (4–8) reads:

> *Charity suffereth long, and is kind; charity envieth not; charity vaunteth not itself, is not puffed up./Doth not behave itself unseemly, seeketh not her own, is not easily provoked, thinketh no evil;/Rejoiceth not in iniquity, but rejoiceth in the truth;/Beareth all things, believeth all things, hopeth all things, endureth all things./Charity never faileth.*

Of course, the four cardinal virtues and the three theological virtues mentioned so far are not the only virtues. Others include: kindness, friendliness, honesty, patience, dedication and industriousness. However, what about wit, good humour and charm? Are these virtues? Some might think they are not, yet Hume willingly thought of them as virtues (which was why they were mentioned above in Hume's explanation of why we have reason to cultivate the virtues). He did so because it is clear that we can admire people for possessing such traits of character and we can wish to acquire them for ourselves. Perhaps Hume was right to think that it is, in the end, not really so important whether we think of a given trait of character as a virtue or just say that we like people (including ourselves) to possess that trait.

Aristotle's view was also much like Hume's in this regard. In fact, the Greek word, *arete*, that we translate as 'virtue' in reality means 'excellence', and Aristotle was therefore concerned with what he called a person's 'excellences', some of which were excellences of character and some excellences of the intellect. Some of the excellences Aristotle discusses are not traits of character that we would naturally or usually think of as virtues, for example, ambition, wit and magnificence (the spending of money on large and noble projects).

We can say the same about the vices. Cruelty, meanness and spitefulness are vices; but are dull-wittedness and humourlessness? Again, we do not really have to decide whether the latter two are really vices or not, but we can be sure that we have reason to wish to avoid having them.

review activity

1. Name the four cardinal virtues and describe how they might be manifested.

2. What account of charity (love) does Christianity give?

Advantages of virtue theory

As I said earlier, virtue theory is very popular amongst philosophers at present and it is not difficult to see why.

Emotions in virtue ethics

1. In its emphasis upon the emotions as well as on rational thought virtue theory seems in many ways more realistic than utilitarianism and Kantianism. That is, it connects well with an important everyday and easily recognisable feature of our life. After all, we do normally think that it is important not simply to act and think well but also to have the right or appropriate emotions.

Pleasure and the exercise of the virtues

2. There is something very appealing in the idea that it is a mark of a good person to take pleasure in acting virtuously. If you help me dig a ditch in my garden, for example, I shall be pleased if you *want* to help me and *enjoy* doing so. Or if a married couple are faithful to one another it is good to think that they are *pleased* to remain faithful, not that they do so, so to speak, with gritted teeth simply because they are morally required to do so.

Moral education

3. Virtue theory has a good understanding of the notion of a moral education. It places given moral decisions concerning what to do, such as those I mentioned earlier that face the doctor and the theatre director, in the context of the whole of a person's life, seeking to explain how and why he makes the specific decisions he does make. It explains how one can receive a moral education and outlines how this education is to take place. In doing so, it also relates the moral life of a given individual to that of others in a very concrete and realistic way, for

example, through its emphasis on the importance of imitating others, and on teachers, in order to learn morally.

Consideration of life as a whole

4. Related to this is the ability of virtue theory to consider a person's life as a whole. For example, it emphasises the importance of virtue to happiness, but will grant that happiness is something which is true (or not) of a life as a whole. As Aristotle said (Aristotle 1985: 1098a:19–21): 'One swallow does not make a spring, nor does one day; nor, similarly, does one day or a short time make us blessed and happy'. Even if it is true, as virtue theory claims, that the virtuous life is the happy or fulfilled life, the theory can also grant that it is very likely that there will be unhappy days in the life of the virtuous person. This is why Aristotle said, following the words of the wise man Solon, that we should call no man happy until he is dead, that is, until his life is complete and we can consider it as a whole.

No decision procedure

5. Those who accept virtue theory take it to be an advantage of the theory that, unlike utilitarianism, it provides no decision procedure for the resolution of moral problems. They see this as an advantage of the theory because they understand life, and moral life, to be so complicated that any theory that attempts to provide such a procedure must be by that fact prone to simplify and distort morality. For, argue those who accept virtue theory, there could not be a proper understanding of morality which sought, as utilitarianism does, to reduce all moral principles to one principle. Think of the great variety of moral situations in which one might find oneself, argue the virtue theorists, and of the great variety of moral notions one might use to think about them: for example, honour, obligations, piety, dignity, duty, integrity, decency, honesty, meanness, deceit, rights and so on. Further, we might think of describing persons and their deeds as 'cowardly', 'noble', 'honourable', 'vicious', 'base', 'generous' and so on. The virtue theorist says that it is absurd to try to reduce all of these, and many others, to some single criterion or some single description, and that it is an advantage of virtue theory that it does not seek to do so. Stuart Hampshire has expressed this point in this way:

Utilitarianism as moral Esperanto

A single criterion morality, such as classical utilitarianism, deliberately makes an abstraction from standard action descriptions as morally irrelevant except as indicating consequences . . . [I]f the single criterion in ethics is accepted by someone, that person decides to restrict the peculiar powers of his intelligence and of his imagination; and he decides to try to set a final limit to the indefinite development of moral intelligence when he prescribes the single criterion to others . . . Utilitarian thinking is a kind of moral Esperanto.

(Hampshire 1983: ch.2, 23; 28–9)

It may seem odd to suggest that it is an advantage of virtue theory not to have a decision procedure. After all, earlier I indicated that for utilitarians it is a strength of a moral theory if it does offer a decision procedure. This disagreement brings out something very important about philosophical disputes. This is that one and the same feature of a theory can seem to some philosophers one of the theory's strengths and to others one of its weaknesses.

Notice that a lack of decision procedure does not mean that virtue theory must altogether do without rules or principles. On the contrary, it can uphold rules or principles of behaviour, for these will be summaries of wise particular choices made by human beings in certain kinds of situations. However, practical wisdom will be required to see whether such rules can be applied in a given situation and, if so, in what way.

review
activity

What does Hampshire mean by saying that utilitarianism is a kind of moral Esperanto? How does this claim, if correct, support virtue theory?

Difficulties for virtue theory

The wicked who are happy

1. Virtue theory claims that (providing one has a certain amount of good luck as well) the life of virtue is the happy life. Is this always true? Surely there are people who have led wicked lives or lives that in some respect are morally questionable and yet are happy. For example, without doubt Napoleon led a flourishing life, yet he was far from morally good, leading many men and women to destruction in pursuit of his own greater glory. Similarly, there are surely at least some people who are made miserable by being virtuous, for in some deep sense they would really like to cast aside their virtue and express themselves in a different, less virtuous way.

The significance of the fact that not all individuals are virtuous

2. Suppose we agree that virtue is something we value. For we do like people to be kind, generous, patient and so on. But consider now the character Catherine in François Truffaut's film *Jules et Jim*. At one point, her husband, Jules, describes her as a *real* woman. He is right: she is tremendously captivating, a woman of complexity, depth and interest. Yet she is in many ways vengeful, aggressive and impulsive. She even tires of her husband because he is so patient and understanding of her. Yet we can be glad that such a person as Catherine exists, even though she far from virtuous, for she contributes to a sense of the excitement and vitality of life.

Again, consider Stefan Zweig's observation (Zweig 1999: 141–2) that amongst the kind of people he found most appealing were confidence tricksters, those addicted to morphine, those with a generally bad reputation and those who 'handled their life, their time, their money, their health, their good reputation in a squandering and almost scornful manner'. He loved them, he says, for the fact that they were passionate and obsessive in their desire simply to exist for the sake of existing, without any goal.

One could think of many such examples and they all help us to see something important, namely, that we can very often be glad that people are *not* always virtuous, for we are often attracted to people who have some kind of qualities that give them a kind of vitality, and make them exciting to be with, even though these same qualities are, from the point of view of virtue, anything but commendable. It is not absurd to think that, without such people, life would be in many ways extremely dull. For the same reason we could even be glad if we were to live intensely but not so virtuously. (Bertrand Russell made a dry observation (Russell 1950: ch.IV, 74) that perhaps explains why virtue theorists (and others) have missed or ignored the points just made: 'Philosophers, for the most part, are constitutionally timid, and dislike the unexpected. Few of them would be genuinely happy as pirates or burglars.')

The significance of the vices in the economy of the soul

3. A related problem for virtue theory is that sometimes people have traits of character that clearly are not virtues – or are even vices – but which lead them to do great or good things. For example, people of an envious nature are sometimes stimulated to seek to emulate those who have completed some great achievement and in doing so achieve something great for themselves. For example, many writers are envious of those who are successful in their writing and this envy is one of the things which stimulates them to write books which we can enjoy and from which we can learn a lot. Something similar can often be said of inventors or businessmen or sportsmen.

The virtues and cultural relativism

4. Another difficulty which virtue theory has is that different cultures and societies value different character traits as virtues. Sometimes they even disagree over whether a given trait of character really is a virtue or a vice. For example, in Christian thought pride is a vice, for it involves the failure to recognise the fact that we have nothing by right and that we owe everything to God. However, in the thought of Aristotle, pride is the central or crowning virtue, and he gives a memorable description of the proud or great-souled man:

Aristotle's great-souled man

The great-souled man is concerned especially with honours and dishonours. And when he receives great honours from excellent people, he will be moderately pleased, thinking he is getting what is proper to him . . . But if he is honoured by just anyone, or for something small, he will entirely disdain it; for that is not what he is worthy of . . . The great-souled man wishes to be superior . . . When he meets people with good fortune or a reputation for worth, he displays his greatness, since superiority over them is difficult and impressive, and there is nothing ignoble in trying to be impressive with them. But when he meets with ordinary people he is moderate, since superiority over them is easy . . . He stays away from what is commonly honoured, and from areas where others lead; he is inactive and lethargic except for some great honour or achievement. Hence his actions are few, but great and renowned. Moreover, he is open in his hatreds and his friendships . . . He is concerned for the truth more than for people's opinion. He is open in his speech and actions, since his disdain makes him speak freely. He cannot let anyone else . . . determine his life. For that would be slavish . . . He is the sort of person whose possessions are fine and unproductive rather than productive and advantageous, since that is more proper to a self-sufficient person . . . He has slow movements, a deep voice and calm speech. For since he takes few things seriously, he is in no hurry, and since he counts nothing great, he is not strident.

(Aristotle 1985: 1124a5–1125a15)

It goes without saying that, like Christians, many modern people would not see much virtue in Aristotle's great-souled man. In fact, they might see a lot of vice in him. And one central reason for this is that the moral thinking of modernity has been decisively shaped by Christianity, even for those who do not accept that system of belief.

Worldliness and other-worldliness

We can put the disagreement between Aristotle and the modern view in this way. Aristotle's view is deeply and profoundly *worldly*: it articulates the idea that how one appears before one's peers is of enormous importance, and it places great emphasis on honour, public acclaim and glory. The virtues he emphasises go with such a worldly view: pride, valour on the battlefield, magnificence. Moreover, he insists that if, for example, one is ugly, one cannot fully have a flourishing life. Christianity, however, is profoundly *otherworldly*: it emphasises humility, meekness, selflessness and so on. How one appears before others does not matter. What matters is purity of motive, and the last thing that could be relevant to one's true worth is one's physical appearance: it is the beauty of the soul that counts in Christianity.

A virtue theorist might simply accept that different cultures have different sets of virtues. However, another response that the virtue theorist can offer is to suggest that it is in principle possible to defend the idea that, whatever differences there may as a matter of fact be between cultures, there is a range of virtues which it is possible to defend as being the ones necessary for a culture to embody so that its members might flourish as human beings. Martha Nussbaum has offered such an argument (Nussbaum 2001). Her view is, roughly, that there are features of life to which each human being, regardless of place or time, has to respond. These include: that we are mortal; that we each of us have a body with the needs this has, for example, for nutrition; that we all experience pleasure and pain; that we can all think; that we can all plan our lives in better or worse ways; and so on. Moreover, we all of us, says Nussbaum, have to make decisions about how to think of our own worth; about our attitudes to the way others treat us, for example, when we are insulted; about what understanding we are to have of good and ill fortune, both that of others and our own; and so on. Nussbaum argues that, if we reflect on the different human responses to these 'constants' and debate and discuss with others, both from our own and other cultures, concerning better and worse ways of responding to them, then we shall be able to come to certain virtues for each constant, or, at any rate, a certain limited range of virtues for each constant, which indicate the best way of responding to that constant. For example, some ways of responding to the pleasure we take in eating and drinking can be thought of as manifesting mistaken understandings of what is good for human beings. Thus, there are ways of responding to such pleasure that show no moderation and hence a distorted sense of its importance in human life. However, there might reasonably be different virtuous ways of responding to the fact that we experience pleasure: thus there will some 'leeway' for different individuals to cultivate different virtues in this area of life, but some ways of responding will be mistaken.

Moral worldviews

It is hard to assess Nussbaum's view without a thorough investigation of different ways of life that human beings have followed. But it is arguable that she is overly optimistic in thinking that there is an acceptable range of ways of responding to the constants of human life which allow a human being to flourish or be happy. The main reason for this is that what one counts as flourishing depends a lot on one's general moral point of view. For example, a Christian will have a different conception from an atheist of what it is to flourish, and a Christian and an atheist are thus likely to disagree very deeply about the 'correct' attitude to what Nussbaum thinks of as the constants of human life. Thus, a Roman Catholic might think that a life devoted to child rearing is the noblest life there could be, because life is a gift from God and there could be nothing greater than creating life; whereas an atheist might see this kind of life as mere drudgery and a form of slavery. Thus, it seems that Nussbaum fails to see there can there can be conflicting moral world-views, and that the existence of such world-views stands in the way of achieving the kind of agreement Nussbaum claims is, in principle, possible.

Goodness beyond virtue and evil beyond vice

5. Another difficulty for virtue theory is that it seems to leave out so much of what is relevant to the moral life. For example, as Hannah Arendt suggested, reflection on the virtues seems unable to provide us with a proper understanding of what she called goodness beyond virtue and evil beyond vice (Arendt 1990: 81-2).

This can be seen in, for example, Aristotle's work, who seems to have had some sense of states beyond vice, which he called 'bestial' or 'diseased'. However, when he gives examples of such states he lumps together 'the female human being who is said to tear pregnant women apart and devour the children . . . [and] the person who sacrificed his mother and ate her [with the person who enjoys] chewing [his] nails'

Hannah Arendt (1906–1975)

Hannah Arendt was unquestionably one of the greatest political theorists of the twentieth century. She was born in Hanover, Germany, and studied with two of the leading German philosophers of the twentieth century, Martin Heidegger (1889–1976) and Karl Jaspers (1883–1969). As a Jew, she had to flee Germany on Hitler's rise to power, going first to France and then to the United States, where she settled. She wrote a great deal, some of her works being extremely controversial. Amongst these, probably the most significant is *Eichmann in Jerusalem: a Report of the Banality of Evil*, a book that documented the trial in Jerusalem of Adolf Eichmann, one of the architects of the mass deportation and slaughter of the Jews during the Second World War. One of the things that made the book so controversial was that she believed that, when at his trial Eichmann claimed that he had not been driven by hatred of the Jews, he had been telling the truth. She interpreted his evil as banal in that it was driven, not by anything 'satanic', but by sheer *thoughtlessness*: being a Nazi had just been, at his time and place, the 'way to 'get on in life'. Amongst her other works, mention should be made of *The Human Condition*, a profound exploration of modern life in which she contrasts modern political life unfavourably with the politics of ancient Greece.

125

(Aristotle 1985: 1148b; 20ff.). But to class together the cannibal and the nail biter shows the weakness in Aristotle's account of anything we might recognise as evil.

Of course, the fact that Aristotle did not make much sense of evil does not mean a virtue theorist could not. But if a virtue theorist were to make sense of evil then he would need more conceptual resources than those provided by the vices, for we are dealing here, as indicated, with evil beyond vice.

But it is not just the notions of good and evil that virtue theory seems to leave out of its understanding of ethics. There are plenty of other concepts about which virtue theory seems to be able to say nothing at all, too little, or the wrong things. For example, there is little, if any, discussion in virtue theory of a person's spirit and sensibility (where these are different from, and not reducible to, character traits); of the *mystery* of birth and death; of fate; of the notion of a vocation or a calling; of the nature of wholly conflicting moral world-views; of the vanity of life; of the importance of individual style for moral matters; of a form of wisdom that is not merely *practical* wisdom; and of the meaning of life. No doubt virtue theory will, indirectly, have something to say about some of these, but, apart from the fact that they are, in general, very rarely discussed by virtue theorists, it is extremely unlikely that enough could be said about them using only the conceptual resources available within virtue theory.

A sceptical note: do we really need a moral theory?

In a way, the last criticism of virtue theory was a little unfair. This is because it is not only virtue theory that says nothing about the topics mentioned in the criticism. Neither utilitarianism nor Kantianism has anything to say about them either. In fact, the philosophical mainstream tends to ignore them altogether. But what this suggests is that *no* moral theory is, perhaps, properly able to be responsive to the features of human life indicated. In fact, many philosophers do now think that we do not need, and could not have, any moral theory at all. This is because they believe that any theory will close down the resources of the moral imagination by limiting the range of moral concepts that the theory makes available for thought and experience, in just the kind of way that Hampshire said utilitarianism does. In that sense, utilitarianism would be just the extreme of a tendency found in all moral theories. In other words, life is simply too complicated and too rich to be understood in the kind of systematic way that any moral theory must aim for.

However, even if we were to think that we cannot have a moral theory, it does not follow that we cannot learn a lot from the theories that there are. On the contrary, thinking them through, seeing their strengths and limitations, not only sharpens the intellect, but can also, perhaps, help with better understanding moral life.

some questions
to think about

1 How far would you agree with Anscombe that we should seek to give up the notion of moral obligation?

2 Do you agree that the central question of ethics should be 'how should one live?'

3 Is it true that all individuals could acquire the virtues, or are individuals' characters not malleable enough for his claim to be, in general, true?

4 Could there be one list of virtues for all human beings?

5 Is it true that virtue is central to human happiness or flourishing?

6 To what extent do you agree with the claim that we do not need moral theories?

further reading

▶ Statman (ed.) 1997 is an excellent reader on virtue ethics. Foot 1978 is also an excellent collection. MacIntyre 1985 is a wide-ranging and quite brilliant, though partisan, work on the virtues. Casey 1992 is an interesting and easy read. On Aristotle's ethics, I recommend Urmson 1988.

IV Practical Ethics

Key topics in this chapter

- The nature of practical ethics
- The moral problems surrounding abortion, euthanasia and the treatment of animals

Abortion: the expulsion (either spontaneous or induced) of a foetus from the womb before it is able to survive.

Acts and omissions doctrine: the theory that there is, in general, a significant moral difference between doing an act with certain consequences and allowing the same consequences to occur.

Euthanasia: the termination of the life of a person who is suffering. Euthanasia can be *voluntary*, which means it is requested by the patient; *non-voluntary*, which means that the patient is not capable of requesting it; and *involuntary*, which means that the patient has requested that it not be carried out.

Prior existence utilitarianism: the theory that the interests of only those sentient creatures now in existence must be taken into account in the utilitarian calculus.

Total utilitarianism: the theory that the interests of all sentient creatures presently in existence and those not yet in existence must be taken into account in the utilitarian calculus.

Vivisection: the carrying out of experiments on living creatures.

What is practical ethics?

Practical ethics is the area of moral philosophy that is concerned with the discussion and exploration of specific moral problems, such as euthanasia, abortion, animal welfare, capital punishment, war, famine, suicide and so on. In this chapter we shall explore the first three mentioned. Where appropriate, we shall explore the relevance of the moral theories we have discussed to such issues but we shall also look at other arguments philosophers have offered in consideration of such issues. The aim of such discussions is to clarify our thinking about these issues and, if possible, to come to conclusions concerning what to do in certain situations where they arise.

Abortion

Of all contemporary moral debates, abortion raises some of the deepest passions. To some, abortion is clearly morally appalling, whereas others fail to see that it raises profound moral issues. We shall look at these and other responses to it.

The *Oxford English Dictionary* defines abortion as 'the expulsion (either spontaneous or induced) of a foetus from the womb before it is able to survive'. Clearly the moral problems surrounding abortion are raised where the expulsion of the foetus from the womb is induced, and it is as such that I shall discuss it.

The gradual development of the foetus

When does a foetus become a human being?

One difficulty arises in the abortion issue because the development of the foetus is gradual. Everyone will agree that the fertilised ovum (egg) just a few minutes old is not a creature that is conscious of its surroundings. On the other hand, everyone will also agree that a healthy baby born at nine months is, and that the fertilised ovum develops into the baby. So is the fertilised ovum a human being? If it is not, when does it become one? There are commonly thought to be four points at which it might be right to say the fertilised ovum has become a human being. These are: birth, viability, quickening and the capacity to feel pleasure and pain (consciousness).

Birth

It is hard to believe that birth marks the point at which we should say that the fertilised ovum has become a human being. After all, it would be odd to think that a baby in the womb at eight months and three weeks was not a human being but that a week later, when born, it is.

Viability

Viability marks the point at which the foetus can survive by itself outside the womb. Peter Singer gives a reason why it looks odd to say that viability marks the point at which a foetus becomes a human being (Singer 1993: 140). Thirty years ago a baby born at six months would have died. Now, thanks to medical technology, it might well survive. Should we say that a baby born this prematurely 30 years ago was not a human being but now is? Surely not. Or again, a woman in England might give birth to a baby that, thanks to the technology available there, can survive. However, if she had given birth to the same baby in a less well-developed country the baby would have died. Should we say that the baby is a human being in England but would not have been in the less well-developed county? This surely is implausible.

Quickening

This is the point at which the mother first feels the foetus move in the womb. It is hard to believe that this marks the point at which a foetus becomes a human being. For one thing, quickening does not always takes place at the same stage of pregnancy in the case of all foetuses. For another, the sheer capacity to move seems irrelevant to whether something is a human being: an adult who suffers an accident which completely paralyses him for a week does not cease to be a human being during that week.

The capacity to feel pleasure and pain

There is something to be said for the idea that the capacity to feel pleasure and pain marks the point at which the foetus becomes a human being. The trouble is, no one really knows at what stage in the foetus's development this happens. In any case, even if a foetus can feel pain very early on it is not clear what significance this should have for the issue of abortion, for, even if it is agreed that the foetus is a human being from that early point when it can feel pain, defenders of abortion nonetheless think that it is legitimate to kill this human being in certain cases. After all, adult human beings can feel pain, too, but only absolute pacifists think they should never be killed.

review
activity

What are the four stages at which one might suppose the foetus has become a human being? What is wrong with each of these as a criterion of this change?

Human beings and persons

Some philosophers who recognise the difficulties in drawing a line at the point at which the foetus becomes a human being think that this is because the term 'human being' is unclear. They draw a distinction between the concepts of a *human being* and a *person* and define each in a special way.

Human beings

According to these philosophers, a human being is a member of a given species, the species to which you, the reader of this book, and I, its writer, belong, namely *Homo sapiens*. This is a *biological* classification. A creature that is a member of the species *Homo sapiens* is a human being.

Persons

A person is a being that has certain capacities or properties. Not all philosophers agree on exactly the same list of capacities or properties that a person has. John Locke (1632–1704) defined a person as 'a thinking, intelligent Being, that has reason and reflection, and can consider it self as it self, the same thinking thing in different times and places' (Locke 1984: II, xxvii, §9). Many philosophers have followed Locke fairly closely in his definition and have thus claimed that the two key notions in understanding the concept of a person are rationality and self-consciousness.

Rationality

It is very hard to say what, exactly, rationality is, but, at the very least, a rational being has some capacity for problem solving, however exactly we should understand that, and for adopting beliefs on the basis of appropriate reasons.

Self-consciousness

A *self-conscious* being is a being that is aware not merely of its surroundings but also of itself. For example, you are conscious, and at the moment what you are conscious of is the book you are reading. You are also conscious of other things. For example, if you are sitting, you are conscious of the feel of the chair in which you are sitting, and you are conscious of the amount of light available by which you are reading and so on. You are also *self*-conscious. That is, you are not merely conscious of this book but also conscious of yourself reading the book: you are aware of yourself *as* reading this book. Further, a self-conscious being is aware of itself as a distinct entity, one entity amongst others, and as existing over time. You are aware of what you did yesterday and can make plans for yourself for tomorrow. You can do this because you are not merely conscious but self-conscious.

Many beings are, it seems, conscious but not self-conscious. For example, a rabbit is certainly a *conscious* creature, aware of its surroundings, seeing and hearing things and so on, but it is unlikely that it is *self*-conscious, that is, aware of itself *as* seeing and hearing and so on.

A person, then, is a rational and self-conscious being; a human being is a member of a certain species.

In these terms, not all members of the species *Homo sapiens* are persons. That is, not all human beings are persons. For example, newly born babies are certainly members of this species, but they are not persons, for they are not rational or self-conscious. On the other hand, there might be some creatures which are not members of the species *Homo sapiens* but which are persons. For example, Peter Singer (Singer 1993: 110ff.) has argued that chimpanzees, whales and dolphins are persons because they are rational and self-conscious, but they are clearly not members of our species. He also suggests that cats and dogs might be persons (Singer 1993: 119). It is hard to know whether this is correct, for it is hard to know whether a creature that has no language is self-conscious, for it is primarily through a creature's use of language that we can be sure that a creature is self-conscious. Still, for the moment we need not worry about whether there are non-human persons, that is, persons that are not members of the species *Homo sapiens*. We shall return to this issue when discussing animal welfare.

review activity

1. Explain the difference between a conscious and a self-conscious creature.
2. Explain the distinction some philosophers draw between human beings and persons.

The status of the foetus

These reflections about persons allow us to assess the status of the foetus.

From the moment of conception the foetus is clearly a member of the species *Homo sapiens*. This is because it has the genetic make up which renders it so. At some stage in its development a foetus becomes conscious. No one knows when this point is reached, but clearly at conception a foetus is not conscious of anything and at birth at nine months it is. However, philosophers such as Singer argue that a foetus, even just before birth, is neither rational nor self-conscious. This means that it is not a person according the criteria discussed.

Non-conscious, conscious and self-conscious entities

A principle for treating creatures

Philosophers who draw the distinction between persons and members of the species *Homo sapiens* do so because they believe that a particular principle should govern the way we treat any object or creature, be it a stone, a flower, a tree, a cat, a monkey or a human being. This principle is that we should treat the object or creature according to its capacities or properties. For example, a stone does not have the capacity to feel pain, so it does not matter if I kick it. However, a rabbit can feel pain, so I should not kick it. (That is, *other things being equal* I should not kick. For example, suppose for some reason the only way I can save your life is to kick a rabbit, then I should be justified in kicking it.) Further, a person – you for example – can suffer pain not merely in the way a rabbit can, but also in a deeper, more intense or more complex fashion. Thus, if I kick a rabbit and break its leg I will have hurt it, but if I kick you and break your leg then I will not merely have hurt you but also destroyed some of your plans for the future – say your walking holiday next week in Wales.

So, in general, a self-conscious, rational being (a person) can suffer more than a conscious being. Moreover, some conscious beings can suffer more than others. For example, a dog, which has a much more complex central nervous system than a fish, can presumably suffer more intensely than a fish, even though (I am assuming) they are both conscious, but not self-conscious creatures. Of course, a pain inflicted on a self-conscious being might be less than one inflicted on a conscious (but not self-conscious) being, as when you experience a mild pin prick on your finger and a cat is run over by a car, but this has to do, not with the creature, but with the type of pain inflicted.

There is a further important difference between a self-conscious being and a merely conscious one in terms of capacity to feel pleasure and pain. This is that a self-conscious being, because it is aware of itself as existing over time, can want to go on existing. A conscious being cannot want this because it cannot have a conception of itself as existing in the future, say in two days' time. This means that a self-conscious being can suffer if it is killed in a way that a conscious, but not self-conscious, being cannot, because the former, but not the latter, will, if it is killed, have its desire to go on living frustrated.

The morality of abortion: the utilitarian approach

We have seen that, according to the reasoning offered so far, a foetus is a member of the species *Homo sapiens* at all stages of its development; that it becomes conscious at some stage of its development; but that even at birth at nine months it is not a person. For those philosophers who offer the kind of arguments I have been explaining so far, these facts offer a particular way in which to understand the morality of abortion. We shall look first at the utilitarian view. I take as representative of this view the arguments of Peter Singer, since he is the utilitarian who is most well-known for his work on this issue.

Peter Singer's arguments

According to utilitarianism, the only criterion by which the morality of any deed is to be judged is the consequences of the deed for the happiness or satisfaction of interests or preferences of those affected. Singer is an interest utilitarian. However, I shall discuss utilitarian views on abortion in this chapter indifferently in terms of happiness, interests or preferences as seems appropriate: nothing of any substance will turn on the use of any specific terminology.

It is evident that the happiness or interests of the mother and the father are directly relevant to the issue of whether a given foetus is to be aborted. There may be others whose happiness should be taken into account. For example, suppose a woman is contemplating having an abortion and we know that she could carry the baby to term and have it adopted by a couple who wish to adopt a baby and give him a secure home. In this case, for a utilitarian, the happiness of the couple who wish to adopt is relevant to the decision the woman makes whether to have the abortion or not. Evidently, if she does not have an abortion and she allows the baby to be adopted she will contribute to the happiness of the couple, whereas, if she does have an abortion, then she will contribute to their unhappiness (or frustration of their happiness).

Leaving aside such complications, however, let us look at the foetus itself. At a very early stage of its development – say up to three months – it is probably barely conscious and hardly able to feel pleasure and pain at all. Singer claims that such a foetus shows fewer signs of consciousness than a fish (Singer 1993: 151). (In the first edition of his book, Singer claimed that a foetus before three months shows fewer signs of consciousness than even a prawn. However, he has clearly changed his mind about this, since he excised that claim from the second edition of his book.) Therefore, Singer claims, there is nothing seriously morally wrong with aborting it. Even when it is older, its consciousness further developed and it is capable of feeling pleasure and pain Singer argues that this will still be so in such a rudimentary way that the serious interests of the mother should override those of the foetus if she wishes to have it aborted. As the foetus is at no point of its development self-conscious, and therefore cannot want to go on existing, the interests of the mother can continue to override those of the foetus in a morally acceptable manner. Singer sums up his view by saying that 'even an abortion late in pregnancy for the most trivial of reasons is hard to condemn' (Singer 1993: 151).

So, we can say that, other things being equal, if a pregnant woman wants to have an abortion at any stage of pregnancy then there will very rarely be anything (seriously) wrong with her procuring one. Thus there is, for the utilitarian such as Singer, no significant moral difference between a woman who wishes to have an abortion as a result of rape or because the foetus is deformed or simply because she finds it inconvenient to carry a baby to term.

review activity

Explain in your own words Singer's argument that abortion presents no serious moral problems.

The potential of the foetus

One objection to this argument is that the foetus has the potential to become a fully self-conscious person. Barring misfortune, it will develop into a person and surely it is this potential, one might argue, which means it should not be aborted, or at least not for reasons that one might regard as trivial.

Singer is quick in response to this argument. He says that although it is true that the foetus is a potential person it is not a person, and so should not be treated *now*, as a foetus, as if it were. Similarly, he says, a prince is a potential king but that does not mean he should be treated now, whilst a prince, as if he were a king (Singer 1993: 153).

review activity

Why does Singer reject the idea that the potential of the foetus is relevant to the issue of abortion?

Replaceability

Many people will disagree with Singer's views, and we shall come back to what might be said against them. But before we do, we need to note a complication in the utilitarian position. Consider the case where the foetus is disabled. A utilitarian will agree that a foetus that is so severely disabled that, if allowed to develop, it would have a life full of misery and suffering, should, other things being equal, be aborted. However, what of a foetus that is also disabled but whose disability will cause it some suffering but not be such that its life will be a complete misery? A utilitarian will say that if the balance of pleasure against pain is likely to be in favour of greater pleasure then the foetus should not be aborted, whereas if the balance tips in the direction of pain then it should be aborted.

At this point a utilitarian is likely to offer a subsidiary argument. For suppose that a foetus is likely, if allowed to develop, to have a net balance of pleasure over pain but nonetheless have a great deal of pain. Suppose also that the mother in question is determined to have just one baby. Then the utilitarian could propose the following. As what matters is to increase the happiness in the world, the mother in question could do this by aborting the foetus and conceiving another that would not be disabled. In other words, she could *replace* the disabled foetus with a normal one and this would lead to a greater amount of overall happiness.

Underlying this argument about replaceability is what is called the 'total version' of utilitarianism. I explain what that is later in the context of euthanasia.

A reply to the replaceability argument

Rosalind Hursthouse has argued that this argument about replaceability fails. Her argument goes as follows (Hursthouse 1987: 151). If one is a utilitarian one is supposed to aim at increasing overall happiness. However, in the kind of situation described where two foetuses are conceived, each of which can be expected to have a net balance of pleasure over pain (though the life of the first will contain a lot of pain), the way to increase overall happiness will *not* be to replace the one foetus by another but to have two babies. Certainly the first, disabled, foetus will be less happy than the second, normal one, but, other things being equal, the overall happiness of the world will be greater if the two are born than if one is.

Of course, if in such a case the mother only wishes to have one baby, and if she sticks by this, then Hursthouse's argument will fail. Nonetheless, the consistent utilitarian should think that it is better if the mother has *both* babies, and he should probably try to encourage her to do so. He will think her in the wrong to have only the one baby.

review
activity

1. What does it mean for a utilitarian to say that the foetus is replaceable?
2. Explain Hursthouse's argument against the claim that a foetus could be replaceable.
3. In which cases would Hursthouse's argument fail?

An objection to the utilitarian argument

A critique of Singer's utilitarian position on abortion

Return now to Singer's claim that, because the foetus is certainly not self-conscious, and is only conscious towards the end of a pregnancy, and even then to a limited degree, it is permissible to kill it if one wishes. It seems that there is a fundamental objection to the argument even on Singer's own utilitarian terms, and it is once again articulated by Hursthouse (Hursthouse 1987: 155ff.). If we kill a foetus then we know that this, other things being equal, will be to kill a being that, had it not been killed, would have lived happily for 70 years or so. So surely it must be wrong on utilitarian grounds to kill it. We have here two situations: one (situation A) in which the foetus is killed, thus depriving the world of the increase in overall happiness that it would have had if the foetus had not been killed; and another (situation B) in which the foetus is not killed and the world's happiness is correspondingly increased. Surely the utilitarian should prefer B. However, this means that he should favour a rather restrictive abortion policy, and not the extremely liberal one that Singer offers. It surely means that the utilitarian should only be in favour of abortion in those cases where to allow the foetus to develop and not abort it will bring overall more *un*happiness into the world than happiness, where to measure this we shall have to consider the happiness of the foetus from the moment of conception to death in, say, 70 years' time, along with the happiness of the mother and father, and so on.

What has gone wrong with Singer's argument? The difficulty is that a utilitarian must be concerned about the consequences – *all* the consequences – of any given act. However, Singer overlooks the consequences of any given abortion and simply says that we should treat the foetus according to the properties it possesses at a given stage of development. This is a mistake, even on his own terms. The fact that the foetus is not self-conscious, is not rational and can hardly feel pain when in the womb does not mean, even for a utilitarian, that we can ignore the consequences of killing it, that is, that it will not experience any happiness at all since if aborted it will no longer exist. Even for Singer, the fact that *at the time it is killed* it can feel no (or little) pain and is neither rational nor self-conscious ought to be irrelevant to the issue of the morality of killing it. In short, Singer treats the foetus as if it were never going to develop, and this is clearly a mistake. Consider an analogous case. If you are anaesthetised you are not self-conscious, not rational and can feel no pain. In such a case, if someone were to kill you he could hardly defend himself by saying that *at the time you were killed* you were not self-conscious, were not rational and could feel no pain. The point is that, after the anaesthetic had worn off, you would have been self-conscious, would have regained your rationality and would have been able to feel pain, and the fact that this is so is surely a good reason not to have killed you. Singer would certainly agree with this last point. So he ought also to agree that, other things being equal, there are good utilitarian grounds not to carry out abortions.

review
activity

Explain in your own words Hursthouse's objection to Singer's view on abortion.

The morality of abortion: rights

Tooley's argument

There are, of course, approaches to the abortion issue that depart somewhat from utilitarianism. In particular, the utilitarian argument makes no mention of *rights*, either of the foetus or the mother. We shall now look at two arguments which do just this.

Michael Tooley has offered the first argument (Tooley 1992). He suggests that we distinguish, in the kind of way already seen, between the concept of a person and the concept of the species *Homo sapiens*. His definition of the concept of a person is complicated but, roughly speaking, he has in mind the kind of concept of a person we have already considered: a person is an entity that has a conception of itself, that is, which is self-conscious. He then says that only a person can have what he calls a 'serious right to life'. A foetus, Tooley says, is not a person in the sense under consideration, from which it follows that it has no serious right to life. Therefore, Tooley concludes that killing the foetus, that is, abortion, is morally acceptable or morally neutral.

The foetus as a potential person

Tooley, like Singer, considers the objection to his argument that the foetus is nonetheless a potential person and thus now has a serious right to life even before it has become a person. To counter this objection he imagines that a chemical has been developed which, if it is injected into the brain of a kitten, will ensure that the kitten will develop into a cat whose brain, unlike that of a normal cat, is rather like that of a person. Such a cat would be self-conscious, could think, use language and so on.

Imagine now that a kitten is accidentally injected with such a chemical. Tooley says that the fact that the kitten will develop into a person does not mean that it *now*, before the process of transformation begins, has the serious right to life that a person has. However, the injected kitten, he says, is just like the foetus. So he concludes that the foetus no more has a right to life than does the injected kitten, even though both are potential persons.

Before considering the plausibility of Tooley's argument I wish to outline a second argument that draws on the concept of rights.

Thomson's 'violinist' argument

Judith Jarvis Thomson offers the argument. Thomson imagines the following situation (Thomson 1992). Imagine you wake up one morning to find yourself plugged into a famous violinist. He has a fatal kidney disease, and a Society of Music Lovers has found out that you are the only person who has the right blood type to help him and has kidnapped you and plugged you into the violinist. If you remain plugged into him for nine months then he will be cured. If you unplug yourself now, he will die. Thomson says that, although it would be kind of you to stay plugged into him, you have the right to unplug yourself and he has no right that you stay plugged into him. The case of this kidnapping is supposed to be like that of rape, and Thomson says that, just as the violinist has no right to the use of your body, neither has a foetus that is there as a result of rape a right to use a woman's body.

Thomson's 'person-seed' argument

Thomson has a second argument to show, she claims, that abortion is justified also in cases other than rape. Imagine, she says, that there are person-seeds that float through the air like pollen. If one of these seeds floats into your house it will take root in the upholstery and grow into a person. As you do not want this to happen, you fix up screens at the window of your house. However, as occurs on very, very rare occasions, one of the seeds manages to get into your house because one of the screens is defective. Does the person-plant that starts to grow have a right to use your house? Thomson says that it does not as you took precautions against its implanting itself. She claims that this case of the damaged screen is analogous to the case of contraceptive failure: if a woman has taken all reasonable precautions against pregnancy but becomes pregnant nonetheless, then the foetus has no right to use her body, just as the person-plant has no right to use your house.

review activity

1. Why does Tooley deny that a foetus has a serious right to life?

2. What is Thomson's violinist example and what is it supposed to show?

3. Explain Thomson's seed argument. What does she think it shows?

Criticisms of Tooley and Thomson

Rights, virtues and vices

There are specific criticisms that one might make of the arguments that Tooley and Thomson offer.

For example, even if Tooley is right that a foetus has no right to life it does not follow from this that to abort a foetus is not, sometimes, a mean, selfish or wicked thing to do. Suppose, for instance, that a woman is seven months pregnant. Let us imagine she then wins a competition, for which she entered before she was pregnant, and the prize is a walking holiday in Nepal. She would love to go, but cannot as she is pregnant. Let us imagine that she agrees with Tooley that her foetus (or baby, as it would be more natural to call a foetus of seven months) has no serious right to life and she has it aborted so that she can go on the holiday. Even if we agree that she has not violated any rights, few people would doubt that she had done something selfish.

Abortion and infanticide

If this seems unfair to Tooley, consider the following. An infant of, say, one month of age is no more a person in the sense we have been discussing than is a baby in the womb at seven months. Suppose the woman in the example had a baby of one month old and then won the competition. On Tooley's principles, there would be no violation of the rights of the baby if the woman decided to kill it so that she could go to Nepal. Perhaps even a baby of six months is not a person and therefore to kill it would violate no rights it has, so if the woman killed her six-month-old baby to go to Nepal that would also violate no rights the baby has. However, surely we should want to say that a woman who did this showed herself to be at least brutal and selfish – many would judge that she had done something evil.

Such examples are important because Tooley is, in fact, quite explicit that he believes that infanticide is morally acceptable – because a baby is not a person, killing it violates no rights. Of course, he grants that no one knows when a foetus or baby becomes a person since its development is gradual. So he would say that if a baby becomes a person after one month then it should not be killed after it is a month old. If it does not become a person until six months of age, then it should not be killed once it has reached six months. None of this, of course, affects his main point.

In fairness to Tooley, it should be said that he is principally interested in justifying infanticide in cases of, for example, serious deformity of the baby. However, his own argument, if accepted, clearly justifies more than this. That is, it justifies the kind of case already mentioned of the woman who would like to go to Nepal (cf. Hursthouse 1987: 119–23).

Similar points might be made against Thomson. Even if it violates no rights to abort a foetus, as the person-seed argument is meant to show, we might still wish to say that the behaviour of a woman who did abort a foetus simply because, say, she could not be bothered to go through with the pregnancy, was heartless.

Are the kinds of examples and arguments of Tooley and Thomson irrelevant?

However, there is a more fundamental objection to the kinds of arguments offered by Tooley and Thomson. For it will have been noticed that they have a 'surreal' or 'science-fiction' quality: injected kittens, kidnappings, person-seeds – none of this is anything like the experience of women who actually are faced with the dilemma of whether to have an abortion or not. Some philosophers think that because such examples are disconnected from such experience they are useless for enabling us to understand the ethics of abortion or helping us to think constructively about the political implications their proposals would have, if embodied in our institutions. What kind of society would we have if infanticide and abortion were regarded as Tooley would have us regard them? This is not a question to which Tooley ever addresses himself, but it is evidently an extremely important one, and one that cannot be ignored. And Bernard Williams has criticised Tooley's argument for ignoring it. He thinks that Tooley's arguments should be rejected on the grounds of their 'sheer frivolity . . . which lies in their refusal to engage with the only two things that matter: the politics of trying to make rules for such situations, and the experience of people engaged in them' (Williams 1995: 221, fn.10).

How should we understand that experience? Here is a suggestion.

The human experience and understanding of pregnancy is connected with the fact that human beings are sexual beings. Through their sexuality human beings can express some of deepest and most tender emotions and also some of their most brutal and violent (as in rape). Further, our understanding of pregnancy is deeply coloured by the fact that only women can get pregnant and that it transforms their bodies in ways that can be painful but which we can also see as beautiful. We can also see the changes in the body, and the very fact of birth itself, as strange and mysterious. Even people who are not religious very often see here a sense of mystery and are touched by a sense of wonder. In addition, the human experience of pregnancy is connected with our understanding of what it is to have a child, and to see him or her grow up and develop over a long period of time, during which time the child needs a great deal of love and care. Further, our sense of what a human baby is, is of a creature that has before it a life that is like a *journey* or *adventure*: things could go well in it, or everything could go wrong, and one way or another it will be marked by joy and disappointment, hope and despair, success and failure.

None of these ideas can lead us to conclude that abortion is always wrong or always right; nor can they lead us to a firm decision that it is wrong in such and such circumstances and right in some other circumstances. But what they suggest is that any discussion of abortion that does not take into account such experiences of human sexuality, of the differences between men and women, of the strangeness and mystery of birth and so on *has not properly understood the kinds of experiences which make abortion the kind of moral problem that it is.* But if this is so, then any such discussion cannot hope to provide any wise guidance concerning the morality of abortion.

Problems with the person/Homo sapiens distinction

We might say something similar about the distinction which theorists make between the concept of a person and that of a member of the species *Homo sapiens*. A pregnant woman, however much or little she wants the child growing in her, *never* thinks of it *merely* as a member of a certain species. Whether she wants to keep it and cherish it or whether she resents it and would like to be rid of it, her understanding of what it is that is in her depends upon the kinds of facts I mentioned above. To insist, as Singer and Tooley do, that the foetus is *just* a member of a certain species is to *fail* to understand what it is. It is to fail to understand the *human significance* of a foetus.

We might compare Singer and Tooley's view concerning the foetus with many other areas of life where what we see before us depends upon the human significance of the thing in question. Consider, for example, the concept of a painting. A painting is something that has a human significance because it exists as something that can be created to express the deepest emotions of a human being, can look beautiful to us, can seem to articulate a whole sense of life, can demand from us that we cherish it and so on. If someone said that a painting was merely a load of blobs of oil on a canvas and therefore it did not matter whether it was thrown into an incinerator or not then any sensitive person would see immediately that this view involved a failure to understand what a painting is. Such a way of speaking is an attempt to destroy the *human significance* of painting.

In general, then, we can say that, within human concerns, things matter to human beings in ways not reducible to their material or biological properties.

This argument suggests, therefore, that to insist that a foetus is merely a member of the species *Homo sapiens* and is therefore of no serious moral consequence is to wish to *destroy the human significance* of a foetus. To do that is to *misunderstand what a foetus is* and thus to fail, once again, to be able to provide any wise guidance concerning the morality of abortion. This is why the arguments of Singer and Tooley 'solve' the problem of abortion so easily: they do so by leaving out pretty much everything which makes abortion a problem in the first place.

review
activity

On what grounds might one argue that thinkers such as Singer, Tooley and Thomson fail to understand the nature of the problem of abortion?

Virtue theory and abortion

The criticisms just offered of the kind of arguments given by philosophers such as Singer are similar to some criticisms suggested by Rosalind Hursthouse in a paper on virtue theory and abortion (Hursthouse 1997). Hursthouse in fact argues that the issue of the status of the foetus, when approached in the kind of way that Singer and Tooley approach it, is *irrelevant* to the issue of abortion because the moral nature of abortion could not depend upon 'fancy philosophical sophistication' (Hursthouse 1997: 235). The kind of way in which, she argues, the status of the foetus is relevant is in the way I suggested in the previous section – that the foetus is produced (leaving out cases such as *in vitro* fertilisation) by sexual intercourse, that only women, and not men, can become pregnant, that childbirth is usually a physically painful experience, and so on.

Virtue theory, we recall, does not attempt to offer a decision procedure for ethical matters, and so it cannot hope to offer the kind of thing that a philosopher like Singer wants to offer, that is, a set of clear guidelines about when abortion is, and when it is not, morally acceptable. What virtue theory can do is to help us to understand in a sensitive manner the value and nature of childbearing in a person's life and the kinds of things that we might wish to say about specific cases of abortion. For example, Hursthouse says that virtue theory helps us recognise that some cases of abortion might show the woman concerned (and man, where he is involved in the decision) to be 'callous or light-minded; others might indicate an appropriate modesty or humility . . . and others would reflect a greedy and foolish attitude to what one could expect out of life' (Hursthouse 1997: 241).

Someone might respond to this by saying that we did not need virtue theory to tell us this, in which case it is not clear why we have need of the theory at all in considering the morality of abortion. However, this is to miss the point that someone like Hursthouse is making. For the virtue theorist can certainly think that it is possible for someone to *mis*understand the moral nature of abortion or of a given abortion. Such a theorist will emphasise the fact that not everyone has the virtues and is wise, and that any given person might be virtuous in some ways and not others, wise about some things in life and not others. Moreover, virtue theory also claims that such virtue and wisdom as one does have come from experience of life and from a kind of reflection and thought on life that are quite different from that which is offered by philosophers such as Singer, Tooley and Thomson.

Euthanasia

We now turn to consider the moral problems surrounding euthanasia. As it is now understood, euthanasia is the deliberate ending of the life of one person by another in order to end the former person's suffering. Such a killing is intended to be an act of kindness to the person killed. The moral problem of euthanasia arises because people disagree about when, if ever, it is right for one person to kill another in this way. The problem is complicated by the fact that we can distinguish three forms of euthanasia: voluntary, involuntary and non-voluntary.

Voluntary euthanasia

Living will

Voluntary euthanasia is euthanasia carried out at the request of the person killed. This could be a request made during an illness, or it could be what is called a 'living will', that is, a document drawn up by a person whilst in good health stipulating that if he is ever to end up in a state of painful terminal illness or incapacity then he wishes to die.

There are various practical difficulties in this area. For example, if a person expresses a wish to die whilst in a great deal of pain, this may not be his considered or settled judgement. Or again, someone might make a living will indicating that he would like to be allowed to die should he ever be in a coma from which he has no prospect of waking. The difficulty is that medical opinion can be divided on whether a given person will ever wake from a coma. However, these practical difficulties do not affect the fundamental issue of whether or not it is right to kill a person who is in a comatose state from which he will, indeed, never wake.

Justifying voluntary euthanasia: (i) utilitarianism

On what grounds, if any, could one seek to justify voluntary euthanasia? From a utilitarian point of view it seems that there is little problem here. If, for instance, a person has said that he wishes to die because he is in acute pain and there is no reasonable hope that the pain will cease then it increases his happiness, or, rather, decreases his unhappiness, and satisfies his interests or fulfils his preferences, if he is killed. Of course, a utilitarian will also have to take into account the happiness of the person's relatives and the like, but this does not alter the case in principle.

Justifying voluntary euthanasia: (ii) autonomy and rights

Voluntary euthanasia might also be justified on the grounds that each person has the right to lead his life as he wishes, to live in accord with his autonomous decisions, that is, in accord with decisions that he makes free from any coercion by others. In this case, if a person wishes to die because he is in incurable agony then it respects his rights if he is helped to die.

review activity

1. What is voluntary euthanasia?
2. How might one seek to justify voluntary euthanasia?

A slippery slope?

It is sometimes argued that allowing voluntary euthanasia by law would be the beginning of a slippery slope which leads to the elimination of those who do not wish to die but who are considered in some way to be 'socially undesirable'. The Nazis, for example, sought to eliminate individuals they thought of in this way, and they tried to disguise this as euthanasia. Could we not end up in the same place if we were to legalise euthanasia?

There seems something mistaken in drawing a parallel between what happened in Nazi Germany and what the proponents of voluntary euthanasia are suggesting. In fact, the Nazi programme was not really euthanasia at all. In reality it was simply murder, dressed up as euthanasia; there was no sense in which those 'treated' consented to what happened to them. However, this may not seem to remove the worry for it might be thought that there is a danger in relaxing restrictions on killing. Could this not lead to a more general acceptance of killing in cases that have nothing to do with euthanasia? The evidence from the Netherlands, where since the 1980s doctors have had the right to assist a patient to die, even if that meant giving the patient a lethal injection, is that this is not so. This is no doubt at least in part because there are strict guidelines in Holland on when voluntary euthanasia is acceptable. These are that it is permitted only if:

- it is carried out by a physician;
- the patient has explicitly requested euthanasia in a manner that leaves no doubt of the patient's desire to die;
- the patient's decision is well informed, free, and durable;
- the patient has an irreversible condition causing protracted physical or mental suffering that the patient finds unbearable;
- there is no reasonable alternative (reasonable from the patient's point of view) to alleviate the patient's suffering;
- the doctor has consulted another independent professional who agrees with his or her judgement. (Quoted in Singer 1993: 196.)

Whether these safeguards would be enough to convince those who are otherwise opposed to voluntary euthanasia is a moot point, for the fact remains that some are opposed to it for a variety of reasons, many of them religious. A religious perspective on euthanasia may not be very widespread in modern Western liberal societies but it is important to see that it is not *absurd* to think that voluntary euthanasia is a rejection of God's gift of life and that it is our duty to accept the suffering that comes to us with good grace. Someone who looks at things this way is, perhaps, not easily going to be convinced that talk of justifying voluntary euthanasia on utilitarian grounds or on the grounds of respecting a person's rights or autonomy gets to the heart of the matter. What this shows is that what one's views on voluntary euthanasia are will depend as much on one's general outlook on life as on what one thinks about specific cases where individuals request that their life be terminated.

Non-voluntary euthanasia

This is the case where the individual in question is not capable of understanding the choice between life and death. This kind of case is usually encountered with babies who are born with disabilities such a cerebral palsy, Down's syndrome, spina bifida and so on. What the utilitarian will say about such cases depends on a variety of things. For example, the interests and preferences of the parents are important here: if the parents wish to look after even a severely disabled child then this is no doubt enough for the utilitarian to think that euthanasia is not a serious option here (though, of course, the utilitarian calculus could, in principle, go the other way, even in such a case). Leaving aside the interests of the parents and considering the infant alone, how will the utilitarian think about such issues?

In order to answer this question, we have to understand a distinction that

Peter Singer has drawn in this context (Singer 1993: 102ff). This is the distinction between what he calls the 'prior existence' version of utilitarianism and the 'total' version of utilitarianism.

Prior existence and total utilitarianism

Prior existence utilitarianism

Imagine the following situation. A couple has two children, and the family as a whole is happy. The couple are wondering whether to have another child. They know that if they do not then they will have more money available for holidays, their children's education and so on. On the other hand, they also know that if they have another child, this child will also be happy and will contribute to the happiness of the family overall. For the utilitarian, the question is: should the couple have the third child?

For the so-called *prior existence* view, the answer is 'no'. For this view says that what counts is increasing the happiness of those who already exist, and there can be no reason to bring extra beings into the world. This is because this view thinks that there is no one to benefit who does not already exist. For example, before the conception of the third child, there is no third child to make happy, and so any considerations about the happiness of this child are nonsensical, because it does not exist. How, after all, can one make someone happy who does not exist?

However, now consider this case. The situation is as before, but the child to be conceived would be extremely unhappy – for example, the parents might know that it would be born with spina bifida. If it is nonsensical to think of making a non-existent child happy, then surely it is also nonsensical to think of making a non-existent child unhappy. In this case, there would seem to be no reason why the couple should *not* go ahead and conceive the child who will have spina bifida. Yet most people would say that this should not be done. So it seems that one can, after all, bring happiness or unhappiness to an as yet non-existent child by conceiving it.

Total utilitarianism

This last view is the *total view*, because it says that the utilitarian should be concerned with the happiness of those creatures who already exist *and* those who do not yet exist.

Before returning to the issue of euthanasia, we should note that the total view seems to have some odd consequences. For example, it seems to suggest that we should breed as many human beings and other creatures as possible in order to increase the happiness of the world, at least up until the point at which a further increase in population would put such a strain on limited resources that the total happiness would be reduced rather than increased by a further increase in population. Or should we have as many pets as possible? I have a corner of my study where I could set up a cage for half a dozen mice. They would probably be happy there (it is nice and quiet as I read and write) and I could, no doubt, become used to them. I might even grow to like them. It seems that total utilitarianism tells me that I am doing something wrong in not breeding mice. This seems very odd indeed.

activity

Explain in your own words the distinction between prior existence and total utilitarianism.

Prior existence utilitarianism, total utilitarianism and non-voluntary euthanasia

Consider now the following case. A baby is born with haemophilia. Severe as this disability is, it is no bar to being happy. Should the baby be killed? Prior existence utilitarianism would say 'no': the child exists and will be happy, so it should live on. Total utilitarianism will, however, suggest that this baby could be replaced with another, which is not a haemophiliac, provided it has reasonable prospects of being happy.

Infanticide

On the total view, creatures that are not self-conscious are replaceable because they cannot have a conception of themselves as existing through time and therefore, in that sense, wish to go on living. On the total view, therefore, human infants are replaceable.

What this means is that, other things being equal, total utilitarianism supports infanticide, that is, non-voluntary euthanasia for disabled infants. However, the utilitarian will agree that it there should be restrictions on infanticide in order to be sure that we do not kill any persons (in the technical sense) – it should be forbidden when the baby reaches, say, one month of age (Singer 1993: 172).

Total utilitarianism will also, other things being equal, support non-voluntary euthanasia of adult human beings who are no longer rational, self-conscious or autonomous – say, as the result of an accident. But other things may not be equal. For example, old people who are ill and *in danger* of losing their rationality, self-consciousness and autonomy might fear that, because non-voluntary euthanasia is carried out on those who have lost these, they will be killed even if they do not, in fact, lose them. This may be, Singer says, an irrational fear, but if there is no way of removing it then non-voluntary euthanasia should not be practised except on those who have never been able to make a choice about life and death, that is, human infants

I noted earlier that, other things being equal, Tooley is in favour of infanticide, even where the baby is healthy, because, he argues, it violates no rights of the baby if it is killed. In fact, he says that those who object to infanticide are, in general, just accepting a taboo rather than a rational prohibition (Tooley 1992: 59). Singer, we have seen, is also in favour of infanticide, other things being equal, and not merely in the case of disabled infants. After all, he says that a late abortion for trivial reasons is morally acceptable, and even after the birth of a child killing it would not be to kill a person, so, other things being equal (the parents do not want it, no one wishes to adopt it and so on), killing it is not a morally grave offence. For sure, Singer thinks there should be restrictions on infanticide, but only so that we make no mistake in killing persons or in killing babies who are actually wanted by their parents. There is, he says, *intrinsically* nothing wrong with it.

Objections to Tooley and Singer on infanticide

The most fundamental objection to this view is that, as in the case of abortion, the arguments Singer, Tooley and others give for infanticide are completely insensitive to the human significance of childbirth and the nature of the human infant. They can only talk as they do because *they have left out of all consideration how it is that parents and others actually feel about infants and children*, whether those infants and children are disabled or not. It is not possible to do this and yet be sensitive to the moral problems that infanticide raises because it is the way people feel about infants and children that raises the problem in the first place.

Involuntary euthanasia

Involuntary euthanasia is euthanasia where the person killed is capable of consenting to his own death but does not do so. Even here a utilitarian might think that it is justified to kill the person – for example, if he were in extreme agony, had no prospect of ever being released from this agony, were incapable, on account of his torments, of doing anything but live with his agony, and so on. In such a case it might be said that killing him would reduce the unhappiness in the world, and this should be done from a utilitarian point of view. However, if this person could consent to his death but did not do so, then this is surely an indication that he believes his life worth living, in which case the utilitarian ought not to kill him. Further, considerations of personal autonomy and rights count against killing this person. There seems to be no justification for involuntary euthanasia.

Active and passive euthanasia

We have so far ignored a distinction that is important in discussions of euthanasia. This is the distinction between active and passive euthanasia. This distinction has been discussed James Rachels (Rachels 1992).

Active euthanasia is where a person intervenes to kill someone who is suffering from a great pain; passive euthanasia is where a person allows someone who is suffering from a great pain to die. Rachels gives this example: a patient is dying of incurable cancer and the pain can no longer be alleviated. He is certain to die in the next few days even if the present treatment is continued. He would rather die now and avoid the pain. He asks the doctor to end his suffering. The doctor can do this either by withdrawing treatment or by administering a lethal injection. In either case, she wishes to reduce the patient's suffering. However, if she withdraws treatment he will live longer and suffer greater pain than if she administers the injection. The former (withdrawal of treatment) would be passive euthanasia; the latter (lethal injection) would be active euthanasia. Given that the doctor's aim is to reduce the patient's suffering, Rachels argues, it is morally better for her to commit active rather than passive euthanasia.

activity

Explain the difference between active and passive euthanasia.

Acts and omissions

You might think you could argue against Rachels by pointing out that there is a great difference between active and passive euthanasia: in active euthanasia the doctor *does something* (administers the lethal injection) and in passive euthanasia she merely *allows something to happen.* You might say that this makes active euthanasia morally worse than passive euthanasia.

In fact, normally, people *do* think that there is a big difference between active and passive euthanasia because they think there is a great moral difference between *doing something* and *letting something happen.* We normally think, that is, that there is great difference between *acts* and *omissions.* For instance, recall the example where I buy an ice cream instead of giving the money to Oxfam for relief of the poor. In this case, someone might say that I *let other people die* by not donating the money but that this is not the same as *killing those people.* There is all the moral difference in the world between eating an ice cream, even if I could donate the money to charity for the relief of the poor, and putting a gun to someone's head and shooting him. Another example where this important difference may be seen was that of Jim and the Indians.

Those who believe that there is a great moral difference in such cases believe in what is called the *acts and omissions doctrine.*

Rachels's example Rachels rejects the distinction between acts and omissions. He gives an example to try to show this. Situation A: Smith stands to gain a large inheritance if his six-year-old cousin dies. The child is one evening having a bath and Smith goes into the bathroom and drowns him. Situation B: Jones stands to gain a large inheritance if his six-year-old cousin dies. The child is one evening having a bath and Jones goes into the bathroom to drown him. At that moment, the child slips, hurts his dead and falls under the water and drowns. Jones watches all this happening, standing there ready to push the child's head under the water should he recover. In the event, Jones does not need to do this.

Rachels says that Jones is clearly as culpable as Smith. Yet Smith killed his cousin (an act) whereas Jones lets him die (an omission). Therefore, Rachels concludes that there is no significant moral distinction between acts and omissions and, therefore, that there is no significant moral different between active and passive euthanasia. Consequently, he argues that, if we accept passive euthanasia – which many do; and it is (in general) not illegal in the UK – then we should also accept active euthanasia.

activity

1. What is the acts and omissions doctrine?
2. On what grounds does Rachels reject the acts and omissions doctrine?

Criticism of Rachels's argument

Rachels's argument shows that there are *some* cases where there is no morally significant distinction between acts and omissions. That is, the argument shows that there are *some* cases where the acts and omissions doctrine collapses. However, it does not show this for all cases. The main reason for this is that in Rachels's example Smith and Jones *wanted* the cousin to die. However, in the ice-cream case this is not so: if I eat an ice cream part of my motivation is *not* that I want people in some poor country to die. Motivation counts for a lot in our assessment of moral matters.

What about the case mentioned before where a man is dying of cancer? Is Rachels right to suggest that there is here no moral difference between acts and omissions and hence that active euthanasia is better than passive euthanasia?

It seems that Rachels's argument can only work if the case in question is more like that of Smith and Jones than like the ice-cream case. But is it? It would be if the motivation of the doctor in each case were the same, that she wants the same thing in each case. Rachels thinks she does because what she wants is to relieve suffering. However, she may want something else as well. She may want to *let him die,* and, if that is so, then *killing him* will, obviously, not be any way to achieve that (cf. Campbell and Collinson 1992: 136). There is no reason why she should not think that it makes all the difference whether she does something or lets something happen: the intentions with which she acts may make all the difference to her sense of what the situation is. (Of course, if she does not think her intentions are relevant in this way then she may well agree with Rachels's conclusion, in which case he has nothing to prove against her.) However, Rachels can only secure his conclusion against the doctor who thinks that the intentions with which she acts are relevant to what she does if he can give some general reason why the intention with which one performs an action is irrelevant to the morality of that action, but it is not possible to show such a thing without begging the question against those who disagree with that claim.

review activity

On what grounds might one argue that Rachels is mistaken to reject the acts and omissions doctrine?

Animal welfare

We now move on to consider issues surrounding the treatment of animals. The main issues arise here because we use animals in many ways – for example, for food, for the testing of medicines and cosmetics, in sports (fox hunting, bull fighting) and as pets. What principles should govern the way we treat animals?

Can animals feel pain and suffer?

However, before we tackle that question, we ought to ask a prior question. This is: can animals suffer and feel pain?

Some philosophers have denied that animals are conscious. One of these is Descartes. However, I do not want to discuss his argument because it depends on views of his about the relation between the mind and body which are too complex to be discussed here. Moreover, those views are, it seems, open to certain fatal objections. Descartes' theory on the relation between mind and body is discussed in the chapter in this book devoted to his *Meditations*.

Instead of discussing Descartes here, I wish to look at a modern argument that has been offered that purports to show that animals are not conscious. If this argument is correct, then animals cannot, of course, feel any pain and thus we shall, perhaps, have no reason to think that we have any special duties to them.

Carruthers' argument that animals are not conscious

The argument in question has been offered by Peter Carruthers (Carruthers 1994: ch.8). Carruthers asks us to consider the following case. Abbie is driving along thinking about her next holiday. Her thoughts are not on the road at all. Suddenly she 'comes to' and returns her attention to the road. She realises that she does not have the faintest idea what she has been doing for the last few minutes. Yet clearly, even when she was thinking about the holiday, she must have been aware of the road otherwise she would have crashed into the car parked at the side of the road half a mile back. Obviously, she had pulled out to avoid it. Carruthers says that such experience as Abbie has of the road is *non-conscious* experience.

What, then, is a conscious experience? Carruthers's answer is complicated, but, roughly speaking, he says that a conscious mental state is one that is available to conscious thought (Carruthers 1994: 180). In other words, to have a conscious mental experience is to have an experience that can itself be thought about. A conscious creature, on this account, thinks things to itself.

It is possible, therefore, says Carruthers, that a creature could be aware *of* the world, without being conscious, as Abbie was aware of the parked car without being conscious of it. In fact, Carruthers does not at all deny that animals are aware of the world. What he denies is that they have *conscious* mental states. They are all, he suggests, like Abbie when she was aware of the parked car: aware of the world, but not conscious. This is because he thinks that 'no one would seriously maintain that dogs, cats, sheep, cattle, pigs or chickens consciously think things to themselves (let alone that fish or reptiles do)' (Carruthers 1994: 184).

Is it really plausible to say that an animal's experience of pain is non-conscious? Carruthers argues that it is logically possible that there be non-conscious experience of pain. Given that this is so, pain, he says, admits of non-conscious and conscious varieties. So he argues that, if it is true, as he has already suggested, that animals cannot think thoughts to themselves 'their pains must all be non-conscious' (Carruthers 1994: 189).

Carruthers thus concludes that, in treating animals badly (as we now see it), we are not being cruel at all. In fact, he thinks that 'it ought to be impossible to feel sympathy for animals, once the true nature of their mental lives is properly understood' (Carruthers 1994: 192). He urges caution, however, since he says that his arguments are not conclusive: there may be reasons for thinking that animals are conscious after all.

What are we to make of Carruthers's claims? The first thing to be said is that even if he is right that animals are not conscious it certainly does *not* follow that our treatment of them cannot be assessed morally. He argues that, just as it is mistaken to think there is any real cruelty in children who pull the wings off flies because flies are not conscious, so there would be no cruelty in someone who (as we now put it) harms, say, a dog, because dogs are not conscious (Carruthers 1994: 57; 192). But he is, surely, mistaken in what he says about flies. The principal reason it is cruel to pull the wings off a fly is not that the fly feels pain (even if it does), but that to do so is *wilful destruction of life*. Similarly, we might think someone brutal and insensitive if he simply destroyed some beautiful flowers, or if he destroyed a beautiful part of the inanimate natural world, without any belief that he had damaged anything that was conscious. What is wrong here is the *wilful destruction of something beautiful*. It makes perfect sense to think this morally reprehensible. I am not saying one would *have* to think this: I am simply saying that it makes sense to think this. Carruthers is not even aware of the issues here, however.

Is Carruthers right to say that animals are not conscious? There are many objections that can be made to his view. First, one could simply deny that the kind of experience on which he builds his case, that is, the kind of experience Abbie had of the parked car and, more generally, of the road, is non-conscious. As Norman Malcolm (1911–90) has said (Malcolm 1977a: 57):

> [S]uppose that as you pass an acquaintance he says 'Hello' to you, and you respond in kind. Did you think to yourself, 'He said "Hello"'? Suppose you did not. Would it be true, therefore, that you were not conscious of his greeting? Of course not.

Here is another example. As I sit here writing, my thoughts are taken up with a certain philosophical issue. My experience of the temperature of, and the light in, the room; of my physical state (a bit tired, somewhat hungry, slightly cold); of the particular clothes I am wearing – these are all what Carruthers would call non-conscious mental states. Yet they are not, it seems to me, non-conscious. There is a real difference from the inside between how my experience is now and how it is when I sit here writing, concentrating on a philosophical issue, and the room is a different temperature, the light is different, I am not at all hungry, and so on. In other words, an experience might not be available to consciousness in the way Carruthers has in mind, yet still be a genuine conscious experience (and not a mere awareness of something). That is, such an experience can be like something from the inside.

Secondly, Carruthers's view would require us to reject all the behavioural evidence that we have that animals are conscious. It would also require us to suppose that the anatomical similarities between animals and us were completely misleading from the point of view of consciousness. And it would also require us to suppose that, even though we are related to other animals through evolution, consciousness first emerges with us, thus denying evolutionary continuity.

Thirdly, we should ask the following. Can we be *more sure* of Carruthers's philosophical argument than we are of the idea that animals are conscious? Surely not: if an argument has a consequence that goes against everything that common sense, biological and anatomical research, and evolutionary theory suggest, then it is far more reasonable to reject the argument than to reject all that other evidence.

review
activity

1. Explain Carruthers's argument for the claim that animals are not conscious.

2. What reasons can be given to show that animals are conscious, despite Carruthers's denial that they are?

Utilitarianism

Let us grant, then, that animals are conscious and can experience pain and suffering. How should we treat them?

The most well-know utilitarian understanding of the treatment of animals is due to Peter Singer (Singer 1984, 1993). Roughly, he argues as follows.

Equal consideration of interests

The crucial issue is whether a being – whether a human being or a rabbit – has interests or preferences. Utilitarianism says that if a being has interests then these should be satisfied, other things being equal. The more interests satisfied, the better. What matters is not the species to which a creature belongs. A human baby might get a certain pain from a light slap across the bottom. A full-grown horse might get exactly the same sensation of pain from a hard whack across its hindquarters with a stick. However, the pain is the same in either case. If we think that it is wrong to slap the baby we should think it wrong to hit the horse so as to produce the same pain. One could only deny this if one thought that the pain of the baby was more important than that of the horse. Why should this be so? The case here between the horse and baby is analogous to that between a white person and a black person. If a white person is struck and feels pain and a black person is struck and feels the same pain, then each pain is as bad as the other. If a white person thinks the pain of white people is worse than that of black people simply on the basis of race, then this is *racist*. Similarly, if a man thinks the pain of men more important than the pain of women on the basis of sex, then this is *sexist*. So, if a human being thinks the pain of a human being is more important than the pain of an animal on the basis of species, then this is *speciesist*. Singer thinks that, if we reject racism and sexism we should reject speciesism. He thus concludes that 'all animals are equal'. This does not mean that we should treat all animals – whether human or non-human – equally in the sense of giving them the same things. A human child needs to learn to read and write, whereas a horse does not need this. The point is rather that we should give *equal consideration to the interests of all animals*. For example, just as a human being has an interest in learning to read and write, a cow has interest in being able to move around freely, eat suitable fodder and so on.

activity

1. Why does Singer think that all animals are equal and what does he mean by this?

2. What, according to Singer, is speciesism?

Practical implications

Singer draws some radical conclusions from his reasoning. Consider modern farming conditions. Very many animals, such as pigs, chickens and veal calves are bred and raised in conditions which do not allow them access to space to move, to fresh air, to food sufficiently rich in the vitamins and minerals they need and so on. This is a frustration of their interests. Now consider the interests human beings have in eating animals. Singer says that the interests of ours that are satisfied in eating meat are far outweighed on utilitarian grounds by the interests animals have in not being raised in factory farms. He thinks that therefore we should not eat meat from such farms.

What about meat from free range farms? Here Singer refers to distinctions we have already seen him draw. He thinks that lots of non-human animals are persons, that is, self-conscious, rational and so on, and therefore should not be killed for their flesh for they have an interest in continuing to live. However, some animals are not persons – perhaps chickens. Singer says that it is morally in order to kill and eat such animals so long as the pleasure we get from eating them is greater than the pleasure they lose in being killed. He doubts, in fact, that the utilitarian calculus will come down in our favour. However, he grants that chickens, because they are not persons, are *replaceable*. Of course, in accord with the total version of utilitarianism, he thinks, as have seen, that we should, other things being equal, breed as many such creatures as possible and keep them as happy as possible. However, suppose that on economic grounds we could not keep any more chickens then we have anyway. Then, if their interests are satisfied, that is, they have space to roam and so on, it is in order to kill them and eat them as long as they are replaced.

Overall then, utilitarianism would like us to give up eating practically all meat.

Similar considerations apply to animal experimentation or vivisection. Vivisection is the carrying out of experiments on living animals. There are, basically, two types of vivisection: for research into products we use, such as shampoos, cosmetics, washing-up liquids and the like; and for medical research into how to cure, or prevent, diseases, such as cancer.

According to Singer, the interests human beings have in having cosmetics, washing-up liquids and so on (especially when so many are already available) cannot be greater than the interests animals have in not having such things rubbed into their eyes to see if they are blinded. Such experiments should be stopped immediately. With experiments for medical purposes, things might be different. Theoretically, it is possible to think that an experiment is justified if it leads to greater overall satisfaction of interests, in which case it would be justified on utilitarian grounds. However, Singer thinks that this is most unlikely and that, since we can never tell in advance that a test will be beneficial in this way, we should err on the side of caution and pretty much abandon animal experiments.

Criticisms of Singer's argument

Most people who have read Singer's book *Animal Liberation* would probably agree that he has done a great deal to expose the truth about the infliction of a huge amount of pointless and stupid cruelty on animals. Moreover, it is possible to agree with Singer that becoming a vegetarian is a good way to respond to this. Yet, one could think all that and yet disagree with his philosophical position.

The deepest criticisms of Singer's position are those given by Cora Diamond (Diamond 1996: ch.13) and, implicitly, by Raimond Gaita (Gaita 1991: esp. 117–21). Basically, what they argue is as follows.

Singer does not see that the most fundamental reason why we do not eat *each other* is not because we have 'interests' that should be respected. Therefore, he is mistaken when he says that it is because of their 'interests' that we should not eat animals. Certainly it is true that, if some of us decided we would eat some other human beings, this would cause a lot of distress. But the distress would itself be because *a human being is not something to be eaten*. This has to do with a number of things. Two of the most important of these are our sense of human individuality and the significance of the human body. This individuality hangs together with the fact that we each have a *name*, and not a number. It has to do with the fact that each human being *leads a life* as no animal does. However clever it is, an animal just lives, and this is not true of a human being. For a human being struggles to find his life meaningful; can believe that his life has been wasted; can curse the day he was born. None of these apply in the case of an animal. We cannot *tell the story of an animal's life*: an animal *has no biography* in the sense in which a human being has.

As to the significance of the human body, what is important here is that, as Wittgenstein (1889–1951) put it: 'The human body is the best picture of the human soul.' Wittgenstein did not mean that human beings have a soul that is a kind of ghostly thing that can leave the body after death. The sense in which he meant that human beings have a soul is the sense brought out when we speak of a kind of work as soul destroying; or when the Greeks said that a man or woman lost half his soul when he or she became a slave; or when we say that someone has sold his soul to the devil for success and worldly prestige. But, Wittgenstein suggests, we could not speak in these ways if we could never see someone's soul in his face, as we can: in his eyes, in his facial expressions, and so on. The fact that we *look* as we do is thus much more important for our sense of each other than Singer allows.

We could sum up these points by saying that the reason we do not eat one another has to do with our sense of human fellowship. And, in general, it is this sense of fellowship that is crucial in structuring and giving sense to the ways in which we treat one another. Simplifying somewhat, we can say that a racist is someone who lacks this sense of fellowship with races other than his own. And Diamond argues that, if we are to treat animals better than we do, then we should seek to extend a sense of fellowship to other animals. To some extent we do this anyway in that we have pets. It is by expanding this kind of understanding that we shall come to treat animals better. Yet Singer's arguments involve absolutely no sense of this fellowship, either amongst human beings or between human beings and animals. To this extent, Diamond argues, they fail completely to engage with the reality before us when we think about the treatment of animals. As can be argued is the case in his arguments concerning abortion, what Singer has to say concerning our treatment of animals can only seem to provide a 'solution' to the issue by leaving out the main aspects of the problem that, properly considered, lead to a deeper understanding of just what the difficulties in this area are.

review activity

Explain in your own words Diamond's objections to Singer's arguments concerning the equality of all animals.

Kant and Regan on the treatment of animals

According to Kant, only rational creatures can be the proper object of a *direct* moral concern. For Kant thinks that only rational beings are entitled to be treated as ends in themselves. This suggests that, for Kant, we may treat animals as we wish. However, Kant does think there is some *indirect* reason to treat animals well. He suggests that those who are cruel to animals will tend to cultivate their cruel dispositions and that this might lead them to be cruel to persons. As this is contrary to the moral law, it is forbidden, he says, to be cruel to animals, and, indeed, we should seek to be kind to them as this nurtures dispositions which are, as he puts it, 'serviceable to morality' (Kant 1993: 238 [443]).

Tom Regan on animal rights

Some philosophers have argued, however, that animals have rights. Prominent amongst these is Tom Regan (Regan in Cohen and Regan 2001). Regan's argument grows out of Kant's position. Regan argues that Kant's moral theory is incapable of making sense of the fact that we do not think that 'late-term human fetuses, infants, children throughout several years of their life, and all those human beings, whatever their age, who, for a variety reasons, lack the intellectual capacities that define Kantian personhood' may be treated simply as a means and not as an end (Regan in Cohen and Regan 2001: 200). Regan suggests that, to make up this gap in Kant's account, we should think that what grounds rights is not that a being is rational in the Kantian sense but that it is what Regan calls a 'subject-of-a-life'. What he means by 'subject-of-a-life' is a creature that has feelings, beliefs and desires, a creature that has experience of the world. He then suggests that a creature that is a 'subject-of-a-life' has inherent value and that this enables us to say that infants, children and the rest of those human beings whom the Kantian position cannot think of as being ends can be thought of as possessing inherent value and rights. However, this also means that animals have rights, because an animal, too, is a 'subject-of-a-life'. Regan believes that this means that the farming of animals and vivisection should be totally abolished: it is no good giving animals used in experiments anaesthetic or giving farm animals more space. Rather, these practices must be completely eradicated.

Regan's argument may be challenged in at least two ways.

First, Diamond has argued that Regan is guilty of the same kind of misunderstanding of the nature of human beings and animals of which she thinks Singer is guilty. For example, Regan says that 'subjects-of-a-life' have a biography: but this is not so in the case of animals, Diamond argues.

Secondly, someone might argue, in a more strictly Kantian fashion than does Regan, that it is only persons who have rights because it is only persons who are members of a moral community. This is basically what Carl Cohen argues in his response to Regan (Cohen in Cohen and Regan 2001: 247ff.). Cohen argues that only those who are members of a moral community have inherent value and thus have rights, not those who are 'subjects-of-a-life'. Much the same point is made by Roger Scruton (Scruton 1996, esp. 59–69). Nonetheless, Scruton does not deny that we have a duty of care for animals because they can suffer. What this care for them will be will depend on our relation to them: our care for pets, for example, will be different from that for animals raised for meat. Nonetheless, Scruton suggests that Singer is right to think that much of our treatment of animals is cruel and ought to be abandoned or modified (Scruton 1996: 69–96).

It should be pointed out, however, that Regan has a powerful point in suggesting that the Kantian position cannot make sense of the idea that human infants and the other human beings he mentions have rights or should be treated as ends even though they are not persons in the Kantian sense. However, perhaps the problem is that the Kantian position does not have the resources to capture what it is that makes us care for human beings or why we should care for them. That, at any rate, would seem to be the implication of Diamond's work on the nature of animals and human beings. But then, if Diamond is right, neither does Regan's positions have such resources.

review activity

1. Explain in your own words Regan's reasons for thinking that animals have rights.

2. On what grounds could Regan's view be criticised?

some questions to think about

1 To what extent would you agree with Rosalind Hursthouse that thinking clearly about the problem of abortion does not require any of the kind of philosophical speculation of the type offered by Singer, Tooley and Thomson?

2 What do you think of Tooley's claim that our reluctance to accept infanticide is a taboo for which we have no rational grounds?

3 'Since the "total" version of utilitarianism leads to the idea that we should be filling up the world with happy creatures, then this just shows that the theory is absurd.' Is this claim correct?

4 'If someone wants to die because of his suffering, no humane person could reasonably say he has no right to have his life terminated.' Do you agree with this?

5 Should we, in general, abandon the acts and omissions doctrine?

6 'If we were to legalise voluntary euthanasia we would be on the slippery slope to the elimination of the "socially undesirable".' What is there to be said for and against this claim?

7 Cora Diamond has said that the *differences* between humans and animals are not great, but that there is nonetheless a great *difference* between human beings and animals. What do you make of this claim?

further reading

▶ A well-known and helpful book on many aspects of moral theory and medical ethics is Beauchamp and Childress 2001. A helpful reader is Kuhse and Singer (eds) 1999. Glover 1982 contains good discussions of abortion, infanticide and euthanasia.

▶ On the treatment of animals, see Clark 1977 and Regan 1984. Scruton 1996 is a stimulating read.

V

Meta-ethics

Key topics in this chapter

The nature of meta-ethics

- The principal meta-ethical theories of emotivism, prescriptivism, intuitionism and realism
- The 'fact-value' and 'is-ought' distinctions
- Relativism, nihilism and related issues

Realism and cognitivism; irrealism and non-cognitivism

Suppose you and I are talking in one room and I ask you how many chairs there are in the room next door. You say you do not know whilst I say I think there are three. Even before we go next door to look, one thing is certain: it is a *fact of the matter* that *either* there are three chairs next door *or* there are not. It is either straightforwardly *true* that there are three chairs there or it is not.

Suppose now that you and I continue our conversation and we start discussing the morality of slavery. I ask you whether slavery is evil. You say you do not know. I then say that I think it evil. Can we say that it is a *fact of the matter* that *either* slavery is evil *or* is not evil, in the kind of way that we can say that it is a fact of the matter that *either* there are three chairs in the next room *or* are not? Is it a *fact of the matter* that slavery is evil or is not evil? Is it a fact of the matter that fox hunting is cruel or is not cruel? And is it a fact of the matter that lying (perhaps in a given concrete situation) is contemptible or not contemptible? Are these judgements straightforwardly true or false? And so on for all moral judgements.

Suppose a philosopher believes that it is a *fact of the matter* whether slavery is evil or not, just as it is a fact of the matter whether there are three chairs in the room next door or not. This philosopher, who believes that there are moral facts of the matter, is a moral *realist*. Further, his claim that there are moral facts is a *metaphysical* or *ontological* claim because it is a claim about the way the world is. Moreover, he thinks that when a person makes a moral judgement (for example 'slavery is evil', 'lying is contemptible') this person is articulating a *belief* about the way the world is. The claim that a person who is making a moral judgement is articulating his *beliefs* is called *cognitivism*. This is because he is in a particular *cognitive* state. Some philosophers, in fact, use the terms 'realism' and 'cognitivism' interchangeably.

Suppose a philosopher believes that it is *not* a fact of the matter whether slavery is evil or not and that it is *not* a fact of the matter whether lying is contemptible, and so on. This philosopher, who believes that there are no moral facts of the matter, is an *irrealist* (or an *anti-realist* or a *subjectivist*). Further, his claim that there are *no* moral facts is a *metaphysical* or *ontological* claim because it is a claim about the way the world is. Moreover, he thinks that when a person makes a moral judgement (for example, 'slavery is evil', 'lying is contemptible') this person is *not* articulating a belief about the way the world is. Rather, this person is doing something else – perhaps, for example, expressing his emotions. The claim that a person who is making a moral judgement is not articulating his beliefs about the way the world is, is called *non-cognitivism*. Some philosophers, in fact, use the terms 'irrealism' and 'non-cognitivism' interchangeably.

The nature of meta-ethics

Meta-ethics discusses the kinds of issues just mentioned. That is, meta-ethics discusses such issues as whether there are moral facts of the matter and what someone is doing when he makes a moral judgement – is he articulating a belief about the way the world is, or is he expressing his emotions or is he doing something else? It discusses the nature of moral judgements and thus the meaning or significance of calling something right or wrong, good or bad.

First- and second-order moral reflection

This means that meta-ethics does not aim to provide a way of thinking about ways to act, feel and be, as do the moral theories of utilitarianism, Kantianism and virtue theory; nor does it aim to provide answers to moral questions, as does practical ethics. It aims to stand above such disputes (which is where the 'meta' comes in, for *meta* is Greek for 'above' or 'after') and achieve clarity on the very concepts that are used in making the kinds of judgements that utilitarians, Kantians, virtue theorists and others make. Meta-ethics seeks, that is, to be completely neutral between all competing moral theories. This is why meta-ethics is sometimes thought of as moral reflection of the 'second-order' and the theories of utilitarianism, Kantianism and virtue theory are thought of as 'first-order' moral theories.

review
activity

1. What does it mean to say that a claim is an ontological or metaphysical claim?
2. Describe in your own words the issues with which meta-ethics deals.

Hume's sentiments

I explained above that the irrealist thinks that there are no moral facts. Why might someone think that? A famous answer is found in the following famous passage written by David Hume (1711–76):

> *Take any action allow'd to be vicious: Wilful murder, for instance. Examine it in all lights, and see if you can find that matter of fact, or real existence, which you call vice. In which-ever way you take it, you find only certain passions, motives, volitions and thoughts. There is no other matter of fact in the case. The vice entirely escapes you, as long as you consider the object. You will never find it, till you turn your reflexion into your own breast, and find a sentiment of*

disapprobation, which arises in you, towards this action . . . It lies in yourself, not in the object. So that when you pronounce any action or character to be vicious, you mean nothing, but that from the constitution of your nature you have a feeling or sentiment of blame from the contemplation of it.

(Hume 1980: III, 1, §1)

According to Hume, we experience a sentiment of approbation or disapprobation when we see certain actions and events in the world. These actions and events do not themselves have any moral properties; rather, it is because we have various sentiments that we see the actions and events as good or evil, noble or base.

The fact-value distinction

One way of putting the point which Hume is making in the passage quoted is to say that he is suggesting that there is a realm of facts that is quite separate from the realm of values. For example, the *facts* are that one man took a knife, had the motive of wanting to harm another man, plunged the knife into the other man's chest, and so on. The *value* (or *disvalue*) of the act is not there in the act itself, as we have seen, but is contributed by the spectator.

Here are other examples of facts: Mozart wrote lots of music; I am sitting at a computer writing a book; you are reading a book; it has just stopped raining; London is about 60 miles from Cambridge; Birmingham is in the Midlands; and so on. And here are some examples of values: Mozart's music is *beautiful*; keeping your promises is *good*; Birmingham is an *ugly* city; Cambridge is an *elegant* city; and so on. We can investigate the world with our five senses and with the methods of science and find out lots of facts of the kind mentioned. Where do values fit into this? As Hume says, they do not seem to be anywhere in the facts, for we cannot sense them with our five senses and they are not revealed by the methods of science. So we seem to have what philosophers call the *fact-value distinction*: the world of facts is, as such, free of any values; the values are just our attitudes towards the facts.

If the fact-value distinction is correct, then certain things follow from it. First, it is possible to agree with another person on all the facts of a case and disagree with his moral judgement of it. Secondly, from *no* description of the *facts* of a case can we *deduce* an evaluative conclusion, for example, a conclusion containing any moral terms. It will always be possible to grasp all the facts and deny a moral conclusion. For instance, in Truman Capote's book *In Cold Blood* two men steal into a family's home during the night, tie up the father, mother, son and daughter, and then shoot them all. These are the *facts*. If the fact-value distinction is correct, then these facts are, as such, value free. So, you cannot deduce from these *facts* about what the two men did that they did something *wicked* or *evil*. Hence, it is always possible to deny that what they did was wicked or evil without making any error of reasoning.

The is-ought gap

The fact-value distinction: metaphysical

The fact-value distinction is a claim about the nature of the world: it is a *metaphysical* or *ontological* claim. This distinction is closely related to another distinction, which is called the *is-ought distinction* or the *is-ought gap*.

The claim that there is an is-ought distinction is a claim about the *logic of moral discourse*. Once again, the distinction was introduced by Hume. In a famous passage he writes:

> *In every system of morality, which I have hitherto met with, I have always remark'd, that the author proceeds for some time in the ordinary way of reasoning, and establishes the being of God, or makes observations concerning human affairs; when of a sudden I am surpriz'd to find, that instead of the usual copulations of propositions, is, and is not, I meet with no proposition that is not connected with an ought, or an ought not. This change is imperceptible; but is, however, of the last consequence. For as this ought, or ought not, expresses some new relation or affirmation, 'tis necessary that it shou'd be observed and explain'd; and at the same time that a reason should be given, for what seems altogether inconceivable, how this new relation can be a deduction from others, which are entirely different from it.* (Hume 1980: III, 1, §1)

There has been a great deal of discussion amongst philosophers about what exactly Hume meant in this passage and about what significance his thought is meant to have for moral philosophy generally, but the most common interpretation can be illustrated by the following examples.

Consider first the following argument:

Premise i): Each of Henry James's novels is complicated
Premise ii): This book is a novel by Henry James
Conclusion iii): Therefore, this book is complicated

This argument is clearly valid. There is no problem about the deduction because the premises and the conclusion are purely factual. That is, they are all 'is'-statements. Further, if you accept i) and ii) then you *must* accept iii). Philosophers put the fact that you must accept iii) if you accept i) and ii) by saying that i) and ii) *entail* iii).

Now consider another argument:

Premise a): God is the creator of human beings.
Premise b): God is the promulgator of the moral law.
Conclusion c): Therefore, human beings ought to obey God's moral law.

In the premises a) and b) we have two statements that are 'is'-statements; they are merely factual, and state what *is* the case. But c), the conclusion of the argument, is not merely factual. It states what we *ought* to do. And Hume's argument is normally taken to be saying that such a conclusion does not follow from the premises. That is, you could accept a) and b) and deny c). That is, a) and b) do not *entail* c).

Of course, we could make the argument valid by adding a third premise thus:

b[1]) A creature ought to obey the moral law that its creator promulgates.

This would make the argument valid. But the problem now is that we need to show that b[1]) is true. We shall not be able to do this by appealing to merely factual premises. So the upshot of Hume's argument is that no *moral* conclusion – or, more generally, *evaluative* conclusion – can be validly drawn from any set of premises that are merely *factual.*

Both the fact-value distinction and the is-ought distinction are very important in moral philosophy. In particular, irrealism accepts both distinctions. We shall discuss two forms of irrealism: *emotivism* and *prescriptivism*.

Emotivism

The theory of emotivism is particularly associated with the English philosopher A.J. Ayer and the American philosopher C.L. Stevenson (1908–79). We shall look in turn at their versions of the theory.

A.J. Ayer

A.J. Ayer's account of emotivism – a simple version of the theory – is set out in Chapter 6 of his book *Language, Truth and Logic*, first published in 1936.

A.J. Ayer (1910–89)

Consider the judgement: 'You acted wrongly in stealing the money'. Since emotivism, as a form of non-cognitivism, denies that moral values are part of the world, it claims that if you offer the judgement in question then it cannot be that you are saying anything about the world. The *wrongness* of stealing the money is no fact of the matter. So, when you say 'you acted wrongly in stealing the money', you cannot be reporting the *fact* that stealing the money was wrong, because there is no such fact. The only fact is that the person in question stole the money. What, then, does emotivism say you are doing when you utter the statement mentioned?

Moral judgement as the expression of the emotions of approval and disapproval

According to emotivism, if you say (A) 'you acted wrongly in stealing the money', you are not stating anything more than if you said (B) 'you stole the money'. What, then, is the difference between the two statements (A) and (B)? Ayer says that (A) expresses your emotion of disapproval or disapprobation of the fact that the person in question stole the money. It is, he says, as if you had said 'you stole the money' in a particular tone of horror, or as if you had said 'you stole the money!!', where the exclamation marks show that your feeling of disapproval is being expressed.

Expressing emotions and describing emotions

Note carefully that Ayer says that in making a moral judgement you are *expressing* your emotions. You are not *describing* your emotions. The difference can be seen in this way: if you are feeling very angry you could tell me you are angry, but you might do so in an extremely calm manner. This would be a case of *describing* your emotion, not *expressing* it. On the other hand, I might express my anger by saying nothing at all, but merely by screaming loudly.

Emotivism, then, says that when you make a moral judgement you are expressing your emotions. However, it claims that you are doing something else as well. That is, according to emotivism, you are not only expressing your feelings – you are also trying to arouse the feelings of your hearers in order to stimulate them to act in certain ways. For instance, if I say 'you act wrongly in stealing the money' I am trying to get you to feel the same way about the act as I do. I do this because I want you to act in a certain way – say, not steal any more money.

Types of command

Furthermore, Ayer goes on to say, some moral utterances are something like commands. For example, if I say, 'it is your duty to help that old lady across the road' then I am expressing my approval at the prospect of your helping the old lady across the road and I am hoping to stimulate in you the same kind of feeling so that you do help her across the road. But I am also, according to Ayer, issuing you with some kind of *command,* such as 'help that old lady across the road'. Again, if I say, 'you ought to help that old lady across the road', I am also expressing and seeking to stimulate feelings, and there is also a command here, but it is less emphatic than in the previous case. And if I say 'it is good to help that old lady across the road', the feelings are still there in the same way, but the command is very weak indeed.

review
activity

1. According to Ayer, if I say that it was wrong of you to cheat in the examination, what am I doing?

2. How does Ayer analyse:

    a) it is your duty to be kind to your parents;

    b) you ought to be kind to your parents; and

    c) it is good to be kind to your parents?

3. What is the difference between these, according to Ayer?

A criticism of Ayer's emotivism

The boo-hurrah theory

The most obvious problem that emotivism has to face is that it seems to make moral disagreement impossible. For example, suppose a woman you and I know has an abortion. I say, 'she acted wrongly in having an abortion', whereas you say 'she acted well in having an abortion'. In each case, according to emotivism, the factual content of what we say is the same, namely, 'she had an abortion'. We just disagree in the emotions we express towards the fact that she had an abortion. It is as if I said 'she had an abortion – boo!' and you said 'she had an abortion – hurrah!'. This is why the theory has been known as the 'boo-hurrah theory of ethics'. However, if all that is going on is that I am saying 'boo' to something and you are saying 'hurrah' to the same thing, where is the disagreement? There would seem to be no more disagreement here than if, when someone handed me a cup of coffee, I expressed pleasure ('hurrah!'), and, when he handed you a cup of coffee, you expressed displeasure ('boo!').

An absence of moral agreement

In fact, Ayer says that *there are no* substantive *moral* disagreements, and in his saying this we see most clearly his espousal of the fact-value distinction. For he says that what look like moral disagreements are, in reality, disagreements about the facts of the matter (none of which, of course, for emotivism can be moral facts). Return to the example where we differ in our response to the woman who had an abortion. We might have been unclear about how old the foetus was when it was aborted; or about the woman's age at the time of the abortion; or whether the foetus was healthy or handicapped and, if so, in what way; or about the woman's domestic situation (whether she is married, whether she has other children and, if so, how many); or whether this was her first abortion or not; or how she became pregnant (whether she was raped, for example); or about her attitude to the abortion; and so on.

Certainly we might have had different feelings about the case because we disagreed about the facts. However, Ayer claims that, if we are completely clear about the facts and agree on what they are, then there can be no real disagreement left: what we are left with (if we are left with it) is each party simply expressing his feelings about the case.

This position is, however, surely very implausible. For there surely are examples where we can agree about all the facts of a case and be left with a genuine moral disagreement, that is, a disagreement that is not simply the expression of a 'boo!' or a 'hurrah!' (which is, of course, as we have seen, no real disagreement at all). A central reason for thinking this is that what one *counts* as a fact in a moral situation will often depend upon one's moral outlook. Thus, some philosophers, such as Peter Singer, as we have seen, think that it is a *fact* that the human foetus is *merely* a member of the species *Homo sapiens* and that killing it raises few moral problems at all. However, some people – for example, Christians – think that this is *not* a *fact* at all. They think that the foetus is one of God's creatures, fashioned by God's hand and destined to grow into his image, and with the task ahead of it in life of worshipping its creator. A philosopher like Singer and the religious believer disagree about what the facts are, and they do so because they have different moral outlooks.

review activity

1. Why is Ayer's view known as the 'boo-hurrah' theory?

2. Ayer denies that there are any genuine moral disagreements. What problems does this view face?

C.L. Stevenson

Meaning and use

A second, more sophisticated version of emotivism was propounded by C.L. Stevenson (Stevenson 1937). Stevenson draws a distinction between the *meaning* of a word or sentence and its *use*. We can *use* a word or sentence to do many things. Stevenson gives the example of the sentence 'I am loaded down with work'. We can *use* this sentence to do any number of things, for example, to drop a hint that we need some help or to arouse sympathy in our hearer. Clearly, neither of these *uses* gives us the *meaning* of the sentence. Such uses of words or sentences Stevenson calls 'dynamic uses'.

According to Stevenson, when we use a word or a sentence dynamically we are trying to *influence* our hearer in some way, getting him to *feel* something or to *do* something.

Dynamic and descriptive uses

Stevenson distinguishes the *dynamic* use of a word or sentence from the *descriptive* use. Thus the sentence, 'I am loaded down with work' can be used *dynamically*, as we have seen, but it can also be used *descriptively*, as when I utter the sentence to another simply in order to let him know how things are with me.

Emotive meaning

Stevenson says that there is a kind of *meaning* of a word or sentence which he calls the 'emotive meaning'. He describes emotive meaning in this way:

The emotive meaning of a word is a tendency of a word, arising through the history of its usage, to produce (result from) affective responses in people. It is the immediate aura of feeling which hovers about a word.

(Stevenson 1937: 23)

For example, the word 'nigger' is a word that has an emotive meaning because it carries with it an idea of contempt for black people.

According to Stevenson

certain words, because of their emotive meaning, are suited to a certain kind of dynamic use – so well suited, in fact, that the hearer is likely to be misled when we use them in any other way. The more pronounced a word's emotive meaning is, the less likely people are to use it purely descriptively.

(Stevenson 1937: 23)

The analysis of 'good' Stevenson suggests that an example of such a word is 'good'. He argues that when one says, for example, 'this is a good book', then the emotive meaning of this is to be understood in something like the following way: 'I like this book'. However, precisely because the word carries this strong emotive meaning, it is fitted very well for dynamic use, and, as we have seen, when we use a word or sentence dynamically we are trying in some way to *influence* our hearer. Hence, our analysis of 'this is a good book' as 'I like this book' is incomplete: there is, as yet, no element in the analysis that captures the influence we are trying to exert on our hearer. Hence the complete analysis or definition must be something like: 'I like this book; do so as well'. And in general, of course, the analysis of 'X is good', or 'this is a good X' will be 'I like X; do so as well'.

Stevenson says that this definition is not perfect because there is no real imperative contained in the original sentence ('X is good') as there is in the definition ('do so as well'), but he suggests that the definition is nonetheless adequate for clarifying the meaning of 'good'.

The example given is, of course, a non-moral example, but Stevenson says that the analysis of 'good' will apply just as much to moral as non-moral cases. Further, he says that the major use of all ethical terms is that in which we seek to influence others' interests.

Stevenson's theory can make sense of ethical disagreement in a way that Ayer's could not. For Ayer, as have seen, once all the facts of a case are known the disputants are left simply with the expression of their own feelings – 'boo!' or 'hurrah!' as the case may be. There is no *arguing* with someone who simply says 'boo!' or 'hurrah!' Stevenson has a richer picture to offer. This is because he has a richer understanding of the concept of an emotion than does Ayer. Stevenson emphasises the way in which people's emotions are rooted in their temperament or depend (at least in part) on their living in a certain social *milieu*. For example, you might feel cold towards the idea of redistributing wealth to the poor because you are generally a cold kind of person; or you might feel cold in this way on account of your never having been poor. Because Stevenson emphasises such aspects of people's emotions he is able to make sense of attempts to change the way people feel, for one can do so by, for example, seeking to change their temperament through the expression of one's own emotions. And in changing someone's temperament, one can change his emotions.

review

activity

1. What does Stevenson mean by:

    a) the descriptive use of a word or sentence;

    b) the dynamic use of a word or sentence;

    c) the emotive meaning of a word or sentence?

2. What, according to Stevenson, is the relation between the dynamic use and the emotive meaning of a word or sentence?

3. How does Stevenson analyse 'this book is good'? What problem does he see for this analysis?

Difficulties for emotivism

1. Both Ayer's and Stevenson's emotivism rely on the fact-value distinction. If this distinction can be shown to be mistaken then the theory collapses. I shall give some reasons to doubt this distinction below after I have described another meta-ethical theory, prescriptivism, which also relies on the fact-value distinction.

2. Both Stevenson and Ayer claim that in making moral judgements one is seeking to influence others' feelings or actions. It is possible to agree that this is *often* so, but also to think that it is not *always* so. For if someone possesses a highly individualistic moral view then he may very well not want everyone to approve of the things of which he approves. It is possible, for example, to think that life is all the richer because different people have different moral views and thus not wish to influence anyone on certain moral matters.

    Further difficulties for emotivism as a form of non-cognitivism will become apparent when discussing what realists take to be the advantages of their theory (below).

Prescriptivism

The theory of prescriptivism is closely associated with the work of R.M. Hare (1919–2002). I shall focus here on Hare's views as they appear in his two books *The Language of Morals* and *Freedom and Reason*. I indicate this because he changed his opinion – or, at any rate, changed the emphasis of his opinions – on a number of issues since writing these books: this new emphasis can be found in his book *Moral Thinking: Its Levels, Method and Point*, part of which is discussed above in the chapter on utilitarianism.

The action-guiding force of morality

A central focus of Hare's theory is the *action-guiding force* of morality. According to Hare, if someone who is a competent speaker of English says that it is *good* to keep one's promises but shows no tendency actually to keep his promises we should think that he was being insincere in what he said. The same applies if he says that it is *right* to keep one's promises or that one *ought* to keep one's promises.

'Ought' and prescribing

Hare concentrates in the first instance on the way in which the word 'ought' functions in moral contexts. If I say to you 'you ought to keep your promises' it is clear that I am urging or encouraging or recommending you to behave in a certain way. Hare says that what I am doing is *prescribing* a particular kind of behaviour to you by issuing you with a *prescription*. We see here the emphasis on action: in saying you ought to keep your promises I trying to get you to *do* something.

Sometimes, of course, one says to oneself 'I ought to do X', and in this case, Hare suggests, the action-guiding element of what is said is captured by some such *imperative* as 'let me do X'.

Hare suggests that the moral words 'right' and 'wrong' can perhaps be explained in terms of 'ought': a right action is one that one ought to do; a wrong action is one that one ought not to do.

Universalisability and overridingness

We have already seen one feature of the way in which, according to Hare, 'ought' functions in moral contexts: it functions as a prescription. But he says that it has two further important characteristics in such contexts. These are: universalisability and overridingness.

If I say that you ought to be kind to your mother then, according to the universalisability thesis, I am committed to the belief that *anyone* exactly like you, or like you in the relevant respects, who is in exactly the same situation, or a situation relevantly similar to yours, ought to be kind to his mother. The reason for the qualification 'relevantly similar' is because, as Hare notes, no two situations are, in fact, ever exactly the same.

Universalisability looks very complicated but what it comes down to is the simple idea that in morality *it is wrong to make an exception for oneself or for others*: if you ought to do some action then so ought I and everyone else to do it if we find ourselves in the same situation. Hare himself puts this in Kant's language of maxims, writing that when one is thinking about what to do one should ask oneself: 'What maxim . . . can I accept as of *universal* application in cases like this, whether or not *I* play the part in the situation which I am playing now?' (Hare 1963: 72).

Hare also suggests that moral judgements are overriding. That is, they take precedence over other judgements or are superior to or more authoritative than other principles. Hare gives the following example (Hare 1963: 168). Suppose Hare's wife has given him a magenta cushion to go on his sofa in his College rooms. His sofa is scarlet. Suppose also that, as an aesthetic principle, he holds the view that one ought not to juxtapose scarlet and magenta. However, he holds the moral principle that one ought not to hurt the feelings of one's wife, and therefore that he ought to place the cushion on the sofa. This shows the way in which, according to Hare, moral principles override non-moral principles.

But what about the situation where moral principles themselves clash? For example, suppose I hold the moral principle that one ought not to lie.

However, I may also hold the moral principle that I ought to protect innocent people from injury when I can. Suppose I am in a situation where the only way to protect an innocent person from injury is to lie. Then my two moral principles will clash. According to Hare, I will have to adjust one (or both) of the them. For example, I might change one of the principles to: 'One ought never to lie *except* when one can thereby protect an innocent person from injury'. This is not a case of one moral principle overriding another, but of qualifying the principle one holds by making it more subtle. Hare thinks that this gradual process of refining one's principles is the key notion in what it is to become morally wiser.

Commendation
We have seen that Hare claims that the words 'right' and 'wrong' can perhaps be understood in terms of 'ought'. What of that other important word, 'good'? Hare argues that when we say something is good – for example, a motor-car, a cricket-bat, a watch or whatever – then we are *commending* that thing. He links the idea of commending with that of *choice*. What this means is that if, for example, I say, 'this is a good watch' then this is like saying 'if you want a watch, choose this one'. Similarly, if I say, 'this is a good watch', then I am committed to choosing this watch, should I have the choice, over a watch that I thought not to be so good.

Functions
We have criteria by which we judge whether a watch is a good watch. This is because a watch has a *function*. It is designed to do something, and if it does not do it then it is not a good watch. For example, a watch must tell the time accurately and not be too heavy to wear or carry. If it grossly inaccurate and too heavy to carry then it is not a good watch. Something analogous can be said of cricket-bats and motor-cars. In all these cases we have criteria for what makes an X a good X.

We can sometimes speak about human beings in a similar way. Thus, if I say that a man is a good plumber then this is something that I judge by certain criteria – he can see quickly what is wrong with the plumbing, can fix burst pipes quickly, plumb in a washing machine without destroying the wall to which he attaches it, and so on – and so if I say that Ludwig is a good plumber I mean to be commending him and saying that if you want a good plumber, choose Ludwig.

However, sometimes we say that someone is a good man or a good woman and we do not mean that he or she fulfils some social role or task (such as plumbing) very well. Hare gives the example of St Francis, whom one might call, simply, a good man. This is clearly a moral context. How should we understand what is being said?

Ideals
Hare says that we are dealing here with an *ideal* of a way of life. In his very early work, Hare thought that if one said sincerely that St Francis was a good man then one was committed to the attempt to try to become like St Francis. Clearly this is an exaggeration: I can think St Francis a good man and know that it would be absurd for me to try to become like him. In later work Hare saw this, and he argued that if we say of individuals such as St Francis that they are good then we are using 'the acts of [such] supremely virtuous men as examples, but only in so far as the traits of character which they exemplify fit into a coherent ideal which we find ourselves able to pursue' (Hare 1963: 155).

There are, of course, many words of moral assessment and evaluation other than 'ought', 'right', 'wrong' and 'good'. Here are some examples: 'cowardly', 'brave', 'foolhardy', 'noble', 'generous', 'mean', 'sordid', 'unkind', 'forgiving', 'courageous', 'gentle', 'honest', 'greedy', 'just'. We could easily add to this list, of course. What analysis does Hare give of these kinds of words?

Descriptive and evaluative meaning

To understand the analysis Hare gives, we first need to distinguish between the notions of *descriptive* and *evaluative* meaning.

A word like 'horse' has only a *descriptive* meaning. This is because it picks out or refers to certain objects in the world, that is, horses. To understand the meaning of 'horse' is to grasp the things in the world it picks out.

A word like 'good' has *evaluative* meaning because, as we have seen, to call something good is to commend it in some way.

Secondarily evaluative meaning

Consider now the kinds of words just mentioned – 'brave', 'meek' and so on. These words have *descriptive* meaning. This is because they are tied to or pick out certain kinds of persons and actions in the kind of way that the word 'horse' is tied to or picks out certain objects in the world. For example, it would not make sense to describe a man who scaled Mount Everest alone, pulled a burning man from the wreck of a car and confronted an aggressive employer with the dissatisfactions of his colleagues as 'meek'. Such a man is courageous, not meek. The word 'courageous' picks out only certain kinds of people and behaviour and therefore has a *descriptive* meaning. However, such words ('meek', 'courageous' and so forth) also have an *evaluative* meaning, for if I say that someone is courageous you know that I approve of him. One can thus use such words to *commend* certain actions, which involves prescribing to others that they be brave and accepting for oneself some such imperative as 'let me be courageous'. Nevertheless, because words such as 'courageous' are tied to particular kinds of people and actions, Hare says that their *descriptive* meaning is primary and their evaluative meaning secondary. Hare thus says that such words have a *secondarily evaluative meaning*.

In the case of a word like 'good', things are otherwise. About the word 'good' Hare says that

> the evaluative meaning is constant for every class of object for which the word is used. When we call a motor-car or a chronometer or a cricket-bat or a picture good, we are commending all of them. But because we are commending all of them for different reasons, the descriptive meaning is different in all cases.
>
> (Hare 1952: 118)

Primarily evaluative meaning

What Hare means by this is that the features that make a cricket-bat good are very different from those that make a motor-car good. Thus the word 'good' is not tied strongly to any particular things. We might therefore say that the descriptive meaning of 'good' is weak because we can call all sorts of different things 'good' and what makes them good will be very different in each case. However, as we have seen, according to Hare, whenever we say that something is good we are commending that thing. Thus Hare says that a word like 'good' has a *primarily evaluative meaning*.

Inverted commas sense

Notice that throughout his discussion Hare relies on the possibility of separating off the evaluative meaning of a word from its descriptive meaning. What this means is that Hare is relying in his discussion on the fact-value distinction. This is because the properly moral meaning of a word is its *evaluative* meaning, which comes to the fore when the word is used to commend. According to Hare, even secondarily evaluative words can be used without commending. For example, one could use the word 'brave' of a certain action *without* thereby commending it. Thus one might see a soldier creep up on his opponent and shoot four enemy soldiers and say that what he did was brave. But in saying this, one might be using the word 'brave' in what Hare calls an *inverted commas sense.* That is, in using the word one might intend to say that, according to the society in which one lives, such an action is brave. However, because one disagrees with these standards one cannot commend such an action. If one thinks this, then one will not think the action brave, but 'brave'. In this way, the evaluative meaning of the word could *come apart from* its descriptive meaning. This is another way of talking of the fact-value distinction.

We can also see Hare's support for the fact-value distinction in his claim that the ultimate principles by which one lives are a matter of *choice* (Hare 1952: 69). This means that one could choose *any* principles by which to live, just so long as one was prepared to treat them as being universalisable, overriding prescriptions. If someone decided that clapping his hands three times an hour was his morality, then, according to Hare, he can do so: there is nothing about morality to stop this. His choice would simply be unusual, that is all.

review activity

1. According to Hare, what do I mean if I say you ought to keep your promises?

2. Give the three features of 'ought' that, Hare argues, are its characteristics when it is used in a moral context, and explain them.

3. How does Hare understand clashes of moral principles?

4. What does Hare think I am doing if I say that a particular watch is a good watch?

5. What, according to Hare, is the difference between saying that this watch is a good watch and this man is a good man?

6. What does Hare mean by saying that some terms are primarily descriptive and some primarily evaluative? Give examples of each.

7. What does Hare mean by the 'inverted commas' use of moral terms?

8. In what way can one best see that Hare's position depends upon the fact-value distinction?

Criticisms of Hare

Hare's views have been widely discussed and very many criticisms of his views have been offered. I discuss here some of the criticisms that seem to me to be the most pressing.

Universalisability 1. Hare's universalisability thesis might be questioned. Remember that the thesis says that if I judge that some person A in a given situation X ought to do action Y then I am committed to judging that anyone relevantly similar to A in a situation relevantly similar to situation X ought to do Y. The problem comes in when we ask what 'relevantly similar' means. Hare himself says (Hare 1962: 49) that the way a situation strikes a person may make all the difference to whether the situation *is* relevantly similar in each case. However, this comes down to saying that the fact that a different individual is present in each of the situations seems enough to make the situations not relevantly similar. And if that is so then the universalisability thesis turns out to be empty, that is, not applicable to any situation in the real world.

Preferring bad things   2.   Hare, as we have seen, claims that if one calls something good – say a hotel – then one is commending this hotel in a way that means that one is committed to choosing this hotel if one is faced with a choice between this hotel and some other hotel that one considers to be not so good. However, this does not seem right: it is possible to think that some hotel is good and to prefer to stay in a hotel that one thinks is not so good. As Bernard Williams has pointed out: '"I simply don't like staying at good hotels" is an intelligible thing to say' (Williams 1985: 125). Similarly, someone might like to listen to music that he knows is, in fact, bad music, and so on.

Self-addressed   3.   Related to this is a point made by Philippa Foot (Foot 1978: ch.VIII, 124).
imperatives   Hare, we have seen, claims that what it is to think someone courageous, for example, is to be committed to a *commendation* that involves accepting the imperative 'let me be brave'. However, Foot says that I could sincerely think someone courageous without having any intention of becoming less cowardly myself and without making any resolution to reform.

Moral principles as not   4.   It seems false to claim, as Hare does, that moral principles are overriding
overriding   for those who accept them. Consider his example of the clash between moral and aesthetic principles. It seems not to be true that, for those who accept morality, moral concerns will always override aesthetic concerns. For example, however much we care about human welfare, we do not usually think that we can simply destroy great and beautiful old buildings in the name of human welfare. It might be said that this is because we know that human beings enjoy such buildings, so we are, after all, concerned about them from a moral point of view. But this thought is merely a subterfuge that secures its point by turning everything we care about into a moral issue. In truth, we think of aesthetic value as having a serious value that, at least on occasion, may compete successfully with our moral concerns.

One cannot value just   5.   Hare's argument, as we have seen, relies on the fact-value distinction. A
anything   critic of Hare's in this regard is, again, Philippa Foot.

Recall that the fact-value distinction implies that, whatever the facts of a case before us, we are free to have whatever moral attitude towards it we like. This is because the world is value-free: the value comes in through our attitudes to the facts. It is a corollary of this that we can, if we wish, ascribe value to anything whatever. Foot argues that this is mistaken. For example, she says that one cannot be proud of just *anything:* no one could just be proud of the sky or the sea. (Foot 1978: 113–14). Similarly, she argues that it is not possible to think that clasping one's hands three times an hour could be, as such, a morally good action (Foot 1978: 118–20). One is simply not free to think that this is morally good. The realm of facts is not entirely separate from the realm of values.

This view is one that underlies the meta-ethical theories we shall now consider.

review
activity

1. Explain the central problem with Hare's universalisability thesis.

2. Is Hare right to say that one can value anything?

3. What is questionable about the claim that moral principles override all other principles for those who take them seriously?

Intuitionism

The theory of intuitionism is most closely associated with G.E. Moore, whose work we have already come across in connection with utilitarianism, with H.A. Prichard (1871–1947) and W.D. Ross (1877–1971).

'Good' and 'yellow'

In his book *Principia Ethica*, first published in 1903, Moore drew an analogy between 'good' and 'yellow'. Consider the latter first. If someone does not already know what yellowness is, then one cannot explain it to him. Of course, it is true that we can give an account of why an object is yellow in colour by explaining how it is that the object reflects light in a certain way because its surface has a certain structure and thus absorbs and reflects light in a particular manner. Yet a blind person who grasped this explanation but who had never had sight would still not know what yellowness is. In this sense, 'yellow' cannot be *defined* or *analysed*. Furthermore, yellowness is a *simple* notion: it cannot be broken down into its constituent parts.

Goodness as simple and indefinable

Moore says that 'good' is like 'yellow'. That is, he says that if someone does not already know what goodness is then one cannot explain it to him. 'Good' is *indefinable* or *unanalysable*. Moreover, goodness is a *simple* notion, that is, it cannot be broken down into constituent parts. What arguments does Moore give for this view?

Moore thinks that goodness must be either i) a simple unanalysable (indefinable) property or ii) a complex analysable (definable) property or iii) it is nothing at all (Moore 1984: 15-17).

The open-question argument

First, Moore tries to show that it is not ii). Suppose, he says, that we tried to define 'good'. We might, for example, try to define it as 'pleasure'. But Moore says that this definition cannot be right because we can always ask whether pleasure is good. And, he says, we could not do this if goodness and pleasure were one and the same, which, he claims, is what they would be were 'good' definable as 'pleasure'. When we think of goodness and pleasure,

Moore says, 'we have two different notions before our minds' (Moore 1984: 16). The same might be said of any putative definition of 'good'. Of any definition we offer for 'good' it will always be an open question whether that thing is good. This is known as Moore's *open question argument.*

Note carefully that Moore is *not* denying that pleasure can be good or that good things are pleasurable: it can be both good and pleasurable to learn philosophy, for example. What he *is* denying is that goodness and pleasantness are one and the same property.

The naturalistic fallacy

Moore, we have seen, thought that 'good' could not be defined. However, he was well aware that many philosophers have tried to define it and he spends a great deal of time in his book dissecting their arguments. For us, what is important is to see that all such attempts commit what he called the *naturalistic fallacy.* Moore seems to have meant a number of things by this fallacy, but the basic idea is that the fallacy consists in supposing that goodness is identical with anything else that can be defined.

Goodness not a natural property

He used the term 'naturalistic' because he wanted to deny that the goodness was a natural property at all. This makes it unlike yellowness, which certainly is a natural property of objects, for example, of buttercups and dandelions.

Moore has said, then, that 'good' cannot be defined. He concludes that goodness is therefore not a complex analysable property. That is, he rejects ii), above. He also rejects iii). He thinks that goodness must be something, otherwise we should not, for example, have the sense that when we think of goodness we have something distinct before our minds. Moore thus concludes i), that is, that goodness is a simple indefinable property. We have also seen that he thinks it a non-natural property. So we are told by Moore that goodness is a *simple, indefinable (unanalysable) non-natural property.*

Moore thinks that it is a *fact of the matter* that certain things are good. We have already noted in the chapter on utilitarianism that he thinks that the contemplation of beauty and the enjoyment of personal relationships are good in themselves. In other words, he is denying here the fact-value distinction: some things *just are* good, and their goodness is one of their properties just as much as their size or shape or weight, although it is, we remember, a non-natural property.

Goodness as self-evident

How, according to Moore, are we ever aware of the presence of goodness? In answering this question his intuitionism comes to the fore. For what Moore says is that, because goodness is a simple, indefinable non-natural property, it cannot be seen with the eyes. In fact, it seems that in calling goodness a non-natural property Moore was thinking of it as something that could not be detected by the senses. So how does one detect that something is good? Moore said that we *cannot give any reason* why this or that thing is good. He also said that such claims were *self-evidently* true or false (Moore, 1984: 143–4). So he is relying on the idea that *we simply know by intuition* that something or other is good: we simply *see* (although not with the eyes) that something is good, in the kind of way that we can just see that $2 + 2 = 4$. And this is what intuitionism in meta-ethics means: it is the belief that we cannot provide reasons for moral judgements, the belief that they are self-evidently true (or false).

The self-evidence of our duties

Moore denied (Moore 1984: 148) that we could just see, intuitively, that one had an obligation to do some action, for example, to keep one's promises, or to keep a promise in some specific situation; for Moore, it was only of attributions of goodness to something or other that we could be intuitively certain, that is, only such attributions are self-evidently true. However, other intuitionists thought that we could intuit such things as the rightness or wrongness of an action. Prichard (Prichard 1949: ch.1, 8) makes this point (in, it must be admitted, a rather convoluted manner).

> *We recognize, for instance, that this performance of a service to X, who has done us a service, just in virtue of its being a performance of a service to one who has rendered a service to the would-be agent, ought to be done by us.*

In other words, because, say, Jean has done us a service we recognise that we ought to do Jean a service. Prichard goes on to say that our apprehension of this

> *is immediate, in precisely the sense in which a mathematical apprehension is immediate, for example, the apprehension that this three-sided figure, in virtue of its being three-sided, must have three angles.*

Morals and mathematics

We also find this analogy between morals and mathematics in the work of Ross, another intuitionist. Ross stresses the belief shared by all the intuitionists that we do not, of course, know intuitively what is good or what is obligatory from the beginning of our lives. We have to learn what is good and bad, what right and wrong, just as we have to learn mathematics. But, according to Ross, once we have learnt certain moral principles or rules (such as that we ought to keep our promises) we can simply see that they are correct and binding on us, just as, once we have learnt that 2 + 2 = 4, we can just see that this is correct (Ross 1930: 19; 32–3).

Prima facie obligations

In fact, Ross's view is slightly more complicated than that, for he draws a distinction between obligations and *prima facie* obligations (*prima facie* literally means 'arising at first sight' or 'based on the first impression'). A *prima facie* obligation is an obligation to do something that may be overturned by another obligation which is more pressing. For example, according to Ross, if I have made a promise to someone then I have an obligation to keep the promise. However, if I find that a person is in distress and I can help him only by breaking my promise then I am permitted to break the promise. This shows that the obligation to keep the promise in the first place was only a *prima facie* obligation.

Ross gives a list of actions which he thinks are self-evident *prima facie* obligations: fulfilling a promise, effecting a just distribution of goods, returning services rendered, promoting the good of others, promoting the virtue or insight of the agent. About these *prima facie* obligations he says:

> *The moral order expressed in these propositions is just as much part of the fundamental nature of the universe . . . as is the spatial or numerical structure expressed in the axioms of geometry or arithmetic.* (Ross 1930: 29–30)

Because in a given case we might for one reason or another be required not to perform a duty – say when there is a conflict of obligations (as in the example about promising, above) – Ross says that we are certain of our *prima facie* obligations in a way that we are not certain of our actual (and non-*prima facie*) obligations. Thus, for instance, the general rule or principle: 'One ought (*prima facie*) to keep one's promises' is intuitively certain in way that 'I ought to keep *this* promise to *this* person in *this* situation' is not. It is the general rules or principles of morality – along with goodness – which are, according to Ross, self-evident.

review
activity

1. What does Moore mean by saying that goodness is a simple indefinable non-natural property?

2. Explain Moore's 'open question' argument.

3. Explain the naturalistic fallacy.

4. What does Ross mean by a *prima facie* obligation?

5. According to Ross we can be intuitively certain of some but not all obligations. Of which can we be certain, and why? Of which can we not be certain, and why?

Difficulties in intuitionism

How can we know intuitively what is good or our duty?

1. The most fundamental problem for intuitionism is simply that it can give no account of *how* it is that we are intuitively aware of the presence of the goodness of some situation or of the obligatoriness of some act. We cannot see it with our eyes and we cannot use our other senses to perceive it. So how do we know it? We have no special faculty for seeing it. So it is mysterious how it is that we are supposed to intuit the truths of morality.

Moral and mathematical training

2. The analogy between seeing the goodness of some deed and seeing the truth of an arithmetical proposition such as $2 + 2 = 4$ is weak. This is because we have a much clearer understanding of what it is to receive a training in mathematics than in morality. Further, we have a much better understanding of what it is to make a mistake in mathematics than in ethics. If someone thinks that $2 + 2 = 5$ then he is just wrong and anyone who is competent in mathematics knows this. Things in morality are not like that, however. Some people, for example, hold the moral belief that all human beings are equal, whereas others deny this. Even if you believe that all human beings are equal, however, it would not be right to say that those who disagree with you are just wrong in the way they would be if they thought $2 + 2 = 5$.

Morality and the giving of reasons

3. This problem is connected with a further difficulty. This is that two people who are equally morally sensitive can disagree with one another about whether some deed really is obligatory or some situation really is good. Yet how are they even to go about settling their dispute on the intuitionists' picture? We have seen that the intuitionists claim that we can give no reasons for our views on the goodness or rightness of certain situations or actions: such things are supposed to be self-evident. But if we can give no reasons for such views then we are helpless if we want properly to discuss our views with others and seek to convince them of

173

our opinion. Similarly, no one else would be able to give us reasons to make us change our mind.

This is serious problem, for it seems, in fact, to belong to the very logic of moral beliefs that we have reasons for our moral opinions. If I like coffee then I do not have to give you a reason why I do. But if I think that abortion is dreadful then I *must* have some reason for my view. This is one of the great differences between preferences and moral opinions.

review activity

1. Why does the analogy between mathematics and ethics raise problems for intuitionism?

2. Describe in your own words one other problem that intuitionism faces.

Realism

Intuitionism is a form of moral realism; it claims that there are moral facts of the matter. However, we have seen some reason to think it weak in certain key ways, and intuitionism as a distinctive theory lost favour amongst philosophers after about 1940. Nevertheless, there is a modern form of intuitionism that is now accepted by many philosophers and that is, like intuitionism, a form of moral realism. In fact, this form of realism is simply called 'moral realism'. This might seem confusing, given that intuitionism is also a form of realism, but it is not really, as when philosophers talk about moral realism these days they do not have intuitionism in mind but the modern form of realism.

Modern moral realism claims, then, that there are moral facts of the matter and that moral claims can therefore be properly understood to be true or false. Thus Mark Platts has written:

> [M]oral judgements are . . . factually cognitive . . . *presenting claims about the world which can be assessed (like any other factual belief) as true or false, whose truth or falsity are as much possible objects of knowledge as any other factual claims about the world.*
>
> (Platts 1979: 243)

Realists about moral value are also realist about aesthetic value – that is, they believe that there are facts about whether a particular piece of music or a sunset is beautiful or not; or a building is elegant or not; or a poem ugly or not; and so on (cf. McNaughton 1996: 55).

Moral realists have suggested at least two ways in which we might think of there being moral facts of the matter.

Moral properties and secondary properties

One is an analogy between secondary properties (qualities) like colour, smell and so on and moral properties of people, deeds and so on (cf. Wiggins 1987: ch.III, 106–8). Recall that our experiencing secondary properties depends partly upon the way the world is and partly on the way we are. If we take secondary properties as a model for moral properties then we can say that moral properties depend partly on us and partly on the way the world is. This has some plausibility. For example, if we say that it is a fact of the matter that pulling the wings off a fly is a cruel thing to do, then we do not expect a bee to be able to *see* this cruelty, no more than we expect a bee to be able to see a rose as the same colour as we do. However, as we saw when discussing secondary properties, secondary properties are nonetheless genuine properties of objects: a rose *really is* red (or yellow or whatever) even though a creature needs our kind of visual equipment and brain to see this redness (or yellowness or whatever).

A second analogy that has been proposed is that between moral properties and mathematics (cf. Wiggins 1987: ch.IV, 153). However, I shall not discuss this further here, as we have already looked in some detail at what the intuitionists had to say about the analogy between morals and mathematics.

review activity

Explain in your own words the analogy moral realists draw between secondary properties and moral properties.

Arguments for moral realism

Denying Hume

1. Realists argue that the idea that there are moral and aesthetic facts of the matter fits well with our experience of moral and aesthetic value. For example, they claim that when we look at a sunset we see its beauty; or that when we come across a group of boys pouring petrol over a cat and setting the animal alight that we see the cruelty of what they do. In other words, they deny that the kind of account that Hume gives of wilful murder (see above) and of other moral and aesthetic cases is correct. Realists say that the Humean account is wrong when it claims that we do not see the viciousness of the deed. The Humean account, they say, distorts our experience of the world.

Moral mistakes

2. Realism seems to make sense of the fact that we can *make mistakes* in moral matters. Consider again the irrealist view that moral judgements are expressions of emotion (emotivism), or ultimately rest on principles we choose (prescriptivism). Now imagine that you are wondering what to do in some morally tricky situation – say whether to agree to euthanasia being performed on a relative of yours. The realists say that, as you think about what to do in this case, you are concerned to *get things right*, to *make the right decision*. That decision cannot rest, they say, on whether you happen to have particular emotional responses to the situation or on your choice of fundamental principles by which to live. Suppose you said, for example, that your fundamental principles forbade your thinking the euthanasia morally acceptable. Then you could come to think it acceptable by simply changing your principles. However, you cannot solve moral dilemmas so easily, say the realists. According to them, there is a fact of the matter about whether euthanasia in this situation is right or not, and you cannot get round this by *choosing* to think one thing or the other, no more than you can tell me how many

chairs are in the other room by *choosing* to think that there shall be three there. Realism makes sense of the idea that when you think about some moral problem *you are trying to find the right answer,* and that that answer exists independently of what you or anyone else happens to feel or the moral principles one might choose.

It is important to note that the realist does not think that it is always *easy* to see moral properties. On the contrary, realists usually stress that it is, in general, very hard to see moral properties. We might require a great deal of discussion with others about a given situation and have to attend patiently to the situation and be imaginative and open-minded in order to see its moral properties. Further, we might only be able to see the moral properties of a case if we have had a certain moral education.

review activity

Why might moral realism be thought to be better able than irrealism to give an account of the fact that one can make mistakes in one's moral judgements?

Difficulties in moral realism

1. One problem for moral realism is in the analogy between secondary qualities and moral properties. It is, after all, very easy to experience secondary qualities: we just open our eyes and see colours, sniff the flower and smell its scent and so on. But with (putative) moral properties things are not like this: as we have seen, moral realists usually stress that it is hard to see moral properties. Similarly, training in the ability to use secondary quality predicates ('red', 'bitter', 'sweet' and so on) is much better understood than is the moral education required to use moral predicates ('cruel', 'generous' and so on). In fact, the two kinds of training seem very dissimilar and this reduces the force of the analogy between the two sets of properties.

2. There is a related problem in that in the case of secondary properties there are not the same disagreements that occur in the case of ethics. For example, we know that we can agree on what colour objects possess. True, there are cases where we might not be sure whether a colour is, say, blue or black, but this unclarity depends upon the fact that we do agree on the central cases of the application of colour predicates. But there seems to be nothing like this in morality: for every moral claim someone makes there are, or have been, equally morally competent persons who disagree with that claim.

Realism and moral motivation

3. Realism has a problem explaining the nature of moral motivation. What this means is as follows. Consider this case: you want (desire) an apple and believe that there is an apple in the fruit bowl. The combination of your desire and belief motivates you to go to the fruit bowl. Suppose, however, that you did not want an apple. You might still believe that there is an apple in the fruit bowl, but in this case you would not go to the fruit bowl. The belief that there is an apple in the bowl is not

enough, by itself, to motivate you to go to the bowl: for that, you need also the desire for an apple. Without the relevant desire you are simply indifferent to whether there is an apple in the fruit bowl or not. However, with the desire and the belief, one can explain your going to the fruit bowl as *rational motivation*. This account of motivation can be generalised and is known by philosophers as the *belief-desire model of rational action*.

Consider now the fact that moral realism claims that when we make a moral judgement we are expressing a belief. For example, you might be able to help your friend and believe that to do so would be generous. The difficulty for moral realism is this. Just as you can *believe* that there is an apple in the fruit bowl and be indifferent to this fact unless you *want* an apple, you could, it seems, *believe* that to help your friend was generous without being motivated to help her. Unless you *want* to help her the mere fact that you believe helping her is generous provides you with no motivation to do so. So, it seems that according to moral realism you could have many moral beliefs without being motivated to do anything in particular. For that, you would need also the relevant desires.

For some realists this might be no problem at all. They might be happy to accept the thought that one could believe some act generous and have no motivation to do it, or believe some act spiteful and have no motivation to desist. But the difficulty here is that we normally think that morality is not like this: we normally think that to believe some act is generous just is to have some kind of motivation to do it: we do not need to have a separate desire to motivate us.

A realist response   One response that a realist might make to this is to deny the belief-desire model of rational action. He could say that, at least in many moral cases, to have some moral belief *is* to be motivated to act in a certain way. Consider a non-moral case. Suppose you detest jazz and only like classical music, and have a friend who loves jazz. How might you come to understand what your friend sees in the music? One possibility is that your friend could begin from music you like, pointing out passages in it that have a 'jazz' feel. For example, she could play you, say, Shostakovich's Thirteenth String Quartet, which, although 'classical' music, contains an extended jazz-like section. If you are receptive to that she could, perhaps, play you pieces of jazz that have a certain feel of classical music. And so on. The point in all this is that your friend will be trying to get you to look at the world from her point of view as far as music is concerned: when you come to see how things look in the light of her interests you will come to see why it is that she wants to listen to jazz. This need not mean that you too will want to listen to jazz, but you will at least see what she sees in it (or, rather, hear what she hears in it).

We could put this point by saying that the beliefs your friend has about the music can explain why she is motivated to listen to it.

If this is the right way to describe things then it is arguable that it is mistaken to think that what it is for a person to like jazz is to hear the same thing as the person who does not like it and that it is just that the first person has a certain kind of desire that the second lacks. The desire, as an independent element in explaining why the person listens to jazz, drops out: to hear the music as she does is to understand why she is motivated to listen to it.

If this model could be applied to moral matters then the belief-desire model of rational action could be abandoned and the realist would be able to secure the claim that moral beliefs (or, at any rate, some of them) can motivate to action.

review
activity

1. Explain why there are problems in the analogy between secondary properties and moral properties.

2. Explain in your own words, using your own example(s), the belief-desire model of rational action.

3. Why does moral realism have a problem on the belief-desire model of rational action? What response can it offer to this problem?

Irrealism and moral motivation

It might be worth making clear why irrealism has no problem explaining moral motivation. It has no such problem because for the irrealist there are no genuine moral beliefs. It is perhaps simplest to see this in the case of emotivism.

According to emotivism, when we say that we believe that some action is good what we really mean is that we feel a certain way about the action. And (many) emotions and feelings themselves incorporate desires. For example, my feeling of fear in the face of a vicious dog incorporates the desire to get away from the dog; my hope that you will find this book helpful incorporates the desire that you find this book helpful; and so on. The same can be said of moral cases: my feeling that to help you would be generous can be understood to incorporate the desire to help you.

For prescriptivism there is also no problem about moral motivation. This is because, as we have seen, prescriptivism claims that the ultimate moral principles by which one lives are principles that one *chooses*. However, to choose some way of living involves having a desire to live in that way and thus there is no problem for prescriptivism about moral motivation.

Cognitivism and non-cognitivism: a rejection of the debate?

It is important to note that some – a very few – philosophers think that the whole debate between cognitivism and non-cognitivism is mistaken and ought to be rejected. That is, they believe that *both* views are mistaken and that the whole issue is confused. Raimond Gaita has put forward the most powerful argument for this view (Gaita 1991: esp. ch.16). Roughly, Gaita's argument is as follows.

Everyone agrees that we can say that we have certain moral beliefs and that we might agree that they are true. For example, you say you believe that incest is wicked or that cheating is mean and I might say that what you say is true. The issue between cognitivists and non-cognitivists is whether, when we use the word 'belief' in a moral context, we really do have beliefs. Do we have beliefs in a moral context in the 'strict' sense in which we can have beliefs about tables and chairs, about the colours of objects or about mathematics because there is a truth 'out there' waiting to be discovered? What the non-cognitivist says is that we do not. However, that means that the non-cognitivist thinks that moral speech is *systematically misleading*: it looks as if we can have moral beliefs, but we cannot. What the cognitivist argues, however, is that when we say we have moral beliefs, we really *do* have moral beliefs and that, therefore, moral speech is *not* systematically misleading. However, the cognitivist will grant that it is far from obvious that moral speech is not misleading in this way – otherwise, how could the non-cognitivist case get off the ground at all? After all, the term 'belief' clearly functions in moral discourse in ways unlike the way in which it functions in paradigm cases of discourse where we can get truth, for example, in science, in ordinary empirical investigations of the world (about tables, chairs and so forth) and in mathematics (for example, those trained in the correct way in those three areas will agree on their beliefs, and this is clearly not the case in moral matters). What the cognitivist will say, therefore, is that we need a philosophical argument to show that moral speech is not systematically misleading. So both cognitivist and non-cognitivist believe that moral speech *looks* as if it is about moral facts: the difference is that the non-cognitivist thinks the looks here are deceptive whereas the cognitivist thinks that the looks are not deceptive.

What Gaita argues from here is that both cognitivists and non-cognitivists are holding moral speech up against speech in, for example, science or mathematics, and asking whether moral speech matches up to speech in these other areas. They disagree about whether it does but they agree on what moral speech looks like. However, he argues that this means that both cognitivists and non-cognitivists have simply failed to understand what moral speech is. It is mistaken to think that moral speech looks as if it is like the 'strict' speech of science or mathematics. Moral speech is *just what it is*. And what it is is an extremely rich vocabulary formed by the distinctive kind of life human beings lead with which we can understand one another and what we do as wise, shrewd, naïve, shallow, deep, gullible, foolish, superstitious, insightful, thoughtful, level-headed, sober, rash and so on. These are the concepts that we use in marking what it is to think well or to think badly in moral matters and it is inattention to these terms – and many others – that leads philosophers to get embroiled in the mistaken debate about cognitivism and non-cognitivism, focusing on an extremely narrow range of concepts such as 'belief', 'truth' and 'fact' whose function in moral discourse is, in any case, misunderstood in that debate.

It must said that Gaita is *very* much in the minority in the approach just outlined, although there are other philosophers whose work bears some similarity to Gaita's: these are indicated in the 'further reading' section below. Whether what Gaita says is correct or not, it certainly offers a valuable perspective on the issues under discussion.

The is-ought gap

Moral realism, we have seen, denies the fact-value distinction. We noticed earlier that this has often been allied to the is-ought gap. There have been many attempts to bridge the gap between 'is' and 'ought', that is, to show that conclusions about what one ought to do can be deduced from statements about what is the case. We shall look at just one such attempt. It is offered by John Searle (Searle 1969: ch.8).

Searle's attempt to bridge the is-ought gap

Searle focuses on the making of promises. His argument is that we can derive an 'ought' from an 'is' by considering the following statements.

1. Jones uttered the words 'I hereby promise to pay you, Smith, five dollars'.
2. Jones promised to pay Smith five dollars.
3. Jones placed himself under (undertook) an obligation to pay Smith five dollars.
4. Jones is under an obligation to pay Smith five dollars.
5. Jones ought to pay Smith five dollars.

Here we move from a purely factual premise concerning what *is* the case – namely, that Jones utters certain words – to an 'ought'. Searle grants that various additional steps have to be added in order to make the derivation one of entailment, but these need not concern us. Leaving them aside, then, is Searle's argument valid?

The basic idea behind Searle's argument is that there is a social institution of promising and that, if one takes part in this institution, then one is bound by the rules of the institution. He draws an analogy here between promising and playing a game such as baseball or cricket. If you are playing cricket and are run out and the umpire says you ought to leave the pitch, then you cannot argue with him by saying: 'Look, you can't derive an "ought" from an "is". It's true that I *have been* run out, but this is just a statement of fact and doesn't show that I *ought* to leave the pitch. So, I'm not going.' Clearly, everyone can see that such a way of reasoning is absurd.

Many philosophers have thought that the basic problem here is that, just as one may decide not to play cricket, one may decide not to take part in the institution of promising. In that case, one could avoid the evaluative implications of making promises. However, Searle, in fact, points this out and is happy to accept this point. He grants that one could decide to criticise the whole institution of promising and not make any promises. However, his point is that the traditional argument which claims that an 'ought' cannot be derived from an 'is' has completely failed to understand the institutional nature of obligations – that it is in virtue of institutional facts that it is possible, for example, to make promises at all. Of course, one might criticise or opt out of those institutions, but within them one can derive an 'ought' from an 'is'.

In fact, Searle goes on to argue that just the same point may be made in the case of what one might call the 'colour predicate-commitment gap'. What this means is as follows. Searle notes that Hare claims that if someone – call him Stafford – uses the word 'red' of some object (a pillar box, say) then he is committed to the view that it is correct to use the same word of anything like that object in the relevant respect, that is, in its colour. Yet to say that Stafford is *committed* to doing something is to make an *evaluative* statement, just as it is to say he *ought* to do something (for example, keep his promises). However, Hare says that 'red' is a purely *descriptive* term. So Hare should really say that one cannot derive a 'commitment' from a 'colour predicate', just as he says one cannot derive an 'ought' from an 'is'. He should *deny* that Stafford is committed in that way. Why does Hare not do this? According to Searle, what Hare has missed is that it is only because Stafford accepts the institution of making statements (for example, 'this pillar box is red') that he is committed to the view that it is correct to use the same predicate of the next object which is like the first object in the relevant respect, i.e., in colour. So Searle's argument is that Hare should *either* give up belief in the 'is-ought' gap because, *by his own reasoning*, there is no 'colour predicate-commitment' gap *or* accept that there is no 'is-ought' gap.

Relativism

In this section we shall consider the issue of moral relativism.

There are a number of different versions of relativism. These are: descriptive relativism; moral-requirement or normative relativism; and meta-ethical relativism. Let us look at these in turn.

Descriptive relativism

Some examples

Descriptive relativism is the claim that, as a matter of fact, different groups of people – usually understood as different cultures – accept or have accepted different moral codes, ways of behaving, moral standards and the like. Here are some examples.

The ancient Aztecs believed that the gods needed a regular supply of blood in order to keep the heavens turning. They secured a supply of this blood by practising human sacrifice on a large scale: they required prisoners they captured in war to ascend pyramids where their hearts were torn out while they were alive. The still beating hearts were placed in a special container and the bodies were kicked down the steps of the pyramids where they collected in a bloody heap.

The indigenous North American culture of the Kwakiutl was a culture based on the notion that the point of existence was to glorify oneself and bring shame and humiliation on as many others as possible. Social life was thus intensely competitive. If a person in that culture suffered misfortune, then he would seek to shame or kill another as a way of shoring up his own ego. If someone in the family died, a relative might kill someone – anyone – as a way of 'getting even' for the shameful misfortune: but there was no thought here that the person killed was responsible for the death.

The Asmat tribe in New Guinea have a number of interesting practices. They put the heads of their dead enemies in a fire to remove the skin, and when the skin is torn off, a hole is made in the skull and the brains poured out for the elders to drink. Their enemies' flesh, and sometimes that of their dead relatives, is mixed with sago, wrapped in leaves, cooked and eaten with relish. The young men of the Asmat are subjected to excruciatingly painful initiation rites: stalks of sugar cane are pushed up the nose until it bleeds freely; they are forced to swallow cane until they vomit (and they often defecate in fear); the tongue is pierced; and the penis head is scraped with rough leaves and cut until it bleeds profusely. And amongst the Asmat there is an elaborate system of ritualised homosexuality in which young boys take part as a matter of course; it is believed that unless they absorb the semen of older men when they are young they will not grow into strong warriors.

The ancient Greeks kept slaves; pederasty was widely practised amongst them. The Romans enjoyed gladiatorial combats of immense violence. In Bali cock fighting is widespread. The Spanish still practise bull fighting.

Sharing moral standards

Evidently we are dealing here with some very great differences of moral outlook and practice. Nevertheless, it might be said that all human cultures share, and must share, some standards or they would destroy themselves. This is surely true. For *any* society of people will have to have *some* constraints concerning the requirement to tell the truth, not to steal, to kill, to injure and so on, which constraints must be followed by *most* people *most* of the time if that society is not to collapse (cf. Williams 1985: 193). Moreover, all human societies have to take care of their infants if those infants and the society itself are to survive. However, although all this is true, it still leaves it wide open for different societies to have profoundly different moral codes and systems. After all, the kinds of moral practices previously described are all consistent with the necessary constraints on society just mentioned. Those constraints do not do much to *describe* a moral way of life, for they are extremely minimal. Still less do they *justify* a given such life.

At this point, when we are entering onto questions of justification, we should turn to look at normative moral relativism.

Normative relativism

Normative relativism is usually understood from a social aspect. When so understood, it states that the moral requirements that are binding on a person in some way depend on – that is, in some way are 'relative to' – the group of which that person is a part. For example, on this view, what makes a person obliged to act in a particular way is that the group as a whole believes that this kind of behaviour is required or good. What *makes* the action good is that the society approves of it.

What can be said in favour of this relativism? Evidently it is true that we all absorb moral habits, patterns of feeling and response, characteristic ways of thought and so on from the culture and social world in which we live, whatever form that world might take. This might give us reason for thinking that normative moral relativism is right. But there are at least two major problems with this line of argument.

Problems for normative relativism

The first is that the fact that we do absorb so much from our immediate cultural and moral environment cannot by itself justify normative relativism. For if normative relativisim were true, it would be possible to find out what was right and what wrong simply by consulting the standards of one's society. But that is absurd. For one thing, morality does not have that kind of 'impersonality': finding out what is right and wrong is not *at all* like taking an opinion poll. For another, it is perfectly possible to criticise the standards of one's own culture. To suppose otherwise is to think that a moral education is really indoctrination, where to absorb one's society's standards is to do so in such an unthinking fashion that one could not question them.

The second problem with the proposed line of argument – it is problem implicit in what has just been said – is that it makes out a culture to be much more homogenous than it is. The fact is that there are all kinds of disagreements within the same culture, but normative relativism simply fails to take proper account of this. In fact, it is possible to feel ethically alienated from the members of one's own group whilst finding oneself in great sympathy with the members of another culture. This point has been well made by Peter Winch (1926–97).

> It is . . . misleading to distinguish in a wholesale way between 'our own' and 'alien' cultures; parts of 'our' culture may be quite alien to one of 'us'; indeed some parts of it may be more alien than cultural manifestations which are geographically or historically remote. I see no reason why a contemporary historical scholar might not feel himself more at home in the world of medieval alchemy than in that of twentieth century professional football.
>
> (Winch 1997: 198)

Winch's point is powerful. The fact is that there are all kinds of overlaps between cultures and all kind of subcultures within cultures. To that extent, normative relativism, which proceeds on the assumption that we can speak of what 'we' believe and do and what 'they' believe and do, is an unhelpful way of understanding moral life.

Nonetheless, there clearly *is* a sense in which we are all, to a greater or lesser extent, limited by our cultural horizons. There *is* a sense in which we *can* talk of *our* way of doing things, or of what *we* do or think, or of what *they* do or think. I am no doubt fairly typical of modern Western liberal society insofar as I would be horrified if I were actually to witness a Roman gladiatorial combat, but this thought coexists with the recognition that, had I been the average citizen of the Roman world at the right time, then I would almost certainly have enjoyed the games as pretty much everyone else did. Had I been a member of the Kwakiutl culture I almost certainly would have accepted that culture's way of going about things in terms of self-glorification and humiliation of others.

Does this mean I cannot or should not judge the games or a 'humiliation culture'? This question leads on to the third form of relativism.

Meta-ethical relativism

Some have argued from the fact of cultural diversity in moral matters to the claim that meta-ethical relativism is true. That is, they have argued that the diversity in question shows that there are no truths in moral matters. They have thought this because it is normally taken as a mark of truth that individuals freely agree with one another on what the truth is, or, at any rate, that they can *come to* agree with one another on what the truth is without being coerced. Hence, if there are moral truths, one might expect individuals and societies to converge on those truths. But as they seem to show little sign of doing so, the argument runs, we can infer that there are no moral truths 'out there' (cf. Mackie 1977).

Moral relativism and moral corruption

It is important to see, however, that not just any moral diversity is relevant to such an argument. For example, the sheer fact that another culture goes about things in another way should not, *as such*, be thought to undermine what we believe and make us think that what we believe is not (or might not be) true. Everything will depend on just how they *do* go about things, morally speaking. This is a point that is often missed and it must be stressed. For to miss this point is to confuse moral relativism and moral corruption. The fact that the Nazis believed it right to exterminate six million Jews and others should not, as such, be thought to lend any weight to the thought that perhaps they had got hold of some moral truth. That thought would be no more plausible in the Nazi case than it would be plausible to say that, because a rapist thinks that his raping a woman is good (if he does), for all we know he might have alighted on some moral truth.

How might a moral realist respond to the challenge from reflection on moral diversity that there are no moral truths? One possibility would be to say that there are different moral realities corresponding to different social worlds. The realist is not likely to find this suggestion very helpful (cf. McNaughton 1996: 149ff.). One reason for this is that we do not countenance the idea that there can be different physical realities, and if we are going to have a robust notion of reality in moral matters we should not countenance them there either. Moreover, we earlier discussed in the context of coherentism Donald Davidson's argument that there can only be one coherent account of the world. The basic idea behind that argument is that there can only be disagreement against a background of agreement, for otherwise we could not understand the other group at all. This same argument could be applied in the case of ethics to suggest that there cannot be more than one moral reality, and that our disagreements will take place against the backdrop of agreement. That backdrop of agreement might give the realist hope for convergence on moral truths in the long run.

Extreme and moderate moral realism

An extreme form of realism in this area would be to say that all moral claims are determinably true or false. A less extreme version of moral realism would say that some or most moral claims are determinably true or false. The latter option would itself be a moderate form of moral relativism. However, note that even the defender of the extreme form need not think that each society should have the same practices. This is because a given act in one situation can be very different, morally speaking, from the same act in another situation. For example, the taking of a second wife will be very different in different cultures. Where it is openly practised and fully accepted, it is very different from being the same thing it would be in a society where it has no social expression and is illegal.

Moral progress

An empistemological problem for moral realism

Roughly speaking, a moral realist will believe that it is either true or false that, say, throwing Christians to the lions is good: he will think there is a fact of the matter about whether that is good or not. Even though an entire culture might believe that throwing Christians to the lions is morally acceptable, this does not make it acceptable: there is a truth about the matter one way or another, regardless of what anyone thinks. So a realist will have no trouble saying that there is a moral truth by which all cultures can be judged. Even if we were to accept that, however, there is a further problem here, an *epistemological* one. This is that, even if there is some determinate truth about some moral matter, how do we *know* what it is? Perhaps there *is* a truth about throwing Christians to the lions, as the moral realist says, and that truth is that it is a *good* thing to do. This shows a difficulty that the realist faces (in addition to those we have already discussed in this chapter), namely, that we can have no *guarantee* that our way of doing things is more responsive to the moral truth than the way of doing things prevalent in another culture. In fact, moral realists often seem to rely, implicitly, upon some notion of *moral progress* when discussing their theory. That is, they rely implicitly on the idea that human beings are gradually progressing towards uncovering *the* morally correct way of living. They are not alone in believing this, for it is an idea deep in modern liberal culture, that is, a culture that lays emphasis on (amongst other things) individual rights, freedoms and equality.

Enlightenment This belief in the moral progress of modernity has deep historical roots, roots in the Enlightenment. This was a movement in European thought and culture in the seventeenth and eighteenth centuries, which began in England and developed in France and Germany, though virtually every European country was affected.

The term 'Enlightenment' is meant to carry the idea that what was happening in European thought and life represented an emergence from the 'darkness' of the Middle Ages. One of the most famous statements of the Enlightenment outlook was formulated by Kant, who was himself one of the greatest of Enlightenment thinkers:

> *Enlightenment is the emergence of man from his self-imposed infancy. Infancy is the inability to think for oneself without the help of another. This infancy is self-imposed when the cause lies not in a lack of understanding but in a lack of resolve and courage to rely on oneself without the direction of another.* Sapere aude! *Have the courage to think for yourself! This is watchword of the Enlightenment.*　　　　　　　　　　　　　　　　　　　　　　　　(Kant 1998: 9)

Because the Enlightenment thinkers emphasised this requirement to think for oneself, they were hostile to the idea that, in religious and moral matters, one should accept the pronouncements of authorities, including the authorities of the Church and Bible. Many Enlightenment thinkers were thus atheists or deists, holding to a belief in a kind of 'scientific hypothesis God' who could be used to explain how the world can be understood scientifically but who otherwise had no dealings with the world, for example, through miracles or revelation.

Although there were, of course, deep differences between Enlightenment thinkers, a central idea of the Enlightenment was that reason was man's central capacity, and that it enables him not merely to think but to act correctly.

The Enlightenment belief in reason led many thinkers of the movement to be indifferent to local customs and practices, for they emphasised that what is important in human beings is what they have in common – that is, above all, reason – not what differentiates them in terms of cultural background. They also placed great emphasis on the notion of cultural and moral progress.

Belief in the moral progress of modern liberal culture

Central to this notion of progress was an emphasis on individual liberty and on the equality of all persons before the law. Enlightenment tended also to a belief in the fundamental goodness of man, which was seen as part of what enabled human beings to progress morally: such goodness could be tapped and channelled through education. The belief in such goodness was deeply shaken by the French Revolution, which ended in the so-called 'Terror', the liquidation of all those who were deemed to stand in the way of the achievement of the aims of the Revolution itself. Further, the experiences of the twentieth century, especially the Holocaust, have done much to undermine a sense of man's natural goodness. However, it is arguable that such events have helped to embed still further a notion of moral progress in the culture of the industrialised countries of Europe and elsewhere, because modern liberal culture sees itself as self-consciously repudiating the horrors of the twentieth century and as being in many ways closer to the moral truth now that slavery has been abolished, equal rights have been achieved by women, racism is rejected, war is no longer (generally) glorified and so on.

And there *is* good reason to believe that liberal culture represents moral progress when compared to previous cultures. After all, if we look at the catalogue of human history, there is little doubt that we are confronted with a vast spectacle of pointless and monstrous suffering and cruelty, a great deal of it inflicted on human beings by each other. There is little doubt that, for those of us lucky enough to be living in a liberal society, life is a great deal more humane than it was only a very short time ago. Indeed, human welfare is one of the moral notions that we emphasise very strongly, and is central to our sense that we have made moral progress.

Have we made moral progress?

However, there are reasons to doubt that we should be so sure that we have made progress. For one thing, it is probably true that pretty much every culture that has existed has considered itself in its moral outlook to be superior to most or all other dissimilar cultures, in which case the whole idea of moral progress might be argued to be nothing more than reflection of the old thought that human beings tend to prefer their own way of life. As Michel de Montaigne (1533–92) remarked:

> I find . . . that every man calls barbarous anything he is not accustomed to; it is indeed the case that we have no other criterion of truth or right-reason than the example and form of the opinions and customs of our own country. There we always find the perfect religion, the perfect polity, the most developed and perfect way of doing anything!   (Montaigne 1991: 231)

Montaigne was not, in fact, arguing for relativism, for he wrote this in the course of an essay pleading for tolerance in the face of the customs of those who were then being encountered in the New World for the first time by Europeans. He was, rather, emphasising the fact that we are, as I suggested earlier, in some way limited by our cultural horizons, however much we seek to be free of them. The belief that we have made moral progress may be an expression of that idea.

Christianity, liberalism and moral progress

Moreover, we are not simply heirs to the Enlightenment; we are also heirs of Christianity. Christianity said that all the suffering of this life would eventually be compensated by the beatific vision of God in an afterlife, in which 'God shall wipe away all tears' (Revelation 7: 17). There is within Christianity a teleology, that is, a belief that all is progressing towards a goal, namely, the goal of that vision. However, few in the West really believe this now, and our liberal moral thinking, emphasising, as it does, individual welfare, freedom and so on, has in many ways taken over this idea of teleology, seeing itself as the goal of history. Henry Staten has expressed the point eloquently.

> *Christianity attempted to recuperate the suffering of history by projecting a divine plan that assigns it a reason now and a recompense later, but liberalism is too humane to endorse this explanation. There is no explanation, only the brute fact. But the brute fact we are left with is even harder to stomach than the old explanation. So Left liberalism packages it in a new narrative, a moral narrative according to which all those lives ground up in the machine of history are assigned an intelligible role as victims of oppression and injustice. There is an implicit teleology in this view; modern Left liberalism is the telos [goal or aim] that gives form and meaning to the rest of history.*   (Staten 1990: 78)

Beyond this, however, even if it is true that we have made moral progress, it is certainly true that the emphasis we place on some values leads us to ignore or downplay other values that some have thought just as important. For example, many have thought that, in emphasising welfare, we are, as George Orwell (1903–50) put it, creating 'a civilization in which "progress" is . . . definable as making the world safe for little fat men' (Orwell 1987: 184). In other words, the charge is that we are becoming 'soft', concerned only with making our lives as comfortable as possible. We shall consider this theme a little more later.

Tolerance

One reason why people have been attracted to relativism is that they wish to promote *tolerance* towards the ways of life of other cultures. The idea is that, just because people live in a different way, this does not mean we should judge them to be morally mistaken or try to interfere with their life to change it. This issue has become particularly pressing in the modern world with our increasing realisation that European colonialism did a great deal to destroy much that was of immense value in indigenous cultures.

Relativism and tolerance

The connection between relativism and tolerance might be expressed in a short argument. This argument supports the notion of normative relativism, arguing that what is right or wrong, or good or bad, is relative to any given society. Then it claims that, this being so, it is wrong for members of any one society to condemn the way of life of another society. In other words, each society must tolerate the practices of each other society. Apart from the fact that this argument relies heavily on the idea, which we have already seen to be highly debatable, that each cultural grouping is more or less homogenous,

187

it is weak. The reason is that it claims that each group has its own moral standards and then relies on a non-relative, universal notion of tolerance to reach to its conclusion that groups ought to tolerate each other. Bernard Williams has called this form of relativism 'vulgar relativism' (Williams 1982: 34).

Political stability and tolerance

Modern liberal thought places great emphasis on tolerance. This tolerance grew out of fierce disputes and wars between Protestants and Catholics in the sixteenth and seventeenth centuries over freedom in religious practice and worship. When the attempt to impose a single religion failed, the assumption that a stable society needed agreement in religious matters was replaced by the belief that tolerance was the key to a stable polity. Hence, one of the arguments in favour of tolerance was – and is – that political stability ultimately depends on it, rather than on everyone's sharing the same religious views.

Tolerance is a political and moral virtue in liberal societies. It is, roughly speaking, the virtue of being able to live in a community with others who live in a way that one dislikes or judges to be inferior to one's own or downright bad (you cannot tolerate what you like or approve of). Liberal thought limits the exercise of tolerance to those situations in which individuals respect the rights of others: I do not have to tolerate your behaviour if it directly harms me. There is a great problem here concerning what counts as harm. If, for example, I detest the practice of certain sexual activities, I might believe that the sheer fact that some engage in such practices harms me. Most would regard this as intolerant, but it does reveal how difficult it is to say what counts as harm and what not. This is at least in part because what one counts as harm will depend on one's general moral outlook.

Locke's argument for toleration

We have already seen one argument in favour of tolerance, namely, that it promotes a stable society. The religious disputes that led to a reflection on the nature of, and need for, tolerance, led to a second argument in its favour, namely, that it is futile trying to impose or coerce genuine religious belief. The classic statement of this is to be found in *A Letter Concerning Toleration* by John Locke (1632–1704). Locke argues that it is simply pointless trying to get another to believe by coercion because a belief is not the kind of thing that one can simply choose to have. If I am unconvinced by some religious doctrine, then, however much I am coerced by another, I shall not come to believe it by being coerced, although I may well, of course, *say* I believe. In matters of religion, argues Locke, it is inner conviction that counts.

> *For no man can, if he would, conform his Faith to the Dictates of another. All the Life and Power of true Religion consists in the inward and full persuasion of the mind; and Faith is not Faith without believing. Whatever Profession we make, to whatever outward Worship we conform, if we are not fully satisfied in our own mind that the one is true, and the other unto God, such Profession and such Practice, far from being any furtherance, are indeed great Obstacles to our Salvation.*
>
> (Locke 1999: 143)

Tolerance and pluralism

Tolerance is usually connected with some kind of pluralism. Pluralism is the belief that there is no one single best way of living for human beings, that, in fact, there are many different good ways of living. Some support for this idea comes from the fact of the diversity of human beings. Stuart Hampshire has nicely expressed this in terms of the 'lop-sidedness' of all individuals (Hampshire 1989: ch.1, especially 27–8). What he means by this is that it is of the nature of the human animal that different individuals develop in different ways, with different tastes, outlooks, aspirations and so on. Someone who agrees with Hampshire on this will be inclined to place emphasis on the importance of tolerance in moral and political matters.

It may seem obvious that human beings are lop-sided in the way Hampshire suggests, but, in fact, it is very much a thought of the modern world. Prior to the growth of modern consciousness it was normally taken as read that there must be one true and good way for human beings to live. This is clear in ancient philosophy as well as in Christianity. Indeed, within limits the Enlightenment thought this also – witness Kant's claim to have discovered *the* correct theory about morality.

Tolerance and the fallibility of our beliefs

So far we have looked at three arguments for tolerance: one concerning the necessity of tolerance for political stability; another concerning the futility of trying to coerce genuine religious belief and a third having to do with the diversity of human beings. However, there are other arguments regarding tolerance. One of these concerns the fallibility of our own beliefs – that we are always prone to having false or partially false beliefs, especially concerning the things that matter most to us, like religion, ethics and politics. There are many reasons for this fallibility. One is that each of us is, inevitably, so limited and has so narrow a view on the world that it can seem absurd to claim more than temporary allegiance to any particular point of view. Life is so rich and confusing that an increase of experience of howsoever small a measure can, in a sensitive mind, have a massive impact on, and work great changes in, one's view on things. A second is that human thought is itself so fragile, halting and awkward that it seems foolish to think that one could arrive at anything definitive concerning moral, political and religious matters. Thirdly, it is clear that there are so many thinkers so much greater than oneself who have arrived at conclusions different from, sometimes opposed to, one's own, that it would appear to be foolhardy to suppose that one had alighted on the truth. Fourthly, it just is always possible to find arguments for opposing views on those questions that are of deep and lasting concern to human beings. Under such conditions, tolerance of others and their beliefs and way of life seems the only reasonable option.

Tolerance and individual autonomy

There is another important argument for tolerance. This concerns respect for individual autonomy and freedom of expression. Autonomy is understood in this context as being the ability of persons to make their own decisions and to control their lives without interference from others. There is no question that modern liberal societies value this highly. Roughly speaking, more traditional societies placed more emphasis of the wellbeing of the group as a whole.

Mill and respect for autonomy

A key defence in the history of philosophy of respect for autonomy is provided by J.S. Mill (1806–73) in *On Liberty*. Part of Mill's argument for the tolerance of individual autonomy, that is, tolerance of how others choose to go about their lives, is that, unless we are tolerant in this way, we shall be subject to the coercive power of public opinion. He argued that, unless we tolerated others' 'experiments in living', we would gradually find that conformism would crush all individuality and difference and we would be left living in a society in which genuine differences were frowned upon in such a way as to make them impossible. We shall return to such issues below.

Mill had a second related argument for tolerance, an argument to do with the importance of free expression and hearing others' views. He thought that it was only through vigorous debate that we could arrive at truth. He even suggested that, even where truth on some matter had been established, it was important to keep alive views that suggested that it was *not* the truth; only in this way could it be a *living* truth. As he says:

> [E]ven if a received opinion be not only true, but the whole truth; unless it is suffered to be, and actually is, vigorously and earnestly contested, it will, by most of those who receive it, be held in the manner of a prejudice, with little comprehension or feeling of its rational grounds. And not only this . . . the meaning of the doctrine itself will be in danger of being lost, or enfeebled, and deprived of its vital effect on the character and conduct. (Mill 1991: 59)

There is much in this that is right, but it does rely on the idea that in, say, ethics and religion there is such a thing as *the*, or *a,* truth. It is far from clear that this is so. Some of the reasons for this have been given in this chapter. In fact, it is no doubt true that Mill valued open-mindedness and tolerance for their own sake, as signs of a mature or well-developed mind, regardless of whether such dispositions help us find out the truth.

Mill's limits on toleration

In any case, Mill did not think that we should tolerate free expression in all cases. He distinguished the statement of a view from incitement, and said that the latter should not be tolerated. For example, we should tolerate a journalist writing an account of how a certain businessman is fleecing his customers. However if someone were to daub extracts from the journalist's article about the businessman's activities on placards and wave them in front of an angry mob outside the businessman's front door, this should not be tolerated, for that would amount to incitement to harm. Mill thought that we should be free to do as we wish just as long as we do not harm others. We have already seen that it is very difficult to say just how we should understand the concept of harm.

Nihilism and moral progress (again)

I have already referred to the claim that a problem many have seen in modern liberal society is that we are becoming 'soft', concerned for nothing but comfort and our own welfare. This thought is often accompanied by another idea, one that I have also already mentioned, namely, that a real danger in modern liberal society is that of conformism and reduction of all to the lowest common denominator – that is, to mediocrity.

The fear that we might be slipping towards such a condition is often understood as the fear of nihilism. For nihilism, on one central understanding, is precisely a condition in which, as existentialist thinkers sometimes put it, all has become *levelled*, and mediocrity is the dominant force in a society.

The disenchantment of the modern world

There are various ways of making this thought more precise, most of them having something to do with the decay of religious belief in modern society.

Max Weber (1864–1920), who is often seen as the founder of the discipline of sociology, famously said that the modern world was *disenchanted*. What he meant by this was that the modern age has lost a sense of the grand passions associated with, for example, religion, which has been reduced to a mere private hobby. As he put it, 'the ultimate and the most sublime values have retreated from public life' (Weber 1974: 155). He thought that we lived in an age of bureaucratic rationality, in which, as J.P. Stern put it, we are confronted by 'the atrophy of the heart and the dulling of the senses [because] conformism and commerce, the civil service and bourgeois taboos, have taken the place of heroism and adventure' (Stern 1971: 37). The following is a good description of Weber's view:

> *Weber . . . identifies bureaucracy with rationality, and the process of rationalization with mechanism, depersonalisation, and oppressive routine. Rationality, in this context, is seen as adverse to personal freedom . . . Weber . . . deplores the type of man that the mechanization and the routine of bureaucracy selects and forms. The narrowed professional, publicly certified and examined, and ready for tenure and career. His craving for security is balanced by his moderate ambitions and he is rewarded by the honor of official status. This type of man Weber deplored as a petty routine creature, lacking heroism, human spontaneity, and inventiveness.* (Gerth and Mills in Weber 1974: 50)

Weber was profoundly influenced by Nietzsche, and indeed Nietzsche gave decisive form to the very notion we have of nihilism.

'God is dead' Central to Nietzsche's work is the idea that, as he put it, 'God is dead', by which he meant, amongst other things, that in modern liberal societies most do not believe in God and most of those who say they do are fooling themselves, for they do not lead any kind of life that could be thought of a Christian. For example:

Friedrich Nietzsche
(1844–1900)

Nietzsche was born in 1844, the son of a Lutheran pastor who died when the boy was young. The young Nietzsche was brought up in the company of women – his younger sister, his mother, his grandmother and two aunts. He was educated at one of Germany's leading boarding schools, Schulpforta, receiving a brilliant classical education, and went on to study at the Universities of Bonn and Leipzig. He was made a professor at the University of Basel when only 25. Increasingly tormented by headaches, which were to plague him throughout his life, he eventually had to resign his chair on the grounds of ill health, thereafter living on a small university pension. He spent much of the rest of his life on the move in the south of France and northern Italy, searching for the kind of climate that could free him from his migraines and allow him to work. His early work was written very much under the influence of Schopenhauer (1788–1860), a deeply pessimistic philosopher, and Wagner (1813–83), the composer, with whom he had a deep friendship that ended bitterly. Among his most important works are *Beyond Good and Evil* (1886) and *The Genealogy of Morals* (1887). He went insane in 1889, probably from syphilis contracted from a prostitute whilst a student in Bonn. The intense intellectual pressure under which he lived also almost certainly contributed to his breakdown. He was looked after by his mother and sister, Elisabeth, for the last 11 years of his life. His sister, who was a fascist and deeply anti-Semitic and later became a friend of Hitler's, edited Nietzsche's work in such a way as to make it look as if he too were of such opinions. It is certain that he was not, but Elisabeth did much to damage Nietzsche's reputation.

Where has the last feeling of decency gone, of respect for oneself, when even our statesmen – otherwise thoroughly impartial and anti-Christians in their actions – still call themselves Christians and go to communion? . . . A young prince at the head of his regiments, resplendent in expressing the egoism and superiority of his people – but without any shame declaring his allegiance to Christianity! Whom does Christianity deny? what does it call 'world'? That one is a soldier, a judge, a patriot; that one defends oneself; that one values one's honour; that one wants one's advantage; that one is proud . . . Every action of every moment, every instinct, every value-judgement which issues in action today is anti-Christian: what sort of a monster of falsity must modern man nonetheless be to have no shame in being called a Christian!

(Nietzsche 1990: 160)

Nietzsche was hostile to Christianity at the best of times, but he believed that the decay of Christianity carried with it the possibility of a profound spiritual depression. This was because he thought that Christianity at least gave man a goal in life, and provided him with a sense of the pointfulness and meaning of existence. In the absence of this sense of the meaning of life, we were, he thought, in danger of finding everything pointless and absurd.

One of the things that struck Nietzsche most forcefully about this situation was that, even though Christianity had been decisively rejected by most and had no real meaning for the rest, we struggled hard to keep hold of a fundamentally Christian scheme of values. He thought this attempt was logically absurd, as the following passage brings out. (His comments are directed at the English, whom he especially disliked, but in reality they have much wider reference.)

They are rid of the Christian God and believe all the more that they have to hold fast to Christian morality: that is English consistency . . . In England one must rehabilitate oneself after every liberation from theology by showing in an awe-inspiring manner that one is a moral fanatic . . . It is different with us. When one gives up Christian belief one pulls away the right to Christian morality from under one's feet. This morality is simply not self-evident: one must make this point again and again . . . Christianity is a system, a complete and completely thought out view of things. If one breaks a central concept out of it – the belief in God – then one breaks the whole thing: one has nothing essential left in one's fingers. Christianity presupposes that man does not know, that man cannot know what is good and what evil: he believes in God who alone knows. Christian morality is a command; its origin is transcendent; it is beyond all criticism, all right to criticize; it is true only if God is the truth – it stands or falls with belief in God.

(Nietzsche 1990: 79–80)

'Life-denial' So Nietzsche thought, as I said, that it was logically absurd to seek to hold on to Christian values. He also thought that the attempt to do so was itself part of the nihilism of modern culture. He thought that the attempt to hang on to Christian morality without the religion was likely to lead us towards what he called 'life-denial'. He believed that the modern age was making a fetish out of virtues such as pity, sympathy, industriousness, disinterestedness, friendliness, humility, and the like. He certainly thought that we were often hypocritical in saying we believed in these things, but then he thought that that should give us all the more reason to seek for new forms of ethical under-

standing. In particular, he looked to the ancient world – to Greece and Rome – for inspiration, seeking in his work to explore the importance and meaning of such 'pagan' virtues as pride, desire for glory and worldly honour, magnificence, strength and nobility. Only in recovering these did Nietzsche think that we could avoid descending into nihilism.

Pagan virtues   If thinkers such as Weber and Nietzsche are right, then, the moral climate of modern life, should, at the very least, not be thought of as representing unqualified moral progress. And in truth, each way of life involves costs as well as benefits: there is no possibility that a way of life, whether that be an individual life or the life of a group, can do justice to all that we might find valuable. If the importance of Nietzsche is to be found nowhere else, it is to be found in the fact that he does not let us forget that thought.

review
activity

1. Explain in your own words the concepts of descriptive moral relativism, normative moral relativism, and meta-ethical relativism.

2. What arguments can one give for each form of relativism?

3. What arguments can one give in favour of tolerance?

4. What is nihilism and how is it connected to the decay of religious belief in modern culture?

some questions
to think about

1 'If there are no moral facts then one can think what one likes about moral issues.' How far is this true, and does it show that moral realism must be correct?

2 Do you agree with the claim that if I judge that I ought morally to perform some action then anyone else in the same situation ought to perform the same action?

3 'It's a waste of time trying to argue another person into accepting one's moral views. Either he agrees with one or he does not.' To what extent must a) emotivism and b) intuitionism make this claim?

4 To what extent do you agree with the claim of realism that Hume was just mistaken that one cannot see the virtue and vice in an action?

5 'If realism needs to abandon the belief-desire model of rational action then this shows that it must be mistaken.' To what extent would you agree with this?

6 'Moral relativism is a hopeless position because it does not take into account the moral diversity within different cultures.' Is this true?

7	Is there a danger that modern liberal society is too tolerant?
8	Do we live in an age of moral decay or progress?

further reading

▶ The most useful introduction to the debate between realism and irrealism is McNaughton 1996. McNaughton is deeply indebted to the writings of John McDowell and Jonathan Dancy, references to which can be found in his book.

▶ I have found Baier 1994 very useful in thinking about Hume's moral theory: it is clear and in many ways exciting.

▶ Winch 1972: ch.8 is a brilliant critique of the notion of the universalisability of moral judgements.

▶ On relativism and related topics I recommend the reader edited by Carson and Moser 2001. Levy 2002 is more basic, but useful. A classic early essay on relativism, from which I have quoted in the text, is Montaigne's 'On the Cannibals' in Montaigne 1991. On Roman gladiatorial games I recommend Auguet 1972, which is a fascinating read. On Balinese cock fighting see the classic and brilliant essay by Geertz 1993, ch.15. The Kwakiutl are discussed in Benedict 2001. On the Asmat see Schneebaum 1988. On nihilism, see Nietzsche 1968 and Goudsblom 1980.

philosophy
of religion

Religion, God and Religious Language

important terms

Indexical: an expression that picks out places, times, people etc. in terms of their temporal or spatial relations to the speaker.

Omnipotence: the property of being all-powerful.

Omniscience: the property of knowing everything.

Verification principle: the claim that a proposition has meaning if and only if it is in principle verifiable.

What is religion?

Key topics in this chapter

- The nature of religion
- The attributes of God
- The nature of religious language

Introduction

In one form or another religion has played a role in every human culture with which we are familiar. Some cultures have been *polytheistic* – for example, the Greeks and the Romans believed in many gods. It is typical in a polytheistic culture that the gods and goddesses are associated with specific activities or areas of human life, and this was certainly true of the Greek and Roman gods. Thus, for instance, the Greek goddess Demeter was, amongst other things, a corn goddess, and a patroness of agriculture in general, and Mars was the Roman god of war. Often in polytheistic religions there is a principal god, as Zeus was the principal Greek god and Jupiter the supreme god of the Romans. Some religions are *monotheistic*, such as Christianity, Judaism and Islam, all of which believe in one God. Yet other religions mix both polytheistic and monotheistic elements, as does Hinduism, for example, which has many gods that are seen as aspects of the supreme divinity. There are even some religions that do without a deity or deities at all. This is the case with some forms of Buddhism, for example, such as Theravada Buddhism. Philosophy always takes a greater or lesser interest in religious matters because religion has always been an important concern in human life and culture.

Religion is, of course, not simply a matter of believing in God or the gods. The different religions are connected with such things as religious practices, for example, ritual or sacrifice and worship; with distinctive moral outlooks or perspectives; with particular conceptions of the purpose of human life; with specific beliefs and claims about the nature of the material world; and so on. This means that it is hard to pin down what exactly religion is or to give an exhaustive list of all of religion's features. This is one reason why there can be disagreements about whether something is a religion at all. Some people, for example, have wanted to say that (Theravada) Buddhism is not a religion because it has no god, whereas others have argued that Marxism is a kind of religion since it gives a complete worldview by which to live. Still, it is, perhaps, possible to give some idea of the core aspects of religion, without in any sense trying to *define* what a religion is. In fact, Ninian Smart has described six aspects or dimensions of religion (Smart 1970: 15–25). These are:

1. *The ritual dimension.* Most if not all religions have special places or buildings, such a temples and churches, where ritual can take place. Such ritual often involves worship of God or the gods, prayer, and the making other offerings. Ritual can be extremely complex, as in, for example, the services of the Catholic or Orthodox Church, or it can be simple, as praying is. What ritual should always involve, however, is a particular way of behaving – an 'outer' dimension – which reflects particular thoughts, intentions or feelings – an 'inner' dimension. Sometimes the outer aspect of ritual can become simply mechanical or routine. This happens when the inner aspect goes dead on a person, no longer has meaning for him. Religious rituals very often accompany the most significant events of human life, such as birth, marriage and death.

2. *The mythological dimension.* To say that a religion has a mythological dimension or that it contains myths is to say that it contains stories or narratives which help to articulate its basic elements. Such stories might be those of the Greek gods, or of the Jewish people, or of Jesus. The stories may be true or false: to call them 'myths' is not to say that they are false.

3. *The doctrinal dimension.* A religion will often have a carefully worked out set of doctrines, which are intended to bring system, order and clarity into the religion. These doctrines make up a large part of the *theology* of the religion, and they seek to provide the religion with an intellectual credibility and authority that, for example, its myths may be thought to lack. Thus, for instance, at the beginning of the first book of the Old Testament, Genesis, there is provided a description of God's creation of the universe (in fact, there are two creation stories which run from Genesis 1: 1 to 2: 4 and from 2: 5 to 25). Christian theology and philosophy have long sought to articulate the meaning of this creation story in intellectual terms in order to understand it in a clear, coherent and intellectually satisfying way.

4. *The ethical dimension.* Most religions incorporate a system or code of morality or ethics that aims to regulate the behaviour of individuals and, to some extent, to provide a moral framework within which the society as a whole can function. This latter function can be very important when religions are institutionalised, as they usually are – that is, when they are built into the social structures of a community.

5. *The social dimension.* Religions are usually institutionalised so they can affect the community in important ways. This is not, however, the same as the ethical dimension. For one thing, a religion can have an effect on the community in non-ethical ways, for example, through the dissemination of doctrine. For another, a religion may seek to influence people in their moral behaviour and fail to be completely successful in this. Nonetheless, such an attempt on the part of the religion can have important social consequences. Thus, for instance, Christianity preaches love of one's neighbour, and probably there have been very few individuals in

Christian culture who have come anywhere near living in this way. Nevertheless, Christianity's preaching of this idea has had an extremely important impact on the social structures of cultures that consider themselves Christian.

6. *The experiential dimension.* Religions usually suppose that in some way it is possible for adherents to be able directly to experience God or the gods or some Ultimate Reality. Sometimes this experience is relatively simple and accessible to many believers, for example a sense of the presence of God through the beauty of nature. Sometimes the experience is fundamentally mystical, reserved to very few within the tradition. Moreover, there are many forms of religious experience between these two extremes. However, whatever form the experience takes, religions usually suppose that it is possible for some or all of their adherents to have some kind of experiential contact with the ultimate persons or objects of its devotion and belief.

review activity

State and explain Smart's six dimensions of religion.

Religion and philosophy

Philosophy of religion concerns itself to a greater or lesser extent with all of these six dimensions of religion together with specific issues and problems they raise. However, it will not be possible here to discuss all of them. Nor will it be possible to explore in equal depth those that *are* discussed. Rather, the focus here will be on those topics that are usually taken to lie at the centre of the discipline of philosophical reflection on religion and the nature of the religious life. Moreover, since the life of Jesus of Nazareth, who is believed by traditional Christians to be God incarnate, and the development of Christianity as a distinctive off-shoot from Judaism, the predominant concern of Western philosophy of religion has been with these topics in the context of Christianity. This concern will be reflected in the discussion of philosophy of religion in this book, and the main focus of concern will thus be on Christianity.

The nature of God As was mentioned earlier, Christianity is a monotheistic religion. According to one traditional view in Christianity, God is an eternal, immutable (unchanging) and transcendent person, who is perfectly good, the creator and sustainer of the universe, omnipresent, omnipotent (all powerful) and omniscient (all knowing). What does it mean to think of God in this way?

The attributes of God

Not all the attributes of God, as traditionally conceived, merit the same depth of discussion but all deserve at least some comment.

God as an omnipresent person, the sustainer of the universe

What are the criteria of personhood?

You are a person and so am I. However, the desk at which I am sitting is not a person. Nor are the trees outside. Nor is my pet cat. So what makes you and me persons? What is the property, or what are the properties, that you and I have which make both of us persons but which my desk, the trees and my pet cat do not possess? This is to ask: what are the *criteria of personhood?*

We must ask this question because, if it can be made clear what makes you and me persons, then we shall be better able to understand what it means to say that God is a person.

Many different philosophers have suggested different criteria of personhood. Inevitably, there are disagreements about just what they are. But the following are some of the principal criteria that have been offered by different philosophers.

Reason (rationality)

One concept that seems central in understanding the concept of a person is that of reason or rationality. This, for example, is something we find in the work of very many philosophers. For instance, in the work of Aristotle (384–322 BC) we find the claim made that the distinctive feature of human beings is their reason, and that it is a life which is controlled by reason that is the best kind of life (for example, Aristotle 1985: 1097b, 30f.). The emphasis upon rationality as the distinguishing mark of human beings finds, perhaps, its most significant articulation in the philosophy of Kant; for Kant, what it is to be a person is to be rational, and any being which is rational is, for Kant, a person, regardless of whether that being is a human being or not.

M- and P-predicates

P.F Strawson has drawn a distinction between what he calls 'M-predicates' and 'P-predicates' (Strawson 1984: ch.3, esp. 104ff.). The former are such predicates as: 'weighs 10 stone', 'consists largely of water'. The latter include: 'is smiling', 'is going for a walk', 'is in pain', 'is thinking hard', 'believes in God'. He says that some things can only have M-predicates attributed to them (for example, tables and mountains) whilst some things are such that both M- and P-predicates are applicable to them. Such things are persons. The intuitive idea is clear: persons are things that are *both* material objects *and* can have states of consciousness (and do things that can only be done by things which have states of consciousness). Thus, as I sit here writing this book, I have a certain height and weight, as does the bookcase to my right; but I also have states of consciousness, for example, thoughts about philosophy, a desire to have a short break from writing, a mild feeling of hunger, none of which a mere material object could have (the bookcase cannot have thoughts, desires or feelings).

Strawson's suggestion may be criticised on the ground that there are some beings to which both M- and P-predicates can be applied which are not persons: for example, monkeys, cats and dogs. Persons should, therefore, on

Strawson's account be thought of as a subclass of beings to which M- and P-predicates can be applied.

First- and second-order desires and second-order volitions

Consider the following case. You are on a diet but are tempted to eat a cream cake. You desire (want) the cream cake but you also want to lose weight. Your temptation would go away if you did not want to eat the cake. So, although you want to eat the cake, you would prefer it if you did not want to eat the cake. That is, although you want to eat the cake, you also want not to want to eat the cake. Following Harry Frankfurt, we can say that you have a *first-order desire* to eat the cake (you want to eat it) but you also have a *second-order desire*, that is, a desire *about* your desire to eat the cake. You desire (second-order) that your desire (first order) to eat the cake were not your desire (Frankfurt 1994: ch. 2).

Sometimes a second-order desire is a second-order volition. Frankfurt gives an example. A narcotics physician may want to know what it is like to desire the drugs his patients take. So, he desires to desire the drug. But he does not want actually to take the drug (for he does not want to become addicted). So, even though he has a second-order desire that he desire the drug, he does not want this desire to move him to action, for example, to move him to take the drug. However, another person might have a desire to want to take the drug, and want this desire to move him to action. In this case, the second-order desire is a second-order volition because the person in question desires that he have a desire and that this desire be his will. A second-order volition is, then, a second-order desire that one's first-order desire move one to action (be one's will).

Roughly speaking, Frankfurt argues that it is distinctive of persons that they have second-order volitions, whereas animals have only first-order desires. After all, a cat, for example, can certainly want to eat the food placed in front of it but it hardly seems to make sense to suppose that it could want not to want to eat the food or, indeed, that it could want this desire to move it to action.

Self-consciousness

Another quality that is often thought to be important for understanding the concept of a person is that of self-consciousness. A conscious being is aware of its surroundings, whereas a self-conscious being is aware of itself being aware of its surroundings. Many philosophers have thought this, and it is clearly part of Frankfurt's claims about desire. This is because if, for example, I want to want something, then I have to be aware of myself as wanting whatever it is I want, that is, I have to be conscious of myself – in other words, self-conscious.

Language

Many recent philosophers have thought that it is a distinctive mark of person-hood to possess language. Indeed, once again, Frankfurt's claims seem to support such an idea. The reason for this is that possessing second-order desires involves one taking up a stance towards oneself, asking oneself what one really wants and the like. It is very hard to make sense of an inner life of this kind of complexity without language. This is because, as Daniel C. Dennett has put it in a discussion of Frankfurt's views, an inner life of this kind of complexity seems to involve being engaged in a *dialogue* with oneself (Dennett 1986: 285).

Another way in which we might be able to see the connection between possessing language and being a person is to note some of the ways in which a creature's mental life is expanded by possessing language. Roger Scruton (Scruton 1996: 24–7) has suggested that possession of language allows a creature to:

- express thoughts about the past and future, about generalities, probabilities and possibilities;
- construct abstract arguments;
- engage in social relations involving dialogue and conversation; and
- experience emotions it would not otherwise feel, such as esteem, because these involve complex thoughts, for example that someone is worthy of admiration.

A person is, one might argue, a creature that can do all of these. If possession of language is necessary to do these, then possession of language is necessary for being a person.

Moral judgement

Many philosophers have thought that the capacity to engage in moral life, make moral judgements, discuss moral matters, be held morally responsible for one's actions and the like is part of the concept of personhood.

Persons as natural kind

Finally, we should note that in an important but difficult paper, David Wiggins has argued that persons are a natural kind (Wiggins 1969). That is, he has suggested that a person is a certain kind of *animal* that has certain kinds of capacities. In his words:

> *x is a person if x is an animal falling under the extension of some natural kind whose members perceive, feel, remember, imagine, desire, make projects, move themselves at will and carry out projects, acquire a character as they age, are susceptible to concern for members of their own kind or like species . . . conceive of themselves as perceiving, feeling, remembering etc . . . have, and conceive of themselves as having, a past accessible in experience-memory and a future accessible in intention . . . and so on.* (Wiggins 1969: 161)

Different philosophers disagree with one another about the relative importance of the criteria of personhood just discussed. Some might even deny that certain of them are necessary properties of a person. For example, some philosophers would deny that it is necessary to be able to make moral judgements to be a person. Nonetheless, most philosophers would agree that something like the list of criteria offered is correct.

1. What is the difference between M- and P-predicates? Give some examples of both types of predicates.

2. Explain the notions of first- and second-order desires, and the notion of a second-order volition. Provide an example of each from your own experience or from that of another person (for example, a character in a novel).

3. What is the difference between a being that is conscious and one that is self-conscious?

4. What kinds of capacities might a creature have that possesses language which are not possessed by a creature that lacks language?

The concept of a person is, then extremely complex. How does all this relate to God if he is thought of as being a person?

God's rationality

There should be no problem in supposing God to be rational, though his rationality will differ in many ways from ours. Human reason works in a variety of ways. Very often, we have evidence before us from which we are able to draw specific conclusions. On a traditional picture, God's reason cannot work this way since he has no need to draw conclusions: he knows all there is to know (he is omniscient) and knows it directly. His knowledge is a kind of complete self-awareness that never leaves him (cf. Hughes 1998: 87). And we see in this way that God is self-conscious.

God is not an animal

Clearly, if God is a person then it cannot be right to think of him as an animal, a member of a natural kind, as Wiggins supposes persons to be. Nor, and relatedly, can it be right to apply M-predicates to him: he must be a person to whom only P-predicates apply, because he is a bodiless person.

Does God have desires?

If this is right then God has, for example, desires. This fits with much that believers want to say about God, for example, that God wants us freely to love him. However, God's desires must be unlike ours in many ways. For instance, when our desires go unsatisfied we are often frustrated but it surely cannot be right to think of God as frustrated in this way. Further, and connectedly, granted that God has desires, it seems hard to make sense of his having first- and second-order desires or second-order volitions *à la* Frankfurt unless we suppose that, even though he has such desires and volitions, they can never give rise to conflict within him. Yet clearly – as the cream cake example showed – part of the point of introducing the notion of first- and second-order desires to explain human motivation in the first place was to explain something about the nature of inner conflict for a human being. It is thus unclear what the purpose of speaking of them in connection with God would be.

God is a transcendent being

In fact, the whole idea of ascribing desires to God involves difficulties, because to have a desire is to *lack* something, and on most accounts of God it does not make sense to think of God as lacking anything because God is taken to be perfect. Moreover, if one has a desire and then this desire is satisfied, one has changed. However, God, if he is immutable, cannot change. Similar problems arise when speaking of God as having emotions: could God feel sad, for example? This seems unlikely, because it again suggests a lack in God, which is contrary to the traditional understanding of his nature. One problem here is that when we speak of God's desiring something or feeling something we are confronted by the difficulty of using human language. We learn this language in the context of mundane (earthly) realities, but then wish to use it to speak of a *transcendent* being, that is, a being beyond nature. Perhaps we should say that to speak of God as desiring and feeling emotions is merely to use metaphors. Or perhaps there is some other way in which we can make sense of talk of God. In any case, we shall return later to problems concerning religion language.

God, language and morality

So far as language and morality are concerned, we are faced with similar problems. Both are social phenomena, learned in conjunction with others in a social world of give and take. We cannot think, however, that God learns (or has learned) a language or that he has learnt the capacity to make moral judgements (cf. Holland 1980: 239). Perhaps he just has language and a moral nature. However, it is far from clear how.

review
activity

What difficulties are there in supposing God to be a person?

God as an omnipresent person

God is often understood to be, not simply a person, but an omnipresent person. Clearly, if God is omnipresent then he has no body, that is, he is a spirit, a bodiless person. What does this mean?

What does it mean for a person to have a body?

Richard Swinburne approaches this question by considering what it means for a body to be a given person's body (Swinburne 1993: 104–6). He suggests that in the case of a person who is a human being and thus has a body, this means that:

i)   disturbances in his body cause pains, aches etc. in him;
ii) he can feel the inside of his body, e.g., when he is hungry;
iii) he can move directly parts of the body;
iv) he looks out on the world from where the body is; and
v)   his thoughts and feelings are affected non-rationally by goings-on in this body, e.g., getting alcohol into his body makes him see double (or whatever).

If this is right about what it is to have a body, it helps us to become clear on what it means to say that God is bodiless.

God's limited embodiment

Clearly, God is not embodied in the sense of i) ii) or v). However, God can, Swinburne says, directly move any part of the universe, and this is analogous to iii). Further, although God does not look out on the world from a specific body, he nonetheless knows directly about every state of the universe in something like the way a human person can know much about, for example, the state of room in which he is sitting. Nonetheless, God knows about the universe, of course, without needing to open his eyes (he *has* no eyes), whereas a human being does need to open his eyes to look at the room he is in. In addition, God's knowledge of the universe is complete, whereas that of a human being of the room he is in is limited – for example he might know there is a cupboard in the room by opening his eyes, but it does not follow that he knows what is in the cupboard. Still, there is some kind of analogy to iv) in the case of God. This, says Swinburne, gives God a very limited embodiment. However, God does not need the universe for him to exist, even though he has the limited embodiment to which Swinburne refers: God's embodiment is in that sense wholly dispensable.

review
activity

1. Explain what might be meant by saying that a body is a particular person's body.

2. In what way might God have a limited embodiment, given that the universe exists?

The idea that God controls all things directly and knows about all things is what is meant by God's omnipresence. How should we understand this notion of God's omnipresence?

God as sustainer of the universe

According to St Thomas Aquinas – who is usually referred to as Aquinas or simply as Thomas – God is best understood simply as *He who is*. This is because God is infinite existence or *being itself*. God is present in everything by *sustaining everything in existence:* were he to withdraw his sustaining power from anything, that thing would cease to exist.

God fills everything

So, according to Thomas, God is everywhere, i.e., in every place and thing, first, by making everything what it is; and secondly, by *filling* everything, that is, by giving existence to that thing.

Moreover, God is wholly in whatever he is in, in the way the soul is wholly in every part of the body: every part of a human being is, for example, animated by that human being's soul.

St Thomas Aquinas (1225–74)

St Thomas Aquinas, who is the quasi-official philosopher of the Catholic Church, is regarded by many as one of the greatest of philosophers. He was born in the country we now know as Italy in around 1225, and was sent in 1230 or 1231 to the Benedictine abbey of Monte Cassino, where he lived and studied for about eight years. Later he studied at the University of Naples where he was introduced to the work of Aristotle (384–322 BC). At some time between 1242 and 1244 he joined the Dominicans, amongst other reasons because he was attracted by their ideals of poverty, preaching and teaching. After a period in Cologne, where he was probably ordained to the priesthood, he moved to Paris as a teacher of theology and philosophy, and started writing the works for which he is best known today. He taught in Paris until some time before 1260, spent some time in Orvieto and Rome, and then returned to Paris in 1268. He left Paris again in 1272, going to Naples. He died in 1274.

One of the aims of Thomas's work was to reconcile the pre-Christian philosophy of Aristotle with a Christian view of the world. The greatest of his works that attempts this task – but not by a long way only this task – is the *Summa Theologiae*, a vast work on a multitude of topics. All his work shows a keen sense of man's relation to God, but even for those with no religious belief there is a huge amount to be learned from his thinking.

activity

Explain what Thomas means by the omnipresence of God.

It is important to note, before we move on, that not all thinkers who have defended belief in God have believed God to be a person, and later I shall discuss or draw attention to thinkers who have denied that God is a person.

God as creator of the universe

Traditionally, God has been thought of as the creator of the universe, and the Bible opens in Genesis with God's creation of the universe. There are very many ways in which to understand this creation.

Plotinus on God's creative activity

Some Christian thinkers, for example Plotinus (204/5–270), have believed that God's creation of the universe was a kind of spontaneous overflowing of the fullness and superabundance of his being. This involves no divine decision to create. Rather, it is a kind of unconscious and inevitable pouring forth, in the kind of way that light pours forth from the sun.

Thomas on God's creation of the universe

Other Christian thinkers, such as Thomas, have believed that God made a choice to create the universe. As Thomas believed that God was immutable, he thus thought that the only way of safeguarding God's free choice to create was to suppose him to have chosen eternally to create. However, it would be wrong to suppose that, for Thomas, God could not help but create, for this would suggest that something or other was forcing God's nature. As God is the creator of all, there can be nothing that stands over against God, forcing him to create. Moreover, for Thomas, God does not need creatures: God is essentially what he is quite apart from anything he produces.

In any case, to call God 'creator' is to think that he is the source of the being of all that is. It is because of God's creative actions that there is anything rather than nothing: God is the cause of all that is. Each thing is what it is and as it is because God has created it in that way, including, of course, human beings.

God's goodness

God is always thought of within Christian thought as perfectly or wholly good. But how should we understand this goodness?

Is God morally good?

Many have seen this goodness as moral goodness, which is why God is often thought of as benevolent. However, there is something odd in looking at God's goodness in this way. For, apart from the fact that it hardly seems right to say that God could be morally well behaved, there is the further problem that a being can only be a moral being if it is a member of a community: morality, whatever else it is, depends on learning and growth within a community of moral agents, and God is not a member of such a community. This means that God cannot have moral reasons for doing what he does. Nor can he be assessed in moral terms: one cannot pass a moral judgement on God without committing blasphemy, yet if he were a moral being one certainly *could* pass moral judgement on him. So, one cannot think that God is not virtuous enough, or has not fulfilled his obligations, without insulting God.

If God's goodness is not moral goodness, what is it? What does it mean to say that God is good?

Thomas's account of God's goodness

Thomas, who would have thought it absurd to suggest that God's goodness consisted in his being morally good, says that the goodness of things is what God has brought about. Further, he believes this goodness of things shows us that God is good. But what does the goodness of things consist in? If you want a good carpenter, then what this means is that you are looking for a carpenter who is desirable, that is one who can do the job well. So Thomas says that what it means to say that God is good is to say that he is desirable. But God is not desirable as a kind. That is, God is not a good such and such. If you are told that Wallace is a good plumber then you know what to expect of him in his capacity as plumber. If you are told that Roland is a good farmer, you know the sorts of things to expect from him in his capacity as a farmer. Or if you are told that this is a good watch, you know what kind of thing it does (tells the time accurately, can be easily carried around and the like). However, as God is not a good thing of a kind, to say that he is good is not to expect any particular thing when it comes to God. God, who is good, is more like a light in which one lives than a thing one wants *for* something or other. However, in searching for what is good for one, one is, in fact, searching for what exists firstly or most fully in God.

Omnipotence

Traditionally, God has been thought of as omnipotent, that is, as all-powerful. (The word derives from the Latin *omnipotens*.) The Bible refers to God in this way. Thus, at Matthew 19: 26 Jesus says that 'with God all things are possible'. And in the Old Testament, at Jeremiah 32: 17, we read: 'Ah Lord GOD! behold, thou hast made the heaven and the earth by thy great power and stretched out arm, *and* there is nothing too hard for thee.' At Jeremiah 32: 27 we find: 'Behold, I *am* the LORD, the God of all flesh: is there any thing too hard for me?' So, God is omnipotent. How are we to understand this?

One possibility is the following (using X to stand for any possible being):

1)   X is omnipotent = X can do everything he wants to do.

So, if God is omnipotent, this means he can do everything he wants to do. Thomas discusses this view (Aquinas 1998: 248). He rejects this notion of omnipotence on two grounds: first, those who are dead and enjoying heavenly bliss can do everything they want, but they are not omnipotent; secondly, wise men and women in this life limit their desires to what they are capable of doing, yet this does not make them omnipotent. So Thomas says that 1) is an inadequate account of omnipotence.

We could try a different tack altogether in attempting to explain the notion of omnipotence.

2)   X is omnipotent = X can do everything.

Then we can say: God is omnipotent because he can do everything.

There are problems, however, with this account of omnipotence. The principal difficulty is that it seems unlikely that even God could do the logically impossible – for example, make a square circle or a spherical cube; or make $1 + 2 = 4$; or make it not true that the three angles of a triangle equal two right angles; or make contradictories true, for example, make it both true and false that the world exists. The most significant philosopher who seems to have thought otherwise and to have believed that God could do literally everything is René Descartes (1596–1650). It seems that Descartes thought that even if *we* cannot understand how there could be a spherical cube, this is simply a limitation on our minds and says nothing about the limits of God's powers. Descartes seems to have thought that it would be blasphemous to think of God as lacking infinite power, a mere presumption on our part since we should be supposing that our inability to understand something (for example, how there could be a spherical cube) put limits on God's power. However, I say 'seems' because it is possible that Descartes did not, after all, really think that God could do literally everything: a lot depends here on how one interprets his comments on this issue (cf. Wilson 1986: 121ff.). If God could do everything then, apart from the odd things already mentioned, he could, for example, make it the case that he himself both exists and does not exist. And one can hardly make sense of that: it simply seems an absurdity. In any case, however one interprets Descartes, most philosophers find absurd the idea that God's power is completely limitless and that he can do the logically impossible. It seems absurd to them to suggest that it is really a restriction on God's omnipotence that he cannot do the logically impossible because the idea of doing such a thing makes no sense at all. Consequently, they have sought a different, weaker conception of God's omnipotence.

Here is one possibility:

3)   X is omnipotent = X can do anything logically possible.

So, if God is omnipotent, this is because he can do everything logically possible.

Is it logically possible to bring about the past?

An interesting question here, which has been discussed with great subtlety by Michael Dummett, is whether it is logically possible to *bring about* the past, that is, whether, by doing something *now*, we can bring something about in the past (Dummett 1993). This is not the same as asking whether we can change the past, for this really is logically impossible. For example, if my son has been drowned at sea, then there is nothing I can do to change that. However, says Dummett, suppose I hear on the radio that the ship my son was on sank at sea two hours ago and that there were few survivors. Dummett argues that it makes sense to pray that he should not have drowned. That is, it makes sense to pray to God now that, at the time of the disaster, God should then have made my son not to drown at that time.

Dummett recognises that this looks absurd but he says that it is just like praying for some event in the future. Suppose my son is setting out on a ship to cross the Atlantic. Then I might pray that he will arrive safely. This, says Dummett, is not a prayer that God will bring about the logically impossible, that is, make what will happen not happen. It is simply a prayer that it will not happen. That is, it is a prayer that God will at the future time make something not to happen at that time. And there is no logical absurdity in that.

If Dummett is right, then God can bring about the past because it is logically possible to bring about the past, and the version of omnipotence we are considering is that God can do anything logically possible. Needless to say, Dummett's view is open to dispute (cf. Kenny 1979: 103–9; cf. also Geach 1994: ch.7, esp. 89–91).

Logically possible actions God cannot perform

Still, leaving aside the issue of whether God can bring about the past, there seem to be some feats that it is logically possible to do but which God cannot do. For example, it is certainly logically possible to make a table God did not make – I can, for example. However, God cannot make a table God did not make. Moreover, it is logically possible to cough or to die, yet God surely cannot do these things. And it is logically possible to change, yet God is normally thought of as being immutable – as being unchanging.

Moreover, there is another problem in the present definition of omnipotence. This is the following, known as 'the paradox of the stone'. It is clearly possible for a human being to make a stone or some other object that is too heavy for that human being to lift. But can God do this? That is, can God make a stone too heavy for him to lift (or make rise)? If he can, then there is something he cannot do, namely, lift the stone. If he cannot, well, then, he cannot. Either way, he seems not be omnipotent. So it seems that God cannot be omnipotent in the sense proposed in 3).

Various solutions to this problem have been suggested. George I. Mavrodes has argued (Mavrodes 1996) that we can draw a parallel between the two following descriptions of an action: a) 'X is able to draw a square circle' and b) 'X is able to make a thing too heavy for X to lift'. We have seen that it is no limitation on God's power that he cannot do something that is logically impossible such as that indicated in a). At first blush, b) does not look like a) and, when applied to a human being, this is so: no human being can draw a square circle, but plenty of human beings could make something too heavy for them to lift. However, Mavrodes argues that, *when applied to God,* b), like a), involves a self-contradiction – it is logically impossible. If he is right, then it is no limitation on God's power that he cannot do b).

Mavrodes's argument is as follows. God is either omnipotent or he is not. Let us suppose that he is not omnipotent. In this case, he clearly cannot make a stone too heavy for him to lift. But then we can say that he is not omnipotent. Of course, it must be granted that this was the assumption with which we started, so the argument is trivial. Nevertheless, the argument does nothing to *establish* that God is not omnipotent in the sense under discussion.

We must begin by assuming that God is omnipotent. If we assume this, can we avoid the problems the paradox generates? Mavrodes thinks we can. He says that, assuming God to be omnipotent, the phrase: 'a stone too heavy for God to lift' is self-contradictory for it becomes: 'a stone which cannot be lifted by him whose power is sufficient for lifting anything'. This, says Mavrodes, is self-contradictory, and thus, the fact that God cannot lift such a stone no more tells against or limits his omnipotence than his inability to draw a square circle does.

Richard Swinburne has argued that Mavrodes's solution is no solution at all (Swinburne 1993: 158). He thinks it begs the question. After all, the point of the problem of the stone is to show that the concept of omnipotence (on understanding 3)) is incoherent: it cannot be shown to be coherent by assuming that God is omnipotent, for this just begs the question concerning whether or not it makes sense to suppose he is.

Swinburne considers another solution (Swinburne 1993: 158–60). According to this proposed solution, the proposition: 'X cannot create a stone which X cannot lift' means (that is, is logically equivalent to) 'If X can create a stone, then X can lift it'. And, it is claimed, this latter statement does not entail that God is limited in power.

Swinburne rejects this solution (cf. also Geach 1982: 53-4). He says that the statement 'If X can create a stone, then X can lift it' says that X cannot give to any stone that he creates the power to resist subsequent lifting by X. So, says Swinburne, there is a task X cannot perform: 'to make a stone to which he gives the power to resist subsequent lifting by himself' (Swinburne 1993: 159). If Swinburne is right, this shows a limitation on God's power and thus does not remove the paradox of the stone.

Swinburne's own favoured solution is to grant that God could create a stone that he could not lift, and to say that, if God did create such a stone, he would no longer be omnipotent. However, he says this does not *now* impugn God's omnipotence since the 'fact that God can abandon his omnipotence does not entail that he will' (Swinburne 1993: 162).

Another response to the paradox of the stone is to claim that there is no coherent notion of omnipotence and that we should abandon the idea that God is omnipotent. Peter Geach suggests this (Geach 1982: 46). Instead of God's being omnipotent, we should, Geach says, think of God as almighty and understand God's being almighty, not as the power to do everything, but as possessing power *over* everything. Moreover, he says that the notion of God's being almighty is adequate for 'anything like traditional Christian belief in God'.

Anthony Kenny has suggested that there is, however, a better account of omnipotence available, one that avoids the paradox of the stone (Kenny 1979: 96ff.). He suggests that, instead of focusing on the *deeds an omnipotent being can do,* we should concentrate on the *powers such a being possesses.* According to Kenny, we could try this account of omnipotence:

4) a being is omnipotent if it has every power which it is logically possible to possess.

So, on this understanding of omnipotence, to say that God is omnipotent is to say that he possesses all logically possible powers (and it is *not* to say that he possesses the power to do all logically possible actions).

As Kenny makes clear, 4) will still not quite do because it is a logically possible power to change, to cough, to die, to make a table God did not make and to make an object too heavy for one to lift. We can, however, formulate a weaker form of 4) to arrive at another account of omnipotence:

5) God's omnipotence consists in his possessing all powers that it is logically possible for a being with his attributes as God to possess.

This account of omnipotence does avoid the problems just adumbrated. This can be seen as follows.

The power to change is not a logically possible power for God, since God is immutable.

The power to cough or to die are not logically possible powers for God, since these are only powers that could be possessed by a corporeal (physical or material) creature and a mortal creature. However, God is neither corporeal nor mortal.

The power to make a table one did not make is not a logically possible power for *any* person. It therefore follows that, if that person is God, then it is not a logically possible power for God to have.

The power to create a stone too heavy for him to lift is not a logically possible power for God to possess. This is because it belongs to God's nature to be immutable, and if he were, *per impossibile*, to create such a stone he would have lost his omnipotence (as Swinburne pointed out) and thus would have changed. So, the possession of such a power by an omnipotent being is not logically possible because the description of that power contains, for such a being, a hidden contradiction.

Note that Kenny's solution seems to bear some relation to the one proposed by Mavrodes. However, there is a difference between the two, since Kenny's relies on God's possessing attributes other than omnipotence, whereas that of Mavrodes does not.

review
activity

1. If God can do anything he wants, does this make him omnipotent?
2. What are the objections to saying that God can do anything logically possible?
3. What is the paradox of the stone?
4. State two suggested solutions to the paradox of the stone and the rejoinders that may be given to these suggested solutions.
5. What is the main difference between Kenny's approach to the issue of God's omnipotence and the others discussed?
6. Explain how Kenny's account of omnipotence overcomes the paradox of the stone.

Omniscience

Just as there are difficulties in understanding the notion of God's omnipotence, there are also problems in understanding the notion of his omniscience.

An omniscient being, one might suppose, is one who knows all propositions. However, this is already mistaken, for one cannot know a false proposition.

So we should try saying that an omniscient being is one who knows all true propositions (cf. Hoffman and Rosenkrantz 2002: 112).

Knowledge through the senses

There are difficulties, however, even for this account of omniscience. One of these is that among the true propositions about the world are those concerning empirical facts, for example, that my table is brown, or that this sugar is sweet, or that the light is bright. I can know these sorts of things because I have five senses – eyes, ears, nose, mouth and a body with which I can feel things. However, God does not have senses, so can he know that my table is brown or that the sugar is sweet or the light is bright?

The traditional answer is that he can, but in a way other than that by which I know. What I know through the senses, God knows intellectually, that is, without using any sense or having any sense experience (cf. Kenny 1979: 30). Clearly if this is correct it nonetheless follows that there is some kind of difference between what I know and what God knows in knowing that the sugar is sweet. When I taste the sugar at least two things are happening: i) I am experiencing a sensation; and ii) I am gathering some information about the sugar (namely, that it is sweet). However, in the case of God the first of these must be lacking: God does not have any sensation of the sugar.

Sensations and pleasure and pain

How are we to understand the difference between having a sensation of some object (something that only those with senses can have) and having information about the object (something that both those with senses and God, who knows only intellectually, can have)? Following Aristotle, Anthony Kenny has suggested that the difference lies in the fact that pleasure and pain are attendant on sensations. For example, when I taste the sugar I get some pleasure from the taste of it, whereas God, in knowing that the sugar is sweet, does not have this pleasure. Of course, not all sensations are pleasurable or painful, but, as Kenny says, 'a sense is essentially a faculty for acquiring information in a modality which admits of pleasure and pain' (Kenny 1979: 32). So, God knows what we know when we experience the world through the senses, but he knows this intellectually and without any pleasure or pain.

There are further complications, however. Consider Jones, who is lying in the hospital. Jones is an amnesia case – he has lost his memory. He knows he is in hospital, but what he does not know is that Jones is in hospital, for he has lost his memory and does not know that he is Jones. Other people can know that Jones is in hospital, but it seems that they cannot know what Jones knows. This is because what Jones knows is 'I am in hospital', and no one but Jones can know *that*. So, Jones, who is not omniscient, seems to know something that God does not know.

Indexicals

The reason for the difficulty is that a word like 'I' is what philosophers call an *indexical*. Indexicals are expressions that pick out places, times, people and so forth in terms of their temporal or spatial relations to the speaker. Examples include: 'I', 'now', 'you', 'yesterday', 'tomorrow' and so on. When Jones knows 'I am in hospital' he knows something different from what God (or anyone else) knows in knowing the proposition 'Jones is in hospital': the use of the indexical expressions makes all the difference here.

It may be argued that the problem can be solved by suggesting that, when

Jones knows he is in hospital and when God knows that Jones is in hospital, they know the same thing – it is just that the same piece of knowledge is being expressed in a different way. Richard Swinburne, however, has argued that this response is not adequate (Swinburne 1993: 170ff.). He has suggested that when we think of some individual person, object or whatever, the thing thought about is presented to the thinker in a particular 'mode'. For example, I may think of some individual as having certain specific properties, or as being related to me in some way, for instance, as the person to whom I am speaking. Others can *describe* what I know when the world appears to me in a certain way, but it does not follow from this that they can *have* the knowledge I have unless the world presents itself to them in the same way. Jones, lying in the hospital, knows 'I am in the hospital'; God knows 'Jones is in the hospital'. In each case something different is known because the 'mode of presentation' is different.

Moreover, there are difficulties in this area concerning indexicals to do with time. Consider the following question: Can God know the date and time? The difficulty arises because, as we know, God has usually been thought of as immutable. But if God knows today that it is, say, Friday and tomorrow will know that it is Saturday, it seems that he is subject to change, for he knows one thing today and he will know a different thing tomorrow.

One proposed solution to the problem is the following. We could say that God's knowledge of the date and time is not knowledge which is expressed in propositions. For if he *did* express this knowledge in propositions he would change, thinking, for example, 'It is now 7.50 p.m.', then 'It is now 7.51 p.m.'. But if he does not express his knowledge in propositions, then he can know permanently and unchangingly what, because we are temporal changing beings, we know first in one proposition and then in another. There is no special difficulty about having knowledge that is not expressed in propositions: most of our knowledge is not, and animals have knowledge that they could not express as propositions since they have no language.

As we have seen, this solution involves the idea that God can know eternally and unchangingly what we know in time. However, there is a difficulty in this. The problem is that it can make a very great difference from which point in time one knows the date and time, and if that is so then God cannot know what we know when we know the date and time. For example, suppose it is Friday and I utter 'today is Friday'. On Saturday I utter 'yesterday was Friday'. Do my two propositions express the same thing? Kenny has argued that they do not:

> [W]hat I am glad about when I am glad that today is Friday is not at all necessarily the same thing as what I am glad about when I am glad yesterday was Friday. Perhaps Friday is payday, on which I always go out for a massive carouse with my friends: when it is Friday, I am glad today is Friday, but during Saturday's hangover I am not at all glad that yesterday was Friday.
>
> (Kenny 1979: 46–7)

We seem, then, to be faced with a choice: either we say that God is immutable and does not know dates and times – in other words, is not omniscient in the sense of knowing all true propositions; or we say that he is omniscient and mutable. And the reason why God does not know dates and times (unless he is mutable) is actually analogous to the reason why God does not know what Jones knows when Jones is lying in hospital. In each case the world presents itself to the knower in a way to which God does not have access.

review
activity

1. If God has no organs of sense, how can he know what I know in knowing the sugar is sweet?

2. What is the difference between my knowing that the sugar is sweet and God's knowing this?

3. If Jones is lying in the hospital, what does God not know that Jones knows?

4. How might it be said that God knows eternally and unchangingly what we know as temporal changing beings?

5. If God is immutable, why might it be said that his omniscience must be somewhat restricted?

Omniscience and free will

However, there is further, and more pressing, problem concerning God's omniscience. This is that there seems to be an incompatibility between God's omniscience and human free will. The problem, schematically put, is this.

If God is omniscient then he foreknows all future human actions. If God fore-knows anything, then it will necessarily come to pass. However, if a human action will necessarily come to pass, then it cannot be free.

So, either God is not omniscient; or human beings are not free.

God as timeless   One response here, suggested by Thomas, would be to deny that, strictly speaking, God foreknows anything. This could be done by saying that God's eternality is to be understood as timelessness. Then God, being outside time, could not then *fore*know anything at all. Then it could be said that what we see as events in the past, present or future, God sees in an eternal present. However, a problem with this approach is that it makes all events simulta-neous for God, and it is far from clear how we are to make sense of the idea that, for example, as I type these words, the Second World War is being conducted, the Black Death is sweeping over Europe, the Roman armies are invading Britain and Plato is philosophising in Athens. Indeed, the very idea that all this is going on at the same time seems incoherent (cf. Kenny 1979: 38–9; 54).

A different solution suggested by Thomas has been clearly and helpfully discussed by Kenny (Kenny 1970b). This solution proceeds by way of offering an analysis of the proposition: 'Whatever is known by God must be'. He said that this proposition could be analysed in two ways. It could mean either:

a) 'Whatever is known by God is true' is a necessary truth;

or:

b) Whatever is known by God is a necessary truth.

Now, a) is true, but does not show that acts foreseen by God are not free. It just means: 'Necessarily, if God foreknows anything, it will come to pass'. In fact, the same proposition can apply to anyone, for all it is saying is that you can only foreknow something if it is true. For example, if it is true that I shall lie tomorrow, then I shall lie tomorrow, and you can only know now that I shall lie tomorrow if I do lie tomorrow. But I am free to lie tomorrow or not, as I wish.

On the other hand, b) does rule out free will, for it says: 'If God foreknows anything, it will necessarily come to pass' – in other words, if God foreknows anything then it *must* happen. Thomas then argues that all that is necessary for God's omniscience is a) and thus that such omniscience is compatible with human freedom.

Richard Swinburne has argued, however, that the real problem so far as divine omniscience and human freedom goes lies elsewhere. He argues as follows (Swinburne 1993: 174ff.). If God knows some proposition then he believes that proposition. Now, suppose at time t God believes that person P will do x at time t_1. Then, if P is free, he has it in his power to make what God believes at t true or false by doing, or not doing, x at t_1. However, that means that, if P is free, he can make what God believes at t false. But if P makes what God believes at t false, then God is not omniscient, for an omniscient being would have no false beliefs. The alternative is, of course, to deny that P is free.

Some religious believers have taken the latter option and denied that human beings are free. Others prefer to say that God must be limited in his omniscience. This is Swinburne's preferred solution. He says that God, in creating free human beings, chose to forgo specific knowledge, that is, knowledge of how they would (freely) act. Further, he suggests that this is consistent with the implicit view of God's omniscience found in the Bible or, at any rate, in the Old Testament.

review
activity

1. Explain in your own words how God's omniscience and human free will might be thought to be incompatible.

2. Outline Thomas's proposed solution to this problem.

3. What, according to Swinburne, is the real problem concerning God's omniscience and human free will?

4. What is Swinburne's solution to the problem?

The nature of religious language

The problem of talk of God

Just after Adam and Eve have eaten of the fruit of the tree of knowledge of good and evil, we read that they hid from God, for 'they heard the voice of the LORD

GOD walking in the garden in the cool of the day' (Genesis 3: 8) and they were afraid, since they had done what God had forbidden them to do.

What are we to make of this description of God? He was walking in the garden: so does he have legs (and a body and arms)? And if he walks, could he get out of breath? And why was he walking in the cool of the day? Does he find the heat oppressive? Does he seek the shade?

Anthropomorphism

To say that God has legs, can get out of breath or seeks the shade looks absurd. Yet this kind of description of God is like countless others that we find in the Bible: God is described in human terms. This is called *anthropomorphism:* speaking of something (in this case God) in the image of human beings, ascribing human qualities to the thing being described.

How can we talk of God?

Our words have a home in our mundane reality, and it is because they have a place in this reality that they have meaning and we can use them to refer to things, discuss our experiences, debate, argue, and so on. How then can they be used to talk of God? God is wholly beyond this world, immaterial, invisible, and so on: how, then, can we take the words that have a place in our mundane reality and use them in the context of a being unlike anything in this world? Hence, it is not just in cases where we speak of God as taking a walk that the difficulties arise.

For example, we use the term 'wise' to describe a human being, say Socrates, and it is in the context of human beings and human life that we learn to say that some are wise and some are foolish. How, then, can we say that God, a being so unlike human beings, is wise? The same can be said of our describing God as good or compassionate or vengeful and so on: all of these terms have a place in human life, so how can they be applied to God? In all of these cases we seem to be guilty of anthropomorphism, speaking of God as if he were a human being when he is not, using words that mean something in a human context and applying them outside that context. In that sense, to say that God is wise or good and so forth seems to be no more sensible than saying that he is taking a walk in the garden.

What we need is some way of understanding talk of God in a way that avoids anthropomorphism and yet allows us to speak sensibly of him. Otherwise, talk of God will just be a disguised form of gibberish: we might have the impression that we are speaking sensibly but we shall just be talking nonsense. We need, then, to find a middle ground between anthropomorphism and nonsense.

Why might talk of God be thought to face difficulties?

Logical positivism and the verification principle

Early in the twentieth century, there arose a school of philosophy according to which there is no such middle ground. This was logical positivism, and this claimed that talk of God was simply nonsense.

The logical positivists were a group of like-minded philosophers, many of whom were based in Vienna and formed the so-called 'Vienna Circle'. Members of the Vienna Circle included Rudolf Carnap (1891–1970), Otto Neurath (1882–1945), Moritz Schlick (1882–1936) and Friedrich Waismann (1896–1959). The best known logical positivist in Britain was A.J. Ayer (1910–89). Ayer spent some time at the University of Vienna before the Second World War and in 1936 he published *Language, Truth and Logic*, a kind of manifesto of logical positivism in the English language. In later work Ayer moved away from the main ideas of logical positivism, but his philosophy retained much of the spirit of the movement. Another philosopher with close links to the Vienna Circle was the Austrian Ludwig Wittgenstein (1889–1951). His *Tractatus Logico-Philosophicus,* published in 1921, exercised great influence over the members of the Vienna Circle. His later philosophical work (for example, *Philosophical Investigations,* 1953) is in many ways very different from the early work and has also been enormously influential.

The logical positivists were interested in putting philosophy on a wholly new and secure foundation and science was their model. Suppose you want to know whether the proposition 'It is raining (here, now)' is true or not. The best way to find out is to look outside and see the rain, perhaps feel it with the hand, hear it beating against the window panes, smell its distinctive odour on the dry ground. You could even taste it. If you can verify the presence of the rain with your senses (one or more of them), then the proposition 'It is raining' is true. On the other hand, if you cannot detect the rain with your senses then the proposition in question is false. Of course, you might rely on someone else to tell you about the rain, but he will rely on his senses. Or, if he does not, another person will; eventually someone must rely on his senses to detect the rain or its absence.

According to the logical positivists, a proposition such as 'It is raining' *has meaning because the senses can be used to verify whether it is true or not.*

Now, however, suppose we had some proposition and that we could never use our senses to ascertain whether it was true or false: no sense experiences could tell us either way. According to the logical positivists, *such a proposition has no meaning, it is meaningless.*

The verification principle

The logical positivists expressed these points about the meaning of propositions by formulating the so-called verification principle, also known as the verifiability principle (VP). According to the VP, a proposition has meaning if and only if it is in principle verifiable. That is, a proposition has meaning if and only if it is possible in principle to make observations which would show the proposition to be true or false.

Verification in principle and practice

Why does the VP include the idea that a proposition must be verifiable *in principle?* The reason is this. When A.J. Ayer published *Language, Truth and Logic,* in which he argued for the VP, no one had ever been to the moon and no rocket had been invented in which anyone could go to the moon. Consider now the proposition: 'There are mountains on the far side of the moon'. At that time, 1936, it was not possible to verify this proposition *in practice.* However, it would have been absurd to think it meaningless because it was clear that it could have been verified *in principle,* that is, by inventing a rocket to take a person (or a probe) to the far side of the moon. So, the logical positivists said that a proposition has meaning if it can be verified in principle.

There are two further complications.

Strong and weak verification

1. Consider a proposition such as 'a body tends to expand when heated'. This proposition cannot be verified conclusively because we would need to carry out an infinite number of tests to ascertain whether it was true or false. This is because, even if we had tested, say, five million bodies and found them to tend to expand when heated, we might, if we tested

one more body, find that, if we heated it, it would not tend to expand (perhaps it contracts). A similar point can be made about the propositions 'arsenic is poisonous' and 'all men are mortal'. As Ayer says: 'It is of the very nature of these propositions that their truth cannot be established with certainty by any finite series of observations' (Ayer 1990: 18). So, if we were to insist on a *strong* form of the VP involving *conclusive* verification, we would have to say that propositions such as 'a body tends to expand when heated' are meaningless. However, surely such propositions are not meaningless. Ayer therefore says that we should adopt a *weak* version of the VP that would not rule out such propositions as being meaningless (Ayer 1990: 18). So, we say that a proposition is verifiable if there are observations that are relevant to the determination of its truth or falsehood (Ayer 1990: 20).

2. The second complication is this. Traditionally, some propositions are considered to be analytic, that is, true in virtue of the meanings of the words they contain. An example is: 'All bachelors are unmarried men'. Similarly, some propositions are traditionally taken to be *a priori*, that is, they can be known without recourse to observation of the world. These include truths of logic. Ayer says that all such propositions are tautologies, and that, therefore, no observations are relevant to establishing their truth.

Thus, we arrive at the following: leaving aside tautological propositions, a proposition has meaning if and only if it is possible in principle to verify it in the weak sense of verification – if sense experience (observations) can go at least some way to confirming it.

Only factual or empirical propositions have meaning

This means that only *factual* or *empirical* propositions have meaning. This is why Ayer's statement of the VP runs: '[A] sentence is factually significant to any given person, if, and only if, he knows how to verify the proposition which it purports to express' (Ayer 1990: 16). Ayer (and other logical positivists) were thus able, as they saw it, to use the VP to discredit all theological propositions. Take, for instance, the proposition 'God exists'. According to Ayer, there are no observations that would go to verify this proposition. It is not, therefore, that according to the VP this proposition is false. Rather, it is *meaningless*. And the same would go for all theological propositions: according to the logical positivists, all talk of God is gibberish, just meaningless noise. It is nonsense.

Responses to the verification principle

Can religious claims be verified?

1. In response to the challenge of the VP, John Hick has argued that talk of God is not meaningless because its claims *can* be verified in principle (Hick 1971). He claims that there is a difference between those who believe in God and those who do not in terms, amongst other things, of what expectations they have. For example, the religious person – or, at any rate, a Christian – believes that there will be a final judgement in which the good are separated from the evil, whereas the non-religious person believes that no such event will take place. Hick elaborates this in terms of a parable of two men who are on a road, walking together. One of the men believes that the road leads to a Celestial City and he

thinks of what happens to him whilst he walks as being all part of the striving to get to this city. The other man thinks the road leads nowhere: he enjoys what is good during the walk, and puts up with what is bad. However, when they turn the final corner, one of them will be right and one wrong: there will either be a Celestial City there or there will not. Hick argues, therefore, that theism can rise to the challenge posed by the VP, and that it is possible in principle to verify whether there is a Celestial City or not. Of course, we cannot verify this now, and so Hick's argument depends on its being true that at least one person survive death in order to verify the claim in question. He argues that we can, indeed, make sense of a post-mortem existence. However, we need not explore his argument for such an existence here: suffice it to say that, if Hick is right, then talk of God can be verified in principle.

A problem for the verification principle

2. A quite different response to VP is to point out difficulties in the principle itself. One difficulty is simply that there are some propositions that surely have meaning for a given person without his having any idea what observations would be relevant to establishing the truth or falsehood of the propositions in question. Swinburne gives an example:

> *A man can understand the statement 'once upon a time, before there were men or any other rational creatures, the earth was covered by sea', without his having any idea of what would count for or against this proposition, or any idea of how to establish what geological evidence would count for or against the proposition.*
> (Swinburne 1993: 28–9)

Of course, it might be said that *someone or other* knows what observations would be relevant in such circumstances, even if a given person does not. Yet there are other propositions that are surely not meaningless but which no one knows how to verify. Swinburne gives the example that whilst people are asleep the toys get out of the cupboard, dance around and then get back into the cupboard leaving no trace at all of their nocturnal activities (Swinburne 1993: 28). There seems to be no observation which would be relevant to establishing the truth or falsehood of this proposition. Of course, it is a trivial proposition, but it is not, as the VP would have it, meaningless.

The verification principle as self-refuting

3. Another problem with the VP is it seems to fall foul of itself. The VP says that a proposition has meaning if and only if it is in principle possible to verify it. But how does one verify the proposition 'a proposition has meaning if and only if it is possible in principle to verify it'? There is no way to verify this proposition. Moreover, it is not a tautology. So the VP is itself meaningless according to the VP!

When is a proposition a factual proposition?

4. A further, deeper problem with the VP can be seen in this way. Presumably, Ayer would agree that a proposition such as 'an electron carries a negative charge' – call it p – can be verified and is therefore meaningful: p is surely a factual or empirical proposition. The problem is that p cannot be directly verified by observation (you cannot look and see that an electron carries a negative charge, not least because you cannot look and see an electron). So, how can we explain p being a factual proposition? Only in conjunction with a great many other propositions would p

entail propositions that can be verified by observation (call these propositions 'observation statements'). So, Ayer suggested the following as a way of telling when a proposition is a factual proposition: '[I]t is a mark of a genuine factual proposition . . . that some experiential propositions can be deduced from it in conjunction with certain other premises without being deducible from those other premises alone' (Ayer 1990: 20).

However, there are problems with this. Consider the following propositions:

r: God is in his heaven and all is well with the world;
s: my desk is brown.

Now, clearly, *s* is an observation statement. Consider now the following argument:

Premise 1: If God is in his heaven and all is well with the world, then my desk is brown.
Premise 2: God is in his heaven and all is well with the world.

Conclusion: Therefore, my desk is brown.

This argument is valid. And we have deduced an observation statement, *s*, from a proposition, *r*, in conjunction with one other premise (Premise 1), and *s* is not deducible from Premise 1 alone. This was precisely the test Ayer suggested to find out which propositions are factual propositions. It follows, therefore, that *r* turns out to be an factual proposition. Moreover, it turns out that *any* proposition can be thought of as being factual by running the kind of argument just offered (cf. Harrison 1979: 72–4).

Obviously, Ayer's test is useless. He came to see this, and sought to reformulate the test for factual propositions, but eventually agreed that no satisfactory account could be given. With that, he finally granted that the VP had to be rejected (Ayer 1991: 22–7).

The VP is thus faced with enormous problems. Given that this is so, the claim that the VP makes, that talk of God is meaningless, should itself be rejected.

review activity

1. State the verification principle, explaining the difference between verification in principle and practice and strong and weak versions of the principle.

2. Give two examples of a proposition verifiable in principle but not in practice.

3. Explain Hick's view that (at least some) talk of God is verifiable in principle.

4. Explain why God talk is meaningless according to the verification principle.

5. State and explain two problems with the verification principle.

Religion as inexpressible

The logical positivists thought of themselves as disposing of religion once and for all. But, oddly enough, their claim that we cannot properly make sense of

Moses Maimonides
(1135–1204)

talk of God is itself very like certain claims that particular religious thinkers have made.

A very important thinker in this regard is the Jewish thinker Maimonides.

In the second book of the Old Testament, Exodus 33: 20, we read that God says to Moses: 'Thou canst not see my face: for there shall no man see me and live.' Maimonides quoted this in his *The Guide of the Perplexed*, a tremendously significant work that was published in 1190, for he took it to indicate something very important about our knowledge of God. This was that, although we can know God by his effects, we can say nothing of him that is positive: we can only say what he is not. God is wholly other, not to be comprehended by the feeble human mind. So, for example, if we read that God is merciful to his children, then this does not mean that God is himself experiencing any emotion (say, compassion), but that God is behaving towards human beings as a father behaves towards his children when he does feel compassion for them (Maimonides 1995: 74). The same is true if we say that God is gracious, long-suffering, abundant in goodness and truth, jealous, wrathful or furious: in all these cases we mean that God's behaviour is something like that which that of a human being would be if that human being were to feel such emotions or possess such qualities. However, God does not feel these emotions or possess such qualities. We can only talk of God in negative terms (Maimonides 1995: 79). This is known as the *via negativa* ('the negative way'). Maimonides says that we can know *that* God is but not *what* God is (Maimonides 1995: 80). He expresses this thought in a kind of rapture:

> *Praise be to Him who is such that when our minds try to visualize His essence, their power of apprehending becomes imbecility; when they study the connection between His works and His will, their knowledge becomes ignorance; and when our tongues desire to declare His greatness by descriptive terms, all eloquence becomes impotence and imbecility.* (Maimonides 1995: 82)

It has been objected against Maimonides that, if God cannot be described in positive terms, then we do not know what are talking about when we talk of him (Davies 1993: 27–8). However, this may be somewhat unfair, the result of taking what one might negatively say about God out of the context of the religious ritual, practice and contemplation that would give the *via negativa* its point and focus.

Still, whether or not Maimonides's view can be adequately defended, it is interesting to note two things. First, there is a tendency from the perspective of Maimonides's view for God to lose much of his personal character, that is, there is a tendency to deny that God is a person. This is clear from the fact that God never experiences emotions, for example. Nonetheless, a personal character is retained for God to some extent in Maimonides's view because God still acts on this view for the well-being of his creatures. Secondly, as suggested earlier, Maimonides's view on talk of God bears some relation to that offered by the logical positivists. There is a sense in which Maimonides, like the positivists, sees religion as inexpressible (cf. McPherson 1963). Significant here is the fact that Wittgenstein's *Tractatus* was taken to be a central text of logical positivism, and he argued in that work that in some sense religious talk was nonsense. Nonetheless, Wittgenstein, unlike the logical positivists, thought that the nonsensical propositions of religion gestured towards a profound and irreplaceably important aspect of human life. In fact, it has been argued that for Wittgenstein at around the time of the *Tractatus* the religious notions that could not be said were *more* important than anything factual that could be said (Janik and Toulmin 1973). The issue of how much continuity there is between Wittgenstein's early and late work is controversial, but it is clear that he never lost his respect for religion and as late as 1929 or 1930 was still expressing an idea that had its roots in the *Tractatus*, for he wrote around that time that, although talk of religion (and ethics) was like running up against the boundaries of language, trying to say something that cannot be said, this is, nevertheless, 'a tendency in the human mind which I personally cannot help respecting deeply and I would not for my life ridicule it' (Wittgenstein 1968: 12).

Aquinas and the doctrine of analogy

Historically, the most influential account of the way it is possible to talk of God is to be found in the work of Thomas.

A central concern of Thomas's is to enquire whether we can speak literally of God.

Perfection signified and mode of signification

Consider such propositions as 'God is wise' and 'God is good'. Thomas says (Aquinas 1998: 220) we must distinguish between, on the one hand, a) what perfections the words 'wise' and 'good' express when used of God and creatures and, on the other, b) their manner of expressing them. These can also be called a) the perfection signified and b) the mode of signification, respectively.

1. He says that words such as 'wise' and 'good' express the perfections in question (wisdom, goodness) more properly in regard to God than in regard to creatures because God is more perfect than creatures. For example, God's wisdom is greater and more perfect than that of any creature (say, that of Socrates) because his wisdom *is* complete and perfect. This ultimately depends, of course, on the fact that God himself is perfect.

Literal talk of God

According to Thomas, when we say that God is wise or good we are speaking of him *literally*: he really is, so to speak, straightforwardly wise and good. He is, as one might put it, wise and good, period. However, this does not mean that we can fully understand his wisdom and goodness. In fact, we cannot. This is because our words 'wise' and 'good' ('wisdom', 'goodness') refer primarily to creatures. It is in interaction with creatures that we learn these terms.

2. This last point means that the manner in which the words 'wise', 'good' and so forth express their perfections is different depending on whether we are speaking of God or creatures. Because the words refer primarily to creatures, so far as their *mode of signification* is concerned they do *not* apply literally to God.

To sum up this part of the argument: the same thing (wisdom, goodness) can be said of God and of creatures, but it is said of them in a different manner.

The *thing signified* is the same, but the *mode of signification* is different. We can speak literally of God in the first sense, but not in the second.

Metaphorical talk of God

Note that Thomas's account here only applies to words like 'wise' and 'good' that can sensibly be predicated of something infinite, like God. Some terms, such as 'rock' and 'lion', can only be applied to finite things, that is, to things of this world. If these latter terms are applied to God then they are *metaphors*, that is, have no literal application to him (Aquinas 1998: 219ff.).

Thomas goes on from here to distinguish between terms which are used *univocally* (univocal terms), terms that are used *equivocally* (equivocal terms) and terms which can be used *analogously* (analogous terms).

Equivocal terms

Consider the word 'wing'. This word could be used to refer to a part of a bird's anatomy or to a suite of rooms of a large building or to part of the bodywork of a car. In each case, 'wing' has a different meaning. Hence, in the present case, 'wing' is *equivocal*. To use a word equivocally is to use it in two completely different senses.

Univocal terms

Consider now the word 'cat'. If I say that Cinders is a cat and that Blossom is a cat, and if it is indeed true that both of them are feline animals, then I am using the word 'cat' in exactly the same sense in both cases. Hence, in the present case, 'cat' is *univocal*. To use a word univocally is to use it in one sense of more than one thing. It is to use it to say of two (or more) things that they are exactly alike in the relevant respect: the word has the same meaning when used of more than one thing.

Analogous use of terms

Thomas says that terms such as 'wise' and 'good', when used of God, are used neither equivocally nor univocally but analogously. This last use lies between equivocal use and univocal use because an analogy is a resemblance or partial similarity: it lies between complete dissimilarity (equivocal terms) and complete similarity (univocal terms) (Aquinas 1998: 225).

Thomas distinguishes three forms of analogy. These are: i) analogy of attribution; ii) analogy of proper proportionality; and iii) analogy of improper proportionality (cf. Ross 1998: 114).

Analogy of attribution

Analogy of attribution

Consider the fact that Martha can be called healthy and so can her complexion. Her healthy complexion is a sign or symptom of her general good health. We can call her complexion healthy because it *is* a sign of her healthy body (cf. Mascall 1968). But the primary meaning of the word 'healthy' is found in reference to her body, and not her complexion. When applied to her complexion, the word 'healthy' is used analogously.

In a similar way, the goodness of creatures is a kind of sign of the goodness of God, yet, as we have seen, the perfection signified by the word 'good' has its primary application to God. So, when applied to creatures, the word 'good' is being used analogously.

In both these cases we are dealing with an analogy of attribution.

In the case of Martha, her healthy body is the *cause* of her healthy complexion. However, Thomas rejects the idea that in saying 'God is good' all we are expressing is that God causes goodness. He does so for the following reason. There is goodness in the world and there are material bodies (human flesh and blood, trees and mountains, and so forth) in the world. Now, God causes everything. So, if to say 'God is good' is to say nothing more than that God causes goodness, then we should also have to say 'God is body' because God causes bodies. But God is not (a) body at all. So Thomas says that 'God is not good because he causes goodness; rather because he is good, goodness spreads through things. As Augustine says, *because* he *is good*, we *exist*' (Aquinas 1998: 218–19).

Analogy of proper proportionality

Analogy of proper proportionality

We saw when discussing the possibility of the literal application of terms to God that terms like 'wise' and 'good' apply literally to God when we are using them to predicate a perfection of God. Indeed, they apply primarily to him, because he is perfect, and only secondarily to creatures. But we also saw that the mode of signification of terms like 'wise' and 'good' differs when applied to God from their mode of signification when applied to creatures. We can express these points in such a way as to get the analogy of proportionality. The basic idea is that God and creatures possess certain attributes *proportional* to their nature.

John Hick has articulated this point in a very helpful way (Hick 1990: 83–4). Consider the term 'faithful'. A man or a woman can be faithful, and this shows in particular patterns of speech, behaviour and so on. We can also say that a dog is faithful. Clearly, there is a great difference between the faithfulness of a man or woman and that of a dog, yet there is a recognisable similarity or analogy – otherwise, we would not think of the dog as faithful. Further, in the case of the analogy between human beings and the dog true faithfulness is something we know in ourselves, and a dim and imperfect likeness of this in the dog is known by analogy.

We might also say that God is faithful. In this case, the true form of faithfulness is that which God has, proportioned to the kind of being he is, that is, a perfect being. Then, we cannot really grasp what his faithfulness consists in, but we can know it by analogy to our own faithfulness which is a dim and imperfect approximation to, or likeness of, God's faithfulness.

So we are predicating the same thing of a dog, of us and of God when we say that these are all faithful (the thing signified is the same); but the way in which faithfulness is predicated is different according to the being (dog, human being, God and so forth) to which it is applied (the mode of signification is different).

Analogy of improper proportionality

Analogy of improper proportionality

This analogy is simply that of metaphor, to which reference has already been made. If, for example, we say that God is a rock or a lion, we are using neither analogy of attribution nor analogy of proper proportionality, for we are saying nothing literally true of God.

review
activity

1. In what way does Thomas think that words can be predicated of God literally?
2. In which cases does Thomas think that words cannot be predicated of God literally?
3. State Thomas's notion of analogy of attribution.
4. State Thomas's notion of analogy of proper proportionality.

Aquinas and Swinburne

Swinburne's criticism of Thomas

It is important to note that Thomas's account of religious language does nothing by itself to show that there is something mistaken about the idea that religious language is absurd (as was suggested, as we have seen, by the logical positivists). If the logical positivists' view is mistaken, this is so on the kinds of ground already discussed. Thomas's account depends on the assumption that we *can* and *do* refer to God. His question is rather: Given that this is so, *how* do we refer to God? If someone thinks that all talk of God is absurd, then Thomas's account will not answer this.

Thomas's view has been criticised by Richard Swinburne (Swinburne 1993: 80–1). Consider again the claim 'God is good'. We have seen that Thomas argues that 'good' is predicated analogically of human beings and God. Nonetheless, as we have seen, Thomas argues that it is the very same thing, namely goodness, that is predicated of both human beings and God. In reply, Swinburne argues that, even if the way in which human beings and God possess goodness differs on account of their being very different types of being, given that it is the same thing they possess, there is no reason to speak here of analogy at all. We could just say, Swinburne argues, that the term 'good' 'is being used univocally if it denotes the same property, even if having that property amounts to something very different in different things' (Swinburne 1993: 81). In other words, Thomas could simply have said that terms like 'good' are used univocally of human beings and God, even though they possess goodness in different ways. Thomas's appeal to analogy therefore achieves nothing, suggests Swinburne.

Whether or not this criticism of Thomas is right, one motivation Swinburne has for it is that in his own account of talk of God he claims that some terms can be used of God in a perfectly ordinary sense. This is so, he says, for 'good': in using it of God we are using it in its perfectly ordinary sense. 'The only extraordinary thing being suggested', he writes, 'is that it [goodness] exists to a degree in which it does not exist in mundane objects' (Swinburne 1993: 72–3).

However, Swinburne suggests that there are other terms that are used analogically of God, such as 'person' and 'knows'. His account of analogy is, nevertheless, different from that of Thomas.

Swinburne's account of analogy

Analogy in a non-theological context

The best way to understand Swinburne's account of analogy is by way of an example that he provides (Swinburne 1993: 67–71). He gives an example of words used analogically in a non-theological context. In fact, the context is that of science.

Swinburne asks us to consider the following question: What is light? Until the beginning of the twentieth century there were two views about what light is: either it consists of a stream of particles or it consists of a wave. There was disagreement about which view was correct, but it was thought that one or the other must be correct because nothing can be both a stream of particles and a wave. However, since 1905 it has been thought that neither the one theory nor the other is correct. Rather, both are correct. That is, it has been thought that light is *both* a stream of particles *and* it is a wave. This is because certain ways in which light behaves can only be explained in this way. However, on a traditional understanding of the terms 'particle' and 'wave' nothing *can* be both a stream of particles and a wave. So, if light is thought, after all, to be both, then we have to use the terms 'particle' and 'wave' analogically. As Swinburne says:

> *Light is a stream of 'particles', in a sense of 'particle' in which grains of sand and everything else we would call 'particles' are particles, but in a sense in which some things which we would not call 'particles' are particles. Light is a 'wave', in the sense in which a water wave and everything else which we would call 'waves' are such, but in a sense in which some things which we would not call 'waves' are waves.*
>
> (Swinburne 1993: 68–9)

Analogy in a theological context

So, when we speak of light as 'a stream of particles' and as 'a wave' we are 'stretching' the terms 'particle' and 'wave' away from their normal meaning but in a way that, so to speak, remains in contact with their normal meaning. Just so, Swinburne says, we can 'stretch' the meanings of words like 'person' and 'knows' when applied to God even as they remain in contact with their normal meaning. We have already seen something of this. For example, part of what it is for a human being to be a person is that he can directly move parts of his body at will. This sense of acting is retained in the case where we think of God as a person but is stretched to mean that he can directly move any part of the universe at will.

review activity

1. Explain Swinburne's criticism of Thomas's doctrine of analogy.

2. Using an example, explain Swinburne's account of talk of God as involving analogy.

Religious language as symbolic

In this section, we shall look at one last account of the way talk of God is to be understood. This is the account to be found in the work of Paul Tillich.

Tillich's account of religious language is very complicated and not always clear, and it is embedded in a complex and radical theology. For this reason, only the bare bones of his theory can be discussed here.

According to Tillich, religious language is fundamentally symbolic (though it is not *always* symbolic, as we shall see). He distinguishes symbols from signs. Both symbols and signs point to something beyond themselves, but there is, according to Tillich, an important difference between them. This is that a symbol, unlike a sign, 'participates' in the reality and power of that to which it points. For example, consider a sign at the end of the road telling cars to stop. The sign simply points to the necessity that cars stop at the end of the road, but beyond that there is no relation between the sign and that to which it points. A flag, however, says Tillich, is a symbol: it 'participates in the power of the king or the nation for which it stands and which it symbolizes' (Tillich 1996: 358; cf. Tillich 1968: 136–7).

The nature of symbols in Tillich's account

So, symbols can be understood in two ways.

1. They point to something beyond themselves.
2. They participate in that to which they point.

Tillich gives some further characteristics of symbols.

3. Symbols open up levels of reality which otherwise are closed for us.
4. They also open up levels and dimensions of the soul which correspond to those levels of reality.

In order to explain what he means by 3. and 4., Tillich draws an analogy between symbols and works of art, say, poetry and music. For Tillich says that such works can also open up dimensions of reality and of the soul for us. It is hard to say exactly what he means by this, but he seems to have at least two things in mind.

First, that which the great work of art articulates cannot be articulated in any other way. If someone were to ask what the meaning of a great work of art is, he could be given a paraphrase or an explanation, but the paraphrase would be useless unless the person in question were familiar with the work of art itself. So, in the case of religious symbols, Tillich's point is that they cannot be substituted by anything else if one is to grasp their meaning.

Second, through great art we can achieve a new vision of, or perspective on, life (Tillich 1968: 137). We could think of this in terms of the way in which, say, the novels of Dostoyevsky (1820–81) can open up for us new understandings of the meaning of good and evil. And religious symbols can also give us

Paul Tillich (1886–1965)

Paul Tillich was one of the leading theologians and philosophers of religion in the twentieth century. He was born in Germany in 1886, the son of a Lutheran pastor. He served in the First World War as an army chaplain, and the horror of what he saw led him to become a founder member of Religious Socialism. He had a number of university appointments, but when the Nazis came to power in 1933 he expressed his opposition to their ideology and treatment of the Jews, and was deprived of his professorship at the University of Frankfurt. He fled to the US where he taught at Union Theological Seminary (1933–55) in New York, Harvard University (1955–62) and the University of Chicago Divinity School (1962–5). His works, including *The Courage to Be* (1952) and the *Dynamics of Faith* (1957), made him into one of the leading philosopher-theologians of the second half of the twentieth century. Just before his death in 1965 he completed his massive *Systematic Theology*, one of the landmarks of twentieth-century theology.

new understandings of good and evil and other issues crucial in human life, such as guilt and redemption (Tillich 1958: 277–91). However, at this point, Tillich was also drawing on the thinking of Rudolf Otto (1869–1937).

According to Otto, the root of religion lies in what he called the 'numinous' or the 'Holy'. This is a complicated state of the soul in which one experiences a sense of mystery and awe in the face of the world, a kind of sense of one's own smallness and nothingness that is nonetheless exhilarating and fascinating. It is an experience of the 'wholly other'. And, when Tillich says that religious symbols open up new aspects of reality and of the soul, it is, at least at times, some such experience that he has in mind.

We can now see that, when Tillich says that symbols point to something beyond themselves, what he has in mind in the case of religious symbols is that they point to the Holy.

Tillich indicates two further features of symbols.

Two further features of symbols in Tillich's account

5. They cannot be produced intentionally. They grow from the unconscious mind of man (or from the unconscious of those in a specific culture).
6. They have a place in a culture and grow and die like living things in that culture. They die when they no longer have any meaning or resonance for the members of the culture.

So far as 5. and 6. relate to religious symbols, Tillich wants to emphasise that a religion is something that grows spontaneously as part of a culture, but can lose its cultural significance – as, say, the polytheistic religions of Greece and Rome lost their cultural significance and died.

Being-Itself

As I mentioned above, Tillich's theory of symbols is embedded in general considerations about the nature of religion and God. Central here is his idea that there is, in fact, one way in which we can understand God in a non-symbolic manner. This is when we say that God is 'Being-Itself'. Tillich links this with the notion of the Holy, which has already been mentioned. This is because, as Tillich understands things, the encounter with the Holy is, basically, the encounter with Being-Itself. Being-Itself is the ultimate, the unconditioned, that on which everything else depends for its being. Being-Itself is the ground of all existence. What it is *not* is a person. In fact, Tillich is clear that when we speak of God as a person, this is only a symbol for Being-Itself. Thus God has two sides: a non-symbolic side as Being-Itself and a symbolic side as a person.

The encounter with Being-Itself, says Tillich, is an encounter that must be understood in terms of the truly fundamental 'ultimate concern'. This is, roughly, the meaning of one's life, but Tillich discusses this meaning in terms of a whole range of concepts such as guilt, punishment, salvation, redemption and so on, that is, in terms of notions central to Christian thought.

The way in which Tillich deals in detail with such notions is, however, far from traditional. To see this, let us look at the notion of God's divine law, commanding us to behave in certain ways and threatening us with punishment if we do not. Tillich says that this must be understood in terms of the anxiety of guilt understood in an existential sense. He explains what he means by this:

227

> [C]ondemnation and judgement are obviously not things which judge us from above, but symbols of the judgement we inescapably make against ourselves, of the painful split within ourselves, of the moments of despair in which we want to get rid of ourselves without being able to, of the feeling of being possessed by structures of self-destruction. (Tillich 1958: 289)

So, roughly, the notion of divine punishment is, according to Tillich, a judgement we make against ourselves for our failure to achieve a kind of inner harmony, a harmony that is the fruit of finding some ultimate meaning in one's life.

Criticisms of Tillich's account

We can approach the central criticism of Tillich's account of religious language as symbolic by considering the point made by John Hick that the notion that a symbol participates in that which it symbolises is unclear (Hick 1990: 87). Consider Tillich's example of a flag. In what sense does this participate in the power of a king or of a nation? Is the idea supposed to be that the flag increases the power of the king or nation? If this is the claim, then it does not seem very plausible. After all, although burning the flag of a country can be an act of hatred towards that country, it hardly does anything as such to weaken that country in any literal sense.

Another possibility concerning what it means to say that the flag participates in the power of a king or a nation is that, when a person sees the flag, the king or the country is *presented* to him. And this presentation would involve, for example, that person's experiencing certain emotions, say a kind of rush of love or pride, or of horror or revulsion (cf. Alston 1984: 15).

There is something in this suggestion, but problems remain if we think about religious symbols. Consider the notion of God's love for us. On Tillich's account, to ascribe love to God is to speak symbolically. Therefore, to say that God loves us is also to speak symbolically. Where might one experience God's love? Presumably in love between human beings, which is a symbol for God's love. However, if experiencing something as a symbol of God is having an experience of the numinous or the Holy or Being-Itself, then to speak of the experience of God's love is just to say that in love that one experiences for another person one has a sense that inner depths of one's soul are opened up to Being-Itself.

William Alston has objected that this means that, so far as a statement such as 'God loves his creatures' is concerned, '[t]here is no point in trying to determine whether the statement is true or false, except to determine whether love does work like that for anyone'. He goes on to say: 'From "God loves his creatures" . . . we cannot infer anything about what is in store for us, not even inferences of a very indefinite sort. From the fact that such items [as "God loves his creatures"] are vehicles of an experience of the holy, nothing whatever follows concerning human destiny' (Alston 1984: 16–17).

In other words, Alston's argument is that from 'God loves his creatures' we cannot infer that we shall be saved or forgiven for our sins or spend eternity after our death in Heaven (or Hell, for that matter). On Tillich's understanding of religious symbols, none of these things is *literally* true. None of them is going to happen in the way that it is going to happen that, for example, we shall all die. Thus, Alston thinks that Tillich's view of religious language evacuates it of substantive content. This criticism clearly goes hand in hand with the criticism that God is not, on Tillich's account, really a person at all.

There are responses that one can make to the kind of criticism that Alston offers. However, I shall not do so here, but rather consider these sorts of issues again later when I come to discuss the views of Kierkegaard (1813–55) (by whom Tillich was deeply influenced) and D.Z. Phillips.

some questions to think about

1 Does it make sense to think of God as a person?

2 Does the notion of an omnipotent God make sense, or is Geach right to say that the notion of an almighty God is all Christian belief needs?

3 Is it possible for God to be both immutable and omniscient?

4 Can God be omniscient and human beings free?

5 What does it mean to say that God is good?

6 'It is impossible in principle to use language to speak of a God who is beyond our experience.' Is this true?

7 Which is a better account of talk of God: by analogy or symbolically?

further reading

▶ Peterson *et al.* (eds) 1996, and Davies (ed.) 2000 both contain many good articles in philosophy of religion. Davies 1993 is a short and accessible introduction to the philosophy of religion. See also Helm (ed.) 1999.

▶ Bowker 1997 is an excellent book on the world's religions. It contains a useful bibliography.

▶ Kenny 1979 is at times a difficult read, but is probably the best and most cultivated book on God's nature as the mainstream of philosophy has often understood it. Stiver 1996 is the best one-volume work on religious language that covers all the main theories.

The question of God's existence

11

important terms

Contingent existence: a being exists contingently if its non-existence is possible.

Deductively valid argument: an argument in which the premises entail the conclusion. If the premises are true, the conclusion is true. Example: P1: All men are mortal; P2: Socrates is a man; C: Socrates is mortal.

Inductive argument: a *good* inductive argument is one in which the premises do not entail the conclusion but make it probable or highly probable. The conclusion could be false even if highly probable. Example: we have repeatedly seen water below a certain temperature freeze, and never seen it not freeze below that temperature, therefore all water freezes below that temperature.

Necessary existence: a being exists necessarily if it could not fail to exist – in other words, if it *must* exist.

Predicate: a word that refers to the properties of things. For example, 'is tall', 'has a headache'. Predicates are said to 'apply to' or 'be true of' objects.

Sound argument: an argument which is valid and in which all the premises are true.

Valid argument: an argument in which the conclusion follows from the premises.

Key topics in this chapter

- The argument from design
- The cosmological argument
- The ontological argument (Anselm)
- The argument from religious experience

I n this chapter we shall consider four different types of argument for the existence of God.

The argument from design

In this section we shall consider the claim that it is reasonable to infer the existence of God from the fact that the world is as it is. More specifically, we shall consider the argument that the world seems designed in some way and that it is therefore reasonable to infer that there must be a designer of the universe. That designer is God.

The argument from design is sometimes known as a *teleological argument*, from *telos*, Greek for 'aim' or 'goal' or 'purpose'. This is because the argument from design suggests, as we shall see, that natural things in the world, such as the human eye, are designed to fulfil certain purposes, just as a watch is designed to fulfil a certain purpose.

Note that calling the argument 'the argument *from* design' actually begs the question, because the point of the argument is to show that we have good reason to think that the universe *is* designed. Still, to call it 'the argument from design' is traditional practice, and I shall follow this practice.

More than one teleological argument has been offered. We shall consider two versions of the argument.

The argument from design is an *a posteriori* argument. That is, it is one based on experience of the world, or, more strictly, that the world exists in a particular way. Moreover, it is an *inductive* argument. This means that the premises of the argument at best make the conclusion of the argument *probable* even *highly probable*, but do not entail the conclusion.

The argument from design (i)

The most well known version of the argument from design is due to William Paley.

Paley's example

Imagine that you are walking across a heath and stumble over a stone. If asked how the stone got there, you might say that it always had been there. But suppose you stumbled on a watch on the ground. You would not think that the watch had always been there. The reason for this is that the watch is of immense complexity, with cogs, wheels, springs, hands, a face and the rest, and it is clear both that individually these have a purpose as part of the whole and that together they have a purpose (namely, to tell the time). Hence, you would not believe it possible that the watch could owe its existence to chance. Rather, you would suppose that some intelligence must have designed and made it.

William Paley (1743–1805)

Paley then says that the universe is like a watch. When we look at the universe we see the same kind of thing that we see when we look at a watch, namely, that the universe is of immense complexity, and that the parts fit together, and work together, extraordinarily well, each having a purpose within the overall scheme. Thus, Paley says, we can infer that there must have been a designer at work who made the universe. That designer is, of course, God.

Hume's account of the argument from design

The same argument is offered by Hume, who, as we shall see, goes on to offer some strong criticisms of it.

> *Look round the world: Contemplate the whole and every part of it: You will find it to be nothing but one great machine, subdivided into an infinite number of lesser machines, which again admit of subdivisions, to a degree beyond what human senses and faculties can trace and explain. All these various machines, and even their most minute parts, are adjusted to each other with an accuracy, which ravishes into admiration all men, who have ever contemplated them. The curious adapting of means to ends, throughout all nature, resembles exactly, though it much exceeds, the productions of human contrivance; of human design, thought, wisdom, and intelligence. Since therefore the effects resemble each other, we are led to infer, by all the rules of analogy, that the causes also resemble; and that the Author of Nature is somewhat similar to the mind of man; though possessed of much larger faculties, proportioned to the grandeur of the work, which he has executed. By this argument a posteriori . . . do we prove at once the existence of a Deity, and his similarity to human mind and intelligence.*
> (Hume 1994: II [109])

This passage comes from Hume's *Dialogues Concerning Natural Religion*, a work which, as the title indicates, is cast in the form of dialogues. There are three speakers, Demea, Cleanthes and Philo. Since Hume wrote all the parts, it can sometimes be difficult to know which character is speaking for Hume himself. However, in what follows we need not be too worried about this. When I say that Hume offers such and such criticisms, I just mean that they are to be found in the *Dialogues*, whether or not Hume himself accepted them.

The design argument and a sense of wonder at the world

The argument from design is, of course, principally an argument from analogy, that is, it is an argument that claims that there is an analogy between nature and man-made artefacts. However, Hume's presentation of the argument from design brings out one further aspect of it that is important. This is that present in the argument is a sense of wonder in the face of the world. We shall later see what importance, if any, attaches to this aspect of the argument.

review
activity

Explain in your own words the argument from design.

Having presented the argument from design in his *Dialogues*, Hume offers a number of criticisms of it. I shall concentrate on the key ones.

Hume's criticisms of the argument from design

Is the analogy between the world and human artefacts good?

1. One of Hume's arguments is simply that the analogy between the universe and human artefacts is not a good one. He writes:

    If we see a house, we conclude, with the greatest certainty, that it had an archi-tect or builder; because this is precisely that species of effect, which we have experienced to proceed from that species of cause. But surely you will not affirm, that the universe bears such a resemblance to a house, that we can with the same certainty infer a similar cause, or that the analogy is here entire and perfect. The dissimilitude is so striking, that the utmost you can here pretend to is a guess, a conjecture, a presumption concerning a similar cause.
    (Hume 1994: II [110])

    In other words, when we come across a house, we can infer that there was a designer because we have a great deal of experience of houses being designed, built and the rest. However, we have no experience of universes being designed and built. This would not matter so much if the universe were very like a house, for then we could say that, although

David Hume (1711–76)

Hume was born at Edinburgh in 1711. His father died whilst the young Hume was still an infant. In 1723, when not quite 12 years old, Hume went to the University of Edin-burgh, stayed for about three years and left, as was quite common then, without taking a degree. It was planned that he would become a lawyer, but he became averse to any form of study but that of philosophy in the broadest sense, and when he was about 18 years old he won through to the philosophical ideas for which he has since become famous. During this period he worked so intensely that he suffered something like a nervous breakdown, and had to give up study for a while. In 1734 he went to Bristol to work as clerk in a firm of sugar-merchants. He left after only four months and went to France, where he wrote most of his *A*

Treatise of Human Nature (1739–40). When it was published it was not the great success for which Hume had hoped, and he eventually recast it in the form of his *Enquiries Concerning Human Under-standing and the Principles of Morals* (1748–51). Having failed to obtain a professorship at the University of Edin-burgh, he became a tutor to the Marquis of Annandale, and later performed diplo-matic duties in Vienna and Turin. He subse-quently became the Librarian to the Faculty of Advocates at Edinburgh and wrote a six-volume *History of England* (1754–62), which brought him fame and wealth. In 1763 he went to Paris, in 1766 returning to England, accompanied by Jean-Jacques Rousseau (1712–78), with whom he quar-relled. He returned to Edinburgh and died there in August 1776.

we have no experience of universes being designed and built, the universe is, in fact, very much like a house, and so the analogy between houses and the universe would hold and we could suppose there to have been a designer of the universe. But the universe is not much like a house.

The uniqueness of the universe

So the key problem in this objection is that the universe is *unique*. As Hume says:

When two species of objects have always been observed to be conjoined together, I can infer . . . the existence of one, whenever I see the existence of the other: And this I call an argument from experience. But how this argument can have place, where the objects, as in the present case, are single, individual, without parallel, or specific resemblance, may be difficult to explain. And will any man tell me with a serious countenance, that an orderly universe must arise from some thought and art, like the human; because we have experience of it? To ascertain this reasoning, it were requisite, that we had experience of the origin of worlds; and it is not sufficient surely, that we have seen ships and cities arise from human art and contrivance.

(Hume 1994: II [115])

So Hume's point is that we cannot arrive at any conclusions about the origins of a unique object; the universe is a unique object; so we cannot arrive at any conclusions about the origins of the universe.

A multiplicity of possible causes?

2. A second important point Hume makes against the argument from design is to say that there might be any number of causes for the apparent design of the universe. For example, Hume suggests that since

the universe bears a greater likeness to animal bodies and to vegetables than to the works of human art, it is more probable, that its cause resembles the cause of the former than of the latter, and its origin ought rather to be ascribed to genera-tion of vegetation than to reason or design. (Hume 1994: VII [138])

Hume's point that the universe bears a greater resemblance to animal bodies or to vegetables than it does to human artefacts surely has some plausibility. So it does not seem absurd to infer that the 'cause . . . of the world, we may infer to be something similar or analogous to genera-tion of vegetation' (Hume 1994: VII [138]). Indeed, perhaps the universe was spun out from the bowels of an 'infinite spider' (Hume 1994: VII [142]). Hume, of course, does not seriously entertain the idea that the universe is of such an origin; he just means to be saying that we have as much evidence that it is as that it was created by an intelligent God.

Hume's principle of causality

3. A third argument that Hume offers is dependent on his principle that '[w]hen we infer any particular cause from an effect, we must proportion the one to the other, and can never be allowed to ascribe to the cause any qualities but what are exactly sufficient to produce the effect' (Hume 1985: 136). In other words, if we are to infer from what we see around us to a designer, then the designer can only be thought to have the quali-ties or properties necessary for creating the world as it is. Here is an analogy. Imagine that I visit a garden and find that it is laid out in exquisite taste, with flowers, shrubs and bushes finely arranged; with the

correct proportion of shade and light for the climate; with fountains and arbours cool. If I am told that one man designed and created all this, I can reasonably infer something about him, say that he has extraordinary skill in wielding gardening tools; a fine sense of balance; and so on. However, I could not infer that, for example, he is a kind and generous man, or that he is also skilled in poetry or music.

So, given the world as it is, what could we infer about its designer, supposing it to have one? For one thing, we would have no good reason to think that the designer was infinite: a finite being could have accomplished the creation of the finite things we see about us. Secondly, we could not think of the designer as perfect, for this world is manifestly not perfect. 'There are', Hume remarks tersely, 'many inexplicable difficulties in the works of nature' (Hume 1994: V [129]). Further, it perhaps took some God many attempts to make a world as good even as this world is. In Hume's words: 'Many worlds might have been botched and bungled, throughout an eternity, 'ere this system was struck out: Much labour lost: Many fruitless trials made' (Hume 1994: V [130]). And beyond all this, we could not rule out the idea that many gods had co-operated on the construction of the world or that the God who created the world is now dead. Indeed, given the evidence of the world as it is, we cannot even rule out the idea that the Deity might 'have eyes, a nose, mouth, ears etc.' (Hume 1994: V [130–1]).

review
activity

1. Why does Hume think that, because the universe is unique, we cannot come to any conclusions concerning its origins?

2. Why does Hume believe that we cannot rule out the idea that the cause of the universe is some kind of vegetable generation?

3. Explain Hume's principle concerning inferences from effects to causes, giving an example to illustrate it.

4. What does Hume think the use of this principle shows about the designer of the universe, if there is one?

How successful are Hume's criticisms of the argument from design?

Richard Swinburne has carefully replied to all of Hume's criticisms (Swinburne 2000).

1. It is mistaken, Swinburne says, to argue that, because the universe is unique, we cannot arrive at any conclusions concerning its origins or about its nature as a whole. In fact, cosmologists *are* reaching well-tested conclusions abut the universe as a whole, and physical anthropologists are reaching such conclusions about the human race, yet we only know of one human race (and there may only *be* one human race). Moreover, and this is an important point, things are not simply unique or not unique. Things are unique or not under some description. And indeed,

everything can be unique under some description. For example, my computer is not unique *qua* computer (there are thousands like it) but it is unique *qua* the only computer on my study desk.

2. Swinburne argues that Hume's claim that the universe could be produced in the kind of way vegetables are produced could not explain the fact that there are laws of nature that operate temporally – in other words they hold across time. A vegetable only grows, for example, because the laws of biochemistry hold. *That* those laws hold, and *that* the vegetable therefore grows, cannot be explained by the generation of the vegetable in the first place.

3. Swinburne grants that the argument from design cannot give good grounds for saying that there is a designer who is totally good, omnipotent and omniscient. Nonetheless, he says that the causal principle on which Hume relies for his third criticism is simply false. He says that it is not, for example, a principle that is observed in science. Indeed, if it were, he claims, science would be abandoned. The reason he gives is that '[a]ny scientist who told us only that the cause of E [some effect] had E-producing characteristics would not add an iota to our knowledge'. And he goes on: 'Explanation of matters of fact consists in postulating on reasonable grounds that the cause of an effect has certain characteristics other than those sufficient to produce the effect' (Swinburne 2000: 281).

Even if Swinburne is right, however, the difficulty is, as we have already noted, that the argument from design takes us nowhere near the existence of a God who is omnipotent, omniscient and wholly good. Nor can it get us to the idea that there is only one designer of the universe. It seems that Hume's substantive point in his third criticism remains, even if the principle to which he appeals is incorrect.

Darwin and the argument from design

Swinburne has his own design argument, and we shall return to him, but for the moment we should take note of the fact that many people think that Darwin's theory of evolution shows that any kind of design argument is destroyed. This is because Darwin showed that plants and animals in the world have the properties they have as a result of natural selection. Briefly, what the theory of natural selection says is that living things are engaged in a struggle to survive, and those that are best adapted to the environment do in fact survive. These living beings then pass on their genes to their descendants, who accordingly inherit the characteristics that are useful for survival. The beings not well adapted to the environment die off. Hence, what explains why living beings have the properties they do is not that they have been designed but that gradually, over millions of years, they have evolved to fit their environment. This is the work principally of chance.

Let us grant that Darwin's theory is correct. Does it, then, as many suppose, refute the argument from design?

James A. Sadowsky has suggested that there is no incompatibility between God's having designed the world and evolution (Sadowsky 1988). He points out that the argument from design need not claim that *whenever* there is adaptation to the environment we must think that this is the result of the immediate action of an intelligent being (God). On the contrary, the argument from design can claim that the *ultimate* explanation for adaptation is found in an intelligent being. In other words, the argument from design is not threatened by the theory of evolution. One can consistently believe *both* that something can arise by mechanical forces, that is, by the blind workings of nature, *and* that it can arise by design. God sets the parameters and the initial conditions and then things evolve from there. An omniscient God will know exactly what is going to happen (at least until human beings, creatures with free will, appear on scene). On this picture, evolution is God's mode of creating. In fact, as Sadowsky points out, even a *creationist*, i.e., someone who believes that every member of a given species is either directly created or is a descendant of a member of that species, does not believe that *his* eyes are designed. What he believes is that the eyes of the *first* human beings were designed. Thereafter, the creationist believes, 'the bodies of all but the most remote of his human ancestors were the result of blind activity', so coming to accept that we have discovered the mechanism by which this blind activity takes place, i.e., evolution theory, should not change what he believes (Sadowsky 1988: 97).

In reply to Sadowsky, it might be said that all his argument shows is that we cannot rule out the possibility that evolution is God's mode of creating. However, it hardly shows that it is. For all Sadowsky says the argument from design might be false, even if consistent with Darwinism. Indeed, he acknowledges this himself. But any rate, if he is right, Darwin did not, as such, do anything that should be thought to undermine the design argument itself. That itself is an interesting result.

review activity

1. Why have some thought that Darwin's theory of evolution refuted the argument from design?

2. What reasons are there for thinking that, in fact, the theory of evolution does not refute the design argument?

The argument from design (ii)

I turn now to discuss Swinburne's design argument (Swinburne 1991: ch.8). It should be noted, however, that this argument is very complicated, and I give it here in a simplified form.

Spatial and temporal order of the universe

Swinburne says that those who wish to offer a design argument can appeal either to what he calls the *spatial order* of the universe or to what he calls the *temporal order* of the universe. An example of the former would be a town with all its roads at right angles to each other. An example of the latter is the behaviour of objects in accord with the laws of nature.

Paley's argument, the one rejected by Hume, is a design argument concerning spatial order. Swinburne wishes to offer one concerning temporal order.

Swinburne draws to our attention the fact that there is a tremendous order-liness in the universe. It is not just that there are laws that govern the way in which bodies behave, it is also that most of what happens happens according to simple laws that we can understand and use to predict the future. Moreover, it is not the case that the temporal order of the world has held up to now but might not in the future. Rather, we are justified in believing that these laws will continue to hold. These laws are part of nature herself: they are not some invention of human beings. It is, says Swinburne, both surprising and wonderful that the universe displays such temporal order.

Now, some people argue against this that there is, in fact, nothing surprising in the fact that human beings find order around them, because, if there were no order, they would not exist: they can only exist in an orderly environment. Swinburne has a reply to this in the form of an analogy that, it seems, absolutely destroys the objection.

> *Suppose that a madman kidnaps a victim and shuts him in a room with a card shuffling machine. The machine shuffles ten packs of cards simultaneously and then draws a card from each pack and exhibits simultaneously the ten cards. The kidnapper tells the victim that he will shortly set the machine to work and it will exhibit its first draw, but that unless the draw consists of an ace of hearts from each pack, the machine will simultaneously set off an explosion which will kill the victim, in consequence of which he will not see which cards the machine drew. The machine is then set to work, and to the amazement and relief of the victim the machine exhibits an ace of hearts drawn from each pack. The victim thinks that this extraordinary fact needs an explanation in terms of the machine having been rigged in some way. But the kidnapper, who now reappears, casts doubt on this suggestion. 'It is hardly surprising', he says, 'that the machine draws only aces of hearts. You could not possibly see anything else. For you would not be here to see anything at all, if any other cards had been drawn.' But of course the victim is right and the kidnapper wrong. There is indeed something extraordinary in need of explanation in ten aces of hearts being drawn.* (Swinburne 1991: 138)

God as an explanation for the temporal order of the universe

So Swinburne says that the temporal order of the universe needs to be explained. Science itself cannot explain this, because science cannot explain why it is that all bodies do possess the same very general powers and liabilities. He thus says that the temporal orderliness of the universe 'cries out for explanation in terms of some single common source with the power to produce it' (Swinburne 1991: 145). Swinburne says that the *simplest* explanation is to be found in supposing that it is God – a being of infinite knowledge, power and freedom – who is responsible for the temporal order of the universe.

Mackie's criticisms of Swinburne's design argument

Swinburne's argument has been criticised by, amongst others, J.L. Mackie (Mackie 1982: 146ff.). One problem, says Mackie, is that Swinburne does not show that there might not be, as Hume suggested, a plurality of gods. There are, after all, many laws that hold in the universe and it could be that each deity is 'responsible' for some of the laws.

However, the major problem with Swinburne's argument, according to Mackie, is that to introduce God to explain why laws hold as they do is not, as Swinburne claims, to adopt a simple explanation at all. The concept of

God is so contested and unclear that to resort to him to explain why laws hold is to make matters more complicated. It might be more rational to live with an absence of explanation of why fundamental laws hold than it is to appeal to God.

The design argument and wonder at the world

Before leaving the argument from design, we should return to the point that, as we noted earlier, the argument expresses in some way a sense of *wonder* at the world. This sense of wonder need not be undermined *at all* by the kinds of points that Hume makes against the argument. In fact, it may be that the argument from design is an attempt to capture in *intellectual* terms a fundamentally *spiritual* sense of the world. But the argument does not really succeed in doing this, and this is why the sense of wonder can survive the criticisms levelled at it. Of course, there is an important and big step from the sense of wonder in question to belief in God, but we can nonetheless say that the failure of the argument (if it fails) need not be thought to remove any grounds one might have for religious belief if that belief is nourished by a sense of wonder at the world (cf. Kemp Smith 1967).

review activity

1. Why does Swinburne think that the temporal order of the universe needs explanation?

2. In what way does Mackie criticise Swinburne's explanation of this order by appeal to God?

The cosmological argument

We shall now consider a second *a posteriori* argument for the existence of God. This is the cosmological argument, and we shall focus here on the cosmological argument that is offered by St Thomas Aquinas (1225–74). In his *Summa Theologiae* Thomas offers five ways to prove the existence of God. The first three are usually taken to comprise the cosmological argument. They are: the argument from change or motion; the argument from cause; and the argument from contingency. The first two are very similar to each other and can be dealt with together. The third is a little more complicated.

The arguments from change (motion) and cause

1. Things we observe around us change. They change in part because they have the *potential* to change. For example, a cold piece of wood has the potential to become hot. The potential for change in some thing must be actualised by some other thing that already *actually* has the relevant property. Thus, the wood is cold but potentially hot. Its potential to become hot is actualised by the fire that already actually is hot. Nothing can be in a state of potentiality and actuality in the same respect at the same time. Nothing can therefore be self-changing; nothing can move itself. So each thing that is changed is changed by something else. If we are to avoid an infinite regress of changers or movers we must suppose there to be a first changer or mover. This would be an 'unmoved mover'. Such a being is God.

Some have said that this argument is weak because it is false that nothing can change itself or move itself. Cannot people and animals do this all the time? But Thomas does not mean to deny that animals and people can move themselves at will, for example. His point can be seen if we consider an example. Suppose I open my mouth to speak. Then I have changed. But how have I done this? I can only start speaking in virtue of my not having been speaking up to the moment when I begin to do so. Hence, there must be some aspect of me that brings about the speaking. In other words, some *part* of me causes another part of me to do something. In this sense, I do not cause myself to speak, and indeed, generalising, we can say that nothing changes itself. But that is Thomas's point.

2. In the world around us we see that everything that happens has a cause. For example, the wind causes the leaves to fall off the tree. Each cause itself is caused. Nothing ever causes itself, for a cause always precedes its effect, and for something to cause itself it would have to precede itself. The series of causes must have some terminus, some first cause. This first cause is God.

Horizontal and vertical causal series

Note that to say that God is the first mover or cause, is not to say that God is such a cause in a temporal or chronological sense. Thomas is not thinking of a long series of causes stretching back in time with God at the beginning, that is, of what one might call a 'horizontal' chain of causes. He could not be thinking of this, for that would make his argument absurd. The absurdity would be that he would then be saying that everything is caused by something else and then conclude that there is an exception to this, namely God. The conclusion of the argument would therefore contradict one of the premises. What Thomas has in mind is something else. He is thinking of a first cause that operates *here and now* to sustain a given causal chain in existence. He is thinking of what can be called a 'vertical' series of causes.

Causes in fieri

Here is an analogy. A temporal cause would be this: the relation a person has to his parents. They caused him, but their continued presence is not necessary for him to continue living. For they can die and he live on. This kind of cause is called a cause *in fieri*. The kind of cause that Thomas has in mind can be illustrated by the relation between the electricity supply to my computer and the image on the monitor. The electricity supply keeps the image on the screen in the sense that the supply has to be there continuously here and now to keep the image there.

Causes in esse

If the supply is cut off the image will go. This kind of cause is known as a cause *in esse*. This is the sense in which Thomas argues that God is the first cause: he is needed as a constant presence to keep all causal chains working.

Note also that we can distinguish at least four senses of cause or four answers to the question 'why?' – four 'becauses'.

a) Material cause. In this case, we might want to explain why something happened by referring to the material of which a thing is made. We might answer the question 'why did this object break?' with 'because it was made of glass'.

b) Formal cause. Here we explain why something happened by referring to the kind of thing it is. We might answer the question 'why does this plant thrive in the pond (and other plants would not)?' with 'because it is a lotus'.

c) Final cause. In this case, we explain something by referring to a goal that is being aimed at. We might answer the question 'why are you staying up so late?' with 'to finish this book'.

d) Efficient cause. An appeal to an efficient cause answers the questions 'what did that?' or 'what keeps that going?' For example, we might answer 'what broke the window?' with 'the brick being thrown at it'.

It is with efficient cause that Thomas is concerned in his argument.

review activity

1. Describe in your own words Thomas's first argument for God's existence.

2. In Thomas's second argument for the existence of God, he speaks of God's being a first cause. In what sense does he mean this?

3. Explain the following, giving your own example of each: material cause; formal cause; final cause; efficient cause.

The argument from contingency

The things we see around us exist contingently. That is, although they exist, their non-existence is possible. Contingently existing things might not have existed. For example, the plants in the garden exist, but they might not have, for they might not have been planted in the first place, or they might not have grown through a lack of rain. Each contingent thing once did not exist. So, if we suppose that everything is contingent, then once there was nothing. But if that were so, then there would be nothing now, because something that does not exist can only be brought into existence by something that exists. However, there is something now – indeed, there are lots of things. Therefore, there must be something that does not exist contingently. Such a thing would exist necessarily, i.e., it could not fail to exist. God is such a being, who therefore exists necessarily.

Assessment of Thomas's cosmological argument

The cosmological argument demands an explanation for the existence of the universe. Some have rejected this demand. Thus Bertrand Russell (1872–1970), when asked about a possible explanation for the existence of the universe, crisply said: 'I should say that the universe is just there, and that's all' (Russell and Copleston 1964: 175).

Russell's comment came in the course of a debate on the existence of God with F.C. Copleston (1907–94). The point they were debating at that moment concerned the so-called 'principle of sufficient reason'. Leibniz (1646–1716) gives a classic statement of this principle. The principle of sufficient reason is, he says, that principle 'in virtue of which we hold that no fact could ever be true or existent, no statement correct, unless there were a sufficient reason why it was thus and not otherwise' (Leibniz 1998: 272). Or again: '[N]othing comes about without a sufficient reason; that is . . . nothing happens without its being possible for someone who understands things well enough to provide a reason sufficient to determine why it is as it is and not otherwise' (Leibniz 1998: 262).

> RUSSELL: *So it all turns on this question of sufficient reason, and I must say you haven't defined 'sufficient reason' in a way that I can understand – what do you mean by sufficient reason? You don't mean cause?*
>
> COPLESTON: *Not necessarily. Cause is a kind of sufficient reason. Only contingent being can have a cause. God is His own sufficient reason; and he is not cause of Himself. By sufficient reason in the full sense I mean an explanation adequate for the existence of some particular being.*
>
> RUSSELL: *But when is an explanation adequate? Suppose I am about to make a flame with a match. You may say that the adequate explanation of that is that I rub it on the box.*
>
> COPLESTON: *Well, for practical purposes – but theoretically, that is only a partial explanation. An adequate explanation must ultimately be a total explanation, to which nothing further can be added.*
>
> RUSSELL: *Then I can only say that you're looking for something which can't be got, and which one ought not to expect to get.*
>
> COPLESTON: *To say one has not found it is one thing; to say that one should not look for it seems to me rather dogmatic.*
>
> RUSSELL: *Well, I don't know. I mean, the explanation of one thing is another thing which makes the other thing dependent on yet another, and you have to grasp this sorry scheme of things entire to do what you want, and that we can't do.*
>
> (Russell and Copleston 1984: 173)

Russell surely has a point. If, for example, you want to explain why, say, Hitler invaded Poland in 1939, you might refer to his ambition for living space for Germans in the East, his hatred of the Poles, his hunger for power and the like. If someone said that none of that explained why he invaded Poland, then you might refer also to the economic and political conditions of Germany and Austria after the First World War, seeking to explain how those conditions helped to bring Hitler to power and set him on the road to war. If someone insisted that we *still* did not have an adequate explanation, you might refer to the condition of Germany before the First World War and try to explain more deeply how that war came about and led to the rise of Hitler. But surely at some point we have got an explanation. It is not as if we need an entire history of the world to explain why Hitler invaded Poland in 1939. Yet it looks as if Copleston is saying that only such a total explanation would be adequate, and that demand looks far too strong.

The problem here is that what Copleston is looking for is an explanation of the universe in its entirety, and that may just be an unreasonable demand.

The point was well expressed by Hume:

> *But the WHOLE, you say, wants a cause. I answer, that the uniting of these parts into a whole, like the uniting of several distinct counties into one kingdom, or several distinct members into one body, is performed merely by an arbitrary act of the mind, and has no influence on the nature of things. Did I show you the particular cause of each individual in a collection of twenty particles of matter, I should think it very unreasonable, should you afterwards ask me, what was the cause of the whole twenty. That is sufficiently explained in explaining the cause of the parts.* (Hume 1994: IX [150])

Could something come into existence without a cause?

Hume has a further objection. This is that there is no *logical* absurdity in supposing that something could come into existence without a cause. He writes:

> *[A]s all distinct ideas are separable from each other, and as the ideas of cause and effect are evidently distinct, 'twill be easy for us to conceive any object to be non-existent this moment, and existent the next, without conjoining to it the distinct idea of a cause or productive principle. The separation, therefore, of the idea of a cause from that of a beginning of existence, is plainly possible for the imagination; and consequently the actual separation of these objects is so far possible, that it implies no contradiction nor absurdity.* (Hume 1980: I, 3, §1)

So, according to Hume there is no *a priori* reason why something may not simply come into existence with no cause. But if that is so, then the premise of the cosmological argument that every event must have a cause is false. And if that is true, the whole argument collapses.

Anscombe's criticism of Hume

G.E.M. Anscombe (1919–2001) has challenged Hume (Anscombe 2000). Anscombe argues as follows. We could interpret the claim that something can come into existence (or change) without a cause to be the claim that, of any *given* thing which comes into existence, it might not come into existence through some *specific* cause. Thus, we can say: 'I know what it would be like to find the kettle boiled without a fire'. And this is true, for there might be some *other* cause of its boiling (say, the heat from the sun). But this does not mean that something could come into existence with *no* cause.

So, is there some other way of arguing for Hume's claim? Anscombe says this:

> *[W]hat am I to imagine if I imagine a rabbit coming into being without a cause? Well, I just imagine a rabbit coming into being. That this is the imagination of a rabbit coming into being without cause is, as it were, the title of the picture. Indeed I can form an image and give my picture that title. But from my being able to do that, nothing whatever follows about what is possible to suppose 'without contradiction or absurdity' as holding in reality.* (Anscombe 2000: 238)

If Anscombe is right, then Hume is wrong. And if Hume is wrong, it seems that the claim the cosmological argument makes that every event has a cause is vindicated.

review
activity

1. What is the principle of sufficient reason?

2. In what way does Copleston think this principle important for proving God's existence?

3. What is to be said in favour of Russell's rejection of the demand for the kind of total explanation Copleston wants?

4. Why does Hume think that it is not logically absurd to suppose that something can come into existence with no cause?

5. What is Anscombe's argument against Hume's claim?

Let us now consider briefly the argument from contingency. This argument, it will be remembered, claims that, if all that exists existed contingently, then there would be nothing now. Why does Thomas claim this? His thought seems to be that a contingent thing needs to be *generated*: it depends on something else to bring it into existence. If absolutely everything depended on something else for its existence, then it seems that we could not make sense of the fact that there is anything at all. Why? Brian Davies puts it thus:

> If absolutely everything would not be there but for the activity of something else, then nothing would be there since everything would then depend for its being there on something and since the something in question would be part of what we mean when we speak of absolutely everything. (Davies 2002: 47)

So, there must be something that does not depend on anything else for its existence, that is, there must be something that exists necessarily. And that thing is God.

This argument can be challenged by suggesting it is mistaken to deny that everything could exist contingently. The idea would be that there could be an infinite chain of contingently existing things. On this picture, the mistake Thomas makes is to suppose that, from the fact that each thing exists contingently, we can infer that all things did not once exist *at the same time*. If that were true then we could not make sense of there being anything at all. However, we could instead say that, even if everything exists contingently, this just means that each thing might not exist at *some time other*, but that at any given time there will be *some* contingently existing thing or things in existence. This or these could give rise to some other contingently existing thing or things and so on to infinity. Whether we appeal to causes *in fieri* or causes *in esse* the opponent of Thomas will make the same argument.

Could there be an infinite series of causes?

Clearly this response depends on the idea that an infinite series of contingently existing things makes sense. Of course, if it does then fundamentally the same criticism applies to Thomas's first two ways as to the third. But is it true? Unfortunately, there is no agreement on this point amongst philosophers. To some it seems clear that there could be no infinite chain of contingently existing things; others find it does make sense. We cannot enter into this debate here: suffice it to say that some think that the issue remains a live one in contemporary philosophy.

In any case, the argument from contingency ends in the conclusion that God is a necessary being, a being who could not fail to exist. The next argument we shall look at seeks to prove God's existence as such a necessary being without appealing to the way the world is but simply by appealing to the very concept of God.

The ontological argument (Anselm)

Anselm (c.1033–1109)

We turn now to an *a priori* argument for the existence of God, the ontological argument. The argument explores the traditional conception of God; if valid and sound it establishes that God understood in this way exists. It is not, like the argument from design and the cosmological argument, an argument that makes the existence of God probable or highly probable. That is, it is a deductive argument. If it works, we know that God exists.

Various philosophers have offered an ontological argument for the existence of God. It is traditional to focus in the first instance on the versions offered by Anselm and by Descartes.

I shall discuss Descartes' version of the argument in the chapter of this book devoted to his *Meditations*. In this section, I shall concentrate on the argument offered by Anselm. However, there is a complication here. This is because, although Anselm's argument is usually interpreted as an ontological argument, it can be doubted whether the argument he offers *is* an ontological argument. Accordingly, I shall first discuss Anselm on the assumption that he is offering an ontological argument. Then I shall discuss the alternative interpretation of his argument.

Anselm's argument as an ontological argument

Anselm presents his argument in Chapters 2 and 3 of his work *Proslogion*, written in about 1078. The exact relation between the argument of the two chapters is a matter of debate amongst scholars. I shall offer here a common interpretation to the following effect:

The argument of Proslogion

- *Proslogion 2* seeks to prove that God exists;
- *Proslogion 3* seeks to prove that God cannot possibly fail to exist – in other words, that God's existence is necessary.

The argument of *Proslogion 2*

Anselm starts by defining God. God, he says, is *that than which nothing greater can be conceived.* In saying this he means that God is greater in value than all else. He also means that whatever qualities God has – such as omnipotence, omniscience and so on – he has to the maximum degree.

Anselm now quotes from Psalm 14 in which we read: 'The fool hath said in his heart, *There* is no God.' However, although the fool has said that there is no God, when he hears of 'something than which nothing greater can be conceived', he understands what this means. This means that, although the fool denies that God ('that than which nothing greater can be conceived') exists in reality, he cannot deny that God exists in his, the fool's, mind or understanding. That is, the fool must have some idea of God in his mind in order to deny God's existence in reality, for if he did not have such an idea of God he would not know what he was talking about when he denies that that being exists in reality.

So, God exists in the mind or understanding – even in the mind or understanding of the fool who denies that God exists in reality. Does God exist in any other way, or does he exist only in the understanding? Anselm says that if that than which nothing greater can be conceived exists *only in the understanding* then there is, after all, something greater than that than which nothing greater can be conceived. For if something exists in reality *as well as* in the understanding, then that thing is greater than the thing that exists *only* in the understanding.

Anselm then argues: it is absurd to suppose that there exists something greater than that than which nothing greater can be conceived. For if there is something *greater* than that than which *nothing greater* can be conceived, then that than which nothing greater can be conceived is also *not* that than which nothing greater can be conceived.

Thus, in order to avoid this absurdity, we can conclude that that than which nothing greater can be conceived must exist *in reality as well as in the understanding*. Therefore, that than which nothing greater can be conceived must exist in reality. But God is that than which nothing greater can be conceived. Therefore, God exists in reality. Therefore, God exists.

This argument, as we have seen, claims that something that exists in reality as well as the understanding is greater than the same thing that exists only in the understanding. But if that is so, then the argument is relying on the idea that that which exists in the understanding lacks the *attribute* or *property* that that which exists in reality possesses, namely, *real existence*.

To see this, compare two things: a) the idea of God in your mind; b) God as a real being. What are the properties of God in your mind? They will include: omnipotence, omniscience and perfect goodness. What are the properties of God in reality? They will include: omnipotence, omniscience and perfect goodness. But is there, then, no difference between the two? Surely not. The idea of God in your mind lacks something that God as a real being does not lack. The God in reality has a property that the God in your mind does not have. That property is: existence. So, we can say: the God in your mind has the following properties: omnipotence, omniscience and perfect goodness. And the God in reality has the following properties: omnipotence, omniscience, perfect goodness and existence. As we have seen, it is the fact that the real God has the extra property of existence that makes him greater than the God who only exists in the mind or understanding. Thus, as we have also seen, Anselm draws the conclusion that God really exists.

Existence as a 'great-making' property

So, to repeat, Anselm thinks that existence is a property and that when something exists in reality it is greater than the same thing that exists only in the mind or understanding. Existence is a 'great-making' property.

By this stage in his argument, Anselm has therefore concluded that God exists.

review
activity

1. What is Anselm's definition of God? What does he mean by this definition?

2. Why does Anselm think it clear that the fool must have an idea of God in his mind?

3. Why, according to Anselm, must that than which nothing greater can be conceived exist not merely in the mind or understanding but also in reality?

4. What view of existence underlies Anselm's argument?

The argument of *Proslogion 3*

Anselm's argument is not yet over, however. So far he has argued that that than which nothing greater can be conceived (God) exists. However, many things exist: my books exist, the trees in the garden exist, clouds exist. Is there anything special about God's existence or the way he exists? Anselm thinks there is, and the argument of *Proslogion 3* is designed to show that there is.

Grant that it is established that God really exists. Then we can say that that than which nothing greater can be conceived exists. However, if this being really is that than which nothing greater can be conceived, what must it be like? Suppose we ask this question: Could we conceive that that than which nothing greater can be conceived could not exist? Could we conceive of it as, for example, coming into existence from non-existence? Or as ceasing to exist?

Let us concentrate on the latter.

Suppose we can conceive this: that than which nothing greater can be conceived *is able* to go out of existence. But we can also conceive of the same thing ('that than which nothing greater can be conceived') in this way: it *is not able* to go out of existence. Which of these is greater? In other words, which is greater: God ('that than which nothing greater can be conceived') that *can* go out of existence; or God ('that than which nothing greater can be conceived') that *cannot* go out of existence? Anselm says that clearly the latter is greater. So, he concludes that to conceive that that than which nothing greater can be conceived is able to go out of existence is a contradiction, because we can conceive of something *greater* than that, namely, that than which nothing greater can be conceived as *not* being able to go out of existence. It follows, says Anselm, that that than which nothing greater can be conceived cannot go out of existence.

Exactly the same argument can be run (*mutatis mutandis*, that is making the necessary changes in wording) concerning conceiving that than which nothing greater can be conceived as coming into existence.

The conclusion Anselm draws is that that than which nothing greater can be conceived cannot be conceived either as coming into existence or going out of existence. This being therefore *must* exist: it cannot *not* exist. That is to say that this being exists necessarily. That is to say, God exists *necessarily*.

Anselm rounds off this argument by saying that everything but God exists *contingently*. God therefore, exists, says Anselm, in 'the truest and greatest way'.

review activity

1. Anselm wants to show in *Proslogion 3* that God exists necessarily. What does it mean to say that something exists necessarily?

2. What does it mean to say that something exists contingently? Which things, according to Anselm, exist contingently?

3. What is Anselm's argument for the claim that God exists necessarily?

Gaunilo's island

Gaunilo's criticism of Anselm's argument

Anselm's arguments were criticised in his time by a monk called Gaunilo, about whom very little is known. Anselm replied to Gaunilo's criticisms and directed that both criticisms and replies should be printed together with the main argument of the *Proslogion*. One of Gaunilo's criticisms is especially famous. He suggests that Anselm's reasoning for the existence of God could be applied to show that the perfect island must exist. After all, says Gaunilo, we each understand what is being said by talk of a perfect island. Could one then reason as follows?

> *You cannot any more doubt that this island that is more excellent than all other lands truly exists somewhere in reality than you can doubt that it is in your mind; and since it is more excellent to exist not only in the mind alone but also in reality, therefore it must needs be that it exists. For if it did not exist, any other land existing in reality would be more excellent than it, and so this island, already conceived by you to be more excellent than others, will not be more excellent.*
> (Gaunilo 2000: 316)

Gaunilo says that anyone who thought he could argue in this way to show that the perfect island must exist would surely be joking: it is absurd to argue from the fact that one has the idea of a perfect island that that island must exist. And if the person who offered such an argument were not joking, Gaunilo says, he would surely be a fool. Moreover, anyone who accepted the argument, he goes on, would also be a fool. But if the reasoning is so bad in the case of the island, then surely it is also in the case of God. So we should reject Anselm's argument for the existence of God.

However, things are not yet at an end. This is because Anselm can provide two replies to Gaunilo. The first reply needs two notions. The first is that the perfect island is the greatest conceivable island. The second comes by drawing on Anselm's reasoning in *Proslogion 3*. There, as we have seen, Anselm distinguished between God, who exists necessarily, and all other things, all of which exist contingently. And that is the second notion needed in Anselm's reply to Gaunilo: only God exists necessarily; everything else exists contingently.

Responses to Gaunilo's criticism

Using these notions, then, Anselm can reply to Gaunilo as follows. The perfect island, if it exists, must exist contingently. That is, it must depend for its existence on whatever it was that created it – a volcanic eruption, or whatever. However, the perfect island is the greatest conceivable island. What is it to be the greatest conceivable island? It is to exist *necessarily*, for that is what it is to be the greatest conceivable thing of whatever sort. But no island can exist necessarily. Only God exists necessarily. Therefore, the very definition of the greatest conceivable island is a contradiction, because it is the definition of a contingently existing thing as existing necessarily (cf. Davis 1997: 30–1).

There is, however, a second reply that Anselm can make to Gaunilo's island example. Consider again the notion of the greatest conceivable island. Such an island would possess all the properties that make an island great. What are these? Let us say that they are beautiful scenery, sunlight, adequate shade, white sands, fresh running water and the like. But the greatest conceivable island would have such properties in the greatest conceivable way. But this seems incoherent. There are two closely connected reasons for this. First, how would we decide what the greatest amount of sunlight is, or what the greatest conceivable scenery is? There seems no way to do this, not least because people disagree about such things. Secondly, it seems that however great the greatest island is, it could always be greater. This is because, as Alvin Plantinga has said, there is no intrinsic maximum to such things as the amount of sunlight, or beautiful scenery.

> *No matter how great an island is, no matter how many Nubian maidens and dancing girls adorn it, there could always be a greater – one with twice as many, for example. The qualities that make for greatness in an island – number of palm trees, amount and quality of coconuts, for example – most of these qualities have no intrinsic maximum. That is, there is no degree of productivity or number of palm trees (or of dancing girls) such that it is impossible that an island display more of that quality. So the idea of a greatest possible island is an inconsistent or incoherent idea; it's not possible that there be such a thing.*
> (Plantinga 1977: 90–1)

So Gaunilo's criticism of Anselm's argument seems to fail: the greatest conceivable island cannot even possibly exist, whereas this cannot be said of God.

review activity

1. What is Gaunilo's argument against Anselm's ontological argument?

2. What reply can Anselm give to Gaunilo?

Kant's criticisms of the ontological argument

Probably the most famous criticism made of the ontological argument is that offered by Immanuel Kant (1724–1804). In his *Critique of Pure Reason* he wrote:

> 'Being' is obviously not a predicate; that is, it is not a concept of something which could be added to the concept of a thing. It is merely the positing of a thing, or of certain determinations, as existing in themselves . . . If, now, we take the subject (God) with all its predicates . . . and say 'God is', or 'There is a God', we attach no new predicate to the concept of God, but only posit the subject in itself with all its predicates, and indeed posit it as being an object that stands in relation to my concept. The content of both must be one and the same . . . Otherwise stated, the real contains no more than the merely possible. A hundred real thalers [a unit of currency] do not contain the least coin more than a hundred possible thalers.
>
> (Kant 1985: 504–5 [A598-9/B626-7])

Is existence a predicate?

What is Kant saying? What is his criticism of the ontological argument? His point is often put in this way: existence is not a predicate. In other words, it is not a property of something that it exists. If, for example, we are asked to list the properties of something and we say that it is green, large and furry, it would be odd if the person who had asked us to list the object's properties said that we had left one out, namely, its existence. Or consider the following. It makes sense to say: 'my future house will be a better one if it is insulated than if it is not insulated'. But it hardly seems to make sense to say: 'my future house will be a better house if it exists than if it does not' (Malcolm 1965: 143). Again:

> A king might desire that his next chancellor should have knowledge, wit, and resolution; but it is ludicrous to add that the king's desire is to have a chancellor who exists. Suppose that two royal councilors, A and B, were asked to draw up separately descriptions of the most perfect chancellor they could conceive, and that the descriptions they produced were identical except that A included existence in his list of attributes of a perfect chancellor and B did not. (I do not mean that B put non-existence in his list.) One and the same person could satisfy both descriptions. More to the point, any person who satisfied A's description would necessarily satisfy B's description and vice versa!
>
> (Malcolm 1965: 144)

So far it seems, then, from such cases that existence is not a predicate. That is, existence is not a property. But, as we saw, Anselm's argument seems to rely on precisely the idea that existence is a property. Given that this is so, it seems that the argument fails.

However, note that it only fails if it is true that existence is not a property – and that can be questioned. Stephen T. Davis has said, for example, that to say that a given thing exists can in some cases 'expand our concept of it' (Davis 1997: 34). If, for example, he says, he found out that the Loch Ness Monster really exists, his concept of this monster would change. Moreover, even in the case of the councillors, things might be more complicated than Malcolm allows. There might, for example, be someone in a novel who satisfies all the attributes on B's list but who does not exist (because he is a fictional character) and therefore does not satisfy all the attributes on A's list. Again, there might be someone who has died who satisfied all the attributes on B's list but not all those on A's (Davis 1997: 34-5. Cf. Alston 1967).

Whether Kant and those who think like him are right, or whether those who think that existence can be a property are right, is too big a question to try to settle here. Suffice it to say that there is no agreement amongst philosophers on this question.

activity

1. Kant argues that the ontological argument fails because it treats existence as a predicate. Explain what this means and why it might be thought to show that the ontological argument fails.

2. What reason might there be to say that existence can after all, be a predicate?

Anselm's argument as a non-ontological argument

One way in which Anselm could avoid the whole problem over whether existence is a property is if he did not appeal to the idea that it is in his argument. For if he did not, then his argument would not involve the claim that existing in reality is one of the properties that make something great. However, if that were so, his argument would not be an ontological argument at all.

Now just this has been argued by G.E.M. Anscombe in a paper entitled 'Why Anselm's Proof in the *Proslogion* Is Not an Ontological Argument' (Anscombe 1985). The paper is difficult, and only the bare bones of what it argues can be given here.

The key to Anscombe's interpretation is the translation of an important sentence in *Proslogion 2*. The sentence can be translated from the Latin in one of two ways. The sentence prior to the one in question runs: 'And for sure that than which a greater cannot be conceived cannot exist only in the intellect.' Then the key sentence can be translated either as:

1. For if it is only in the intellect, it can be thought to be in reality as well, which is greater; or as:
2. For if it is only in the intellect, what is greater can be thought to be in reality as well.

Now, the difference between these is crucial. The first really does involve the idea that existing in reality is a great-making feature of something, and thus that existence is a property. This is how the sentence is usually taken. Then Anselm's argument is an ontological argument and open to Kant's objection. But the second translation does not commit Anselm to the idea that existence is a property. If it is right to read Anselm in this second way, then we have a quite different argument altogether.

On this different argument, it would have to be something *other* than the fact that it exists in reality that makes something that exists in reality greater than the same thing that exists only in the intellect.

What is the argument on Anscombe's reading? This can best be seen by a parallel (Anscombe 1993: 502). I can think of a pain more intense than can be survived. This thought is simply in my mind or understanding. Suppose now that someone has witnessed another suffer such a pain: obviously, the person suffering the pain died. So now the witness has a thought of a pain – an actual pain – more intense than can be survived. Now, one might say that the pain that he, the witness, can think of is more intense than the pain I can think of, even though we both think of a pain more intense than can be survived. One might say that the description of a pain more intense than can be survived that the witness can give is real, whereas the description I can give of such a pain is imaginary. We could also say: the witness's thought is greater than my thought.

Suppose now that there could be a thought like the thought that the witness had, but that one did not have to witness a real pain more intense than can be survived in order to have it. It is just that the thought itself is greater in virtue of being of something greater, even though, as said, the corresponding real pain was not witnessed. Anscombe suggests that something like this idea is going on in Anselm's argument. The fool has a thought of that than which nothing greater can be conceived. However, there is a thought of something greater, something that really exists – in other words, something that exists outside the mind or understanding. This latter thought is greater than the thought the fool has of that than which nothing greater can be conceived. However, that shows that the thought the fool has is not, after all, of that than which nothing greater can be conceived.

But if it is not the *existence* of that than which nothing greater can be conceived that is the source of the maximal greatness of the thing existing in reality, what is it? Anscombe suggests that it is that that thing, which exists, exists necessarily. For a thing that exists necessarily is greater than a thing that exists.

What does Anscombe's version of Anselm's argument show? Anscombe says she is not sure. In fact, she says she does not know whether it is a valid argument (Anscombe 1993: 500). But if she is right about what Anselm is arguing, then she has established an extremely important result: Anselm's argument is not an ontological argument.

The argument from religious experience

We must now consider one last argument for God's existence. This is the argument from religious experience.

Features of religious experience

The term 'religious experience' has a wide range of reference. It 'can be applied to any experiences one has in connection with one's religious life, including a sense of guilt or release, joys, longings, and a sense of gratitude'. (Alston 2000: 382). However, it is usually used in philosophy to refer to occasions when a person (subject) takes himself to be directly aware of God or some other Ultimate Reality (nirvana, for example).

Private and public perceptions

Even with its range thus narrowed down, the term still covers many different types of experience. Richard Swinburne has sought to provide a taxonomy or classification of different types of religious experience (Swinburne 1991: 250–1).

First, he distinguishes between public and private perceptions (Swinburne 1991: 248–9). Roughly, if an object *x* causes normal perceivers under normal conditions who are rightly positioned to enjoy an experience of *x*, then *x* is a public perception. For example, roughly speaking, if ten individuals who are sober, possess properly functioning eyes, are standing close to one another in good light and facing the same way all have an experience of a tree, then the experience of the tree is a public perception. However, if under the kinds of condition previously described it is *not* the case that all normal subjects enjoy an experience of *x*, but rather that only one or some such subjects enjoy an experience of *x*, then the experience of *x* is a private perception.

Five types of religious experience

Having distinguished public from private sensations, Swinburne then goes on to suggest that there are five ways in which one might have a religious experience.

1. The subject perceives a perfectly ordinary non-religious public object but when he does so he has an experience of God. For instance, he might experience part of the natural world in this way. He might, Swinburne says, suddenly experience the night sky as God's handiwork. Here is another example: 'There was a mysterious presence in nature . . . which was my greatest delight, especially when as happened from time to time, *nature became lit up from the inside* with something that came from beyond itself' (Alston 2000: 383, quoting Beardsworth 1997: 19).

2. A very unusual public object is perceived and in perceiving this object the subject has a religious experience. For example, in Luke 24: 36–49, after Jesus' crucifixion, when Jesus was thought to be dead, a man looking like Jesus appeared to the disciples and ate some fish and honey. In seeing him, they took him to be the risen Jesus Christ, and in this sense they were having a religious experience. Someone else might have seen this man and not taken him to be the risen Christ. This person would, therefore, have seen the same object that the disciples saw (that is, the man who looked like Jesus) but not have had a religious experience.

3. Someone has a private experience of certain sensations that he takes to be a religious experience, but this private experience can be described in perfectly normal vocabulary. For example, at the beginning of Matthew's Gospel we read that Joseph is disturbed by the fact that Mary is with child although they are not yet married. Then we read (Matthew 1: 20): '[T]he angel of the Lord appeared unto him in a dream, saying, Joseph, thou son of David, fear not to take unto thee Mary thy wife: for that which is conceived in her is of the Holy Ghost.'

4. The subject has a private experience of certain sensations analogous to, but not the same as, ordinary sensations (as when one sees or hears a public object) that he takes to be a religious experience but that cannot be described in normal language. We might speak here is a 'sixth sense'.

5. The subject has a private experience which he takes to be a religious experience but in which he has no sensations. There are two types of case here. a) Those in which the subject experiences God as a 'nothingness' or 'darkness'. b) Those where someone is convinced that God is

telling him to do something or other (for example, follow a certain vocation) but experiences no sensations.

Presumably, the following from St Teresa (1515–82) is an example of this last kind of religious experience.

I was at prayer on a festival of the glorious Saint Peter when I saw Christ at my side – or, to put it better, I was conscious of Him, for neither with the eyes of the body nor with those of the soul did I see anything.

(Quoted in Peterson *et al.* (eds) 1996: 7)

All of the cases Swinburne describes are, of course, of religious experiences, but it seems that we can understand some religious experiences as mystical experiences. That is, mystical experiences seem to be a subclass of religious experiences. It is hard, perhaps impossible, to provide a clear set of distinguishing features for mystical experiences. Mystical experiences seem to be different from other religious experiences in being more extraordinary. Sometimes they are taken to involve the obliteration of distinctions in the kind of way described as follows.

Suddenly, at church, or in company, or when I was reading, and always, I think, when my muscles were at rest, I felt the approach of the mood. Irresistibly it took possession of my mind and will, lasted what seemed an eternity, and disappeared in a series of rapid sensations which resembled the awakening from anaesthetic influence. One reason why I disliked this kind of trance was that I could not describe it to myself. I cannot even now find words to render it intelligible. It consisted in a gradual but swiftly progressive obliteration of space, time, sensation, and the multitudinous factors of experience which seem to qualify what we are pleased to call our Self. In proportion as these conditions of ordinary consciousness were subtracted, the sense of an underlying or essential consciousness acquired intensity. At last nothing remained but a pure, absolute, abstract Self. The universe became without form and devoid of content. (J.A. Symonds, quoted in James 1971: 371)

Mystical experiences are the kinds of experiences sought by those in different religious traditions who actually embark on a regimen or kind of training in order to achieve mystical insight. Such training often includes asceticism (self-denial), breathing exercises, physical exercise of various kinds (such as yoga) and the like. It seems that Swinburne's categories 4 and 5a are the most likely to be accounted mystical experiences.

Swinburne claims that his list is exhaustive and exclusive, that is, that it covers all the cases of religious experience and that each case of religious experience can be fitted into one, and no more than one, of the five categories. However, there are some religious experiences and some mystical experiences that it is hard to fit into one or other of his categories. For example, the following is clearly a religious experience: 'God surrounds me like the physical atmosphere. He is closer to me than my own breath. In him literally I live and move and have my being' (Quoted in James 1971: 86.) This does not really seem to fit properly any of Swinburne's categories, although 1 seems the most likely.

There are also some mystical experiences that it is hard to fit clearly into one or other category. For example, the case I have already quoted from Symonds seems like this. It is not quite clear whether this should go into category 4 or 5. From one perspective it looks as it fits into 5, because the writer refers to an absence of sensation. However, when the writer says that all that was left in his experience was that of 'a pure, absolute abstract Self', it is hard to know whether this was an experience of a 'something' or a 'nothing'. It strongly suggests a 'something', a positive presence, but then the references to the formlessness and lack of content of the universe suggest a 'nothing', so the situation is unclear.

Another example of a mystical experience that does not obviously fit neatly in any one of Swinburne's categories seems to be provided by the Christian mystic St John of the Cross (1542–91). Speaking of the contemplation in which he experienced God, he writes:

> *Contemplation is secret and hidden from the very person that experiences it; and ordinarily, together with the aridity and emptiness which it causes in the senses, it gives the soul an inclination and desire to be alone and in quietness, without being able to think of any particular thing or having the desire to do so . . . [T]he soul . . . can find no suitable way or manner or similitude by which it may be able to describe such lofty understanding and such delicate spiritual feeling . . . A person contemplating can only say that he is satisfied, tranquil, and contented, and that he is conscious of the presence of God, and that, as it seems to him, all is going well with him; but he cannot describe the state of his soul, nor can he say anything about it save in general terms like these.*
>
> (Quoted in Kenny 1987: 97–8)

As in the case from Symonds, it is far from clear whether this should go into category 4 or 5, for it is unclear whether St John really experienced any sensations here (and if he did of what kind they were) or whether his sense of God was that of a 'nothing'.

Still, it is, perhaps, not terribly important whether Swinburne's taxonomy is correct as or not, just so long as it helps us have a good sense of the kinds of things religious and mystical experiences are.

review activity

State and explain Swinburne's five categories of religious experience.

William James, from whom I have quoted some of the examples of religious experience that have been given, suggested four distinguishing features of mystical experience (James 1971: 367–8). These are:

Four features of religious experience

1. *Ineffability.* According to James, mystical experiences are ineffable: those who have them cannot adequately describe in words what it is that they experience in this way. James draws an analogy between the ineffability of mystical states and the experience of music or the experience of being in love. Just as it is possible for some people to be dead to music or certain kinds of music so that they cannot hear the value of, say, a particular symphony; and just as it is more-or-less impossible to understand

William James (1842–1910)

what it is to be in love if one has never been in love; so, he says, only those who have had mystical experiences can really understand what it is to have such experiences.

2. *Noetic quality.* Mystical states seem to give those privy to them an insight into the true nature of reality: they seem to be states of knowledge about the way the universe is. We shall return to this at length below.

3. *Transiency.* Not always, but in general, says James, mystical experiences are not sustained for long: it is rare for them to last more than half an hour. (Note, however, that whilst undergoing a mystic experience the subject might well feel that the experience is lasting a very long time, even if it is not. The example from Symonds, above, illustrates this sense that the mystical experience can be very prolonged.)

4. *Passivity.* When the mystic has a mystical experience he feels that his will is in abeyance: he is in the grip of something else, which controls him. This is true even where mystics train in order to have mystical experiences: they can try to produce the correct conditions for such an experience to come, but when it does come it is not something over which the mystics have control.

Are religious experiences ineffable?

Richard M. Gale has objected to the idea that mystical experiences should be thought of as ineffable in some way in which other experiences are not. On the contrary, he argues, mystical experiences are, if ineffable, ineffable in just the way that many other experiences are. Therefore to say that mystical experiences are ineffable is to make a 'trivial claim'. He writes:

> *No concepts can completely describe any direct experience; they can never serve as substitutes for such experiences. My concept of a loud, deafening noise is not itself a loud deafening noise. Our experience of yellow is just as unique and ineffable as a mystical experience; we cannot define the color yellow in terms of anything more basic or simple.*   (Gale 1982: 116)

Nonetheless, Gale does draw an analogy between aesthetic experiences and mystical experiences, as does James, although in a somewhat different way. Thus he says that the experience of the second movement of Beethoven's Seventh Symphony is both tragic and joyous, and this contradictory description is also true of mystical experiences, which mystics often describe as being 'passive and active, personal and impersonal, full and empty, containing a multiplicity of objects and still being a Oneness without parts, etc.' (Gale 1982: 117). We might note here in passing that the fact that mystical states can be, and often are, described in contradictory terms is one reason why Swinburne's classification of religious experiences was found in some ways wanting, as was pointed out earlier.

review activity

1. State and explain James's four features of mystical experience.

2. What does it mean to say that mystical experiences are ineffable and what is Gale's objection to saying this?

Religious experience and the existence of God

Granted, then, that we understand something of the nature of religious experiences, we must ask what the relevance of these is to the existence of God.

Are religious experiences ever veridical?

It will be clear from all that has been said so far that there is supposed to be an analogy between sense experience, such as seeing a tree in front of one, tasting pineapple and so forth, and experience of God. In the case of sense experience, we have an experience and it is an experience *of* something – *of* a tree, *of* a pineapple, as the case may be. The existence of the tree or the pineapple explains the corresponding sense experience and it does so because it *causes* that corresponding sense experience. Clearly, religious experiences are genuine experiences in the sense that subjects have them. But the question is: are they experiences *of* anything? Thus, a mystic might have an experience that he takes to be of God, but *is* it really *of* God? Is it *caused* by God in the way that the experience of a tree is caused by the tree or the experience of the pineapple is caused by the pineapple? That is, is it *veridical?*

Here is another way to put the question. We can distinguish between sense experiences such as those of trees and sense experiences such as those of headaches. In the normal case, a sense experience of a tree has an object, namely, the tree. However, a headache has no object: it is not *of* anything. True, it is caused by something – say a lack of blood flowing to the brain – but it is still not *of* anything in the way an experience of a tree is *of* a tree (not even of the lack of blood in the brain). So is a religious experience analogous to the sense experience of a tree or to the sense experience of a headache? If it is analogous to the former we can say it is of something (namely, of God); if it is analogous to the latter it will be caused by something but not be *of* anything (cf. Wainwright 1982).

So, the key question is: Are mystics and others who have religious experiences right to think they are experiencing God? Does the occurrence of religious experiences support the claim that God exists? Or is there some other explanation of religious experiences? If mystics are right to say they are experiencing God, this clearly gives us good grounds for thinking that God exists, just as our experiences of trees give us good reason for thinking trees exist. But if there is some other explanation of mystical experiences, this will clearly weaken the claim that such experiences can justify belief in the existence of God.

In the following two sections I shall, first, give the main reasons against thinking of religious experiences as experiences of God and then, secondly, suggest some reasons why we might, after all, think that they are or, at any rate, why they lend some support to rational belief in the existence of God.

Religious experience as experience of God: the arguments against

Religious experiences, we have seen, are supposed to be forms of awareness of God that are analogous to forms of ordinary perceptual awareness. So, to see if the analogy works, we have to understand something about our ordinary sense experiences of public objects such as trees, desks, cats and mountains.

Consider the following features of our perception of public objects (cf. Alston 1983: 121):

1. There are standard ways of checking the accuracy of a perception of a public object. This is so in at least two ways. First, one mode of sense experience (for example, sight) can be checked against another (for example, touch). Thus, if I see a piece of material or cloth before me I might suspect that it is velvet or has the feel of velvet, but not be quite sure. I can touch it to corroborate (or subvert, as the case may be) the evidence of my eyes. Secondly, if I am not sure what it is before me I can get others to take a look, feel it, taste it or whatever (cf. Martin 1963: esp. 86–8).

2. We can, through observing public objects, discover regularities in the way they behave and come to be able, to a greater or lesser extent, to predict the way they will behave in certain circumstances. For example, we can predict what will happen to a wooden chair if thrown on a bonfire; or what will happen to the oil if poured into this other liquid (water); or (more loosely) that if there are clouds in the sky and other conditions are fulfilled then it will rain; and so on. Further, and connectedly, sense experience is continuous and regular whilst we are awake.

3. All normal human beings have the capacity to perceive (can see, taste, smell, touch, hear) public objects. Deviations from this, such as blindness, or lack of a sense of smell, can be readily and uncontroversially explained.

4. All normal human beings in all cultures see public objects in much the same way (they use the same 'material object conceptual scheme').

Many philosophers have argued that none of these conditions holds for religious experience. From this they have concluded that sense experience and religious experience are *dis*analogous and thus that we have no good grounds for thinking that someone who claims to experience God is really experiencing God as we have good grounds for thinking that someone who claims (under normal conditions) to be experiencing a tree in front of him is experiencing a tree in front if him.

Let us look at the alleged disanalogies.

First, it seems that we lack checking procedures for putative religious experiences. If you are not sure what it is that you see in front of you, you can ask someone else what he can see at the same place. If the object is a public object, there is no problem here about checking up. However, it seems, we do not have the same thing in the case of religious experiences. If a person claims to have seen God at a certain place, one cannot go there and check whether God is to be seen there. Moreover, whilst a person is undergoing a religious experience he can hardly ask someone in the vicinity to check that what he is experiencing is, indeed, really there.

Secondly, although we can predict the way public objects will behave in given sets of circumstances we cannot predict how God will behave – whether, when and to whom he will manifest himself. Religious experiences are not at all continuous or regular whilst we are awake.

Thirdly, it is not true that all normal human beings have religious experiences as they all have sense experiences of public objects.

Fourthly, different cultures have very deep differences in terms of their religious conceptual schemes: there seems to be no universal religion as there is a universal conceptual scheme for public objects.

Related to this fourth issue is the fact that religious experiences have been reported of many different, sometimes mutually incompatible gods. For example, as Antony Flew has said,

The varieties of religious experience

> *the varieties of religious experience include, not only those which their subjects are inclined to interpret as visions of the blessed Virgin or senses of the guiding presence of Jesus Christ, but also others more outlandish presenting themselves as manifestations of Quetzalcotal [an Aztec god] or Osiris [a god of ancient Egypt], of Dionysus [an ancient Greek god] or Shiva [a Hindu god].* (Flew 1966: 126–7)

Moreover, the kind of god that someone sees in a religious experience seems to depend heavily upon that person's interests, character, background and expectations (cf. Flew 1966: 126). Thus, for example, a Roman Catholic monk is hardly likely to have a religious experience of Dionysus. This suggests that the subject of the religious experience sees what he sees in the experience because he already believes in the god or in God, and not because the god, or God, is really presenting himself to the subject (cf. Mackie 1982: 181).

Together, these points all suggest that religious experiences are not veridical. That is, what is going on in a religious experience is *not* that God is presenting himself to the subject; there must be some *other* explanation of what is going on. This other explanation would be a purely human or naturalistic explanation, that is, one that does not appeal to anything transcendent. Perhaps, for example, the mystic thinks he sees God because he *wants* to see God; or because he is uncritical in what he believes (he is gullible); or because his unconscious mind is working to make him think he sees God – he has subconscious motives to have the experience (cf. Mackie 1982: 181), and so on. In short, religious experiences do nothing to establish the existence of God. Moreover, even if we accepted that the subject really has seen God in a religious experience, it does not follow from this that he has seen the God of traditional theology, that is to say, an omnipotent, omniscient, wholly good (and so forth) being (cf. Mackie 1982: 182).

review
activity

1. State four features of our everyday sense experience of public material objects.

2. State and explain four disanalogies between such sense experience and religious experience.

Religious experience as experience of God: the arguments for

There are several possible lines of response to the above criticisms of the worth of religious experience in establishing, or helping to establish, the existence of God.

Religion as a key element in human life

1. One response is to point out that religion constitutes a central and dynamic aspect of the history of human life, and that religious experiences have been one very important element in nurturing that aspect of human life. We thus need very good reason to dismiss the value of religious experience in its claim to give us some insight into the nature of the transcendent, for if we do dismiss it in this way we are saying that, in the end, there is *nothing* of truth in such experiences (cf. Smart 1969: 120). This may, of course, be correct, but it is wise to be cautious here: if millions of people have thought that religious experience does give us some understanding of the transcendent it would be well to look carefully at whether there is not, after all, something in what they say.

The principle of credulity

2. Richard Swinburne has formulated and defended what he calls the 'principle of credulity' (Swinburne 1991: 254ff.). This is the principle according to which when a subject takes himself to be presented with some object *x* then probably *x* is present. That is, what one perceives to be so is probably so. We use this principle for sense perceptions of public material objects, and so we should also, says Swinburne, in the case of God.

Defeating conditions

Of course, there are restrictions on this principle – that is, cases where we should say that, even if it seems to some subject that *x* is present then *x* is nonetheless probably not present. Swinburne discusses four of these *defeating* conditions. They are: a) the apparent perception was made under conditions or by a subject found in the past to be unreliable; for example, the subject is an inveterate liar or was under the influence of LSD; b) the subject claims to have perceived an object of a certain kind in circumstances where similar perceptual claims have proved false – for example the subject did not have the necessary experience to make reliable perceptual claims in such instances; c) the subject claims to have perceived *x* but we have independent evidence that *x* was probably not present to the subject at that time, such as when you think you see Rudolf in Cambridge, but I have good grounds for thinking that Rudolf was in London at that time; d) whether or not *x* was present, it was probably not *x* that was the cause of the subject's perception – for example, if an actor is dressed like Fyodor the subject might believe that he had perceived Fyodor in seeing the actor but would in fact have no good grounds for believing that he had perceived Fyodor.

We could argue that these four defeating conditions do not in general apply to cases of religious experience and thus that we have good grounds to believe those who claim to have perceived God. Thus, usually most of those who claim to have had religious experiences are not liars and have not been under the influence of drugs; secondly, there is no reason to doubt that someone could recognise God if God presented himself to him (one could recognise an omnipotent God by hearing his voice, for example); thirdly, God is everywhere (omnipresent), so, for the third defeating condition to apply we should have to show that very probably there is no God, and this has not been shown; fourthly, even if it is claimed that the (putative) experience of God is actually caused by something else, that is, can be explained by being given a naturalistic account, we do not in general have such an account (cf. Alston 2000: 385).

Of course, sometimes, one or more of the defeating conditions will apply and we shall say that a subject did not really have a religious experience. But this will only be so on occasion and thus, in general, we have reason to believe those who claim to have perceived God.

The negative principle of credulity

However, there is a reply to Swinburne's argument. Michael Martin has suggested this reply by formulating what he calls a 'negative principle of credulity' (Martin 1996: 52–3). He says that, just as we could say that, other things being equal (if the defeating conditions do not apply), we have good reason to believe that if a subject says he has perceived *x* then *x* was present, we could also say that if it seems to a subject that he does not perceive *x* then *x* is not present. Very many people – perhaps most people – do not take themselves to have perceived God, so this, says Martin, is a good reason for thinking that God is not present.

Do the disanalogies between sense experience and religious experience matter?

3. We could argue that, although it is true that we have no checks for religious experience as we have for sense experience of public objects, this does not matter because the objects in each case (God; trees, tables, mountains and so forth) are so different (Alston 1983: 129). Roughly, the claim is that if God is as he is traditionally thought to be, then:

a) he is very different from created beings;
b) we can only attain a very sketchy idea of what he is like; and
c) (plausibly) he has decreed that it is only under very special and difficult conditions that he might be perceived.

Hence, a) will explain why there is a difference in predictability between God's behaviour and that of public objects; b) will explain why different cultures have different conceptions of God (whereas they do not have different conceptions of public objects); and c) will explain why the capacity to perceive God is rare amongst human beings.

It is appropriate here, in the light of b), to add some further comments on the fact that different cultures have different religions. Some, as we have seen, suggest that this fact undermines the claim that a given religious experience can be veridical because different such experiences would seem to support belief in different, sometimes conflicting, religious creeds. However, this is only so if one believes that the different religions must ultimately conflict with one another. This is too big and deep a question to go into at length here, but it should be noted that it can be argued that the different religions – at any rate, Judaism, Christianity and Islam – are different ways of thinking about and experiencing the same Ultimate Reality (see, for example, Hick 1993: ch.9). There are several reasons for thinking this: there is a great deal of overlap in the moral teaching and outlook of these religions; they often draw on the same or similar stories in their account of human life and its purpose; and they share in many ways a core understanding of the nature of God. Not everyone will agree with this. Perhaps the greatest objection is the idea that Jesus of Nazareth was God incarnate, and that only through him is anyone saved: James Borland has argued that anyone who does not believe in Jesus as the Christ (the anointed one) is damned (Borland 1996: 495–502). Others have argued that we need to give up the idea that Jesus was God incarnate (see, for example, the essays in Hick 1977).

Are there checks on religious experiences?

4. We could say that there are, after all, checks when a person claims to have had a religious experience (Wainwright 1982: 127–8). It must be considered whether:

a) the effects on the person are good, for example in terms of renewed virtue or goodness;

b) the effects on the community are good – for example, does the person have a good effect on his community as a result of his religious experience?;

b) the person can speak with more depth and authority than before the experience;

d) what the person says agrees or not with what the orthodox of his religion say;

e) the person's religious experience resembles other such experiences had by members of the religious community in question;

f) the authorities in the religion (such as a spiritual director, guru, bishops and so forth) are inclined to believe the individual's report on his religious experience or not.

Evidently a) to c) depend on a conditional: *if* God is good, holy and so forth, then we should expect the individual who has had a genuine religious experience of God to be increased in his virtue, benefit his community in a new or fresh way, and speak with depth and authority. In the case of d) to f), these tests only apply if one already accepts the tenets of some specific religious authority.

Religious experience and its effect on a person

Some philosophers have denied absolutely that the effects on a person – goodness, way of speaking and so forth – who claims to have had a religious experience are of any relevance at all in judging whether the experience was genuinely of God. This is because they claim that the experience might not have been of God at all and yet still have these good effects (Flew 1966: 127–8). However, it is far from clear that such philosophers are right.

Consider the following comment made by Rush Rhees:

I knew a woman . . . who maintained . . . that she had had just such an experience [a religious experience] herself. And I do not believe it. I believe that she had the vision or the dream she described. But it was nothing of the sort that Paul's and Simone Weil's experiences were. And I say this categorically because I think that if it had been, then she and her life would have been impressive in a way they were not. I do not mean that she would have said illuminating things about religion. I mean that it would have shown in what she said about the lives and affairs of people in this world. (Rhees 1997: 339)

In this passage, Rhees is contrasting the woman in question with St Paul and Simone Weil.

Rhees's point is well taken. Very often it is extremely important in moral and religious matters whether we think that a person can stand behind his words, speak with authority and not simply mouth what he has been told by others or has simply absorbed from the society in which he happens to find himself. Such a person resists clichés and hackneyed ways of expressing himself and describing the world. Of course, we would only think someone such a person if we could see that his behaviour had the same kind of integrity as his speech, if, indeed, his speech and deeds reflected one another. In speaking of the woman he knew as he does and in saying that she had nothing significant to say about the lives and affairs of people in this world, Rhees is making the point that she lacked authority in what she said; she did not speak out of what one might call a disciplined individuality. Yet he obviously felt that this individuality could be found in Paul and in Weil. It is such people who can sometimes make us see the sense and meaning of a way of speaking and a way of living that before had seemed meaningless to us or to which we had been indifferent. We can in this way learn through others' example. If someone speaks with the kind of authority in question and this is connected with his having had a religious experience, this might enable us to come to believe that he had genuinely experienced God or, at the very least, to keep an open mind about God's presence to him.

Of course, some people might simply insist that they will never believe that someone could have had a veridical religious experience and they will not distinguish, as Rhees does, between those whose religious experience one can take seriously and those whose religious experience one cannot take seriously. As J.J.C. Smart has said, 'someone who has naturalistic preconceptions will always in fact find some naturalistic explanation [of a religious experience] more plausible than a supernatural one' (Smart in Smart and Haldane 1996: 50). This may be true. But part of the problem with Smart's comment is that, as we have already noted, we have no real idea what such a naturalistic account might be

Simone Weil (1909–43)

Simone Weil was a teacher, political activist and mystic. She was born in Paris in 1909 into a non-orthodox Jewish family. She was educated at the Lycée Henri IV and the Ecole Normale Supérieure, training to become a teacher. After graduation, she taught at various schools, but also worked on farms and at the Renault car factory, her political views leading her to want to experience life as the working class did. In 1936 she went to Spain to join the anarchist militia in the Spanish Civil War. She did not want to fight, but she showed in her temperament a keen desire to seek out extreme situations, partly as a way of testing her own limits and partly as a way of experiencing what the weakest in society had to endure. She returned to France after being burned in an accident. In 1938 at Solesmes Monastery she had a mystical experience. In a later mystical experience she said that 'Christ himself came down and took hold of me'. In 1940 she settled briefly at Marseilles, leaving France for the US on 17 May 1942. She returned to Europe, to England, late in the same year in order to serve under the French provisional government. Whilst in England she refused to eat more than her compatriots in occupied France had, and this weakened her already failing health. She died in August 1943 in Ashford, Kent. Her major works include *Gravity and Grace* (1947), *Waiting on God* (1951), a collection of letters and essays, and *The Need for Roots* (1943).

like. Moreover, the issue here is *never* simply one of intellectual conviction: if one supposes that there *must* be a naturalistic explanation this will be because one cannot take seriously the idea that a religious experience could be veridical (cf. Davis 1997: 132). This is why Richard Gale is surely right to say:

Conceptions of reality as conceptions of value

> The question, 'Which is the true *reality*, the one revealed to us in *mystical* experiences or the one revealed to us in our *non-mystical* experiences?,' is really a value question and cannot be settled by any logical means. What a man takes to be the really *real* is a value judgement expressive of what experiences have the greatest significance for him.
>
> (Gale 1982: 122)

And for those who are not determined that they already know what they think about religious experiences, it is possible that one learn from the authority of another as Rhees clearly took himself to learn from St Paul and Simone Weil. This would not provide a 'proof of God's existence', but it would form part of the case to be made for his existence.

some questions to think about

1. 'We cannot but think of the universe as orderly: but that is quite different from thinking of it as designed.' Is this right?

2. What does it mean to say that something is *designed*?

3. Does it make sense to ask for a reason why the universe as a whole exists?

4. Is Hume right to say that something could come into existence without a case?

5. 'The universe just exists, and that's that.' Discuss.

6. If existence can be shown in some cases to be a property, would this show that the ontological argument was correct?

7. Do we have an adequate enough understanding of God to argue that he necessarily exists?

8. What is a religious experience? Can believers of different faiths have the same religious experience?

9. Can a human being have an experience of God?

10 How could one know that what one takes to be an experience of God really is an experience of God and not of something else?

further reading

▶ Hick (ed.) 1964 contains all the most important readings on the question of God's existence. Davis 1997 is an excellent book on the proofs for the existence of God. Mackie 1982 and Swinburne 1991 fight it out over God's existence, without, it seems, being able to convince each other of anything at all. An excellent book on the ontological argument is Hick and McGill (eds) 1968.

▶ Weil 1977 contains her spiritual autobiography, in which she describes her mystical experiences. Kenny 1987: ch.6 is a good, although sceptical, discussion of the mysticism of St John of the Cross.

11

Divine command theory: the claim that what makes something good or right is God's commands.

Fideism: the claim that reason is irrelevant to, or opposed to, religious faith.

Free will defence: an attempt to argue that it is logically possible that God's omnipotence and goodness is consistent with the evil of the world on account of the free actions of rational beings.

Theodicy: the attempt to 'justify the ways of God to man'. The attempt to give the reason or reasons why there is evil in the world despite God's goodness and omnipotence.

Faith, reason, belief and the implications of God's existence

Key topics in this chapter

- Pascal's wager
- Plantinga and reformed epistemology
- Kierkegaard, Wittgenstein and Phillips on the nature of religious belief
- The problem of evil
- Miracles
- The relation between religion and morality

Pascal's Wager

One of the most famous attempts to show that it is rational to believe in God is to be found in Pascal's wager.

Blaise Pascal (1623–62)

Blaise Pascal and his two sisters were brought up in the Catholic faith by their father, the mother having died when Pascal was only three years old. The boy was educated rigorously by his father, and showed early great brilliance of mind, especially in mathematics. Physically he was of a sickly constitution, something that led to him being somewhat pampered in the family and left him with a lifelong dislike of displays of physical affection. He published his first work in 1640 when he was still hardly more than a boy, and went on to make significant contributions to hydraulics, calculus and probability theory. Pascal had always retained his Catholic faith, but his life was changed by a mystical experience he had on the night of 23 November 1654, when God appeared to him in the person of Jesus Christ. This led to his becoming deeply involved with the Jansenists, a Catholic order with whom he had previously had some significant contact, and who occupied the buildings of a former Cistercian convent, Port Royal, south west of Paris. The Jansenists, followers of Cornelius Jansen (1585–1638), a Dutch Roman Catholic theologian, were deeply opposed to the Jesuits, another Roman Catholic order, and this opposition created a deep split in Catholicism in seventeenth-century France. Pascal contributed to the split, writing the *Provincial Letters* (1656) in defence of the Jansenists and against the Jesuits, whom he thought of as forces of evil, but he is best known for his *Pensées*, published posthumously in 1670. This work is his philosophically most important and contains his famous wager argument.

The wager is a kind of bet on the existence of God, and Pascal aims to show that it is rational to 'bet' that God exists, even if – in fact, *because* – one cannot *prove* that he exists. Thus the wager is addressed to someone who is rational and self-interested and is undecided about the existence of God. In fact, Pascal supposes for the purposes of the wager that 'we do not know either the existence or the nature of God' (Pascal 1966: 149). He also assumes that to believe in God is both to believe that he exists and to live in a religious manner (cf. Davis 1997: 158). Living in a religious manner involves going to Mass, following the moral teachings of Jesus and the Church, and so on. From here, Pascal argues as follows.

One is faced with this choice: either one believes in God or one does not; there is, says Pascal, no third alternative. Of course, it might *seem* that there is there is a third option, since one could suggest that it is possible simply to refuse to choose or decide one way or another. However, Pascal points out that to refuse to make any decision here is, in effect, to decide against God, and surely he is right about this. After all, to refuse to decide will involve *not* going to Mass, *not* following the teachings of the Church and so on, and this amounts to a decision against God.

The wager for God

Suppose, then, that I am faced with believing in God or rejecting belief in God. Suppose I wager for God. Then, there are two possible outcomes here: I could be right, and I could be wrong – God might exist, or he might not. Suppose that, having bet on God, it turns out that I bet correctly: God exists. In this case, I shall be extremely glad I bet on God (even though I shall, of course, have had to lead a religious life, forgoing pleasures and experiences that I might otherwise have had but which are forbidden by God's law and the teachings of Jesus and the Church). For, by betting on God and finding that my bet was correct, I shall gain the infinite blessedness of an eternal life in the presence of God after my death.

Suppose, however, that, having bet on God, it turns out that God does not exist. Then I shall have lost very little. That is, I shall have lost the pleasures and experiences I might have been allowed as a non-believer, but this loss is small compared to the gain I would have made had I believed correctly that God exists. In fact, Pascal thinks of the loss here as nothing at all, because it amounts to nothing when compared to an infinite happiness lasting to infinity, which is what I would have had if God had existed and I had bet on his existence.

The wager against God

Suppose, now, that I wager against God. Once again, there are two possible outcomes: I could be right and I could be wrong – God might exist and he might not. Suppose that, having bet against God, it turns out that God exists. Then, it is true, I shall have gained the pleasures of a life free from having to obey Christian principles and laws but what I lose is enormous, indeed, infinite, for I shall spend an eternity separated from God in Hell as a result of my rejection of God. And, once again, Pascal thinks of what I have gained here as nothing compared to the infinity of misery that will be mine, having bet against God only to find out that he exists after all. If it turns out, however, that God does not exist, and I have bet against him, then I shall have gained the pleasures of leading a non-religious life, but this is a tiny gain (if any real gain at all) compared to that which I would have lost had it turned out that God exists.

So, to summarise:

Suppose I wager for God. Then a) I could be right, in which case I get infinite reward; b) I could be wrong, in which case I have lost (more or less) nothing.

Suppose I wager against God. Then a) I could be right, in which case I have gained (more or less) nothing; b) I could be wrong, in which case I am condemned to Hell for ever.

According to Pascal, it is thus clear that it is rational to believe in God, even if one is motivated only by self-interest.

Pascal considers the following objection that someone might offer. Let us suppose that I am convinced by the argument. Nonetheless, it does not follow from this that I am psychologically capable of believing. That is, even if I agree that it is rational for me to believe, it does not follow from this that I will believe. So the question arises: How can I get myself to believe?

Pascal's answer to this is that I can do so by trying to live a religious life, 'taking holy water, having masses said, and so on' (Pascal 1966: 152). Gradually, Pascal says, I shall come to believe.

Note that Pascal is not saying here that one can simply *decide* to believe in God. This idea would, in fact, make no sense. I can no more *decide* to believe in God than I can *decide* to believe that it is raining when it plainly is not. Rather, his point is that, by living in a certain way, it is possible gradually to become convinced of something of which one was not previously convinced.

review activity

Explain Pascal's wager in your own words.

Objections to Pascal's Wager

Several objections have been raised to Pascal's argument.

1. One obvious objection to the Wager is that it is evidently powerless against someone who simply does not care about the long-term consequences of his actions. We might think such a person foolish but he is not strictly irrational: if someone genuinely believes he could end up in Hell but does not care then there is probably nothing more to be said to him.

The appeal to self-interest

2. Some have thought that the appeal to the self-interest of the person who is undecided about God's existence in order to make him try to believe is misplaced. To believe for reasons of self-interest, it is said, is to believe for all the wrong reasons: belief should be from, say, a sense of the goodness of the world, not from self-interest. This point was put extremely forcefully by William James:

We feel that a faith in masses and holy water adopted wilfully after such a mechanical calculation would lack the inner soul of faith's reality; and if we were ourselves in the place of the Deity, we should probably take particular pleasure in cutting off believers of this pattern from their infinite reward.

(James 1956: 6)

James's point, however, whilst powerful, may not be wholly correct. If we place Pascal's wager in the context of Pascal's whole view of life then James's objection seems less powerful.

For Pascal, man is in a state of wretchedness. We are driven hither and thither by our vanity, ambition and greed in a ceaseless, restless pursuit of things that we believe will satisfy us but fail to do so: social status, wealth, power and the like. Further, we cannot bear even our own company, and constantly seek to distract ourselves from ourselves and from our condition by filling our time with trivial distractions such as business activities, soldiering, flirtations, hunting or gambling. In all of this we are pursuing our self-interest, but fail to see directly – though we dimly recognise – that our self-interest is not at all served by such activities for they do not fill the spiritual void in our lives. Indeed, they leave us feeling even more wretched than we otherwise would have.

Whether or not one agrees with this view of man's condition, the fact that Pascal accepts it helps to make sense of his appeal to self-interest to motivate one to seek for belief in God. This is because Pascal thinks that, in the case of someone who is in such a condition and is thus constantly on the lookout to find something that will satisfy him, there is nothing but self-interest to appeal to in order to get him to seek for God. The person who distracts himself from his own wretched condition by gambling, for example, can, perhaps, be brought to enjoy the gamble on God. Pascal thus wants to appeal to psychological features of each person that he already possesses. It is as if he said: 'You like gambling, don't you? Well, here's a massive gamble, more thrilling than any you have made so far.' To this extent, Pascal is trying in his wager simply to be psychologically realistic about what could motivate someone to belief in God: just preaching Hell and damnation will, as such, he thinks, have no effect. One has to take people as they are if one wants to change them.

Pascal did not think, then, that the appeal to self-interest was good: it was, rather, so to speak, making the best of a bad job. As J.H. Broome has said, for Pascal the appeal to self-interest 'may not be very satisfactory, but in this desperate situation, it is the best that can be done, and there just is not a viable alternative' (Broome 1965: 163). So, Pascal would have agreed with James that the appeal to self-interest was far from ideal but he would have said that it was better than nothing.

Belief and intellectual integrity

3. An objection to Pascal related to the one just considered has been offered by J.L. Mackie (1917–81). Mackie argues that to try to make oneself believe in God when one does not is to lack intellectual integrity; it is a kind of self-deception. Mackie writes:

Deliberately to make oneself believe, by such techniques as he [Pascal] suggests . . . is to do violence to one's reason and understanding . . . [I]n deliberately cultivating non-rational belief, one would be suppressing one's critical faculties.

(Mackie 1982: 202)

However, as Stephen T. Davis has said (Davis 1997: 162), Mackie's criticism is based on a misunderstanding of Pascal. Mackie takes Pascal to be saying that one should try to cultivate belief even if one thinks there is good reason *not* to believe in God. However, this is not so. Rather, as we have seen, Pascal is saying that it is in one's self-interest to seek to believe in God where there is no more evidence for his non-existence than for his existence. In such a case, one is not suppressing one's critical faculties in seeking to believe in God because one has no more reason to think he does not exist than to think that he does exist.

The 'many gods' objection

4. The most widely accepted objection to Pascal's argument is the so-called 'many gods' objection (see, for example, Flew 1976: 66–8; Davis 1997: 164–6). The problem is that Pascal offers us just two options: either the God of traditional Christian belief who rewards believers and punishes atheists or nothing. However, in fact, given that Pascal assumes that we are in a state of total ignorance concerning the existence of God and his nature, he cannot assume that the choice is between the two options, and only the two options, he indicates. There might be any number of gods between which we have to choose, and we have no idea how they might punish or reward us. Perhaps a god exists, for example, who rewards those who do not believe in him if they are sincerely and genuinely convinced that there are no good grounds for believing in him. Some god or other might, for example, think that such a person is praiseworthy because he is using his intellectual faculties as they ought to be used – he withholds assent from that of which he is not convinced (cf. Mackie 1982: 203). Or again, perhaps the idea that a God of love would punish *anyone* for an eternity is just mistaken: it is, for sure, hard to make sense of the idea that he would. Clearly, such problems could be multiplied. They can summed up by noting that Pascal offers us the choice not merely between Christianity and nothing, but between a very specific form of Catholic Christianity and nothing. And, as already noted, this seems simply to limit our options in a way that is not justified by Pascal's insistence that we know neither whether God exists nor, if he does, what his nature is.

review
activity

1. Explain James's criticism of Pascal's Wager. How successful is his criticism?

2. Explain in your own words the 'many gods' objection to Pascal.

Is religious belief properly basic?

In recent English-speaking philosophy of religion there has been growing interest in the idea that religious belief does not depend on the kind of arguments for the existence of God that are characteristic of natural theology – for example, the cosmological argument or the ontological argument. Instead, there has been discussion of whether religious belief can be basic. The most well known defender of this way of looking at faith is Alvin Plantinga, and I shall discuss his views in this section.

Plantinga's approach is known as Reformed epistemology, since it is rooted in the thinking of such Reformation thinkers as John Calvin (1509–64) and others. This epistemology involves a rejection of the claims of classical foundationalism, specifically of the claim made by classical foundationalism that foundational or basic beliefs must be self-evident or incorrigible or infallible. Plantinga thinks that this opens up room for saying that a belief can be basic or foundational for other beliefs without being self-evident or incorrigible or infallible. He suggests that religious belief can be one such basic belief. That is, belief in God can be basic for a person. In this case, a person can be rationally justified in believing in God even if he has no good arguments of the natural theological kind for the existence of God and, in fact, even if no such arguments exist (Plantinga 1983: 65). Indeed, Plantinga goes so far as saying that such a person can *know* that God exists.

Plantinga discusses a number of aspects of his view (Plantinga 1983: 74ff.). We shall look at three of them.

The great pumpkin objection

One immediate problem is that it seems there could be any number of beliefs that someone might claim are basic. For example, if one person claims that belief in God is basic, why could another not claim that belief in voodoo or astrology can be basic beliefs? Or what about the belief that the Great Pumpkin returns every Hallowe'en? Could that be basic?

Plantinga's response to this is bullish. His response is to say that, although the Reformed epistemologist can think that belief in God is basic, it simply does not follow that he has to accept any number of other beliefs as basic. He says that, although belief in God is properly basic, such belief has *grounds*, whereas belief in the Great Pumpkin does not.

The grounds for religious belief

Suppose you see someone in front of you displaying typical pain behaviour – moaning and groaning, clutching his foot and so on. Then, you have the belief that this person is in pain. This belief is typically taken to be a basic belief. However, the behaviour of the person in question is not *evidence* for the belief that he is in pain and you do not infer the belief that he is in pain from other beliefs. Nevertheless, the belief that he is in pain is not groundless. On the contrary, it has *grounds* – most crucially, that you are perceiving the person in question manifesting pain behaviour. So a basic belief can have grounds; it can be justified.

Plantinga says that belief in God is like this: it is a basic belief but has grounds and can be justified.

What grounds or justification might there be for belief in God? Plantinga gives some examples. The sense that the universe is wonderful to behold can give rise to the belief that it was created by God; reading the Bible can lead one to believe that God is speaking to one; a feeling of guilt for having done something bad can give rise to the belief that God disapproves of what one has done; and so on (Plantinga 1983: 80). Note that in each case we have a *justifying* or *grounding* situation (seeing the universe as beautiful; reading the Bible; feeling guilty) which gives rise in each case to a *belief* (that the universe was created by God; that God is speaking to one; that God disapproves of what one has done). In each case the justified belief is not, in fact, directly that God exists; it is rather the belief that the universe is created by God, and so on. So Plantinga suggests that a basic religious belief may not be that God exists but that God has created the universe, and the like. However, because the latter belief entails the former, we can continue speaking as if the basic belief is that God exists.

Is argument irrelevant to basic belief?

Plantinga's answer is no. Just because belief in God is properly basic it does not follow that argument is irrelevant to religious belief. For example, someone might have been brought up to believe in God and thus have a basic belief in God. However, the pain and suffering in life might seem to him to suggest that there is no God after all. Then argument, for example, reflection on the problem of evil, is relevant to exploring his (now questioned) belief. Such reflection may uphold the belief or destroy it. Either way, argument is relevant to the belief.

Similarly, someone who does not believe in God might come through rational argument to accept that there is a God. After all, Plantinga's Reformed epistemology does not claim that one *ought* not to believe on the basis of argument. It simply says that one *does not have to have* arguments in order to believe.

One of the undoubted advantages of Plantinga's approach is that we believe a whole host of things that can be no more easily be proven – justified through purely rational argument – than can belief in God. Such beliefs include the belief that the world has existed for more than five minutes. Everyone believes this, but no one can prove it. Again, almost everyone in the West, and many others elsewhere, believe in human rights, but no one knows how to prove that such a belief is justified. Plantinga wants to say that, so far as proof goes, religious belief is no better and no worse off than the kinds of beliefs just mentioned.

However, there is a difficulty here: it is the old problem of the Great Pumpkin (cf. Van Hook 1996). For it is not clear that Plantinga has disposed of this objection. *He* may not think that a belief in the Great Pumpkin can be properly basic, but someone else might. Indeed, whole cultures have believed in witches or gods Plantinga would reject (for example, the Greek and Roman gods). Belief in witches or in other gods could be basic for a whole culture. Surely Plantinga would not be happy to accept that, yet it seems he must be committed to doing so. Surely, by his own standards, such beliefs would be rational. But this means that there is no special reason to accept Christianity rather than any other system of belief – and that means that a Reformed epistemologist who claims to *know* that God exists has not justified this claim. Plantinga has, in fact, replied to this objection (Plantinga 1996). He says that it does not follow from the fact that he cannot convince everyone of the existence of God that he does not know that God exists. There might be any number of reasons why he cannot convince everyone. He singles one out: sin. For, in the Reformed tradition within which Plantinga is working, human sin explains why it is that many people do not believe in God: their sin stands in the way of their accepting God, for sin *is* a rejection of God. (He is at pains to point out that a non-believer or others who find belief in God difficult are not to be thought of as in some way especially sinful. Disease, he says, is also the result of sin, but the diseased person need not be more sinful than someone with glowing health.)

It is hard to feel completely convinced by Plantinga's reply, although he is certainly right to say that one can know something even if one cannot prove it to everyone, or even to most people. What his account needs is, perhaps, a way of making sense of the idea that religious belief can deepen a person and that it is when it does that we might be able to say that someone knows God. This way of looking at things is close to the next view on religious faith we need to discuss.

Religion as a form of life

A view somewhat similar to that of Plantinga is to be found in a number of other philosophers, and in this section we shall discuss this way of looking at faith. However, it should be noted that one important difference between Plantinga's view and that of those we are to discuss in this section is that the latter group of thinkers do not talk of religious belief as basic. Rather, as we shall see, they understand religious belief to be a *way of living* or a *form of life*.

The view in question is to be found in the work of Wittgenstein, and has been developed by other thinkers, particularly D.Z. Phillips, Norman Malcolm and Gareth Moore. However, Wittgenstein was deeply influenced in his thinking on religious matters by the work of Søren Kierkegaard, and thus it is appropriate to turn to consider the work of the latter, albeit briefly, before moving on to look at Wittgenstein and the development of his thinking more directly. It should be noted, however, that there is much disagreement amongst commentators on how to interpret Kierkegaard. What I say here presents one view of his work, though certainly not a wildly unusual view.

Kierkegaard's attitude to the traditional arguments for the existence of God

It is helpful to take the starting point of Kierkegaard's explorations of the nature of religious belief to be his recognition that the traditional arguments for the existence of God, such as the ontological, cosmological and teleological arguments, are too riddled with weaknesses to be convincing to those who do not already believe. In fact, he makes the point that the only reason people have ever believed these arguments is because they already believed in God, and that in the absence of such belief they would not have found the arguments intellectually convincing. Similarly, if someone does not believe, then he will not be brought to believe by the arguments. Kierkegaard expresses this as follows:

If . . . the god does not exist, then of course it is impossible to demonstrate it. But if he does exist, then it is foolishness to want to demonstrate it, since I, in the very moment the demonstration commences, would presuppose it as not doubtful – which a presupposition cannot be, inasmuch as it is a presupposition – but as decided, because otherwise I would not begin, easily perceiving the whole thing would be impossible if he did not exist. (Kierkegaard 1985: 39)

Inwardness

Since, then, the traditional arguments for the existence of God are, according to Kierkegaard, irrelevant to why anyone believes in God in the first place, there must be some other way of understanding faith. Now, Kierkegaard emphasises that faith is paradoxical; to try to make faith rational is to take away its very nature as faith. If someone thinks that he has a rational argument for the existence of God then he has lost the dynamic, inward side of faith. Faith, says Kierkegaard, is a matter of *inwardness*. What he means by this is, roughly, that it is a matter of the whole of one's way of living. Faith cannot be a matter of believing a number of propositions – such as that 'God is being with such and such properties who is related to the world in such and such a way'. Someone could believe all that and still have no real faith: his faith might be *dead, fake*, mere words. In fact, Kierkegaard thought that this was the case with most believers, like those who go to church every week but whose lives are otherwise just the same as any non-believer.

Truth is subjectivity

On the other hand, it is possible to come across someone who has never heard of the Christian God but who lives with a kind of intense and *living* inwardness in such a way that it would make sense to say of him (even if he could not and would not say of himself) that God is alive in him. Kierkegaard sums up this idea by saying that *truth is subjectivity* (Kierkegaard 1974: 169ff.). He goes on to say: 'The objective accent falls on WHAT is said, the subjective on HOW it

Søren Kierkegaard (1813–55)

Søren Kierkegaard is often taken to be the founding father of the philosophical movement known as existentialism, although he did not describe himself in this way. What he did do was to object very strongly to a style of philosophising that lacked connection with everyday experience and lost sight of the individual in vast philosophical systems. For Kierkegaard, the prime exponent of that way of doing philosophy was Hegel (1770–1831), whom he never tired of attacking. In accord with his idea that the individual ought to stand at the centre of philosophical reflection, Kierkegaard included in his work reflection on all kinds of topics the discussion of which was very rare in philosophy at his time, such as love relations between men and women (which interested him not least on account of his disastrous broken engagement to Regine Olsen), despair, anxiety, self-loathing and the like. He often wrote under pseudonyms, the reason for which is a matter of dispute, and often his works have one pseudonym introducing the work of another, who talks about that of another and so on. In fact, his work often straddles the borders between philosophy and literature, abounding as it does in places in the appearance of quasi-literary characters, and it often contains irony, jokes and puns. His most accessible works are probably the two volumes that make up *Either/Or* (1843), which contrast the different world-views of aestheticism and morality, and *Fear and Trembling* (1843), a philosophical discussion of God's command to Abraham to sacrifice his son Isaac (Genesis 22: 1–13). In his later works Kierkegaard claimed that he had always been writing in the service of Christianity, although it is unclear whether this is so or not. He denied, in any case, that one could *be* a Christian (as one can *be* a member of a Church, for example). At most, one's Christianity could consist in a struggle to come to know God and live a life like that of Christ.

is said' (Kierkegaard 1974: 181). What he means by this is that two people could believe the same thing, for example, that God exists, but that there could be a fundamental difference between them in the *way in which they believe,* or the *spirit in which they believe*: for one of them, belief might be just an empty formula which has no essential connection with his life, whereas for the other it is alive and extends throughout his life, transforming his sense of things and his relations to both others and himself. We could put the point this way: it is possible to have a religious belief but to remain a shallow and stupid person, in which case one's belief would be worthless, however sincerely one assented to belief in God's existence. On the other hand, a religious belief can deepen a person, making him a person of wisdom and allowing him to live in a spirit of generosity.

Kierkegaard not a
fideist

How could one acquire such a deepening religious belief? Kierkegaard spoke of a 'leap of faith', and he has often been taken to mean that one should just believe blindly, irrationally. If this were so, then there could be, according to Kierkegaard, no rational discussion of religion at all. Some critics of Kierkegaard have taken him to be saying just that: *either* you believe *or* you do not, and that is all there is to be said; there can be no rational discussion on either side (cf. Mackie 1982: 210–16). Such a position has often been called 'fideism': reason is irrelevant to religious faith and should be rejected in the name of such faith. However, this is not what Kierkegaard means and Kierkegaard is not a fideist. The *only* sense in which Kierkegaard thinks that rational discussion is useless is, as we have already seen, in the case of the 'proofs' for the existence of God. But the sense of rationality that is relevant here is simply *one*, very *narrow* conception of rationality, a conception according to which one's experience of life, for example, is wholly irrelevant to what one believes with respect to religion. Kierkegaard's whole point is that this *narrow* conception of rationality is too limited to have anything substantial to say about religious belief. For Kierkegaard, whether one believes or not really does have to do with one's experience of life. For example, and speaking very roughly, someone might come to believe as a result of a growing sense of the beauty and goodness of the world; another as a result of the suffering he has had to endure; another because he is bearing witness to the goodness he sees in the life of another (say, in a monk or a nun); another as a result of living amongst people who believe and who worship and/or being brought up amongst such people; and so on and on. (Kierkegaard himself explored all of these and more, although he emphasised the issue of suffering.) None of this means that the belief of such people cannot be criticised or rationally discussed, but the notion of rationality here must be broader than that found in the usual 'proofs' of the existence of God. For example, one might wish to criticise someone who comes to believe as a result of the suffering he has endured on the grounds that one judges his faith to be merely self-serving. Indeed, this whole point was implicit earlier in the discussion of Kierkegaard's distinction between WHAT a person believes and HOW a person believes: both belief and unbelief can be deep, sensitive, insightful and the like, and both belief and unbelief can be foolish, gullible, shallow and the like. It is possible for both believers and unbelievers to *live in the truth*. Those philosophers who criticise Kierkegaard for constructing a view of faith that leaves no room for rational discussion are themselves insensitive to the lived experience of faith and its connection with the rest of life. And both those philosophers who write in defence of religious belief and those who write against it far too often leave that connection out of account, which is why, as Kierkegaard pointed out, their discussions often seem so sterile. It is even arguable that there is something absurd in such philosophy (cf. Mulhall 1994: ch.3).

We can understand in greater depth this way of looking at faith if we turn to the work of Wittgenstein on religious belief and the use made of his thinking on this by other thinkers.

Wittgenstein's point of departure is that the evidence there is for the existence of God is extremely weak. Moreover, religious believers, he suggested, do not come to their belief because they neutrally survey the evidence for God's existence and then come to believe. Rather, they come to their belief in the kind of ways indicated above.

Language games   Wittgenstein argues that here, as in other areas of life, believers use a specific language, the language of belief, and that when one comes to accept religious faith one also learns how to use this language. Wittgenstein spoke in this connection, as in others, of 'language games': there is a language game of religion, another of morality, another of science and so on. These games are *played,* and a believer in God plays the language game of religion. In order to understand religious belief, we need to understand the language game of religion.

One way that Wittgenstein does this is to draw our attention to features of the way people speak in the religious language game. For example, he imagines the following situation. If one person says to another that he believes he hears a German aeroplane overhead and the other says, 'Possibly. I'm not so sure', then the two are quite close to one another in what they believe. However, if one person says to another that he believes in the Last Judgement and the other says 'Possibly. I'm not sure', then the two are very far apart: there is a gulf between them (Wittgenstein 1966: 53). The idea of belief in the case of ordinary, everyday empirical matters (for example, tables, chairs, aeroplanes and so forth) is unlike the idea of belief in religion. In the case of religion we are dealing with *a whole way of living* or *a form of life.* That is, we are dealing with a *picture* in the light of which the believer thinks of, and judges, his life. A person who says he believes in God does not *contradict* a person who says he does not believe in God in the way that a person who says that there are three chairs in the room *does contradict* a person who says that there are not three chairs in the room. To come to faith in God, Wittgenstein suggests, is to have one's life changed (Wittgenstein 1966: 57); whereas to come to believe that there are three chairs in the room is not at all like that.

Some philosophers have thought that Wittgenstein and those who have been influenced by his work have wanted to suggest that the language game of religion is a kind of self-contained game that is sealed off from the rest of life and thus cannot be criticised (Nielsen 1982). This is, once again, the charge of fideism, that is, the charge that there is no rational debate to be had about religious belief. You either play the religious language game or you do not, just as you might play golf or not: religion is just a kind of hobby. However, the charge of fideism is a mistake. D.Z. Phillips has developed Wittgenstein's views at great length, and he has emphasised the connections between religious belief and the rest of life. For example, praying often only makes sense if there are connections between prayer and one's relations with other people. Moreover, Phillips has emphasised that a given person's religious belief can be criticised in the kind of way discussed above: religious belief can, in Wittgenstein's view, be open to criticism as foolish or self-serving or shallow or whatever, and so can the religious way of life of a whole people (see especially Phillips 1971; 1981b; 2001: 25–30 and also below).

What kind of God is implicit in, or implied by, the arguments we have considered in this section? In order to show the nature of God on the understanding of religious belief that Phillips and others offer, I shall concentrate on Phillips's view in just one of his books, *Death and Immortality* (Phillips 1970).

Here is a common way to think of the soul. The soul is a wholly immaterial thing that sees, hears, feels and so on, and is what a person really is. The body is then extrinsic to the person, like a suit of clothes. Just as a suit can be discarded, so can the soul discard the body and survive. Immortality would then be the survival of the soul after the death of the body in the way that the body itself can survive the shedding of a suit of clothes.

Phillips argues that, if we think of the soul this way, talk of the immortality of the soul is to be construed as talk of the *literal* survival of the soul after the death of the body. However, the survival of the soul in this way would solve no puzzles at all: the eternal survival of the soul in the sense under discussion would be as puzzling as this life is anyway. Moreover, we simply have no good reason to think that the soul *could* survive in this way.

Phillips therefore suggests that there is another way to think of the soul. We can understand this other way if we pay attention to the various ways in which we speak of the soul. For example, we might say of someone that he had 'sold his soul for money'. In this sense of 'soul', to talk of a person's soul is to talk of his *moral condition*. To have a soul in this sense is not like having a heart: the soul is not a *thing*.

In general, 'terms like "the destiny of the soul", "losing one's soul", "selling one's soul", "damning one's soul", etc. are all to be understood in terms of the kind of life a person is living' (Phillips 1970: 45). We can begin to understand the notion of eternal life, then, if we see that, for a Christian believer, the important issue concerning his soul has to do with the reality of goodness. As Phillips says: 'Eternal life is the reality of goodness, that in terms of which a human life is to be assessed' (Phillips 1970: 48). In other words, for the Christian, eternal life is connected with the extent to which he lives in the light of true goodness or whether his concerns are those of getting on in this world, satisfying his desires, achieving his ambitions and the like. 'Eternity is not *more* life, but this life seen under certain moral and religious modes of thought' (Phillips 1970: 49).

However, this is not all. To live in the light of moral goodness can be the beginning, but it cannot be the end, of making sense of the idea of the immortality of the soul. Beyond this, Phillips suggests, immortality involves a notion of 'dying to the self'. This notion involves a number of things. It involves possessing a sense that we have nothing by right and that we have no claim on the universe that we should continue: our own existence is not necessary and we are entirely dependent on external circumstances for our continued existence. The universe can crush us at any moment and we have no right that it not do so. To die to the self is to live fully in the light of such ideas. Dying to the self thus involves a sense that all that we have we have as a gift from God and that nothing is ours by right or necessity. In this way, death is overcome: the overcoming of death is thus a way of living this life, and has nothing to do with going on existing after one's death.

God is not a person

This way of looking at things leads to a radical and new understanding of God. On this account, to think that all that one has is a gift from God, and that one has nothing by right or necessity, involves learning to be able to worship God, to speak of the love of God, and to learn what 'contemplation, attention, renunciation, what forgiving, thanking, loving, etc. mean in [religious] contexts' (Phillips 1970: 55). But to learn these things is to participate in the reality of God and, indeed, this is what is meant by God's reality. God is not some object or being, another thing in the universe. Rather, the reality of God *is* the reality of participation in the life of worship, prayer and so on. Aside from this life there is no God. Gareth Moore has expressed a similar point by saying that God is not a person (Moore 1988).

review activity

1. Explain in your own words the notion of fideism.

2. What does Kierkegaard mean by 'truth is subjectivity' and that what matters is *how* one believes religiously?

3. What does Wittgenstein mean by speaking of a religious language game?

4. If immortality of the soul does not mean that a separable part of a person lives on after death, how, according to Phillips, are we to understand this idea?

5. According to Phillips, how should we understand the reality of God?

The problem of evil

One of the most obvious facts about existence is that it presents the spectacle of a great deal of human suffering. Not only do human beings inflict a great deal of suffering on one another but they are also subject to all kinds of natural evils: earthquakes, illness and disease, mental suffering and so on. It is hard enough to make sense of all this suffering and evil anyway, but it seems that the attempt to do so is even more difficult for a religious believer, such as a Christian. After all, if God is omnipotent, it seems that he could stop the suffering. If he is perfectly good, it seems he would want to stop the suffering. So why does the suffering continue? It seems that to explain this we must say either that God is not omnipotent after all; or that he is not perfectly good. Neither view is likely to appeal much to the theist, the believer in God. The theist is thus faced with the *problem of evil*. How is one to show that the suffering in the world is consistent with the existence of a God who is perfectly good and omnipotent? If the problem of evil can be answered then this would be to provide a theodicy, a justification of the ways of God to man. (The world 'theodicy' comes from two Greek words: *theos*, meaning 'god' and *dike*, meaning 'justice'.)

Natural evil and moral evil

Note that a theodicy has to explain the existence of two types of evil: *natural evil*, such as earthquakes, volcanoes, disease and the like; and the evil that human beings inflict on one another, or *moral evil*.

In what follows, we shall look at some answers that have been offered to the problem of evil. I shall begin by considering the work of two early Christian thinkers, Augustine and Irenaeus, presenting their views as these have been understood by modern philosophy. As we shall see, such a way of understanding their thinking is open to challenge. For the moment, however, we can leave this concern aside.

Augustine

Everything is created good

The starting point for Augustine's theodicy is the claim that everything that is created is created good.

Augustine thought this because he thought that it made no sense to think of God as having created anything evil: God is himself wholly good, there could be no possibility of evil in him, so anything he creates is also good. Moreover, this way of looking at things is encouraged by the beginning of the Bible when God looks at his creation and declares that what he has created is good.

A hierarchy of beings

The universe is, of course, teeming with different plants and creatures, and Augustine interprets the goodness of the world to mean that there is a hierarchy of beings. He describes it thus:

> Now among those things which exist in any mode of being, and are distinct from God who has made them, living things are ranked above inanimate objects; those which have the power of reproduction, or even the urge towards it, are superior to those who lack that impulse. Among living things, the sentient rank above the insensitive, and animals above trees. Among the sentient, the intelligent take precedence over the unthinking – men over cattle. Among the intelligent, immortal beings are higher than mortals, angels being higher than men.
>
> *This is the scale according to the order of nature.*   (Augustine 1984: xi, 16)

St Augustine (354–430)

Each plant and creature, then, has a place in the hierarchy of being, and is good. To be lower down the scale of being – as, say, a worm is lower than a cat, and a cat lower than a human being – is not to be evil, but simply to possess goodness in a lesser degree.

Augustine thinks that everything that exists is good, so he is committed to a belief in the identity of being and goodness.

Evil is a privation of good

If, then, all creation is good, how does it come about that evil exists at all? Augustine's answer is that evil is nothing positive but simply a privation (lack or absence) of goodness; evil is *privatio boni*. Evil enters the world when something turns away from its proper place in the hierarchy of being and thus renounces its proper role in the divine scheme. It ceases to be what it is meant (by God) to be. Moreover, because, as we have seen, Augustine believed that being and goodness are identical and also that evil is a privation of goodness, it follows for Augustine that nothing could be wholly evil. This is because if something were, *per impossibile*, to be completely evil it would cease to exist. Evil is, in Augustine's view, parasitic on good.

Note that, when Augustine says that evil is *privatio boni*, he does not mean this in an everyday, empirical sense. In *that* sense, evil is something real and positive. When Augustine says that evil is a privation of goodness he means this in a *metaphysical sense*. That is, roughly speaking, he means it in the sense of an account of what evil ultimately is, as it is in itself. He does not mean it in the sense of how we actually *experience* evil. For, as we have noted, we experience evil as something positive and dreadful not as a mere absence of goodness.

The exercise of free will as the source of evil

What, then, according to Augustine, is the explanation for some created thing's turning away from its proper role in creation? The answer is: the exercise of free will. In other words, of the creatures God has made some – the angels and human beings – have free will, and it is in the exercise of this will to turn away from God that evil enters the world. It is the turning itself that is evil. Or, as Augustine puts it: '[W]hen the will leaves the higher and turns to the lower, it becomes bad not because the thing to which it turns is bad, but because the turning is itself perverse' (Augustine 1984: xii, 7). The name of this turning is *pride*: the angels and human beings who turn away from God do so because they prefer themselves to God – they prefer a lesser to a greater good. Pride is the sin of supposing one's good to lie with oneself, rather then with God.

What, then, makes a free being turn from a greater to a lesser good? Again Augustine appeals to the doctrine of evil as *privatio boni*, although there remains a deep mystery here.

> *For to defect from him who is the Supreme Existence, to something of less reality, this is to begin to have an evil will. To try to discover the causes of such defection – deficient, not efficient causes – is like trying to see darkness or to hear silence. Yet we are familiar with darkness and silence, and we can only be aware of them by means of eyes and ears, but this is not by perception but by an absence of perception.* (Augustine 1984: xii, 7)

So, Augustine claims that evil enters the world through the exercise of free will on the part of free rational beings. Moreover, he thinks this provides an account not simply of moral evil but also of natural evil. His ground for thinking this is that it is fallen angels – Satan and his cohorts – who cause natural evil. These are free beings who seek to wreak havoc with God's creation wherever they can, and the result is natural evil.

The world as an object of aesthetic contemplation

To complete the account of Augustine's theodicy, we should note that there is also in Augustine's work the idea that evil is only evil from our perspective. In the sight of God all things, even in the world as it is, are good. Augustine likens the universe to a work of art. Some parts of a work of art might seem ugly when seen close up or looked at in isolation – say, some blobs of black on a canvas – but when they are viewed in the context of the work as a whole we see that they are necessary to the overall beauty of the work. Similarly, what looks evil to our limited perspective is necessary for the overall beauty of the world in God's eyes. Thus he writes:

> *For you [Lord] evil does not exist, and not only for you but for the whole of your creation as well, because there is nothing outside it which could invade it and break down the order which you have imposed on it. Yet in the separate parts of your creation there are some things which we think of as evil because they are at variance with other things. But there are other things again with which they are in accord, and then they are good. In themselves, too, they are good.*
> (Augustine 1961: vii, 12)

A problem for Augustine's theodicy

There is certainly something moving in Augustine's attempt to preserve a sense of the goodness of all things and yet explain the existence of evil, but how successful is his theodicy? Among the problems that beset it, the key one is this: How are we to explain how it is that a creature created good turns away from God? There seems to be no answer to this question. For if an angel really is good, as Augustine's doctrine of creation claims is the case, then he surely could not turn from God. If an angel does turn from God then he must have some flaw in his nature. How could he have a flaw if created by God and all created things are good? As John Hick says:

> *The basic and inevitable criticism [of Augustine's theodicy] is that the idea of an unqualifiedly good creature committing sin is self-contradictory and unintelligible. If the angels are finitely perfect, then even though they are in some important sense free to sin they will never in fact do so. If they do sin we can only infer that they were not flawless – in which case their Maker must share the responsibility for their fall, and the intended theodicy fails.*
> (Hick 1979: 68–9)

review activity

1. Explain in your own words the problem of evil.

2. Why does Augustine say that all created things are good?

3. What does Augustine mean by saying that evil is a privation of good? What is the difference between a metaphysical and an empirical interpretation of this idea?

4. How does Augustine think evil can be explained?

5. What is Augustine's analogy between art and the universe, and why does he draw it?

6. What seems to be the basic flaw in Augustine's theodicy?

Irenaeus and 'the Irenaean theodicy'

Like Augustine, Irenaeus believed that human beings have free will, but in many respects his theodicy is very different from that offered by Augustine.

According to Irenaeus, man was not made perfect from the beginning. As part of explaining this, Irenaeus draws a distinction between the image of God and the likeness of God in man. He says that man is made in the image of God, but as he is not yet perfect he does not yet possess the likeness of God. He

Irenaeus (c.130–200)

thinks that, because all things are possible to God, God could have made man perfect but he says that man, when created, was like an infant, and as such could not receive the perfection God could have bestowed on him.

For as it is certainly in the power of a mother to give strong food to her infant [but she does not do so], as the child is not yet able to receive more substantial nourishment; so also it was possible for God Himself to have made man perfect from the first, but man could not receive this [perfection], being as yet an infant.
(Irenaeus 2001: 31)

Since Irenaeus sees man as having been created in a state of immaturity from which he has to develop, he does not see Adam and Eve's sin as a catastrophe in the same kind of way Augustine does, that is, as an appalling event that upsets God's plans. Rather, he sees it as a kind of childish mistake, something born of immaturity and naïveté. Further, Irenaeus sees the trials and difficulties of life as a kind of testing ground in which human beings may struggle for the perfection that would mean they possessed the likeness of God, not simply his image.

'Vale of soul-making theodicy'

Irenaeus's approach to the problem of evil has been taken up and developed by John Hick: he calls his approach the 'vale of soul-making' theodicy (Hick 1979: 289), a phrase which occurs in one of John Keats's letters (Hick 1979: 295, fn.1). Hick speaks in this context of the 'Irenaean theodicy'.

The basic idea behind Hick's approach is the one that lies behind the work of Irenaeus: the trials and tribulations of life exist because they help us develop from immaturity to maturity. It is a mistake of antitheistic writers, says Hick, to suppose that God's concern for us as his creatures or children would be best displayed by his making this world as comfortable and cosy as possible. That way of looking at things sees God's relation to us on the analogy of a human being making a cage for a pet, for if we do this and wish the pet well then we shall, of course, seek to make the cage as cosy as possible (Hick 1979: 292–3). The correct analogy, says Hick, is rather that of parents to their children. Certainly parents want their children to have pleasure, but they also want them to grow up to be ethically mature, to possess 'moral integrity, unselfishness, compassion, courage, humour, reverence for the truth, and perhaps above all the capacity for love' (Hick 1979: 294). However, children can only develop such qualities if they do not lead lives devoted solely to pleasure; they must confront difficulties from time to time and learn to overcome them, and parents will be glad, in the long run, if this happens – much gladder than if their children remained immature through being cosseted.

Accordingly, God has arranged the world in such a way that human beings can develop, and this involves the world's containing much that seems to frustrate man's purposes and aims. However, by facing such frustrations, human beings can develop: their souls can grow and they can move towards God.

The hidden God

Of course, the fact that the world does, indeed, contain so much that frustrates man's purposes makes it seem to many that there is no God. However, Hick argues that it is part of God's plan to be a hidden God, not known directly. Indeed, he says the world must be set up 'as if there were no God' (Hick 1979: 317). Since this means that we lack immediate consciousness of

God Hick says that we stand at an 'epistemic distance' from God (Hick 1979: 317). If we did not, says Hick, our love for him, supposing we achieve that, could not be freely given, and a love that is not freely given is not true love.

Dysteleological suffering

However, even if we were to accept Hick's account so far, the truth is that a great deal of the suffering to which human beings are subject is quite simply pointless: it does not contribute to the growth of the soul. Hick himself is quite clear about this: '[F]rom our own observations, even when supplemented by the entire scroll of recorded history, we are not entitled to say . . . that all suffering is used for good in its final issue' (Hick 1979: 375). Hick says that this kind of pointless suffering – he calls it 'dysteleological suffering' – remains a mystery: we cannot, here and now, understand its purpose.

Soul-making after death

Consequently, his theodicy is by no means complete at this stage of his argument, for the aim of a theodicy must be, of course, to show how it is that we can make sense of suffering within the context of God's loving care for his creation. So Hick says that we must here invoke the idea that soul-making goes on, not simply in this life, but also after death. This will allow us, he says, to 'affirm in faith that there will in the final accounting be no personal life that is unperfected and no suffering that has not eventually become a phase in the fulfilment of God's good purpose' (Hick 1979: 376). In other words, the meaning and point of suffering is that it contributes to the soul-making of those who have to bear it. However, it is clearly the case that in this world lots of suffering does not do this. So Hick says that the Christian must affirm that, if all souls are to be perfected, the soul-making will continue after death. And once this has been achieved? Hick writes:

> The Christian claim is that the ultimate life of man . . . lies in that Kingdom of God which is depicted in the teaching of Jesus as a state of exultant and blissful happiness, symbolized as a joyous banquet in which all and sundry, having accepted God's gracious invitation, rejoice together. And Christian theodicy must point forward to that final blessedness, and claim that this infinite future good will render worth while all the pain and travail and wickedness that has occurred on the way to it.
> (Hick 1979: 376)

How satisfactory is this view? The fundamental difficulty seems to be, as Kenneth Surin has pointed out (Surin 1986: 95), that the idea that soul making goes on after death cannot do anything to guarantee that there will not be pointless suffering in a post-mortem state. That is, could there not be pointless suffering after death in the soul-making that takes place then? Perhaps Hick would say there could not be. If that is so, then the soul-making process after death will be much easier than the same process this side of death, and in that case we should have to face the problem of why there is or needs to be pointless suffering in this world. To that question there seems to be no clear answer within Hick's terms.

There is a further problem with Hick's argument. This is simply that there seems to be something grotesque in the idea that the bliss of Heaven, however great it is, could compensate for the sufferings that some have undergone. Could we ever really say that some future state of happiness would render Hitler's extermination camps *worthwhile*? Surely, anyone who thinks this has lost grip on the real issues here, that is, has lost (or never had) a proper understanding of the kinds of sufferings that many have endured. This point, to which we shall return in some detail below, raises a problem for the whole notion of a theodicy.

review
activity

1. Why does Irenaeus think that God did not create man perfect from the beginning?

2. What role does Hick believe is served by the pain and suffering of life?

3. What does Hick think happens after death?

A different view on Augustine and Irenaeus on the problem of evil

Before looking at some further attempts to cope with the problem of evil in the kind of form in which we have been discussing it hitherto, we should note that it is possible to understand Augustine and Irenaeus in a way significantly different from that already presented. I have presented the views of Augustine and Irenaeus very much in the kind of way that those views have been understood within modern philosophy – that is, within philosophy since about the seventeenth century. That understanding may be mistaken.

An alternative way of understanding Augustine and Irenaeus on the problem of evil has been suggested by Kenneth Surin, and we should briefly look at his account (Surin 1986: 10ff.).

Surin argues that, in the case of Augustine, it is a mistake to see him as attempting a general theodicy of the kind we have been exploring so far – that is, an attempt to render consistent a belief in the existence of a perfect, omnipotent God with a recognition of the existence of evil. Rather, says Surin, Augustine was concerned with the *psychological hold* that evil could have over a person – for example, that, having done something wicked in the past (stealing, for instance), the memory of the thrill and pleasure of the deed could be what helped to ingrain in the agent a *habit* to do such things. Thus, what Augustine was concerned about in the 'problem of evil' was the process of conversion, that is, a person's being freed through God's grace from the propensity or habit to do evil. Thus, there can be, for Augustine, no such thing as a solution to the problem of evil for someone not in the right kind of spiritual and psychological state – for someone who has not been freed from his propensity to do evil. However intellectually gifted a person is, if he is himself unconverted then what he has to say about the mystery of evil will be 'doomed to be self-defeating . . . Only faith in Christ makes possible the cleansing of our vision . . . which enables us, damaged souls that we are, to discover the true answer to this most perplexing of questions' concerning evil (Surin 1986: 11). A solution to the problem of evil is thus, for Augustine, not primarily an *intellectual* or merely *theoretical* matter at all, but a *practical* and *spiritual* matter, that is, one concerning what to make of, and how to be freed from, one's own evil and sin. It is only when the mind and soul have been illuminated by God's revelation of himself that the mystery of evil can be accepted: outside this revelation, there can be no understanding of evil – no solution to the problem of evil.

Surin argues that Irenaeus has to be understood, like Augustine, as not proposing a 'theoretical' response to the problem of evil. In the case of Irenaeus, Surin suggests that the real focus of Irenaeus's concern was to combat the Gnostics, an early Christian sect. The Gnostics argued that we should distinguish between two godheads, a lower Demiurge, who had created the world, and the Supreme God, who was responsible for the redemption of existence. They had identified the lower Demiurge with the God of the Old Testament and the Supreme God with the God of the New Testament. Irenaeus wanted to show that there was, after all, only one God and that the God of the New Testament was also the God of the Old Testament. Thus, Irenaeus wanted to establish a continuity between the works of the Bible and argue that there was just one creation in which human beings advance towards salvation. Irenaeus thought that to accept that there was, as he believed, just one God, was to be presented with a profound mystery about the nature of God, and that it was tempting to accept the Gnostic view, even though this view was false, for it removed the mystery of God by splitting him into two. For Irenaeus, therefore, the problem of evil was not one in which there is a difficulty about whether certain propositions ('God is wholly god'; 'God is omnipotent'; 'evil exists') can be shown to be consistent with one another. Rather, the problem was one of coming to accept the mystery of the *one* God. The way to do that was to come truly to love Christ, a struggle that, whilst being in part intellectual, is primarily a practical and spiritual task. As with Augustine, in Irenaeus the problem of evil has to do with one's *spiritual orientation,* an orientation that allows one to accept the mystery of God and his work of salvation.

If Surin is right, then the presentation of the problem of evil in Augustine and Irenaeus that was offered earlier in this chapter was mistaken, for, roughly speaking, it failed to be responsive to the *spiritual* nature of the task of coming to accept evil in and through a love of God and Christ. In seeing Augustine and Irenaeus as trying to offer an *intellectual* response to the problem of evil, modern philosophy has failed properly to understand these two early Christian thinkers.

Let us return to the problem of evil as this is discussed in the mainstream of modern English-speaking philosophy.

Plantinga and the 'free will defence'

One of the most widely discussed modern thinkers who has written about the problem of evil is Alvin Plantinga, and we shall now look briefly at his work on this issue (Plantinga 1977; 1994).

Plantinga's approach is to try to show that the proposition

a) God is omnipotent and wholly good

is logically consistent with the proposition

b) Evil exists.

In order to do this, Plantinga says that we need to find some third proposition which is consistent with a) and is such that a) and this third proposition entail b). The third proposition in question is:

c) Evil exists on account of the actions of free, rational creatures.

The difference between a defence and a theodicy

Plantinga says that a *theodicy* will attempt to show that c) is *true*. A theodicy will attempt to show that c) tells us the *real reason* why evil exists. But Plantinga does not wish to offer a theodicy in this sense. He does not want to say that he can show that c) is true, or even that c) is plausible. All he wants to show is that c) is *logically possible*. For if c) is logically possible then it will be true to say that a), b) and c) are not logically inconsistent – that is, that the existence of an omnipotent, omniscient and wholly good God is *logically consistent* with the evil of the world. This is why Plantinga calls his approach a 'defence' and not a 'theodicy' (Plantinga 1977: 26ff.).

Plantinga's argument proceeds through use of what is called 'possible world semantics'. The details of this need not detain us: it is enough to know that a possible world is a way things are or might have been. Thus, for example, there is a possible world in which everything is as it is in this world expect that my shoes are brown instead of black. Or there is another possible world in which everything is as it is except that you are not reading this book at the moment but doing something else instead. Possible worlds can be quite near to (quite like) the actual world, as in the two examples just given, or they can be very unlike the actual world – as is the possible world where elephants can fly, worms are two metres thick, and everyone is happy. This world – our world – is, of course, a possible world: it is a possible world that is actual, which is to say really exists.

Consider now two worlds, W and W*. W is the actual world. W* is a possible (non-actual) world. Imagine now that Smedes, the Director of the Highways Agency, has just bribed Curley, the mayor of the city, for £35,000, so that Curley will drop his opposition to the building of a new motorway. This is what happens in W. Smedes now wonders whether Curley would have taken a bribe of £20,000 and dropped his opposition. In W*, Curley would have accepted the bribe if Smedes had offered him £20,000. That is, in W* the following proposition:

a) Smedes offers Curley £20,000 and Curley accepts it

is true. W* is, of course, a possible (but non-actual) world. So, we can say that the following proposition

b) If W* were actual, Curley would accept £20,000

is true.

Could God make (Plantinga says 'actualise') W*? Well, God is omnipotent, so he could. But notice now that, if God were to actualise W*, then, in W*, Curley would have no choice but to accept the £20,000 since in W* he does take the bribe. In other words, if God actualises W* he thereby deprives Curley of his freedom. So, it cannot be that God actualises W* and Curley remains free concerning whether or not to take the bribe. This is so even if God does not want Curley to take the bribe – even if God wants Curley to do good (Plantinga 1977: 45–7).

However, if God cannot actualise W* with Curley remaining free, is this not a limitation on God's omnipotence? In fact it is not, because it is not logically possible for God to actualise W* and leave Curley free. This is not a limitation on God's omnipotence, since it is mistaken to think that God's omnipotence extends to doing what is logically impossible, as our earlier discussion of omnipotence showed.

This may seem enough to vindicate the free will defence, but it is not. The reason was suggested by John Mackie in a well-known article on the problem of evil (Mackie 1994). Mackie argued that, if it is possible for a person who is free to do the right or good thing on one occasion, then it is possible for a person to do the right or good thing on all occasions on which he could do something right or good (that is, not do the bad action). So why, asked Mackie, could God not have created a free human being who always did the right or good thing? (Mackie 1994: 33–4). If this were possible, then Plantinga's argument would be undermined.

In order for Plantinga to rebut Mackie's argument, what he has to show is that it is *possible* that God could not have created beings who are free but never do anything wrong. He does not have to show that this is *in fact* the case (Plantinga 1994: 102). Recall that he is not attempting to provide a theodicy but just a defence: and all he has to show is that there is nothing logically inconsistent in the existence of a wholly good, omnipotent God and evil.

Transworld depravity

By way of reply to Mackie, then, Plantinga introduces the notion of *transworld depravity*. A free creature suffers from transworld depravity if it is such that, if it is actualised (created), it will freely do wrong on at least one occasion. That is, in whatever world this creature existed it would do wrong at least once.

Now, there is nothing logically inconsistent in the notion of transworld depravity. Moreover, it is possible that all free creatures suffer from transworld depravity. However, given that this is possible, it is possible that God could not actualise a world in which any free creature always did the right action. If that is possible, then 'it is possible that God could not have created a world containing moral good but no moral evil' (Plantinga 1994: 105). This would not be a limitation on God's omnipotence, because if all free creatures suffer from transworld depravity it is not logically possible for God to create free creatures who always do what is right: it is not limitation on God's omnipotence to be unable to do what is logically impossible – a thought we have already met in our exposition of Plantinga's argument.

Note that Plantinga is not claiming that all human beings *do* suffer from transworld depravity. He is simply claiming that it is logically possible that they all do. However, if it is logically possible that they all do, then it is logically possible that God cannot create free human beings who always do what is right. And that is all he needs to show that the existence of at least some evil is logically consistent with the existence of God.

Plantinga's argument so far shows that it is logically possible that a wholly good, omnipotent God and *some* evil exist. However, there is a great deal of evil in the world. Is the existence of a wholly good, omnipotent God consistent with the *amount* of evil there is? Plantinga replies that we must look at the balance of moral good to moral evil in the world, not simply at the evil. What he says about this is that it is logically possible that this world contains a better balance of moral good to evil than any other world – that any world that contained less moral evil would be deprived of even more moral good.

Lastly, Plantinga's argument has to cope with the problem of natural evil. His answer is that it is logically possible that the natural evil of the world is caused by free spirits, that is, by devils (Plantinga 1977: 57–9).

So Plantinga thinks that the free-will defence is successful, provided only that the notions of free agency and transworld depravity are logically possible, and that God has some purpose in creating a world with free human beings in it. How successful, then, is Plantinga's argument?

Problems for Plantinga's defence

One difficulty is that, even if one thinks the argument entirely successful in its own terms, it still remains a defence and not a theodicy. This is to say that a believer might well be interested in something more than simply being assured that the existence of a wholly good, omnipotent God is *logically consistent* with the existence of evil. Of course, the reason why Plantinga sets his sights on a mere defence rather than a theodicy is that those atheists who have discussed the problem of evil have generally argued that there is a logical inconsistency in supposing there to be a wholly good, omnipotent God even as evil exists. So Plantinga thinks that his task is to show that *that* is mistaken. However, it is reasonable for a believer who is genuinely troubled about the existence of evil to be dissatisfied with what Plantinga has to offer. Such a believer may want to know *what the reason is* for so much suffering, not what the reason *might be* from the point of view of *logical possibility*. Indeed, a non-believer may want that too. For example, Pablo Casals (1876–1973) tells us that, when he was a young man, he was suddenly struck by

> *how much ugliness there was [in the world]. How much evil! How much pain and travail! I would ask myself: Was man created to live in such squalor and degradation? All about me I saw evidence of suffering, of poverty, of misery, of man's inhumanity to man. I saw people who lived in hunger and had almost nothing to feed their children. I saw beggars in the streets and the age-old inequality of the rich and the poor . . . Day and night I brooded on these conditions. I walked the streets of Barcelona feeling sick and full of apprehension. I was in a pit of darkness, at odds with the world . . . I could not understand why there was so much evil in the world, why men should do such things to one another, or what, indeed, was the purpose of life under such circumstances.*
> (Casals 1970: 50)

Casals goes on to say that he

> *turned to religious mysticism. I would go to a church near school after my classes, and I would sit in the shadows, trying to lose myself in prayer, trying desperately to find consolation and an answer to my questions, searching for calm and some easement of the torment afflicting me . . . But to no avail.*
> (Casals 1970: 51–3)

Could Casals have had his worries calmed through being convinced by Plantinga's argument? Evidently the thought that he could is ludicrous. So it seems there must be something amiss in Plantinga's argument. Plantinga, however, would say that this criticism mixes up two things that should be kept apart: a theodicy or defence on the one hand, and help with coping with evil when faced with it, on the other (Plantinga 1977: 63). Nevertheless it is arguable that, in drawing this distinction, Plantinga has failed to understand the problem of evil. I shall return to this issue later.

In any case, there seem to be other problems with Plantinga's free-will defence. One of the most significant of these is that the God who appears in Plantinga's argument seems to bear little, if any, relation to the God of Christian belief, practice and worship. That God is one who is three persons in one – God the Father, God the Son and God the Holy Spirit; a God who was incarnated as the Second Person of the Trinity as Jesus Christ who suffered and died on the cross; a God who fills the life of the believer as a living presence in the great and small things of life; a God who wishes us freely to love him for the gift of life he has bestowed on us; a God to whom the believer can turn in prayer; and so on. This God seems utterly unlike Plantinga's God, who by comparison seems to be nothing more than an abstract metaphysical entity with no serious or clear connection with the realities of the life of faith and worship. The believer might with justice feel that, even if one can make sense of how Plantinga's God can allow evil, his argument leaves it unclear how the Christian God can allow evil.

One final criticism of Plantinga should be mentioned. This is that he supposes in his argument that one can sensibly balance up the moral good and evil in the world. But there is a criticism of this move analogous to the criticism made of Hick earlier in his claim that Hitler's concentration camps can be made worthwhile by a final beatific vision of God for all. For Plantinga wants to say that we should seriously look at Auschwitz and wonder whether it was worthwhile because greater counterbalancing good was (or will be) present in the world than would have been present had there been no Auschwitz. One might feel that this way of looking at things involves a grave loss of moral sensitivity.

review
activity

1.   Explain in your own words the idea of a possible world.

2.   Why does Plantinga offer a defence rather than a theodicy? What is the difference between the two?

3.   What reasons does Plantinga give for saying that the existence of evil is logically consistent with the existence of a wholly good, omnipotent God?

4.   What does Plantinga mean by 'transworld depravity' and why does he invoke this idea in his argument?

5.   Why does the example from Casals suggest that Plantinga has not properly understood the problem of evil?

6.   Give in your own words one other criticism of Plantinga's argument.

Swinburne on natural evils

Swinburne, like Plantinga, supports the free will defence in his reflections on the nature of evil. However, he thinks that the idea that natural evil is caused by devils is not wholly convincing because we have no independent evidence of the existence of such devils – independent, that is, of the role they play in helping the theist out who wants to claim that natural evils are caused by such devils (Swinburne 1991: 202). Swinburne therefore proposes to offer a different argument that will explain the existence of natural evil.

Swinburne's argument, which he elaborates in some detail, is, in essence, fairly straightforward. As we have already noted, he accepts the freewill defence. This means that he thinks it is good that human beings have free will and, relatedly, that God has good reasons for allowing human beings to have free will. However, human beings need to know what kinds of consequences their freely done actions have if the exercise of their free will is to have any point: if they did not know the consequences, they could not know what reasons there are to exercise their will in one way or another. How are human beings to know what kinds of consequences the exercise of their free will is likely to have? Swinburne says that this can only be from experience. '[W]e can', he writes, 'only know that certain of our actions will have harmful consequences through prior experience (in some degree) of such harmful consequences' (Swinburne 1991: 206). For example, human beings have to learn, both as individuals and as a race, what the consequences are of, for example, drinking eight double whiskies, or administering cyanide to others, or allowing rabies to enter a country, or getting an arm caught up in a dangerous machine in factory, or building a city on fault-line where earthquakes might occur (the examples are all Swinburne's). Sometimes this experience will be an experience one undergoes oneself, for example drinking the whisky; or that one sees another undergo, for example the administration of cyanide: I could hardly learn anything useful for later life by administering cyanide to myself!

In other words, the natural world has to operate according to *law-like regularities in nature* for human beings to learn about the consequences of their actions (Swinburne 1991: 210). We have to learn from experience that cyanide kills, that fire maims, that earthquakes cause devastation and so forth, so that we can judge how to exercise our free will when dealing with cyanide or with fire, or when building cities, and so on. As Swinburne says: 'There must be naturally occurring evils (i.e. evils not deliberately caused by men) if men are to know how to cause evils themselves or are to prevent evil occurring' (Swinburne 1992: 207). Thus, I could not know what I was doing (freely choosing to do) in dousing a cat with petrol and setting it alight unless there were natural evils connected with fire, for example, that fire maims and kills. In short, natural evils serve, on Swinburne's account, to give us knowledge so that we can properly exercise our free will.

There are two problems with Swinburne's account – problems that are connected with one another. The first is that some human beings learn about the consequences of actions by seeing the suffering of *others*. For example, the present generation in England is, let us suppose, much more wary about war because of the suffering we have seen in the two world wars

– and numerous other conflicts – in the twentieth century. However, many countless millions of human beings suffered in those wars. Does there not seem something unjust in a 'system' that allows some to learn about evils at the expense of others, as it might be said we have learnt about wars at the expense of those millions slaughtered in the conflicts of the twentieth century?

A central part of Swinburne's response to this problem is to argue that we should remember that the relation of God to human beings is like that of parents to their children. Parents, says Swinburne, have a right to allow one of their children to suffer *somewhat* for the good of their other children. This is because parents are responsible for the existence of all their children. As God is so much more the author of our existence than parents are of the existence of their children, God has a right, argues Swinburne, to allow some human beings to suffer for the good of others (Swinburne 1991: 217).

There is, however, something rather odd in this response of Swinburne's. This is that it is far from clear that it makes sense at all to ascribe rights to God. Rights, whatever else they are, are claims that some have against others, claims that others have the duty to observe. For example, if I have a right not to be harmed as I walk down the street, you have the duty to observe my right by refraining from attacking me. Rights seem to be the kind of thing that only beings within a moral community can have. Yet, as we noted earlier, clearly God is not a member of any moral community, still less a member of the moral community of human beings. So, it seems that the idea that God has rights, including a right to inflict harm, does not make sense at all.

The second difficulty with Swinburne's theodicy is that concerning the amount of evil and suffering in the world. After all, even if we were to agree with Swinburne's argument as he presents it, the fact remains that it seems there is far more – indeed, vastly more – suffering and evil in the world than is necessary for us to have knowledge of the good and evil consequences of our actions. Could God not have made things so that the natural world was able to inflict some, but less, suffering on us, so that we were able to inflict some, but less suffering, on each other? In response to this concern, Swinburne says that it misses the point that the fewer natural evils there are, the fewer the opportunities man has to exercise his freedom and responsibility. Thus, the great amount of suffering there is is necessary for man to have the knowledge necessary for the proper exercise of that freedom and responsibility. The idea that there should be suffering, but less of it, he dismisses by saying:

> *What in effect the objection is asking is that God should make a toy-world, a world where things matter, but not very much; where we can choose and our choices can make a small difference, but the real choices remain God's. For he simply would not allow us the choice of doing real harm, or through our negligence allowing real harm to occur. He would be like an over-protective parent who will not let his child out of sight for a moment.*

> (Swinburne 1991: 219–20)

Hence, Swinburne concludes that 'Hiroshima, Belsen, the Lisbon Earthquake, [and] the Black Death' are for the good in the long run (Swinburne 1991: 219).

We seem here once again, as in the case of Hick and Plantinga, to have in Swinburne the same questionable idea that the monstrous sufferings of some can be justified in the long run, an idea that, as I have already noted, seems to show a lack of moral sensitivity. In any case, there is another problem with Swinburne's account of why there is so much evil and suffering. This can be seen by asking the following question. Assuming Swinburne is right about the need for a huge amount of suffering so that we can exercise our free will and be responsible, why does God allow so *little* suffering? After all, God could have made us so that it was much *easier* to inflict much *more suffering* on each other than it is. If he had made us this way, we would have had much *greater* opportunities for exercising our free will and responsibility. Suppose, for example, that it was genuinely possible to make voodoo dolls or effigies of those whom we dislike, stick pins in them and thus cause real suffering to those of whom we had made an effigy. Many people would no doubt be tempted to do this – much more tempted than they are, say, to go out, buy a gun, and shoot someone through the head. Moreover, it would be much more difficult for the police to catch those who killed or maimed using voodoo effigies. In other words, in such cases one could both commit and get away with evil much more easily than at present. That being so, if God had made it possible for us to harm one another with voodoo effigies he would have allowed us a far greater range for our exercising our free will and responsibility. Thus, on Swinburne's account, there seems no good reason why there is so little suffering. On his account, there should be much *more* evil and suffering if God's purposes in his granting us free will are to be achieved. Yet this is clearly absurd. So, if what has been said in reply to him is correct, Swinburne's argument should be rejected.

review activity

1. Why does Swinburne think that the natural world must operate in a law-like manner for human beings to learn about the consequences of their actions?

2. If it is true that the natural world must operate in a law-like manner for human beings to learn about the consequences of their actions, what relevance has this to the problem of evil?

3. How and in what way does Swinburne argue that God has a right to inflict harm on human beings? What objection might one raise to this argument?

4. In what way does Swinburne argue that there is not too much suffering in the world? In what way might one argue against this conclusion?

The problem of evil revisited

I have three times suggested – in connection with Hick, Plantinga and Swinburne – that the claim they make that evil can be justified by being counterbalanced by good displays a lack of moral sensitivity. I shall conclude this discussion of the problem of evil by making some more general comments on these lines, aiming to make clear why it is that some philosophers believe that the approach to the problem of evil taken by such thinkers as Hick, Plantinga and Swinburne is quite mistaken (cf. Holland 1980: ch.15; Surin 1986; Mulhall 1994: esp. 17–19).

The play *Shadowlands* by William Nicholson, based on true events, tells the story of the relationship and marriage of C.S. Lewis and Joy Gresham. Lewis was an Oxford don in his fifties when he met Gresham, an American divorcée in her late thirties. At the time of their meeting, Lewis was leading a very traditional life at Oxford, safe in the protective world of academic life. He was a devout Christian, who had thought a lot about the problem of evil, trying to understand why it is that there is so much suffering in the world. At the beginning of the play, Lewis is giving a lecture on the problem of evil, articulating a position that had become his standard view. His view is very much like that of Swinburne. He even says at one point: 'God loves us, so he makes us the gift of suffering. Through suffering, we release our hold on the toys of this world, and know that our true good lies in another world' (Nicholson 1992: 2).

Lewis and Gresham fall in love, and marry. Shortly thereafter, Gresham is diagnosed with cancer, and Lewis finds that his whole world is beginning to collapse. At one point, after she is diagnosed with the illness, Lewis is giving his usual lecture on the problem of evil, but there are signs that he is beginning no longer to believe his usual line on it. Later on, after his wife has died, Lewis, devastated by what has happened to the woman he loves, has a conversation with Warnie, his brother, in which he says that he is beginning to think that there is no meaning to suffering, no point in it, no purpose behind it: it is just suffering, and that is all. Right at the end of the play, he is giving again his old lecture on the problem of evil. The stage direction reads: 'His words are a version of the talk he has given earlier, now transformed by his own suffering' (Nicholson 1992: 53).

Amongst other things, then, the play is about the problem of evil and one man's response to it. It contains an implicit critique of the work of thinkers like Hick, Plantinga and Swinburne, and, indeed, of those who argue against such thinkers on the same terms, such as Mackie. So far as the problem of evil is concerned, the point of the play is this. At the beginning, when Lewis is talking about the nature of evil and suffering, he does not know what he is talking about. His beliefs about evil are merely intellectual and have no connection with wider life. In particular, what he says has no real authority because he has not suffered at all in his life: he is just mouthing words. Moreover, and connectedly, he has no right to say what he says about suffering, because he does not know what it is to suffer. In the course of the play he comes to realise this: he comes to learn what it really is to suffer and that what he previously thought was simply empty rhetoric. That is what it means to say that his words at the end are transformed by his suffering.

The problem of evil: a practical and spiritual, not merely intellectual problem

All of this, as I said, has relevance to Hick *et al.* For Lewis's problem was that he treated the problem of evil as a *theoretical* problem to be solved by the resources of the intellect and nothing else. He came to see that the problem of evil is not that kind of problem at all. To speak of one's own and others' sufferings is *to articulate a moral point of view*, and this moral point of view can range between the extremes of being complacent, shallow, self-satisfied and thoughtless on the one hand, and being insightful, deep, generous and sensitive, on the other. And those who adopt a purely theoretical approach to the problem of evil, as if it were a strange puzzle that needs to be solved, have by default adopted a moral point of view. This is why I suggested earlier that those who say that Auschwitz is justified by a greater good have lost their moral sensitivity on this topic: to speak as they do is, at the very least, to insult those who were exterminated in the concentration camps. Nothing could *justify* the concentration camps. Moreover, as Stephen Mulhall has pointed out (Mulhall 1994: 19), those who say that Auschwitz can be justified also insult God when they say this, for they imply that Auschwitz is part of God's overall plan for the world. That is to see God as a criminal, and, as Mulhall says, is little less than blasphemy.

It should be clear that Surin offered the same kind of criticism of the 'standard' way of reading Augustine and Irenaeus on the problem of evil: for Augustine and Irenaeus, the problem of evil was not a purely intellectual problem, but a practical and spiritual problem.

None of this is to say that the problem of evil is not a real problem, but it is to say that if one is going to have anything worth saying on it one will need to draw on much more than mere intellectual reflection of the narrowly academic kind. This is why I suggested that, when Plantinga draws a sharp distinction between the theoretical justification of evil and the possibility of consoling someone faced with evil, he did not understand the problem of evil. This is because if someone does have anything worth saying on the problem of evil then it must at least aspire to say something that might console someone faced with evil. For sure, someone might think he has something to say about the problem and we might judge that he does not. Moreover, if someone does have something serious to say about it, then the chances are that it will be expressed in the form, not of an argument, but of a story; this is one reason why Jesus often spoke of people's suffering in parables. Beyond all that, one should also not forget that there will be some people's suffering that is so great that it could be an insult even to attempt to offer consolation. Having something to say in such cases could be, as it were, to have nothing to say. One might need in such cases simply to keep silent, or just to listen. Wittgenstein wrote in a quite different context: 'Whereof one cannot speak, thereof one must remain silent' (Wittgenstein 1990: §7). This is often the right thing to remember in the face of much of others' suffering.

review activity

1. In what way could one argue that the problem of evil cannot be treated simply as an intellectual problem?

2. If the problem of evil is not simply an intellectual problem, how should we understand it?

Miracles

It is sometimes said that Christianity stands or falls with the truth or falsity of the claim that Jesus rose from the dead. If he did not rise from the dead, then Christianity must be at an end. This is to say that the truth or falsity of Christianity depends on whether a miracle took place. Moreover, the Bible is full of stories of miracles other than the resurrection of Jesus. What are miracles? Can they, or do they, really take place?

What is a miracle?

There are different views on how we should understand what a miracle is. I shall start with the traditional or mainstream understanding of a miracle as this is found in the philosophical literature. Having discussed this, I shall move on to look at one or two less common understandings of the concept of a miracle.

A miracle as a violation of a law of nature by God

On the traditional understanding, then, a miracle involves a violation of the laws of nature, a violation brought about by God, where the laws of nature tell us how bodies *must* behave under certain conditions. For example, speaking roughly, the laws of nature tell us that *whenever* a brick is dropped from such and such a height onto a sheet of glass at such and such velocity the glass *must* shatter. So, 'a miracle [is] a violation of the laws of nature, that is, a non-repeatable exception to the operation of these laws, brought about by God. Laws of nature have the form of universal statements "all As are B", and state how bodies behave of physical necessity' (Swinburne 1983: 186). Again, Hume defines a miracle as 'a transgression of a law of nature by a particular volition of the Deity' (Hume 1985: 115, fn.1). And J.L. Mackie says that a miracle is

> *a violation of a natural law . . . [by] divine or supernatural intervention. The laws of nature . . . describe the ways in which the world – including, of course, human beings – works when left to itself, when not interfered with. A miracle occurs when the world is not left to itself, when something distinct from the natural order as a whole intrudes into it.*   (Mackie 1982: 19–20)

Now, given this view of what a miracle is, we can ask whether it is reasonable to believe in them – to believe that they have taken place or do take place. The place to start is Hume's famous discussion in his *Enquiries Concerning Human Understanding and the Principles of Morals* (1748–51).

Hume: miracles are impossible

It is not always entirely clear just what Hume is arguing in his essay. At times he seems to be saying that a miracle *could not* happen. His argument for this is that our only source for what the laws of nature are is experience. However, when our experience of the past has been, in a certain respect, always the same – when our experience of the past has been, as Hume puts it, uniform – then we have what amounts to *proof* that the future will resemble the past. Thus, we have experience 'that all men die; that lead cannot, of itself, remain suspended in the air; that fire consumes wood, and is extinguished by water' (Hume 1985: 114). This means that we have what amounts to *proof* that all men die; that lead cannot, of itself, remain suspended in mid-air; and so on. Hume suggests that an event would only be called or considered a miracle when we have the evidence of the *uniform* experience of nature *against* it happening. However, if we *do* have such experience of nature, then there *could not* be such an event as a miracle – that is, a miracle is *impossible*, for that is what it *is* to have such experience of nature. In Hume's words:

There must . . . be a uniform experience against every miraculous event, otherwise the event would not merit that appellation. And as a uniform experience amounts to a proof, there is here a direct and full proof, from the nature of the fact, against the existence of any miracle.   (Hume 1985: 115)

There is a problem for Hume's argument. To see this, consider the fact that when Hume says that miracles are impossible, what he has in mind is *physical* impossibility. After all, there is nothing *logically* impossible about, say, a man's curing another's blindness by spitting on his eyes (Mark 8: 22–6). But the problem for Hume is that what counts as physically impossible changes over time. For example,

Hume could have said (with complete justification) that it was physically impossible, according to the best laws of nature at his disposal, for a man in England to be able to talk to and see a man who is at the same time in America. Now if he had taken this to mean 'it could not happen that . . . ' then we would simply retort it has *happened.*   (Gaskin 1988: 163–4)

In other words, there are plenty of things of which we have had no experience but that *could* happen and so our experience of the uniformity of nature cannot be used to rule out miracles as impossible. Moreover, there are times when the laws of nature are revised because some event takes place that those laws had indicated was impossible: this is a normal part of scientific progress. If Hume were right in saying that any violation of a law of nature is impossible, then there could not be scientific progress in the way there is.

review

activity

1. What is Hume's argument that a miracle is impossible?

2. What problems are there for this argument?

Hume: miracles are highly unlikely

I mentioned above that it is not always clear what exactly it is that Hume is arguing. This is because he often seems to retreat from the very strong claim that miracles are *impossible* to the claim that it is *highly improbable* that any have taken place. And when he is looking at things from this point of view, he is mainly interested in the testimony that others might give of their having witnessed a miracle. The question is therefore: Should we believe them?

Hume suggests that we should only believe them if it is more likely that the miracle took place than that they are lying, mistaken, exaggerating or the like. In Hume's words: '[N]o testimony is sufficient to establish a miracle, unless the testimony be of such a kind, that its falsehood would be more miraculous, then the fact which it endeavours to establish' (Hume 1985: 116).

Hume on testimony of others

However, Hume argues that there are four reasons why we should not accept the testimony of others that they have witnessed a miracle. I give them in summary form, and then make some comments on them.

1. Rationally or reasonably to believe in the testimony of others that they have witnessed a miracle, we need to have confidence in those making

the testimony. We can only have this confidence if the persons concerned are 'of such unquestioned good-sense, education, and learning, as to secure us against all delusion in themselves'. Moreover, they would have to have integrity and be of good reputation. Further, the testimony would have to be from a 'sufficient number' of such persons. Hume says, however, that we have no such testimony (Hume 1985: 116–17).

2. Human beings have a natural love of 'surprise and wonder' and this inclines them to believe in reports of miracles and spread them further. To this must be added the fact that some religious persons may knowingly spread lies about the occurrence of some miracle in the belief that this promotes a holy cause (Hume 1985: 117–19).

3. It is chiefly among 'ignorant and barbarous nations' that there is widespread belief in miracles. (Hume 1985: 119–21).

4. Hume starts in his fourth point from the idea that the different systems of religion – Christianity, Islam, Hinduism and so on – cannot all be correct. Either they are all mistaken, or one of them is correct. Now suppose we try to support the claims of these religions by reference to the alleged occurrence of miracles. More specifically, let us suppose, as is the case, that certain miracles are alleged to have taken place and to support Christianity. Let us also suppose that certain miracles are alleged to have occurred and to support Islam, as Muslims usually claim. Then, argues Hume, the one set of testimonies (in support of Christianity) cancels out the other set of testimonies (in support of Islam) and *vice versa*. In this case, we have no more reason to believe in Christianity on the basis of miracles then we have to believe in Islam on the same basis and so we should believe in neither on the basis of the alleged miracles. The case, says Hume, is like that in a law court: if two people say that they saw the accused at the scene of the crime whilst two others say that they saw him somewhere else at the same time then, other things being equal, the testimonies of the first two witnesses destroy those of the latter two, and *vice versa*, leaving us none the wiser about where the accused was at the time of the crime. (Hume 1985: 121–2)

Responses to Hume There appear to be problems with Hume's four grounds for not accepting the testimony of others that they have witnessed a miracle. One is that he does not tell us what is to count as a 'sufficient number' of putative witnesses of the kind he has in mind. Moreover, some of those who have reported miracles have certainly been of good sense, education and learning (some of the most insightful, brilliant and learned men and women have been religious believers). Again, it is true that human beings have a love of surprise and wonder, but there is no clear reason for thinking that religious people give themselves up to this love and are especially prone to being unable to distinguish the true from the false in reports of certain happenings. Further, whilst it may be true that belief in miracles has been most widespread amongst 'ignorant and barbarous' nations, such belief is certainly not confined to such nations. Finally, there are reports of miracles that could be seen as evidence for more than one religion. Certainly this will depend on one's general view of the relations between different religions. No doubt it is true that in

Hume's day it was generally believed that, if Christianity was true, then Islam, Hinduism and other religions were false. However, we need not take this view: it is possible to see all the great religions as articulating different perspectives on the one Ultimate Reality. If one does think that, the miracles that seem to support one of these religions might well be thought to support the other religions.

review activity

1. Explain in your own words why it is that Hume thinks that we never have adequate grounds to trust the testimony of others that they have witnessed a miracle.

2. What objections are there to Hume's arguments concerning the unreliability of the testimony of others to have witnessed a miracle?

Holland's view of miracles

We saw earlier that Hume's argument that the uniformity of the operations of nature makes miracles impossible is weak. It would, nonetheless, be in the spirit of Hume's claims about the uniformity of nature to suggest that if we came across what seems to us to be a violation of the laws of nature we should adjust the laws of nature to take account of this new phenomenon. The suggestion is that what looks like a violation of a law of nature cannot be thought of as such: it is just that our understanding of the laws of nature is not yet comprehensive enough to take account of all eventualities (cf. Mackie 1982: 24–6).

R.F. Holland has argued against this view (Holland 1980: ch.12). Imagine, he says, a horse that has been normally born and reared. Suppose now that this horse is deprived of all nourishment but continues to thrive, and that an examination of the horse's digestive system reveals no abnormality. That is, this horse is just like all other horses in the relevant respects but does not need food to survive. Should we say that our knowledge of the laws of nature as they apply to horses and their nutrition is mistaken and needs to be revised? We could do that, but Holland suggests that to do so would be to pay too high a price. We cannot, says Holland, in the face of the one case of the self-sustaining horse, just throw away our knowledge of the nature of horses

> not when it rests on the experience of generations, not when all other horses in the world are continuing to behave as horses have always done, and especially not when one considers the way our conception of the needs and capacities of horses interlocks with conceptions of the needs and capacities of other living things and with a conception of the difference between animate and inanimate behaviour quite generally. These conceptions form part of a common understanding that is well established and with us to stay.   (Holland 1980: 182)

Holland: the conceptually impossible can be empirically certain

In other words, Holland argues that it is better to leave an inconsistency in our knowledge than abandon what we know about horses and other creatures in the light of the self-sustaining horse. There could be, he says, events which are 'empirically certain and conceptually impossible' (Holland 1980: 184).

297

Note that the case of the self-sustaining horse is not, as such, a case of a miracle. A miracle, says Holland, when it involves a violation of a law of nature, must involve more than that. Specifically, it has to be connected in some way with religious thought more generally and with human good and evil. For example, if someone rises three feet into the air, and this is a violation of the laws of nature, this can only be seen as a miracle against a religious background and if some good is brought about in this way – say, that the person who rises this way escapes a certain death.

Holland is not arguing that violations of the laws of nature take place. He is arguing, rather, that there could be certain circumstances in which there are no *philosophical* objections to saying that they have taken place – for example, the case of the self-sustaining horse. However, this means that there could be circumstances in which there was no *philosophical* objection to saying that a miracle had taken place. Consider, for example, the story in St John's Gospel where Jesus turns water into wine (John 2: 1–11). Holland says that this constitutes a violation of the laws of nature. However, given his argument, he can say that, if someone chooses to see the turning of the water into wine as a miracle, there can be no objection from philosophy to his doing so (Holland 1980: 184).

Miracles with no violation of a law of nature

Holland's point that it is only against a religious background that we can speak of a miracle comes out also in a case where what is seen as a miracle does not violate any laws of nature. He imagines the following case. A child is riding his toy motor-car. He strays onto a railway line, and one of the wheels gets stuck down the side of one of the rails. An express train is bearing down on him. As the boy is at a curve in the line, the driver of the train cannot see him in order to brake in time. Nonetheless, the train comes to a halt just in front of the boy: the driver has fainted and fallen on the brake (Holland 1980: 169–70).

There is no violation of a law of nature here. Yet the mother of the boy continues to think of what happened as a miracle. This only makes sense because something good happened. It will also only make sense if the mother is religious or, at least, open to religion. Otherwise, she might simply say that what happened was just a piece of extraordinary luck. Indeed, in such a case what a non-religious person thinks of as luck is thought of by a religious person as a miracle of God.

review activity

1. Explain in your own words why it is that Holland thinks we might sometimes have to accept a contradiction in our experience concerning the laws of nature. When could such a contradiction be seen as a miracle, according to Holland?

2. In what kind of circumstances does Holland think that it might make sense to see something that is not a violation of a law of nature as a miracle?

Gareth Moore and the problem of God's intervention in the world

If we take it that God intervenes from time to time in the workings of the natural laws of the world, that is, performs miracles, then presumably he does so, on a traditional picture, in order to save some human beings from suffering. If that is so then we cannot overlook the fact that there is a great deal of suffering to which God does not respond with a miracle. How, then, are we to explain God's seemingly arbitrary interventions in the world? Does this not show that God only cares for some – for those for whom he performs a miracle? What about the others? Does he not care for them?

One interesting answer is provided by Gareth Moore (Moore 1988: ch.7). Recall that on Moore's account, God is not a person (see above). In line with this, he says that what it is to say that God performed a miracle is not to say that some invisible agent performed some act. Rather, it is to say the *no one* performed the act. That, he says, is what we *mean* by calling something a miracle. If, for example, someone goes to Lourdes and is cured of some illness and some want to speak of a miracle in connection with this cure, the aim is not to find out that *someone or other* – some invisible agent – effected the cure. In Moore's words:

> *Think of the shrine at Lourdes, where, it is claimed, people are sometimes miraculously cured of their diseases. Often close to death, they are suddenly restored to health. Brain tumours shrivel, cancers disappear, and the recovery is claimed as a miracle. How are such claims investigated, and what is taken to establish that a recovery is indeed miraculous? Much of the investigation is concerned with* ruling out *possible causes for the cure, showing what has not caused it; and it is certainly not* proved *to be a miracle by the discovery of the cause for the cure and its subsequent identification as God.* (Moore 1988: 226)

God as no one

According to Moore, therefore, to say that God intervenes in the world is *not* to say that *someone* intervenes in this way. It is to say that *no one* did. Similarly, to say that God watches over us, or looks after us, or helps us out and the like, is not to say that *somebody* is watching over us, or looking after us and so on. If it *were* the case that God's concern for us was a concern that *somebody* has who is watching over us, then it would be reasonable to ask why he does not make a better job of it. Why, for example, does he not intervene more often? However, because on Moore's account God is *not a somebody*, these questions *make no sense* with respect to God. If that is correct, then we can say that the problem of why God does not intervene more is, not solved, but *dissolved*: for the believer who thinks as Moore does, the question concerning why God does not intervene more than he does is empty and pointless (Moore 1988: 233–4).

review
activity

Gareth Moore claims that we can explain why God does not intervene more than he does to alleviate human suffering. How does Moore's understanding of God as not being a person support this claim?

Religion and morality

Introduction

One of the most interesting and thorniest issues in philosophy of religion is the relationship between religion and morality. Most people have some sense that there is *some* kind of connection between religion and morality, and even those who say that there is not usually feel that they have to show this, and that it cannot just be taken for granted. What exactly that connection is, or why there is, after all, no such connection, is extremely hard to say. In this section we shall look at a few of the problems and issues in this area.

One important reason why it is difficult to say just what the connection is between religion and ethics is that both concepts are themselves in various ways unclear. We noted this at the beginning both of the section of this book devoted to philosophy of religion and of that which deals with moral philosophy. Obviously enough, if two concepts – indeed, areas of life – are unclear, then it is not going to be easy to say just what the relation between them is. And just as we have a problem in understanding the relation between religion and morality, we have a problem in understanding the relation between morality and politics, or between morality and aesthetics. There is, in this sense, nothing especially odd in the fact that the relations between religion and morality are unclear.

To add to these difficulties, we should note that many cultures have made no serious distinction between the moral life and the religious life. Where God, or the gods, are thought to be present in all aspects of life, then the religious element of life is not going to be clearly separable from the rest of life. 'In Classical Greece', writes Michael Morgan, 'everything – politics, ethics, science, painting, music, dance, drama, agriculture – had a religious character' (Morgan 1992: 228). In such a culture, it is mistaken to think that one could separate out religious from ethical notions in any especially helpful manner. The same is probably true of European culture during the periods when Christianity was a dominant force. Indeed, there is thus something to be said for the idea that it is only in the modern age, where religion has for many people and cultures become more or less marginal, a merely private affair, that the relation between religion and morality becomes one on which it even makes sense to try and get philosophical clarity.

Still, with these caveats entered, we can take a closer look at what has been said by some philosophers on the connection between our two notions.

In what sense might morality be related to religion?

In a helpful paper, William Frankena distinguishes three ways in which morality might be dependent on religion: historically or causally; psychologically or motivationally; or logically (Frankena 1981). He himself is most interested in the last of these – that is, in the question whether morality is logically dependent on religion. However, there are important connections between the different kinds of dependence indicated.

Morality as historically dependent on religion

So far as *historical* dependence goes, there can be little doubt that the modern liberal morality of Western Europe, North America, Australia and so forth is the way it is largely on account of the impact and influence of Christianity. For, although fewer and fewer individuals in these areas believe in God – and many who say they do lead nothing remotely resembling a genuinely Christian (or Christ-like) life – some of the basic moral ideas by which we live have come to us from Christianity. Thus, for example, modern notions of equality, tolerance and freedom all have their roots in Christian thinking, and the value modern moral life places (if only in theory) on the virtues of cooperation, kindness, generosity, helpfulness, social utility and the like also have a deeply Christian provenance.

Moral obligation as logically dependent on religion

This kind of historical dependence of morality on religion has important consequences for the *logical* relations between religion and morality. Thus Elizabeth Anscombe argued that the concepts of *moral* obligation, the *moral* law, the *moral* ought and *moral* duty only make proper sense within a conceptual system in which there is belief in a God as a law giver. She suggested that in modern Western culture we no longer seriously believe in such a law giver, but the moral notions in question have survived the decay of this belief. They thus make no proper sense in modern culture. The situation is, she says, rather like how things would be 'if the notion "criminal" were to remain when criminal law and criminal courts had been abolished and forgotten' (Anscombe 1958).

A fuller discussion of Anscombe's argument can be found at the beginning of the chapter in this book on virtue ethics. For now, we should look at an argument concerning the relation between religion and morality that is heavily indebted to, though somewhat different from, Anscombe's argument. It is given by Alasdair MacIntyre (MacIntyre 1985, esp. ch.5).

MacIntyre starts by noting that in the ethical thought of Aristotle the basic structure is given by a relation between three components: man-as-he-happens-to-be; man-as-he-could-be-if-he-realised-his-essential-nature; and ethics itself. This looks complicated, but it is, in fact, fairly simple in outline. The basic idea is that man has a nature that can be developed through the course of a life, and that it is the job of an ethical education to do this. Human beings start out untutored, and the task of an ethical education is to develop their reason, their emotional life and their capacity to act so that they acquire the virtues and thus can get as close as possible to perfecting their nature. The achievement of that perfection would be the achieving of rational happiness. To fail to be ethically educated is to have one's nature frustrated and left incomplete. It is also to fail to be happy in the distinctive way in which a human being, endowed with reason and reflection, can be happy.

Underlying this scheme is a belief in what would count as the best or perfect way of life for a human being – a life, as Aristotle put it, 'complete and lacking in nothing'. What Aristotle believed that such a life was is a matter of dispute amongst scholars of his work, but, roughly speaking, he thought of it as involving, in a proper balance, the activities of citizen, soldier and the philosopher. His view on this may be mistaken, but much more important for our purposes is the basic scheme within which he was working, that is, a scheme involving man-as-he-happens-to-be, man-as-he-could-be-if-he-realised-his-essential-nature, and ethics itself.

This basic scheme, says MacIntyre, was complicated but remained fundamentally the same with advent of Christianity. Thus, within Christianity, man has a nature that has been given by God and it is the task of ethics to indicate how man might be perfected. Unlike the case with Aristotelian ethics, this perfection, and the happiness it involves, will now lie beyond this life in a final beatific vision of God, but that there is a perfection for human nature in the Christian scheme is an idea this scheme shares with Aristotle's account.

In both the Aristotelian and Christian scheme there is a *telos* or goal or aim to life, that is, a conception of what perfected human nature would be.

In the modern age, argues MacIntyre, and as a result of the decay of Christian belief, we have lost a sense of a *telos* for life, that is, we have lost a sense of what man's perfected nature might be like. Consequently, we are left with only two of the three parts of the original scheme: man-as-he-happens-to-be, and ethics itself. We now can no longer make sense of morality, for we have lost that third part of the scheme – man-as-he-could-be-if-he-realised-his-essential-nature – to which ethics was originally a bridge. We thus no longer have a proper understanding of the *point* of ethics or moral thought. In other words, the decay of Christian belief has left modern morality in a mess, for we can longer understand the point and nature of the moral life. We can perhaps see here, if MacIntyre is right, one reason why it is that some people in the modern world have a hostile attitude to moral notions in general: they do not believe that morality itself can be necessary to a full achievement of the *telos* or goal of a human life, whether this be in this world, as in an Aristotelian scheme, or in another, as in a Christian scheme.

It may be that MacIntyre's argument is wrong in some of the details, but it is, at any rate, a serious attempt to do justice to the truth that our morality is in many ways historically dependent on religion.

Morality as psychologically dependent on religion

For some there is also a *psychological* dependence of morality on religion. That is, some just do feel that morality depends in some way on religious thought and experience, and that without a religious backing morality does not properly make sense. This may be connected with a more general sense that in the absence of God life itself becomes pointless or meaningless. It is possible for someone to fail to possess the requisite *psychological motivation* to observe moral requirements if he thinks that morality only makes sense against a religious background but he cannot, for whatever reason, believe in God. Others are not like this at all, and do not lack such motivation even in the complete absence of religious belief: for such persons, morality and religion have little to do with one another.

review activity

1. According to MacIntyre, what purpose was ethics thought to serve in Aristotelian and Christian thinking?

2. In what way, according to MacIntyre, has the modern age lost the Aristotelian and Christian conception of the purpose of ethics?

The *Euthyphro* dilemma

Philosophers have, however, often discussed the relation between religion and morality in a sense narrower than that already discussed. Their concern has been with a problem concerning the *logical relations* between morality and religion that is raised in Plato's dialogue *Euthyphro*.

Divine command theory

The problem concerns the relation between the commands or laws of God (or the gods) and morality. It can be seen in this way. Suppose we say that what we ought to do, and what is right and good, depends on God's commands – an idea known as the 'divine command theory'. Then it seems that whatever God commands would be good. However, suppose, for example, God were to command that a certain act of killing was right, say that a certain man should kill his son. Then this would mean that this act of killing was right. Indeed, if God were to indicate that rape and torture were good then these things would become good. This is surely implausible.

Suppose, then, that we say, as seems more plausible, that rape and torture, for example, are evil. Then, whatever God thinks about them is irrelevant. Moreover, if rape and torture just are evil, then there is nothing God can do about changing that, and this seems to imply a limitation on his omnipotence.

So, God's commands seem one way or another irrelevant to morality: it cannot be that his commands make some action right simply because he commands them; but if certain actions are right or wrong independently of God's commands then we have no need of God for finding out what is right or wrong, good or evil.

Evidently, those who believe in God would not be happy with this result, for they have usually thought that somehow or other God's commands must be relevant to morality. On the *Euthyphro* argument they are not, and God has no serious or substantial connection with morality.

review activity

Explain in your own words the *Euthyphro* dilemma.

Responses to the *Euthyphro* dilemma

Geach's response to the Euthyphro dilemma

Peter Geach has sought to give an answer to the *Euthyphro* dilemma, showing that God is not, after all, irrelevant to morality (Geach 1994: ch 9).

Geach begins by denying that all our moral knowledge comes from God. He says, for example, that we know without any command from God that lying is bad. He does not mean that we know that we should *never* lie. On the contrary, perhaps sometimes we should: it is sometimes a necessary evil. Geach says, however, that we know that lying is, indeed, an evil.

Geach says, however, that we do need knowledge of God (and his commands) to know that we may not do evil that good may come of it. Geach gives the example of adultery. He says that we can know rationally that adultery is *generally* undesirable, that is, that we can know by rational reflection that it is *generally* a good thing that adultery not be committed. This, says Geach, seems to leave *some* occasions when it would be a good thing to commit adultery. When are those occasions? Under what conditions, or in what circumstances, is adultery the right thing to do? Geach says that we simply cannot know when it would be good to commit adultery. But, he says, if this is so, then our knowledge that adultery is *generally* undesirable is of no real use to us. This means that if it is thought that God gave us knowledge *merely* that adultery is *generally* undesirable then God has left us without any substantial guidance at all. This, says Geach, is an absurd view of God: we cannot suppose that God left us bereft in this way of being able to judge and know what to do, and what the truth is, concerning adultery.

Geach thus says that the only way in which our knowledge that adultery is *generally undesirable* is of real use to us is that this knowledge is *in fact* a promulgation of the Divine law that *absolutely forbids* adultery. Thus Geach says:

> *The rational recognition that a practice is generally undesirable and that it is best for people on the whole not even to think of resorting to it is thus in fact a promulgation to a man of the Divine law forbidding the practice, even if he does not realise that this is a promulgation of the Divine law, even if he does not believe there is a God.* (Geach 1994: 124–5)

Supposing we accepted this argument so far, we need to ask the question: Why should we obey God's commands? Geach's answer is that we should do so because otherwise we shall be punished by God. Hence, for Geach, the reason we should obey God's commands is because of God's *power*, which instils in us a fear of God. Geach then considers an objection and reply to this claim:

> *I shall be told . . . that since I am saying not: It is your supreme moral duty to obey God, but simply: It is insane to set about defying an Almighty God, my attitude is plain power worship. So it is: but it is worship of the Supreme power, and as such is wholly different from, and does not carry with it, a cringing attitude towards earthly powers.* (Geach 1994: 127)

D.Z. Phillips has criticised Geach's view by saying that he does nothing to show that worship of God on account of fear of him does not display a cringing attitude towards God (Phillips 1970: 36). In any case, such fear, says, Phillips, can hardly be thought of as the beginning of wisdom, as Geach claims it is. Further, Richard Swinburne has suggested that it is not because of God's power that we should obey him, but because he has created and sustains us, and also because he has created and sustains the rest of the universe (Swinburne 1993: 211–12).

Swinburne's response to the Euthyphro *dilemma*

Swinburne has himself offered a reply to the *Euthyphro* dilemma in the context of a naturalistic moral theory – a moral theory that claims that the moral properties of, e.g., actions, depend on their natural properties (Swinburne 1993: ch.11). This last point will become clear in what follows.

First, Swinburne draws a distinction between what he calls *necessary moral truths* and *contingent moral truths*. A necessary moral truth is understood to involve a specific relation between the natural properties of, for example, some action, and the moral properties of that action. Thus, for example, if an action has the *natural properties* of being the application of intense pain to another for one's own pleasure and for no other reason despite the desire of the other that one not inflict such pain, then that action *necessarily* has the *moral property* of being wrong. Any action that had the natural properties in question (the infliction of pain for one's own pleasure and so forth) would have the moral property of being wrong.

A contingent moral truth is a truth made so by the way the world happens to be. For example, suppose it is true that I should pay £10 to the bookshop. This is a *contingent* moral truth since it depends on my having ordered £10 worth of books which have now been delivered – for, after all, I might not have ordered the books, in which case it is not the case that I should pay £10 to the bookshop.

Note that the *contingent* moral truth that I ought (here and now) to pay the bookshop £10 depends on a *necessary* moral truth that I ought to pay the bookshop £10 whenever I have ordered £10 worth of books and they have been delivered. In fact Swinburne suggests that this necessary moral truth depends on some other necessary moral truth, such as that one ought to pay one's debts. Necessary moral truths are thus general principles of conduct (Swinburne 1993: 192–3).

Swinburne's proposed solution to the *Euthyphro* dilemma then goes like this. He says that *some* actions are obligatory or wrong independently of what anyone commands and *some* are made obligatory or wrong by divine command. Here are some examples of the first: genocide and torturing children. These are wrong independently of any command. Here are some examples of the second: attending Mass on Sundays or caring for the sick in Africa. These are dependent on divine command for their being obligatory.

The actions that are obligatory or wrong independently of any divine command are the necessarily true moral judgements. They could, says Swinburne, no more be false than such mathematical propositions as $7 + 5 = 12$ could be false. But this means that God's command could not make genocide and torturing children right. Does this not imply a limitation on God's omnipotence? Swinburne says that it does not, for it is no more a limitation on God's power that he cannot make genocide and torturing children right than it is a limitation on his power that he cannot make it true that $7 + 5 = 11$. This is because, if Swinburne is right, it is necessarily true that genocide and torturing children are wrong, just as it is necessarily true that $7 + 5 = 12$.

Phillips on God as Father

D.Z. Phillips has offered a different perspective on the relevance of Divine commands to morality (Phillips 1981a). Phillips argues that we should focus on the concept of a father if we want properly to understand the issues surrounding the *Euthyphro* dilemma. For example, within the context of a family, saying 'He's your father', or 'Because he's my father' can give a good reason for doing something. Phillips suggests two reasons for this. First, one owes one's existence to one's father. Secondly, the institution of the family itself generates obligations to one's father: there is no question here that what generates obligations to one's father is that one has *decided* that to obey one's father is good. Of course, it certainly does not follow from Phillips's view that he thinks that one will or should always think one ought to do what one's father commands or suggests. There can be conflict with one's father, but what gives this conflict the very importance and poignancy it has is that one does have obligations here that one has not chosen – even if one decides not to follow them.

Phillips argues that similar considerations apply to those who think of God as their Father. To think of God as one's Father just is to think that one has reason to obey what he commands. However, it does not follow, Phillips argues, that someone who thinks of God as his Father will or should believe that he must always do what God commands. There can be, says Phillips, a clash between the will of God and moral requirements: obligations to God and moral obligations are not one and the same, and the two can conflict. A good example is found in the Old Testament story of Abraham and Isaac (Genesis 22: 1–13). In this story, Abraham is commanded by God to sacrifice his son, Isaac, as a sign that he, Abraham, is faithful to God. Abraham leads Isaac out and prepares to sacrifice his son, at which point God stays his hand and provides a ram in Isaac's place: Abraham has done enough to show his faith in God. Phillips refers to Kierkegaard's discussion of this story, which says that ordinarily one is tempted to go against morality by, for example, desire, but in this case one is tempted to go against morality by a command of God.

None of this means that there are not connections between morality and religion on Phillips's view. On the contrary, there are many points of contact between them. For example, someone might pray for forgiveness but often his need for forgiveness will only arise on account of what has happened in his relationships with others, and will be, in part, an expression of what he hopes for in those relationships.

Phillips's view does not 'solve' the *Euthyphro* dilemma. It is not intended to. Rather, his argument suggests that there is, as such, no theoretical or intellectual solution to the problem. Instead, a believer simply has to live with the tension that could crop up for him between religious commands and morality. In that sense, the only 'solution' to the *Euthyphro* dilemma is one achieved through living a life in which one believes in God. However, this may well be one that involves great cost – as it was for Abraham, whose actions, whilst in accord with God's commands, were, from a moral point of view, certainly wicked.

review activity

1. Why does Geach think that our knowledge that some action is generally undesirable is, in fact, knowledge that this action is absolutely forbidden by God?

2. Explain in your own words Swinburne's distinction between necessary and contingent moral truths.

3. How does Swinburne propose to use the distinction between necessary and contingent moral truths to solve the *Euthyphro* dilemma?

4. Why does Phillips believe that thinking of God as one's Father gives one reason to obey his commands?

some questions to think about

1. What kind of understanding of God is implicit in Pascal's Wager? Does his understanding of what God is discredit his claim that we should believe in him?

2. Does Pascal's Wager encourage self-concern? If it does, what kind of self-concern is it, and does it matter that the Wager encourages it?

3. Could belief in God really be basic? Could any belief be basic? If not, which beliefs could not be?

4. Are the traditional proofs of the existence of God pointless?

5. Is there really a problem of evil? If so, what is it?

6. Can God be omnipotent and wholly good?

7. Is there any point in supplying a free will *defence* rather than *theodicy*?

8. In what sense, if any, are all things good?

9. Is there any sense in which evil can be said to derive from God?

further reading

▶ The best collection of essays on Pascal's Wager is Jordan (ed.) 1994.

▶ Kierkegaard 1974 is hard, but very powerful. Secondary literature on Kierkegaard is, in general, disappointing. An exception is Mulhall 1994, but this is less of an introduction than an exercise in thinking with Kierkegaard.

▶ An excellent reader on the problem of evil is Larrimore (ed.) 2001. Very good articles on this problem can be found in Adams and Adams (eds) 1994. Hick 1979 offers wide and deep discussion on the problem of evil, and is not a difficult read: I recommend it highly. Surin 1986 is also excellent. Holland 1980: ch.15 is the best single article on the problem of evil I know. It demands a lot of thought, but the thought is well worth it.

▶ A good collection of essays on divine command theory is Helm (ed.) 1981.

PART 2
texts

Plato: *Republic*

Plato's life and works

Plato (c.428–348 BC)

Plato is one of the most important philosophers in the history of Western philosophy. He was an Athenian, and of noble descent. At the time when he lived, there was no unified state in the region of present-day Greece. Rather, there were many Greek city states, the most important of which were Athens and Sparta. These states were often at war with one another, except when they united to face a common enemy. This they did against the Persians who sought to expand their enormous empire westwards by an invasion of the Greek mainland at Marathon in 490. Despite the strength of the Persian forces, the Athenians defeated them, and eventually, by the middle of the fifth century, the Athenians were the leaders of Greece, having founded a naval empire in 478. However, from about 460, Athens and Sparta were locked in a series of wars – the so-called Peloponnesian Wars – which dragged on until 404 and signalled a serious and lasting downturn in the importance of Athens.

Map showing the Greek mainland, the Mediterranean and Persia in the 4th century BC

Socrates (469–399 BC)

Athens was a democracy from 508 to 322, with the exception of two short periods in 411 and 404 during which short-lived oligarchies – that is, systems of rule by a few, very powerful men – took control. Plato himself developed a deep dislike of democracy from at least around 399 when his teacher, Socrates – whom he had met in around 407 – was condemned to death on a charge of disbelieving in the city's gods, introducing his own gods, and corrupting the youth of Athens.

Socrates wrote no philosophy at all. He simply talked to people about philosophical matters, principally those concerned with ethics and the nature of the good life for human beings, asking 'what is beauty?' and 'what is goodness?' Not surprisingly, he found that those with whom he talked could not answer these questions. At best, they could give him examples of beautiful or good things, actions and the like, which was not what he was after. What we know of Socrates we have from a number of sources, in particular from his appearance in Plato's works. Plato wrote many philosophical dialogues in which Socrates appears as the central character. The dialogues are fascinating from both a philosophical and literary perspective, containing not simply arguments but jokes, irony, a host of interesting characters in discussion with one another and with Socrates, and much else besides. They are normally divided into three groups, early, middle and late, although there is some dispute about which dialogues fall into which group. It is generally thought that the early dialogues represent (more or less) the historical Socrates as Plato saw him, whereas from the middle dialogues onwards Socrates becomes a mouthpiece for Plato's views that he developed in independence of Socrates, though always with Socrates' life and example in the background. In our discussion I shall sometimes refer to what Socrates says or thinks, and sometimes to what Plato says or thinks, according as to whether the context makes the one or the other seem more suitable. In both cases I mean to be referring to Plato's views.

The Parthenon still stands on the highest part of the Acropolis in Athens, the city's fortress and sanctuary. It was the temple of the Greek goddess Athena. Work on erecting it was begun in 447 BC, and continued until 432 BC. Part of the frieze and some other figures and parts of the Parthenon can be seen in the British Museum in London. They are known as the Elgin marbles after the seventh Earl of Elgin who had them removed in the early nineteenth century and brought to London.

The *Republic* is one of the middle dialogues, and is concerned with justice – the term is discussed a little below – and the ideal community. The Greek word for 'community' is *polis*, and this is variously rendered by different translators as 'state', 'city-state', or 'city'. Usually I use the term 'community' in what follows, but not much hangs on the choice of word as long as it is borne in mind that Plato's image of community life depended, amongst other things, on his experience of life in the Greek *polis*. The title of the dialogue – the *Republic* – is the English form of the Latin title supplied by Cicero (106–43 BC), a translation of the Greek title *Politeia*, which is related to the word *polis*.

The decline of Athens' splendour, which, as we have seen, began during the period of the Peloponnesian Wars, together with Socrates' execution by democratic Athens, were the principal motivations Plato had in trying to work out an ideal form of state. Aware that greatness in the community was possible, but dissatisfied with democracy, Plato set himself the task of trying to think through to a better form of political association.

Shortly after Socrates' death, Plato began a series of travels which lasted 12 years, and when he returned to Athens he founded a school for philosophy, known as the Academy. His most famous pupil was Aristotle (384–322). Plato spent the second half of his life involved with this school, whose aim was to teach the kind of studies that were thought to be necessary for future statesman and politicians. He died in Athens in about 348.

A note on the translation

The translation of Plato's *Republic* to be used in this chapter is that made by Desmond Lee, published by Penguin. There are plenty of other translations available, and different commentators on the text refer to different translations, as well as sometimes making their own translations. It is often a good idea to compare different translations of key passages, even if you can read the original Greek, because comparing these different translations can help to give a good idea of Plato's meaning, which is not always clear. However, in this chapter I shall not compare different translations, leaving this exercise to the reader. In any case, Lee's translation contains many footnotes that help explain why he has translated things as he has and alert us to the difficulties of translating from Ancient Greek into modern English. When reading Lee's translation it is highly recommended to pay attention to these and the rest of his footnotes, because they all help with gaining a deeper understanding of what Plato is doing in the *Republic*.

The *Republic* V, 474c – VII, 521b: the context

Plato's *Republic* is divided into ten Books and further subdivided into page numbers known as 'Stephanus pages'. This pagination derives from an edition of Plato's works published in 1578 by Henri Estienne ('Stephanus' is the Latinised version of 'Estienne'). Each page of the Stephanus edition was subdivided into approximately equal segments, indicated by the letters a–e. Different editions of the *Republic* have the Stephanus pages and subdivisions printed in the margins. This means that, whatever translation is used, it is possible to find the place in Plato's text to which reference is being made.

In this chapter we shall be discussing in detail the stretch of the Republic from Book V, 474c to Book VII, 521b. In order properly to discuss this part of the text, however, it is important to have some idea of what goes on either side of it, and especially of what goes on before it. Accordingly, I shall give here a brief account of the content of the *Republic* both before and after the section of the text with which we shall be especially concerned. This will allow us to set our passage in the right context.

The *Republic* was completed in about 374–370; it is set in about 420. As mentioned above, most of Plato's works are in the form of dialogues, and the *Republic* is no exception. The central character is Socrates, who is the narrator. The other principal characters are Glaucon and Adeimantus, who were the elder brothers of Plato; Polemarchus, at whose house the dialogue takes place; Cephalus, the father of Polemarchus; and Thrasymachus.

The subject of the Republic

The subject of the dialogue is justice or right (good) conduct: the Greek word is *dikaiosunē*, and it can be translated as 'justice', 'doing right' or the like according to whether the context makes the one or the other suitable, though 'justice' is the traditional translation (cf. Cross and Woozley, 1964: vi–vii; Annas, 1981: 10ff.) The interlocutors want, amongst other things, to answer two questions: 'what is justice?' and 'why should one be just?' However, the distinction between these questions is not always maintained in the discussion. Let us look at how the conversation develops.

The participants consider the view, suggested by Cephalus, that justice consists in being truthful and in returning things we have borrowed (331a–d). Socrates has little trouble in showing that this is inadequate because it would not be right to return a weapon to a friend from whom one borrowed it if, in the meantime, the friend had gone mad. Further, one should not always tell the truth to a madman, because, for example, knowledge of the truth might lead him to harm others (331c–d). Next, Polemarchus suggests (331e) that justice consists in giving every person his due, which is taken to mean that one should help one's friends and harm one's enemies (332a–c). Socrates has a number of objections to this definition. We need not concern ourselves with the nature of these objections, which run from 331e–336a. Suffice it to say that Polemarchus takes himself to be defeated in argument. This enrages Thrasymachus, who believes that Socrates is playing tricks on his interlocutors and being dishonest (337a). Thrasymachus goes on to give his own view of what justice is. It is not entirely clear what he takes it to be, and his comments are subject to differing interpretations but, roughly, he thinks that being just to others is a mug's game: if you are strong and can get away with it, you have no reason to be just to others. Justice is for the weak; the strong, who need not fear others, have no real reason to care about justice.

Socrates seeks to show that Thrasymachus is mistaken, and he does so to his own satisfaction, although his arguments have been found weak by many commentators. Thrasymachus himself is not convinced by Socrates, but he can no longer be bothered to discuss the issue, and he retreats, full of contempt for Socrates (354a).

What Socrates wants to show in all this is that it is far from foolish to be just. On the contrary, he would like to show that the just person is happier than the unjust. But it is not only Thrasymachus who wishes to question this claim, for at this point, after Thrasymachus has retreated, Glaucon takes up the case. He, too, questions Socrates' claim that the just are happier than the unjust. In order to do so, he tells the story of the ring of Gyges (359c–d).

The story of Gyges, king of Lydia

The possessor of such a ring can make himself invisible, and Glaucon wants to know why, if one had such a ring and could thus escape detection for doing bad things, one should not do bad things which are to one's own advantage. Glaucon emphasises the story by imagining two men, one thoroughly just who has a reputation for injustice and one thoroughly unjust who has, nonetheless, a reputation for being just. In such a case, there are no rewards or honours for being just, but rather shame and contempt, whilst the unjust man is lauded and praised because it is believed that he is just. In such a case, of what advantage is it to be just? (360e–361d). Adeimantus agrees that this is the challenge that Socrates faces: to show how being just is in the interests of the just man and being unjust is to the disadvantage of the unjust man, 'leav[ing] out the common estimation in which they are held' (367b).

Gyges (c.685–657 BC) was the favourite officer of king Candaules of Lydia and became himself king of Lydia by murdering Candaules. The Greek historian Herodotus (c.490-425 BC) tells one version of the story in his *Histories*. According to Herodotus, Candaules was extraordinarily proud of the beauty of his wife, the queen, believing her to be the most beautiful woman in the world. Candaules was insistent that Gyges should fully appreciate the queen's beauty, and he instructed Gyges to hide himself in the queen's chamber so that he could watch her undress and verify her beauty for himself. Gyges was horrified at the proposal, but in the end was unable to avoid doing as the king insisted. He duly hid and watched the queen undress. When she had done so, he left the room. However, the queen had seen him. She said nothing however, and called for Gyges the next morning. There she told him that he must either die for what he had done or kill Candaules, take her as his wife, and become king himself. He took the latter course.

Plato presents the story of Gyges through the mouth of Glaucon. Glaucon says that Gyges was a shepherd who found a ring that could render the wearer invisible. It was with the aid of this ring that he was able to kill the king. Glaucon says nothing about Candaules' vanity or the queen's beauty.

The bulk of the rest of the *Republic* is taken up with responding to this challenge. Socrates' procedure is the following: he proposes to try to find out what justice is in the community and then, using what is discovered there, see if this helps in finding out about the nature of justice in the individual and whether, and to what extent, it benefits him (368e–369a). The thought is that if we can find out what justice on a large scale (that is, the community) is like we can then see better what it is on a small scale (that is, in the individual). So Socrates proceeds to construct an account of the perfectly just community (*polis*) and then use this to understand justice in the individual.

At about this point, the dialogue-nature of the *Republic* changes: although formally still a discussion, the rest of the *Republic* consists very largely in Socrates' laying out his understanding of the nature of justice. He meets little resistance from his interlocutors, Glaucon and Adeimantus, who are the sole respondents after Book I.

According to Socrates, the ideal community is one in which there are three classes of citizens: Guardians, Auxiliaries and the Producers. Plato says that each class will consist of members who are responsible for specific activities: the Guardians are the rulers proper, the Auxiliaries are basically warriors, and the third class, the Producers (or Business class) are, as the name suggests, primarily responsible for the more (in Plato's eyes) menial tasks which keep the community going, such as trade and agriculture.

Socrates is most interested in the Guardians, and he spends a great deal of time explaining the nature of their education (376c–412a; 521c–541b). In fact, the Guardians' education is designed to ensure that they are true lovers of wisdom, that is, philosophers – the Greek *philosophos*, from which we have the word 'philosopher', means 'lover of wisdom'. In other words, Plato argues that in the truly just community those who are the rulers must be philosophers and that it is only when those who are philosophers become rulers that there will be true justice in the community.

According to Socrates, the Guardians constitute the class that most has the wellbeing or interest of the community at heart. Socrates says that the Guardians must propagate amongst the populace belief in a 'noble lie' or 'magnificent myth' – which they themselves should believe if possible (414b–c). (The translation 'noble lie' is the traditional one: for the view that it is mistaken see Arendt 1967: 108.) According to this myth, the members of the community are born with different metals in their souls – either gold, or silver, or iron and bronze – and this is what fits them to occupy a given class: the Guardians have gold in their soul, the Auxiliaries silver, the Productive class iron and bronze (415a–c). According to this myth, individuals might be able to move between the classes. For example, a child with a golden soul might be born to members of the Productive class, and in this case this child would be promoted to the class of Guardians. However, the divisions between classes themselves would be rigorously enforced.

Socrates goes on to say that the Guardians will have no private property and will live in common, in a kind of camp (426d–417b). They must preserve the community at the right size and prevent extremes of wealth or poverty amongst the citizens. Later on he says, amongst other things, that, in the ideal community, the family will be abolished (457c–462a); women of any given class will assume all the roles that men in that class do (451d–457b); and reproduction will be severely regulated (there will be mating festivals (459e–460b)).

In the meantime, Plato has said that we can now see what justice in the community is: this is when the members of each of the three classes get on with their own jobs without interfering with other people (433a–b; 434c). Justice in the community means that the three classes do what they are supposed to do and thus consists in the harmonious functioning together of all three classes.

Plato now draws a parallel between justice in the community and justice in the soul. He argues that the soul has three parts: reason, desire and, between them, 'spirit'. Plato's discussion of these three is complex but, for our purposes, we can take the first two to be tolerably clear on an intuitive understanding. The notion of spirit is rather unclear, however. What Socrates seems to mean by this covers many psychological attributes. For example, spirit involves a tendency to aggression, violence and assertiveness, but it is also that part of the soul that delights in winning and receiving honours. But we need not be too worried here about what exactly Plato means by this. It is more important to note that Plato pairs off the classes in the community with the parts of the soul thus: Guardians/reason; Auxiliaries/spirit; Producers/desire. This then allows him to say that, just as justice in the community consists in harmonious relations between the three classes, justice in the (individual) soul consists in harmonious relations between the parts of the soul: reason is to rule, aided by spirit, and desire, which would otherwise be unruly, must accept the governance of reason. Then, Plato continues, the reason why it is an advantage to be just is that, in being just, a person has a harmonious soul, which Plato thinks of as being the ideal condition to be in.

There are many difficulties in Plato's arguments thus far, but I shall not discuss them because we are at the moment doing nothing more than giving a brief overview of the arguments in the *Republic* prior to the section with which we are properly concerned. Before moving on to that, I shall very briefly say something about what comes in the *Republic* after the section at which we shall be looking in detail.

As mentioned above, Plato has already spent some time describing the nature of the education of the Guardians, who, as we have also noted, turn out to be philosopher-rulers (or philosopher-kings, as is sometimes said). From 521c Plato continues this description of the philosophers' education. From 543a, he describes a number of imperfect societies, as a contrast to his own ideal community, and the kinds of character that go with such imperfect societies. Then he picks up and continues a discussion of the nature of art that was begun in Book III when first discussing the Guardians' education. Finally, the *Republic* ends with a discussion of the immortality of the soul.

The Republic: 474c–521b

Introduction: first attempts at describing the nature of the philosopher

As we have seen above, Socrates claims that the ideal community will only come into being when the Guardians of the community are philosophers. In order to explain what he means, Socrates must give an account of what he means by 'philosopher', and at 474b–c he says that this is what he intends to do.

Central to Socrates' account is the claim that if someone has a love or passion for a kind of thing then he will pursue everything of that particular kind (475b). For example, if someone has a passion for young boys then he will always be pursuing such boys (474d–475a); if he has a passion for wine, he will always be trying out different wines (475a); if he has a passion for honour, then he will always seek out those things in life that bring him honour (475a–b); and so on.

Before exploring the philosophical implications of this claim, we should pause a moment and consider these examples, for they might seem peculiar. Why does Socrates choose these examples?

The answer is that the kinds of things in question were very important in Greek life at his time. For example, in fourth and fifth century Greece homosexual relations between older men and young boys were very much part of normal life for free males. This went hand-in-hand with a sense of the importance of education, for the older man would educate the boy as part of their relationship. Moreover, wine was very important in the Greece of the time: there was a god, Dionysus, who was the god of wine and revelry – and also of various festivals, Dionysia – and free Greek males would often meet for drinking parties, which might last all night. Indeed, one of Plato's dialogues is entitled the *Symposium,* and 'symposium' means 'drinking party'. In addition, fourth and fifth century Greece was a time when individuals laid enormous importance on public reputation and honour: much more than we do, they craved the respect and

The Greek god Dionysus – as a baby – with Ino

admiration of their fellows. So Plato chooses the examples he does because they come readily to his mind.

The philosopher is a lover of wisdom

Socrates, then, says that a passion for some kind of thing will mean that one pursues this kind of thing. The philosopher's passion is for wisdom, because he has a taste for all kinds of learning and is never satisfied (475c). Glaucon takes the wrong cue from Socrates' comments: he thinks that the philosopher is therefore some kind of dilettante, a sort of frivolous person who likes to get a taste of everything without knowing much about anything in detail. (Note here (475d) the reference Glaucon makes to Dionysia, which picks up on the earlier reference to wine: Glaucon is perhaps taking Socrates' initial comparison of the philosopher with the lover of wine rather too literally!)

The philosopher cares for truth

Socrates corrects Glaucon: what the philosopher is interested in, he says, is truth (475e). It is at this point that the hard philosophy begins.

Socrates first distinguishes beauty and ugliness, justice and injustice, good and evil. He says that 'each of them is single'. However, as they appear in the world they are 'everywhere in combination with actions and material bodies and with each other' (476a). What does this mean?

What Socrates is doing in speaking of beauty, ugliness, justice, injustice and so forth as 'single' is drawing attention to what Plato calls the 'Forms'. (Older translations referred to the Forms as Ideas: this terminology is now usually not used.) I shall discuss the notion of Forms in more detail below and for now shall simply state baldly the basic idea.

The Forms

In the world as we see it there are many things which are beautiful, many other things which are ugly, many just people, many unjust people, and so on. What is it that makes all beautiful things beautiful? For example, we might have before us several Greek urns that are beautiful but that are in other respects different: one might be for wine, one might be for mixing water and wine, another for olives, and they will all be correspondingly different in size, style, design and so on.

So what makes them all beautiful even though they differ in so many other ways? Plato's idea is that in some way they *share in* or *partake of* the quality of beauty. This quality is the Form – and we can thus speak of the Form of Beauty. The Form of Beauty is not the beauty of this or that urn, but Beauty *Itself*. On a traditional understanding, this Form is non-material, really exists, and is fully or completely beautiful. It is not in the least subjective or dependent on the mind for its existence: it exists independently of mind and thought. It is timeless and non-spatial. Further it is unique, a single 'one'. It cannot be seen with the eyes, but it can be seen with the mind's (or soul's) eye, although, Plato says, it takes a great deal of intellectual training to come to see it.

Just as there is a Form of Beauty, there is, according to Plato, a Form of Justice, a Form of Good and so on. In these cases we have Justice Itself and Good Itself: these Forms, like all the Forms, have the kind of character – independence of thought and so forth – that, we have seen, is possessed by the Form of Beauty.

Are there 'bad' Forms?

Plato entertains the idea that there are Forms also of Ugliness, Evil and Injustice, just as there are Forms of Beauty, Good and Justice (see, for example, 476a). However, this suggestion drops out as the argument of the *Republic* progresses, and it is clear that Plato is not in the least concerned to emphasise the possibility that there are 'bad' Forms in the sense indicated. In his dialogue *Parmenides* Plato has doubts about whether there are Forms of 'hair or mud or dirt or any other trivial and undignified objects' (130c–d). So it seems likely that he would also wish to deny that there are, after all, Forms of Ugliness and the like. In any case, I shall not discuss them further in what follows. (For some other comments on 'bad' Forms see White 1979: 41, 161–2 and 180.)

Socrates says that philosophers are to be distinguished from 'sight-lovers'. Sight-lovers are those who love 'beautiful sounds and colours and shapes' (476b) along with the rest of the world of appearances, but who cannot see and delight in the Form of Beauty or any of the other Forms. In fact, he suggests that those who do not believe in the Forms are living as if in a dream, whilst those who see and delight in the Forms are properly awake (476c). Those who are properly awake are the philosophers.

So the philosopher is the person who can see and delight in the Forms.

At this point, I shall leave explicit discussion of the Forms, returning to it later, as I said. For now, we need to pursue Socrates' line of thought in a different, though related, direction.

review
activity

1. To explain what does Plato introduce the notion of the Forms?

2. What are the most important properties of the Forms?

Knowledge and belief

From 476d–480 Socrates draws crucial distinctions between knowledge and belief.

Consider the following. If I say that I *know p* (where *p* is some proposition, such as 'it is raining'), then we would naturally think that I could not be mistaken about this. If I know *p*, then *p* is the case. On the other hand, if I *believe* it is raining then I can be mistaken: it is perfectly possible for me to believe that it is raining and it not be raining. For example, I might look out of the window and think there is rain trickling down the windows and I then come to believe that it is raining. However, in fact my next door neighbour is watering his lawn and has got some water from the hose on my windows, and it is not raining at all. From my belief that it is raining we cannot infer that it is raining.

It is true, of course, that I cannot say 'I believe it is raining, but it is not raining'. However, this does not alter the fact that I can grant that my belief that it is raining could be wrong. Indeed, we are all aware that we believe lots of things that might be mistaken: only a madman thinks that none of his beliefs could be mistaken.

Knowledge is infallible   Plato puts these points by saying that knowledge is *infallible*, whereas belief is *fallible* (477e). However, his presentation is in at least one important respect significantly different from what has just been said. For I put the issue in terms of knowledge of propositions, that is, in terms of *knowing that* (for example, knowing that it is raining).

Plato's concern: knowing what

We can also think of *knowing how* (for example, knowing how to ride a bicycle) and *knowing an object* (for example, knowing a city or a person). But Plato's emphasis is not on any of these. He is interested in *knowing what*. That is, he is interested in the notion of knowing what a thing is, knowing what it *really* is. This means that he is interested in knowledge as *understanding*, that is, in the kind of knowledge we have when we can explain why something is as it is, giving reasons why it is as it is. For example, if two people, one of whom is a violinist and one of whom is not, consider a violin, the musician will know why it is that the instrument's being put together in such and such a way, and why its strings being of such and such differing thicknesses, and so on, enable it to produce a good sound when appropriately played. The non-musician will not. In this sense, the musician will understand in a way the non-musician does not what the instrument is: he will have a deeper understanding than the non-musician.

review activity

Plato is interested in knowledge as knowledge what. Explain what this means and give an example of your own to illustrate the point.

Objects of knowledge and effects of knowledge

Plato thinks of knowledge in terms of *knowing what*, so it is natural for him to think in terms of the *object* of knowledge, a thing known. He is helped in this view by the idea that knowledge is a 'faculty' or 'capacity' or 'ability' or 'power' of the mind (*dunamis* in the Greek). As he understands the situation, a faculty is distinguished by two criteria: a) its *objects* and b) its *effects* or the *state of mind it produces*. The objects of the faculty of knowledge are things known; the effect of the faculty is the state of knowledge (477c–d). Plato does not argue for the idea that knowledge is a faculty: he just assumes it, and Glaucon accepts the introduction of the notion of a faculty into the conversation without demur (477b).

Knowledge, then, is a faculty. But then so is ignorance. So we can ask: What is the object and what is the effect of ignorance? The effect is clearly that of knowing nothing, being ignorant; the object is 'sheer blank nothingness, the non-existent' (Cross and Woozley 1964: 146). It is not at all clear that this notion of the object of ignorance really makes sense, but this does not really matter, because Plato is not especially interested in ignorance and does not here discuss it at any length.

Belief is of what is and what is not

What he *is* interested in, however, is what lies *between* knowledge and ignorance. He says that there must be a faculty lying between knowledge and ignorance: this is the faculty of opinion or belief (477b). This faculty must have its own objects and its own effect. The effect is clearly the state of mind of belief. But what is its object? If the object of knowledge is *what is*, and the object of ignorance is *what is not*, then the object of belief must be *what is and is not,* that is, 'something that has its share of being and non-being, and cannot be said to have the characteristics of either without qualification' (478d).

There is a great deal of controversy amongst commentators concerning what exactly Plato means by talking of what is and what is not, or of what is both being and non-being without being exclusively one or the other.

Three senses of 'is' The difficulties here are compounded by the fact that when we talk in English of what is, we might have any or all of the following in mind: a) what *exists* (as in 'God is', which means 'God exists'); b) what is *true*; c) what *is something or other*, such as big or small or good or just. These three are respectively a) the *existential* use of 'is'; b) the *veridical* use of 'is'; c) the *predicative* use of 'is'. (This term, 'predicative' comes from the fact that to say that some object x is F – say, that a boy is brave – is to *predicate* bravery of the boy.) In Plato's Greek, however, there was only one word to cover the existential, veridical and predicative uses of 'is'. This raises the following problem: which of these did Plato have in mind when saying that belief (or opinion) concerned what both is and is not? As I have already mentioned, philosophers disagree about the answer to this question. What can be said for and against each position?

review
activity

1. Why is there a problem over the interpretation of what Plato means by saying that the object of belief or opinion both is and is not?

2. What are the three possible interpretations of what Plato means by this?

The existential use

According to this interpretation, what Plato has in mind in saying that the object of belief is that which has its share in being and non-being is that there are degrees of existence: some things do not exist at all, some exist fully and some – the objects of belief – exist to some degree. The difficulty that most commentators see with this is that it is far from clear how the notion of degrees of existence is supposed to make sense at all. Surely, one might think, either something exists or it does not: one thing cannot exist *more* than another. The grass on the lawn outside, the fox sunning himself on it, the water in my glass, the computer before me, my body – these things all exist, and there is no sense in saying that some of these exist more than others. Even God, if he exists, exists as I exist: he does not *exist* more than I do, despite the fact that he has many properties that I lack, such as omnipotence and omniscience.

For this reasons, some philosophers who think that Plato did have in mind the existential use of 'is' believe that he was confused in doing so because the idea of degrees of existence does not make sense (see, for example, Cross and Woozley 1964: 162ff.). Others agree that the idea does not make sense and that therefore Plato could not have had in mind a notion of degrees of existence at all (see, for example, Vlastos 1965).

Certainly the argument we have considered is powerful, and it *is* extremely hard to understand the idea that there might be degrees of existence. On the other hand, it is also true that many thinkers have thought they *did* understand such a notion, usually in a ethico-religious context – in a context that concerns ethics or religion or both. For example, we have a reasonably good grasp of the idea that some people are more *alive* than others, in the sense that they live with a greater vitality or intensity than others. There is a sense of degrees of existence in such a notion. Moreover, it is certainly true that Plato's philosophy was deeply influenced by Greek religious ideas and mysticism (cf. Morgan 1990, esp. ch.5; 1992) and had a mystical dimension (cf. Taylor 1960: 231). So perhaps there is some sense in which Plato could be interpreted as holding to the existential use of 'is', so long as we allow that this would make sense from a ethico-religious or mystical perspective. Of course, this would not be possible if we insist on being able to understand Plato in a way that has no truck with such a perspective, that is, a way of understanding him that does not depend on our possessing or empathising with such a perspective: to some philosophers, the idea that you would have to have a religious or mystical perspective to understand a given idea shows that that idea is deeply questionable.

It must be pointed out, however, that if Plato is interpreted as using 'is' in its existential sense and that this only makes sense in a ethico-religious context, then clearly what he has in mind is a notion of being in an *evaluative* sense. In fact, he definitely thought that the things of this world are so much trash and rubbish: nothing is of any lasting value and what most people chase after in their life – money, possessions and so on – is all empty and pointless. This is why he talks of this 'twilight world of change and decay, [where] it [the mind] can only form opinions, its vision is confused and its opinions shifting' (508d; cf. 515d).

The veridical use

Some philosophers support a reading in terms of veridical use (see, for example, Fine 1978). In favour of this interpretation is that this makes good sense: after all, it is not at all contentious that knowledge is of what is true. On this reading, when Plato says that belief is of what is and what is not, he means that, whereas knowledge puts us in touch only with truths, belief relates us to both truths and falsehoods. But there may be problems with this interpretation. For example, Julia Annas has suggested (Annas 1981: 198) that when Plato talks of that which is and is not, he must, on the present interpretation, be committed to the idea of degrees of truth. However, Annas suggests that such an idea makes no more sense than that of degrees of existence, and therefore we should reject the veridical use of 'is'.

The predicative use

This is the most popular interpretation. According to this account, when Plato says we can only know what fully or really is, what he means is that we can only know what is fully or completely F – where F is just, or good or whatever. Then, talk of what is and is not is talk of what is F and not F. For example, on this reading, one could have *belief* about an action that is just and also not just, or kind and also not kind.

So which 'is' is the one of which Plato makes use? It may be that we cannot say definitively. For it may be that Plato himself had all three in mind and that he stressed one or the other according to whether the context suited what he wanted to say. Still, it will not be too misleading for Plato's thought as a whole if we follow up the predicative interpretation. Obviously, we then need to find out which kinds of things are fully *F* and which are both *F* and not *F*. For, so far, all we have learnt from Plato is that knowledge is of things that are fully or completely *F* and belief is of things that are *F* and not *F*. But what kinds of things does he have in mind?

review activity

Explain in your own words the three different interpretations of what Plato might mean by talking of what is and is not:

a)   the existential use;

b)   the veridical use;

c)   the predicative use.

The Forms

The answer is that the Forms are fully or completely *F*.

The best way to see what Plato is trying to say, and to deepen our understanding of Plato's concept of Forms, is to consider what Socrates says in Book V at 479a–b and what he takes this to imply.

At 479a–b Socrates persuades Glaucon to agree that any beautiful object in the world (a painting, a vase, a landscape, a woman and so on) can also seem ugly. Similarly, for example, a just act can seem unjust, and a righteous act can seem unrighteous. What does this mean?

Basically, what Socrates is trying to say is this: a vase may be beautiful, but its beauty will be limited in some way. Thus, it might be beautiful in shape, but have garish colours. Or it might be beautiful compared to some other vase, but not compared to my vase. Or it may be beautiful now, but later will not be (it will decay). And so on. (Cf. Vlastos 1965: 10ff.; Nehamas 1999 ch.7.) This means it is not completely or fully beautiful.

Socrates says that the same kind of considerations apply to terms such as double, half, large, small, light and heavy (479b). Thus, four is double two, but half eight. So, from one perspective it is double, from another half. Or again, a large mouse is small compared to a cat. So, from one point of view it is large (when compared to other mice) and from another it is small (when compared to a cat).

The result of this line of reflection is that we cannot say of anything in the world – that is, of any *sensible particular* – that it is *unqualifiedly* beautiful, just, right-eous, double, half, large, small, light or heavy. This line of argument will apply to all sensible particulars to which opposite epithets may be given, such as those already discussed: hence it is often known as the 'Argument from Opposites' (see, for example, Allen 1972).

Although it lies beyond the section of the Republic with which we are principally concerned in this chapter, we should briefly note that Plato has a similar line of reasoning in Book II, from 523a–524d.

At 523a–b Socrates says that some perceptions do, and some do not, call for any further exercise of thought. For example, when a person holds up a hand to us, or we look at one of our own hands, we see the fingers and we have no doubt that we are, indeed, seeing fingers. However, if we look at the middle finger, the third finger and the little finger, we see that the third finger is small compared to the middle finger and big compared to the little finger. So here, says, Socrates, the mind is puzzled (524b): from one perspective the middle finger is big, from another, small. He says the same kind of considerations apply to thickness, thinness, hardness and softness (523e–524a). Hence, we again find that certain sensible particulars can have opposing predicates or epithets applied to them.

In both of these cases, that is, in Book V and Book VII, Plato assumes that there must be something to which the predicates in question – double, half, large, small, just, beautiful and so on – apply unqualifiedly. These things are the Forms. So, the Form of Beauty is unqualifiedly beautiful; the Form of Justice unqualifiedly just; the Form of Double unqualifiedly double; and so on. There is no perspective from which, for example, the Form of Beauty is not beautiful, as the beautiful vase we considered earlier is not beautiful (that is, ugly) from some perspective. The Form of Beauty is always and fully beautiful.

review activity

1. What does it mean to say that a Form is unqualifiedly *F*?

2. What does it mean to say that any sensible particular is only qualifiedly *F*?

Why does Plato postulate the Forms?

Plato never gives thorough arguments in favour of the Forms. Nonetheless, there are many reasons why he postulated them. In the *Republic*, there are at least two main reasons.

A foundation for ethics

1. Plato was deeply concerned about the possibility of establishing that there is a firm foundation for ethical values. As we have already seen, Plato was bothered by the fact that one kind of action – say, returning a weapon one has borrowed to a friend – can be just or good in one case and unjust or bad in another. Is there anything that is simply just – just, that is, always and everywhere – or do we always have to take the context into account in thinking about justice? Is there an ultimate standard for justice? Further, Plato was worried that if we could not find an account of justice as such, then we would have no response to those who claimed, as Thrasymachus claimed, that being just was a game for fools and that, if you could get away with it, you should do exactly what

Puzzles about experience

2. As we have seen, Plato wanted to be able to solve what he saw as puzzles about sense experience that, he thought, was in some way in conflict with the intellect. If our experience of the beauty, justice, largeness and so forth of sensible particulars led to such confusion as he clearly thought it did – a confusion, that is, in which some such particular can both be beautiful and ugly, large and small and so on – then, he believed, there must be some way of clearing up the confusion. Further, as we have seen, it is clear that there is a distinction between knowledge and belief and Plato thought that he must be able to find the objects of knowledge and belief. He thought he could solve both of these problems by appeal to the notion of the Forms.

you want to do. For Plato, the Forms provide the foundation to ethical thought and experience that could allay such worries.

review activity

For what two reasons does Plato postulate the Forms?

What sorts of things have Forms associated with them?

As we have already seen, in Books V and VII of the *Republic,* Plato seems to envisage there being Forms of those sensible particulars that can have applied to them opposing predicates. However, in Book X, 596a–b, Plato seems to suggest that there are many more Forms, including Forms of Bed and Table. This certainly strikes the reader as bizarre, and, moreover, it is very hard to make this idea consistent with the understanding of the Forms recovered from Books V and VII. In fact, it has been suggested (Griswold 1981) that Plato was here being ironic and making a joke, and that he did not really think that there were Forms of Bed, Table and the like. Fortunately, we need not worry about this problem here, but it is in any case a reminder that one of the things that makes Plato's philosophy interesting and difficult to interpret is that we have to be aware of its distinctively literary qualities, such as irony.

The relation between Forms and sensible particulars

As Plato understands things, the sensible particulars which have Forms are as they are – that is, beautiful or just or whatever – because they are in some way related to the relevant Form. It is unclear just what that relation is. Sometimes he says that sensible particulars are 'copies' or 'imitations' of the Forms. In Plato's dialogue *Phaedo,* in which he discusses the Forms at some length, Plato says that the particulars 'fall short' of the Forms (for example, 74d), or 'strive', unsuccessfully, to be like the Forms (for example, 75a–b).

We have already seen what he might mean by this: no sensible particular is ever unqualifiedly *F*, meaning that it is *F* now in one respect but not in some other respect; or is *F* now, but will not be later; and so on.

A different possibility is to argue that when Plato says that sensible particulars fall short of being *F*, he means that they never are completely *F* in any respect even at a given time. Thus, on this view, what stops a vase, for example, from being completely beautiful is not that it is beautiful in one respect, for example shape, but not in another, for example colour, but that even its beautiful shape is not completely beautiful, right here and now. This view has, however, recently been subjected to some strong criticisms (Nehamas 1999; cf. also Gallop in Plato 1983: 127ff.).

Plato also says that sensible particulars 'participate' in the Forms (see, for example, Phaedo 101c). Philosophers disagree about what exactly Plato had in mind in saying this.

Universals   One possibility is to interpret Plato as saying that the Forms are *universals*. What is a universal?

Consider all the red things in the world – pillar boxes, (some) roses, blood and so forth. Some philosophers think that when we refer to the redness of pillar boxes, or roses, or blood, there is an entity – *redness* – which is being referred to and which explains how it is that all red things are, in fact, red. Such an entity is a universal.

We can think of a universal as existing in one of two ways: a) either as not in space and time, and as distinct and separable from all red things; or b) inseparably from all red things, so that if there were no red things then there would be no redness.

It is very common to think that Plato's Forms are universals in the sense a). Then, when we say that particulars 'participate' in Forms we mean that the Form can inhere in particulars as redness inheres in red things or, as it is often put, we mean that the particular *exemplifies* or *instantiates* the Form.

The 'third man'   However, there is a problem with this interpretation. Sensible particulars are
argument   beautiful in virtue of partaking in the Form of Beauty. Now, Plato, we remember, says that the Form of Beauty is itself beautiful. But then the Form of Beauty and sensible particulars which are beautiful are all beautiful. So in virtue of what are the sensible particulars and the Form of Beauty beautiful? Presumably, there will be a second Form of Beauty – call it Form[1] of Beauty – in virtue of which the Form of Beauty and the beautiful particulars are beautiful. But the Form[1] of Beauty is itself beautiful. So, in virtue of what are sensible particulars, the Form of Beauty and the Form[1] of Beauty all beautiful? Presumably, there will be a Form[2] of Beauty that explains this. Clearly, the argument could be extended to show that we have an *infinite regress* of Forms of Beauty. This would be to reduce the notion of Forms to absurdity since they could not explain that which they were introduced to explain.

This argument is known as the 'third man argument' because Aristotle formulated it in his *Metaphysics* using the concept of man (in place of the concept of beauty we have used). Plato was aware that there was a problem of this sort, and he discussed it in his dialogue *Parmenides*.

One basic feature of this argument is that the Form of Beauty is said to be beautiful *in the same sense* as sensible particulars are said to be beautiful. That is, 'beautiful' is *univocal* as applied to the Form and particulars. So one way to avoid the problem would be to say that the term 'beautiful' as applied to Forms and particulars is *equivocal,* that is, that it is being used in two different ways when applied to Forms or particulars.

R.E. Allen has suggested just this (Allen 1965a). His idea is that we should think of a Form as a paradigm or standard – and this is, in fact, language that Plato often uses. Then, when we say, 'the Form of Beauty is beautiful' we are *not* predicating beauty of the Form but rather making an identity statement. What this means is that to say 'the Form of Beauty is beautiful' is to say that 'the Beautiful is the Beautiful' – that is, we are saying what it is. However, when we say that, for example, a vase is beautiful, we *are* predicating beauty of the vase. So, 'beautiful' is used in each case in a different way (cf. also Meinwald 1992).

Note that on Allen's account Forms are not universals *in the sense recently explained.* He agrees that they *are* universals in the sense of being 'One over Many', as it is often put: there is *one* Form (say, of Beauty) for the *many* beautiful things. However, he thinks the best way to understand this is to say that particulars are like reflections of a single thing, in the kind of way that we could have one scarf which is reflected in ten mirrors. So, on Allen's account, this is the kind of way in which we should understand the notion of a particular's participating in a Form – as a kind of reflection.

review activity

1. What is a universal?

2. If Plato's Forms are universals, in what sense are they so?

3. Explain in your own words the third man argument and what it claims to show about the Forms.

4. In what way might it be possible to avoid the problems of the third man argument?

The two worlds theory

As we noted earlier, Plato aims to uncover the objects of knowledge and belief. The Forms, which are completely *F*, are the objects of knowledge, and it is the philosopher who has knowledge of such objects. What are the objects of belief? Opinions are divided on this. Clearly Plato means that those sensible particulars to which opposing predicates can be applied – such as just actions or beautiful vases – are the object of belief. However, does he mean to include *all* sensible particulars as being the objects of belief and not knowledge? If he does, then we seem to have 'two worlds': a) a world of *Forms* that are the object of *knowledge* and that the *philosopher* knows; and b) a world of *sensible particulars* that are the objects of *belief* and that are the concern of the *lover of sights,* that is, of the ordinary non-philosophical person. If this is what Plato means, then he has, perhaps, not properly argued for it, for he has only shown that *some* sensible particulars generate Forms, namely, those that can have opposing predicates applied to them. However, often he seems to have in mind a much more thoroughgoing two worlds theory: for example, he seems to have this in mind in the image of the cave, which we shall consider shortly.

Nevertheless, if there are two worlds, then there must be some kind of bridge between them, because Plato clearly thinks that knowledge of the Forms and, in particular, of the Form of the Good, can illuminate experience of the everyday world. Hence he says (520c) that once the philosopher has acquired true knowledge of the Forms – especially of the Form of the Good – he will see the things of this world 'a thousand times better' than do those who have no knowledge of such things. More generally, without there being such a bridge and such illumination, Plato could not even think it makes sense for the philosophers to be Guardians, because otherwise they could not apply what they know to the everyday world, that is, could not be rulers at all in the sense in which Plato thinks of them. As Julia Annas has rightly said:

> [E]ven if knowledge requires grasp of Forms, it must be applicable to experience in such a way as to guide the person [who has knowledge of the Forms] to make good particular choices; it must enlighten the process of moral development that he or she actually goes through, and be of use in particular cases.
>
> (Annas 1981: 261)

What this suggests is the following. When Plato says that there can only be belief or opinion concerning sensible particulars, he has in mind those who have no knowledge of the Forms. Those, however, who have knowledge of the Forms – the philosophers – see sensible particulars (the world of everyday experience) in a wholly new way and with new understanding. On this interpretation, then, there are not two worlds, but one world seen from two perspectives. This seems to make best sense of Plato's views, even if it must be granted that he is less than clear that he really had this interpretation in mind.

review activity

1. Explain in your own words the two worlds theory.

2. Why does the two worlds theory signal problems for Plato's account of the Guardians in the *Republic*?

3. In what way could the two worlds theory be avoided?

The philosopher

So, Plato proposes that philosophers should be the Guardians of the community because they have knowledge of the Forms which they can use as the model or guide for the ideal community. However, knowledge by itself does not make for good rulers, and so Plato says that he will describe the other qualities of the Philosopher-Guardians.

The key qualities of the Guardians Plato mentions are: truthfulness (485c); lack of interest in physical pleasures and money (485d–e); self-control (485e); an absence of meanness, pettiness or cowardliness (486a–b); greatness of mind and breadth of vision (486a); fearlessness in the face of death (486b); modesty (486b); justice and easiness to deal with (486b); swiftness in learning, and a good memory (486c); a sense of taste or style and of proportion (486d); and maturity (487a).

It is sometimes said that Plato is arguing in these sections that to have knowledge of the Forms is to possess the qualities Plato lists, so that if someone gets the knowledge in question he comes in this way to possess the indicated character traits. However, it is said, is there not 'massive evidence that people absorbed in cerebral pursuits can still prove as susceptible as anyone else to lust and greed'? (Pappas 1995: 114). If so, Plato has missed something fundamental and his argument is weak, for it is certainly true that intellectual or academic work in general is perfectly consistent with meanness, smallness of mind and other vices.

Knowledge of Forms:
not a purely intellectual
activity?

However, this criticism of Plato is, perhaps, misplaced. For it presupposes that what Plato has in mind is simply the acquisition of knowledge of the Forms and that, once one has that knowledge, one somehow thereby develops the character traits in question – greatness of mind and the rest. However, this may not be what Plato is arguing at all. Rather, Plato may be trying to suggest that there can be no knowledge of the Forms *unless one has* the kind of character traits in question. In other words, Plato may be suggesting that knowledge of the Forms *is not a purely intellectual activity* but rather also involves being truthful, greatminded and so on. It is not that one *first* goes through an intellectual exercise to come to knowledge of the Forms and *then* this brings with it development of one's moral or ethical character. Rather, coming to knowledge of the Forms is a development of the *whole* ethical-intellectual character, and without ethical development there can be no such knowledge. This might be why Plato talks of *love* of the Forms (485a–b) and describes knowledge of the Forms in fundamentally mystical terms (for example, 490b; 500b–c). We shall return to this point later.

In any case, Plato certainly thinks that the true philosopher must have the kinds of character traits in question. This shows that, whatever he means by 'philosopher' he certainly does not mean what *we* mean by 'philosopher', that is, a person paid to teach the subject at a college or university, or who writes books on the subject. This is because it certainly *is* true that the kind of training individuals have to become philosophers in the modern world has nothing whatsoever to do with their moral nature. There is no inconsistency between being a very important philosopher – even a very important *moral* philosopher – in the academic world and being mean, ungenerous and cowardly. In fact, it is possible to be a very important philosopher and have little understanding of life – be shallow, foolish and wicked – just so long as one is good at finding arguments for one's views (cf. Gaita 1991: 323ff.). For Plato, however, this is impossible: in Plato's eyes such a person would not be a true philosopher.

Asceticism and other-
worldliness

We should also note that there is a strong element of *asceticism* in Plato's philosophers: they do not care for the pleasures of this world – those of the body, for example, or of money – and, as we noted earlier, they live together in a kind of camp, having no personal possessions. This asceticism signals a strong *other-worldly* or *religious* element in Plato's philosophy.

Note also that the philosopher is not afraid of death. This is a large theme in

Plato's work, and it has to do with his belief in the immortality of the soul. However, but it is also connected with his emphasis upon the idea that the philosopher is a *contemplative,* that is, someone who spends a great deal of his time in beholding the Forms, particularly the Form of Good, which will be discussed further below. In fact, in his dialogue *Phaedo,* Plato says that philosophising is itself a preparation for death (67d–e) because through philosophical contemplation the philosopher focuses his mind and soul on things beyond the vicissitudes of everyday life and thus prepares himself for release from that life.

The prejudice against philosophy

At this point (487b) Adeimantus interrupts Socrates: he says that what Socrates has argued sounds all well and good, but, in reality, philosophers are 'very odd birds, not to say thoroughly vicious' or, at the best, 'useless' in the community (487d).

To Adeimantus' surprise, Socrates agrees with him: in present-day society the philosopher is thought to be useless and vicious. So far as his uselessness is concerned, Socrates explains the point through the analogy of the ship.

The ship analogy The community or state, he says, is like a ship. The people in the state are like the captain of the ship, who is larger and stronger than the crew, but a bit myopic and deaf. Politicians are similar to the crew, and they vie with each other for the captain's favour, grouping themselves into cliques to enable them to oust their rivals. None of them has any real idea how to navigate a ship, and they despise those who have studied the art of navigation and hence are the real experts at guiding a ship to port.

Plato's story suggests that, just as there can be experts in navigation, so there can also be experts in political matters. Such experts are the philosophers, and these, like the experts in navigation, are (mistakenly) ignored in society because they are thought to be useless.

Plato's claim that true philosophers are like experts in navigation assumes that politics is a skill (*technē*) in the way that navigation can be. This notion has often been criticised because it is far from clear that there can be political experts in the way that there can be experts in navigation. There are several reasons for this. The most significant is that there are agreed standards on what would count as (acquiring) expertise in matters of navigation but this is not so in the case of politics. In the case of navigation, when confronted with a choice about what to do there is, in principle, a single correct answer, or, at the very least, a number of correct answers between which to choose and on which experts can agree. In the case of politics, however, this is not so, for equally competent politicians can disagree about what to do in a given situation.

Here is another way of putting the difference. In navigation, we can all agree what the aim is, namely, to get the passengers safely to their destination. However, in politics we can all – and politicians can all – reasonably disagree about, so to speak, what the correct destination is (for example, capitalism, communism, socialism and so forth). So Plato's analogy seems to break down (cf. Bambrough 1975).

Plato's distrust of democracy

However, beyond this, the analogy articulates a deep distrust of the democratic politics of Plato's time (remember the dialogue is set in about 420BC). Moreover, it goes further than that and involves a critique of democracy as such, a critique to which Plato returns, and that he fills out, later in the *Republic* (555b–562a). It suggests that the people do not really understand themselves and what it is they really need in order to flourish or lead a good life, and that democratic politicians are merely opportunists who pander to what the people *think* would be good for them. As Plato puts it later, in a democracy it does not matter what quality of men and women are politicians, just so long as they can convince the citizens that they are the people's friends (558b–c). Indeed, left to their own devices the people and politicians make a mess of the politics of a community and of their own lives: they waste their time in pointless pursuits and petty rivalries, unable to see beyond their immediate situation. The root problem here, Plato thinks, is lack of discipline: there is no need in a democracy to bow to authority (557e), and the individual's soul is weak and frivolous, for he indulges himself in now this activity, now that activity, with no thought for the overall direction his life is taking (561c–e). The democratic individual indulges his desires with no thought for whether satisfying them is necessary or is really good for him, or for whether they are shameful or extravagant (560e-561a). Further, the democratic individual cares too much for money and the things it can buy (561a–b).

Despite all this, Plato certainly sees that democracy can be thought appealing because in a democratic society the two ideals most valued are those of liberty (557b) and equality (558c). So far as the former is concerned, however, he thinks that too much liberty leads to a lack of discipline of the kind described. In the case of equality, he simply does not believe that human beings are equal. Indeed, a central reason why Plato wants to see the rule of the wise and knowledgeable is that he believes in what one might call an aristocracy of the spirit, that is, in the idea that individuals, far from being equal, are of profoundly different quality and worth. As far as Plato is concerned, most people are simply too apathetic and indifferent, too sunk in their own concerns, to care about anything of lasting significance, and he thinks that such people should not have power over those who are sensitive and insightful, such as the philosophers he is describing.

Many find offensive what Plato says about democracy, yet it is certainly true that he articulates some thoughts that many – both from a conservative and from a left-wing perspective – have had about democratic politics and a democratic society. Many from both the right and the left are disgusted by what they see as the vulgarity, the low moral standards, and the permissiveness, hedonism and materialism of modern democratic life. Moreover, many have thought that where what the majority of people think and want has great influence over the political process then the tastes and concerns of the 'lowest common denominator' are bound to prevail. This is often said about modern democracies, for example, where many think that television, newspapers, cinema, theatre and so on cater in the main to cheap and coarse tastes, and politicians have to appeal to the selfish interests of the population to stand any chance of being elected.

Plato's thoughts on this come out further when he goes on to consider the way in which potential philosophers are corrupted (491b–495c). He argues that those individuals who might seem to have all the makings of philosophers are liable to be corrupted by the mass of thoughtless people. If someone has the makings of a philosopher and thus has a place in the public life of a democracy, he will find that, in order to preserve his position and popularity, he will have to accept the mass of people on *their* terms, not his, with the consequence that his nature will be corrupted because he will have to ingratiate himself with them despite the shallowness and foolishness of what they want (492b–493a).

The sophists

Socrates compares such a corrupted philosopher to a sophist (493a). The sophists were itinerant teachers who went from city to city and gave lessons, for which they charged. They claimed to be able to teach virtue or excellence and, in particular, offered lessons in the art of rhetoric or public speaking, because the ability to speak well was very important in Greece at that time for a political career, which itself brought with it power, fame and fortune. Socrates loathed the sophists whom he thought of as charlatans without any real wisdom but who claimed, nonetheless, to be wise. Usually, he is scathing about them when he discusses them, but here he sees them as less to blame for the state of society than the people are themselves (492a). In a memorable image (493a–d) he says that the sophists merely pander to the crowd. They are like a man who is in charge of an animal and who learns to anticipate its moods, desires and reactions and thus keep it satisfied. Such a man cannot question whether what the animal wants is good or bad; he simply has to seek to keep it satisfied. Similarly, say Socrates, the sophists have no knowledge of whether what the people want is good or bad, shameful or admirable: they just seek to satisfy their desires. Again, many would see a parallel with modern democracy, arguing that politicians and others who are influential in public life seek to pander to the people.

Socrates goes on to say that when true philosophy is abandoned bogus philosophers rush in and start talking and acting as if they were really philosophers: only in very rare cases does a true philosopher emerge, someone who has not been corrupted and who does not seek merely to ingratiate himself with the people.

Philosophy as a vocation

Before moving on, it is important to note that Socrates' attitude to philosophy only really makes sense because he thought of it as a *vocation*. That is, he thought of it as something one should *serve*, something therefore which one can *betray*. For him, it could not be a profession or a career at all, something that one could do during work time and then stop doing, for example, in the evenings or at weekends, as, say, people stop and relax after work in the office. This is not to say that he was philosophising all the time. It is to say that philosophising was not for him a mere intellectual pursuit but rather something in which every aspect of his soul participated in a striving for self-knowledge and integrity. For Socrates, philosophy and life were one, and the idea that one could be 'interested' in philosophy in the way that one might be interested in tennis or chess would have made no sense to him at all: he would have seen that as a betrayal of philosophy. Very few philosophers look at philosophy this way, but in modern times Kierkegaard (1813–55), Nietzsche (1844–1900) and Wittgenstein (1889–1951) are examples of those philosophers who have. Like Socrates, they were all thinkers of tremendous integrity, whether or not one agrees with their specific ideas, because for them there was no point in doing philosophy if it did not bring one to deeper honesty about life itself. Hence Wittgenstein, having commented in a letter on how difficult philosophy is, continued:

> *But it is, if possible, still more difficult to think, or try to think, really honestly about your life and other people's lives. And the trouble is that thinking about these things is* not thrilling, *but often downright nasty. And when it's nasty it's* most *important.* (Quoted in Malcolm 1989: 94).

Socrates would certainly have agreed with that.

review activity

1. Describe in your own words Plato's analogy of the ship and the state and what it is intended to show.

2. What seems mistaken in Plato's comparison of philosophers to experts in navigation.

3. What is Plato's view of democracy?

4. Who were the sophists and why did Socrates despise them?

5. What kind of view of philosophy did Socrates have?

The rational community

Having discussed the state of contemporary philosophy, Plato insists that the philosopher ruler is not impossible. And here he says something very important and interesting. He notes again that the philosopher has knowledge of the Forms and says that these give him a 'divine pattern' (500e) for society. He then compares the philosopher to an artist who works on a canvas. An artist obviously needs a clean canvas on which to work, and Plato says that the philosopher is the same: he must 'wipe the slate of human society and human habits clean' (501a). Later he gives this idea a practical dimension: the first generation of those trained to be Guardians would send away all those in the community over ten years old, leaving the children, whom they would educate to be citizens of the new community (540e-541a).

This idea that it is possible to reorganise a society from the ground up and place a community on a wholly new footing has been a recurrent hope of radical thinkers since at least the time of Plato. Many thinkers have been opposed to this as a belief in the name of which all kinds of forms of violence and destruction seem to be justified. The French Revolution provides a classic example of this, when the original aim of putting society on a wholly new footing of rational order gave way to the destruction of those who were deemed to stand in the way of this project – the so-called 'Terror'. Thus, in the name of *liberté, égalité* and *fraternité* many thousands of people were guillotined. More generally, opponents of the 'rationally organised society' (see, for example, Oakeshott 1991: esp. ch.2, 5–42) argue that it is true, as the 'rationalist' says, that there is an absence of order and coherence in human affairs, but that the attempt to organise society along rational principles that aim to remove this disorder can only result in the destruction of society. This is because they think that society, if it is to remain healthy, must be allowed to develop from within and grow after its own manner, rather than being forced into the straitjacket of explicitly formulated rules, regulations and principles. Needless to say, whether this view is correct, or whether there is some middle ground between it and the 'rationalist' position, is a hotly disputed issue.

The sun and the Form of the Good

Plato now moves on to say that the highest form of knowledge is that of the Form of the Good (505a), the Form that is itself the highest of all the Forms. Socrates says that he cannot say what exactly this Form is (506d–e), although it is neither pleasure, because there are bad pleasures (505c), nor knowledge, because the only knowledge here in question could be knowledge of the Good, and this explanation is hopeless because it does not tell us what the Good is, which is what we want to know (505b). The best Socrates says he can do is to provide an analogy to the Form of the Good in order to help us see what it is. In fact, he provides three images to help in this: the sun, the line (also known as the 'Divided Line') and the cave. These images are amongst the most famous in Plato's philosophy, indeed, in Western philosophy as a whole.

The sun and the Form of the Good

Socrates asks us to consider the faculty of sight (507b–508d). In order to see, there must be three things: an object to be seen, the eyes, and the medium of light. It is the sun that provides this light. This applies to the visible realm, that is, to the realm of things in this world that we see. Socrates now says that we can apply it to the mind (508d–509c). Just as in the *visible* world there are *objects* to be seen by the *eye*, which has need of the medium of *light* provided by the *sun*, so in the *intelligible* world there are *Forms* to be seen by the *mind's (soul's) eye*, which has need of the medium of *knowledge and truth* provided by the *Form of the Good*. Moreover, as the *sun* is responsible for the *growth* of things in the visible world, so the *Form of the Good* is responsible for the *being and reality* of the Forms.

What does Plato understand by the Form of the Good? As it is, indeed, a Form, he clearly means that the Form of Good is itself good, and it is good *unqualifiedly*. Some philosophers doubt whether this makes sense, because they believe that nothing can be simply good, that is, good as such, or good *simpliciter*, as philosophers sometimes say. They think that if something is good it must be good in some specific, qualified way – for example, it is *a good x* because it fulfils its specific purpose well (for example, the knife is good because it cuts well) or it is *good for* y (for example, jogging as exercise is good for this person to keep him healthy, but bad for that person because he has a weak heart).

Still, leaving aside such concerns, we note that Plato claims that the Form of Good illuminates things in the intelligible world. What this means is that Plato thinks that it is only in the light of the Form of the Good that anything can be known at all. Thus, Plato believes that a full knowledge of reality ultimately has a moral or ethical dimension. In other words, Plato thinks that it is not possible properly to understand the world except from a moral perspective – except through knowing the Form of the Good.

This view, it seems, conflicts with the standard modern opinion that it is perfectly possible to know things regardless of any ethical perspective. For example, it seems nothing more than common sense to say that one can know that, for example, the sky is blue, regardless of one's ethical perspective. Moreover, scientific investigations seem to be perfectly possible without any commitment whatsoever to an ethical point of view, let alone one concerned with the Good in Plato's sense. So is what Plato claims overblown or even absurd?

A teleological conception of nature

Plato's way of understanding science certainly was very different from the modern way, but it may not be so absurd. Several commentators (for example, Taylor 1960: 294; White 1979: 179–81; Sayers 1999: 117–9) suggest that what Plato had in mind was a teleological conception of the world. 'Teleological' comes from the Greek *telos*, meaning 'goal' or 'aim'. The idea is that everything in nature tends towards a certain end, which is the Form of the Good.

To understand what this means, consider a modern scientific notion of explanation. According to this account, the world functions purely mechanistically, and what causes anything to be the way it is is that at some previous time an event has taken place that simply produces a certain effect. For example, if the wind causes a tree to fall down, then we have a cause (the wind blowing) and an effect (the tree falling down) and the cause mechanically produces the effect from 'behind', a kind of 'pushing'.

On Plato's account, we are dealing with a different kind of cause. Taylor gives a helpful example (Taylor 1960: 294). Modern biology explains why it is that creatures have the features they have by reference to their adaptation to the environment. For example, some birds (for example, the ibis) develop an extremely long, narrow and delicate beak because such a beak enables them to tap a food supply that is present in the environment and which would otherwise elude them. Other birds (for example, the parrot) develop a short, powerful beak because this enables them to tap a different food source. Now, if a biologist explains how an organism achieves adaptation to the environment in this way, then we can see this as the organism *aiming* at something, namely, the *best* fit it can achieve to the environment. The organism's *aim* or *goal* is what is best for it: and here we thus have a *teleological* explanation.

The 'best' here is only *relative to the environment:* given a different environment then different adaptations would occur – for example, birds would develop different beaks.

This principle of adaptation can be applied to all the other plants and creatures as it can be to birds.

But, now, if we consider *everything there is* (not just this or that bird or this or that species) taken together then we can ask: what is the environment for that? Plato says that because each thing is aiming at its best, then the environment as a whole is aiming for the best. And that best is the Form of the Good: the environment for everything taken as a whole is, so to speak, the Good, at which everything thus aims.

So, on Plato's account, all things together aim at the realisation of the Good. And we thus see in this way that a knowledge of science is inseparable from moral or ethical notions, because, in Plato's view, to understand something is to understand its contribution to the realisation of the Good. Hence, knowledge of things is at the same time knowledge of their value or worth.

Some scientists would, of course, reject the idea that in adaptation anything is being aimed at: they would say that it is by chance that creatures develop the specific features they need for survival. For example, amongst a group of birds of the same species with a short beak some may, by chance, have a slightly longer beak that enables them to tap a particular food source better than other birds of the same species. These birds with the slightly longer beak flourish better than the others and reproduce, whereas the less well-adapted birds die out. Over an extremely long period of time the beaks of the well-adapted birds become longer until eventually a new species of bird develops, which has a long beak. In this, nothing is aimed at and all happens by chance: we can dispense with the teleological explanation.

review activity

1. Explain in your own words Plato's analogy between the sun and Form of the Good.

2. Plato has a teleological view of science. What does this mean, and how exactly did Plato understand this teleology?

3. In what way might some scientists reject Plato's view of science?

Obviously we cannot settle the issue here concerning the correctness or otherwise of Plato's conception of the Good and its relation to scientific explanation. However, it is important to see that Plato's understanding of the importance of the Form of the Good can be approached from a different, distinctively moral or ethical direction. For the Form of Good must enable those who understand it to recognise good actions, people and so on, and to act better and be better individuals themselves. It does not make known just the things of the intelligible realm but also gives understanding to the individuals who have seen this Form in the everyday world, allowing them to see things that are genuinely good (genuinely participate in, copy, or reflect the Form of the Good) and to distinguish them from those things that are not. This way of understanding Plato's conception of the Good has been developed in the work of the contemporary philosophers Raimond Gaita (Gaita 1991 and 2000), R.F. Holland (Holland 1980) and Iris Murdoch (Murdoch 1986).

Here, then, is roughly the perspective on Plato's thinking on the Form of the Good suggested between them by the three thinkers mentioned.

Beauty, love, and the Form of the Good

Plato's dialogue the *Symposium* is about love and beauty, and suggests that coming to see the Form of Beauty is the work of love: starting out from love of individuals in their physical being it is possible to progress beyond this to love of the soul of individuals, through to love of institutions, thence to love of morality and the sciences, until at last one can love the Form of Beauty itself. What this suggests is that, just as love can lead to knowledge of the Form of Beauty, so love is also important in leading to knowledge of the Form of Good. Indeed, this view is confirmed by the reflection that, as

Taylor has pointed out (Taylor 1960: 231; 287), the Form of Beauty and the Form of Good are really expressions for the same thing. So we can say that there can be no knowledge of the Form of the Good without *loving* this Form. This, indeed, might be another way of putting the point I made earlier that there can be no knowledge of the Form of Good aside from a specific ethical perspective.

There are many types of love, but the highest notion of love we have is one that involves selflessness: to love is to care for the object of love in a selfless way.

Plato occasionally talks about love in the *Republic* but he tends to put things somewhat differently in this dialogue. In fact, his training for the Guardians that they might see the Form of Good involves a great deal of study in mathematics (524d–531d). Clearly, part of what he has in mind here is the fact that mathematical knowledge is abstract knowledge, and this helps prepare the mind to turn away from the everyday world to acquire knowledge of the Forms. However, learning mathematics also involves a kind of selflessness; what one has to learn in learning mathematics is a discipline in something that teaches one a certain selfless humility because there is nothing one can do to change or manipulate the object of learning – one must bow to its demands. The same kind of selfless humility is central to the highest kind of love we know.

There is no doubt that Plato's sense of what it is to love the Form of the Good involved him in many ways in a disgust with the everyday world and with everyday experience. This is analogous to the way in which many Christian thinkers have found the world disgusting, just so much trash compared to the vision of God. However, it is surely correct to think that someone who loves the Form of Good will love the things in the world that partake in this Form, in the kind of way that Christian love of God can lead to a greater love of the world (cf. 485a). In any case, there would certainly be something bizarre in someone who loved the Good, but was completely indifferent to its manifestation in the material world. In fact, the Guardians try to model the community as much after the Good as possible (484c–d), which means that it is hard to resist the thought that in some sense they *must* love the Good as and when it appears in the world.

Goodness beyond virtue

The Good, when it appears in the world, is not the ordinary run of virtues – kindness, generosity, courage and so on – but something that is beyond virtue (Gaita 2000: ch.1; cf. also Holland 1980: 92–109), something whose presence in the world is fleeting and gone almost the moment it appears (cf. Arendt 1958: 73–8). It has a fineness that makes all talk of virtue seem inadequate. It is hard to find examples, but Raimond Gaita has drawn attention to one to be found in Primo Levi's work (Gaita 2000: 150–1).

Levi was an Italian who was deported to Auschwitz in 1943 and stayed there until the end of the war. He only managed to survive because he contracted scarlet fever towards the end of the war and was transferred to the camp sanatorium. One of the prisoners in the sanatorium was Lakmaker, a Dutch Jew, aged 17. He had been in the sanatorium for three months and had had typhus and scarlet fever together with a serious cardiac illness. In addition, he was covered in bedsores so bad that he could only lie on his stomach.

Primo Levi (1919–87)

One night towards the end of the war after the Germans had fled the camp Lakmaker threw himself from his bed. Another prisoner, Charles, Levi writes

climbed down from his bed and dressed in silence. While I held the lamp, he cut all the dirty patches from the straw mattress and the blankets with a knife. He lifted Lakmaker from the ground with the tenderness of a mother, cleaned him as best as possible with straw taken from the mattress and lifted him into the remade bed in the only position in which the unfortunate fellow could lie. He scraped the floor with a scrap of tinplate, diluted a little chloramine and finally spread disinfectant over everything, including himself.

I judged his self-sacrifice by the tiredness which I would have had to overcome in myself to do what he had done.   (Levi 1998: 173)

As Gaita says, this is 'goodness to wonder at', something beyond mere kindness or generosity. And this kind of deed is surely one kind of way in which we might come into contact with the Good if we ever do. Both Socrates and Plato would surely have agreed.

review
activity

1. What is the connection between the Form of the Good and the notion of love?

2. What does it mean to say that there is a Goodness beyond virtue?

Whatever we think of such moral examples, however, we recall that Plato also insisted that knowledge of anything requires knowledge of the Good. What could this mean for our knowledge that the sky is blue or for more specialised scientific knowledge?

We all think, of course, that we know what 'blue' or 'red' means and how to pick out blue or red things in the world. However, Iris Murdoch has suggested that even here knowledge – true knowledge – could be dependent on love. She wrote: 'Why not consider red as an ideal end-point, as a concept infinitely to be learned, as an individual object of love? A painter might say, "You don't know what 'red' means".' (Murdoch 1986: 29).

Notice that implicit in Murdoch's way of putting things is the idea, which we have already mentioned, that knowledge for Plato is knowing *what something is*. Thus, we are not really concerned here with knowing that something is red but with knowing the (nature of the) red of that thing. Similarly, if Plato wishes to talk of some such example as that the sky is blue and to bring the Form of the Good into this, then he must be thinking in terms of knowing the true nature of the blue of the sky.

Perhaps all our concepts can be thought of in the way Murdoch thinks of red, for we can find wonderful many of the things in nature, and such a sense of wonder is, to speak in a Platonic way, the offspring of the Good. Of even a banal concept like *down* it is possible to acquire a deepened understanding by being brought up against its strangeness. This, at any rate, seems to be the thought behind something Cora Diamond has written:

I once stood on a ledge behind a waterfall, where all I could hear was the water thundering down, *all I could see in front of me was thousands of gallons hurtling* down. *The experience I had I could only describe by saying something like 'Now I know what "down" means!'* (Diamond 1996: 233)

It is perhaps possible that even in science we can think we understand a concept but not do so because we do not really *see* what is before our eyes. Perhaps, as I said, it is possible to come to a deepened understanding of *any* concept, in the kind of way that the painter might come to a deepened understanding of *red*. After all, who would have thought that one could come to a deepened understanding of *down*? Yet it is clearly possible.

review
activity

In what way might one defend the claim that even to know that, for example, the sky is blue, one needs knowledge of the Form of the Good?

I noted earlier a reason why Plato takes it that the study of mathematics helps with coming to see the Form of the Good: the abstract nature of the subject and the demands it makes turn the learner away from concern with himself and with the things of this world. However, there is another reason why Plato was interested in mathematics in this regard, a reason well brought out by Holland.

Geometry and good and evil

First of all, we should remember that when Plato spoke of mathematics, he primarily had geometry in mind. Holland notes (Holland 1980: 131) that in Plato's dialogue *Gorgias* Socrates criticises Callicles' moral attitude by saying: 'You neglect geometry' (508a). But, of course, one wants to ask what geometry has to do with morality. Holland says this:

> *In the dialogue in which he alludes to the power of geometry, Plato says that it is better to suffer evil than to do it. In this fundamental ethical proposition it is the sense of 'better' that he believes geometry might help us to understand. When you see that in doing such-and-such a thing you will be harming someone you are brought up against a limit. Evil is the unlimited range of points lying outside the circle of action drawn by the geometry of goodness.*
>
> (Holland 1980: 134)

In other words, the power of geometry is like the power of morality: they both set absolute limits to what can be done, and this is one reason why Plato was interested in it from a moral point of view.

Someone might say that what I have suggested, following Gaita, Holland and Murdoch, about the Good sounds as if it has a strong mystical element. I think this is true: it has. In fact, Plato's philosophy is deeply indebted to mystical thinking and experience – much more so than a lot of recent commentary on his work would lead one to notice. This lack of interest in the mystical side of Plato's work lies, perhaps, in the fact that an understanding of the Good, given that it is partly a mystical notion, depends, as Plato says, upon personal experience, and that there can be no adequate description or conceptual understanding of what it is. As Taylor says (Taylor 1960: 231), referring to the apprehension of the Good: 'Either a man possesses it and is himself possessed by it, or he does not, and there is no more to be said.' In Plato's Form of the

Good, philosophy as a logical and conceptual investigation dependent upon argument finds its limit: only experience – and *not* argument – will make one think that anything lies on the far side of philosophy or not.

activity

What is the connection between ethics and geometry on Holland's account of Plato?

The line

Having discussed the simile of the sun, Socrates goes on to provide two further analogies. The first is the line, which he says is a continuation of the sun analogy (509c). He asks us to draw a line divided into four segments thus:

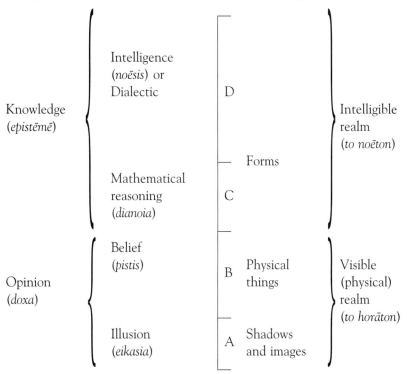

Plato's line

Socrates says (509e–510a) that the lowest segment (A) contains shadows and images. The next segment up (B) contains the objects of which (A) contains the shadows and images, such as plants and animals (510a–b). Above that, (C) uses as images the objects contained in (B): the objects in (C) are mathematical objects (510b-511b). Finally, the topmost segment (D) contains the Forms (511b-e). Further, in (D) we have what Plato calls 'dialectic' (511b), a fuller account of which he gives later (531d-534e). By dialectic he means, roughly, philosophy.

What is the purpose of the line? Plato tells us explicitly that it is supposed to be a continuation of the sun (509c). In this case, it seems clear that we are supposed to understand the two lower segments (A + B) as the visible world and the top two segments as the intelligible world (C + D). Then there would be an analogy between the visible world (A + B) and the intelligible world (C + D).

However, things are more complicated than this, because Plato says that each segment of the line is associated with a special cognitive state (that is, state of mind). Thus, the cognitive state relevant in (A) is that of illusion (*eikasia*); in (B), that of belief (*pistis*); in (C), reasoning (*dianoia*); and finally in (D), intelligence (*noēsis*). Then, corresponding to A + B as a whole there is opinion (*doxa*); and to C+D knowledge (*epistēmē*). (Note that some translators render the Greek terms in slightly different English terms.) Corresponding to these cognitive states there are, of course, the objects of those states we have already noted.

It seems, then, that Plato is not interested only in the analogy of the visible to the intelligible world but also in a series of steps by which the mind is led to greater knowledge. However, because Plato wants the line to do two things as once – that is, to provide an analogy of visible to intelligible world and to show the series of steps in question – problems are created in understanding the line. One of these is that the lowest segment (A) does not seem correctly to capture a special state of mind from which one might ascend, since we do not in our lives spend any significant amount of time in the state of looking at shadows and images, only later ascending to see the 'originals' of such shadows and images, i.e., animals and plants. Rather, we learn about shadows and images *at the same time* as we learn about animals and plants.

Given this problem, it is perhaps better to understand the lower segments of the line, (A) and (B), as concerned not so much with the visible world as with the whole world of second-hand opinions about all manner of things. Plato even seems to suggest this (510a), in which case the distinction between the objects in (A) and (B) is not very important. However, if this is so, it is unclear why Plato draws this distinction in the first place.

What of the upper two segments? Here we are concerned with knowledge. Plato suggests that the objects in both (C) and (D) are the Forms (510d). This already suggests a difference in situation from (A) and (B), since there we were told that each of these had different objects – shadows and images, and 'originals' of these images, respectively. (However, as we have seen, this distinction may not have been very important to Plato anyway.) In any case, Plato is not really interested in the difference between the objects in (C) and (D) – the Forms – as in different ways of understanding them. In (C), the Forms are approached via mathematics; in (D) they are approached directly, so to speak.

Plato says that (C) suffers from two weaknesses. First, in mathematics reasoning takes place from hypotheses that are assumed but not proven (510c–d); secondly, mathematicians are forced to use 'visible figures', that is, drawings and the like (for example, of squares and circles), in their reasoning, even though, as we have noted, what they are really concerned with is the Forms (for example, the Form of Square, the Form of Circle). (D) is an improvement on (C) in that, in philosophy, arguments depend upon no assumptions or hypotheses as do those in (C). Philosophy, in other words, comes to complete and full knowledge or understanding: philosophy proceeds to a 'first principle', which we may take to be the Form of the Good. We may do so because knowledge of this Form provides an understanding of the whole and, as we have seen, it is that for which the whole aims.

review activity

1. What is in each segment of the line A, B, C and D?

2. How should we understand the two segments of the line A + B and C + D?

3. What two jobs does the line have to do? Why does this create difficulties?

The cave (I)

After discussing the line, Plato goes on to describe his third simile, the cave, which is intended to continue and complete the similes of the sun and the line (517b). The cave is probably the most famous image ever created by a Western philosopher.

Plato asks us to imagine a number of prisoners chained in a cave. Their chains hold them fast so that they are able to see only the back wall of the cave. On this back wall is a kind of screen. Behind the chained prisoners a fire is burning, and between them and the fire men carry figures along such that the shadows of these figures are projected onto the screen at the back of the cave.

The prisoners take it that the shadows are real things. Moreover, if the men carrying the figures talk to one another, the prisoners take this for speech of the shadows.

We are to imagine that one of the prisoners is let loose and turns around to see the figures. He finds it difficult to believe that these figures are more real than the shadows. Further, if he were made to look at the fire, his eyes would hurt. He is then led out to the real world, where he is dazzled by the light. At first he cannot look at anything other than shadows, but then he gets used to this. Gradually he comes to be able to look at real objects, then at the heavenly bodies by night, and finally at the sun itself.

Clearly, Plato intends the simile of the cave to parallel that of the line and the sun. Lee, in his translation, offers this in explication of the parallel:

The cave and the line

Tied prisoner in the cave – illusion

Freed prisoner in the cave – belief

Looking at shadows and reflections in the world outside the cave and the ascent thereto – reason

Looking at real things in the world outside the cave – intelligence

Looking at the sun – vision of Form of the Good

The cave and the line

It is clear that Lee captures Plato's fundamental idea concerning the relation between the prisoners in the cave and the line. However, there are difficulties. One is that Plato says that the prisoners in the cave are 'drawn from life' or 'like us' (515a). However, if this is so, then there seems to be a severe disanalogy between the cave and the line. In the line, belief was what we obtained by looking at ordinary objects. However, belief in the cave, according to Lee's account, is looking at figures. Figures are not real objects at all: a figure of a tree is not a tree, for example. Further, when the prisoner is released and looks at the figures he cannot say what they are. However, when we look at trees and the rest, we have, in general, no problem in saying what they are. So belief outside the cave is not really like belief inside the cave.

There are also problems about how to understand the figures and their shadows. They are said to be made of wood, stone and other materials (524e–515a), and it clearly makes sense to think that such things could cast shadows. However, later it turns out that there are shadows of justice (517d–e), so clearly the things that cast shadows are not simply material objects.

Part of the problem here is that Plato obviously wants to show how the whole of everyday life is lived as if in a cave if we have no knowledge of the Forms and of the Good. In fact, in a way it seems that the specific details of the sun, line and cave do not matter so much to Plato as the general point he is trying to make, and that to press his similes too far is simply to be overly fastidious.

The message of the cave

What, then, is Plato's general point? It is that most people spend most, if not all, of their time in a miserable state of ignorance and confusion, unable properly to understand themselves, their fellow men and women, or the world around them. They are lazy and thoughtless, concerned only for shallow and evanescent goods. Moreover, it is clear that Plato thinks that people who are in such a state *enjoy* being like this: they *like* it. This is clear from the fact that they do not, in fact, *want* to be released from their captivity in the cave (517a).

So, we see once again that Plato belongs to those who believe in what I called earlier an 'aristocracy of the spirit'. He does not believe in equality, and does not believe most people are able to strive for things of genuine worth or things that will genuinely make them happy. Of course, this view is, as we have already noted, offensive to modern moral tastes, but even those who agree with Plato that most people do not know what they are doing with their lives might disagree with the idea that they should be controlled as Plato thinks. Perhaps, after all, there is value in a person's being free to mess up his own life, rather than having another putatively more fulfilling life thrust upon him.

review activity

1. What kinds of difficulties are there in supposing an analogy between the line and the cave?

2. What is the overall point that Plato is trying to make in his simile of the cave?

The cave (II)

The cave simile is not, however, quite over yet. For the released prisoner returns to the cave. There he has no interest in what passes for honour and glory amongst the prisoners – say in remembering which shadows had passed and predicting which were to come – for he can see the limitations and foolishness of their concerns (516c–d). In any case, he would no longer be much good at discriminating between the shadows, because he has grown accustomed to the sight of the sun. The other prisoners would accordingly think that his journey to the outside world had ruined his eyes, and that he was foolish to have left them in the first place.

Again we see Plato's conviction that most people *like* their limited and benighted state: they do not *want* to see and think more clearly than they do. In fact, they would willingly kill anyone who sought to drag them from their blinkered state – and here Plato almost certainly had the execution of Socrates in mind.

Plato goes on to articulate his view that the person who has had a taste of true understanding, that is, of the Form of the Good, will be unwilling to get involved in the everyday affairs of those who have not been in 'the realm above' (516d–e; 517c–e). However, we recall, precisely those who have knowledge of the Good are the philosopher-rulers, so they must take part in the everyday business of political life. And this poses a problem for Plato, for he sees that such individuals must be *compelled* to return to the cave: they would much rather spend their time in contemplation of the Good and in thought and reflection. Yet, because Plato's concern is with the good of society as a whole, and because the Guardians have been 'bred' (520b) and educated to be who they are with their vision of the Good, it is, says Plato, only right and fair that they should take part in the dull business of politics.

When he is presenting his belief that each philosopher must play a role in ruling, Plato makes the point that if the job of ruling is left in the hands of those who *want* to govern then bad government is bound to ensue (520d; 521a–b), for such persons will scrabble amongst themselves for the positions of greatest prestige, influence and power. Better government comes if those who govern do not really wish to do so. This is an important and interesting point, and there certainly is much to be said for this view.

The 'problem of dirty hands'

One way of looking at what Plato says in this regard is to note that, as has been recognised since more or less the beginnings of thought, political life sometimes, perhaps even often, requires those who rule to lie or do evil to protect both their own position and the position and life of their community. The obvious case of this is war, but even day-to-day government requires politicians to do much that is morally dubious. This is often known as 'the problem of dirty hands': a politician must be the kind of person who is willing to get his hands dirty by doing things that those not involved in political life do not have to do. Given that this is the case, the kind of person who is likely to be attracted to politics and to flourish in political life is also likely to be someone who has a rather weak conscience or is even fairly ruthless. This is one of the things that Plato has in mind when he says that those who *want* to rule should not rule. What Plato wants is a political life which is wholly subservient to moral or ethical thinking, that is, to the Form of the Good. That is, what Plato wants is a political life that dispenses with the need for politicians to do morally dubious things and with politicians who are prepared to do such things. Many would be inclined to regard this as merely utopian thinking. But even if it is, it stems from a real and important insight.

review
activity

Why does Plato think that those who want to rule should not do so?

some questions
to think about

1 Plato says that it is by the Beautiful that beautiful things are beautiful. What does he mean by this, and what problems are there for the claim?

2 Do you think there is any real way of making sense of the idea of degrees of existence?

3 How plausible do you find Plato's claim that the best community will not exist until kings are philosophers or philosophers are kings?

4 To what extent would you agree with Plato's criticisms of democracy?

5 Is Plato's teleological conception of nature defensible?

6 Plato says that the simile of the cave represents our state with respect to education and the lack of it. How, in Plato's opinion, does it do this?

7 'Plato's presentation of the relations between the line and cave is so unclear that these images are useless.' What is there to be said for and against this claim?

further
reading

▶ It is important for understanding Plato to have some sense of his historical and cultural context. The best short general account is *The World of Athens* (Cambridge: Cambridge University Press, 1984) produced by the Joint Association of Classical Teachers. For general background on Plato's ethical context see the distinguished Dover 1974. Burkert 1985 is a masterpiece, which contains some discussion of Plato and much else besides. Dover 1978 is fascinating on one important aspect of Greek life. Howatson (ed.) 1997 is a treasure trove of interesting articles, which help to situate Plato in context.

There are many introductions to Plato's *Republic*. Annas 1981 is detailed and contains lots of close philosophical argument. The same is true of White 1979. Cross and Woozley 1965 is a little dated in parts, but an accessible and helpful read. Sayers 1999 and Rice 1998 are more sweeping in their approach. Another useful introductory book is Pappas 1995. Taylor 1960, although originally published in 1926, retains a tremendous freshness and is written in a noble style befitting work on Plato. In addition, it draws attention to features of Plato's work often missing in the work of modern commentators.

Extremely useful collections of articles on the major topics in Plato's philosophy are Vlastos (ed.) 1972a and 1972b, and Fine (ed.) 1999a and 1999b. Another useful collection of articles is Kraut (ed.) 1992.

Morgan 1990 pays close attention to the religious influences on Plato's work and is a very enjoyable read.

Irwin 1979 presents the moral theory of the *Republic* as marking an important break in Plato's work. A dense work, it is nonetheless rewarding.

On the theory of the Forms see Allen 1972; Cherniss 1965, reprinted in Vlastos (ed.) 1972a; Griswold 1981; and Wedberg 1955 ch.3, reprinted in Vlastos (ed.) 1972a. On the concept of 'faculty' see Hintikka 1973, which is a brilliant and fascinating article.

Rutherford 1995 is good on Plato's style. On this see also Frede 1992.

11

important
terms

Causal adequacy principle: the principle that there must be at least as much reality in the efficient cause and the total cause as in the effect of that cause.

Eminent possession: to possess a property F eminently is not to have the property F but instead to have some grander or more excellent property G.

Formal falsity: the judgement that something not existing does exist.

Formal reality: something possesses formal reality simply in virtue of existing.

Material falsity: the falsity involved in having an idea of, or a desire for, something that does not exist.

Natural light: the natural or intrinsic power of knowledge in all human minds.

Objective reality: the representational content of an idea.

Descartes: *Meditations on First Philosophy*

Life and works

Descartes was born on 31 March 1596 in a small town now called La-Haye-Descartes into a family that belonged to the lesser nobility. In 1604 he entered the Jesuit college of La Flèche at Anjou, which had only opened that year, and later continued his studies at the University of Poitiers. In 1618 he joined the forces of Maurice of Nassau, Prince of Orange, who was the general of the army of the United Provinces (the Netherlands), but he remained something of a gentleman soldier for he saw no action. He had enlisted, in fact, in order to gain some experience of practical affairs rather than to fight. During the 1620s he travelled a lot, and from 1628 to 1649 he lived in Holland, which was a comparatively liberal society. Descartes had an illegitimate daughter, Francine, who was born in August 1635. She died in 1640 and it is said that Descartes felt the blow severely.

In September 1649 he went to Sweden where he became personal tutor to Queen Christina. The philosophy lessons took place at 5 a.m. and this, together with the cold weather, took its toll on his health, and he died of pneumonia on 11 February 1650.

Descartes is often thought of as the founding father of modern philosophy, because he rejected in his work many of the ideas that had dominated philosophical thought since the time of Aristotle. His most famous work is the *Meditations on First Philosophy* (1641), which was published with a set of objections to Descartes' work written by other philosophers and theologians, together with Descartes' replies. What he means by 'first philosophy' is metaphysics, the study of the fundamental nature of reality. Other important works of his include *Discourse on the Method* (1637) and *Principles of Philosophy* (1644).

Third Meditation

We have already looked in some detail at Descartes' reflections in the first two meditations. In this chapter we shall, therefore, pick up Descartes' thought from the *Third Meditation*.

René Descartes (1596–1650)

The main topic of this *Meditation* is God, whose existence Descartes will seek to prove. However, before Descartes starts on the proof, he deals with a number of other things.

He begins by reminding himself that he is so far certain of nothing but that he exists as a thinking thing. He also knows something about what thinking involves – affirming, doubting, denying and so on.

Given that Descartes *is* certain that he is a thinking thing, he can ask the following question: 'Do I not therefore also know what is required for my being certain about anything?' (CSM II: 24/35). In other words, given that he has arrived at certain knowledge that he exists, there must be some way of extracting from this a *criterion* or *rule* for what it is to be certain, not just about the Cogito, but about anything. Descartes says there is, and he suggests what that criterion or rule is:

Clarity and distinctness as a criterion of truth

> *In this first item of knowledge [that I exist as a thinking thing] there is simply a clear and distinct perception of what I am asserting; this would not be enough to make me certain of the truth of the matter if it could ever turn out that something which I perceived with such clarity and distinctness was false. So I now seem to be able to lay it down as a general rule that whatever I perceive very clearly and distinctly is true.* (CSM II: 24/35)

In other words, Descartes says that the criterion or rule for whether something is true is whether his perception of it is *clear and distinct*. For it was the fact that he clearly and distinctly perceived that he is a thinking thing that was the basis for the truth of that claim. Thus, Descartes says, whatever is clearly and distinctly perceived is true.

The will and assent

There is a problem here for Descartes. This is: how are we to recognise when our perceptions are clear and distinct? In general, Descartes seems to have thought that he could not give any general account of how we are to recognise when our perceptions are clear and distinct. He seemed to think it possible that his readers could learn to recognise when their perceptions are clear and distinct through examples he gives of what he says he perceives clearly and distinctly (we shall be looking at some of these in this chapter). However, he does suggest, in the *Fourth Meditation*, that a mark of a clear and distinct perception is that the will is compelled to assent to it. That is, when a perception is clear and distinct one's will cannot be indifferent to, or uncertain about, the perception. Nonetheless, this still leaves open the question of whether we can be mistaken in whether the will is compelled. In fact, Descartes seems to have no answer to this problem. In general, it is surely possible for the will to be compelled but fail to be perceiving something clearly and distinctly; and, conversely, also possible genuinely to be perceiving something that is clear and distinct and yet not be paying attention to it in the right kind of way, so one's will is not compelled as it should be. (Cf. Hatfield 2003: 200)

review activity

1. What is Descartes' criterion or rule for accepting something as true?

2. To what problems is this criterion exposed?

It will be recalled that in the *First Meditation* Descartes had imagined there to be a deceiving God (later elaborated as the malicious demon) who led him into radical doubt. So great was this doubt that Descartes said that, whilst prey to it, he could not even be sure that he could properly carry out simple mathematical operations such as adding two and three or counting the sides of a square. Here, in the *Third Meditation*, Descartes repeats this point (CSM II: 25/36). But then he goes on:

> Yet when I turn to the things themselves which I think I perceive very clearly, I am so convinced by them that I spontaneously declare: let whoever can do so deceive me, he will never bring it about that I am nothing, so long as I continue to think I am something; or make it true at some future time that I have never existed, since it is now true that I exist; or bring it about that two and three added together are more or less than five, or anything of this kind in which I see a manifest contradiction. (CSM II: 25/36)

In this passage, Descartes is likening the certainty of the Cogito to mathematics, suggesting that one can no more doubt the truth of mathematics than one can doubt one's own existence. So why is it that he suggested in the *First Meditation* that the deceiving God could make him doubt the truths of mathematics?

The answer seems to be that Descartes draws a distinction between the different forms of attention that we can give to mathematical truths. When we think of such truths directly and 'attend to the arguments on which our knowledge of them depends', then we cannot doubt them. On the other hand, when we are not thinking of such truths directly, but are merely remembering having thought them and seen the arguments for them, then the deceiving God hypothesis is enough to make us doubt them (CSM II: 104/146).

review
activity

In what way does Descartes think that we can and cannot be mistaken about mathematical truths?

Classification of thoughts

Descartes now turns to a classification of his thoughts. His reason for doing so is to 'ask which of them can properly be said to be the bearers of truth and falsity' (CSM II: 25/36-7). He distinguishes two main groups of thoughts: a) ideas; b) those thoughts with 'various additional forms'. What he means by the latter he explains by saying that, when willing, fearing or affirming, 'there is always a particular thing which I take as the object of my thought, but my thought includes something more than the likeness of that thing' (CSM II: 26/37). Examples of thoughts with 'various additional forms' include volitions, emotions and judgements.

Ideas, he says, are 'as it were the images of things'. The 'as it were' signals that not all these are strictly imagistic, for he gives angels and God as examples of ideas, yet he did not think one could have a sensory image of angels or of God. His point is rather that the idea of God, like the idea of a table, represents a particular individual, and represents him or it as having various properties.

The thoughts from the second group also represent individuals in some way, but go beyond this. An example will clarify what Descartes means. If I want to eat a cake then I must have some kind of idea (representation) of the cake, but my desire goes beyond this: it is the 'additional form' that is part of the mental state that leads me to eat the cake. Further, deciding to eat the cake, which also goes beyond having an idea of the cake, is an act of volition (will). And judgements, which are also mentioned in the second group of thoughts, affirm or deny something.

Material and formal falsity

Descartes notes that I can have an idea of some individual that does not exist, just as I can desire something that does not exist. For example, I can have an idea of a cake that does not exist, just as I can have one of a cake that does exist; or I can desire a cake that does not exist, just as I can desire one that does exist. Such ideas and desires have what Descartes calls 'material' falsity. However, this is not strict or 'formal' falsity. This kind of falsity can only occur in judgements. For example, if I have an idea of a hippogriff (a mythical monster with the head and wings of an eagle and the body of a horse) then this idea is not strictly (formally) false. What is (formally) false is my judgement if I think that there is a hippogriff in front of me. Similarly, if I desire to eat a cake that is non-existent, then the desire is only materially, but not formally false. But if I judge that I can eat a cake that is non-existent – say because I think there is a cake in the tin, but there is not – then my judgement is formally false (cf. CSM II: 26/37; 30/43).

review activity

1. What are the two groups into which Descartes classifies his thoughts?
2. What does Descartes mean by 'material' and 'formal' falsity?
3. Why does Descartes think that, strictly speaking, it is only judgements that can be formally false?

The sources of ideas

Descartes says that his ideas seem to have three sources: some are innate, some adventitious, and others have been invented by him. Innate ideas have already been mentioned, and we shall return to them. Adventitious ideas are those that come 'from things which are located outside me' – though Descartes adds 'or so I have hitherto judged' since, as yet, he is still unsure of the existence of the external world. Such ideas include his ideas of the sun or the fire in front of him. Invented ideas include those of the hippogriff.

What really interests Descartes at this stage is whether he has any reason to think that the adventitious ideas he takes to be of things outside him a) really are derived from such objects; and b) resemble those objects. He gives two reasons to say that he cannot be sure that they are derived from things outside him and one to show that, even if they are, they may not resemble those things. First, although he has a strong natural tendency or impulse to believe that the ideas in question come from things outside him, natural impulses in general cannot be trusted. After all, he has often had a natural impulse to do something that he did not judge to be good, so why should natural impulses that lead him to believe that his ideas come from the external world be any more reliable than his natural impulse to do things?

Secondly, although adventitious ideas do not depend on his will in the sense that when he opens his eyes he sees what he sees and has no choice in the matter, it does not follow that these ideas come from external objects. Might there not be some other cause? Such seems to be the case in dreaming, where the ideas he has do not depend on his will but do not come from external objects. Thirdly, even if his adventitious ideas are caused by external objects, they may well not resemble those objects. He has two ideas of the sun. According to one of these ideas the sun is, say, about the size of a coin. According to the other, derived from astronomical reasoning, the sun is vast. Which is more likely the correct idea? The latter. But which is the adventitious idea? The former.

review
activity

1. What are the three sources Descartes gives for his ideas?

2. What reasons does Descartes give for saying that he cannot be sure that his adventitious ideas are derived from objects external to him?

3. What reason does Descartes give for saying that he cannot be sure that his adventitious ideas, even if they are derived from external objects, resemble those objects?

'Natural light' Note that in this discussion Descartes refers to 'natural light'. What he means by this is the natural or intrinsic cognitive power – that is, power of knowledge – in all human minds. He will use this notion soon.

Formal reality At this point Descartes makes a distinction between two kinds of reality. These are 'objective reality' and 'formal reality' and, in using these terms, Descartes is expressing his distinction between two kinds of reality in the terminology of scholastic philosophy – the philosophy of the thirteenth to the fifteenth centuries. We need to see what Descartes means.

According to Descartes, something has formal reality simply in virtue of existing. In this sense, all ideas possess formal reality, as do all material objects.

Objective reality Objective reality is more complicated. To see what it means, consider an example.

Ideas, we have seen, have, for Descartes, representational content. When Descartes talks of the objective reality of an idea he has in mind this representational content of the idea. For example, suppose you have an idea of St Paul's Cathedral. Your idea represents it as, say, tall. Then tallness is said to be present 'objectively' in your idea. Note that an idea can have objective reality in this sense whether or not there is an object in the world that it correctly represents. My idea of a hippogriff can have objective reality in Descartes' sense. Hence, this sense of 'objective' or 'objective reality' has nothing to do with the modern notion of objective reality, for the modern notion applies to independent objects outside the mind.

Descartes also thought that we could speak of things as having more or less reality. This idea, it seems, depends on the distinction between substance and mode that we have already mentioned. What Descartes says is that modes have less formal reality than substances because they depend on substances for their existence. Further, a finite substance has less formal reality than an infinite substance (should such exist). Consequently, an idea of a mode (such as a shape) has less objective reality than an idea of a finite substance, and an idea of a finite substance has less objective reality than an idea of an infinite substance.

review activity

1. What does Descartes mean by 'natural light'?
2. What does Descartes mean by 'formal reality'?
3. What, according to Descartes, has objective reality? What does this term mean?
4. How are Descartes' notions of substance and mode related to the idea of degrees of reality?

The proof of God's existence (i)

Descartes actually seeks to give two proofs of the existence of God in the *Third Meditation*. In this section we shall consider the first; in the next, the second.

The trademark argument

The proof Descartes offers has come to be known as the 'trademark argument' because it invokes the idea that God has placed within us the idea of himself 'to be, as it were, the mark of the craftsman stamped on his work' (CSM II: 35/51). This idea of God is innate (CSM II: 35/51).

The causal adequacy principle

The argument starts with Descartes invoking a principle that, he says, 'is manifest by the natural light'. This principle is that 'there must be at least as much reality in the efficient cause and the total cause as in the effect of that cause' (CSM II: 28/40). Let us call this the 'causal adequacy principle' (cf. Cottingham 1986: 49).

Efficient cause and total cause

By 'efficient cause' Descartes means what actually produces an effect. The 'total cause' must include everything needed to produce its effect. Descartes gives an example. 'A stone . . . which previously did not exist, cannot begin to exist unless it is produced by something which contains either formally or eminently everything to be found in the stone' (CSM II: 28/41).

Eminent reality

The notion of the thing that causes the stone to exist having as much formal reality as the stone should be clear given what we have said above about formal reality and its relation to the concepts of substance and mode. It means that, as Descartes puts it, the cause of the stone must 'contain in itself the same things as are in the stone' (CSM II: 28 fn.2/41). The notion of eminent reality can be seen in this way. Suppose God made the stone. The stone is a material object. But God is not material. So God can create a material thing even though he is not material. Hence, the reality of matter would be in God eminently, but not formally. Descartes says that if what causes the stone contains eminently all that the stone contains then it contains 'more excellent things' than the stone (CSM II: 28 fn.2/41). As Anthony Kenny succinctly puts it: '[T]o have a property F eminently is not to have the property F but to have instead some grander property G' (Kenny 1968: 141).

Now, Descartes says that the causal adequacy principle can be applied to ideas just as much as it can to objects such as stones. Thus he says:

> [I]n order for a given idea to contain such and such objective reality, it must surely derive it from some cause which contains at least as much formal reality as there is objective reality in the idea. For if we suppose that an idea contains something which was not in its cause, it must have got this from nothing; yet the mode of being by which a thing exists objectively in the intellect by way of an idea, imperfect though it may be, is certainly not nothing, and so it cannot come from nothing. (CSM II: 28-9/41)

What he means is this: if an idea represents some object which has some property, then the cause of the idea must have as much of that property as exists 'objectively' in the idea. Descartes gives an example in the *Principles*.

> [I]f someone has within himself the idea of a highly intricate machine, it would be fair to ask what was the cause of his possession of the idea: did he somewhere see such a machine made by someone else; or did he make such a close study of mechanics, or is his own ingenuity so great, that he was able to think it up on his own, although he never saw it anywhere? All the intricacy which is contained in the idea merely objectively – as in a picture – must be contained in its cause, whatever kind of cause it turns out to be; and it must be contained not merely objectively or representatively, but in actual reality, either formally or eminently. (CSM I: 198–9/11)

Descartes now considers the ideas that he has. One of these is that of God, who is 'eternal, infinite, immutable, omniscient, omnipotent, and the creator of all things' (CSM II: 28/40). Later Descartes says that this idea of God is also of God as 'supremely intelligent' (CSM II: 31/45). The question that this raises is: Where did he get this idea?

As Descartes is not eternal, infinite and so forth, indeed, because he is imperfect in all sorts of ways (CSM II: 32/46-7), he could not be the cause of the idea of God who possesses the kinds of attributes listed. 'All these attributes are such that, the more carefully I concentrate on them, the less possible it seems that they could have originated from me alone', a claim that follows from the causal adequacy principle (CSM II: 31/45).

Could it be that the idea of God comes from nothing – that it is materially false? This could not be so, he says, because the idea of God 'is utterly clear and distinct, and contains in itself more objective reality than any other idea; hence there is no idea which is in itself truer or less liable to be suspected of falsehood' (CSM II: 31/46).

Could it be that we arrive at the idea of God by taking one's understanding of one's own limitations – finitude, limited knowledge and so forth – and, by some process of abstraction, getting to a notion of the unlimited nature of God? Descartes insists not.

> I must not think that, just as my conceptions of rest and darkness are arrived at by negating movement and light, so my perception of the infinite is arrived at

not by means of a true idea but merely by negating the finite. On the contrary, I clearly understand that there is more reality in an infinite substance than in a finite one, and hence that my perception of the infinite, that is God, is in some way prior to my perception of the finite, that is myself. (CSM II: 31/45-6)

The only conclusion, then, is that God is himself the cause of Descartes' idea of God. 'So from what has been said it must be concluded that God necessarily exists', he writes (CSM II: 31/45).

How good is Descartes' argument? One problem is this, raised by Margaret Dauler Wilson (Wilson 1986: 137–8). Even if we accept the causal adequacy principle, it seems arbitrary to say that there must be as much *formal* reality in the cause of an idea as there is *objective* reality in the idea itself. Objective existence is, after all, it seems, something less than formal existence, because it possesses reality in a comparatively less perfect mode of actual existence. So why could not a *lesser formal reality* cause a *greater objective reality*? If it can, then, even if it follows from the causal adequacy principle that Descartes has a creator, his creator could be less than perfect, despite the perfection of his idea of his creator.

Problems with the causal adequacy principle

There are also problems with the causal adequacy principle itself. For there seem to be cases of causation where the cause does not have either formally or eminently all the features found in the effect. John Cottingham has given a simple but telling example of this (Cottingham 1986: 51). A sponge cake has a characteristic sponginess. However, this sponginess was not in the ingredients from which the cake was made – eggs, flour, butter and so on. One might reply that the sponginess might have 'potentially' been in the ingredients. This is true in some sense, but to invoke this idea wherever there is a problem with the causal adequacy principle would be to make it trivially true, as Cottingham points out. In any case, Descartes' argument for the existence of God could hardly work if we were to say that the cause of his idea of God contained *potentially* all the things the idea contains (cf. CSM II: 35/51).

review activity

1. What is the causal adequacy principle?

2. Explain the notion of eminent reality as Descartes uses it.

3. Why does Descartes think that the idea of God could only be in him as a result of God placing it there?

4. What is Wilson's objection to Descartes' argument for the existence of God?

5. Why does the sponginess of a cake present problems for Descartes' argument for the existence of God?

6. Why might one say that the notion of degrees of reality makes no sense?

In any case, Bernard Williams has suggested that the causal adequacy principle is 'unintuitive and barely comprehensible', going on to say that it is astonishing that Descartes could 'unblinkingly accept [it] as self-evident in the light of reason' (Williams 1987: 135). Part of the problem is that the idea of degrees of reality seems unclear. Either something exists or it does not, so the thought goes, and if God exists and a human being exists they both exist equally, regardless of the fact that God is infinite and the human being finite. The whole notion of degrees of reality seems not to make sense.

The proof of God's existence (ii)

We now come to Descartes' second proof of the existence of God in the *Third Meditation*.

The argument begins with Descartes asking himself whether he could exist if there were no being more perfect than he is. Supposing there were no such being, then the question arises: from whom would he derive his existence? Basically, Descartes' argument works by seeking to eliminate any answers other than God. And the answers he eliminates are: a) himself; b) his parents; c) some other source less than God.

Descartes divides the first suggestion, that he derives his existence from himself, into two possibilities, depending on whether he had a beginning or not. Supposing he did, then he argues then he could not have brought himself into existence because, had he done so, he would have given himself 'all the perfections of which I have any idea, and thus I should myself be God' (CSM II: 33/48). After all, he says, if he had enough power to bring himself into existence, he would have no great difficulty in giving himself all perfections.

One odd thing about this argument is, as Kenny has pointed out, that '[p]arents are able to bring children into existence, but they cannot endow them with omniscience . . . [or] with every perfection of [physical] strength and beauty that they might wish' (Kenny 1968: 143). Descartes' answer to this, as Kenny says, would have to be that parents do not really bring their children into existence: both thinking and material substances are brought into being by God.

The second possibility concerning his bringing himself into existence Descartes puts in terms of his always having existed. This will not mean that he does not bring himself into existence because 'a lifespan can be divided into countless parts, each completely independent of the others, so that it does not follow from the fact that I existed a little while ago that I must exist now, unless there is some cause which as it were creates me afresh at this moment – that is, which preserves me' (CSM II: 33/49). In other words, Descartes is saying that, even if he had always existed he would still need to have the power to keep himself in existence – to bring himself into existence at each moment. However, Descartes says that he is not aware that he has such a power.

Let us leave aside the question about whether Descartes is right in saying that a life can be divided up in the way he suggests, debatable though this is. Still, we might reply to Descartes' argument by saying that even if Descartes is not aware of having the power in question, he might nevertheless have such a power. And that would mean that he is preserving himself in existence.

Descartes now considers whether his parents could be the cause of his existence. Or perhaps some other source less than God is the source of his existence? Descartes says this cannot be so, since the supposition in question would lead to an infinite regress. Let us suppose that he was produced by his parents (the same considerations would apply if we were to consider some other source less than God as the cause of his existence). Under the supposition in question we should have to ask what (or who) it was that produced his parents. Then we should be led to ask who produced that producer of his parents, and so on. So eventually, says Descartes, we shall be led back to God, that is, to something that 'has the power of existing through its own might' (CSM II: 34/50). What underlies this argument is ultimately the causal adequacy principle, as Descartes points out (CSM II: 34/49).

Before leaving this topic, it is worth noting that commentators are divided about the relation between the two arguments for the existence of God in the *Third Meditation*. Some have seen the second as a continuation of the first, for which they have the support of the point just made concerning the causal adequacy principle. In addition, this is how Descartes seemed to see the matter. Having referred to the two proofs, he says that, concerning the second, 'my purpose here was not to produce a quite different proof from the preceding one, but rather to take the same proof and provide a more thorough explanation of it' (CSM II: 77/106). Still, E.M. Curley is surely right in suggesting that the presentation of the second argument 'strongly suggests that he [Descartes] thought of the two arguments as distinct and independent of one another' (Curley 1978: 137). In any case, on either interpretation the argument seems not to work because, as we have seen, Descartes has not shown that he is not the cause of himself. In the *Fifth Meditation* Descartes will offer another argument for God's existence, and this will quite definitely be a different argument from what is offered in the *Third Mediation*.

review
activity

1. Why does Descartes think that he could not be the cause of his own existence?
2. Why does Descartes think that he does not have the power to sustain himself in existence?
3. Why, according to Descartes, could his parents not be the cause of him?

The Cartesian circle

The deceiving God banished

At the end of the *Third Meditation*, Descartes says that, having proved the existence of God, he is now able to banish the idea of a deceiving God as this has been with him since the *First Meditation*. For if God exists and is perfect then it follows, says Descartes, that God is no deceiver, because God's perfection excludes deception.

This raises a problem. For Descartes had appealed to the natural light, or the faculty of clear and distinct perception, to prove the existence and non-deceptiveness of God. If he had not done so, he could not have grasped the argument he gave. However, now when he says God is not a deceiver, this is meant to vindicate his ability to rely on clear and distinct ideas. This looks like a circular procedure. If that is so, either the proof of God's existence is unnecessary, because Descartes can rely on clear and distinct ideas anyway, or the proof is impossible. Thus, the argument can only work, it seems, by relying on something that it is supposed to show, namely, that one can rely on clear and distinct ideas.

This is a famous objection to Descartes – the 'Cartesian circle'. Descartes himself seems to make it inescapable when he says in the *Fifth Meditation*:

> *I have perceived that God exists, and at the same time I have understood that everything else depends on him, and that he is no deceiver; and I have drawn the conclusion that everything which I clearly and distinctly perceive is of necessity true.* (CSM II: 48/70)

Descartes was certainly aware of the problem of the circle, for it was raised as an objection for him by Antoine Arnauld (1612–55) in the *Fourth Set of Objections*.

> *I have one further worry, namely how the author avoids reasoning in a circle when he says that we are sure that what we clearly and distinctly perceive is true only because God exists. But we can be sure that God exists only because we clearly and distinctly perceive this. Hence, before we can be sure that God exists, we ought to be able to be sure that whatever we perceive clearly and evidently is true.* (CSM II: 150/241)

Descartes' reply was to refer Arnauld back to the response that he had made to the same objection in the *Second Set of Objections*. That reply reads:

> *[W]hen I said that we can know nothing for certain until we are aware that God exists, I expressly declared that I was speaking only of knowledge of those conclusions which can be recalled when we are no longer attending to the arguments by means of which we deduced them.* (CSM II: 100/140)

And in the reply to Arnauld he says:

> *I made a distinction between what we in fact perceive clearly and what we remember having perceived clearly on a previous occasion. To begin with, we are sure that God exists because we attend to the arguments which prove this; but subsequently it is enough for us to remember that we perceived something clearly in order for us to be certain that it is true. This would not be sufficient if we did not know that God exists and is not a deceiver.* (CSM II: 171/246)

Descartes' reply, then, seems to be drawing on the kind of distinction drawn earlier concerning attention to mathematical truths. We saw that Descartes said that he cannot doubt mathematical truths just so long as he is attending to the arguments on which our knowledge of them depends. However, he also said that, when we are not thinking of such truths directly, but are merely remembering having thought them and seen the arguments for them, the deceiving God hypothesis is enough to make us doubt them.

Descartes' solution to the circle

Descartes' route out of the circle seems, then, to be this. There are certain things that we cannot doubt even when subject to the deceiving God hypothesis *as long as we are attending to them*. These include the truths of mathematics. They also include the Cogito. And they include the ideas needed to prove the existence of a non-deceiving God.

Stability of knowledge and God

The reason we need to prove the existence of God is that once we have done so we can achieve stability in our knowledge, for we shall have God's guarantee that the ideas in question are clear and distinct even when we are *not* attending to the arguments on which our knowledge of them depends. What we achieve, therefore, is *stability* in our knowledge. This seems to be Descartes' point in the *Fifth Meditation* when he writes:

> [M]y nature is such that so long as I perceive something very clearly and distinctly I cannot but believe it to be true. But my nature is also such that I cannot fix my mental vision continually on the same thing, so as to keep perceiving it clearly; and often the memory of a previously made judgement may come back, when I am no longer attending to the arguments which led me to make it. And so other arguments can now occur to me which might easily undermine my opinion, if I did not possess knowledge of God; and I should thus never have true and certain knowledge about anything, but only shifting and changeable opinions.   (CSM II: 48/69)

As Kenny puts it: 'The veracity of God . . . is brought in not in order to prove the truth of what I intuit, but in order to show that I shall never have reason to change my mind about what I have once intuited' (Kenny 1968: 193).

Further support for this interpretation comes from Cottingham, who suggests that if we were to suppose that doubt extends even to one's present intuition of clearly and distinctly perceived truths such as those of mathematics, then the meditation could not even get started. This is because the meditator has to be able to trust the fundamental intuitions of the intellect to get things going, for example, know what is meant by 'thought' and 'doubt' (Cottingham 1986: 70–1). We have, indeed, already seen that Descartes does not doubt that, for example, he can reason through the *Meditations*, for if he did his mind would simply be empty.

This solution to the circle has been criticised by Wilson. She argues that the problem with it is that, whilst it might be true that we cannot *doubt* the truths of mathematics whilst attending to them even under the deceiving God hypothesis, it does not follow from this that under such conditions we *know* these truths. And it is only if we have knowledge that we achieve the truth that Descartes is after (Wilson 1986: 133).

review
activity

1.   Explain on your own words the Cartesian Circle.

2.   Describe one way in which the circle might be solved. How might this solution be criticised?

Fifth Meditation

The main topic of the *Fifth Meditation* is the existence of God. However, before he proceeds to this topic, Descartes picks up the reflections of the *Second Meditation* concerning the nature of material objects.

In the *Second Meditation*, Descartes had said that reflection on a piece of wax shows us that bodies are known by the mind, meaning that their true nature is known by the mind rather than by the senses. In the *Fifth Meditation* Descartes follows this up by considering the *ideas* he has of material body. In considering these ideas, he says that he sees that quantity (or 'continuous' quantity) belongs to bodies. By 'quantity' he means 'extension'. Extension is, in fact, as we have already noted when discussing the *Second Meditation*, the essence or principal attribute (sometimes Descartes says 'nature') of material bodies. Extension can be characterised by various modes, such as 'sizes, shapes, positions and local motions; and to the motions I assign various durations' (CSM II: 44/63). Moreover, Descartes thinks that there is just *one* material substance and thus that individual objects, such as trees, cats and tables are modifications of this single extended substance. This is a position that contrasts sharply with other views of substance, according to which individual objects, such as trees, cats and tables are *themselves* individual substances. Further, Descartes says that a substance is that which is capable of existing on its own. Strictly speaking, it is only God who is a substance in this sense, since he is the only substance that has the power of sustaining himself in existence: everything else requires the power of God to stay in existence, as we saw when discussing Descartes' argument for the existence of God in the *Third Meditation*. But, aside from this qualification, material substance depends on nothing for its existence. (The other such substance is mind or mental substance.)

Problems in Descartes' account of the material world

There are various problems associated with Descartes' account of the material world. One is that it led him to deny that there can be any such thing as a vacuum. This comes out in *Principles* II 11, which is entitled 'There is no real difference between space and corporeal substance', in which he says that 'the extension constituting the nature of a body is exactly the same as that constituting the nature of a space' (CSM I: 227/46). Hence: 'The impossibility of a vacuum, in the philosophical sense in which there is no substance whatsoever, is clear from the fact that there is no difference between the extension of a space, or internal place, and the extension of a body' (CSM I: 229–30/49). Even God, says Descartes, could not make a vacuum – an extraordinary claim given the fact that Descartes may well have thought that even the laws of logic and mathematical truths depend on God's will.

Another curious aspect of Descartes' view on matter is that it does not seem to explain how it is that there are different things in the world – trees, cats and tables, for example. As Cottingham says, Descartes' account of the material universe 'seems to give us nothing more than an entirely bland and homogeneous universe – a kind of universal, impenetrable three-dimensional dough' (Cottingham 1986: 87). Descartes' answer to the problem, according to Cottingham, is that portions of matter 'move at different speeds from other portions, and this is enough to give differentiation and variety to the universe' (Cottingham 1986: 87). Whether Descartes' account at this point suffices to explain what it is supposed to explain seems doubtful, as Cottingham implies.

Having considered the nature of material bodies, Descartes goes on to say:

> [T]he truth of these matters [concerning material bodies] is so open and so much in harmony with my nature, that on first discovering them it seems that I am not so much learning something new as remembering what I knew before; or it seems like noticing for the first time things which were long present within me although I had never turned my mental gaze on them before.
>
> (CSM II: 44/63–4)

Descartes is claiming that his knowledge of the essence of the material world is innate: it is not something drawn from observation of the material world. It is the *a priori* discipline of geometry that gives us knowledge of the material world. This is why Descartes refers in the last sentence of the *Fifth Meditation* to 'the whole of that corporeal nature which is the subject-matter of pure mathematics' (CSM II: 49/71). And God has imprinted on our minds this innate knowledge of the material world. As Descartes writes in *Discourse on the Method*:

> I have noticed certain laws which God has so established in nature, and of which he has implanted such notions in our minds, that after adequate reflection we cannot doubt that they are exactly observed in everything which exists or occurs in the world. (CSM I: 131/41)

Immutable essences

From here, Descartes proceeds to consider what he calls the 'immutable natures' or 'immutable essences' of particular things. The example he gives is that of a triangle, and he thinks that the triangle has an immutable nature even if no triangles 'exist anywhere outside me' (CSM II: 44/64). For example, it is part of the immutable nature of the triangle that its three angles equal two right angles. This is not something that depends on the human mind for its truth, for, says Descartes, he clearly recognises this property of the triangle whether he wants to or not (CSM II: 45/64). However, could he not have obtained the idea of a triangle from observation of many triangles and from there deduced its essential properties? If so, this would undermine the claim that his knowledge of the triangle is innate. No, he says, for he has the ideas of many figures that he has never seen in the world, and with these too it is possible to demonstrate their essential properties. Descartes' rationalism, his belief that our own reason and reflection are the sources of knowledge, is very much to the fore here.

review
activity

1. Explain in your own words Descartes' account of material substance.
2. Why does Descartes think there could not be a vacuum?
3. How does Descartes explain the variety of things we see about us in the world?

The ontological argument for the existence of God

The scene is now set for Descartes' ontological argument for the existence of God.

Descartes inspects his idea of God, just as he inspected his idea of a triangle. What he finds is that, just as the triangle has an immutable nature, so too does God. A key element in that immutable nature is God's existence. That is, just as the idea of a triangle cannot be separated from the fact that its three angles add up to two right angles, which tells us of the immutable nature or essence of the triangle, so the existence of God cannot be separated from the essence of God. It would be a contradiction to think of a triangle in which the three angles did not add up to two right angles. Similarly, it would be a contradiction to think of God without existence. It is the essence of God to exist. God could not *fail* to exist: he exists necessarily.

Why is it the essence of God to exist? Descartes' answer is that God is perfect and existence is a perfection. As Descartes says: '[I]t is just as much of a contradiction to think of God (that is, a supremely perfect being) lacking existence (that is, lacking perfection), as it is to think of a mountain without a valley' (CSM II: 46/66). And 'existence', he explicitly states, 'is one of the perfections' (CSM II: 46/67).

Descartes immediately raises two objections for himself. One is: how can we be sure that it is necessary to ascribe all perfections to God? Descartes' answer is basically that one should attend closely to one's idea of God and one will see that perfection is essential to him (CSM II: 46–7/67). The other is: it is true that a mountain cannot exist without a valley but it does not follow from this that there is any mountain in the world. So, 'similarly, it does not seem to follow from the fact that I think of God as existing that he does exist. For my thought does not impose any necessity on things' (CSM II: 46/66). But Descartes rejects this last challenge. He does so by repeating the point that 'existence is inseparable from God, and hence . . . he really exists' (CSM II: 46/67).

Descartes' ontological argument is open to some much-discussed objections. One is that it takes it that existence is a property, or, as it is often put, that 'existence is a predicate'. I shall not discuss this objection here because it is covered in some detail in the section of this book dealing with Anselm's argument for the existence of God, and the reader is referred to that discussion.

A second objection is the following. Even if we grant that existence is one of the perfections to be ascribed to a perfect being, it still does not follow that such a being exists. Johannes Caterus (d. 1656) made this point in the *First Set of Objections*:

> *Even if it is granted that a supremely perfect being carries the implication of existence in virtue of its very title, it still does not follow that the existence in question is anything actual in the real world; all that follows is that the concept of existence is inseparably linked to the concept of a supreme being. So you cannot infer that the existence of God is anything actual unless you suppose that the supreme being actually exists; for then it will actually contain all perfections, including the perfection of real existence.* (CSM II: 72/99)

Caterus' point can be seen better with the help of some comments by G.E.M. Anscombe (1919–2001) on Descartes' argument (Anscombe 1985).

Anscombe says that we should distinguish between *being a living thing* and *being alive*. That it belongs to the concept of something to be a living being does not prove that it is alive. Consider the dodo. It is part of the concept (the essence) of the dodo to be a *living being*. However, it is a living being of an extinct species. So, being a living being and being alive are not the same thing.

Similarly, *existing everlastingly* or *being the kind of thing to have an everlasting existence* is not the same as *being extant* or *always being extant*. It can be part of the concept of something to have everlasting life, but this does not prove that it is extant. So, it can be part of the concept of God to exist and yet God not exist.

As Caterus says, if he exists, he exists with all perfections, including the perfection of existence (if existence is a perfection). But this does not show that he *does* exist.

review
activity

1. Why does Descartes think that simply by reflecting on the idea of God we can prove that he exists?

2. What is Caterus' objection to Descartes' ontological argument?

Sixth Meditation

We turn now to the last of the *Meditations*. The *Sixth Meditation* contains a wealth of material and some of Descartes' most interesting ideas. We shall pick out and discuss a number of the key topics.

Imagination

Imagination establishes the probable existence of bodies

Reflection on the imagination is, Descartes says, helpful in establishing the *probable* existence of material objects. He begins by distinguishing the imagination from pure understanding or the intellect. He says that when imagining something one has an image of that thing before one's mind's eye. Thus to imagine a triangle is to 'see the three lines with my mind's eye as if they were present before me' (CSM II: 50/72). In the case of the intellectual apprehension of a triangle there is, presumably, no imagery. This introduces a limitation in the imagination *vis-à-vis* the intellect: the image before the mind in acts of imagination may be vague, as when I imagine a chiliagon (a figure with a thousand sides). In this case, I could not have a mental image of a 1000-sided figure that was clearly distinguishable from a mental image of a figure with, say, 999 sides.

This difference between the imagination and the understanding prepares the way for a more crucial point that Descartes wants to make. This is that 'this power of imagining which is in me, differing as it does from the power of understanding, is not a necessary constituent of my own essence, that is, of the essence of my mind' (CSM II: 51/73). Descartes says that he would remain the same individual even if he lacked the imagination. This allows him to say that the imagination seems to depend on 'something distinct from myself'. What could that something be? Descartes' answer is: the body. This is signalled right at the outset of the *Sixth Meditation*: 'For when I give more attentive consideration to what imagination is, it seems to be nothing else but an application of the cognitive faculty to a body which is intimately present to it, and which therefore exists' (CSM II: 50/71-2).

Why does Descartes think that the imagination involves – more strictly at this stage, *probably* involves – the body? The answer may lie in his claim that 'imagination requires a peculiar effort of mind which is not required for understanding' (CSM II: 51/73). The idea seems to be that because it can be *difficult* to imagine something – for example, a 1000-sided figure – imagination depends on something outside the mind for its operations. As he says: when the mind 'imagines, it turns towards the body and looks at something in the body which conforms to an idea understood by the mind or perceived by the senses' (CSM II: 51/73). We should not perhaps take the metaphors of 'turning towards' and 'looking at' too literally, but the basic point seems to be that if the imagination depends in some ways on the body for its operations then this could explain why it can be difficult to imagine things.

But in what sense *is* it difficult to imagine things? Is not intellectual thought sometimes more difficult than imagining? The answer is that, although Descartes would grant that intellectual effort can be just that – effort – and that it is easy to imagine some things, there is nonetheless a kind of immediacy and stability about the intellect that the imagination does not have. If, for example, I am asked to imagine a pentagon, this is easy. But the image can very easily 'slip away' from me or otherwise become unclear: the mind is, so to speak, easily distracted when imaging things, even things that in themselves are easy to imagine.

At any rate, Descartes thinks that the operations of the imagination give us *some* reason for thinking that material objects exist.

review activity

1. In what way does Descartes distinguish the imagination from the understanding?
2. What does he take this difference to suggest, and why?

Proof of material things and further reflections on their nature

Reflection on the imagination, we have seen, can only *suggest* that there are material objects. In this final *Meditation*, however, Descartes also gives a full argument to this conclusion.

He begins by noting that he experiences sensations which do not have their source in him, for they are 'produced without my cooperation and often even against my will' (CSM II: 55/79). He is just thinking here of the fact that if, for example, you open your eyes you simply see what is there, and have no choice in the matter. Descartes says that, because he is not the source of these sensations, there must be some source outside him. He makes three suggestions: a body, material in nature; God; or some creature nobler than a body – he probably has angels in mind. In the terminology previously explained, if it is body, then the cause will contain formally all that can be found objectively in the idea (effect); and if it is either God or some creature nobler than a body, the cause will contain eminently all that is in the idea (effect).

Descartes rules out the idea that the cause of his sensations of objects could be God. The reason he gives is that God is no deceiver (this was previously established). And God has given him no faculty for recognising God himself as the source of the sensations in question. However, God *would* be a deceiver if he caused such sensations and gave no faculty for recognising him to be such.

So God is not the cause of these sensations. The same considerations rule out the idea that some creature nobler than a body is the cause: God has given us no faculty for recognising such a creature to be the cause. Thus Descartes concludes: 'So I do not see how God could be understood to be anything but a deceiver if the ideas were transmitted from a source other than corporeal things. It follows that corporeal things exist' (CSM II: 55/80).

review activity

Why does Descartes rule God out as a cause for our sensations of material objects?

Descartes immediately goes on to note that, even though corporeal things exist, they may not all exist in a way that corresponds to the way in which his sensations of them reveals them to be. And this is, indeed, what Descartes believes to be the case: our senses reveal objects to have certain properties that are not 'in' those objects.

This is what Descartes is suggesting when he says that he has been 'taught by nature' to believe that 'any space in which nothing is occurring to stimulate my senses must be empty; or that the heat in a body is something exactly resembling the idea of heat which is in me; or that when a body is white or green, the selfsame whiteness or greenness which I perceive through my senses is present in the body; or that in a body which is bitter or sweet there is the selfsame taste which I experience, and so on' (CSM II: 56-7/82).

Later Descartes explicitly says that 'there is no convincing argument' to support any of these beliefs (CSM II: 57/83). In fact, he thought those beliefs all false. For example, as we saw when discussing the *Fifth Meditation*, he thought that there could be no vacuum: what seems to us to be a vacuum is, in fact, a space filled with fine matter, known as aether. Similarly, he thought that our sensations of the weight, hardness, colour and the like of material objects are misleading. As he says in the *Principles*:

> [T]he nature of matter, or body considered in general, consists not in its being something which is hard or heavy or coloured, or which affects the senses in any way, but simply in its being something which is extended in length, breadth and depth. For as regards hardness, our sensation tells us no more than that the parts of a hard body resist the motion of our hands when they come into contact with them. If, whenever our hands moved in a given direction, all the bodies in that area were to move away at the same speed as that of our approaching hands, we should never have any sensation of hardness. And since it is quite unintelligible to suppose that, if bodies did move away in this fashion, they would thereby lose their bodily nature, it follows that this nature cannot consist in hardness. By the same reasoning it can be shown that weight, colour, and all other such qualities that are perceived by the senses as being in corporeal matter, can be removed from it, while the matter itself remains intact; it thus follows that its nature does not depend on any of these qualities.
>
> (CSM I: 224/42)

*Primary and secondary
qualities*

Descartes is here articulating the distinction common to thinkers of his time between primary and secondary qualities. These have already been discussed at some length above, and so here I shall just draw attention to two interesting differences between Locke's account of primary and secondary qualities and Descartes' account.

The first is that Descartes does not, as Locke does, consider *solidity* a primary quality, a point made clear in the previous quotation.

The second difference is that Descartes does not accept the claim which Locke was later to make that, although our ideas of secondary qualities do not resemble anything in objects, our ideas of primary qualities do. That is, Descartes thought that even in the case of primary qualities our ideas of such qualities do not resemble the objects at all. He argues this in a work entitled *Optics* in which he discusses the fact that 'the perfection of an image often depends on its not resembling its object as much as it might' (CSM I: 165/113). The example he gives is that of

> *engravings: consisting simply of a little ink placed here and there on a piece of paper, they represent to us forests, towns, people, and even battles and storms; and although they make us think of countless different qualities in these objects, it is only in respect of shape that there is any real resemblance And even this resemblance is very imperfect, since engravings represent to us bodies of varying relief and depth on a surface which is entirely flat . . . Thus it often happens that in order to be more perfect as an image and to represent an object better, an engraving ought not to resemble it. Now we must think of the images formed in our brain in just the same way.* (CSM I: 165–6/113)

So it is clear that our ideas of objects do not resemble them. What is important in perception is not that our ideas resemble objects, but that we obtain the correct information about objects when we perceive them. Note that Descartes thinks that, although there is thus a sense in which our perceptions of material objects are misleading, for they have to be corrected by what the intellect tells us about the real nature of objects, such perceptions are perfectly adequate for everyday purposes:

> *For the proper purpose of the sensory perceptions given me by nature is simply to inform the mind of what is beneficial or harmful for the composite of which the mind is a part; and to this extent they are sufficiently clear and distinct.* (CSM II: 57/83)

Locke, unlike Descartes, did not believe in innate ideas. However, the fact that Descartes did raises an interesting issue in this area. For, if properties like colour are, for Descartes, not really 'in' external objects, then what is going on when we see colours? According to Descartes, God has decreed it that when a certain stimulus from an external object occurs then a certain idea will arise in the mind. However, this means that, according to Descartes, there is a sense in which *all* our ideas are innate. This, as well as the previous point about the lack of resemblance between our ideas and the objects that cause them, comes out in the following passage from a paper of Descartes' entitled *Comments on a Certain Broadsheet*:

> *[I]f we bear well in mind the scope of our senses and what it is exactly that*

reaches our faculty of thinking by way of them, we must admit that in no case are our ideas of things presented to us by the senses just as we form them in our thinking. So much so that there is nothing in our ideas which is not innate to the mind or the faculty of thinking, with the sole exception of those circumstances which relate to experience, such as the fact that we judge that this or that idea which we now have immediately before our mind refers to a certain thing situated outside us . . . Nothing reaches our mind from external objects through the sense organs except certain corporeal motions . . . But neither the motions themselves nor the figures arising from them are conceived by us exactly as they occur in the sense organs, as I have explained at length in my Optics. Hence it follows that the very ideas of the motions themselves and of the figures are innate in us. The ideas of pain, colours, sounds and the like must be all the more innate if, on the occasion of certain corporeal motions, our mind is to be capable of representing them to itself, for there is no similarity between these ideas and the corporeal motions.   (CSM I: 304/358–9)

review
activity

1.   Why does Descartes deny that solidity is a primary quality?

2.   What reason does Descartes give for thinking that *all* our ideas are innate?

The argument for the mind-body distinction

The first argument for the mind-body distinction

It is customary to look at two versions of the argument for the distinction between mind and body that Descartes gives, and we shall also do so. The first is found, not in the *Meditations*, but in the earlier *Discourse on the Method*. It runs:

> I examined attentively what I was. I saw that while I could pretend that I had no body and that there was no world and no place for me to be in, I could not for all that pretend that I did not exist . . . From this I knew I was a substance whose whole essence or nature is simply to think, and which does not require any place, or depend on any material thing, in order to exist. Accordingly this 'I' – that is, the soul by which I am what I am – is entirely distinct from the body . . . and would not fail to be whatever it is, even if the body did not exist.
>
>   (CSM I: 127/32-3)

The argument relies on doubting, for it claims that, from the fact that I can doubt the existence of the body whilst being unable to doubt the existence of the 'I', the thinking self, then the thinking self and the body are distinct. And the problem is that there are lots of things one could doubt which in fact are not the case. For example, I could doubt that George Eliot, the author of *Middlemarch*, is Marian Evans. But, in fact, they are one and the same person. Or I could doubt that the angles of a triangle add up to two right angles because I have not learnt any geometry. So, from the fact that I can doubt that my body exists whilst being unable to doubt that my mind exists shows nothing about whether the two really are distinct.

In the Preface to the *Meditations*, Descartes sought to respond to this objection:

> *My answer to this objection is that in that passage [of the* Discourse*] it was not my intention to make those exclusions [of anything physical from my essence] in an order corresponding to the actual truth of the matter (which I was not dealing with at that stage) but merely in a order corresponding to my own perception. So the sense of the passage was that I was aware of nothing at all that I knew belonged to my essence, except that I was a thinking thing, or a thing possessing within itself the faculty of thinking.* (CSM II: 7/8)

Descartes is claiming that the argument of the *Discourse* was intended to establish nothing more than his subjective sense of the relation of mind and body. However, he clearly thinks he can do better than this, for he ends the passage just quoted by saying that 'I shall, however, show below [in the *Meditations*] how it follows from the fact that I am aware of nothing else [than thought] belonging to my essence, that nothing else does in fact belong to it.'

The second argument for the mind-body distinction

So let us now turn to the argument of the *Meditations*. This runs as follows:

> *I know that everything which I clearly and distinctly understand is capable of being created by God so as to correspond exactly with my understanding of it. Hence the fact that I can clearly and distinctly understand one thing apart from another is enough to make me certain that the two things are distinct, since they are capable of being separated, at least by God . . . Thus, simply by knowing that I exist and seeing at the same time that absolutely nothing else belongs to my nature or essence except that I am thinking thing, I can infer correctly that my essence consists solely in the fact that I am a thinking thing . . . I have a clear and distinct idea of myself, in so far as I am simply a thinking, non-extended thing. And accordingly, it is certain that I am really distinct from my body, and can exist without it.* (CSM II: 54/78)

Clearly there is one way in which this argument is different from that in the *Discourse*: whereas the latter depended on doubt, the former depends on what can be clearly and distinctly perceived, whence it is known as the 'argument from clear and distinct perception'. It involves the idea that one can achieve a clear and distinct perception of one's essence, as one could, so Descartes argued, achieve a clear and distinct perception of the essence of a triangle, or of God. And, of course, one's essence is supposed to be thinking and nothing else.

Indivisibility of mind, divisibility of body

Descartes' view that the mind and body are quite distinct was reinforced by his view that mind is indivisible whereas body is not. He says:

> *[T]here is a great difference between the mind and the body, inasmuch as the body is by its very nature always divisible, while the mind is utterly indivisible. For when I consider the mind, or myself in so far as I am merely a thinking thing, I am unable to distinguish any parts within myself; I understand myself to be something quite single and complete. Although the whole mind seems to be united to the whole body, I recognize that if a foot or arm or any other part of the body is cut off, nothing has thereby been taken away from the mind.* (CSM II: 59/85–6)

Descartes is surely right that there is something odd about the idea that the mind could be divided: the notion of having half a mind in a literal way seems to make no sense. On the other hand, we are used to the idea that the mind may contain many different parts, some of which – for example, unconscious motives – are hidden from us. Descartes would have disagreed with this, saying that the mind is 'transparent' to itself. However, the mind could be a thinking thing and yet still not be wholly transparent to itself.

The most serious problem with Descartes' view in the previous quotation is that, although it is true that one can lose a foot without losing the mind, it is far from clear that one can lose one's brain without losing the mind. Thus, if I lost half a leg my mind would survive, but if lost half my brain my mind would not survive as it is now. Given this, it seems highly likely that if my brain were destroyed then my mind would cease to exist altogether. This, however, is not accepted by Descartes: he thought that the mind could survive the total destruction of the body.

Let us return to Descartes' main argument in the *Meditations* for the 'real distinction', as it is often put, between mind and body.

In the *Fourth Set of Objections,* Arnauld raised the following objection to Descartes' argument. In a right-angled triangle the area of the square on the hypotenuse is equal to the sum of the areas of the squares on the other two sides. This is known as Pythagoras' theorem. Now, it is certainly true that someone could clearly and distinctly perceive that a given triangle was a right-angled triangle, without clearly and distinctly seeing that Pythagoras' theorem applies to it – say, because he has not done much geometry. If so, could he argue that it does not belong to the essence of a right-angled triangle that this theorem applies to it? It seems to follow on Descartes' reasoning that this would be so. But that is absurd.

So, in short, the objection is that from the fact that Descartes can clearly and distinctly see that he could exist without a body, it does not follow that he could exist without a body. Perhaps he needs a body in order to exist. Indeed, this is precisely what many or even most people now believe, for there are good reasons to think that the existence of the human mind depends on the brain.

Descartes never managed to answer the objection that has been raised. He continued to believe that a human being is made up of a non-extended immaterial thinking substance (mind) and an extended material non-thinking substance (body). In the next section we shall see how he thought they are related.

review activity

1. What are Descartes' arguments for the real distinction between mind and body?

2. What mistake does Descartes seem to make in his arguments for this distinction?

Relations between mind and body

It is a common experience of everyday life that body and mind are in causal interaction. This causal interaction can go from mind to body, as when your desire (mental event) to eat an apple leads you to move out your arm (physical event) towards the fruit. Or it can go from body to mind, as when a kick on your shin (physical event) causes you to decide (mental event) to run away.

Descartes was well aware, of course, not merely of these facts but also that there is, so to speak, a peculiar *intimacy* between a given person's mind and body. Descartes expresses this in one of the most famous passages of his work.

> *I am not present in my body as a sailor is present in a ship, but . . . I am very closely joined and, as it were, intermingled with it, so that I and the body form a unit. If this were not so, I, who am nothing but a thinking thing, would not feel pain when the body was hurt, but would perceive the damage purely by the intellect, just as a sailor perceives by sight if anything in his ship is broken.*
>
> (CSM II: 56/81)

Body and soul are intermingled

Descartes also mentions the experience of hunger and thirst as showing how 'intermingled' body and mind are (CSM II: 56/80; cf. 52–3/76). There is no doubt that what Descartes writes here is correct. I am not in my body as a sailor is in his ship. But this raises two key questions for Descartes.

Remember that Descartes has said that a human being is made up of an immaterial, non-extended thinking mind and a material, extended thoughtless body. So the first problem is this. Why is my experience of being in my body as it is? If I am a purely thinking thing, then what one would expect is that I *would* be in my body as a sailor is in his ship (Descartes' words in the last quoted passage suggest as much). If my foot were damaged, for example, I would notice this as a sailor might notice some damage to the hull of his ship. There would be cause for alarm in both cases, but in both the perception of the damage would be, so to speak, purely intellectual. There would not be the *experience*, the *felt quality*, of the pain. But things are not like that, for, of course, Descartes is right: when my body is damaged I *feel* the pain. My apprehension of my pain is not purely intellectual.

It seems that Descartes' official view that mind and body are independent substances cannot make sense of the fact that mind and body are, as he says, 'intermingled'.

How can mind and body interact?

However, there is a second, more fundamental problem. This is that, given Descartes' account of mind and body there seems no way in which they can interact with one another. How can a non-extended, immaterial thinking substance interact with an extended, material non-thinking substance? How *can* a mind so conceived make the body move? And how *can* the mind be affected by goings on to and in the body? Mind and body are defined as being so utterly unlike one another that it is hard, to say the least, to see how they can interact.

Descartes was never able to explain how mind and body interact, lamely remarking that, even though he had no answer to the problem, we can be sure from experience that mind and body do interact. In fact, so severe is the problem of mind-body interaction on Descartes' principles that a later follower of his, Nicolas Malebranche, suggested that it is the will of God that explains how mind and body interact: when, for example, I want (mental event) to eat something, my arm moves out (physical event) to pick up, say,

Nicolas Malebranche
(1638–1715)

some bread because God wills that my arm should move consequent on my having this desire.

Occasionalism and 'the ghost in the machine'

This doctrine is known as 'occasionalism' because such an event as my having a desire is the *occasion* for God's willing that something move, for example, that my arm move. The theory is extremely extravagant and hard to accept, especially perhaps in the modern age, but in many ways it ties in neatly with Descartes' view that any created thing only remains in existence because of God's sustaining power. Yet the persistent failure to solve the problem of how mind and body interact on Descartes' account of them led eventually to Gilbert Ryle (1900–76) dubbing Descartes' view the theory of the 'ghost in the machine' (Ryle 1949).

The pineal gland

We note in passing that, although Descartes acknowledged that he could not explain *how* body and mind interact, he nonetheless thought he had explained *where* they interact. For he believed that the point of interaction was the pineal gland, a small gland situated in the centre of the brain. Unfortunately, it remains unclear how it could be that mind, as Descartes conceived it, could have any spatial location at all, because it is non-extended and immaterial. To be able to say *where* a non-extended, immaterial substance is seems to be bordering on the unintelligible – whether the location be one gland or the whole body, as the intermingling thesis would have it.

review activity

1. What does Descartes mean by saying that I am not in my body as a sailor is in his ship?

2. Why are mind-body interactions difficult to explain on Descartes' view of mind and body?

Sensory error and the goodness of God

In the *Fourth Meditation* Descartes had worried about how it is that God's goodness is consistent with the fact that I make errors of judgement from time to time. If God is good – no deceiver – and has made my mind, why is it that my mind can go astray at times? Would a good God not have made me with a mind that always arrives at the truth? Descartes' answer to this question is that it is through the free exercise of our will which, so to speak, 'outruns' our judgement, that we can make errors in understanding.

In the *Sixth Meditation* Descartes raises the same problem in the area of sensory experience: how is it that human beings can make mistakes in their sensory judgements? For example, someone who is ill with dropsy wants drink when to drink would be harmful. Or someone else feels pain in an amputated limb. Why did God not make us such that if we are ill with dropsy we do not want to drink or that if we lose a limb we can never feel pain in it? Would a good God not have made us in that way?

Descartes assesses one possible answer to this. He considers a clock that tells the wrong time because it is broken in some way. In this case, the parts of the clock still obey all the laws of nature, but the clock departs from its intended function – the function that the clockmaker intended for it.

Perhaps a diseased human is like the inaccurate clock. Such a body will still follow the laws of nature laid down by God, but has malfunctioned – has departed from fulfilling the function God intended for it. So if the dropsical person wants a drink, God cannot be held responsible for this.

Descartes rejects this answer on the grounds that this solution depends on considering the body by itself, rather than when the soul is intermingled with it. What makes the dropsical person want drink is not simply that the body is malfunctioning but that the mind reacts to the body in a certain way. This is what he seems to mean by distinguishing two senses of 'nature': the first is with reference to the body only, which he calls 'merely . . . an extraneous label'; the second refers to the mind and body together, which is 'a true error of nature' (CSM II: 59/85). It is the latter kind of error that needs to be explained.

Descartes' answer to the problem is as follows. The mind and body interact at one point, namely, the brain or one part of the brain (CSM II: 59/86). Because this is so the brain has to rely on 'signals' arriving from the nerves. These nerves are made from matter. Suppose now that a stab in the foot causes a 'motion' in the brain. The signal for this has to travel up the foot, through the nerves in the leg and spinal cord, and to the brain. Suppose now that the subject feels a blow to the leg. Then the same nerves will be activated as are activated when the foot is damaged. It is thus possible that, from a blow in the leg, the subject could feel a pain in the foot. Similarly, the stomach may cause nerves to be activated in such a way as to make someone want to drink even though drinking is in fact harmful.

So, nerves can be activated midstream, so to speak, and thus give misleading information. Why did God design things so? Descartes' answer is that overall this design is the 'best system', even though it sometimes goes wrong. This is because each motion of the brain has just one meaning. As Descartes says:

> [A]*ny given movement occurring in the part of the brain that immediately affects the mind produces just one corresponding sensation; and hence the best system which could be devised is that it should produce the one sensation which, of all possible sensations, is most especially and most frequently conducive to the preservation of the healthy man.* (CSM II: 60/87)

In other words, nearly always when we feel thirsty it will be good for us to drink and it is best that things be set up in this way. Occasionally things go wrong, but no better system could be designed.

review activity

1. Why is it a problem for Descartes that we can make sensory errors?
2. What solution does Descartes give to this problem?

The removal of scepticism

Descartes ends the *Sixth Meditation* by saying that now his earlier thoughts about the dreaming hypothesis seem to him to be 'laughable'. He sees that he can, after all, tell the difference between sleeping and waking experience. This is partly, he says, because so much of what goes on in dreams is weird. But could he not be dreaming, yet his dream not be weird at all? This is no longer a real option for Descartes, for God's goodness guarantees that he can believe what all his senses, working with memory and intellect, tell him (CSM II: 62/90). Here, as elsewhere in Descartes' philosophy, we depend in the end on God for our knowledge.

some questions to think about

1   Does Descartes' method of clear and distinct ideas answer the hyperbolical doubt?

2   How important is God in Descartes' philosophy?

3   Does Descartes have a good answer to the problem of the Cartesian circle?

4   How plausible is Descartes' claim that God has provided us with innate knowledge of the material world?

5   How good is Descartes' argument for the existence of material objects?

6   Could it be true, as Descartes suggests, that *all* our ideas are innate?

7   What can be said in defence of Descartes' claim that there is a real distinction between mind and body?

8   How satisfactory is Descartes' explanation of how we make sensory errors?

further reading

▶ Hatfield 2003 is a very detailed introduction to Descartes' *Meditations*, with lots of useful material concerning Descartes' intellectual background. Kenny 1968 is good and clear. Wilson 1986 is also helpful. Mention should be made of the following collections of essays on Descartes: Doney (ed.) 1967; Rorty (ed.) 1986; Cottingham (ed.) 1992; Cottingham (ed.) 1998. See also the further reading section of the chapter on the theory of knowledge in this book.

Marx and Engels: The German Ideology

important terms

Alienation: a term used to indicate some form of a sense of meaninglessness by which individuals are afflicted in their activities.

Base: the forces of production and the relations of production that together determine the superstructure. The forces of production themselves determine the relations of production.

Bourgeoisie: the ruling class under capitalism; the owners of the forces of production.

Civil society: trade and industrial relations, as well as more informal forms of association, between people.

Forces of production: the equipment necessary for making things, for example, machines and raw materials.

Ideology: a set of ideas – the dominant ideology is the ideology which serves the interests of the dominant class.

Proletariat: the working class under capitalism.

Karl Marx (1818–83)

Marx: life and works

Karl Marx was born in Trier in Germany in 1818. He studied at the universities of Bonn and Berlin, completing a doctoral thesis that was accepted at the university of Jena. He had hoped to get a university post in order to pursue an academic career, but, failing in his attempt to do so, turned to journalism instead. He became the editor of the *Rheinische Zeitung* and then of the short-lived *Deutsch-Französische Jahrbücher*, which was published in Paris where Marx lived from October 1843 to January 1845. In the meantime he had married Jenny von Westphalen. Around this time his collaboration with Engels began and in 1846 Marx and Engels set up a network of communist correspondence committees to keep German, French and English socialists informed about each other's activities. In June 1847 the Communist League was set up.

When Marx was expelled from Paris for his radical views, he went to live in Brussels. In 1848 there were revolutions in France and Germany. Marx had supported the revolutionary movement by publishing a radical newspaper in Cologne, the *Neue Rheinische Zeitung*. However, the revolutions were more or less crushed by the summer and Marx decided to leave for London. In London, he lived with his family in a variety of places. He had very little money and got by thanks to gifts from Engels and through journalistic work, including being European correspondent for the *New York Daily Tribune*, although his English was, at first, so poor that Engels wrote many of the articles for him, which Marx then sent off under his own name. However, he spent most of his time researching in the British Library.

In 1864 Marx inherited some money and moved with his family to Haverstock Hill. From the same time he was heavily involved in the International Working Men's Association, an organisation that dissolved in 1872 owing to an argument between Marx and Mikhail Bakunin (1814–76), an exiled Russian anarchist.

Marx's wife died in 1881. Marx himself died in 1883. He is buried in Highgate Cemetery in London.

Principal works: *Economic and Philosophical Manuscripts* (1844); (with Engels) *The German Ideology* (1846); (with Engels) *The Communist Manifesto* (1848); *Grundrisse* (1857-8); *Capital* (1865–) (the three volumes were never completed).

important terms

Relations of production: the social arrangements of a given period of history, specifically those having to do with who owns what.

State: political organisation of a body of people for the maintenance of order. The liberal state has the task of guaranteeing that all have the same basic rights and are equal before the law. According to Marx and Engels, the state will wither under communism.

Superstructure: the legal, moral, political and religious aspects of society. It is also often taken to include forms of social organisation such as the family.

Friedrich Engels (1820–95)

Engels: life and works

Friedrich Engels was born in Barmen, a highly industrialised part of Germany near Düsseldorf, in 1820. His father was a wealthy businessman, owning factories in both Germany and Manchester. Engels left school at the age of 16 in order to enter the family business, the training for which he received in Barmen and Bremen. In April 1841 he left Bremen to do his military service in Berlin, which lasted a year. In 1842 he travelled to Cologne to meet the editors of the *Rheinische Zeitung*, for which he was writing, and met Marx for the first time. The meeting was rather inauspicious, but when they met again in 1844 they got on very well, and thus began their lifelong friendship.

Engels worked from 1842–4 at his father's factory in Manchester, which furnished materials for his book *The Condition of the Working Class in England,* and then, from 1844–7, he lived in Brussels, close to Marx. The two friends made a trip to England in 1846, with Engels acting as a guide.

After the failed revolutions of 1848, Engels made a walking tour of France, heading for Switzerland, where he remained until mid-January 1849. From November 1850 he worked for his father's factory in Manchester, using his spare time to support the communist movement. He found business boring, and retired early in 1869. In 1870, he moved to London, living about 15 minutes' walk from Marx. The two men saw each other regularly. Engels continued to work for the communist cause, in 1888 visiting the US for two months. He died in 1895. His body was cremated and his ashes were scattered off Beachy Head in Sussex.

Principal works: *The Condition of the Working Class in England* (1845); (with Marx) *The German Ideology* (1846); (with Marx) *The Communist Manifesto* (1848); *Anti-Dühring* (1877-8); *The Origin of the Family, Private Property and the State* (1884).

A note on the text

The German Ideology (hereafter, GI) was written largely between the end of 1845 and the middle of 1846. Marx and Engels could not find a publisher for the work, and it was not published until 1932, long after they were both dead and by which time parts of the text were lost. The original manuscript was written in Engels' hand, largely because Marx's handwriting was almost completely illegible. It is not certain what the exact contribution of each man was to the ideas of the text, though in general Marx provided the intellectually more powerful side of their writing partnership. The text in the German original is around 700 pages long, and most of it is of merely historical interest. The English version of the text, which forms the basis of the discussion in this chapter, is an abridged version, edited and introduced by C.J. Arthur, and published by Lawrence & Wishart. This includes the philosophically most interesting parts of the book as well as the 'Theses on Feuerbach' which Marx wrote alone in 1845 before work was begun on GI.

Hegel and Feuerbach

In order properly to understand *GI* – indeed, the work of Marx and Engels as a whole – it is important to have some understanding of the work of Hegel and Feuerbach, because both of these thinkers had a profound effect on Marx and Engels.

The philosophies of Hegel and Feuerbach are extremely complicated, however, and thus only a very brief overview of the key points necessary for understanding their impact on Marx and Engels can be given here.

Mind

Hegel was very interested in history. In particular, he was interested in the development in history of what he called *Geist*. *Geist* may be translated as 'Spirit' or 'Mind'. There is a great deal of controversy amongst scholars of Hegel concerning just what he meant by Mind. In some way Mind resembles the God of Christian theology, but it is not clear how far Hegel meant such an identification to be taken, for he sometimes seems to understand Mind as the world as a whole – a view that is usually called 'pantheism'. At any rate, he certainly thought of Mind as different from individual human minds, such as my mind and your mind: Hegel's concept Mind seems to be some kind of universal Mind.

G.W.F. Hegel (1770–1831)

The separate minds of individual human beings are, according to Hegel, manifestations or aspects of universal Mind.

Mind, as Hegel understands things, and as one can guess from the term itself, is non-material: it is not a thing one could point to as one can point to tables and chairs, to human beings and animals. Yet this non-materiality of Mind does not make it unimportant in Hegel's eyes. On the contrary, the nature of Mind forms, in one way or another, the central concern of his philosophical work. Indeed, according to Hegel, the change and progress of history is best understood as the change and progress of Mind.

What Hegel means is roughly the following. The aim of Mind is to come to know itself, that is, to come to know its own being or nature. An analogy may help to understand this. An artist, we often think, expresses himself in his work. For example, a poet may express his feelings or moods in a poem that he writes. But sometimes he does not know before he writes the poem exactly what it is that he is feeling. He might have a vague feeling of uneasiness or sadness, for example, but not know exactly what the uneasiness or sadness is. Then, as he writes the poem, he gradually comes to a true realisation of just what his feeling is. This is why, when the poem is finished, he will be able to say that through the writing of it he has finally understood exactly what it is that he is feeling. A reader of the poem may have the same experience. He, too, feels sad or lonely but does not really know what that sadness or loneliness is, and then he read the poet's work and exclaims: 'Yes, that's it! That's just how I feel!' In this case, both the poet and the reader come to understand better the nature of their own mind through expression; the poet by directly expressing his mind, the reader by seeing that what the poet has written is the best expression of what he too is feeling. In general, we can say that one often comes to know one's own mind better by expressing it in some way.

Mind's self-expression Hegel thinks of Mind as working in something like this way. He thinks of Mind as expressing itself in the world in order to come to know itself as the poet expresses his mind in his poetry and thus comes to understand himself better. There are two ways in which Mind thus expresses itself: in nature and in history. We can concentrate on the latter.

Alienation According to Hegel, the different historical epochs, with all their differences from each other and all their turmoil and change, constitute Mind's attempt to come to know itself. The way in which it tries to come to know itself involves the overcoming of conflicts or obstacles. For example, in history we see a great deal of conflict in which individuals seek to destroy or otherwise triumph over other individuals – wars, power struggles and so on. In such conflict, one individual is an obstacle to another. However, as we have already noted, individual minds are, for Hegel, aspects of the universal Mind. What this means is that Mind is in conflict with itself on account of the conflict between individual minds. This state of self-conflict Hegel calls *alienation*: Mind is alienated from itself insofar as it is in conflict with itself.

The movement of history is, as already noted, Mind's attempt to know itself. When it does finally come to know itself, conflict is ended. When conflicts end – for example, when wars end – we usually experience a sense of freedom. So, Hegel says, the end of Mind's conflict with itself involves the beginning of true freedom for human beings. So we can say that Mind aims through history to overcome its alienation from itself and to come to self-knowledge and freedom. The freedom and self-knowledge of Mind is the freedom and self-knowledge of individual minds – that is, of human beings.

For Hegel, the path of history thus makes sense; it is rational. Moreover, Hegel's conception of history is *teleological*, for it has a *telos* (Greek for 'goal' or 'aim').

One odd consequence of Hegel's theory is that Mind has come finally to know itself in Hegel's own writings. The goal of history, which is Mind's knowledge of itself, occurs in Hegel himself. In this sense, Hegel seemed to think that history had come to an end in his work, which heralded the beginning of a realm of freedom for mankind.

Since history reaches its goal when Mind comes to know itself in the kind of way described, the basic motor of history on Hegel's account is *thought*. In other words, according to Hegel, it is *ideas* and their change and development that we must understand if we wish to understand history and the individual human beings who make up history. (This does not mean that, on Hegel's account of history, we can ignore the material world. It just means, as we have seen, that we have to understand the material world in a particular way.)

review activity

1. What does Hegel mean by Mind?

2. Explain in your own word Hegel's conception of alienation.

3. What, according to Hegel, happens when Mind comes to know itself?

Right Hegelians and Left/Young Hegelians

Hegel had an enormous influence on German philosophy at the time, and he had plenty of followers. However, after his death his followers split into two camps. The so-called Right Hegelians believed that Mind had come to know itself in the contemporary Prussian state. The so-called Left or Young Hegelians believed that this was not so. They believed that human beings had not fully achieved freedom. The Young Hegelians believed that human beings were still in a condition of alienation. One of the most important of these Young Hegelians was Ludwig Feuerbach (1804–72), and he attempted to describe this alienation as he understood it.

God as a projection

In order to do this, Feuerbach turned to reflect on religion. In a traditional philosophical account of Christian belief, God is the creator and sustainer of the universe, wholly good, omniscient (all-knowing), omnipotent (all-powerful) and immutable. According to Feuerbach, there is no such God, but this left him with the problem of explaining how it is that human beings acquire the idea of such a God if he does not exist. Feuerbach argues that God is, in fact, the projection of all of the ideal qualities of human beings onto a mythical being. That is, God is just a fictitious being who unites in himself the idealised features of human nature. The consequence is that man is aware of himself as being far from wholly good, limited in his knowledge and strength, and subject to all kinds of changes and fluctuations in his nature. At the same time, he is aware of God as perfect. The consequence is that man is divided against himself: he measures himself in all the frailty of his nature against a perfect being, who is nothing more than an idealisation of himself, and can only conclude that he is contemptible in comparison with God. This division of man against himself, Feuerbach says, constitutes man's alienation, and Feuerbach argues that for man to overcome his alienation he must understand what God really is, that is, a projection of the idealised qualities of man.

Feuerbach certainly believed that there was some important connection between thought, including religious thought, and the material conditions of life, for example people's relations with each other, the food they eat, what they drink and so on. However, it is possible to interpret Feuerbach as failing to have a proper understanding of these connections and as thus holding to the view that, ultimately, man's alienation lies in his thought, in his having false beliefs and ideas. This, at any rate, was the way Marx and Engels read him (cf. Wartofsky 1982: 20–1; cf. also Marx's Ninth Thesis on Feuerbach, discussed in more detail later).

review
activity

1. Explain in your own words Feuerbach's notion of God.

2. What does Feuerbach mean by 'alienation'?

Marx and Engels' critique of the Young Hegelians

In *GI*, Marx and Engels took over an interest in history from Hegel, as well as the belief that man is alienated from himself, although they altered his understanding both of history and of alienation, as we shall see. However, as I hinted above, they rejected Feuerbach's central idea as they interpreted it, namely that man can cure his alienation by adjusting the way he *thinks* about himself in the world, that his problem is that he has false *beliefs*. In fact, they saw all the Young Hegelians as caught up in this mistake. This is, indeed, the German ideology: according to Marx and Engels it is a piece of ideology on the part of German thinkers to suppose that it is by adjusting or changing his beliefs that man can overcome his alienation. This is why the book carries the title it does. One of the aims of *GI* is to break with this way of looking at things. For this reason, Marx and Engels speak at the outset of *GI* in mocking tones of the revolutions that are 'supposed to have taken place in the realm of pure thought' (*GI:* 39). They believed that all of this was fantasy, because the Young Hegelians had remained trapped in the basic premise of Hegel's philosophy, which is that 'the relationships of men, all their doings, their chains and their limitations are products of their consciousness' (*GI:* 41), that is, that what men and women *think and believe* determines how they behave and relate to one another and the world. This was an idea which Marx and Engels rejected.

In fact, Marx and Engels go further than this, for they believed that the Young Hegelians had remain trapped in religious thought. This view receives some support from the fact that two of the Young Hegelians they had in mind, David Friedrich Strauss and Feuerbach himself, had devoted themselves to an elucidation of the meaning of religious thinking, Strauss in *The Life of Jesus* and Feuerbach in his *The Essence of Christianity.*

David Friedrich Strauss
(1808–74)

Strauss and Feuerbach were sceptical about religious belief in various ways. We have already seen something of this in connection with Feuerbach, and in the case of Strauss this comes out in the fact that in his book he interprets the life of Jesus in mythic terms, stripping many of the events of Jesus' life of their literal meaning (in fact, Strauss lost his post at the University of Tübingen after publishing his book because it was so unorthodox). Nonetheless, Marx and Engels claim that the Young Hegelians saw too many of man's relations and activities – such as politics and morality – fundamentally in religious terms. They believed that the Young Hegelians thought that the fundamental aspect of individuals' relations to one another and to the world was religious. To Marx and Engels, the Young Hegelians' *criticisms* of religion only confirmed the idea that they, the Young Hegelians, were trapped in the toils of religious thought. This comes out in their criticism of another of this group, Max Stirner (1806–56), whose real name was Kaspar Schmidt.

Most of Marx and Engels' criticisms of Stirner have been excised from the text edited by C.J. Arthur because, as Sidney Parker remarks in his introduction to a recent edition of Stirner's main work, *The Ego and Its Own,* Marx and Engels' attack on Stirner 'is undoubtedly one of the most indigestible pieces of polemical vituperation ever composed' (Stirner 1982: ix). Nonetheless, it is worth saying a few brief words about their attack on him.

Marx and Engels often refer to Stirner in their text as 'Saint Max', 'Sancho' and 'the Unique'. The reason for the last epithet is to be found in the final chapter of Stirner's book, which is entitled 'The Unique One' and refers to Stirner himself. 'Sancho' is the name of Don Quixote's companion in the famous novel *Don Quixote* by the Spanish writer Cervantes (1547–1616). Marx and Engels wanted to ridicule Stirner as the companion of the feckless and rather absurd Don. As to calling Stirner 'Saint Max', this derived from the fact that Stirner saw 'the Holy' everywhere. That is to say, he believed, as did the other Young Hegelians, that human beings have hitherto 'constantly made up false conceptions about themselves, about what they are and what they ought to be', which they took to be holy and accordingly they 'have bowed down before their own creations' (GI: 37). For Stirner, it was not just that human beings had invented a notion of God before whom they bowed down; Stirner rejected anything and everything that stood over against the individual, including not simply religion but also morality, politics and the demands of society. Nonetheless, Marx and Engels believed that Stirner had not released himself from religious thought because, as they read him, he thought that mankind could release itself from its worship of its own creations by *thinking correctly* about what these creations are, that is, seeing them as they really are, namely false creations of the human mind. So, when Marx and Engels called Stirner 'Saint Max' they did not mean simply to say that he basically saw religious categories everywhere but also that he remained trapped in such categories on account of his faith in the power of thought to release human beings from their wretched state.

Marx and Engels were themselves certainly hostile to religious belief, but they did not believe that human beings could overcome their alienation simply by divesting themselves of such belief. This is because they thought that the reason why human beings resort to religious belief is that their ordinary, everyday life is full of contradictions and conflict. This is the point that Marx makes in his Fourth Thesis on Feuerbach (GI: 122). So, for Marx and Engels, it is not merely necessary to cast off religious belief. It is also necessary to cast off the conflicts of secular, everyday life. What these conflicts are we shall see throughout our discussion of GI.

review
activity

1. What, according to Marx and Engels, is the German ideology?

2. In what way did Marx and Engels think the Young Hegelians had remained trapped in the categories of religious thought?

State and civil society

Before going any further we should clarify the notions of state and civil society. In liberal political theory there is an important distinction between these two. The state has the task of making and enforcing laws and ensuring the maintenance of basic political rights. In a liberal state, everyone is politically equal in that, in principle, all have the same basic rights and are equal before the law. All are *citizens* of the state. Civil society is made up of all those relations between individuals that involve informal relations, as well as relations in trade and industry. Morality is seen as part of, and emergent from, civil society.

In an early essay, 'On the Jewish Question', Marx had argued that there is a problem in the way liberal political thought conceives of the state and civil society (Marx 1977: 39–62). In declaring the members of the state to be citizens and in thinking of them as equal in this way, he thought, the state ignores their real differences. These differences – differences in wealth, education, religion, race and so on – are deemed irrelevant to their being citizens and are thus thought of simply as features of their existence as members of civil society. However, according to Marx, this leaves civil society as a realm of domination, exploitation and conflict. Another way to put this point is to say that the notion of citizenship and egalitarianism in a liberal state is almost entirely abstract. This leaves the real problems of association between human beings unaddressed and thus unsolved.

Materialism

Marx and Engels'
materialism

In claiming, as we saw earlier, that it is mistaken to suppose that what human beings think and believe determines how they behave, Marx and Engels had something very specific in mind. They could not seriously have denied, of course, that, for example, the fact that you *want* a glass of water and *believe* you can get one by going into the kitchen explains why it is that you go into the kitchen to get water from the tap. In this sense, they would not have denied that things that go on in the mind influence how people behave, for it is clear that your desire for water and your belief that you can get some by going into the kitchen are things that go on in your mind that lead you to behave in a certain way. What they were interested in was, rather, how it is that people come to have the kinds of desires and beliefs they do have. That is, they were interested in answering the question: Where do beliefs and desires come from? Of course, Marx and Engels would not have claimed that they could explain where every single individual belief or desire that anyone has comes from (for example, my desire now to eat, say, an orange). What they thought they could explain was where the most important or fundamental desires and beliefs which people have come from – for example, moral and political beliefs and desires. They claimed to be able to do this by considering the *material* conditions of human beings' life. This is why their view is called *materialism*.

When Marx and Engels spoke of materialism, they had a number of things in mind. Two of the concepts central to Marx and Engels' materialism were labour and action.

Labour

Labour

Marx and Engels suggest that if we are properly to understand human life, we must start by a consideration of how it is that human beings acquire the kind of necessities they need to survive from one day to the next. This involves a consideration of their material conditions in the sense of how it is that they labour to gain food, shelter and so on. In fact, Marx and Engels see this as the key to the difference between man and animals: man must *labour* to gain his subsistence, whereas this is clearly not the case so far as animals are concerned. Hence they wrote: 'Men ... begin to distinguish themselves from animals as soon as they begin to produce their means of subsistence' (*GI*: 42). It is labour which makes human beings what they are. Thus: 'The nature of individuals ... depends on the material conditions determining production' (*GI*: 42).

Action (praxis)

Marx and Engels' account of sensuousness

Labour involves action or praxis. Marx and Engels thus see man's actions as crucial in order to understand him. As we have seen, they believed that it is no good trying to understand human beings by seeing what they *think;* one must try to see what they *do.* This is what Marx means in criticising Feuerbach in the first of his theses on him. In that thesis, Marx complains that Feuerbach believes that human beings show themselves as they truly are when they *contemplate* ideas and the world around them. Apart from the fact that, as far as Marx is concerned, this *directly* leaves out the labouring activity of men and women, this also, Marx believes, fails to acknowledge that material objects only exist for contemplation because they are there as a result of human labour. This is what Marx means in the Fifth Thesis by saying that Feuerbach 'does not conceive sensuousness [that is, seeing material objects] as *practical,* human-sensuous activity' (*GI*: 122). Thus, Marx and Engels mention the fact that if, for example, one were to contemplate the material existence of a cherry tree in the sense of looking at it, then one should not forget that there are cherry trees in Western Europe only as a result of human labour: the cherry tree was imported from abroad and is not native to Western Europe (*GI*: 62). To see a cherry tree and fail to see it in the context of human labour is to fail to grasp properly what it is, for what it *is,* is given in part by its place in this context. The same might obviously be said of tables and chairs, but also, less obviously, of forests, rivers and mountains: for these have all been, to a greater or lesser extent, modified by the hand of man. As Marx and Engels point out, there is hardly any part of nature that has not been so modified: exceptions, when they were writing, might have been parts of Australia (*GI*: 63), but perhaps even this would be doubtful now.

We saw earlier that Marx and Engels believed Feuerbach's materialism was inadequate. We can now see more clearly why. For Marx believed, as he put it in the Ninth Thesis on Feuerbach, that Feuerbach's materialism was merely a 'contemplative materialism' because it leaves out 'practical activity' (*GI*: 123).

review
activity

1. Explain in your own words Marx and Engels' conceptions of

    a) labour

    b) praxis.

Materialism as Marx and Engels understand it involves at least two other notions besides labour and action. These are: the relation between base and superstructure; and the scientific status of their views. We shall defer discussion of these until later.

The materialist conception of history

Historical materialism

Marx and Engels were not simply interested in materialism, however. They were, as already mentioned, also interested in history, that is, in discovering how and why history changes. Thus their materialism is, in fact, *historical materialism*, and GI gives the first statement of historical materialism in the work of Marx and Engels, though some of the details remained to be worked out in later writings. The theory consists of a number of different ideas related together in sometimes complex ways and in one way or another the rest of our discussion will concern itself with Marx and Engels' historical materialism. ('Historical materialism' is not a term that Marx and Engels used, but it has now become common practice to use this term in the context of their work.)

Forces of production

In any given society human beings have to produce the things that satisfy their wants and needs, for example, things that satisfy their hunger and thirst, their need for shelter and so on. In order to produce these things, they make use of what Marx and Engels call *forces of production* or *productive forces*. Examples of productive forces include natural resources (such as coal, oil and trees); raw materials (such as wood and cotton); and the machines necessary to produce things people want (such as steam engines, turbines and looms). Productive forces also include the labour of individuals. Examples of labour include physical exertion (such as is necessary when working on a building site) and technical know-how (such as an understanding of how computers work, how to programme them and so on).

Relations of production

I use here the term 'relations of production' because this is the term that Marx and Engels later used. However, the same notion is meant by their use in GI of 'forms', 'modes', 'relations' or 'conditions' of intercourse, as C.J. Arthur remarks in a footnote in his edition of the text (GI: 42–3). (Note that the German given at GI 42–3 is incorrect: 'form of intercourse' should read *Verkehrsform*, and 'relations (conditions) of intercourse' should read *Verkehrsverhältnisse*.)

The relations of production are the relations that individuals stand in relative to the forces of production. For example, a slave might use implements of agriculture (a hoe or a shovel, for example) to work the land, but he does not own or even, ultimately, control the implements he uses. The control over the implements rests with the slaveowner. Similarly, the slaveowner actually has control over the labour of the slave, because he can direct the slave to do particular tasks and so on.

It is a slight simplification, but helpful nonetheless, to conceive of relations of production in terms of who owns the forces of production.

Class

Capitalist division of labour

A class is a group of people who stand to one another in the same relations of control or ownership with regard to the forces of production. For example, Marx and Engels distinguish in capitalism the class of the bourgeois from the class of the proletarians. The former class is the group of people who own the forces of production (for example, they own factories); the latter class is the class of people who do not own the forces of production but work on or with them (for example, by turning the handles on a machine). An economic system that is based on the distinction between bourgeois and proletarian is typical of the capitalist economic system. Other examples of classes include slaves, serfs and landowners.

The ruling class in a given society is that group of persons who collectively exercise control over the means of production in that society.

Division of labour

There results a division of labour, that is, a state of affairs in which different individuals work on different tasks, from the fact that different classes of people stand in different relations to each other and to the forces of production. In fact, one way of understanding the concept of division of labour is to see it roughly as another way of expressing the notion of class, because the class to which any given individual belongs involves his being required to perform certain kinds of labour. For instance, it is because a proletarian does not own the factory or even some proportion of it that he is required to work in it; whereas the bourgeois does not have to work in the factory because he does own it. Thus Marx and Engels say that the 'various stages of development in the division of labour are just so many different forms of ownership' (*GI*: 43). As already noted, we can conceive of ownership in terms of relations of production, so we can thus think of division of labour, ownership and relations of production as roughly picking out the same phenomena.

Marx and Engels describe various forms of ownership. These are: a) tribal ownership; b) communal and state ownership; c) feudal ownership; and d) manufacture, which Marx and Engels subdivide into di) early manufacture, dii) commerce and trade and diii) capitalism.

Tribal ownership

Tribal ownership is the most primitive form of ownership. Tribal ownership involves a very elementary division of labour, for societies organised on a tribal basis live 'by hunting and fishing, by the rearing of beasts or, in the highest stage, agriculture' (*GI*: 44). Marx and Engels draw a parallel here between the division of labour typical of a tribal society and what they see as the division of labour in the family. Indeed, they see the division of labour in a tribal society as an 'extension of the natural division of labour existing in the family' (GI: 44), going on later to suggest that the most primitive form of division of labour is that which obtains in the family since, in general, men and women have by nature different 'natural predisposition[s] (e.g. physical strength), needs, accidents [= qualities], etc. etc.' (GI: 51), and this allots men and women to different roles in family life. So, Marx and Engels' idea seems to be that there is a division of labour in the family, with the (traditional) family consisting of (1) a father who dominates, (2) a mother who is subordinate to him, and (3) children who occupy the lowest place. This corresponds in tribal society to the (1) chieftains, (2) the members of the tribe, and (3) the slaves (cf. Hearn 1991: 228ff.).

Tribal ownership began to break down as tribes, either willingly or through war, started to group themselves into unions (cities) of several tribes.

Communal and state ownership

The second form of ownership is communal and state ownership. Here Marx and Engels have in mind the kind of political entity they took ancient Greece to exemplify, although they also refer to ancient Roman society in this context (GI: 44–5). Ancient Greece was divided into a number of city states – Athens and Sparta were two of them. In such city states there was, Marx and Engels suggest, a greater division of labour than in the tribal societies. For example, there was a clear distinction between citizens and slaves. Free male citizens in Athens, for example, were not required to labour: indeed, they despised labour as being unfit for a free man and as something to be avoided as beneath their dignity. Slaves laboured for them so that they could be free to pursue the life of citizens, engaged in the political life of Athens. Further divisions of labour are apparent, according to Marx and Engels, in the fact that within the city states some work on the land and some in the town (they describe this as an 'antagonism of town and country' – GI: 44).

With the end of the Roman Empire, populations were scattered over a much wider area, that is, over the countryside, rather than being more concentrated in towns.

Feudalism

This scattering of the population in the countryside led to the third form of ownership, namely, that of feudalism, a system of division of labour characteristic of the Middle Ages. The most fundamental division of labour here was that of the landowner or master – the nobility – and the peasantry or serfs. Serfs worked on the land for their masters; they differed from slaves in a number of respects, but most importantly the master was limited by law in his right of disposal of his serfs, that is, in what he was allowed to do with them.

Although the economy of the Middles Ages was based on the country, Marx and Engels note also that, corresponding to the groupings of serfs under a given master, was the establishment in the towns of guilds (GI: 46). A guild was basically a body of individuals who grouped together for mutual support and aid. Very often, a guild was made up of a group of professional craftsmen who all shared the same craft. Thus, there were guilds of cobblers, carpenters, blacksmiths and so on. A very long apprenticeship was necessary in order to become a master of a particular craft and there were some who, though they had qualified, worked for another. These were the journeymen.

Marx and Engels mention that a house and the tools of the trade were amongst the craftsman's capital (*GI*: 71).

Feudalism began to break down with the invention of machines for manufacture and the expansion of commerce.

Manufacture

The final form of ownership that Marx and Engels mention is that of manufacture. As we have already noted, Marx and Engels subdivide manufacturing into three elements.

Early manufacture

What Marx and Engels mean by manufacture is a form of production that involves the development of machines. The example they give is that of weaving which, they say, 'was the first and remained the principal manufacture' (*GI*: 73). In fact, as one historian has said, 'the cloth industry was the basic industry of the Middle Ages' (Southern 1970: 45). What made weaving so important, according to Marx and Engels, is that, through the invention of machines that could allow weaving to be carried out by those with little skill, the demand for cloth could be satisfied, a demand that was growing on account of an increase of population. This had the effect of beginning to break up the guilds since the guilds had been, as we have seen, groupings of highly skilled craftsmen. Now it was becoming possible to manufacture on a fairly large scale without the long training required under the old guild system. This gradually weakened the power of the guilds and began the development of independent manufacturers which was to reach its apotheosis in capitalism.

Along with the gradual collapse of the guild system in towns, the feudal system of serfs and landowners in the countryside began to break down. Marx and Engels trace this to a number of factors, including improvements in agriculture (*GI*: 73). The collapse of the feudal system brought with it vagabondage – that is, the growth of large numbers of dispossessed and more or less destitute individuals wandering the land.

Commerce and trade

The rise of manufacturing depended upon increased trade, since markets had to be supplied with the goods they needed. According to Marx and Engels, from the middle of the seventeenth century until almost the end of the eighteenth century commerce, which had always gone along with manufacture, became more important. This was largely because a world market for goods was developing along with the development of colonies by West European powers (*GI*: 75). This growth in a world market finally led to the development of a full-blown capitalist system.

Capitalism

As we have already seen, capitalism is a form of economic relationship in which the primary division of labour is between those who own the means of production and those who work in or with such means, that is, between the bourgeois and the proletariat.

Alienation

Like Hegel and Feuerbach, Marx and Engels believed that man was alienated. However, they had their own conception of that alienation. Marx and Engels saw the source of alienation in all societies hitherto in the relations in which individuals stood to the forces of production, that is, in what they owned. We can see this best by taking the capitalist system as an example.

Under capitalism, there are very few people – the bourgeoisie – who own the forces of production, whereas the majority of the population – the proletariat – do not own, but work in or with, the forces of production. In *GI* Marx and Engels see alienation in this in three key ways.

Specialisation and routine of work

First, each person works in a highly specialised way. That is, individuals are farmers or fisherman or writers to the exclusion of doing other things and this involves a stunting of the potentialities that individuals have to pursue a variety of occupations and activities in life (*GI*: 54). Related to this is the fact that work in modern capitalist societies is routine, boring and soul-destroying. Marx and Engels put this by saying that work in such societies 'has lost all semblance of self-activity' (*GI*: 92; cf. *GI*: 71).

Market not planned

Secondly, no one has control over what happens in the market. This is because the market is not planned or regulated but rather operates in terms of supply and demand.

Consider a contemporary example, very simplified. In some parts of London, the price of houses and flats is far too high for most people on even a reasonably good income to be able to afford to buy a property. A central reason for this is that these parts of London are very pleasant to live in, and so those who already own property there can charge very high prices when they sell, because they know that there will always be a demand for their property. The consequence is that prices continue to rise in such areas. This means that those who already have property in these areas, that is, who are already wealthy, become wealthier, perhaps so much so that they can buy a second or even third property in a desirable area.

Those who do not have wealth, however, are more or less permanently excluded from buying property in the areas concerned. Such individuals are forced to live in areas in which they would prefer not to live. Those individuals who are without wealth are, therefore, Marx and Engels would say, subject to a power – namely, the power of the market – which is alien to them since it thwarts what they would like to do. This, say Marx and Engels, is a form of alienation (*GI*: 54–5).

However, even those who seem to have power in the market place may be mistaken and thus prey to the forces of the market. For example, someone who owns a shop can be making a good profit but if a supermarket opens next door to his shop then he will find it hard to make a living and, in all likelihood, will be forced out of business (cf. *GI*: 81). The market is, fundamentally, in the control of no one.

Private property   Thirdly, alienation exists in capitalist society through the existence of private property or accumulated labour (*GI*: 91; cf. *GI*: 68). Thus, suppose a given bourgeois owns a factory and the workers labour in it. The workers need to complete a certain amount of work to satisfy their needs. Under the capitalist system, they do not stop working once they have done so. They continue to work, and anything they produce once they have covered their needs goes to the factory owner in the form of goods which he can sell for profit. So he owns the products of the workers' labour over and above the labour they complete for themselves. In later work Marx calls this *surplus* labour; in *GI* Marx and Engels call it *accumulated* labour or, more simply, *private property,* for that is the form in which the surplus labour accumulates for the factory owner. Now, the workers could make as much use of their surplus labour as the factory owner does, but, as we have seen, it does not rest with them but goes instead to the factory owner. Thus, the workers are alienated from the products of their labour, because they are taken from them as soon as produced and these products serve, not to benefit them, but to benefit the bourgeois.

Thus, Marx and Engels conclude that, as long as private property exists, alienation is inevitable.

So far we have only discussed the alienation of workers under capitalism. Marx and Engels did, however, also think that capitalism involved the alienation of the bourgeoisie. Implicit in their discussion in *GI* are at least two forms of such alienation.

First, the bourgeoisie, like the workers, are highly specialised in their activities. As in the case of workers, this involves a stunting of human potential.

Secondly, the capitalist suffers from an impoverishment of his human relations. Under capitalism, Marx and Engels argue, 'all relations are subordinated in practice to the one abstract monetary-commercial relation' (*GI*: 109; cf. *GI*: 102). This means that for the bourgeois 'only *one* relation is valid . . . [that is] the relation of exploitation' – either in reality or in imagination (*GI*: 110). In other words, Marx and Engels argue, the capitalist loses all proper individual relations with others (*GI*: 102) because his way of relating to others involves a view of both them and himself as there merely to increase profit.

review activity

Describe in your own words the various ways in which both proletariat and bourgeoisie are, in Marx and Engels' view, alienated in the capitalist system.

Transition from one form of ownership to another: the progress of history

We have already noted some of the ways in which Marx and Engels suggest that one form of ownership was replaced by another in the course of history.

However, they have a much more general account of such historical change, which we must describe because it lies at the heart of their materialist conception of history.

The most concise and famous account of historical development to be found in Marx's work is not, in fact, in *GI* – though there is an account in *GI* on pages 86–7 – but in the Preface to his *A Critique of Political Economy*. The account in the Preface runs as follows:

Marx and Engels'
account of historical
change

> *In the social production of their life, men enter into . . . relations of production which correspond to a definite stage of development of their material productive forces . . . At a certain stage of their development, the material productive forces of society come in conflict with the existing relations of production or – what is but a legal expression for the same thing – with the property relations within which they have been at work hitherto. From forms of development of the productive forces these relations turn into their fetters. Then begins an epoch of social revolution.* (Marx 1977: 389)

What this means is as follows.

In any given society certain forces of production are available. For example, in the modern age coal, oil and gas are available, whereas in a feudal society this was not so. Corresponding to the available forces of production in any given society is a set of relations of production, for example, the relations of master and slave, or landowner and serf, or capitalist (bourgeois) and proletarian. In fact, the relations of production are *determined* by the forces of production. In other words, given certain forces of production a given set of relations of production *must* develop; they are *forced* to develop. For example, given the type of farming methods available during the Middle Ages, together with an absence of developed machinery and so on, then the relation of landowner and serf *must* arise. It would not be possible, for example, to have available in a given society only a set of productive forces typical of the Middle Ages and for the relations of production to be those of the bourgeois and proletariat. As Marx puts is at one point: 'The hand-mill gives you society with the feudal lord; the steam-mill, society with the industrial capitalist' (Marx 1977: 202).

Now, Marx and Engels believed the following:

1. That the productive capacity of human beings tends to grow in time, that is, that human beings have a tendency to improve their forces of production. Thus, they invent new tools (for example, the spinning jenny and computer), synthesise new materials (for example, polythene and nylon), increase their scientific understanding and so on.

2. That human beings have a tendency to make as full a use as possible of the productive forces that are available at any given time.

3. That different relations of production differ in their ability to make use of the forces of production available at any given time.

Relations of production
as a fetter on forces of
production

If 1., 2., and 3. are true then, Marx and Engels thought, the relations of production of any given society will come under increasing pressure from the gradually developing forces of production until the relations of production in the society become useless because they can no longer make full use of the forces of production. The relations of production will be a *fetter* on the further use and growth of the forces of production. At this point there will be an overthrow of the now outmoded relations of production, which will be replaced by the new such relations that are capable of making full use of the available forces of production. Hence they write that 'all collisions in history have their origin . . . in the contradiction between the productive forces and the form of intercourse' (GI: 89). For example, and simplifying somewhat, when the kind of machinery or technology typical of capitalism is introduced into a feudal context the relations of production typical of feudalism (nobility and serfs) will not be able to make full use of this technology. Thus, the feudal relations of production will be replaced by a new set of relations of production (bourgeois and proletarian) which can make use of the new technology.

Marx and Engels believe that it is in this kind of way that relations of production have changed from tribal to communal to feudal to capitalist.

This all looks complicated, but a simplified analogy may help to make things clear.

Imagine an old-fashioned railway station. At this station, tickets are issued by being written by hand, train time information is available only in large books of train running times and not on computers, there are no loudspeakers or electronic boards to announce arrivals and departures, the drivers and guards do not have mobile telephones for communicating with one another, and there are no automatic gates to check the validity of passengers' tickets. Imagine now that the management gradually introduces these things. We could imagine that some of the staff could continue working and yet ignore the innovations. For example, many of the staff might be able to get by without using the computers so long as the books of running times are available. Or they might be able to continue to issue hand written tickets even after the introduction of machine produced ones. But eventually any staff who have not learned how to cope with the new technology will simply not be able to work at the station. For example, when the automatic gates are introduced, the hand-written tickets will not function in them and thus any ticket salesman or saleswoman who cannot issue machine produced tickets will not be able to do his or her job. Eventually, therefore, the new technology available will *force* the management to retrain their staff and sack those who cannot or will not learn to manipulate the new technology. They will *have* to do this in order to keep the station working at all. They will *have no choice* if the station is to function at all. So here we have an example of the introduction of new technology forcing a change in the way in which the individuals who work at the railway relate to one another.

This analogy is in many ways highly simplified. For example, it leaves out, amongst other things, any mention of what the passengers' demands are and whether they want the new technology, as well as any general consideration of the market, the introduction of technology elsewhere and so on. Further, it does not involve a change in ownership, for it illustrates a change *within* a given set of relations of production. Nonetheless, it does show, as we have already noted, how it is that human beings collectively engaged in some enterprise will be *forced* to behave in new ways towards one another as the result of the introduction of new technology in the field of that enterprise. It is Marx and Engels' contention, as we have seen, that large-scale changes in ownership (relations of production) are forced on individuals in this kind of way, that is, through the introduction of new forces of production.

Revolution   Marx and Engels called the large-scale change in relations of production brought about by changes in the forces of production a *revolution*. We have already seen examples of such revolutions, for these took place in the change from the tribal to the communal system, in the shift from the communal to the feudal system, and in the change from the feudal system to that of capitalism. Hence Marx says in the Third Thesis on Feuerbach: 'The coincidence of the changing of circumstances [that is, roughly, the forces of production] and of human activity or self-changing [that is, roughly, the relations of production] can be conceived and rationally understood only as a *revolutionary practice* (*GI*: 121).

Marx and Engels believed that the development in history of new relations of production from the tribal to the capitalist was *determined*. That is, they believed that history *had* to develop this way; it could not have developed otherwise. Hence they can say that 'revolution is the driving force of history' (*GI*: 59).

review
activity

1. What do Marx and Engels mean by saying that at given points of history the relations of production become fetters on the forces of production?
2. Why do the relations of production become fetters in this way?
3. What happens when the relations of production become fetters on the forces of production?

Base and superstructure

I earlier deferred discussion of two key concepts of Marx and Engels' materialism, that is, base and superstructure, and the scientific status of their claims. In this section, I deal with the first of these. In the next, I shall deal with the second.

As we have seen, Marx and Engels believed that the productive forces of a given society determine the relations of production in that society. However, this was actually part of a larger claim they made. This was, roughly, that the material conditions of life determine the non-material conditions of life. The material conditions, including the relations of production, they called the 'base' or 'basis' and the non-material conditions the 'superstructure'. The superstructure includes moral, religious and political beliefs and ideas. It is often supposed to include also such forms of social organisation as the family. In *GI* the distinction between base and superstructure appears in a number of places. For example, it is intended in the comment: 'Life is not determined by consciousness, but consciousness by life' (*GI*: 47). It is also being invoked when Marx and Engels say that 'starting out from the material production of life . . . as the basis of all history . . . [we can] explain all the different theoretical products and forms of consciousness, religion, philosophy, ethics etc. etc. and trace their origins and growth from that basis' (*GI*: 58). However, the most succinct account of the relation between base and superstructure is to be found in a letter Marx wrote to Annenkov, a wealthy Russian acquaintance of his:

> *Assume a particular state of development in the productive forces of man and you will get a particular form of commerce and consumption. Assume particular stages of development in production, commerce, and consumption and you will have a corresponding social constitution, a corresponding organization of the family, of orders or of classes, in a word, a corresponding civil society. Assume a particular civil society and you will get particular political conditions which are only the official expression of civil society.* (Marx 1977: 192)

Ideology So, according to Marx and Engels, the situation is this: the forces of production in a given group of people determine the relations of production amongst those people. These relations of production determine the civil society in which these people live. This civil society determines the political form of life amongst those people. Thus, according to Marx and Engels, a given state of the productive forces always ultimately gives rise to particular moral ideas, political ideas, religious ideas and so on. Marx and Engels call all such ideas an *ideology*, and write:

> *Morality, religion, metaphysics, all the rest of ideology and their corresponding forms of consciousness, thus no longer retain the semblance of independence. They have no history, no development; but men, developing their material production and their material intercourse, alter, along with this their real existence, their thinking and the products of their thinking.* (*GI*: 47)

The only real history is that of changes in material conditions of life: if we can explain these – as Marx and Engels believe they can – then we can explain changes in ideology.

This kind of approach is know as *reductionism* or *reductivism*, because it aims to reduce an understanding of one phenomenon (in this case, morality, religion and so forth) to another (in this case, the material conditions of life).

review
activity

1. What do Marx and Engels mean by 'base' and 'superstructure'?
2. How do they think of base and superstructure as related?

A good example of the relation between material conditions and ideology is given in Marx and Engels' discussion of Kant's moral philosophy. They claim, for example, that when Kant suggested that the good will is good regardless of what it achieves in the real world this was merely a philosophical expression of the social and economic class to which Kant belonged, namely, a class that was unable to make itself felt in the world through its actions (*GI*: 97).

A second example of the relations between ideology and the material conditions of life is to be found in Marx and Engels' comments on utilitarianism.

According to Marx and Engels, the idea central to utilitarianism that all moral decisions can be reduced to a calculation concerning *one* measure – namely, which actions promote utility or happiness – is simply an expression of the fact that in modern capitalist society relations between individuals have been reduced to *one* measure – namely, how significant they are for a market where all is measured in terms of financial loss and gain – that is, money. Marx and Engels see exploitation at the root of utilitarianism, just as they see exploitation at the root of capitalism (*GI*: 109–14).

Marx and Engels do not simply believe that the ideology of a given society is as it is as a result of the forces of production in that society. They also believe that the ideology is always that of those in the society who constitute the ruling class. That is, the ideology serves the interests of the ruling class. It is a system of belief whose aim is to justify and legitimise the fact that some particular individuals are in effective control of the forces of production whilst others are not. This helps the ruling class keep their control over the forces of production and over those in the dominated or lower class or classes. This is what Marx and Engels mean by writing:

> The ruling ideas are nothing more than the ideal expression of the dominant material relationships, the dominant material relationships grasped as ideas; hence, of the relationships which make the one class the ruling one, therefore, the ideas of its dominance (*GI*: 64).

Here is an example. In the feudal system the real reason why the nobility or landowners are in a position of dominance over the serfs is that the development of the forces of production at that point in history ensures that some individuals constitute the nobility and others constitute the peasantry. However, the dominant ideology in the society might be that some are nobles or landowners, and others serfs, because God has allotted each man and woman to a specific place in the social hierarchy. The nobles believe this not because it is true – in fact, Marx and Engels would say that it is false – but because it protects their position in society. If they can get the serfs to believe this as well, then their position will be all the more secure. Such religious ideas are thus an ideology – a mask to cover up the real interests of the nobles.

Marx and Engels' reductionism has another feature. This is that people think as they think and behave as they behave simply in virtue of the material conditions of their society. A good example of this is Marx and Engels' view of the great artists of the Renaissance, who were determined to paint as they did on account of the material conditions of life prevailing at that time and place (*GI*: 108–9). Further, Marx and Engels' reductionism means that communists 'do not preach morality at all . . . They do not put to people the moral demand: love one another, do not be egoists, etc.; on the contrary, they are very well aware that egoism, just as much as self-sacrifice, *is* in definite circumstances a necessary form of self-assertion of individuals' (*GI*: 104-5). Exhorting people to do certain things in the name of morality is a waste of time. The only way to get people to behave differently is to change the material conditions of their life. This is the core of what Marx means in his Eleventh Thesis on Feuerbach when he says that 'philosophers have only *interpreted* the world, in various ways; the point is to *change* it' (*GI*: 123).

review
activity

1.   What do Marx and Engels mean by an 'ideology'?

2.   Whose interest does an ideology serve?

3.   Why do Marx and Engels think that appeals to morality are a waste of time?

The scientific status of Marx and Engels' claims

The relation between Marx and Engels' work and philosophy

It follows from this that it is a mistake to call Marx and Engels' ideas an ideology. An ideology, we have seen, seeks to justify the position of the ruling class in society. But Marx and Engels did not want to do that. Furthermore, they would have rejected the idea that their views constitute a morality or political philosophy at all, since these are just ideologies. On the contrary, they believed that, in seeing how history works, they had stepped outside any such way of approaching things at all. They believed that their views did not constitute a philosophical view at all, but a view *outside* philosophy. Hence they explicitly say that it is important to leave philosophy behind because philosophy cannot understand reality (*GI*: 103). In fact, they claim that once philosophy is given up in favour of the kind of view they espouse then 'every profound philosophical problem is resolved' (*GI*: 62). Truth resides, Marx writes in the Second Thesis on Feuerbach, not in philosophical reflection but in action (*GI*: 121). This is why he mockingly refers to such thought as *scholastic* – a reference to the kind of philosophy pursued in the Middle Ages when abstruse questions concerning, for example, how many angels could stand on the head of a pin were discussed (cf. also the Eight Thesis which makes a similar point).

But if Marx and Engels' views are not philosophy, what are they? The answer is that Marx and Engels believed they were doing *science*.

What they mean by this can be seen by taking an example of a piece of knowledge that is genuinely scientific. As is well known, chemistry has shown that water is made up of molecules, specifically, that a molecule of water consists of two atoms of hydrogen and one of oxygen (H_2O). Anyone with the requisite scientific training knows this to be true. A scientist (or anyone else, come to that) who believes that water is H_2O does not believe this on account of his political, moral or religious views. Nor does he believe it because it is convenient to believe it or because he wants to believe it. Neither does he believe it because he has been indoctrinated or brainwashed to believe it. He believes it because it is true, quite independently of all political, moral and religious thinking, and quite independently of his desires and so on.

Now, what Marx and Engels think is that their view of history is as scientific as is that which the scientist believes about water, namely, that it is made up of H_2O molecules. They do not believe what they believe because it fits in with their moral, political or religious views or because it is convenient for them to believe or because they have been brainwashed. They believe what they believe because it has been scientifically established in the kind of way it has been scientifically established that water is H_2O. They believe it, in a word, simply because it is *correct*. One way to put this would be to say that Marx and Engels believed in *laws of history*. We have already seen this, for we have seen that they believed that history had to develop from a tribal to a communal to a feudal to a capitalist order. They confidently believed that the next *inevitable* stop on this road – which would bring history as hitherto known to an end – was communism.

review
activity

1. Why do Marx and Engels claim that their view is not a philosophical view?

2. Explain what is meant in saying that Marx and Engels thought their view to be scientific.

The communist revolution and the overthrow of capitalism

Communism would come about through a revolution through which the proletariat would appropriate the forces of production. As we have seen, Marx and Engels believed that revolutions come about when the relations of production become a fetter on the further growth and use of the forces of production. This would happen in the late stage of capitalism because capitalism would ensure that more and more individuals would be forced to become members of the proletariat and wealth would be concentrated in the hands of fewer and fewer bourgeois. They thought that capitalism would develop in this way for they believed that, because capitalism is by its nature competitive, most people would be driven by it into being 'propertyless', thus destitute. However, they also believed that the communist revolution would take place, and would have to take place, as a result of the development of a world market, that is, not simply when the proletarians in one or two countries had become destitute, but when the proletarians in all nations simultaneously had become destitute. In other words, they believed that the communist revolution would occur across the globe in all nations, failing which local revolutions would be unsuccessful (*GI*: 55–6).

Life under communism

According to Marx and Engels, communist society would involve some profound differences from capitalist society. In fact, communism would constitute a new age in the history of humanity. The key features of communist society according to Marx and Engels are the following.

Abolition of the state

Marx and Engels did not believe in a 'communist state'. On the contrary, they believed that there would be no state under communism. As they famously put it, under communism the state would wither. And with this withering of the state the relation between state and civil society, which, as we saw earlier, Marx and Engels thought to be fraught with difficulty in a liberal society, would be overcome.

Abolition of private property

According to Marx and Engels, in a communist society there would be no private property. This is because, so Marx and Engels believed, the communist revolution would involve the appropriation of the means of production by the proletariat as a united force, thus abolishing private property (GI: 93).

Another way to look at this abolition of private property is to remember that, according to Marx and Engels, private property is simply accumulated labour and arises from the expropriation of the surplus labour of the proletarian by the bourgeois. With the end of the relations of production typical of capitalist society, such expropriation would cease. This is because under communism production would be centrally regulated.

The overcoming of man's alienation

This centrally organised production would be but one aspect of the end of man's alienation. It would involve the end of the subjection of individuals to forces of the market over which they have no power and whose workings are obscure to them. Consider again the example I gave earlier concerning the property market in London. Suppose that the market I described there were replaced by a regulated market in which both those who were wealthy and those who were not co-operated in order to provide each person with what he needs to live. Then there could be investment in all areas such that they all become desirable as places in which to live. This would abolish the subjection of individuals to the market, that is, their alienation in this regard, and bring to end the fact that under the capitalist system some (very few, according to Marx and Engels) individuals get what they want whereas most are excluded from this.

The end of the division of labour

Alienation would also be overcome in that under communism there would be an end to specialisation in work, that is, division of labour. Thus, Marx and Engels write that

> *in communist society . . . it [is] possible for me to do one thing today and another tomorrow, to hunt in the morning, fish in the afternoon, rear cattle in the evening, criticise [that is, practise literary criticism] after dinner, just as I have a mind, without ever becoming hunter, fisherman, herdsman or critic.*
>
> (GI: 54)

This end of specialisation would again be the result of the central regulation of production. The idea is once again that individuals would co-operate in order to rationalise production and share out the burden of different types of work to be done.

A planned economy

Beyond this, individuals would have more time to devote to things they wish to do and which have little, if anything, to do with producing the means of subsistence. This is because, Marx and Engels believed, the competitive system of capitalism is wasteful in the way in which a planned economy is not. There would be an abundance of goods for all under communism. This can be see by taking a simplified example.

We all need clothes to wear. Under capitalism, the production of clothes is dominated by fashion. We usually throw out old clothes, not because they are worn out, but because they are no longer fashionable. Moreover, most people have lots of clothes at home in cupboards which they never or very rarely wear, despite the fact that they are perfectly serviceable, simply because they have grown bored with them. Further, and connectedly, because there are so many different styles of clothing that can be bought, there are far more clothes circulating in the market than we could possibly need. For these and other reasons the production of clothing in capitalist societies is extremely wasteful, both in terms of the materials used in their production and of the time individuals have to spend on designing them, fabricating them and so on. Something similar could be said about the production of a great many other products in capitalist societies.

Suppose now that the production of clothing and other goods were centrally regulated. Then we could get rid of a great deal of waste, thus freeing up materials and time for other activities. People would be free to do lots of things for which they at present have neither the material resources nor time. Moreover, people would be able to spend time doing the kind of activities they *wish* to do. Hence, communistic regulation would involve the end of the necessity for specialisation of activities, that is, alienation.

It should be clear from what has already been said why it is that Marx and Engels thought that communist society would also end human beings' alienation in that exploitation of some by others would come to an end with co-operative, regulated production.

Freedom The end of alienation would mean that individuals could at last achieve freedom in the full development of their faculties and abilities. In fact, the communist society would be a society where human freedom was for the first time made real and concrete. Under communism, individuals could at last have room to develop freely.

One way Marx and Engels put these points about the end of man's alienation is to say that in a communist society it is not simply that there would be an end to the division of labour. More important is that Marx and Engels believe that communist society would abolish labour itself (*GI*: 82; 85; 94). What this means is that the activities people would pursue in a communist society would be more or less what we now think of as hobbies (cf. Arendt 1958: 128).

According to Marx and Engels, communism would involve the end of man's alienation, so they saw in such a society a truly human society. This is what Marx means in the Tenth Thesis on Feuerbach when he says that his form of materialism involves the creation of 'human society, or social humanity'. The kind of materialism defended by Feuerbach would not be able to make sense of this, the same thesis suggests, because it adopts the point of view of civil society. By this Marx means that Feuerbach's materialism does not show how individuals could live together in such a way as to have a common purpose (as would be the case under communist society, where co-operation would be the basis of human interaction). Rather, it adopts the point of view of a society where conflict continues because persons in such a society interact with one another as individuals with their own interests which they try to satisfy even at the expense of the satisfaction of others' interests.

An end to human selfishness

As we have seen already, Marx and Engels believed that the way people behave is determined by the material conditions of their life. They believed that self-ishness and egoism was simply what people manifested in their behaviour under certain conditions and that, were the conditions changed, they would behave in a selfless or generous way. Moreover, they thought that under the communist system individuals would stop behaving selfishly and would start behaving selflessly and kindly to each other.

Underlying this idea is a belief about human nature. That is, Marx and Engels believed (at least in GI) that there was no such thing as human nature (except insofar as man ia s social animal). What we are is determined by the conditions of our life, and therefore we cannot suppose that different individuals living under different material conditions (for example, feudalism or capitalism) share the same nature. This is why Marx and Engels criticise others, and parti-cularly the Young Hegelians, for talking about the nature of 'Man' as if they had discovered something about the nature of all human beings independently of their conditions of life. What the Young Hegelians had done was rather to think that the individuals around them in their society were typical of human beings everywhere (GI: 83; 93–4). Hence, Marx says in the Sixth and Seventh Theses, Feuerbach had thought that he was speaking of a human essence or nature when he analysed religion, but actually he had at best been speaking of the kind of human being present in his society at his time – that is, one which was the product of specific material conditions. What Feuer-bach had done, according to Marx, was to ignore these conditions and thus arrive at an abstracted, but unreal, human being in his analysis of religious sentiment. And, says Marx, *the* religious sentiment, no more exists than does a human being outside a given society: there can only be different forms of reli-gious sentiment, forms that are as they are on account of their place in different societies (GI: 122).

According to Marx and Engels, similar mistakes about human nature were also made by the so-called 'true' socialists (GI: 119–20), that is, those socialist thinkers who thought that to bring about a socialist society it was important to make moral demands on the individuals of society to seek to improve things. This is what Marx and Engels mean when they say that the 'true' socia-lists had proclaimed 'the universal love of mankind' (GI: 120). Marx and Engels thought such a demand absurd, of course, and indicative of the fact that the 'true' socialists had 'lost all revolutionary enthusiasm' (GI: 120).

review activity

1. In what ways do Marx and Engels believe that communism will overcome man's alienation?
2. Why did Marx and Engels think that human beings would no longer be selfish under communism?

Criticisms of Marx and Engels

Marx and Engels' theories have been subjected to a great deal of critical exploration, both by those sympathetic to them and by those opposed to them. In this section I discuss briefly some of the most pressing difficulties to which their theory as we have explored it in this chapter is exposed.

The relation of base and superstructure

Critics of Marx and Engels have questioned whether it can really be true that the material conditions of life determine the non-material conditions of life without the latter also having an important effect on the former. For example, it is surely true that the ideas people have affect the machines they build, which in turn affect the ideas they have, and so on. If this is so, then it is mistaken to suggest that ideas play no role in shaping society but are determined by the forces of production, as Marx and Engels often insist.

After the death of Marx, Engels insisted that what he and Marx had meant was that the forces of production were only *one* of the factors determining the non-material conditions of life, but were in some sense the most fundamental such factor. The trouble is, if this is all the forces of production are, then much of what is distinctive about Marx and Engels' theory is lost, because no one should disagree that the material conditions of life play some significant role in the development of ideas. The difficulty is to understand what the extent of that influence is, and Engels' more 'softened' approach does not help solve that problem at all.

It is important to see that, even if Marx and Engels' specific claims about the relations of base and superstructure are questionable, it does not follow that they are completely wrong to lay emphasis on the material conditions of life as having an important influence on moral thinking, religious consciousness the like. Moreover, it is almost certainly true that a great deal of, for example, moral philosophy and philosophy of religion has been insensitive to this fact. So, even if what Marx and Engels say is not the whole truth, it may contain a grain of truth to which we should pay attention.

Apart from the problem for the relation between base and superstructure that has already been mentioned, there is another difficulty in this area. This concerns the fact that the relations of production are said to become fetters on the growth and use of the forces of production. This could only happen if the relations of production were in some degree independent of the forces of the forces of production, that is, not completely determined by them. However, Marx and Engels claim that they are so determined. What this means is that the relations of production could not become the fetters on the forces of production as Marx and Engels claim, which means that their explanation of historical change cannot be correct (cf. Plamenatz 1975: 24).

A further worry that arises in this area is that, if it is true that consciousness is determined by material conditions, how it is that Marx and Engels could know what they claim to know. After all, they did not live in a communist society, but a capitalist one, so how is it that their thinking is not determined by the forms of consciousness that a capitalist society produces?

Marx and Engels actually answer this objection (GI: 87–8). They argue, roughly speaking, that changes in the relations between forces of production and relations of production take place at different rates in different places. This means that pockets of consciousness can develop here and there before that consciousness establishes itself in general.

Communism as the goal of history

Marx and Engels' theories are also questionable so far as their scientific status is concerned. In fact, many have argued that we should not accept their claim that they had discovered the 'laws' that underlie the development of history and lead to communism as its goal. The reason for this is that Marx and Engels acquired their idea that specific laws underlie history, not from their study of history, but from philosophy, specifically, from Hegel's philosophy. They believed, as many did in the nineteenth century, in the idea that history was progressing and that mankind was gradually improving. In fact, many have suggested that the experiences of the twentieth century – two world wars, the Holocaust, Stalin's dictatorship in the Soviet Union, not to mention the collapse of Soviet communism and countless other examples of human cruelty, barbarity and evil – give us good reason for thinking that the belief that history has a goal and that mankind is improving are little more than wishful thinking. Perhaps, then, it is true that Marx and Engels' reading of history was made to fit in with their system rather than being a dispassionate exploration of historical phenomena and events (cf. Taylor in Marx and Engels 1985: 11).

Many have thought that the fact that first communist revolution took place in Russia – in a country that did not have a capitalist system – shows that Marx and Engels' theories are mistaken. It is said that this is clear because Marx and Engels, as we have seen, thought that there were laws of history which were followed *en route* to communism, and it seems clear that Russia bypassed these laws. However, this should not be possible if Marx and Engels are right that they have discovered genuine laws of history. So their position on history seems to be mistaken.

David Conway has argued that Marx and Engels can be defended here (Conway 1987: 63–8). This is because Marx did in fact explicitly envisage the possibility that Russia might pass to communism without going through a capitalist stage. How was this possible if the laws of history were as he said they were? The answer is that Russia possessed at that time a very particular institution of communal property in the form of the communal village (the *mir* or *obschina*). This, together with the fact that Russia was tied into a world market which was capitalist and could thus appropriate from capitalist states what Marx called 'the positive results from this mode of production', meant, according to Marx, that Russia could pass to the communal life of communism without having to pass through a capitalist phase. One might say: if Marx and Engels had discovered the laws of history, these laws could manifest themselves in different ways against different backgrounds and in different conditions.

Human nature

Marx and Engels are by no means alone in denying that there is any such thing as human nature. But it is a belief which is highly questionable. Perhaps the best reason for thinking that human beings have a nature has been offered by Mary Midgley (Midgley 1979). This is that we recognise that different species of animals each have a nature: cats have a certain nature, dogs another, and so on. If it is true, as seems overwhelmingly likely, that human beings are related by evolutionary processes to the rest of the animal kingdom, it seems implausible to suppose that we have no nature. Otherwise we should have to postulate a break between us and the rest of nature which is implausible. On the other hand, even if we think that human beings do have a nature, we can also grant that it is more flexible than that of most animals, for we are creatures who need culture to complete us, as Midgley suggests (Midgley 1979: ch.12; cf. Geertz 1993: ch. 2).

If we believe that human beings have a nature, then we shall not be able to think that human beings behave in ways which are wholly determined by the kind of society in which they find themselves, as Marx and Engels supposed. In particular, it will be hard to believe that, however flexible our nature might be, we could become as selfless and generous as Marx and Engels supposed we would in a communist society.

The end of the division of labour

Marx and Engels, we have seen, believed that communist society would end the division of labour. They believed that such division inhibited the full flourishing of human potential. We may readily agree that the way work is organised in the modern world, and the way it was organised in previous ages, does, and did, a lot to inhibit the developing of all the talents that given individuals might have by constraining them to work in one kind of way or at one kind of activity. Nonetheless, it is far from clear that it is always as bad as Marx and Engels assume to be specialised. For one thing, there are some disciplines in life – such as artistic endeavour or the pursuit of philosophy – where one can only really achieve much by a great deal of specialisation: only very few would be able to achieve anything great in more than one of these areas. For another, there is no reason why specialisation in one such area should be found dissatisfying: indeed, someone who feels that, say, music or intellectual endeavour is his vocation would feel stunted and poorly nourished were he *not* able to concentrate most of his energies on such disciplines. This is, in fact, why we can speak of such things as music as a vocation in the first place (cf. Cohen 2000: 350–1).

The abolition of labour

We have seen that, according to Marx and Engels, a communist society would abolish labour and that this would mean that the members of such a society would pursue their activities much as we now pursue hobbies. What this surely comes to, as David Conway has suggested, is that 'communism permits each individual to do what he likes, as he likes, when he likes during the period of work' (Conway 1987: 47). However, the central problem with this is that it is completely unclear how it is that in a society where people were able to do this there could be any central planning of the economy at all. If everyone were free to do what he wanted the result would simply be chaos. It is surely not possible for labour to be abolished in the way Marx and Engels suggest and have much of an economy left at all.

There is a second problem with the abolition of labour, a more philosophical problem. This is that Marx and Engels insist that it is through labour that man distinguishes himself from animals (*GI*: 42) and yet suppose that man will only be fully man in a communist society in which labour is abolished. As Hannah Arendt has remarked, this contradiction leaves us 'with the rather distressing alternative between productive slavery [under capitalism] and unproductive freedom [under communism]' (Arendt 1958: 105).

Morality

We have seen that Marx and Engels deny that their theory makes appeal to morality. However, it is clear that their work is suffused with a very strong sense of the injustice and evil of the fact that many have to labour most of their life so that a fortunate few can live in comfort. So is there not a contradiction here? Steven Lukes has argued that Marx and Engels can be cleared of such a contradiction (Lukes 1990).

Lukes says that we should distinguish between the morality of *Recht* and the morality of emancipation. The former is the kind of quasi-legalistic morality that Marx and Engels thought of as being at home in bourgeois society. This kind morality is concerned with rights, justice and fairness. Marx and Engels rejected this sort of morality as being nothing more than the ideology of capitalist society. However, Lukes argues, they did not reject the notion of a morality of emancipation, which would signal in its triumph the end of exploitation and would, indeed, herald the end of capitalism and the triumph of communism.

review activity

1. Why does it seem that Marx and Engels' account of the relation between base and superstructure is mistaken?

2. What reasons are there for thinking that communism could not be the goal of history?

3. How plausible is Marx and Engels' denial that human beings have no human nature?

4. What problems are there for Marx and Engels' idea that under communism there would be no division of labour?

some questions to think about

1 To what extent would you agree that the collapse of communist régimes in the Soviet Union and elsewhere shows that Marx and Engels' theories are false?

2 Is it true that men and women are alienated in capitalist societies on account of the work they do?

3   Is it plausible to think that history has a goal to which it is progressing?

4   How far would you agree with the claim that specialisation in work stunts human potential?

5   To what extent do you think moral and religious consciousness and the like is influenced by the material conditions of individuals' lives?

6   Is the description Marx and Engels give of communist society anything more than wishful thinking?

7   If it were true that human beings had a nature, would it still be possible to think that a communist society was a real possibility?

further reading

The best selection from Marx's voluminous works is Marx 1977, edited by McLellan. McLellan 1974 is a very good introduction to Marx. Other helpful introductions include Singer 1986 and Eddy 1979, an unusual book which is written in the form of a dialogue. Conway 1987 is hostile to Marx, but clear and useful. Cohen 2000 is a rigorous and sometimes difficult book, but rewarding. Tucker 1969 is in some ways eccentric, but it is very interesting and clearly written. Carver (ed.) 1991 contains some useful papers. On Engels, see McLellan 1977.

IV

Jean-Paul Sartre: *Existentialism and Humanism*

Sartre's life and works

Jean-Paul Sartre, who was born in 1905 in Paris, was one of the most influential philosophers of post-war France. His father died when the young Sartre was only about a year old, and Sartre later claimed that this was a blessing in disguise because it left him free to be who he wanted to be without having the pressure of a father figure. In 1928 he failed his *agrégation,* the highest examination for teachers in France. The next year he was placed first in the same examination, having reconciled himself to presenting more traditional philosophical ideas. Simone de Beauvoir, a fellow student, was placed second. She and Sartre had a life-long relationship, though they never married and both had other lovers. From 1929 to 1931 he did his military service, and from 1933–4 he studied in Berlin, though until the mid-1940s his main work was as a teacher in various *lycées.* He was conscripted during the Second World War and was taken prisoner, managing to get released by posing as a civilian. The first of his major works of existentialist literature and philosophy, *Nausea* (1937) and *Being and Nothingness* (1943), were published around this time. From the beginning of the 1950s Sartre became more and more interested in Marxism, and this led to his gradual abandonment of existentialism as the problems of social existence moved closer to the centre of his concerns, supplanting his earlier interest in the individual. This interest in Marxism coincided with a deep involvement in radical left-wing politics, which included, amongst other things, editing, and writing for, various radical publications. In 1964 he was awarded the Nobel Prize for Literature, which he refused on the grounds that it represented bourgeois society's desire to 'forgive' him for leading such a rebellious life. From about 1971, when he suffered a heart attack, his health began to decline, although he continued to write and to be politically engaged. He died in 1980. Besides those already mentioned, his main works include the *Critique of Dialectical Reason* (1960), various intellectual biographies, such as *Saint Genet, Actor and Martyr* (1952) – Jean Genet (1910–86) was a friend of Sartre's – and *The Idiot of the Family* (1971-2) on Gustave Flaubert (1821–80), numerous plays and novels, and the autobiographical *Words* (1963).

Jean-Paul Sartre (1905–80)

The roots of existentialism

Existentialism is a distinctive philosophical movement, which has its roots at least as far back as the work of the Danish philosopher Søren Kierkegaard (1813–55), who is often seen as the founding father of existentialist philosophy. Kierkegaard's thinking is extremely complicated, but most fundamentally it articulates the idea that philosophers, particularly the philosophers of the Enlightenment, had lost sight of the *individually existing human being* from their reflections. They had done so, Kierkegaard thought, on account of their emphasis on reason and their belief that reason could solve all the substantial problems of life, including those of morality, religion, politics and art. This led them to construct huge systems that purportedly explained everything, but in which, Kierkegaard thought, it was impossible for the individual to find a place. In other words, such systems were cut off from life as it is actually lived, and were lifeless and abstract, in the worst sense of the term.

Kierkegaard was himself a Christian thinker, but even here he was opposed to systems, and this led him into conflict with the established Church, which he thoroughly despised. He objected to the unthinking acceptance of dogma and to the idea that one could become a Christian simply by being baptised or christened and living in a Christian country. For him, the issue in Christianity was not *what* one believed, but *how* one believed, and thus the real issue was one of how to live in a certain way and what difference Christianity made to one's life. In this sense, he thought that no one could actually *be* a Christian: at best, one could *seek* to be a Christian.

Kierkegaard's work has influenced many other thinkers in both theology and philosophy, and, as I said, was one of the main sources of the movement in European thought known as existentialism. As the name and what has been said about Kierkegaard suggest, existentialism places great emphasis on the individually existing human being. There have been other existentialists who, like Kierkegaard, worked from a Christian perspective, and others who were atheists. One of the most important of these atheistic existentialists was Sartre, and one of his most accessible works is his *Existentialism and Humanism,* which I shall henceforth refer to as *EH.*

Existentialism and Humanism

The original French title of Sartre's *EH* is *L'Existentialisme est un humanisme.* This means that a more literal translation of the title would be *Existentialism is a Humanism.* Sartre uses this title in order to make clear that his version of existentialism is humanist: he is not at all a Christian existentialist as, for example, Kierkegaard was.

Sartre's book was originally delivered as a lecture in Paris on 29 October 1945 and published in 1946 in French. It was first published in English translation in 1947. Because it is a lecture, it is somewhat popular in form, and therefore lacking in parts in a certain precision and clarity. This means that properly to understand the text it is important to fill in some of its ideas by reference to some of Sartre's other work, especially his massive *Being and Nothingness,* which he published in 1943, and which I shall henceforth refer to as *BN.*

One of the really interesting things about Sartre's version of existentialism is that central concepts in it include those of *anguish, abandonment* and *despair*. These are in many ways unusual concepts for a philosopher to be interested in, but they also seem in some ways indicative of a negative or pessimistic philosophy. Sartre was well aware that some people thought of his philosophy in this way, and he gave the lecture in order to try to dispel this sense of thinking.

Hostility to Sartre's existentialism

The main criticisms which Sartre outlines at the beginning of the text and which he would like to rebut come from communists and Christians.

The communists' criticism of existentialism

According to communism, history will one day issue in a society in which human beings will treat one another with mutual respect and in which individuals will be able to lead fulfilled lives, free of the waste and grind that characterise capitalist societies. According to communism, this state can be brought about more quickly by individuals' engaging in political action. However, in order for individuals to do this they have to believe that their actions can be, or have a good chance of being, efficacious, that is, of achieving what they set out to achieve. It is clear that a philosophy that emphasises anguish, abandonment and despair might therefore seem from a communist perspective to undermine communist hopes and action, and to be a kind of self-indulgence that fails to motivate people to do anything to bring about much-needed change in the world. For communists, existentialism provides no sense of solidarity amongst individuals who could then work together to bring about a better world. Such, Sartre says, is the communists' complaint against existentialism.

The Christians' criticism of existentialism

According to Sartre, another set of criticisms of his existentialism comes from the Christians. For Christians, life is a gift from God; life is something beautiful that is to be treasured. Sartre's existentialism might seem to undermine this sense of life, this joyful attitude to things, and lead people to focus on the bleak and depressing side of life. Furthermore, Sartre thinks that the Christians believe that existentialism, in denying the existence of God and of his moral law, destroys all moral values and leads to a kind of anarchy in which no one is entitled to criticise the behaviour of anyone else from a moral point of view. Finally, like the communists, the Christians claim that existentialism denies any proper room for human solidarity.

We shall have to investigate later whether Sartre manages to show that these criticisms of his view are mistaken or not.

review activity

Explain in your own words the criticisms that the communists and Christians level against existentialism and why they do so.

Existence and essence

Sartre draws a sharp distinction between two kinds of beings: those whose essence precedes existence, and those whose existence precedes their essence.

In *EH* Sartre considers some article of manufacture, such as a paper-knife. Sartre says that even before such an object comes into existence – is manufactured or produced – the maker of this object, the artisan, has in his mind an idea of what the object must be like. This is because, in order to make the paper-knife, the artisan must know fairly exactly how much it must weigh, what its width, length and breadth should be, how long the blade must be, what sort of shape the handle must be if the knife is to be effective, and so on. In short, the artisan must know in advance of making a paper-knife what its properties must be. If the artisan did not know these things then he could not make the knife.

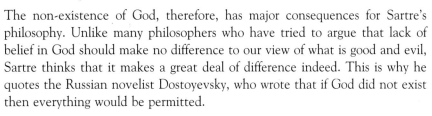

The paper-knife: essence precedes existence

Sartre says that the idea of the paper-knife in the artisan's mind reveals the *essence* of the paper-knife, for the properties it is to have *determine what kind of thing it is*. Further, Sartre says that because the artisan must have an idea of the properties of the paper-knife *before* he makes it the *essence* of the paper-knife *precedes* its *existence*.

Human beings' existence precedes essence

Sartre then goes on to draw an analogy between the artisan in such a case and God as an artisan. On a traditional account of God and his relation to human beings, God created us with a particular nature and with a particular purpose in life. That purpose is to follow God's commands and freely to love God in preparation for a life beyond this after death. Sartre says that if there were such a God then we could say that, for human beings, just as for paper-knives, essence precedes existence: just as the artisan has an idea in his mind of what the paper-knife must be before it exists, so we could say that God has an idea in his mind of what we are before we exist. However, Sartre says that God does not exist and that therefore in the case of human beings their essence does not precede their existence. On the contrary: their existence *precedes* their essence. What this means is that we find ourselves in existence and we have no nature that could determine what it is that we should do with our lives. We are free to find that out for ourselves.

The non-existence of God, therefore, has major consequences for Sartre's philosophy. Unlike many philosophers who have tried to argue that lack of belief in God should make no difference to our view of what is good and evil, Sartre thinks that it makes a great deal of difference indeed. This is why he quotes the Russian novelist Dostoyevsky, who wrote that if God did not exist then everything would be permitted.

Sartre's view is thus that we are completely free: God does not exist to tell us what to do and how to live, and we have no human nature which could guide us as to what the right kind of human life is.

Fyodor Dostoyevsky (1821–81)

review
activity

1. What does Sartre mean by saying that for a paper-knife essence precedes existence?

2. Under what conditions would it be true to say of human beings that their essence precedes their existence?

3. Why does Sartre think that in the case of human beings their existence precedes their essence?

Is it true that there is no human nature?

It might be said as an objection to Sartre that even if God does not exist this does not mean that there is no human nature. For, it might be argued, we do after all have a nature, and we get it from our basic biological (genetic) and physical make-up. For example, we can think of ourselves as having a particular nature when we remind ourselves that we are creatures who are mortal; who experience hunger, thirst and sexual desire; whose bodies can be easily damaged by material objects; who need to sleep; and so on. These conditions to which all of us are to a greater or lesser extent exposed, and it is plausible to think that they together give us a particular nature. Moreover, we can add to this the fact that, although there are exceptions to this, human beings in general are social animals who need the company of others for physical security as well as for emotional support. As Aristotle remarked, human beings need friends if they are to live a good and excellent life.

Should we think, therefore, that Sartre is denying that we have a nature in this sense?

In *EH* it looks as if Sartre does deny just this. However, this would make his view seem extremely implausible. In fact, this is one of those points where what Sartre says there needs to be supplemented by what he says in *BN*.

Facticity and the human condition

In *BN* Sartre discusses what he calls our 'facticity'. What he means by this can be illustrated by examples: a person's facticity includes, amongst other things, his physical constitution (height, weight, hair colour and so on); his living in a certain physical environment (which consists of a certain set of material conditions of both a natural and man-made form, such as climate and landscape, buildings and streets); and his being engaged on certain activities at a given moment (such as writing a book, which involves, in the present case of my writing *this* book, using the material objects of a computer, a desk and so on). It will also include the fact that we need to eat, drink and sleep and so forth; and that most people at any rate need the help and support of others through life (or some part of it).

Facticity   In *EH* Sartre describes human beings' facticity by drawing a distinction between human nature and the human condition (*EH*: 45f.). There is no human nature, he says, in the sense of an essence that can be found in each and every human being. Nonetheless, there is a universality of *condition*. Sartre says that this condition consists of 'the necessities of being in the world, of having to labour and to die there' (*EH*: 46).

The human condition

This is his version, so to speak, of the idea that there is a human nature. And he argues that, although the necessities in question are fixed, there are differing ways of *living* them. What does he mean by this?

What Sartre is getting at here is that *nothing about our facticity (condition) determines for us the kind of life we ought to lead,* either as individuals or as a group.

Consider, for example, the fact that a given person might be disabled. This is evidently part of such a person's facticity: there is nothing he can do about changing this. However, Sartre insists that such a person is free to think about his disability as he wishes. This is what Sartre means when he says that 'I choose the way in which I constitute my disability (as 'unbearable', 'humiliating', 'to be hidden', 'to be revealed to all', 'an object of pride', 'the justification for my failures' etc.)' (*BN*: 328).

Attitudes towards one's facticity

Clearly this case can be generalised: Sartre believes that one is free to adopt particular attitudes to one's facticity, whatever that might be. Thus, although each of us has to work in some way in life and many are not free in the choice of work we do – Sartre mentions the case of being born a slave in a pagan society, a condition from which there was (usually) no escape – we can choose our attitude to the work we do. For instance, we can see work as a humiliating necessity (as the ancient Greeks did) or as the place where the true dignity of man shows through (as Marx thought) or we can simply be indifferent to our work. None of these attitudes is itself forced on us by work itself.

So Sartre is claiming that our facticity, whilst it limits us in various ways, does not limit our free choice to view it – or, as Sartre sometimes puts it, to *appropriate* it – in a variety of different ways. In this sense, circumstances do not force us to behave in particular ways.

review activity

1. What does Sartre mean by 'facticity'?

2. What does it mean to say that there are different ways of living one's facticity? Give your own example to illustrate the point.

The for-itself (*pour-soi*) and the in-itself (*en-soi*)

Sartre's distinction between those constituents of the world whose existence precedes their essence (for example, human beings) and those whose essence precedes their existence (for example, paper-knives) corresponds to the distinction he makes in *BN* between the for-itself and the in-itself.

An example of an in-itself that Sartre discusses in *BN* is an inkwell. An inkwell is, Sartre says, wholly coincident with itself. This means that it is an inkwell and wholly an inkwell: its being is simply to be an inkwell and nothing else. Of course, we can use it as, say, a paperweight, but it remains an inkwell, which we are using as a paperweight. We might say: an inkwell is an inkwell through and through.

Human beings are partly forms of the in-itself. For example, they have bodies of given dimensions, proportions and so on. My body is what it is: I cannot alter my height at will, and, although I can alter my body by putting on or losing weight, this is in principle no different in this context from the fact that I can change the inkwell by breaking a piece from it or painting it or the like. However, a human being is also a for-itself. This is because a human being is a conscious being, indeed, a self-conscious being. A for-itself is a consciousness, a mind. Sartre uses the terminology of 'for-itself' because a mind is something for itself since it can reflect upon itself, that is, be concerned about its own operations, processes and so on.

Nothingness   Sartre gives a complicated analysis of consciousness, but central to it is the notion of *nothingness* – hence the title of his book *Being and Nothingness*. What Sartre has in mind here can be illustrated by considering the following example.

Suppose you are working with wood, trying to make the frame for a door of a greenhouse. Within this complex activity certain possibilities are available to you: they are *live* possibilities. For example, you have to measure wood out at the right length; saw it at the right point and in the right way; make a certain kind of joint; use hammer and nails or wooden pins to hold the door together securely; and so on. Each of the tasks presents itself as a *lack,* as something that is *not* the case – as a *nothingness*. The wood has *not yet* been measured or sawn; the joint has *not yet* been composed; and so on. However, these are possibilities only for you (and for anyone else engaged on this activity of door making with you). If I come along I shall see all the pieces of wood lying around, the greenhouse half-finished, but the ensemble of bits and pieces does not present itself to me as a lack, as something that is not the case. For me, they are just bits and pieces. What this means is that *you* are separated from the pieces of wood, the hammer, the nails and the rest by a *nothingness:* the pieces present themselves to you as a something to be done, in short, as a possibility for action. However, they are not this for *me:* I am not separated from them in this way. For me, they are just *there,* lying inertly around, so to speak.

This is typical of human activities. It is only within an ongoing activity for a particular person or a particular group of persons that something or other presents itself as a nothingness. This is rather like the case that Sartre describes of going into the café to see my friend Pierre. I have arranged to meet Pierre at three o'clock and I turn up just after three. I look around the café and see that Pierre is not there: the café contains for me a nothingness, and a very particular one at that. There are plenty of people who are not there, for example, Napoleon or Julius Caesar or Plato. However, the way in which Napoleon (or Julius Caesar or Plato) is not there differs for me profoundly from the way in which Pierre is not there: it is against the background of the activity of my arranging to meet Pierre that he is not there, that I am separated from the café by a nothingness. Napoleon is not there in a quite different way since it never was a live possibility that he be there. Moreover, for you, who do not even know that Pierre exists, Pierre is not absent from the café in the same way as he is absent for me.

review activity

1. What does Sartre mean by the terms 'for-itself' and 'in-itself'?

2. In what way is the notion of nothingness connected with Sartre's account of consciousness? Give your own example to illustrate the point.

Freedom and the fear of freedom

Sartre therefore argues that each for-itself is separated from the world by a nothingness that exists because each for-itself can act in any number of possible ways in the light of its situation in the world. Sartre calls this separation from the world in this way the for-itself's *freedom*. In fact, for Sartre the for-itself has no essential properties other than its freedom: this is why he says that 'man is free, man is freedom' (*EH*: 34).

Radical freedom and the emotions

This freedom is very radical. It includes the idea that we are responsible even for our emotions. Of course, Sartre grants that we often feel that we are overwhelmed by an emotion, but he insists that this is something we choose. He argues for this in an early work entitled *Sketch for a Theory of the Emotions* and he repeats the point in *BN* (445f.) and *EH* (34). His basic idea can be seen through an example he gives (Sartre 1985: 68f.).

Suppose that I am wealthy businessman and I discover that I have suddenly become financially ruined. Then I will need to face this and find other ways of dealing with money (for example, being frugal), other ways of going to work (for example, taking the bus because I have lost my car), consider selling my house and so on. In all of this I could take a practical attitude, and get on with changing my life in the relevant ways. This would be to approach the situation *scientifically* (*BN*: 445). On the other hand, I could become melancholy. Sartre says about this that my

> *melancholy is a method of suppressing the obligation to look for these new ways [of living], by transforming the present structure of the world, replacing it with a totally undifferentiated structure. What it comes to, in short, is that I make the world into an affectively neutral reality, a system which is, affectively, in complete equilibrium...In other words, lacking both the ability and the will to carry out the projects I formerly entertained, I behave in such a manner that the universe requires nothing more from me.* (Sartre 1985: 68–9)

Sartre says, then, that reacting to the situation with melancholy is an attempt to view the world as if it demanded nothing of me, but that this is clearly not the case since the world *does* demand something of me – namely, that I seek to confront my situation. Hence, he argues that the emotion in this case is an attempt to change the world just by *looking* at it in a certain way, that is, as emotionally coloured. This, he goes on to say, is a belief in a *magical transformation* of the world. But this he claims is true of all emotional states. Thus he says that having emotions is a state into which one deliberately puts oneself *in order to change the world by magic*. It is an attempt to evade the fact that the world can be *difficult* for us by pretending to ourselves that we can change it without doing anything except looking at it in a given way.

Sartre's view on the emotions shows how radical his conception of freedom is. Another example is our relation to our own past.

In one sense, one clearly is whatever it is that one has done. Thus I am in one sense a teacher and writer because in the past I have taught many times and because I have written a lot. However, according to Sartre, I cannot actually *be* a teacher and writer in the sense in which the inkwell is an inkwell. This is because I am free at any time simply to throw over my teaching and writing and do something else instead. In fact, whatever I have done in the past is simply part of my facticity to which I am free to take up any attitude I wish: I am not constrained by my past to continue behaving as I did then.

Sartre says that this radical freedom is something of which we are frightened: it scares us to know that we are free to throw over our past and start behaving in a different way. For this reason, we seek to pretend that we are not, after all, free in this way. We try to pretend that we can have the kind of being that an in-itself has. For example, we like to pretend that we simply *are* a teacher or writer or student or politician or waiter. And Sartre gives an example to show how a waiter can pretend to himself that he is a waiter, as an inkwell is an inkwell.

> *Let us consider this waiter in the café. His movement is quick and forward, a little too precise, a little too rapid. He comes toward the patrons with a step a little too quick. He bends forward a little too eagerly; his voice, his eyes express an interest a little too solicitous for the order of the customer. Finally there he returns, trying to imitate in his walk the inflexible stiffness of some kind of automaton while carrying his tray with the recklessness of a tight-rope-walker by putting it in a perpetually unstable, perpetually broken equilibrium which he perpetually reestablishes by a light movement of the arm and hand ... He is playing, he is amusing himself. But what is he playing? We need not watch long before we can explain it: he is playing at being a waiter in a café.* (BN: 59)

Part of what Sartre is getting at here is the idea that the waiter would like to think that he *is* a waiter in the sense that he has no choice about being a waiter. This would relieve him of the burden of recognising that he could simply stop working as he does if he wants to. As it is, he would like to believe that he is a waiter for at least two reasons. First, he has behaved as a waiter in the past, and this helps him towards the belief that he has no choice but to continue being a waiter. Secondly, his customers in the café have certain expectations of him – that he behave in a certain way, look a certain way and so on – because of his social role as a waiter. For them, he is nothing more than a waiter. This makes it easy for him to take on their judgement of him, and helps him believe that he *is* a waiter, that is, that he is nothing more than a waiter.

Bad faith According to Sartre, of course, the waiter can never *be* a waiter. However, insofar as he seeks to live as if he *were* a waiter in the sense in question, he is in a state of what Sartre calls 'bad faith' (*mauvaise foi*). In fact, Sartre thinks that because we are frightened of our freedom we are most of us most of the time in a state of bad faith. That is, we try to behave as if we existed as an in-itself, not as a for-itself. We can never *be* an in-itself, says Sartre, as we have seen, but the futile attempt to do this and thus flee our freedom characterises a great deal of human activity.

One way of putting Sartre's claims here is to say that he believes that we always have some distance from features of our own psychology. We can see this by noting that, just as Sartre thinks that it is impossible ever to be a waiter, he also thinks that it is impossible ever to *be* a coward or a traitor or a mean person. What we can say is that someone might have done lots of cowardly or treacherous or mean deeds, but this does not mean that he is now incapable of not doing such things. There is no such thing, says Sartre, as a cowardly temperament (*EH*: 43): a coward is responsible for his cowardice, that is, for doing cowardly deeds. A coward, in this sense, Sartre claims, 'is guilty of being a coward' (*EH*: 43). The only sense in which someone *is* a coward, then, is that he has behaved in certain ways: no one can be a coward in the sense that he cannot help acting in a cowardly manner. If someone said: 'Well, I did this because I just am a coward. That's the kind of person I am and there's nothing I can do about it', Sartre would say that this person was in bad faith.

review activity

1. In what way does Sartre argue that we are responsible even for our emotions?

2. What does Sartre mean by saying that when we experience an emotion we are trying to transform the world by magic?

3. Explain in your own words Sartre's notion of bad faith. Give your own example to illustrate your account.

'The chips are down'

Sartre's conception of freedom has at least one particularly odd consequence. We can see this in the following way.

Suppose I am confronted by a situation that demands some response of me. For example, I might discover that a friend has betrayed me. There are various ways I could respond: with anger (I want to punish him in some way); with sadness or depression (the meaning seems to have gone out of my life); with self-loathing (I think it must be my fault that he betrayed me); and so on. Further, the situation demands that I do something: I could break off my friendship; I could try to patch things up; I could leave the country; I could plot to have my friend betrayed by someone else; and the like. Suppose I do one thing rather than another. Why do I do this? Well, there must be something about me, about the kind of person I am, that leads me to act as I do (I am a jealous or aggressive or forgiving person, or whatever). Why am I this kind of person in the first place? Sartre says that I am thus because I have *chosen* to be like this: we each of us have an 'original project' or a 'fundamental project', which is the choice of who we are, of our character. Here is the oddity, however. If I have chosen to be a certain kind of person, then when I react in a certain way to my friend's betrayal of me I am simply playing out the fundamental choice that I have made to be a certain kind of person. This means that *I am not really choosing* how to react to my friend's betrayal at all. The choice of how to react was, as it were, made a long time ago when I chose to be a certain kind of person. Moreover, I might not even remember making, or have any sense that I did make, such a choice. But if I have made such a choice then when I react to my friend's betrayal I am not, after all, really free to behave in one way rather than another. This is why Sartre says in *BN* that when I deliberate 'the chips are down' (*les jeux sont faits*) (*BN*: 451). It is also why he says in *EH*:

> [W]hat we usually understand by wishing or willing is a conscious decision taken – much more often than not – after we have made ourselves what we are. I may wish to join a party, to write a book or to marry – but in such a case what is usually called my will is probably a manifestation of a prior and more spontaneous decision. If, however, it is true that existence is prior to essence, man is responsible for what he is.
> (*EH*: 28–9)

It turns out, therefore, that at a given moment of decision we are usually not free. There are exceptions to this, as we shall return to this below. But in the meantime, we need to ask whether there are other problems with Sartre's conception of freedom.

Why does Sartre think that when we choose 'the chips are down'?

Are we as free as Sartre supposes?

One of the basic problems with Sartre's theory of freedom seems to be that we simply do not always have the kind of distance from our own psychology that his theory claims. For example, most people find that they have a certain type of character with certain traits and that at least many of these are pretty much impossible to change or get rid of. This might sometimes be because they are in a state of bad faith, trying to resist responsibility for what they are, but it might be because human beings just do have more fixed psychological traits than Sartre supposes. For example, Samuel Johnson (1709–84), who is probably most widely known for producing the first important dictionary of the English language, but who was also a very great writer and man of letters, spent years trying to combat his tendency to indolence and laziness, with very little success. Johnson, however, was certainly not a man who wished to shirk responsibility for what he was. On the contrary, he made enormous demands on himself to be sincere and open in his dealings with himself and others.

Or consider another case. In a discussion of homosexuality in *BN* (63ff.) Sartre suggests that a homosexual chooses to be homosexual and could thus change his sexual preferences if he wished. (Sartre would also argue the same for a heterosexual, of course.) But is this true? As Gregory McCulloch has written:

> *Do people really choose or have the live possibility of changing their sexuality? Is it not, rather, that some people find themselves sexually attracted to men, others to women and some to both? Certainly, if one is to be straightforward, then sexuality is the sort of thing that has to be taken responsibility for, and this contributes to the sort of person you are. But choice and change are other matters entirely.*   (McCulloch 1994: 67)

One way of putting the criticisms I have made of Sartre is to contrast two conceptions of the self.

Most people believe that the self has very definite traits of character, usually very different from one person to the next. We tend to think, that is, that some people are cowardly, others courageous; some mean, some kind; some people are hard working, whilst others are lazy – although it is not always easy to say what traits of character a person has, even if one knows him very well. It may well be true that we can do more to alter our character than we usually suppose, but we usually think we have a substantial set of character traits. Some moral theories look at things in this way: virtue theory is one of them.

For Sartre, the self is not substantial in terms of having or being made up of character traits. On the contrary, for Sartre, the self is really *empty*: it is nothing but freedom. This is why, as we have seen, he writes that man *is* freedom. You are, in fact, nothing but the possibility of being other than you have been hitherto. And it is this idea that I have been criticising.

If these criticisms are correct, we can say that Sartre has an overly optimistic view of human freedom.

review activity

On what grounds might one say that we are not as free as Sartre supposes?

Anguish

Fear and anguish

Still, whether these criticisms are right or not, Sartre believes that human beings are free in a very radical sense. This, he argues, gives rise to *anguish*. However, his account of anguish in *EH* is slightly different from the account of this that he offers in *BN*.

In *BN* (29ff.) Sartre distinguishes between fear and anguish. He gives the following example. If am walking along the edge of a cliff that has a steep fall and no guard-rail I might be fearful lest I fall: perhaps my foot will slip, or maybe a gust of wind will blow me over the edge. However, I might then realise, not that I might fall, but that I could throw myself off the edge of the cliff. In this case, I see that I am completely free to do this act, and that nothing at all determines me not to throw myself off. When I realise this I am in anguish. So, fear is an emotion that one experiences in the face of a danger that comes to one from without (unstable ground, a gust of wind and so forth); anguish is an emotion one experiences in face of oneself, and specifically, in face of one's freedom.

Action: commitment of all mankind

In *EH*, Sartre's account of anguish is, as noted, slightly different. There (*EH:* 30ff.) he clearly assumes that anguish is, indeed, a response to one's freedom, but he adds something else. This is that when one acts one at the same time commits the rest of mankind to this way of acting. Of course, Sartre does not have in mind here all one's trivial actions, such as eating toast or muesli for breakfast. What he means are the big decisions that commit one to a whole way of life, such as becoming a parent or a communist. Sartre thinks that choosing, not simply for oneself but for all human beings, is a terrible burden, and his name for this is 'anguish'.

Sartre's view here bears some similarities to Kant's view of morality as well as to that of R. M. Hare. According to Kant, for example, one should only act in such a way that one would be willing for others also to act. Let us pursue Kant's thinking on this a little for it will help us in our understanding Sartre.

One of Kant's examples is this: if you are considering lying to a friend, you ought only to do so if you were willing that others also lie. But Kant thinks that you could not will that others lie, and therefore you ought not to lie yourself. Roughly, this is because he thinks that if you lie to your friend then you are relying on your friend believing you. If he believes you this is because he trusts you. Why does he trust you? He trusts you because he thinks that you do not lie; and he thinks this at least in part because people can be relied upon to tell the truth. So, if you lie to your friend, you require him to believe you and are therefore depending upon your friend's belief in the general reliability of people. But this means that in lying to him you rely on something (people being generally truthful in what they say) which you at the same time undermine (by lying). So, for Kant, to lie is *irrational:* it relies on something which it undermines at the same time. This is an example of the way in which Kant thinks that one should only act in a way that one would be willing for others to act.

Kant's argument relies on the idea that we are all rational beings and thus can agree on the way in which we wish to act; for obviously, since the argument depends upon the irrationality of lying, there would not be a problem about lying if we were not rational beings.

Sartre does not place any emphasis upon reason. Unlike Kant, he does not see reason as the crucial aspect of human beings, but rather freedom. Therefore he cannot argue that the reason why we should only act in such a way that we can will others also act is that we are rational beings. What, then, is his justification for saying that when one acts one chooses for all human beings?

Unfortunately, Sartre gives no reason in *EH* for his claim. He simply asserts it. Nevertheless, it has some plausibility. Thus, a person who converts to, say Catholicism, must believe in God, in the general tenets of the Church, in its moral teaching and so on. Further, he must surely believe in some sense that the life of a Roman Catholic, or at any rate that of a Christian or some related religion, is the right kind of life and that those who are atheists are in some sense mistaken. Similarly, a communist must surely believe that those who reject communism and the communist way of life are in some sense mistaken. And so on.

However, Sartre's point has only a limited plausibility. This is because it can make perfect sense for someone to adopt a way of life but not be at all committed to the idea that everyone should live in this way. Thus, to take Sartre's example, a person may marry and have children, but it does not follow that he is thereby committing the whole of mankind to the practice of monogamy, as Sartre claims. He could think that monogamy is right for him and his wife, but also quite sensibly and consistently think it is not right for everyone. He could think that a different kind of person should live in a quite different way; or he may have no opinion on how others should behave with respect to the issue of getting married; or he might think that it makes life interesting if there are people who do not marry and have children, that is, who live in a way different from his own.

Someone might say, in any case, that he does not experience anguish in the way Sartre suggests. However, Sartre would argue that such a person is in anguish after all, but that he is concealing it from himself. And the way he would be doing this would be by being in bad faith, as we have already discussed. We can deny that we bear the kind of responsibility Sartre claims we have, but we cannot in truth escape it: we can only pretend to ourselves that we have.

review activity

1. What does Sartre mean by anguish?
2. What arguments might one give against the claim that in choosing I choose for all mankind?

Abandonment and a moral dilemma

Another term Sartre uses, related to that of 'anguish', is 'abandonment'. What he means by this is simply that, because there is no God we cannot think that values – any values, but Sartre has in mind particularly moral values – are written into the nature of things. There are no values *a priori*. He says rather that one should *choose* one's values. We are abandoned without any guidance from God as to how to live. Further, as we have already seen, Sartre thinks that there is no human nature from which we could derive our values.

This emphasis upon choosing values means that Sartre is an irrealist and a non-cognitivist about morality.

There is something slightly odd here. This is that, although Sartre insists that God does not exist, he never argues that he does not. He clearly thinks that in some sense it is just not possible honestly to believe that God exists, but he does not spell out in his work the reasons for this. Furthermore, right at the end of the book (*EH*: 56) Sartre says that even if God existed this would make no difference from a moral point of view, because one would still have to choose how to interpret God's commands and whether to follow them as thus interpreted. So we are just as abandoned even if God does exist. Perhaps this is why he does not undertake to show that God does not exist.

Art and morality

Sartre's views on the status of values is well brought out in his comparison of art and morality (*EH*: 48–50). He points out there that there are no *a priori* rules for the construction of a work of art. Similarly, Sartre argues that there are no *a priori* rules for morality. Just as the artist must paint a picture without any rules to follow, so when we act morally there are no rules for us to follow, rules, that is, that exist independently of the choices we make. The artist has to decide what to do from one moment to the next, and we cannot tell in advance what he is going to do: that is for him to decide. We are the same when we make moral decision. Moral choice is like constructing a work of art: we have, so to speak, to improvise, use our considered judgement, and we cannot rely in either case upon rules to tell us what to do.

Sartre emphasises that he is not propounding an aesthetic morality. That is, he is not propounding a frivolous morality that would make morality unimportant. Rather, his point is that morality, like the production of a work of art, is creative. In addition to this, by comparing morality to art, Sartre means to be pointing out that, just as the value of a work of art slowly emerges as the work is produced, so the value of a person's life gradually emerges as the person lives his life. It is in what a person does that his value appears: each person is the sum total of his actions and nothing else. We shall return to this point in more detail below.

Moral dilemma and radical choice

Sartre seeks to show the sense in which we have to choose our values through the example of the young man who came to him to ask his advice about what to do in a moral dilemma. The young man did not know whether to go and fight for the Free French Forces, to help the French war effort; or whether to stay at home and look after his old and sick mother.

Sartre argues that any moral system is useless in helping this young man decide what to do. For example, Kantianism says that we should never treat a person merely as a means but always also as an end. However, the problem here is that it is unclear what this tells the young man to do. If he goes away to fight, then perhaps this is treating his mother as a mere means; but if he stays, then perhaps he is treating his potential comrades in arms as mere means. Or again, Christianity says that one should act with charity and love. But does this mean he should stay or that he should go? Which act is really the charitable and loving act? To this, Christianity seems to provide no answer.

The pointlessness of advice

Furthermore, Sartre argues that it is actually useless asking another person for advice about what to do in a moral dilemma. This is because one knows already what kind of advice it is that one will get. If the young man were to ask a priest who was a collaborator, that is, one who supported the Nazis, then he would get one kind of answer; if he were to ask a priest who opposed the Nazis then he would get a different answer. So it is in fact pointless for the young man to ask anyone for advice. He did, of course, ask Sartre for advice. But, believing that asking for advice is useless, Sartre merely said to the young man: 'You are free, so choose.'

Sartre's idea that when confronted with a moral dilemma one can do nothing but choose in the kind of way indicated is known as his theory of *radical choice*.

We noted earlier that Sartre claims that when one makes a decision 'the chips are down'. We noted that there are, Sartre thinks, exceptions to this. The central case of this is the point where one makes a radical choice, as the young man in Sartre's example had to. Here, Sartre thinks, one can genuinely take a decision which is not determined by choices one has made in the past. In this case, one chooses a new 'fundamental project'. As Sartre says:

> *These extraordinary and marvelous instants when the prior project collapses into the past in the light of a new project which rises on its ruins and which yet exists only in outline, in which humiliation, anguish, joy, hope are delicately blended, in which we let go in order to grasp and grasp in order to let go –– these have often appeared to furnish the clearest and most moving image of our freedom.*
>
> (BN: 476)

review
activity

1. What does Sartre mean by 'abandonment'?
2. Why does Sartre think that, even if God existed, we would still be just as abandoned?
3. What is the point of Sartre's comparison between art and morality?
4. What does he not mean in making this comparison between art and morality?
5. Describe in your own words the dilemma of the young man who came to see Sartre. What does Sartre think this dilemma shows?

Is Sartre's account of radical choice plausible?

There seem to be certain problems with Sartre's theory of radical choice (cf. Taylor 1986: 29ff.).

Sartre presents the young man as torn between doing two things, in a situation in which he cannot do both. Both of these things *weigh* with him – that is, are important to him. Clearly he thinks that it is valuable to stay with his mother and also that it is valuable to go off to fight. Each of them has a *claim* on him. However, they can only have this claim on him because he did not *choose* to think they are valuable. They do not present themselves to him in this way, that is, as merely a matter of choice. If they did, then he could also simply choose to regard some other decision as a dilemma of the same magnitude, for example, the decision whether to eat vanilla or chocolate ice-cream. Yet that choice of ice-cream flavour could never present itself to him as the same kind of dilemma as the one of whether to stay with his mother or go off to fight. This is because the choice of ice-cream flavour can never have a *claim* on him as does the dilemma involving his mother or fighting.

So one thing wrong with Sartre's account of the young man's dilemma is that Sartre fails to see that the dilemma is only a dilemma because the young man has not *chosen* to regard staying with his mother or going off to fight as valuable.

There is, however, another problem with Sartre's presentation of the issue. The problem is this. When we have to choose between alternatives we normally weigh up what is to be said for doing one or the other. The young man might, for example, think about what kind of relationship he has with his mother; about whether he could find someone else to look after her if he went off to fight; about what she might think of this if he did; about whether he really could contribute to the war effort; about whether he was really prepared to die in the war; and so on. He will also think about what it is that he in fact *wants* to do. In other words, he will try to find *reasons for acting one way rather than another*. If he thinks about such things, then he does not simply choose in the radical way Sartre envisages. For Sartre envisages him as simply choosing, but *not* on the basis of what is to be said for acting one way rather than another. For the young man, as Sartre presents him, has *no* reasons for acting one way rather than another. Sartre thinks that the choice to act one way rather than another *is* the choice about what to count as reasons for action. According to Sartre, if he chooses to stay with his mother then he will thenceforth be counting fidelity to his mother as a reason for acting; in the absence of having made the choice, fidelity to his mother will not be for him a reason for action. Similarly, if he goes off to fight then he will henceforth think of patriotism as a reason for acting; but he does not think this before going off to fight. However, if Sartre's way of looking at the situation were correct then he could not see what he is faced by as a dilemma.

What all this means is that, on Sartre's presentation of the situation, when the young man chooses he chooses on the basis of nothing whatsoever – he has no reasons and his wishes are irrelevant. But this just means that the choice is a leap into the dark. It would be as if he simply said: 'What the hell, I'll stay with my mother'. To choose on the basis of nothing, however, is not to make a *choice* at all. What Sartre presents as a radical choice is nothing but blind and thoughtless action.

review
activity

What is the key criticism one can make of Sartre's account of radical choice?

Despair

Another notion which is crucial in Sartre's existentialism is that of despair. As he himself says, this is basically quite a simple notion. It means that we should act without hope. That is, we can never be sure that the things we aim for will come to fruition. Further, we cannot rely on others whom we do not know. They might act in any way – for example, in such a way as to undermine the things one is aiming at.

This leads Sartre into a discussion of the importance of action in life. He argues that, for an existentialist, a person can claim no credit for what he might have done but did not do: for it is *action* that counts. In some of his literary writing Sartre explores this issue. For example, in his play *Huis clos* (*In Camera*), three people – Garcin, Inez and Estelle – find themselves after their death in Hell.

Garcin was in life a journalist, working in Rio and running a pacifist newspaper. He thought of himself as a hero, someone who would stand up to oppression and cruelty. For this reason he was able to forgive himself for his cruel treatment of his wife. However, when war broke out he fled by train, afraid to stand up for what he believed in, telling himself he could set up a pacifist newspaper in Mexico. He was caught at the border and shot, facing death, as he puts it 'miserably, rottenly' (Sartre 1982: 215). Now in Hell he is tormented by the fact that he acted in a cowardly manner: it is no use pretending that he was really a hero. His thoughts counted for nothing. What counts are his actions. Now, in death, he is the sum of what he did and nothing else. And what he did was to behave as a coward. What he might have done and what he thought about himself are nothing.

Sartre's responses to the criticisms of the communists and Christians; and the experience of shame

Sartre's existentialism emphasises action, that is, what one does, so he thinks that it is a positive and optimistic doctrine, telling man who he really is and thus helping to make possible for him the kind of life worthy of the free being he is. This is part of his response to the claim of the communists, noted at the beginning, that existentialism is a negative and pessimistic doctrine. The communists also claimed that Sartre's existentialism did not allow for any human solidarity. Sartre says that it does, because it puts man firmly in charge of his own destiny, which means that he is free to co-operate with others with total responsibility for his actions. Moreover, Sartre insists that existentialism posits a true solidarity amongst individuals because 'I cannot obtain any truth whatsoever about myself, except through the mediation of another. The other is indispensable to my existence, and equally so to any knowledge I can have of myself' (*EH*: 45). His thinking here is somewhat obscure, because it is not explained in detail, and once more we need to turn to *BN* in order properly to understand what Sartre means.

Suppose you are alone in a room, looking at the objects in it. The room might be a large room in an art gallery, for example, and you are looking at the paintings on the walls. Suddenly, someone else comes into the room and starts looking at the paintings. When this other person comes in, you realise that these paintings are not simply there *for you*: they are also there *for him*, or, as Sartre puts it, there for the *Other* (the word is usually written with the initial letter as a capital in such contexts). That is, there is a perspective on the room that is the perspective of someone other than you – of the Other.

The Other may now turn to look at you. Then, suddenly, *you* are an object for the Other in the room: your body is just one more thing at which the Other looks. This gives to you a new sense of yourself. For you were simply a consciousness looking at the world (the objects in the room). Suddenly you have become an object for the consciousness of another – of the Other.

Shame   Sartre illustrates this change most dramatically with the following example (*BN*: 259ff.). Suppose I am looking through a keyhole at what is going on in the room on the other side of the door. I am wholly absorbed in this, totally taken up in what it is that I see there. Suddenly, however, I hear footsteps behind me. Then I realise that I am being looked at. I am no longer absorbed in what is going on in the room: I am aware of being an object for the Other. The experience I have is, says Sartre, one of *shame,* for I am ashamed to be caught by the Other looking through the keyhole.

I only experience shame in this way because there is another person there to look at me. This means that my sense of myself is structured at least in part by the Other. *What I am,* my own being, does not simply depend upon myself, but also depends upon the Other.

The example of shame is one of a number of cases where Sartre thinks that one's sense of oneself depends crucially upon the Other's sense of one.

In *EH* Sartre presents this interrelation – or 'intersubjectivity' as he calls it – as part of the idea that existentialism allows for solidarity amongst human beings. However, this is slightly misleading, for in *BN* he presents the idea that what any given individual is depends partly on what others thinks of him as being a source of permanent conflict between individuals.

All human relationships involve conflict

We can see why he thinks this in the following way. Recall that each of us is completely free, according to Sartre. Now, when the Other looks at me, I am just an *object* for him. If I am caught looking through the keyhole I am merely one more thing (an in-itself) in *his* world. Yet, at the same time I remain a free being (a for-itself). This sets up a conflict: I am an object for him, yet I am always more than an object for myself because I am free in the way no object is or could be. This means that my relation to the Other is one of tension or conflict, and in *BN* Sartre presents all human relationships as involving such tension or conflict. So, whilst it is true to say, as Sartre does in *EH,* that I discover myself and the Other together – that is, that I am what I am partly through what the Other is – this kind of solidarity is an odd one: it is a solidarity which involves tension or conflict. To this extent, Sartre's reply to the communists is misleading, for the communists would presumably not value very highly a solidarity amongst human beings which fundamentally involved conflict.

Sartre goes on to discuss the issue of human solidarity in the context of his thinking on the human condition, already mentioned above. We recall that he argues that each human being lives or appropriates his condition in the world in a different manner. Obviously the condition of each human being is itself very different: that of an inhabitant of contemporary England is different from that of someone living in contemporary China; that of a medieval peasant very different from the condition of a denizen of ancient Greece. However, Sartre suggests that one can always understand the way in which another person – however distant in time and space from oneself – appropriates his own condition. This is what he means when he says (*EH*: 46): 'In every purpose there is universality, in the sense that every purpose is comprehensible to every man.'

Once again, Sartre's comments here are somewhat obscure and contentious. It seems that he exaggerates the extent to which human beings are comprehensible to one another. After all, it is a great theme of many human endeavours to try to explore the ways in which human beings are obscure to one another and fail to understand each other's projects and aims. Novels, poetry, history and anthropology, for instance, all explore such things. Furthermore, the issues surrounding moral relativism raise serious problems about whether we can fully understand, say, Aztec practices of ritual human sacrifice; or the exposure of unwanted infants, which was often normal practice in previous ages; or different kinds of punishment, which seem to us barbaric but which other cultures (or our own at a previous time) thought of as quite normal; and so on.

Sartre also wanted to respond to the Christians' criticisms, and in response to them he clearly thinks that existentialism does allow one to see the beautiful and joyous things in life. This is one reason why he says that 'this theory [of existentialism] is alone compatible with the dignity of man' (*EH*: 44–5).

review activity

1.   In what way does Sartre think that the Other is necessary for knowledge of myself?

2.   Why does Sartre think that all human relationships involve conflict?

Judging others

We have seen that, according to Sartre, there are no values *a priori*, and that we must choose our values. However, if this is so, then on what basis can one judge others? Sartre actually thinks that one cannot condemn others so long as they are acting 'on the plane of free commitment' (*EH*: 54). He illustrates this by comparing Maggie Tulliver in George Eliot's novel *The Mill on the Floss* with La Sanseverina in Stendhal's novel *Chartreuse de Parme* (*EH*: 53).

Maggie is in love with Stephen, but he is engaged to another young woman. Maggie chooses to renounce Stephen and thus sacrifices her passion to human solidarity. La Sanseverina looks to be in a quite different position. She believes that it is only through experiencing a great passion that one's life is of value, and she would never have given up a love like the one Maggie had for Stephen so that the latter could live out a boringly conventional life. Sartre says that these two women seem to be acting for quite different reasons, but he claims that this is not so. Both of them, says Sartre, are aiming in their different ways at their own freedom. Thus, it is not possible to condemn either of the women, for they are both acting freely. In this sense, it does not matter what they do, just so long as they are acting freely.

To this one might reply that this might be plausible in some cases, but that it is surely not right in all cases. For example, suppose tomorrow lots of people become fascists. They choose a way of life that involves violence and oppression of others. If we are free to choose our values, how can one judge that what such persons do is wrong? Sartre himself says that if some people choose fascism tomorrow than 'fascism will be the truth of man' (*EH*: 40). So, on what basis can they be condemned?

Sartre actually says that such people cannot be condemned from a *moral* point of view: they are to be condemned for being in bad faith. In oppressing others, fascists are pretending that they themselves have a fixed nature. For, so Sartre's thought goes, when they see the pain they cause to the oppressed in the eyes of the oppressed, they experience themselves as definite, fixed, that is, as having a given nature. This is because when they oppress others they feel that they are *by nature* the strong ones, the ones who *by nature* are in charge. This they can never be, for in Sartre's philosophy no person can have such a nature. In addition, fascists also suppose that others – for example, Jews – have a fixed nature. But, for the same reasons, this is false.

The liberty of others   This argument of Sartre's can be put in another, related way, as Sartre himself does (*EH:* 52). According to Sartre, human beings are free. But this means that each individual must make the liberty of others his goal. The idea is that if I see you for what you really are, then I must see that you are free. But if I see this and behave as if you were not free then I am denying what you really are. This is why Sartre says that 'I am obliged to will the liberty of others at the same time as mine' (*EH:* 52).

Sartre calls those who pretend they are not free 'cowards'; he calls those who pretend that others are not free 'scum'. 'Scum' translates the French word *salauds*, which comes from the French *sale* ('dirty').

There seem to be some difficulties with Sartre's argument here. First, it does seem odd to suppose that one cannot condemn fascists on moral grounds. One could, for example, do so on the basis of certain moral theories – utilitarianism, Kantianism or virtue theory. Sartre would reply that the choice to condemn fascists on the grounds of one of these theories depends upon a choice to believe in such a theory and that this choice is completely free and, from that point of view, no better or worse than that of the choice others make to accept in fascism.

However, there is a second criticism that one could make of Sartre here – a much more serious criticism. This is the following. Suppose we grant that we are all free. Then it is clear why I have reason to wish for a life in which *my* freedom can be expressed and why I want to pursue *my* freedom. It is also clear why you have reason to wish for a life in which *your* freedom can be expressed and why you want to pursue *your* freedom. But why should *I* have reason to wish for a life in which *your* freedom can be expressed? I might see clearly that you are free, but this, as such, does not give me any reason to care about your freedom.

If this seems unclear, consider a parallel case. I might say – and it seems plausible – that each person wants to be happy. In this sense, *I* want to pursue *my* happiness, and *you* want to pursue *your* happiness. But why should *I* want to pursue *your* happiness? Surely I only want this if I have some moral concern for you (unless I am just your friend, but we can leave this case aside). But then we would say that I care about your happiness if I am, at least to some extent, morally good. There is no problem in this. However, there would be if we had no real notion of moral goodness: if we lacked such a notion then we would have no reason for saying that if I am indifferent to your happiness I am morally blameable.

Go back now to the case of freedom as Sartre presents it. In this parallel case there is no notion of moral goodness. Hence, there is no reason to blame me if I do not care about your freedom. I could just say: 'Yes, I see that you are free, but I don't care about that and I am not going to respect your freedom.' We would normally think this morally blameable. However, Sartre cannot because he has no adequate notion of moral praise or blame. To this extent, then, his claim that we are obliged to respect the freedom of those around us is simply an assertion for the defence of which his philosophy has no real grounds.

review activity

1. From what point of view does Sartre think fascism can be condemned?

2. Why does Sartre think that 'I am obliged to will the liberty of others at the same time as mine'?

3. What criticism can one make of Sartre's argument concerning the liberty of others?

Two forms of humanism

Sartre ends his short book by considering two forms of humanism, one of which he rejects and the other of which he accepts.

The first form of humanism involves the idea that man exists as a supreme and wonderful being, the purpose for which all exists – or, as Sartre puts it, 'as the end-in-itself' (*EH*: 54). Sartre rejects this notion of humanism since he thinks that it is impossible and absurd to come to a judgement concerning the value of human beings as such. This is because man is a being that has no fixed nature and thus one cannot say that he is good or bad as such, for he does not exist as a finished being on whom one could cast such a verdict.

The second notion of humanism is one that Sartre accepts. According to this second notion of humanism, what humanism means is that man is always in the process of making himself and there is no one – no God or the like – to tell him how to live. He must and does struggle always for new possibilities, new ways of living. This is what Sartre means by saying that man is 'self-surpassing' (*EH*: 55). It is only by existing this way that man truly exists at all. He must decide for himself how to live: abandoned in a godless world, he must make of life what he will; this is the source of true humanism and, Sartre thinks, an inspiring vision of man.

some questions to think about

1 'Because Sartre simply assumes that God does not exist and does not argue for it, his entire philosophy is undermined.' How far would you agree with this claim?

2 Do you agree with Sartre that one is free to take up any attitude one wishes to one's facticity?

3   Is Sartre right in saying that a coward is responsible for his cowardice?

4   Do you agree with Sartre that we choose our character (fundamental project)?

5   Can Sartre's theory of radical choice be defended against criticism?

6   Is Sartre right to think that all human relationships are fundamentally hostile?

7   'A philosophy that issues in the result that one cannot *morally* condemn the fascist is absurd.' Is this true?

further reading

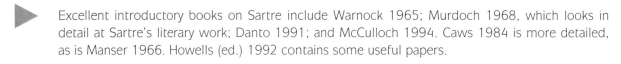

Excellent introductory books on Sartre include Warnock 1965; Murdoch 1968, which looks in detail at Sartre's literary work; Danto 1991; and McCulloch 1994. Caws 1984 is more detailed, as is Manser 1966. Howells (ed.) 1992 contains some useful papers.

bibliography

Acton, H.B. (1970), *Kant's Moral Philosophy* (London: Macmillan).

Adams, Marilyn McCord and Adams, Robert Merrihew (eds) (1994), *The Problem of Evil* (Oxford: Oxford University Press).

Allen, R.E. (1965a), 'Participation and Predication in Plato's Middle Dialogues' in Allen (ed.) 1965, pp. 43–60.

Allen, R.E. (ed.) (1965), *Studies in Plato's Metaphysics* (London: Routledge & Kegan Paul).

Allen, R.E. (1972), 'The Argument from Opposites in *Republic* V' in Anton and Kustas (eds) 1972, pp. 165–75.

Alston, William (1967), 'The Ontological Argument Revisited' in Doney (ed.) 1967, pp. 278–302.

Alston, William P. (1983), 'Christian Experience and Christian Belief' in Plantinga and Wolterstorff (eds) 1983, pp. 103–34.

Alston, William P. (1984), 'Being-Itself and Talk About God' *Center Journal*, **3**(3), 9–25.

Alston, William P. (2000), 'Why Should There Not Be Experience of God?' in Davies (ed.) 2000, pp. 382–6.

Altham, J.E.J. and Harrison, Ross (eds) (1995), *World, Mind, and Ethics: Essays on the Ethical Philosophy of Bernard Williams* (Cambridge: Cambridge University Press).

Annas, Julia (1981), *An Introduction to Plato's* Republic (Oxford: Oxford University Press).

Anscombe, G.E.M. (1958), 'Modern Moral Philosophy' *Philosophy*, **33**(124), 1–19.

Anscombe, G.E.M. (1985), 'Why Anselm's Proof in the Proslogion Is Not an Ontological Argument' *The Thoreau Quarterly*, **17**(182), 32–40.

Anscombe, G.E.M. (1993), 'Russelm or Anselm?' *The Philosophical Quarterly*, **43**(173), 500–4.

Anscombe, G.E.M (2000), '"Whatever Has a Beginning of Existence Must Have a Cause"' in Davies (ed.) 2000, pp. 233–38.

Anton, J.P. and Kustas, G.L. (eds) (1972), *Essays in Ancient Greek Philosophy* (Albany: SUNY Press).

Aquinas, St Thomas (1991), *Summa Theologiae: a Concise Translation* (London: Methuen), tr. and ed. Timothy McDermott.

Aquinas, St Thomas (1998), *Selected Philosophical Writings* (Harmondsworth: Penguin), tr., intro., and notes Timothy McDermott.

Arendt, Hannah (1958), *The Human Condition* (Chicago: University of Chicago Press).

Arendt, Hannah (1967), 'Truth and Politics' in Laslett and Runciman (eds) 1967, pp. 104–33.

Arendt, Hannah (1990 [1963]), *On Revolution* (Harmondsworth: Penguin).

Aristotle (1985), *Nicomachean Ethics* (Indianapolis: Hackett), tr., ed., and notes Terence Irwin.

Armstrong, D.M. (1969), 'Does Knowledge Entail Belief?' *Proceedings of the Aristotelian Society*, **70**, pp. 21–36.

Armstrong, D.M. (1973), *Belief, Truth and Knowledge* (London: Cambridge University Press).

Audi, Robert (1998), *Epistemology: a Contemporary Introduction to the Theory of Knowledge* (London: Routledge).

Auguet, Roland (1972), *Cruelty and Civilization: the Roman Games* (London: George Allen).

Augustine (1961), *Confessions* (Harmondsworth: Penguin), tr. R.S. Pine-Coffin.

Augustine (1984), *City of God* (Harmondsworth: Penguin), tr. Henry Bettenson.

Aune, Bruce (1979), *Kant's Theory of Morals* (Princeton: Princeton University Press).

Austin, J.L. (1964), *Sense and Sensibilia* (Oxford: Oxford University Press).

Ayer, A.J. (1958 [1940]), *The Foundations of Empirical Knowledge* (London: Macmillan).

Ayer, A.J. (1965 [1954]), *Philosophical Essays* (London: Macmillan).

Ayer, A.J. (1984 [1956]), *The Problem of Knowledge* (Harmondsworth: Penguin).

Ayer, A.J. (1990 [1936]), *Language, Truth and Logic* (Harmondsworth: Penguin).

Ayer A.J. (1991 [1973]), *The Central Questions of Philosophy* (Harmondsworth: Penguin).

Bahr, Ehrhard (ed.) (1998), *Was ist Aufklärung? Thesen und Definitionen* (Stuttgart: Reclam).

Baier, Annette C. (1994), *A Progress of Sentiments* (Harvard: Harvard University Press).

Bambrough, R. (ed.) (1965), *New Essays on Plato and Aristotle* (London: Routledge & Kegan Paul).

Bambrough, R. (1975), 'Plato's Political Analogies' in Laslett (ed.) 1975, pp. 98–115.

Beardsworth, Timothy (1997), *A Sense of Presence* (Oxford: Religious Experience Research Unit).

Beauchamp, Tom L. and Childress, James F. (2001), *Principles of Biomedical Ethics* (Oxford: Oxford University Press).

Benedict, Ruth (2001), 'Anthropology and the Abnormal' in Carson and Moser (eds) 2001, pp. 80–9.

Bentham, Jeremy (1962), *An Introduction to the Principles of Morals and Legislation* (Glasgow: Collins), ed. Mary Warnock.

Berkeley, George (1998a [1710]), *A Treatise Concerning the Principles of Human Knowledge* (Oxford: Oxford University Press).

Berkeley, George (1998b [1713]), *Three Dialogues between Hylas and Philonous* (Oxford: Oxford University Press).

Bernecker, Sven and Dretske, Fred (eds) (2000), *Knowledge: Readings in Contemporary Epistemology* (Oxford: Oxford University Press).

Borland, James (1996), 'Religious Exclusivism' in Peterson *et al.* (eds) 1996, pp. 495–502.

Bowker, John (1997), *World Religions* (London: Dorling Kindersley).

Bradley, F.H. (1914), *Essays on Truth and Reality* (Oxford: Oxford University Press).

Broome, J.H. (1965), *Pascal* (London: Edward Arnold).

Burkert, Walter (1985), *Greek Religion* (Oxford: Blackwell) tr. John Raffan.

Cahn, Steven M. and Shatz, David (eds) (1982), *Contemporary Philosophy of Religion* (New York: Oxford University Press).

Campbell, Robert and Collinson, Diané (1992), *Ending Lives* (Oxford: Blackwell).

Carruthers, Peter (1994), *The Animal Issue* (Cambridge: Cambridge University Press).

Carson, Thomas L. and Moser, Paul K. (eds) (2001), *Moral Relativism: a Reader* (New York: Oxford University Press).

Carver, Terrell (ed.) (1991), *The Cambridge Companion to Marx* (Cambridge: CUP).

Casals, Pablo (1970), *Joys and Sorrows* (New York: Simon & Schuster).

Casey, John (1992), *Pagan Virtue* (Oxford: Oxford University Press).

Caws, Peter (1984), *Sartre* (London: Routledge).

Cherniss, H.F. (1965), 'The Philosophical Economy of the Theory of Ideas' in Allen (ed.) 1965, pp. 1–12.

Chisholm, Roderick M. (1966), *Theory of Knowledge* (Englewood Cliffs: Prentice-Hall).

Clark, Stephen (1977), *The Moral Status of Animals* (Oxford: Oxford University Press).

Cohen, Carl and Regan, Tom (2001), *The Animal Rights Debate* (Boston: Rowman & Littlefield).

Cohen, G.A. (2000), *Karl Marx's Theory of History: a Defence. Expanded Edition* (Oxford: Oxford University Press).

Conan Doyle, Arthur (1980 [1928]), *The Complete Sherlock Holmes Short Stories* (London: John Murray/Jonathan Cape).

Conrad Joseph (1989 [1900]), *Lord Jim* (Harmonds-worth: Penguin).

Conway, David (1987), *A Farewell to Marx* (Harmondsworth: Penguin).

Cottingham, John (1986), *Descartes* (Oxford: Blackwell).

Cottingham, John (ed.) (1992), *The Cambridge Companion to Descartes* (Cambridge: Cambridge University Press).

Cottingham, John (ed.) (1998), *Descartes* (Oxford: Oxford University Press).

Crisp, Roger (1997), *Mill on Utilitarianism* (London: Routledge).

Cross, R.C. and Woozley, A.D. (1964), *Plato's Republic: a Philosophical Commentary* (London: Macmillan).

Crosson, Frederick J. (ed.) (1981), *The Autonomy of Religious Belief: a Critical Inquiry* (Notre Dame and London: University of Notre Dame Press).

Curley, E.M. (1978), *Descartes Against the Skeptics* (Cambridge MA: Harvard University Press).

Dancy, Jonathan (1984), 'On Coherence Theories of Justification: Can an Empiricist be a Coherentist?' *American Philosophical Quarterly,* **21**(4), 359–65.

Dancy, Jonathan (1985), *Introduction to Contemporary Epistemology* (Oxford: Blackwell).

Dancy, Jonathan (1987), *Berkeley: an Introduction* (Oxford: Blackwell).

Dancy, Jonathan (ed) (1988), *Perceptual Knowledge* (Oxford: Oxford University Press).

Danto, Arthur (1991), *Sartre* (London: Fontana).

Davidson, Donald (1989), 'A Coherence Theory of Truth and Knowledge' in LePore (ed.) 1989, pp. 307–19.

Davies, Brian (1993), *An Introduction to the Philosophy of Religion* (Oxford: Oxford University Press).

Davies, Brian (ed.) (1998), *Philosophy of Religion: a Guide to the Subject* (London: Cassell).

Davies, Brian (ed.) (2000), *Philosophy of Religion: a Guide and Anthology* (Oxford: Oxford University Press).

Davies, Brian (2002), *Aquinas* (London: Continuum).

Davis, Stephen T. (1997), *God, Reason and Theistic Proofs* (Edinburgh: Edinburgh University Press).

Dennett, Daniel C. (1986), *Brainstorms* (Brighton: Harvester Press).

Descartes, René (1985), *The Philosophical Writings of Descartes Vol. I and II,* tr. Cottingham, Stoothoff and Murdoch (Cambridge: Cambridge University Press).

Diamond, Cora (1996), *The Realistic Spirit* (Cambridge, MA: MIT Press).

Dickens, Charles (1985 [1854]) *Hard Times* (Harmondsworth: Penguin).

Dicker, Georges (1993), *Descartes: an Analytical and Historical Introduction* (New York: Oxford University Press).

Doney, Willis (ed.) (1967), *Descartes: a Collection of Critical Essays* (Garden City: Anchor Books).

Dover, K.J. (1974), *Greek Popular Morality in the Time of Plato and Aristotle* (London: Duckworth).

Dover, K.J. (1978), *Greek Homosexuality* (London: Duckworth).

Dummett, Michael (1993), 'Bringing About the Past' in Le Poidevin and MacBeath (eds) 1993, pp. 117–33.

Eddy, W.H.C. (1979), *Understanding Marxism* (Oxford: Blackwell).

Fine, Gail (1978), 'Knowledge and Belief in *Republic V*' *Archiv für Geschichte der Philosophie,* **60**(2), 121–39.

Fine, Gail (ed.) (1999a), *Plato I: Metaphysics and Epistemology* (Oxford: Oxford University Press).

Fine, Gail (ed.) (1999b), *Plato II: Ethics, Politics, Religion, and the Soul* (Oxford: Oxford University Press).

Flew, Antony and MacIntyre, Alasdair (eds) (1963), *New Essays in Philosophical Theology* (London: SCM Press).

Flew, Antony (1966), *God and Philosophy* (London: Hutchinson).

Flew, Antony (1976), *The Presumption of Atheism and Other Essays* (London: Elek/Pemberton).

Foot, Philippa (1978), *Virtues and Vices* (Oxford: Blackwell).

Ford, Ford Madox (1999 [1915]), *The Good Soldier* (Harmondsworth: Penguin).

Frankena, William (1981), 'Is Morality Logically Dependent on Religion?' in Helm (ed.) 1981, pp. 14–33.

Frankfurt, Harry (1994), *The Importance of What We Care About* (Cambridge: Cambridge University Press).

Frede, Michael (1992), 'Plato's Arguments and the Dialogue Form', *Oxford Studies in Ancient Philosophy,* Supplementary Volume (Oxford: Oxford University Press), pp. 201–19.

Gaita, Raimond (1991), *Good and Evil: an Absolute Conception* (London: MacMillian).

Gaita, Raimond (2000), *A Common Humanity: Thinking about Love and Truth and Justice* (London: Routledge).

Gale, Richard M. (1982), 'Mysticism and Philosophy' in Cahn and Shatz (eds) 1982, pp. 113–22.

Gaskin, J.C.A. (1988), *Hume's Philosophy of Religion* (London: Macmillan).

Gaunilo (2000), 'Gaunilo Argues that Anselm is Wrong' in Davies (ed.) 2000, pp. 313–17.

Geach, Peter (1977), *The Virtues* (Cambridge: Cambridge University Press).

Geach, Peter (1982), 'Omnipotence' in Cahn and Shatz (eds) 1982, pp. 46–60.

Geach, Peter (1994), *God and the Soul* (Bristol: Thoemmes Press).

Geertz, Clifford (1993), *The Interpretation of Cultures* (London: Fontana).

Gettier, Edmund (1963), 'Is Justified True Belief Knowledge?' *Analysis,* **23**(6), 121–3.

Glover, Jonathan (1982), *Causing Death and Saving Lives* (Harmondsworth: Penguin).

Glover, Jonathan (1992), 'It Makes No Difference Whether or Not I Do It' in Singer (ed.) 1992, pp. 125–44.

Godwin, William (1994 [1793]), 'The Archbishop and the Chambermaid' in Singer (ed.) 1994, pp. 312–3.

Goldman, Alvin (1967), 'A Causal Theory of Knowing' *The Journal of Philosophy,* **64**(12), 357–72.

Goudsblom, J. (1980), *Nihilism and Culture* (Oxford: Blackwell).

Grayling, A.C. (1985), *The Refutation of Scepticism* (London: Duckworth).

Griswold, Charles (1981), 'The Ideas and the Criticism of Poetry in Plato's *Republic*, Book 10' *Journal of the History of Philosophy*, **XIX**(2), 135–50.

Guyer, Paul (ed.) (1992), *The Cambridge Companion to Kant* (Cambridge: Cambridge University Press).

Hampshire, Stuart (1983), *Morality and Conflict* (Oxford: Blackwell).

Hampshire, Stuart (1989), *Innocence and Experience* (Harmondsworth: Penguin).

Hare, R.M. (1952), *The Language of Morals* (Oxford: Oxford University Press).

Hare, R.M. (1963), *Freedom and Reason* (Oxford: Oxford University Press).

Hare, R.M. (1981), *Moral Thinking: Its Levels, Method and Point* (Oxford: Oxford University Press).

Harrison, Bernard (1979), *An Introduction to the Philosophy of Language* (London: Macmillan).

Hatfield, Gary (2003), *Descartes and the Meditations* (London: Routledge).

Hearn, Jeff (1991), 'Gender: Biology, Nature, and Capitalism' in Carver (ed.) 1991, pp. 222–45.

Helm, Paul (ed.) (1981), *Divine Commands and Morality* (Oxford: Oxford University Press).

Helm, Paul (ed.) (1999), *Faith and Reason* (Oxford: Oxford University Press).

Hemingway, Ernest (1987), *A Farewell to Arms. Death in the Afternoon. The Old Man and the Sea* (London: Jonathan Cape).

Herberg, Will (ed.) (1958), *Four Existentialist Theologians* (Garden City, New York: Doubleday Anchor Books).

Herman, Barbara (1993), *The Practice of Moral Judgment* (Cambridge MA: Harvard University Press).

Hick, John (ed.) (1964), *The Existence of God* (New York, Macmillan).

Hick, John (1971), 'Theology and Verification' in Mitchell 1971, pp. 53–71.

Hick, John (ed.) (1977), *The Myth of God Incarnate* (London: SCM Press).

Hick, John (1979), *Evil and the God of Love* (Glasgow: Collins).

Hick, John (1990), *Philosophy of Religion* (Englewood Cliffs: Prentice Hall).

Hick, John (1993), *Disputed Questions in Theology and Philosophy of Religion* (New Haven: Yale University Press).

Hick, John and McGill, Arthur (eds) (1968), *The Many-Faced Argument: Recent Studies on the Ontological Argument for the Existence of God* (London: Macmillan).

Hill, Thomas E., Jr. (1992), *Dignity and Practical Reason in Kant's Moral Theory* (Ithaca: Cornell University Press).

Hintikka, J. (1973), 'Knowledge and its Objects in Plato' in Moravcsik (ed.) 1973, pp. 1–30.

Hirst, R.J. (ed.) (1965), *Perception and the External World* (New York: Macmillan).

Hoffman, Joshua and Rosenkrantz, Gary S. (2002), *The Divine Attributes* (Oxford: Blackwell).

Holland, R.F. (1980), *Against Empiricism* (Oxford: Blackwell).

Howatson, M.C. (1997), *The Oxford Companion to Classical Literature* (Oxford: Oxford University Press).

Howells, Christina (ed.) (1992), *The Cambridge Companion to Sartre* (Cambridge: Cambridge University Press).

Hughes, Gerard J. (1998), 'Omniscience' in Davies (ed.) 1998, pp. 86–94.

Hume, David (1980 [1739/40]), *A Treatise of Human Nature* (Oxford: Oxford University Press).

Hume, David (1985 [1748/51]), *Enquiries Concerning Human Understanding and the Principles of Morals* (Oxford: Oxford University Press).

Hume, David (1994 [1779]), *Dialogues Concerning Natural Religion* (London: Routledge), ed. Stanley Tweyman.

Hursthouse, Rosalind (1987), *Beginning Lives* (Oxford: Blackwell).

Hursthouse, Rosalind (1997), 'Virtue Theory and Abortion' in Statman (ed.) 1997, pp. 227–44.

Irenaeus (2001), 'Against Heretics' in Larrimore (ed.) 2001, pp. 28–34.

Irwin, Terence (1979), *Plato's Moral Theory: the Early and Middle Dialogues* (Oxford: Oxford University Press).

James, William (1956), *The Will to Believe and Other Essays in Popular Philosophy* (New York: Dover).

James, William (1971 [1902]), *The Varieties of Religious Experience* (London: Fontana).

Janik, Allan and Toulmin, Stephen (1973), *Wittgenstein's Vienna* (New York: Simon & Schuster).

Jordan, Jeff (ed.) (1994), *Gambling on God: Essays on Pascal's Wager* (Lanham: Rowman & Littlefield).

Kant, Immanuel (1956 [1788]), *Critique of Practical Reason* (New York: Macmillan), tr. Lewis White Beck.

Kant, Immanuel (1983 [1785]), *Groundwork of the Metaphysics of Morals* (London: Hutchinson), tr. H.J. Paton.

Kant, Immanuel (1985 [1781]), *Critique of Pure Reason* (London: Macmillan), tr. Norman Kemp Smith.

Kant, Immanuel (1993 [1797]), *The Metaphysics of Morals* (Cambridge: Cambridge University Press), tr. Mary Gregor.

Kant, Immanuel (1994 [1799]), 'On a Supposed Right to Lie Because of Philanthropic Concerns' in Kant *Ethical Philosophy* (1994) (Indianapolis: Hackett), tr. James W. Ellington, intro. Warner A. Wick, pp. 162–6.

Kant, Immanuel (1998 [1784]), 'Beantwortung der Frage: Was ist Aufklärung? in Bahr (ed.) 1998, pp. 9–17.

Kemp Smith, Norman (1967), 'Is Divine Existence Credible?' in Phillips (ed.) 1967, pp. 105–25.

Kenny, Anthony (1968), *Descartes: a Study of his Philosophy* (New York: Random House).

Kenny, Anthony (ed.) (1970a), *Aquinas: a Collection of Critical Essays* (London: Macmillan).

Kenny, Anthony (1970b), 'Divine Foreknowledge and Human Freedom' in Kenny (ed.) 1970a, pp. 255–70.

Kenny, Anthony (1979), *The God of the Philosophers* (Oxford: Oxford University Press).

Kenny, Anthony (1987), *Reason and Religion: Essays in Philosophical Theology* (Oxford: Blackwell).

Kierkegaard, Søren (1974 [1846]), *Concluding Unscientific Postscript* (Princeton: Princeton University Press), tr. David F. Swenson and Walter Lowrie.

Kierkegaard, Søren (1985 [1844]), *Philosophical Fragments. Johannes Climacus* (Princeton: Princeton University Press), tr. Howard V. Hong and Edna H. Hong.

Korsgaard, Christine M. (1996a), *Creating the Kingdom of Ends* (Cambridge: Cambridge University Press).

Korsgaard, Christine M. (1996b), *The Sources of Normativity* (Cambridge: Cambridge University Press).

Kraut, Richard (ed.) (1992), *The Cambridge Companion to Plato* (Cambridge: Cambridge University Press).

Kripke, Saul (1984), *Naming and Necessity* (Oxford: Blackwell).

Kuhse, Helga and Singer, Peter (eds) (1999), *Bioethics: an Anthology* (Oxford: Blackwell).

Larrimore, Mark (ed.) (2001), *The Problem of Evil: a Reader* (Oxford: Blackwell).

Laslett, Peter (ed.) (1975), *Philosophy, Politics and Society: First Series* (Oxford: Blackwell).

Laslett, Peter and Runciman, W.G. (eds) (1967), *Philosophy, Politics and Society: Third Series* (Oxford: Blackwell).

Leavis, F.R. (ed.) (1971), *Mill on Bentham and Coleridge* (London: Chatto & Windus).

Leibniz, G.W. (1998 [1686–1714]), *Philosophical Texts* (Oxford: Oxford University Press), tr. and ed. by R.S. Woolhouse and Richard Francks.

Le Poidevin, Robin and MacBeath, Murray (eds) (1993), *The Philosophy of Time* (Oxford: Oxford University Press).

LePore, Ernest (ed.) (1989), *Truth and Interpretation: Perspectives on the Philosophy of Donald Davidson* (New York: Blackwell).

Levi, Primo (1998), *If This Is a Man. The Truce* (London: Abacus), tr. Stuart Woolf.

Levy, Neil (2002), *Moral Relativism: a Short Introduction* (Oxford: One World).

Locke, John (1984 [1689]), *An Essay Concerning Human Understanding* (Oxford: Oxford University Press).

Locke, John (1999 [1689]), 'The Futility of Intolerance' in Rosen and Wolff (eds) 1999, pp. 142–5.

Lukes, Steven (1990), *Marxism and Morality* (Oxford: Oxford University Press).

Macdonald, G.F. (ed.) (1979), *Perception and Identity* (London: Macmillan).

MacIntyre, Alasdair (1971), *Against the Self-Images of the Age* (London: Duckworth).

MacIntyre, Alasdair (1985), *After Virtue: a Study in Moral Theory* (London: Duckworth).

MacIntyre, Alasdair (1987), *A Short History of Ethics* (London: Routledge).

Mackie, John (1976), *Problems from Locke* (Oxford: Oxford University Press).

Mackie, John (1977), *Ethics: Inventing Right and Wrong* (Harmondsworth: Penguin).

Mackie, John (1982), *The Miracle of Theism* (Oxford: Oxford University Press).

Mackie, John (1994), 'Evil and Omnipotence' in Adams and Adams (eds) 1994, pp. 25–37.

Maimonides, Moses (1995 [1190]), *The Guide of the Perplexed* (Indianapolis: Hackett), abridged, intro. and commentary Julius Guttman, tr. Chaim Rabin, new intro. Daniel H. Frank.

Malcolm, Norman (1965), *Knowledge and Certainty* (Englewood Cliffs: Prentice-Hall).

Malcolm, Norman (1977a), *Thought and Knowledge* (New York: Cornell University Press).

Malcolm, Norman (1977b), *Dreaming* (London: Routledge & Kegan Paul).

Malcolm, Norman (1989), *Wittgenstein: a Memoir* (Oxford: Oxford University Press).

Manser, Anthony (1966), *Sartre: a Philosophic Study* (London: Athlone).

Martin, C.B. (1963), 'A Religious Way of Knowing' in Flew and MacIntyre (eds) 1963, pp. 76–95.

Martin, Michael (1996), 'Critique of Religious Experience' in Peterson *et al.* (eds) 1996, pp. 41–55.

Marx, Karl (1977), *Selected Writings* (Oxford: Oxford University Press), ed. David McLellan.

Marx, Karl and Engels, Friedrich (1985 [1848]), *The Communist Manifesto*, (Harmondsworth: Penguin), intro. A.J.P. Taylor, tr. Samuel Moore.

Marx, Karl and Engels, Friedrich (1999 [1932]), *The German Ideology* (London: Lawrence & Wishart), ed. and intro. C.J. Arthur.

Mascall, Eric L. (1968), 'The Doctrine of Analogy' in Santoni (ed.) 1968, pp. 156–81.

Mavrodes, George I. (1996), 'Some Puzzles Concerning Omnipotence' in Peterson *et al.* (eds) 1996, pp. 112–15.

McCulloch, Gregory (1994), *Using Sartre: an Analytical Introduction to Early Sartrean Themes* (London: Routledge).

McDowell, John (1978), 'Are Moral Requirements Hypothetical Imperatives?' *Proceedings of the Aristotelian Society,* Supplementary Volume, pp. 13–29.

McDowell, John (1988), 'Criteria, Defeasibility, and Knowledge' in Dancy (ed.) 1988, pp. 209–19.

McLellan, David (1974), *The Thought of Karl Marx: an Introduction* (London: Macmillan).

McLellan, David (1977), *Engels* (London: Fontana).

McNaughton, David (1996), *Moral Vision* (Oxford: Blackwell).

McPherson, Thomas (1963), 'Religion as Inexpressible' in Flew and MacIntyre (eds) 1963, pp. 131–43.

Meinwald, Constance C. (1992), 'Good-bye to the Third Man' in Kraut (ed.) 1992, pp. 365–96.

Midgley, Mary (1979), *Beast and Man: the Roots of Human Nature* (Hassocks: Harvester Press).

Mill, J.S. (1965), 'Permanent Possibilities of Sensation' in Hirst (ed.) 1965, pp. 274–82.

Mill, J.S. (1991), *On Liberty and Other Essays* (Oxford: Oxford University Press), ed. John Gray.

Mitchell, Basil (ed.) (1971), *The Philosophy of Religion* (Oxford: Oxford University Press).

Montaigne, Michel de (1991[1580–92]), *The Complete Essays* (Harmondsworth: Penguin), tr. M.A. Screech.

Moore, Gareth (1988), *Believing in God: a Philosophical Essay* (Edinburgh: T & T Clark).

Moore, G.E. (1984 [1903]), *Principia Ethica* (Cambridge: Cambridge University Press).

Moore, G.E. (1959), *Philosophical Papers* (London: Routledge).

Moravcsik, J.M.E. (ed.) (1973), *Patterns in Plato's Thought* (Reidel: Dordrecht).

Morgan, Michael (1990), *Platonic Piety: Philosophy and Ritual in Fourth Century Athens* (New Haven: Yale University Press).

Morgan, Michael (1992), 'Plato and Greek Religion' in Kraut (ed.) 1992, pp. 227–47.

Morton, Adam (2001), *A Guide Through the Theory of Knowledge* (Oxford: Blackwell).

Moser, Paul K., Mulder, Dwayne H. and Trout, J.D. (1998), *The Theory of Knowledge: a Thematic Introduction* (New York: Oxford University Press).

Mulhall, Stephen (1994), *Faith and Reason* (London: Duckworth).

Murdoch, Iris (1968), *Sartre* (London: Fontana).

Murdoch, Iris (1986), *The Sovereignty of Good* (London: Ark).

Nehamas, Alexander (1999), *Virtues of Authenticity: Essays on Plato and Socrates* (Princeton: Princeton University Press).

Nicholson, William (1992), *Shadowlands* (London: Samuel French).

Nielsen, Kai (1982), 'Wittgensteinian Fideism' in Cahn and Shatz (eds) 1982, pp. 237–54.

Nietzsche, Friedrich (1968 [1901]), *The Will to Power* (New York: Random House), tr. R.J. Hollingdale and Walter Kaufmann.

Nietzsche, Friedrich (1990 [1889–95]), *Twilight of the Idols/The Anti-Christ* (Harmondsworth: Penguin), tr. R.J. Hollingdale.

Nozick, Robert (1981), *Philosophical Explanations* (Cambridge MA: Harvard University Press).

Nussbaum, Martha (2001), 'Non-Relative Virtues' in Carson and Moser (eds) 2001, pp. 199–225.

Oakeshott, Michael (1991), *Rationalism in Politics and Other Essays: New and Expanded Edition* (Indianapolis: Liberty Fund).

O'Neill, Onora (1989), *Constructions of Reason: Explorations of Kant's Practical Philosophy* (Cambridge: Cambridge University Press).

Orwell, George (1987 [1937]), *The Road to Wigan Pier* (Harmondsworth: Penguin).

Pappas, Nickolas (1995), *Plato and the Republic* (London: Routledge).

Parekh, Bhiku (ed.) (1974), *Jeremy Bentham: Ten Critical Essays* (London: Frank Cass).

Pascal, Blaise (1966), *Pensées* (Harmondsworth: Penguin), tr. A.J. Krailsheimer.

Peterson, Michael, Hasker, William, Reichenbach, Bruce and Basinger, David (eds) (1996), *Philosophy of Religion: Selected Readings* (Oxford: Oxford University Press).

Phillips, D.Z (ed.) (1967), *Religion and Understanding* (Oxford: Blackwell).

Phillips, D.Z. (1970), *Death and Immortality* (London: Macmillan).

Phillips, D.Z. (1971), 'Religious Beliefs and Language Games' in Mitchell (ed.) 1971, pp. 121–42.

Phillips, D.Z. (1981a), 'God and Ought' in Helm (ed.) 1981, pp. 175–80.

Phillips, D.Z. (1981b), 'Belief, Change, and Forms of Life: the Confusions of Externalism and Internalism' in Crosson (ed.) 1981, pp. 60–92.

Phillips, D.Z. (2001), *Religion and the Hermeneutics of Contemplation* (Cambridge: Cambridge University Press).

Plamenatz, John (1975), *German Marxism and Russian Communism* (Westport: Greenwood Press).

Plantinga, Alvin (1977), *God, Freedom, and Evil* (Grand Rapids: Eerdmans).

Plantinga, Alvin (1983), 'Reason and Belief in God' in Plantinga and Wolterstorff (eds) 1983, pp. 16–93.

Plantinga, Alvin (1994), 'God, Evil, and the Metaphysics of Freedom' in Adams and Adams (eds) 1994, pp. 83–109.

Plantinga, Alvin (1996), 'On Reformed Epistemology' in Peterson *et al.* (eds) 1996, pp. 330–6.

Plantinga, Alvin and Wolterstorff, Nicholas (eds) (1983), *Faith and Rationality: Reason and Belief in God* (Notre Dame: University of Notre Dame Press).

Plato (1983), *Phaedo* (Oxford: Oxford University Press), tr. and notes David Gallop.

Plato (1986), *The Republic* (Harmondsworth: Penguin) tr. Desmond Lee.

Platts, Mark (1979), *Ways of Meaning* (London: Routledge).

Price, H.H. (1965), 'The Given' in Hirst (ed.) 1965, pp. 108–15.

Prichard, H.A. (1949) *Moral Obligation* (London: Oxford University Press).

Putnam, Hilary (1975), *Mind, Language and Reality: Philosophical Papers Vol. II* (Cambridge, Cambridge University Press).

Putnam, Hilary (1981), *Reason, Truth and History* (Cambridge: Cambridge University Press).

Rachels, James (1992), 'Active and Passive Euthanasia' in Singer (ed.) 1992, pp. 29–35.

Radford, Colin (1966), 'Knowledge – by Examples' *Analysis*, **27**(1), 1–11.

Radford, Colin (1970), 'Does Unwitting Knowledge Entail Unconscious Belief?' *Analysis* **30**(9), 103–7.

Rawls, John (1972), *A Theory of Justice* (Oxford: Oxford University Press).

Regan, Tom (1984), *The Case for Animal Rights* (London: Routledge).

Rhees, Rush (1997), *On Religion and Philosophy* (Cambridge: Cambridge University Press), ed. D.Z. Phillips.

Rice, Daryl H. (1998), *A Guide to Plato's Republic* (New York: Oxford University Press).

Rorty, Amélie Oksenberg (ed.) (1969), *The Identities of Persons* (Berkeley: University of California Press).

Rorty, Amélie Oksenberg (ed.) (1986), *Essays on Descartes' Meditations* (Berkeley: University of California Press).

Rosen, Michael and Wolff, Jonathan (eds) (1999), *Political Thought* (Oxford: Oxford University Press).

Ross, James (1998), 'Religious Language' in Davies (ed.) 1998, pp. 106–35.

Ross, W.D. (1930), *The Right and the Good* (Oxford: Oxford University Press).

Russell, Bertrand (1950), *Unpopular Essays* (London: George Allen and Unwin).

Russell, Bertrand and Copleston, F.C. (1964), 'A Debate on the Existence of God' in Hick (ed.) 1964, pp. 167–91.

Rutherford, R.B. (1995), *The Art of Plato* (London: Duckworth).

Ryan, Alan (1974), *J.S. Mill* (London: Routledge).

Ryle, Gilbert (1949), *The Concept of Mind* (London: Hutchinson).

Sadowsky, James A. (1988), 'Did Darwin Destroy the Design Argument?' *International Philosophical Quarterly*, **XXVIII**(109), 95–104.

Santoni, Ronald E. (ed.) (1968), *Religious Language and the Problem of Religious Knowledge* (Bloomington: Indian University Press).

Sartre, J.-P. (1982), *The Respectable Prostitute. Lucifer and the Lord. In Carrera* (Harmondsworth: Penguin).

Sartre, J.-P. (1984 [1943]), *Being and Nothingness* (London: Methuen), tr. Hazel Barnes.

Sartre, J.-P. (1985 [1939]), *Sketch for a Theory of the Emotions* (London: Methuen), tr. Philip Mairet.

Sartre, J.-P. (1992 [1946]), *Existentialism and Humanism* (London: Methuen), tr. Philip Mairet.

Sayers, Sean (1999), *Plato's Republic: an Introduction* (Edinburgh: Edinburgh University Press).

Scheffler, Samuel (ed.) (1988), *Consequentialism and its Critics* (Oxford: Oxford University Press).

Schneebaum, Tobias (1988), *Where the Spirits Dwell* (London: Weidenfeld & Nicolson).

Schneewind, J.B. (1992), 'Autonomy, Obligation, and Virtue: an Overview of Kant's Moral Philosophy' in Guyer (ed.) 1992, pp. 309–41.

Scruton, Roger (1982), *Kant* (Oxford: Oxford University Press).

Scruton, Roger (1996), *Animal Rights and Wrongs* (London: Demos).

Searle, John R. (1969), *Speech Acts* (Cambridge: Cambridge University Press).

Searle, John R. (1990), *Intentionality* (Cambridge: Cambridge University Press).

Searle, John R. (1999), *The Rediscovery of the Third* (Cambridge, MA: MIT Press).

Sellars, Wilfrid (2000), *Empiricism and the Philosophy of Mind* (Cambridge MA: Harvard University Press).

Sen, Amartya and Williams, Bernard (eds) (1984), *Utilitarianism and Beyond* (Cambridge: Cambridge University Press).

Singer, Peter (1984), *Animal Liberation* (Wellingborough: Thorsons).

Singer, Peter (1986), *Marx* (Oxford: Oxford University Press).

Singer, Peter (ed.) (1992), *Applied Ethics* (Oxford: Oxford University Press).

Singer, Peter (1993), *Practical Ethics* (Cambridge: Cambridge University Press).

Singer, Peter (ed.) (1994), *Ethics* (Oxford: Oxford University Press).

Smart, J.J.C. and Haldane, J.J. (1996), *Atheism and Theism* (Oxford: Blackwell).

Smart, J.J.C. and Williams, Bernard (1985), *Utilitarianism: For and Against* (Cambridge: Cambridge University Press).

Smart, Ninian (1969), *Philosophers and Religious Truth* (London: SCM Press).

Smart, Ninian (1970), *The Religious Experience of Mankind* (London: Collins).

Sosa, Ernest and Kim, Jaegwon (eds) (2000), *Epistemology: an Anthology* (Oxford: Blackwell).

Southern, R.W. (1970), *The Making of the Middle Ages* (London: Hutchinson & Co.).

Staten, Henry (1990), *Nietzsche's Voice* (Ithaca: Cornell University Press).

Statman, Daniel (ed.) (1997), *Virtue Ethics: a Critical Reader* (Edinburgh: Edinburgh University Press).

Stern, J.P. (1971), *Idylls and Realities: Studies in Nineteenth Century German Literature* (London: Methuen).

Stevenson, C.L. (1937), 'The Emotive Meaning of Ethical Terms' *Mind*, **XLVI**(181), 14–31.

Stirner, Max (1982 [1844]), *The Ego and Its Own* (London: Rebel Press), tr. Steven Byington, intro. Sidney Parker.

Stiver, Dan R. (1996), *Religious Language: Sign, Symbol and Story* (Oxford: Blackwell).

Strawson, P.F. (1979), 'Perception and its Objects', in Macdonald (ed.) 1979, pp. 41–60.

Strawson, P.F. (1984), *Individuals: an Essay on Descriptive Metaphysics* (London: Methuen).

Stroud, Barry (1984), *The Significance of Philosophical Scepticism* (Oxford: Oxford University Press).

Stroud, Barry (1985), *Hume* (London: Routledge).

Sullivan, Roger J. (1994), *An Introduction to Kant's Ethics* (Cambridge: Cambridge University Press).

Surin, Kenneth (1986), *Theology and the Problem of Evil* (Oxford: Blackwell).

Swinburne, Richard (1983), *Faith and Reason* (Oxford: Oxford University Press).

Swinburne, Richard (1991), *The Existence of God* (Oxford: Oxford University Press).

Swinburne, Richard (1993), *The Coherence of Theism* (Oxford: Oxford University Press).

Swinburne, Richard (2000), 'God, Regularity and David Hume' in Davies (ed.) 2000, pp. 274–85.

Taylor, A.E. (1960), *Plato: the Man and His Work* (London: Methuen).

Taylor, Charles (1986), *Human Agency and Language: Philosophical Papers I* (Cambridge: Cambridge University Press).

Taylor, Charles (1992), *Sources of the Self* (Cambridge: Cambridge University Press).

Thomson, Judith Jarvis (1992), 'A Defence of Abortion', in Singer (ed.) 1992, pp. 37–56.

Tillich, Paul (1958), 'Existential Analyses and Religious Symbols' in Herberg (ed.) 1958, pp. 277–91.

Tillich, Paul (1968), 'Symbols of Faith' in Santoni (ed.) 1968, pp. 136–45.

Tillich, Paul (1996), 'Religious Language as Symbolic' in Peterson *et al.* (eds) 1996, pp. 357–65.

Tooley, Michael (1992), 'Abortion and Infanticide' in Singer (ed.) 1992, pp. 57–85.

Trilling, Lionel (1967), *Beyond Culture* (Harmondsworth: Penguin).

Tucker, Robert (1969), *Philosophy and Myth in Karl Marx* (Cambridge: Cambridge University Press).

Urmson, J.O. (1982), *Berkeley* (Oxford: Oxford University Press).

Urmson, J.O. (1988), *Aristotle's Ethics* (Oxford: Blackwell).

Van Hook, Jay M. (1996), 'Knowledge, Belief, and Reformed Epistemology' in Peterson *et al.* (eds) 1996, pp. 321–9.

Vlastos, Gregory (1965), 'Degrees of Reality in Plato' in Bambrough (ed.) 1965, pp. 1–19.

Vlastos, Gregory (ed.) (1972a), *Plato I: Metaphysics and Epistemology* (London: Macmillan).

Vlastos, Gregory (ed.) (1972b), *Plato II: Ethics, Politics, and Philosophy of Art and Religion* (London: Macmillan).

Wainwright, William J. (1982), 'Mysticism and Sense Perception' in Cahn and Shatz (eds) 1982, pp. 123–45.

Walker, Ralph C.S. (1982), *Kant* (London: Routledge).

Warnock, Mary (1965), *The Philosophy of Sartre* (London: Hutchinson).

Wartofsky, Marx W. (1982), *Feuerbach* (Cambridge: Cambridge University Press).

Weber, Max (1974), *Essays in Sociology* (London: Routledge), tr. H.H. Gerth and C. Wright Mills.

Wedberg, A. (1955), *Plato's Philosophy of Mathematics* (Stockholm: Almqvist & Wiksell).

Weil, Simone (1977), *Waiting on God* (London: Fount), tr. Emma Crauford.

White, Nicholas P. (1979), *A Companion to Plato's* Republic (Indianapolis: Hackett).

Wiggins, David (1969), 'Locke, Butler and the Stream of Consciousness: and Men as Natural Kind' in Rorty (ed.) 1969, pp. 139–73.

Wiggins, David (1987), *Needs, Values, Truth* (Oxford: Blackwell).

Williams, Bernard (1982), *Morality: an Introduction to Ethics* (Cambridge: Cambridge University Press).

Williams, Bernard (1985), *Ethics and the Limits of Philosophy* (London: Fontana).

Williams, Bernard (1986), *Moral Luck* (Cambridge: Cambridge University Press).

Williams, Bernard (1987), *Descartes: the Project of Pure Enquiry* (Harmondsworth: Penguin).

Williams, Bernard (1995), 'Replies' in Altham and Harrison (eds) 1995, pp. 185–224.

Wilson, Margaret Dauler (1986), *Descartes* (London: Routledge).

Winch, Peter (1972), *Ethics and Action* (London: Routledge).

Winch, Peter (1997), 'Can We Understand Ourselves?' *Philosophical Investigations*, **20**(3), pp. 193–204.

Wittgenstein, L. (1966), *Lectures and Conversations on Aesthetics, Psychology and Religious Belief* (Oxford: Blackwell).

Wittgenstein, L. (1968), 'Lecture on Ethics' *Philosophical Review*, **LXXIV**(1), 3–12.

Wittgenstein, L. (1969), *On Certainty/Ueber Gewissheit*, (Oxford: Blackwell), tr. Denis Paul and G.E.M. Anscombe.

Wittgenstein, L. (1986), *Philosophical Investigations* (Oxford: Blackwell), tr. G.E.M. Anscombe.

Wittgenstein, L. (1990 [1921]), *Tractatus Logico-Philosophicus* (London: Routledge), tr. C.K. Ogden.

Wollheim, Richard (1969), *F.H. Bradley* (Harmondsworth: Penguin).

Zweig, Stefan (1999 [1942]), *Die Welt von Gestern* (Frankfurt am Main: Fischer Taschenbuch Verlag).

index

Page numbers in bold indicate definition of term or biography of person. Page numbers in italic indicate illustration.

UNDERSTANDING PHILOSOPHY

for AS Level